BRUMBACK LIBRARY
3 3045 00091 9411

P9-DBI-205

Woody's Boys

20 Famous Buckeyes Talk Amongst Themselves

Woody's Boys

20 FAMOUS BUCKEYES TALK AMONGST THEMSELVES

by Alan Natali

portraits by Greg Storer

Orange Frazer *Press*

Wilmington, Ohio

Library of Congress Catalog Card Number: 95-70158

ISBN 1-882203-04-6

Published by Orange Frazer Press
37½ W. Main Street
Box 214
Wilmington, Ohio 45177

As always, for Alison

Acknowledgements I would like to thank *Ron Forsythe,* friend and teacher, who has been there, without fail, from the beginning; *John Baskin,* who didn't lose faith even when I did; *the Bucks,* and in particular *Kenny Kuhn,* my fellow traveler; *Miss Betsy,* for her forebearance; *Dr. Bernard De Flippo,* for his insightful comments; the Varsity 'O' Association, especially *Sue Ferguson*; *Steve Snapp* and the Sports Information Office of Ohio State University; and the English Department of California University of Pennsylvania.

—Alan Natali

art direction John Baskin
design Brooke Wenstrup
consultant J Porter
photography and research Chance Brockway
manuscript preparation Beth Dubberley
additional research Dave Stephenson
formatting Kristina Schneider

and portraits by Greg Storer

Contents

I do admit I like to pull the laundered jock up on my legs, and the helmet down over my head. And I like the heft and stink of my shoulder pads—and, damn right, I'll admit it ain't half bad to be knocking people down, on the football field. Man, I've worked hard to be a good lineman, and you, sir, ought to have respect for that.

—Joiner

Woody's Boys

20 Famous Buckeyes Talk Amongst Themselves

Searching *for the* Bucks

FOR NEARLY 18 months, I had been hoping that this moment wouldn't come. When it finally did, I was—oddly—clinging to a passenger's seat aboard a sleek Ski Nautique speed boat that beneath my sunburned feet felt as powerful as a fuel dragster.

The boat was thundering over the Ohio River just off-shore from Parkersburg, West Virginia, and dragging behind it, at the end of a long yellow tow rope, the acclaimed former Ohio State linebacker Tom Cousineau. Leaning casually back at a steep angle, sinewy biceps tight against his polyurethane safety vest, Cousineau was frowning slightly and rolling his eyes toward the cloudless sky. He looked utterly indifferent, despite what seemed to me to be the herculean effort required to surge along at 40 miles an hour atop a single water ski.

Perhaps Cousineau's lack of interest was brought on by the debris that forced him to wear any ski at all. He had wanted to go barefoot. Perhaps a man who is married to a former professional water-skier takes such feats for granted. Whatever the case, Cousineau's skiing was not what prompted the disturbing revelation that I was about to have, even when he began to methodically dip first one shoulder and then the other nearly into the boat's wake in order to carry out a series of swooping arcs, each of which threw a roostertail of spume over his head.

After all, people do learn to ski, even one who is 6-3 and 225 pounds and wears on the inside of one calf a large talismanic tattoo of a leaping shark, the sun setting over a turbulent sea, and a vaporous face blowing storm winds. Cousineau is lean and hawknosed, his skin taut over a framework of lengthy bone and muscle from which all fat has been rendered. He looked capable of skiing any way he chose to. Rather, what caused me to see myself in a new and troubling light happened, quite suddenly, when Cousineau decided to stop riding his ski.

Later, he would say that he felt a slight "pop" in his back and didn't want to risk further injuring the body that he claims is "falling apart" after nine seasons of professional football. He decided to dismount, and instead of just releasing the rope, Cousineau gathered himself, tucked his chin against his barrel chest, and, in a startling compact and controlled movement, executed a graceful forward somersault. For a 150-pound gymnast, the flip would've been impressive. Performed by a man of Cousineau's size, it was nothing short of amazing.

Dumbfounded, I was immediately made to reconsider one entire aspect of my life—the part of me that I had always referred to as "athlete," but in the aftermath of one blasé stunt by Tom Cousineau, demanded to be called by some other name.

I beheld Cousineau's prowess that afternoon because I had been asked to write a book about Ohio State football. I was selected, at least in part, because I played the game, having been a small-college All-American linebacker. Also, Ohio State football had been of particular interest to me since an old high school rival, Fred Pagac, who still coaches at the university, signed to play for the Buckeyes 25 years ago.

The publishers and I looked over the spate of books about OSU football. Finding many of them transparent attempts to turn a quick profit, we decided that an oral history was the only way to know what it was like to be a Buckeye. I would search out the Bucks and talk, seeking their particular impressions of playing football for Ohio State. We would get the true picture of life among the scarlet and gray warriors from the Lords of Discipline themselves, we decided.

I unscientifically jotted down several dozen names and, through the university, came up with a list of addresses. I wrote to the first of my subjects, explaining what I was attempting to do. I would call at some unspecified later date to set up an interview, I advised. I believed I was being courteous to a fault, but I soon found out that my approach had been inadequate. Esco Sarkkinen, former All-American end and head scout and defensive end coach at OSU for 31 years, snarled at me over the phone one evening that he didn't do such interviews, particularly with writers from out of town. Sarkkinen slammed the phone down before I had a chance to voice the purity of my intentions. I felt like a new hire required to cold-call dormant accounts for a second-rate stock brokerage firm.

Although he probably wouldn't like the idea, Sarkkinen did get me "coached up," to use the appropriate football expression. The next day, I put together a bulky packet containing a more thorough explanation of my background and concept, copies of several pieces I had written, and a form that each subject could return in a self-addressed stamped envelope should he agree to be interviewed. I also clipped prominently to the top of the first page of the packet a business card from the time I spent coaching the outside linebackers at the university at which I had played.

To Sarkkinen, I realized, I represented the lowest and most feared of abominations—not just a writer, but one he did not know. I thought that as a former player I didn't deserve such brusqueness. However, I had forgotten that the world of big time sport—at Ohio State and elsewhere—is an insular one inhabited by people who are constantly on the lookout for nosy strangers hoping to dig up dirt. Even Fred Pagac, whom I have known for years, didn't return my calls. Had majoring in English made me a pariah? I wondered. Esco Sarkkinen vividly reminded me of the inbred mistrust between sportswriter and sports figure, two mostly incompatible species who view each other as either geekish scavengers or boorish, unjustly gifted oafs. In the case of OSU football, that rift was widened by Hayes's distaste for the press, a contempt that he passed along to his players.

If Sarkkinen didn't clarify matters enough for me, Champ Henson did. Henson called after receiving one of my elaborate requests.

I was excited at the chance to help tell the tale of a player who, as he was about to take his place in the hallowed lineage of Buckeye fullbacks, lost everything with one unfortunate step.

However, rather than inviting me out to his farm, Henson began to admonish me. He had already been burned by the press, he said as prologue to a bitter litany of gripes. I tried to counter each of his complaints with assurances that I would not misquote him or quote him out of context. He abruptly changed his angle of attack, declaring that it wasn't right that I should benefit from the blood and sweat of those who had played the game. That new tack stopped me cold.

We hung up, and I wrote Henson again, telling him that as I typed, there hung above me a poster-sized photo of two trainers helping me off the field after I ripped a groin muscle, leaving me black and blue from mid-abdomen to mid-thigh. I told him that I can't straighten an elbow that had been shattered and dislocated, can't turn my head to look over my right shoulder, and am given to severe headaches I'm sure are the by-products of collisions with running backs. Even though I collected these infirmities before 6,000 fans instead of 60,000, I said, I felt no compunctions whatever in writing about football.

The letter was more curt than I intended, but I mailed it off, giving up on both the prospect of including Henson's story in the book and the idea that I could reach the Bucks through any kind of unconscious class bondage.

Long afterward, I came home to a ringing phone. It was Champ Henson, and he sounded irked. He wondered where I had been and when I was coming out to Ashville to talk to him. I don't really know why he changed his mind, but months later, I found in an old *Columbus Dispatch* a photo of Henson just after his knee was destroyed early in his junior year, which is remarkably similar to the one of me being toted to the sidelines.

When I drove up the long dirt lane of the farm Henson bought at a sheriff's auction, I noticed the carcass of a deer, fresh-killed but frozen in the November wind, hanging near the barn. We talked for a while, as his three children gamboled around the rustic living room, and he asked me if I were hungry. I was, and Henson hacked the tenderloin from the deer, tossed it into a pan, and roasted it. When the meat was done, I sat at the kitchen table of the home he had built himself around a fancy cutglass door he found at a flea market, washed the still-bloody, succulent venison down with cans of beer, and listened to Champ Henson—bright, innately generous, and at ease with his fate—tell a moving, wise story tinged with wry farmboy humor. Later, he asked to excise from the interview only several snippets of dicey locker room talk that he didn't want his mother reading.

That animosity between athlete and reporter made John Cooper's forthrightness all the more surprising. Cooper, of course, found himself besieged by the media and fans almost from the moment he touched ground in Columbus. At times, he must've felt like a treed boar 'coon back in his native Tennessee hill country. Yet Cooper called me on the very day he received my request and said, simply, "Let's get it done." Surrounded by mounted trophy fish and prominently displayed memorabilia, we talked for several hours in the plush office for which he has also been criticized.

Cooper is a reasonably personable man given to an understated sense of country humor not unlike Henson's and possessed of the clear resolve to do whatever is required of him, if only to preserve what he has worked so hard for—the concrete evidence of just how far he has come from his meager Appalachian roots. He reminded me of the squared-away state trooper who pulls you over on some desolate stretch of I-75, treats you with immaculate politeness, then, just as you think you're going to get away with a warning, writes up the citation—against his own inclination—in strict adherence to the table of speeds and fines, sparing you not a single mile per hour. For the most part setting aside the usual coach's bromides, Cooper discussed the assertion that he is a high-paid mercenary following the money wherever it leads, the uproar over his contract extension, recruiting, the strange and infamous case of Robert Smith, some of the factors that led to the decline of OSU's program. At one point, he shook his head slightly, in an almost imperceptible reflex of wonder, and said of the state's passion for the Buckeyes, "It's Ohio State football; it's Ohio State football; it's Ohio State football."

Something of a hybrid species—part jock, part journalist—I found myself afflicted with reverse discrimination when I talked to former *Dispatch* sports editor Paul Hornung. I'd read his undistinguished, saccharine prose and heard the oft-repeated claim that he'd been nothing more than a sycophant to Hayes and a shill for the university. I was prepared to be scornful of him. We were to meet for lunch at the Refectory, a church that had been turned into a restaurant and a favored haunt of the OSU athletic crowd. I arrived early and found the place closed. A maintenance man told me that the Refectory didn't even serve lunches.

Our appointment had been for noon, and at precisely noon, Hornung pulled into the lot, small behind the wheel of a huge black Buick that crushed the ice rotting in potholes. He was frail. His parchment flesh was shot through with blue veins, and his face was liver-spotted. He wore a belted trenchcoat, a houndstooth chapeau, and an old-fashioned print tie. He looked exactly as I've always thought Grantland Rice or Ring Lardner must have.

I carefully took the hand he offered, afraid, truly, of crushing his brittle bones. His chin was trembling. His eyes were red. Hornung told me only that he'd "been up all night with a family problem." I fatuously asked if I could do anything to help.

"No," he said, a soft air of resignation in his voice. "I suppose when you get to be my age, these things are bound to happen."

I told him that we could postpone the interview, but he said that he didn't want me to have to travel back to town and that we should go ahead and do it. I insisted that we not and arranged to call him again. Several weeks later, when we met at the Jai Lai, where he'd spent so much time with Hayes over the years, I learned that Hornung's brother had died the day before our meeting at the Refectory. He could easily have not shown up that day. He could've left a message on my answering machine or come blasting into the lot, unshaven and wearing a moth-eaten sweater and pajama bottoms, shouting out the window that he had no time for me. But he was punctual, dressed immaculately, and ready to keep his promise. It was something I'd expect Hayes to have done—ignore his grief to meet an obligation. I wondered how I might've reacted in Hornung's position, and I know I wouldn't have cut it.

I thought much differently of Paul Hornung then. The man had more sand than anyone gave him credit for, an assessment borne out as he offered an inside look at the hirings and firings of coaches, as he bemoaned some of Hayes's antics, as he lashed back, in his reserved way, at those who assailed the admittedly partisan position he took in covering the Bucks and Hayes. "People think I supported him because I was stupid or that I didn't know any better, or never thought about what I was doing,"he said. "But I always felt, and I justified myself, if I had to, that I was the sports editor of the biggest newspaper in town, Ohio State football was the biggest thing, by far, in Columbus in the way of sports, and it was wholesome, it was clean, it was uplifting, it was connected to education, it was providing a wholesome outlet for the community, so, therefore, why should I not be what some people derogatorily called a 'cheerleader'?"

There was something unspoken between Hornung and me that day at the Jai Lai. He mused often about old friends who had passed away or become infirm. Somehow, we both knew that he wouldn't live to see the interview in print. Our talk took on the tenor of a coda, a final recapitulation, and what had once sounded smarmy and patronizing in his work now seemed merely quaint, an echo of an older more innocent time, when referring to players by their nicknames in print and cheering in the pressbox were not sins, mortal or venial. Paul Hornung is himself dead now. I'm glad to have known him.

As I talked with the Bucks, I became increasingly conscious of the varied manner in which they said things, of the sound and rhythm of their speech. Cooper telegrams stacatto bursts of colloquialism-sprinkled Tennessee twang: "cain't" and "wadn't" and "gonna git." Likewise, Pete Johnson's thick Georgia drawl forms a kind of verbal scrim between him and the listener. We northerners have always associated such an accent with bumpkinism, but behind the screen, Johnson is sensitive, funny, and has a keen memory for significant details. Cousineau speaks at a measured, contemplative pace, as does Bob Vogel, who upon hearing a question would lean back in his chair for minutes at a time, stroking his salt-and-pepper beard and staring at the ceiling, like a professor of philosophy about to launch into a disquisition on Sarte's *Being and Nothingness.* Cornelius Greene organizes his thoughts into tightly structured paragraphs, and Rex Kern's largely uninflected tone seems modulated to be as soothing as a long doze under a warm towel. On the other hand, the irrepressible Tom Skladany would suck in a deep breath, hold it as if gathering words along with oxygen, then let it all spew out so rapidly that he might've been rushing out to the far hashmark to attempt a last-second field goal against Michigan.

Jim Parker spun colorful tales in the rich, distinctive, and ancient tradition of great rural storytellers. In his dulcet voice, the Rev. Daryl Sanders inquired after my spiritual well-being. The wildest and most fascinating speaker, however, was Jim Stillwagon, Outland Trophy-winning middle guard and jock Jabberwocky. Stillwagon delivers a frequently vulgar and hilarious kind of epic street poetry. His is a frightfully active if undisciplined mind, and he vaults from idea to idea, beginning sentences, dropping them in mid-syllable, spuriously backtracking to pick up a thought discarded an hour earlier.

Wearing an expensive suit, one thumb hooked in a braided leather suspender, Stillwagon talked for almost seven hours in his office in the huge building he owns near Columbus. The office was strewn with the detritus of his many and varied business ventures—tee-shirts, ballcaps, preliminary designs, video tapes, prototypes, prospecti for ad campaigns. Stillwagon turned away appointments and refused phone calls as he held forth. He was puffing a cigar half as thick as my wrist. It went out every minute or so, and he relit it, drawing on the stogie, squinting and scowling, like Edward G. Robinson in *Little Caesar*, as he roared his unbridled, cynical insights into everything from Woody Hayes's travel habits to seasonal affective disorder.

"People want to meet you sometimes so they can see if you're dumb or smart," said Stillwagon, who is quite smart. "They can go back that night and say, 'Boy, I met the dumbest shit in the whole world. You know that fucking guy who played at Ohio State? He's a fucking idiot, but he can do something for me.' They'll let you bullshit them one time, but there comes a time when Joe Blow has to have you make widgets, because that's how he gets paid. He don't give a fuck if you scored a touchdown in the Michigan-Ohio State game. He cares if you can make a widget for him, and it gets down to that."

The memories the Bucks have of their days in scarlet and gray are idiosyncratic. For example, Sanders found nothing amusing about Hayes, while Skladany remembers him as perpetually hilarious, and Tim Fox thought his humor as calculated and well-timed as a late-night TV host's monologue. Fox recalls that away from the locker room nearly everyone went his own way, but Dave Mazeroski, whose bum shoulders relegated him to running opponents' plays in practice for four years, says the Bucks were one big happy family, socially as well as athletically. To Archie Griffin, whose endorsement of everything Hayes and OSU could be dismissed as platitudinous claptrap if he didn't believe so earnestly in every word of it, the Bucks were a cohesive unit dedicated to a single proposition—winning games for the greater glory of Ohio State. Whereas, to Kenny Kuhn, punishing linebacker and team captain in 1975, the squad was divided along clear political lines—those who bought into Hayes and the system without question and those who rebelled against what they saw as his antiquated and sometimes insensitive approach to handling players.

One constant among the Bucks is that they all have trouble remembering specific dates, specific opponents, specific scores, specific statistics, except for Skladany, who in the the way of all kickers can tell you, in order, exactly how far each of his punts traveled in the 1976 Indiana game—both in the air and with the roll. Over the years, more important abstractions have replaced the concrete numbers.

"We had a 15-year reunion for the '74 team, and almost everybody came," Henson said. "It was a wonderful time. They had highlight films there from the games. They had 'em runnin' down on both ends, and you know what? I don't think I saw anybody watchin' 'em. They were talkin': 'Hey, man, what're you doin'?' Like nothing ever changed."

But, of course, things do change, as my visit with Rex Kern demonstrated. Kern's infectious grin, his flaming red hair, the fighter pilot's nerve with which he played the game are among the clear memories of my late adolescence. We met for breakfast at a Bob Evans in northwest Columbus. Kern was dressed like a middle school principal, in a nondescript tan raincoat, double-knit sport coat, powder-blue shirt with long fly-away collars, and colorful tie. His trademark red hair had thinned and faded, as if it had been left too long in the sun. I'm unrealistic enough to have been taken aback at his appearance, as if, like one of the Lost Boys, he should've remained a teenager for nearly three decades.

He's had five back surgeries and a total hip replacement. He said that sitting for too long in one position can leave him bed-ridden. He looked pale. Afraid that pain was causing him to blanch, I suggested that we cut short the interview. Kern, however, insisted we continue talking, and as we did, a remarkable change took place. His cocksure smile came back, the bruise-colored patches beneath his eyes disappeared, the crow's feet around his temples dissolved. Transformed by the intensity of his own recollections, it was as if Kern had taken off a mask that had been intended to age him 20 years. For some reason, I felt reassured.

My plan had been to talk with Buckeyes from over the depth and breadth of the program, those who had played for Earle Bruce and Cooper as well as for Hayes. However, as I should have known would happen, Woody Hayes managed to take control of the narrative. Hayes has indelibly stamped himself on every player I talked to, with the possible exception of Vogel, a thoroughly independent thinker. Remnants of Hayes live in them, almost genetically deep. They speak of him, eerily, in the present tense. It's as if all we had to do was walk over to St. John Arena and climb the winding concrete stairs into the warren of offices, and we'd find him there in the clatter and flicker of a film projector, searching the miniature silverine images for the ill-conceived formation, the revealing stance, the unrecognized tendency that would give his boys the edge against Michigan.

"He magnetized, hypnotized me," said Parker, who was such a favorite of the coach that other players referred to him as "Woody's boy." "He could take a guy with a wooden leg and make him run a hundred-yard dash."

He attracted players from all backgrounds: inner city kids like Griffin, Sanders, and Greene, who developed their skills on Police Athletic League teams; smalltown boys, like Kuhn and Mazeroski, who spent their childhoods in pickup games on grassy playgrounds; farm kids, like Johnson, Henson, and Parker, who tended livestock and played basketball in haybarns. He profoundly affected almost all of them. Greene, from a tough neighborhood in Washington, D.C., was so intimidated by Hayes's demands that he developed an ulcer, the same malady that both Tom Matte and Kern say Hayes helped visit upon them.

Hayes frequently made Stillwagon and Skladany laugh and awed Cousineau so much that the linebacker never felt comfortable in the old coach's presence, even after having been the overall number one pick in the NFL draft. He baffled Sanders, often frustrated Kern, became a second father to Parker and Johnson (although, at one point, Parker was so enraged with Hayes that he planned to murder him), left his distinct mark on Griffin, the player who most completely absorbed his every word, and infuriated Kuhn, who says, "We loved him, and we hated him."

Hayes arbitrarily denied Matte an opportunity to be elected captain, cajoled him into playing a position he did not want to play, and forced him to spend almost every free hour in the coach's company for an entire year. "He was a monster for me," Matte says. During his outstanding 12-year career with the Baltimore Colts, however, Matte would grow quite close to his old coach. "I had the endurance and ability to do what I did in the pros because of Woody Hayes," he reflects. "I can't give him any more credit than that, and this's a guy that gave me ulcers in college."

"We knew when we were there we were playing for a legend," Skladany said. "Not after. We knew right then and there."

My quest had its unusual moments. I got into Baltimore on a Saturday night and as arranged, called Jim Parker. We had planned to meet the next morning at the bar and package store he owns in the city. As we spoke that night, Parker suggested several times that he instead come out to the motel. Far too impatient to wait for anyone, I told him I'd prefer sticking to the plan. He said I could probably not find his place, but I told him all I needed were a few vague directions. He said he'd come out, and I could follow him in, but I didn't think I should inconvenience a Hall of Fame tackle any more than necessary.

The next morning, I had driven for some time around streets filled with well-dressed churchgoers carrying Bibles, before what Parker had been trying to say finally dawned on me. I was, conspicuously, the only white person in dozens of blocks, except for a couple of winos muttering in doorways. The situation didn't bother me at all, however. Nothing promotes harmony—racial and otherwise—like the considerable shared suffering playing football offers. Besides, I'm from a small river town bisected by a single road. In my childhood, one side of the road was peopled by poor Italians, the other by poor blacks. My father, the most tolerant man I've ever known, used to remind me that we were related to everyone on one side of the road and half the people on the other side. Parker's concern amused me.

I stopped the car and got out near the store, recognizable because of the lifesize plastic figure of Parker, in uniform, above the door, as if he had just pulled to lead a sweep through the malt liquor and wine cooler ads. The first people I passed on the street were two men in ankle-length white robes and colorful skull caps. They gave me a sidelong once-over and shortly after I entered the store and found Parker, came in, ostensibly to get change for a dollar, but more, I suspect, to see what I wanted in the neighborhood.

It turned out to be a splendid Sunday. Glasses perched atop his thinning grizzled hair, Parker regaled me with stories for several hours, then sent one of his four sons who work in the store across the street for wonderful, thick deli sandwiches that we shared, as people came in to buy beer, play the lottery, or shoot the breeze.

The obviousness of my skin color seemed to fade very quickly, prompting not even a second glance from most folks. That phenomenon struck me as ironic when Parker said that two decades ago, before the community began to change, some of his first customers would yell at him to keep his black hands off the wine bottles they purchased. Parker told me that he didn't care what the customers said, as long as they cleared the shelves of inventory. He had grown up in poverty, dreaming of earning enough money to get his parents out of their shotgun shack. Now, Jim Parker drives a Mercedes and owns the entire block on which his business is located.

Far more unsettling was my skiing excursion with Cousineau. Late in the afternoon, he directed the friend who was driving the Ski Nautique up a wide slow tributary stream so that Cousineau could do some barefoot tricks—shortline skiing, he called it. Cousineau and his pal began to rig a heavy boom arm that projected at a 90-degree angle from a housing in the middle of the craft. Roasting my fine pale golfer's tan, humiliated by my own pathetic attempts to get up on skis, cowed by Cousineau's tremendous athletic ability, I stood in the bobbing drag racer and watched them assemble the boom.

The boom looked as if it

couldn't possibly hold together, particularly under Cousineau's weight. Lacking any aptitude for mechanics, however, I kept quiet. As Cousineau dangled from the boom like a giant tree sloth, the driver gunned the boat. Cousineau dropped into the water, and the entire contraption flew apart. Cousineau was left behind, but the boom, tethered to the boat by Kevlar cords, leaped from its housing and—an enormous, murderous bola—whipped around, bounced off the shatter-proof windshield, and grazed the top of my head. Three inches lower, and my viscera would've splattered the deck. Cousineau and his chum expressed concern over my brush with decapitation, and, indeed, I'd been given a last-second reprieve from the guillotine. By that point, however, I was so sunburned, embarrassed, and exhausted from being bounced across the water that I didn't care what happened to me.

I suppose it was only natural that, as a former player, I would size myself up against the Bucks while I talked to them. I tried to project back over the chasm of years, erasing laugh lines, paring away excess flesh, coloring hair. How would I have fared at that level, I wondered, against athletes who are so blessed by nature that they make the belief that all men are created equal seem ridiculous?

Having performed in the big time, the Bucks, of course, weren't compelled to do the same with me. But at times, I did feel them probing at me, trying to determine if I really were a bona fide member of the brotherhood. Once in a while, one would say, "You know how it is. You were a player."

I admit I felt a certain pride at those moments. I knew then what Dave Mazeroski meant when he said that the four purgatorial years he spent as a scout team running back were made worthwhile by the occasional compliment he received from players whose names were known across the country. Most of them had been high school stars of such magnitude that they were recruited by every major football power, choosing OSU as if the university were an entrée on the bill of fare of a fabulously expensive four-star restaurant. "I walked into that stadium, and there were 83,000 people, and there was such an atmosphere, such a spirit in the place, I mean, it arrested me," said Daryl Sanders of his recruiting visit to Columbus.

I'll never have that feeling. I do remember standing with other recruits in a pre-game buffet line at the University of Pittsburgh, feeling like a sneak thief because I had lied about my size to reporters who called after I made some all-star teams. The con job went wrong when Pitt, and every major school that contacted me deemed me too small to be a linebacker and too slow to be a strong safety. Coincidentally, Tim Fox, who was not heavily recruited, tried to pull the same scam on Pitt, to the same futile end. Yes, I was small, but I was also terrified of failing. I could never make myself think like Stillwagon, who upon entering the Buckeye locker room for the first time, told a fellow freshman who was gaping at the upperclassmen, "They're no different from us, just asses with a pair of shoes on."

Henson, Fox, Kurt Schumacher, Matte, Cousineau, even the incomparable Griffin, doubted that they were good enough to ever become Buckeyes. They took their chances, though, and discovered, as Mazeroski put it, that the other players weren't "these eight-foot, 400-pound cyclops."

On the other hand, I've seen Tom Cousineau on water skis.

Would I have been happy to run the next opponent's plays for four years? Could I have endured, in the spirit of teamwork, being just another number on the roster while others made All-American, won Heisman Trophies, and went off to the NFL? Mazeroski knew from the first that he would rather serve in heaven than rule in hell. I wasn't so sure.

Whatever level it's played at, the game has to end for everyone, and, for most, that end comes hard. There is an order and security in football that isn't present in the real world, as Johnson noted when he said, "You could just look on either side of you, and you knew that guy was going to give 110 percent."

Because he had made so much money in the NFL, Schumacher had a terrible time finding anyone to hire him when his career ended. Greene counted on a decade of pro ball to give him a start in business. Instead, he was released by the Cowboys and Seahawks—"a letdown as serious as a divorce"—and forced to deal with the awful fact that he would never again be as famous as he was between the ages of 19 and 22.

Whatever his accomplishments, the game drifts away from the player. Invited to speak at the ritual Senior Tackle several years ago, Skladany, who had a distinguished NFL career, felt as if he were talking to a crowd of pampered children, none of whom was listening to him.

Granted, for some the split is easier. A first-round pick of the Lions, Sanders walked away after only four years to take a marketing position, eventually becoming a minister. Vogel played 10 seasons in Baltimore, making All-Pro five times and winning a Super Bowl, then quit and never looked back. He has little interest in football now, keeping his Ohio State tickets mainly for the joy he gets from giving them away. "Once I was done, that was it," he said.

When nagging injuries kept him

from playing as well as he felt was acceptable, Cousineau, one of the few Bucks I talked to who left the game financially secure, retired, which he says has been a mixed blessing: "Sundays have never been quite as exciting, but on Mondays, I always feel much better."

For most players, though, the end is more traumatic. As Fox, who played a dozen seasons for three NFL teams and now works as many as 80 hours a week in sales, puts it, "It's like, everybody knows they're going to die, but people don't always make the best arrangements for it."

When that torn muscle abruptly ended my playing days, I felt like I had been cut away from my moorings. With no knack for figures or using my hands or even getting along in groups, I spent another five years in school, then decided to try to understand some things by writing about them.

It goes without saying that the Bucks have been through their share of life's usual difficulties since leaving the game—the business disappointments, divorces, careers gone awry. However, if Woody Hayes actually did measure his success more by what happened to his players after they left Ohio State than by how many games they won as undergraduates, he can be happy with the men I met. They seemed to have an enviable and nearly uniform sense of values and commitment to family, community, and friends—evidence of Hayes's repeated lectures about life after football.

As I look back at those Bucks I've come to know, Champ Henson is my favorite, although Bob Vogel, who spends his Friday nights in a street ministry in a Columbus ghetto, is the one I most admire. Jim Stillwagon is the most outrageously entertaining, the man you'd most like to have a beer with. Cousineau is the apogee of what I wish I would have accomplished as a player, Jim Parker the most universally and unpretentiously renowned, Pete Johnson the most genuinely congenial, and Rex Kern the one who reminded me most vividly of the inevitability of time (and, thus, of my own mortality).

However, it is Kenny Kuhn—he of the shoulder tattoo of the Marine bulldog surrounded by four roses—with whom I can most identify. We met at a bedraggled sports bar in a small suburban shopping center. In one corner sat "The Temple of Kuhn," a wooden case containing scarred helmets, torn game jerseys, faded photographs, and dogeared game programs, all provided by Kuhn.

Others warned me that Kuhn's psyche was a foul mess of vitriol accumulated over what he believed was shoddy treatment by Hayes and, more particularly, by former defensive coordinator George Hill. Finding happiness elusive, weighed down by the world's contradictions, driven by a need to give shape and meaning to it all, Kenny Kuhn has spent an inordinate amount of time pondering his tumultuous four years as a Buck and the NFL career that never panned out. Kuhn felt as if he were trapped between two conflicting worlds—Hayes's idea of his teams, which, to Kuhn, seemed not to have evolved much since 1958, and the "special, weird time" of the 1970s, an age of shaggy haircuts, Vietnam protests, and the exploding allure of the counter-culture. "I had this idea that I wanted to be a football player, but I didn't want to be the dumb jock," said Kuhn, who wants to write a book, tentatively titled *Four Roses and a Crown of Thorns*, about his time as a Buck. The "Kuhndog," as he was known, is intelligent, archly sensitive, given to a rebellious turn of mind, and compulsively direct. He had never been loath to tell Hayes and Hill what he thought, resulting in a decade's worth of bad blood. Not until he was so overcome by emotion upon hearing of Hayes's death that he had to pull his car off the road did Kenny Kuhn begin to reconcile all he had experienced at Ohio State and afterward.

"I was a little bitter, but I could have changed a lot of things that happened to me by not doing a lot of the stupid things I did," he says now. "But when you're 25 years old, you think a lot differently than you did when you were 19, 20 years old. And you think a lot more differently when you're 39 and have a wife and two little boys."

Even after all the time I've spent talking with the Bucks and mulling over what they said to me, I can't say that I know exactly what it was like to play for Ohio State and for Woody Hayes. I quizzed and analyzed everyone from NFL Hall-of-Famers to sports reporters to fourth-string fullbacks to devoted fans.

I ordered Hayes's favorite dish (beef stew) at his favorite restaurant (the Jai Lai) while talking to one of his favorite people (Hornung). I bought the kind of ballcap Hayes preferred—plain black, emblazoned with a single red block "O"—and wore it into Ohio Stadium for games. I even began to feel that in some strange way Woody Hayes had coached me. But I am still not sure that my goal for the book was realistic. The experience is much clearer to me now, but Esco Sarkkinen was right: I am an outsider. And so I'll have to take Jim Stillwagon's word for it when he says, "When you play at Ohio State, you see how it can be."

Woody *and the* Fall *of* Saigon

HE SEEMED ALWAYS to have been the head football coach at Ohio State University, but when Wayne Woodrow Hayes arrived in Columbus in 1951, he'd already been a football coach for 16 seasons. Scowling, jut-jawed, coarse-featured Woody had won 75 percent of his games at Denison and Miami universities. He'd commanded a destroyer escort in the Pacific and bested a field of impressive candidates in a rancorous campaign for the head coach's position at Ohio State. By 1951, he'd fought often and won wherever he had fought. However, as Woody embarked on the remarkable 28-year odyssey at Ohio State during which he would become both Caesar and scourge, no sports-writer had yet revealed that Hayes had sprouted from a dragon's tooth sown in the soil of Greene County; no supplicant had sung the legend of infant Woody throttling a serpent that had crawled into his crib, although some would declare later that what he accomplished at Ohio State beggars even those marvels.

Hayes appeared in a remote age, one he would wistfully describe years later as when "the air was clean and sex was dirty." The time suited his essentially simplistic view of the world. Outnumbered F-86 Sabres dueled Russian jets over Korea; the French battled Viet Minh rebels in what would later be called Vietnam; and Joe McCarthy confided to the national VFW convention that Secretary of State Dean Acheson had been lax about ridding his department of Communists. One sipped "Coke," called jeans "dungarees," and knew a "joint" was a poolroom on the wrong side of town. The problem Hayes faced was also a simple one: Satisfy the Ohio State fans, who were, as always, rabid for a championship team.

In that distant era, no one joked about the football played at Wisconsin and Northwestern. In fact, Ohio State's program had acquired for itself the sobriquet "Graveyard of Coaches." Through his unique perspective, however, Woody Hayes was one of very few to see Columbus as, potentially, the seat of an empire. Hayes became the Buckeyes' sixth coach in 11 years. His predecessor, Wes Fesler, lasted only four seasons, leaving for the University of Minnesota on the brink of nervous collapse.

Fesler had replaced Paul Bixler, who survived only one year. Bixler had succeeded Carroll Widdoes, who escaped to Ohio University after two seasons. A year after winning the national championship at OSU, Paul Brown joined the navy. Fired in 1940, Francis Schmidt put in two losing seasons at Idaho before his death, hastened, some say, by Schmidt's failure to win in Columbus. Only someone as cussedly brazen as Woody Hayes could proclaim that he "came to Ohio State primarily for opportunity, not security."

In 1951, American universities still reeled from the college basketball betting scandals and the cribbing probe at West Point. The NCAA had laid down a 12-point "sanity code," calling for fewer scholarships and practices and curbs on recruiting. Thirty-three colleges found football either extraneous or too expensive, and dropped the game. Fearing that football's moral backbone had been twisted beyond healing, many educators insisted that "de-emphasis" could be the game's only cure. In Columbus, though, the guiding word remained *win*, and although it wasn't immediately obvious, Buckeye fans had found a coach who knew how to win as well as any in the game's history.

Despite his bluster, Hayes was

not an instant success. During his first tempestuous, mediocre season, when the Buckeyes won but four of nine games, a popular variation on "Carmen, Ohio" urged: *Come let's sing Ohio's praise. Say goodbye to Woody Hayes.* The impatient unbelievers who sang that ditty didn't realize that its subject—although one man—outnumbered them.

Woody's severe discipline and rigorous practices prompted several incipient uprisings. He admitted drilling the squad so hard that they sometimes had barely enough energy to play on Saturday. After a meager two-point victory over winless Pittsburgh, he chided several players as "clowns" and "muscleheads." Illinois earned the Rose Bowl, and Ohio State finished fifth in the conference, despite the talents of Vic Janowicz, recipient of the previous year's Heisman Trophy.

Hayes's $12,500 salary and full-professor's post appeared to be ill-advised investments. Those who had supported Paul Brown, Sid Gillman or Chuck Mather for the Ohio State job shook their heads knowingly. But those heretics had no more chance to overthrow Woody than did the anonymous callers who phoned in the middle of the night to deride him. On October 23, 1954, after two 6-3 seasons that left Hayes even more vulnerable to his critics, the grumbling ceased. Ohio State, ranked number four in the country, was losing 6–3 to number two Wisconsin in the third quarter, and the Badgers were driving toward another score, when Hopalong Cassady returned an interception 88 yards for a touchdown, a twist of fortune that provoked a three-touchdown outburst from the Buckeyes, made Ohio State number one in the country, and seated an emperor.

A month later, Michigan held the ball a foot from the Ohio State end zone, fourth down, score tied, late in the third period. Jim Parker and Jim Reichenbach joined Cassady in stopping the Wolverine fullback short of the goal line. Ohio State then drove the length of the field to win. On New Year's Day, the Buckeyes bludgeoned Southern Cal in the Rose Bowl, and at 41, Woody Hayes had secured the throne he would hold for the next 24 years against insubordination, insurrection, and invasion.

Hayes won 205 games at Ohio State, nearly three times as many as any other Buckeye coach. When he met other Big Ten teams, he won over 79 percent of the time, including a record 17 straight. He won or shared 13 conference and five national championships. Fifteen times his Buckeyes finished among the top 10 teams in the country. He coached 58 All-Americans and won four Rose Bowls. Only Amos Alonzo Stagg, Pop Warner, Bear Bryant, and Eddie Robinson won more games. He reigned for 28 years, two times longer than John Wilce, who before Hayes arrived had the longest tenure of any coach in Ohio State's history.

Woody Hayes cherished victory as a sacred spiritual possession, and like anything holy, victory couldn't be reduced in his eyes by someone else's analysis of it. Winning, he believed, requires no explanation, is its own interpretation, is the very definition of "honor." To him, the concept of winning's relative unimportance was nothing but an excuse for molly-coddles who confused cowardice with egalitarianism. He believed, along with the ancient Greeks and most of Calvinist Western civilization, in the dogma of the deserving sufferer: Prosperity correlates directly with righteousness; failure is a judgment for weakness or sloth; divine decree institutes the contest only as an ordeal though which combatants are weighed in the balance.

Hayes ignored the liberal contention that losers should have a share of the spoils. "Football," he said in 1973 to Robert Vare, author of a controversial book about Hayes and Ohio State football, "is about the only unifying force left in America today. It is certainly one of the few places in our society where teamwork, mental discipline and the value of hard work still mean anything. We stick to the old-fashioned virtues, and if the rest of the country had stuck to them, it would have been a different story in Vietnam." The implied equation was simple and steadfast: Acid rain and the New Morality usurp clean air and dirty sex, and Saigon falls to the Viet Cong.

Woody dominated often and without apology, winning those 205 games by an average score of 30–9. Convinced that the world consists only of winners and those unworthy to win, Woody Hayes never considered negotiation. Even so noble a foe as the Michigan Wolverines, should they come tainted to the trial by combat, could expect no quarter. Having trounced eight consecutive teams by a mean score of 31–15, Ohio State entered the 1968 Michigan game ranked second in the country. The Wolverines were rated number four. Late in the game, ahead 44–14, Hayes became angry when a reserve fullback was halted for no gain at the Michigan two. Hayes sent in starting fullback Jim Otis to score his fourth touchdown of the afternoon, then tried a two-point conversion. After the game, he told a reporter that "50 points and nothing less" was the only safe margin in modern college football.

Ohio State rooters had their champion. And for a city and a state so eager for a winner, Woody Hayes did more than win. Through the social morality play that football has become, he verified the superiority of an entire way of life. His preoccupation with scores and records showed Hayes to be enormously pragmatic. He saw life in concrete terms, yet became a hero/villain through a game that has evolved into a convergence of abstractions. If war is the romance of history, football is the romance of modern America. Football is codified warfare for a people nauseated by actual war, a nation expressing its aggressive instincts through isolated, nonfatal clashes.

In the clashes of autumn, we replace the avoidance of death with the avoidance of defeat. Knowing almost nothing of football's subtleties, we can revel in the spectacle, quaffing liquids to dull our more rational senses, and painting our faces with arcane emblems. In this fantastic tableau, successful coaches are elevated to feudal barons, rulers as well as icons reflecting what we imagine our own finest qualities to be. Certainly, Woody Hayes didn't escape this phenomenon. More than any of his contemporaries—more than any coach in history, save, perhaps, Rockne or Lombardi—Woody was held up as a token.

At one time, this headstrong, rugged son of a school superintendent embodied everything good about life in Mid-America. He worked his way from neighborhood tough to outstanding student at Dension University to naval officer to winning coach. His was a natural-born fighter's visage, as dour, beefy, and pugnacious as Teddy Roosevelt's. High priest of free enterprise, hard and ready defender of the Republic, Woody symbolized the time-honored American verities of industriousness, order, martial virtue, sacrifice, individuality, courage, and patriotism.

With their unerring animal instincts for such matters, politicians courted Hayes. Governors lent a hand in recruiting; presidents embraced him. Every Saturday, Woody's puritanical, republican, "high-button shoe" brand of football made a personal and political statement. That statement struck a sympathetic chord among conservatives, who were reassured by the elemental sight of Ohio State's offense, the basis of which was a powerful fullback "grinding meat" through the middle of an opposing defense. Fullback and offensive tackle were the two positions that came to be identified most strongly with Ohio State football—hard-working, blue-collar positions unsullied by the hype and tinsel surrounding tailbacks at Southern California or quarterbacks at Notre Dame. Hayes was held up as a token, and he often seemed fiercely proud of personifying certain values. When demonstrators protested Kent State and the invasion of Cambodia in 1970, Hayes roamed the campus, lecturing them, certain that a return to discipline and hard work would resolve any problem. Hayes did four tours in Vietnam, supporting the war effort and bemoaning the public timorousness that prevented a swift end to the conflict. Claiming he didn't want to politicize the position he held, Hayes wouldn't greet Lyndon Johnson when the president visited Columbus; yet he exuberantly clasped hands with his friends Richard Nixon and Gerald Ford when they stopped by.

If Woody's methods were sometimes harsh, they were forgiven. *Life* once praised him for cudgeling a player into a better performance, the implication being that Hayes's great demands imbued his young men with characteristics that kept the land safe for democracy, and that sparing the rod could indeed spoil the child. Besides, Woody's record spoke for itself.

Hayes seemed larger than life. Year round, he worked 18-hour days and failed to pay proper attention to the diabetes with which he was afflicted. Money and social trappings didn't concern him. He lived in an unpretentious frame house, worked for 28 years in spartan offices that were little more than a bulge in the concrete corridors of St. John Arena, refused numerous raises, and didn't own a credit card. He ignored even the vagaries of nature. "If it's 30 degrees, Woody will wear one T-shirt. If it's zero, he'll wear two," Jim Parker, the great former OSU guard once said. "Feeling cold is psychological," Hayes declared.

Even when he suffered a heart attack in 1974, Hayes didn't flinch, despite his family's history of heart trouble, and the fact that his brother had died of a heart attack at age 44. The very day after entering the hospital, Hayes dictated a letter to his squad, assuring them he would be their coach that fall. "After my heart attack the doctor said I had to turn over more of the work to my assistants," Hayes said before that season began. "Hell, that lasted about 10 minutes. I don't worry about my heart attack, because as Napoleon said, I'd rather die a winner than live a loser."

Though embarrassed by such evidence of his mortality, he accepted encouragement from Richard Nixon, Gerald Ford, and Bo Schembechler, acquiesced to wear a windbreaker on freezing days, and won another Big Ten title by beating Michigan by two points when, with 16 seconds left, the Wolverine placekicker missed a field goal.

The Woody Hayes legend developed, and as it did, it attracted petitioners. Spectators filled huge stadiums to praise and jeer it. Devotees brought gifts to enrich it. Reporters wrote stories to perpetuate it. Television universalized it. Acolytes learned from it. Strong, swift young men fought for it.

Hayes had unbounded faith in the significance of what he did. He once told a reporter, "I see my job as a part of American civilization and as a damn important part. I see football as being just so much above everything else."

Woody expressed that belief, as he did all of his beliefs, readily and ferociously. But for a man so widely read in history, he appeared to view life as a child does, as a simple world shaded only in whites and blacks. He probably never entertained the idea that no other human endeavor both requires and creates as much emotion as football, yet is of such inconsequence to society and history. The game makes the trivial appear important, the important seem trivial. That it can arouse such passion without doing permanent, widespread damage is both the best and the worst thing about football. And anything capable of conceiving such feeling in its favor can surely raise as much against it.

One knew well on which side of the question Woody Hayes, always terrible in the intensity of his convictions, stood. At the tempestuous center of any confrontation, he remained undeterred, convinced that taking his team to see *Easy Rider* the night before a game nearly cost him a loss, and that watching *Patton* spurred the Buckeyes to one of their greatest efforts.

Convinced that holding his tongue would give him an ulcer, Hayes said just what he thought about officials, opponents, reporters, administrators, peers, freaks, gays, Commies, and anyone else he was of a mind to reprove. He called everything by its right name, or at least the name by which he knew it. After beating USC in the 1955 Rose Bowl, he infuriated the West Coast by commenting that five other Big Ten teams were better than Southern Cal.

Should he have lied to those California reporters, he wanted to know, or gone ahead and told them the truth?

Believing that winners deserve fealty, he saw no reason to be magnanimous in victory. Inconsistently, however, he was rarely gracious in defeat. As much as he detested losing, Hayes found, however it might have shocked him, that winning could be just as dangerous. A commander fixated on kill ratios can outrun his supply columns. Not everyone was as committed to complete victory as was Woody. For years, he and Jack Fullen, executive secretary of the Ohio State alumni association, battled over the part football should play in the university. After routing Michigan in 1961, the Buckeyes were conference champions and ranked number one by UPI. Nevertheless, the faculty council voted 28–25 against Ohio State's attending the Rose Bowl. Angry fans demonstrated for two days, and

Woody hardened in his resolve to maintain the dominance and impregnability of his kingdom. As it turned out, he shoud have taken the faculty's vote as a portent.

The decade wore on, and admiration of success—financial, military, or athletic—began to be tempered. To some, the results of conquest were more repellent that its romance had been attractive. In Vietnam, we wanted an army willing to die but feared having one eager to kill. Hayes's philosophy, centered on a single idea, as it must be, began to offend some. "We're tearing down all our heroes in America," he told Robert Vare. "And I can tell you, a society that's always tearing down its heroes is a suicidal society. A civilization without heroes isn't going to be a civilization much longer."

Hayes, who in the early '60s still piped Mitch Miller music into the locker room, failed to recognize that what had once been heroic had quickly become archaic. On the threshold of a new age, heroes assumed odd forms, emerged from unlikely settings. This was a time when Peter Fonda's Captain American could be every bit as much a hero as George C. Scott's Patton.

In this changing time, itself contradictory, Woody Hayes became a great enigma, a helplessly protean creature whose form was chosen by those who interpreted his actions: benevolent despot and dangerous misanthrope; spokesman for the old verities and cracker-barrel spouter of warmed-over fascist screeds; circuit rider preaching faith in democratic institutions and false prophet calling for prayer and ammunition in the same sermon; a primitive suited only for the barracks-yard and an earnest soldier with the courage of his convictions; a builder of character and a martinet who whipped mercenaries into combat units; erudite friend of distinguished professors and loutish, vulgar jock. He was frank, bold, guileless, daring, fearless, dynamic, caring, charming, witty, scholarly, and creative as well as gruff, scornful, boorish, contentious, willful, egocentric, childish, profane, petty, and antiquated.

The very desire to win that had been his greatest strength and protection was also his tragic flaw. Like Oedipus, he was assailed for doing the very things that had once earned him great praise. Richard Nixon succinctly capsulized the anomalies when, as president, he called Hayes and asked him to direct the Peace Corps, a fitting office given that Hayes had been both born on Valentine's Day and named student instructor of boxing at Denison.

Hayes said that what concerned him about this new America was that each of its citizens had decided to live according to his own rules. The fact is, Woody himself was easily moved to anarchy. He bit the heel of his hand until blood flowed, pummeled himself about the face, smashed film projectors, crushed eyeglasses and watches, struck players, cursed his enemies in public. He said of his temper in 1976, "I probably have more trouble controlling my emotions now than I did when I was a young man in my fifties."

From the first time he faced Michigan, Woody surrounded his career with a pagan frieze of grotesque scenes depicting his frequent titanic rages, the worst of which were called "megatons" by his staff. Early in his tenure at Ohio State, Hayes nearly came to blows with Iowa coach Forest Evashevsky, whom he accused of allowing the grass to grow so long it would hamper the Buckeye running game. He set upon a cameraman after a loss to Iowa in 1956 and a sportswriter and bystander after losing a 1959 game to USC, an act that prompted public censure from the American Football Coaches Association. As he ran off the field following a loss to Michigan State in 1974, a defeat that ended his streak of regular-season victories and spoiled an undefeated year, Woody elbowed a heckler in the mouth. Minutes later, he threatened to ram his fist down a reporter's throat and excoriated the officiating, earning a reprimand from the Big Ten.

In 1977, Big Ten commissioner Wayne Duke placed him on a year's probation for swinging at an ABC cameraman who chose the inopportune moment of a Buckeye fumble against Michigan to record Hayes's reactions. Had he committed any unsportsmanlike act during that final season, Hayes would have been suspended for two games. Characteristically unrelenting, he remarked about the incident, "You get doggone tired of cameras being pushed in your face. I'm fed up with it. I make no apologies."

Some explained Haye's explosions by saying, "That's just Woody." A laconic assumption that some quirk in his make-up, some demon of insecurity, was the real target of his vehemence. Indeed, he often remarked that he'd been the least talented child in his family. At a banquet following his first season at Ohio State, he said, "If people don't criticize me, there's something wrong with them. I passed in front of a mirror this morning and almost took a swing at myself."

When players and coaches seemed inordinately sympathetic with Hayes's outbursts, they were more than maintaining the fraternal barrier between themselves and the civilian population. They were also acknowledging that football forces everyone to the edge, that it can appear to encourage a vicious reaction to almost any situation, that the state of "controlled violence" the game demands is a precarious condition, that anyone can go over the edge given the proper circumstances. Woody's command to his offensive team to abandon all frills and "put the hats on those bastards" ordered his players to reach back to a primal subconscious. The deliberate stimulation of that instinct for pugnacity fascinates the spectator and makes football one of those few games in which the player is in constant peril of serious injury as a direct consequence of the game's specific functions.

Although many of Hayes's malevolent acts couldn't be justified, a system that transforms a game into combat and then persecutes a warrior for excessively desiring victory is fraught with hypocrisy. Regardless of the reactions of those around him, Woody continued to rage, and each time he did, he made himself more of a hero, a villain, an antihero, and a dilemma.

Woody's was a severe world in which he was measured by a game's final score, a season's record. Cultists can glorify such an existence, but few can endure its demands. Tightrope walkers, test pilots, soldiers of fortune, high-rolling gamblers, and big-time criminals know its rigors and attractions. The average fan, though, is hopelessly removed from the kind of life in which one ventures everything on a series of winner-take-all wagers. Hundreds of thousands could examine Woody Hayes each Saturday, then go home, eat dinner, and fall asleep on the couch.

He existed among unforgiving absolutes, not justifying his inflexibility by claiming to act under the aegis of a higher power, preparing no allowances for failure by minimizing the significance of success, refusing to bargain by arranging alternate opportunities, or accumulating wealth. Hayes was determined to thrive or perish in his harsh corner of extreme reality.

The volcanic irascibility that brought Hayes so much attention lay next to a tremendous capacity for kindness and sentiment. At the jointure of those two contradictory sides of his nature, one finds a large part of the phenomenon that was Woody Hayes. He was moved as easily to tears as to anger, caring enormously for those who were faithful to his capricious standards, mercilessly attacking his enemies. On the same day he took the poke at the ABC cameraman, he called a hospitalized Columbus police officer to whom he'd promised the game ball, and apologized for losing to Michigan.

Always the rugged individualist, he sought identity with groups and causes. He expressed the elitist opinion that each should make his own way, but was impulsively generous with his time and possessions. A romantic who believed that within the individual are the resources to accomplish all, he also had a Machiavellian perception of man's inborn weakness. Suspicious of nonconformists, he was himself the exuberant eccentric who'd call an assistant at two in the morning to regale him with passages from James Whitcomb Riley. He paid officials to establish discipline by calling penalties during practice, then shouted at them for making bad calls. Many of his players feared and detested him, and many hoped to become half the man he was. He kept his number in the telephone book, but was uniformly inaccessible to most of the press. He constantly alluded to the military life, studied its history and strategies, but ended his own service career after five years. He espoused democracy and practiced monarchy. Sometimes an aloof bully, he could also rue his isolation: "When you come out of that stadium an hour and a half after a game and there's no one out there to congratulate you, it gets pretty lonely. You love it when a little kid happens to come up and say, 'Good game, Mr. Hayes.'"

Woody had little of the Free Companion in him. Uninterested in securing personal wealth, he seems also to have been too nonmaterialistic to ply recruits with cash and cars, too prudish to procure them girls, and too strong a believer in education to alter transcripts or set up bogus courses. Although he didn't agree that athletic scholarships should be based solely on a player's financial need—a concept that smacked of socialism to him—Hayes's recruiting methods differed from those of many of his contemporaries. While other coaches took to the streets like the seventeenth-century military recruiters who paraded with fifers and drummers, stopping to entice young men by shaking a hat full of silver over a table stocked with food and drink, Hayes seems to have relied on his record, the Ohio State tradition he forged and, he'd occasionally admit, his charisma.

In 1956, Ohio State did receive the most stringent punishment meted out by the conference in 25 years, but judged by today's preposterous standards, OSU's crimes barely qualify as misdemeanors: Woody lending players money from his own pocket or the department finding them campus jobs that required little work. If it seems implausible that Hayes could win so often for so long without soiling his hands on the prosaic realities of big-time college football, it is less likely that he could've managed to cheat for such a time under the tweaked noses of his numerous enemies, who included many members of the press. Hayes had even less aptitude than did Patton for public relations, a skill, to his view, useful only to milksops, and it irritated him that those he thought unfit to judge him scrutinized his every move. To Hayes, freedom of the press was an invitation to sedition.

Blunt by nature, he had difficulty withholding his true feelings, then was furious to find himself revealed in the public prints. His was not an insular wall of silence, but one of contempt. The day before his final game, he ungracefully called the reporters at a press conference "nosy pipsqueaks."

Hayes played out his attitude toward the press in a brief, one-act drama shortly before the 1978 season began. A Columbus television reporter mentioned to Hayes that 56 percent of those responding to a recent survey believed he should retire. Hayes answered with his normal aplomb: "Those 56 percent probably weren't even living when I started winning here. No, I'm not interested. I'm not going to worry about that. Sure, people are fickle, and I don't much care. There's no one in this league or any other league that has won as many games as I have. I'm not going to let their opinion decide this thing. And if you're one of the 56 percent, I don't give a damn about you, either."

He paused in front of the reporter to say, "And if you don't like it, you can go straight to hell."

The reporter started to respond, and Hayes said, "I just wish you were bigger and stronger. I'd take you on."

For 28 seasons, he took them all on. When the media finally saw their chance for reprisal, though, they reacted with all the sanguinary enthusiasm of the Grand Master of Malta, who, in revenge for some atrocities committed by the Turks, massacred all of his prisoners and shot their heads from his cannon into the Turkish camp.

Not just the national press awaited and predicted Hayes's downfall. After the Buckeyes lost the 1976 Rose Bowl to UCLA, a columnist in Ohio State's *The Lantern* criticized Woody's behavior as inexcusable and claimed the coach had become an embarrassment to the University. Many joined the movement to demand his abdication.

But retirement was unlikely for a man who couldn't abide vacations. Woody was, above all else, a combat commander. How could he quit the parades, the rallies, and the midnight victory serenades, blaming his attraction to arms on a certain passing heat in the liver, as Descartes had? Hayes had found time to make few social connections or develop hobbies. Golf, fishing or hunting didn't interest him. It's difficult to imagine him spending a sedentary afternoon casting for bass. He'd either measure every catch against a chart of world records or leap in to meet the slimy buggers nose-to-nose. The prospect of Woody after he dubbed an approach shot to number 17—eyes bulging, jowls purple, neck swollen, seven-iron clutched in meaty paw— would make gathering a foursome impossible. Could he stroll away from that supreme theatre of human strenuousness in which he'd spent most of his life and, like his military heroes, just fade away, distorted by sallow fatness, haunting pep rallies, Rotary luncheons, and press boxes?

He supposedly once said that he preferred to die on the 50-yard line at Ohio Stadium in front of the usual crowd of 87,000, a romantic ending for the legend. At 60, he told Robert Vare he'd know when the time had come and would have enough sense to get up and walk out the door. He said that his record spoke for itself and only the players could fire him. Everyone associated with him knew he'd fought too long and too hard to go gently into any good night. Lombardi died. Frank Howard became infirm. Paul Brown and George Halas slipped upstairs to management. Bear Bryant was ornery enough to say it'd all been a big joke and stroll off chuckling to raise hogs. But they were going to have to kill Woody, or chase him away. He couldn't, as the ancient Macedonians did, simply purge himself of battle lust by cutting a dog in two and marching between its parts while praying to the gods of peace and the hearth.

At least in football Woody had some yardstick by which to measure himself, and he always knew who the enemy was. He never had to be concerned with the creeping sense of purposelessness that has become a chronic ill of a society with no central motivation. The supreme goal was the perfect season, the win over Michigan, the Rose Bowl. His enemy was always easily identified and clear in his intentions. The foe wore maize and blue and sang "Hail to the Victors." He was Bo, Rick Volk, Ron Johnson, Glenn Doughty, Rick Leach. The lines were clearly drawn. But outside of football, pain comes in countless, spurious forms. An unstable white-cell count, a thin-walled blood vessel, a boss in foul temper, a mugger, a false friend, a drunken driver, a doctor who forgets a sponge inside your body after a gall bladder operation—all injure with no warning. Such an enemy doesn't attack in formation or adhere to the rules of the Geneva Convention. Woody's life in football had its pressures, but it also had its certainties. Measurement is reassurance, the unknown alarming.

His final year began badly, with a loss in a Sugar Bowl game that had been billed as the battle of legends: Woody against Bear Bryant, the only active coach to have won more games than he. Between them, Hayes and Bryant totaled 128 years, 65 seasons of college head coaching, and 503 victories. Favored by a point and a half, Alabama dealt Hayes his worst beating in 11 years, 35–6.

When Ozzie Newsome caught a 29-yard pass to put Alabama in position for its first touchdown, Woody ripped off his scarlet windbreaker and slammed it down. Trotting off the field at halftime, head down, he ran into a goalpost. Startled, he threw a left hook at it. Spectators howled. He shook his fist at them. Bear went ahead of Woody by 51 wins. Remarkably candid and self-effacing, Hayes said, "They had half as much material as we did, but we had one-fourth as much coaching."

The year ended worse than it began. By the end of the season, Hayes had four more losses, two on them on national television, giving him seven consecutive defeats before network audiences. He also had much less a sense of proportion. Before the 1978 Gator Bowl, he said, "This game of football used to be pretty important to me. It isn't anymore. Now it's just damn near everything. It represents and embodies everything that's great about this country, because the United States is built on winners, not losers or people who don't bother to play."

Two days later, he was done with football forever.

During a luncheon prior to the Gator Bowl, sportscaster Keith Jackson presented Hayes with a pair of boxing gloves. After the final gun, the joke became an eerily prophetic moment. At a press conference before that game, Danny Ford, not quite 30 and facing his first game as a head coach, said he was tempted to ask Woody Hayes, 65 and facing his 350th game as a head coach, for an autograph. Thirty-six hours later, Ford said he would've been satisfied with an apology.

Prior to kickoff that December 29, Charlie Bauman was a squat sophomore middle guard trying to make Clemson University's first team. By game's end, he'd become one of those innumerable bit players who are swept into history by forces they don't begin to understand, let alone control.

Throughout the 1978 season, Art Schlichter, Ohio State's freshman quarterback, gained notoriety as the one player gifted enough to convince Woody Hayes to abandon his hedgerow-to-hedgerow offense and begin to throw. In the fourth quarter of the Gator Bowl, as a national television audience watched, Schlichter transformed himself into the unwitting agent of destined retribution.

With 1:59 remaining in the game and the career, Woody Hayes's contradictions finally synthesized. Behind 17–15, Schlichter led his team downfield. On third and five from the Clemson 24, he underthrew halfback Ron Springs, and Charlie Bauman intercepted the first pass of his life. The Buckeyes drove Bauman out of bounds in front of Hayes. Woody slugged the player under the chin. In that impulsively violent moment, the puzzle of Wayne Woodrow Hayes, that enigma cloaked in a mystery, forever crystallized, and he froze in time as mastermind, megalomaniac, and martyr. The final image is a strange Laocoön grouping: Three figures—Hayes, Bauman, and another Clemson player trying to intervene—linked by a serpent of flailing arms. It was an act, like Achilles' destruction of the Trojan youths, that couldn't go unpunished, despite the hero's past deeds.

The 1978 Gator Bowl was no place for a soldier to pass, a meaningless working vacation for two also-rans with five losses between them. The Gator was an opening act for the headliner bowls in Pasadena, Dallas, New Orleans, and Miami, a chance for the city of Jacksonville, Clemson, Ohio State, and ABC to have a payday. Two days later, John Robinson's USC Trojans claimed half the national championship by beating Bo Schembechler's Michigan Wolverines on a touchdown that was never scored. Bear Bryant, sans houndstooth hat, seized the remaining half of the title by beating Joe Paterno, who made a crucial mistake by having too many players on the field at a key moment, then said, what the heck, the whole business wasn't so important anyway.

Paterno was probably right. The Jonestown slaughter and a 14.5 percent hike in crude prices by OPEC were still fresh. Just a few days before the Gator Bowl, 90,000 Vietnamese regulars had swarmed into Cambodia, and the Shah had named Shahpur Bakhtiar prime minister-designate, then fled into seclusion. Woody's wasn't even the only peculiar act of violence perpetrated by a coach against an opposing player that season. Fairfield University part-time coach Ed Hall had just seen his team go ahead of Western New England by a point when Jim Brown, Western's star runner, took the ensuing kickoff, eluded tacklers, and raced up the sideline. At midfield, the 48-year-old high school gym teacher made a perfect tackle on the 195-pound Brown.

"Are you out of your mind, Coach?" Brown asked.

"I guess I am," Hall said.

The press treated Hall as a kind of slapstick "Wrong Way" Roy Riegels or a modern Tommy Davis, who came off the Alabama bench to tackle Rice's Dicky Moegle as Moegle streaked for the goal line. Woody Hayes did not receive such light handling. *The Washington Post* went page one with a story and a photo over the caption "Goodbye Columbus." *The New York Times* ran a front-page story and, the next day, another on page one of the sports section. Sportswriters described the incident as everything from a "final pathetic flameout" to "a memorable comedy" to a case of "arrested development." One writer selected Clemson as the nation's number one team, based solely on its part in Hayes's demise. *The Columbus Dispatch*'s headline read, "Woody Hayes Resigns."

Hayes had told Paul Hornung, the paper's sports editor, that he had quit. Actually, Hayes, uncompromising to the end, refused to resign and was fired the morning after the Gator Bowl. The sun didn't turn black, the earth didn't sink into the sea, the old serpent and his brood didn't gnaw through the tree of the universe, Woody Hayes wasn't borne off to Valhalla by the Valkyries. A porno house in Columbus put the epitaph "Bye, Bye, Woody" on its marquee beside a come-on for a Linda Lovelace flick, and Hayes went home to face life without football, but with arthritis and double gall bladder surgery.

At a chamber of commerce luncheon three weeks after the Gator Bowl, Hayes told an audience of 1,200, "I got what was coming to me." He said, "Nobody despises to lose more than I do. That's what got me into trouble over the years, but it also made a man with mediocre ability into a pretty good coach." The crowd, each of whom had paid $15, gave him two standing ovations.

Earle Bruce, once Hayes's apprentice, took the job and went 11-0 in his first season. After an 18–15 comeback win over Michigan, fans took to the streets of Columbus to throw bottles, smash parking meters, tear down street signs, and break windows. Bruce lost the national championship by two points in the Rose Bowl. In subsequent seasons, Bruce listened to complaints that Woody would've done better, before he, too, was fired. His replacement, John Cooper, has listened to the same litany of complaints and suffered by the same comparison.

Hayes, for his part, was lionized and canonized in various ways. Shortly after the Gator Bowl, Senator Thomas Van Meter attempted to introduce a bill in the State Senate commending Hayes for his 28 years of service. Senate President Oliver Ocasek refused to accept the resolution. Upon reintroduction the bill passed. Senator Harry Meshel cast the only dissenting vote. Van Meter retaliated by voting "No" on Meshel's resolution expressing sadness at the death of a former member of the Youngstown City Council.

In 1978, such diverse luminaries as Gerald Ford, Ann-Margret, Shirley MacLaine, Cloris Leachman, Paul Anka, Bud Wilkinson, Don Shula, and Yogi Berra turned up at a $150-a-plate benefit roast of Hayes. *Rocky* producer Gene Kirkwood wanted to film Hayes's life story. Ohio State Trustees approved a resolution changing the name of Stadium Drive to Woody Hayes Drive. Over 450 of Woody's former players came to a 1979 reunion honoring their old coach. In a less obvious acknowledgment of Hayes's achievements, Iowa, Iowa State, Wisconsin, Indiana, and Illinois began to win occasionally in the Big Ten.

The most fitting tribute to Hayes came after his death, not when 10,000 attended a public service at Ohio Stadium, not when Richard Nixon delivered the eulogy at First Community Church, but when dozens of anonymous fans placed red roses on the stadium's turf.

Wayne Woodrow Hayes, the man, probably never lived up to Woody Hayes, the coach. It couldn't have been otherwise. A finite man does not have infinite qualities. He never walked across the Olentangy River, as former Ohio State basketball coach Fred Taylor once joked Hayes had. Grumpy, stubborn, volatile, sentimental, dedicated to battle, disdaining social status, wealth, and liberalism, he came along in a once-upon-a-time.

America had just begun to reexamine the success ethic that had guided her for 175 years. College football was divesting itself of the vestiges of being any uplifting tradition of academic life and was moving toward consumerism and gaudy entertainment for a public increasingly willing to accept the lie, as long as it is nicely packaged. Like Earl Blaik, Bernie Bierman, Frank Howard, Jock Sutherland, Frank Leahy, General Bob Neyland, and Bud Wilkinson, Hayes was gradually fading into the dusty shelves of our archives. His legend has become hazy. Compulsively idolatrous, we quickly create new heroes.

Was he the Congressman Wayne Hayes with the blonde secretary who couldn't type? No. That was Wayne B. He's not that one. And he wasn't Bob, Helen, Elvin, Gabby, nor Isaac (although both his grandfather and brother were), nor Rutherford B., nor Ira M. The first ran faster but didn't cover nearly as much ground. The second acted almost as well. The third played basketball. The fourth, God forbid, made a career out of being the butt of jokes. The fifth was Moses only to blacks. The sixth was a U.S. president (with whom Woody once wished he could claim kinship). The last one was also a hero, but he died a broken man, an ending that Woody did not, for even a moment, consider, nor was it ever considered for him. This one is Hayes, Woody. Look under *Hayes, W.W.* There's only one entry.

Moobie Foobie

HE WAS RAISED in a shotgun shack near Macon, Georgia, one of a trackgang laborer's six children. He was a dreamer searching the sports pages for news of his heroes—Joe DiMaggio, Joe Lewis, Charley Trippi, Vic Janowicz—and imagining that he would achieve such fame. A burst appendix and peritonitis left him, at 15, with "no means, no ends, no physical ability, six feet tall, weighin about 110 pound, 120 pound."

He spent two unremarkable seasons as a "puny" junior varsity lineman, then, planning to join the service, moved to Toledo to live with an aunt. During his final two years of high school, he worked three jobs to support himself ("It was holy hell"). He was woefully unprepared for academics at Ohio State and lacked even the rudimentary skills required of a major college player. He was told by coaches—including Woody Hayes—that only a fixed number of blacks could play at one time and was banned from segregated hotels. Humiliated in his first professional game, he told his coach not to waste a plane ticket on him; he was quitting and would find his own way home.

Nonetheless, the standard analysis of Jim Parker's career holds that Parker was a force of nature, a man so gifted that his becoming one of the celebrated athletes of his generation was as inevitable as a summer thunderstorm.

Hayes chanced upon Parker during a visit to Toledo. He heard that the best player around was jockeying cars at a nearby garage. The impulsive Hayes found Parker and offered him a scholarship. Through he had never owned so much as a bicycle, Parker turned down inducements from cash to convertibles to play for Hayes, who guaranteed him nothing. "I was promised the moon by some," Parker says. "Woody didn't promise me the moon. He said, 'You don't get anything on a silver platter here.' And I didn't."

Parker was the rawest of recruits. Assistant coaches Harry Strobel and Bill Hess endlessly drilled him, Hess's wife tutored him, and Hayes became "something like a father image." And as a sophomore, Parker was a two-way starter on only the third unbeaten team in OSU history. During his three seasons, the Bucks won 17 straight conference games, two Big Ten titles, and a national championship.

Parker's ferocious blocking was even credited with helping to spawn Hayes's notoriously conservative offense. Hopalong Cassady won the 1955 Heisman behind Parker, but regardless of who carried the ball—Jerry Harkrader, Bobby Watkins, Hubert Bobo, Jim Roseboro—300-yard rushing games were common while he played at OSU. However, Parker first came to national attention as a defensive player. In 1954, Michigan had a first down at the OSU three late in a close game. Parker led the stand that stopped the Wolverines a foot from a touchdown. A subsequent 99 2/3 yard scoring drive sent Hayes to his first Rose Bowl, where Parker's fumble recovery set up the Buckeyes's first touchdown of the 20–7 win over USC. He was a twice All-American and Ohio State's first Outland Trophy winner. He would eventually be named to both the all-time NCAA team and to the College Football Hall of Fame.

Before Parker, Hayes's record was so unexceptional that one magazine referred to him as "a bumbling devil incarnate," and his appreciation for the role Parker played in securing his job—along with his tendency to identify with the underprivileged—made Hayes openly fond of his huge prodigy. "If he told me, 'Go out there and move that stadium two inches to the right or four inches forward,' I would do it," Parker says.

The two men demonstrated their mutual loyalty when the Big Ten investigated Ohio State for, among other matters, Hayes's practice of giving money to needy players. Lest he embarrass them, Hayes refused to name the players, while Parker insisted to Commissioner Tug Wilson that he often received money from relatives.

All wasn't uniformly peaceful between Parker and Hayes, however. Hayes inexplicably held him out of a Dad's Day game, the only game Parker missed in three years and the only one his parents could attend. Murder in his heart, Parker barged into the post-game press conference. "I planned to kill him," he says. "I said, 'He's gone, he's gone. That sonofabitch, I'm gonna lay him out.'"

The relationship was patched up, enough so that Hayes would say of Parker, "I'm not sure that there has ever been a greater offensive guard. He was everything an offensive lineman should be," and for Parker to maintain that of everyone he's known, Hayes remains his favorite person.

Drafted by Baltimore, Parker immediately realized that he knew nothing about pass protection. The Colts threw 47 times in his first game, and Parker was embarrassed. He pleaded with defensive linemen to stay after practices so that he could learn to pass block. "That's where it all started from, by workin,' workin' and whuppin,' whuppin,' whuppin,'" he says. "The secret is, I put a lot of work into it."

Parker took extensive notes on pass rushers and developed a library of film clips. His devotion cost him his first marriage but earned Parker a spot on *Sports Illustrated's* all-time NFL team as a pass blocker.

Baltimore's overtime win against New York in the 1958 NFL championship game marked a turning point both in Parker's career and in the public view of offensive linemen. Johnny Unitas completed 26 of 40 passes that day, and fans and writers took note of Parker's epic struggle with Giant end Andy Robustelli. Parker became the archetypal offensive lineman, 275 pounds of speed, strength and technique, a spectre dredged up from a defensive back's nightmares: Parker bearing down, with relish, on a 180-pound safety, massive white helmet like a battering ram, eyes narrowed, hands taped like a boxer's, treetrunk legs churning, Lenny Moore peeping over his ax-handle-wide shoulders. "When I walked on that field on Sunday and I looked at you, it wasn't *if* I was gonna whup your ass, it was *how bad* I was gonna whup your ass," he says.

Parker is the only man on the

NFL's 75th Anniversary team who could well have been the greatest player at either of two positions. In 11 seasons, he made All-Pro four times at tackle, three times at guard and once at both positions. He was elected to the Hall of Fame the first year he became eligible.

Serious, good-natured, and superstitious, Parker—who for obscure reasons was nicknamed "Moobie Foobie" by his Colt teammates—became the subject of numerous amusing stores and the butt of dozens of practical jokes. As he reminisced in the package store he owns in Baltimore, he laughed frequently and heartily. He kibitzed with customers who strolled in for wine coolers, six packs, and boxes of margarita mix, and played the dozens with three of his sons, who chided him about his weight, his horrendous driving, and his receding hairline. Parker's denim shirt hung over faded jeans. Bifocals perched in his grizzled hair. He lisped slightly because his front bridge was shoved under the sun visor in his white Mercedes.

He is a marvelous storyteller who speaks honestly of his accomplishments; nevertheless, Parker seems not quite able to believe that he is even more famous than he imagined he would become. He is, after all, the All-Pro who never brought more than one small bag to training camp, so that if he were released, he could make the next practice with a new team.

"From the time I first stepped on Woody's campus in 1953, I had a dream that I thought I could reach," he says. "I wanted to be the best player in college, and I wanted to be the best player at my position in professional football."

Certainly, a player of his prominence who retired today wouldn't be running a liquor store, but Parker appears content. His vivid, persistent memories of poverty have made him an astute businessman. He enjoys recounting clever real estate deals and remembers gross sales for every year since he bought the business. Memorabilia cluttered the cramped store. Cases of liquor and beer, all of which, Parker said, would be sold in a day, were piled almost to the ceiling. Letters from fans fill his mailbox. Twice a month, he appears at card shows to sign autographs. Admirers beg to purchase his old helmets, spikes, and jerseys. "It seem like the older you get, the more valuable you get," he says.

Occasionally, someone would come into the store to buy lottery tickets. Parker would take the person's list of numbers, cram himself into a cubicle behind the counter and pull his glasses down onto the bridge of his nose. Then he would hunch over the ticket machine and squint as he punched in numbers, dispensing dreams.

Jim PARKER

"MY BROTHER WAS A BIG football hero in Georgia. When his teams played Ft. Valley or any of the other teams in that area, the team bus would stop at our house. We had three rooms that you could look right through, from the front to the back, with an outdoor toilet and outdoor water. They would bring their teams there to eat, and everybody from the neighborhood would flock around because he was home. All the way through high school, he was a sideshow, palmin two balls and everything. I was the third child, I was sittin back and watchin all this notoriety he was gettin, and I wasn't gettin any.

I started dreamin about it, started readin the sports page. I was a dreamer. I was dreamin about how I could get them out of this poverty. We was a family, but what could we do? We had two in college, and I knew they couldn't afford to send me. I wanted to play football, and my mother told me I couldn't.

She didn't want me to get hurt, but my dad said, 'There's no such word in our vocabulary in this house as 'can't.' We're not goin to let you use *can't*.' If I would've stayed in Georgia, I couldn'ta won the scholarship. I knew that, so I went to Toledo. I had gained a little weight, because my mother went to the warehouse and bought three or four cases of grits and oatmeal and told me I could have it anytime I got ready for it. I decided to go north to join the army. We had an aunt and uncle who lived in Toledo. I had given up on the idea of playin football.

I had one year of high school left. That mornin when I got up in Toledo, I went for a walk and I seen the school. I walked in the buildin, and the assistant principal grabbed me, took me by the arm, twisted it, and took me to the office. He said this wasn't the first time he'd seen me walkin the halls, and I tried to explain that I wasn't a student there. He wouldn't listen. He slammed me down in a chair, and when he got the principal, the principal didn't recognize me. I was tryin to explain that I was a visitor, and he said maybe I was right.

After they found out I was a visitor, they introduced me to the coach. He invited me out to practice. He asked me about my schoolin and my transcripts. I said, 'I didn't come here to go to school. I came here to join the army.' We talked about it, and I told him, 'If you help me to make ends meet so I can pay my room and board, I can stay and go to school.'

He got me three paper routes: the *Toledo Blade*, the *Toledo Times*, I believe, and *The New York Times*. I used to get up at 4:30 in the mornin and go through my papers before school, then after school, I had already got me a job downtown parkin cars, and I parked cars until 11 o'clock every night. It was hellish for that year tryin to go to school and work all these jobs. I didn't even go to the prom because I couldn't afford a suit.

I was parkin cars in Toledo at this garage, and Woody came to town. Woody had come to meet some recruits, and a guy told him he was wastin his time with the recruits here; the best ballplayer in the area is parkin cars across the street. So Woody walked across the street to the garage and he met me. Woody and I got to talkin, and Woody said, 'The only thing that Ohio State can guarantee you is an education.'

That left an impression on me. I talked with some other people from Michigan, Michigan State, some other areas, and they had promised about everything, even a new automobile. It was hard not to take that, because I had never even owned a bicycle. I never had a new anything comin up. We never had no toys. Seein this new car parked out there and bein a teenager, it was rough, but it was just something about Ohio State that I loved.

I had two heroes when I was young. Joe DiMaggio was my hero and Vic Janowicz was my hero. Only two people that I ever looked up to, other than Joe Louis. Ohio State got more write-ups in Georgia than the University of Georgia. Every week, they would write about Vic, Vic, and when I finally got to the campus, it was like I knew him personally.

I went to summer school that summer. Woody had just got there. He was just gettin acquainted with the campus and the Quarterback Club, and he needed somebody to confide in. He told me things that I don't think he told anyone else. He told me, 'I can only play three blacks at a time.' He said he had to answer to 20,000 people downtown, that's the Quarterback Club. He locked the door in his office and told me.

That year, we had Jimmy Roseboro, we had Bobby Watkins, and myself. Never more than three of us on the field at a time, but we had Lee Williams, Bill Cummings, we had about ten of us. Only three played that year at a time. He said, 'But next year it'll be different.' And that next year, it was different. My first year, he wasn't satisfied with the control he had and he was new.

Jesse Owens had two daughters on campus who were livin on River Road. Jesse came into town and went to the president's office, and all the black people on campus had bet that they wasn't goin to live on campus. No blacks that I know of were livin on campus. They were the first two. We saw the U-Haul truck run and get all of their things and bring them back over there to Baker Hall right across from the Union.

MY FIRST HOME, after I left Woody's house, was the Tower Club. There were no other blacks in that whole buildin but me. Then me and my best friend, Bill Cummings, moved into a house across from campus. Woody came in the room one night when we went to the Rose Bowl, and Bill was snorin. He took him out of the room and put him down in the basement 'cause he was snorin too loud. I said, 'Ain't this some shit?' I roomed with this man all year on the trips. Home games, we stayed downtown at one of the hotels, and he was my roommate. We came from Toledo together. We were just like *that*. Woody said, 'I don't see how you can sleep through that and play football.' And he put him in the basement.

Me and Bill Cummings would follow this milk truck around, and if he put two cases of milk down, we took one of 'em. We went and got some corn flakes, and we had milk and corn flakes. One day, we didn't have but a dollar or two dollars between us. He said, 'Jim, I'm hungry.'

I said, 'Me too.'

He said, 'Well, what you gonna eat?'

I said, 'There ain't too much we can eat.'

He said, 'Let's make some chicken and dumplins.'

Our upstairs roommates was five guys from China. We went and bought a chicken and put it in the pot, put noodles in it and everything.

When it got done and was coolin down, we went across the street to throw the football around. We came in, and the whole pot was wiped out. Everything was gone. These Chinese guys were sittin at the table eatin. I said, 'Oh my god, we're goin to jail today.' Because I knew what Bill was gonna do. He whipped the shit outta all five of 'em. They were screamin and hollerin, the campus cops came. I knew the chief. He was a good friend of mine. I think his name was Parker, too. I explained to him what had happened, and he didn't make no arrests. That's when Woody stopped likin Bill.

Bill was a good athlete. I thought he was better than me, to tell you the truth. He played tackle. His freshman year, he did the same thing I did. He was a dummy for the varsity. They used to put these big old rubber suits on us so the varsity didn't hurt themselves when they hit us. It wasn't to protect you; it was to protect *them*. They used to put it on you and blow it up like an innertube. They'd put the ball on the one yard line, then they'd run 15, 20 plays, and they couldn't score. Woody would get pissed off, and about then, Bill would start laughin real loud: 'Bring it to 'em, bring it to 'em.' That's when Woody built up this resistance against him. We used to have a lot of fun doin that.

WHEN I MET WOODY, he was something like a father image because he gave me my instructions. He brought me in his office and he would talk to me for hours about his brother bein an athlete and what he expected out of me and I could be one of the all-time greats that came out of this university, and he didn't want me to have a mustache or no side-burns. I couldn't get married, but when I got to be a senior, I challenged that. I got married just to see what he would do. He came on my job and told my supervisor and my boss that he wanted to talk to me. He walked up there—we were buildin a new buildin—and he came up on the job and walked up the scaffold. I started to push the scaffold over on him, because I didn't know what he mighta done there. I told him I was married, and he said, 'Well, who'd you marry?'

I told him, and he said, 'I wanna wish you the best of luck.'

It was something about Woody. He convinced me. I don't know what it was. He magnetized me. I've seen him bust tables open. I don't go near him before a game unless I have a helmet and shoulder pads on. My seat was on the front row for the pregame talk, and I kept my helmet on. I told Bill, 'If you go near him, he's gonna knock your ass out.' He didn't believe me, and he walked by him one day, and Woody popped him and broke his shoulderpads.

After he'd give the speech, he'd look at me, and I'd have to lead the song, 'Drive, drive on down the field.' At that point, he was ready to go. As long as I maintained a certain average, they gave me my out-of-state fee. I had moved to Toledo, but they still charged me my out-of-state fee. They waived that, the vice president's office, and Woody gave me a $600 check to pay my tuition. I went to see Woody one day to get the check. I took the check and went to the bank and got all $1 bills and called my girl and asked her did she want to go to the movies. We used to go to two or three movies in the city of Columbus for free. They let football players in free. But I went to this movie a little ways over so I would have to pay, so I could pull my money out and impress this young lady. I pulled these 600 $1 bills out, picked off two dollars or three dollars or whatever it was, paid, and made sure everybody saw me put it back in my pocket.

I was in the movie about 45 minutes and reached back and didn't feel the money in my pocket. I looked in another pocket, then I started screamin just as loud as I could. Some of the management came down and turned on the lights. They thought I was havin a fit. I said, 'I been robbed!' We looked all under the seats with the flashlights. We couldn't find my money nowhere. I thought the young lady had ripped me off, but she didn't have the money, because I patted her down. The guy sittin back of us was gone.

Now, the big challenge came. I had to face Woody, come back to the office, look him in the eyes, and tell him the money was gone. All the way back up town that was the fearful thing in my heart. I never been so scared in my life. I walked straight up to the Athletic Department, went upstairs, knocked on his door. He said he'd be right with me. I went in and sat down and I told him what had happened. He didn't ask me how did I lose it, why did I lose it. He wrote me another check and handed it to me and never said a word. From that day to this day, if he told me, 'Go out there and move that stadium two inches to the right or four inches forward,' I would do it. I would try. I would believe it could be done. When he didn't question my credibility on that occasion, that was a turnin point in my life.

In the four years I had around Woody, I learned more from him than I did in my whole lifetime. I learned about people, I learned about business. It was more than four years of college, just comin from him. He used to take me down to a place on High Street for breakfast. He would order for you what *he* wanted, then eat what he wanted off of it. Woody loved buckwheat cakes. I didn't like buckwheat cakes. He'd order for me, and he'd order for him. He'd get black coffee and an order of ham. When the buckwheat cakes come—which I didn't eat anyway—he'd end up eatin them off of my plate, watchin his weight. I said, 'I don't want no buckwheat cakes.' But he'd order for me and order for him and end up eatin half of my meal. He would never let you order for yourself.

The kids on the team used to laugh at me a lot and call me 'Woody's boy,' because of all the things I did with Stevie, Woody's boy. Anne would let me have Sunday dinner. She would prepare the dinner, and I could invite as many people as I liked for that dinner. She would always ask me what I want for dessert. I would always say 'watermelon.' When I said that, everybody would laugh and laugh and laugh—Lee Williams, Bill Cummings, Aurealius Thomas, the guys on campus. They would come over and eat with us. She'd say, 'You can have anything you want.' I would give her the menu, and I would always tell her 'watermelon,' and she thought that was just the funniest thing.

WOODY COULD BE HARD. One game he told one of the quarterbacks, 'Don't complete no passes.' But this quarterback set up and saw one of the guys open. He threw the ball, and he completed it. He completed it to the guy from the Illinois team, and he went all the way for a touchdown. That particular player never played again at Ohio State, and he was the best quarterback in the country. Woody wanted things done his way and no other way. You had to do it his way. Woody had good coaches. That was one of things I asked him when I got bold enough: Why didn't he give authority to Bill Hess, to Doyt Perry, to Gene Fekete, to some of his top assistants? 'Why did you do everything yourself?'

He said, 'Jim, let me tell you one damn thing. When they hired me, they hired me to be the head coach of this football team, and when they fire me, they don't fire the assistants, they fire the head man.' Woody, you never knew what he would say to you. One day I was comin out the stadium. I was tired. He put his arms around me. That was unusual, but he put his arms around me. I'm expectin him to say somethin to me that's meaningful, somethin about the game that's comin up. I said, 'Now what in the hell's goin on?'

He said, 'Look up at that stadium, just look at it.'

I looked up at the stadium.

He said, 'Now, what're you thinkin about?'

'It's a funky old stadium,' I'm thinkin to myself.

He said, 'Just look up there and ask yourself are you a better football player today than you were yesterday? Look at the stadium and ask it.'

I looked up and said, 'Am I a better football player today than I was yesterday?' That's what I asked the stadium.

I said, 'It didn't say nothin, Coach.'

He said, 'Well, if it didn't say nothin, if you don't think you're better, take your ass back out there and jog around the field four times.'

See, the practice field was right back of the stadium there. So, every day when I came out past that stadium, I would look up there and think about what he said: Ask yourself if you're better today than you were yesterday. If not, go back and work on your weak things. That stayed with me all my life.

Woody could get 120 percent out of an 80 percent guy. The only time he hurt me was comin up on my senior year. The only thing I ever wanted was to be captain of that football team. I never told this to anyone before. When I went to New York to be honored as All-American, we had our team banquet at the Union Hall that night on campus. I was breakin my neck to get back to Columbus. I was tryin to make contact to get back, but I had spent all the money I had, buyin gifts and souvenirs for my family. I didn't have cab fare to get from the hotel to the airport. I told the cabdriver, 'I'm tellin you now, I don't have but $8 to get to the airport. When the meter gets there, put my ass out, and I'll walk the rest of the way.'

We started to the airport. The meter ran out, but he couldn't turn around because there wasn't anywhere for him to turn around. He said, 'If I go in the airport with my meter down, I'm gonna lose my job.'

I said, 'Whatever I owe you, I'll mail to you. I have these souvenirs with me, you can have them. Just get me to the airport.' Get to the airport, I missed the plane. Now, I'm gettin hungry, ain't got no money to eat with, got two or three hours layover, owe this man money for drivin his cab. I got back to the Union late that night. The banquet was over. That was the night they selected the captain of the team. Woody told me they had made Frank Ellwood and somebody else captain.

He said, 'Well, you didn't need to be captain because you had enough honors already. You're All-American and everything, and I just like to spread things around equally.'

I said okay; I didn't say one word. The first game we had next year, he said, 'I want you to get out there and lead 'em.' I said, 'If they wanted me to lead 'em, they woulda voted for me.' He figured he wanted me to get out there and start hittin hard and leadin hard. I did what he told me to do. I didn't give him no lip about it, but I thought I had the right to be captain. I was the only senior returnin, with more seniority than anybody. I just felt real pissy about it, and I bitched about it all year, and I think it affected my playin.

I finally mailed the cab driver his money after I got back to Columbus, and this guy kept the letter. After I turned pro, he brought the letter down to the stadium in Baltimore for me to autograph.

Woody would provoke the hell out of me. I used to go back when he was coachin. I'd be sittin in the stadium; they'd be practicin. He would call me down, introduce me, and let me talk to the team for five or ten minutes.

Then, again, me and him'd be sittin in the office, he'd look at me and say, 'You know, John Hicks is the best ballplayer I ever coached.'

I'm gettin pissed off, I'm gettin mad, you know, I want to choke the shit out of him. So I say, 'Well, so, who cares?'

I'm sittin there madder than hell. He knew how to control you. I'd say, 'I'll choke the shit out of him.' I'd say, 'Nah, I'm not. It ain't worth it.' Then I'd say to Woody, 'Well, John Hicks's not in the collegiate Hall of Fame. John Hicks's is not in the pro Hall of Fame. I have one distinction that nobody can't never claim—I'm the only player that you coached in both hall of fames and presented.' Nobody can never do that no more 'cause he's gone.

That didn't make any difference. He'd say Hop Cassady was the best athlete that he ever coached, then Archie Griffin came along, and he said Archie was the greatest athlete he ever coached.

I thought after I had left Ohio State, if I had it to do all over again, would it be Ohio State? I said 'no' on one side, because I never got a chance to enjoy my college life. Woody wouldn't let you pledge a frat, I couldn't have a mustache, I couldn't date. On the other hand, would I trade everything I learned from Woody? Everything positive that happened to me came from Ohio State and from Woody. Would I want a campus life? I didn't know anybody on campus. I'd go in classrooms, and the professor would mention football, you outta seen me draw up and gettin small. They'd talk about these dumb football players and how they hated them. My name was James Parker, not no Jim Parker.

I'd go in there and sit down. 'Son, do you play football?'

'Nossir.'

I think I had ten friends on campus. I didn't have no friends that wasn't on the football team. All football and class, football and class. They had a coach who did a roll call. I had to go to school five days a week at University Hall, and I missed one day, I better have a damn good excuse.

YOU KNOW, MOST PLAYERS HATE COACHES. In a coach-player relationship, you just get to the point where you hate him, but Woody was different. He would make you want to *kill* him.

I planned to kill him one time. I said, 'He's gone, he's gone. That sonofabitch, I'm gonna lay him out.'

I had planned this murder plot. What happened was my father had never seen me play football, never in my whole career. On Dad's Day, he came up to see me play. The only game I missed in my whole career at Ohio State was that particular game, the only game I ever sat on the bench for 60 minutes. Woody said I was hurt. I wasn't hurt. We had a pushover that week. We were playin somebody we could kick the shit out of, and he benched me for 60 minutes.

After the game, I proceeded up to where he was holdin his press conference. I said, 'I wanna see you.'

He said, 'Just a moment.'

I said, 'I wanna see you *now*.'

I was gonna kick his ass, we was gonna rumble.

He said, 'I'll be with you in a moment.'

When he finished his press conference, he came over and said, 'I wanna take you and your father and mother out to dinner. After you get dressed, meet me downstairs.' Now, he done talked himself out of this ass-whuppin. I want him to explain to my father and mother why he sat me on the bench for 60 minutes. This is the way he controls you. When we got to the Faculty Club for dinner, I couldn't eat nothin, I was still mad.

He told my mother, 'We're savin Jim for the Wisconsin game, for Alan Ameche. We didn't want to take any chances.'

He told that damn lie—I figured it was a lie—to pacify me. I'm still sittin there with murder in my heart plannin what I'm gonna kill him with. That was the second biggest hurt I ever had, because I was all geared up to have a great game for my parents.

IF YOU CAN FIND ONE PLAY that I played at Ohio State where I loafed, you bring it to me and I'll pay you for it. I had two goals. When I was in collegiate ball, my main goal was to be the best defensive, the best offensive, the best football player in the country. I kept that in the back of my mind. I never told nobody that. I wanted to win the Outland Award; I won that. I wanted to win the Heisman Trophy; I was third or fourth for that. When I came to Baltimore, I wanted to be the best football player at my position in the league, and I was goin to accomplish that. I told the other five tackles at the meetin before the coach came that that was my job, before the season started. I walked up to the blackboard, and everybody started laughin.

I said, 'This'll be my job, and the rest of you all'll be shipped out of here.'

Everybody got a big kick out of that. I was at practice, and they called for the rookies to move the bags and sleds off the field. I said, 'I'm not movin shit. I'm not a rookie. My name is Jim Parker.' This went on to the third ballgame before the season started. I had moved up to number three. Two games before the season started, I was moved up to number one, and when I got to be number one, I went up to Weeb and said, 'I want all them gone. I don't like for nobody to play in back of me.'

He said, 'What happens if you get hurt?'

I said, 'I'm not gonna get hurt.'

He said, 'What about after you run down the field on a long play? Don't you want somebody else to take a turn?'

I said, 'That's just too bad. I'll run back and take my turn.'

He got rid of everybody but one guy, who alternated between the two. I played 11 years and never got hurt. It was in my mind that I was that good.

I remember when I came to Baltimore, Weeb Ewbank came to me and put his arm around me and said, 'Look, rookie, you're startin today.'

I said, 'Well, thank you.'

He said, 'Don't let the crowd bother you.'

I said, 'How many we havin, Coach?'

He said, 'About 42,000.'

I said, 'Hell, we had that many at practice every day at Ohio State.'

He got a big chuckle out of that. We'd have 85,000 at practice, if Woody woulda let 'em in.

When I was in Columbus, I didn't have no high profile. I didn't want nobody to know who I was. A lot of people thought I was white. The first year I was eligible, when I was still playin for the Colts, I was selected into the College Football Hall of Fame. That knocked some people's butt off in Columbus. They didn't realize what was goin on there. They mighta not been noticin, but the people in the nation was noticin. The same thing in professional ball. The same year I became eligible, I went in, on the first ballot. There wasn't no two ballots. Out of 29 votes, I got 28 1/2 votes. Some players wait until they get 70 and 80 years old to get in. That was two of the greatest honors—on the first ballot, the first time. Woody introduced me both times, at the Waldorf-Astoria in New York, and he went to Canton with me. He was right there. You know he got a bigger hand than me? He got a bigger hand than anybody in the parade.

ONE THING I LIKE ABOUT OHIO STATE is when you go to play football for Ohio State, they insist on the best equipment. When I came to the Colts, I asked for some good equipment, and they rejected me. Woody had the best that money could buy. When I came here, I asked for a Rydell helmet, they told me I had to make the team first. Every player at Ohio State's helmet is custom made for his head. You don't have to get somebody else's helmet. When I came here, I told them that, they started laughin, callin me a rookie prima donna and all that shit. I said, 'No way. I want a Rydell helmet and nothin but a Rydell. That's what Woody insisted on, and I never been hurt, never had an injury.'

They told me to go pick one up off the floor. I got in my car and drove back to Columbus. Rosenbloom called me and wanted to know who the hell I think I am. I said, 'I'm not playin in that inferior equipment.' I had helmets Woody have gave me in my garage. I coulda got one of those, painted it white, put a horseshoe on it, and it woulda been the same thing, but I refused to do it. When I came back to camp, a guy from Chicago came in and measured my head. The whole team was watchin him measure my head for this helmet. They was laughin and callin me a prima donna and all that shit, but I never had a head injury. After that, most of the players started havin their helmets made in professional ball.

When I came to Baltimore, I'd always been an offensive lineman;

nobody had ever noticed an offensive lineman. I was gonna make 'em notice an offensive lineman. I wasn't goin to wait till Johnny Unitas or Lenny Moore do somethin outstandin to make people notice 'em. I started a war at tackle, right there on the line of scrimmage, and it got so obvious that they started writin about it: Jim Parker and Doug Atkins—Doug Atkins kicked Jim Parker's ass, Parker kicked Atkins's ass. Go to Detroit, Alex Karras been kickin ass, they want to know how many tackles he's gonna make today, who he's gonna beat up. If you matched up against him, then you whup his ass right down to the ground, and they have to write about it. It got so damn bad my last year in professional football that Don Shula wanted to move me around. Against the Packers, you go against Willie Davis. Whoever you play against, you have to play against the toughest guy.

I PLAYED MY FIRST PRO GAME in an exhibition game against Chicago in Cincinnati, Ohio. I got the shit whipped out of me. I went to the coaches and said, 'This ain't for me. I know an easier way to make a livin than this shit. I'm not gonna want to play pro football. I might's well stay here. There's no sense in you wastin a ticket and a meal.'

They turned a rookie loose against a bunch of pros, and I just got beat on. We had 45 offensive plays, and I got beat on 45 times. I didn't even want to see the films. I was gonna stay in Columbus. Woody came up. He was jokin and goin on, and a guy named Gene Fekete, who was on the staff at Ohio State at the time, came to me and said, 'Look, it ain't the end of the world. They was loadin up on you, and they whupped your ass. You don't know enough about the passin game.' My years at Ohio State, we threw the ball 21 times a year. My first pro game, we threw the ball 47 times. I had to learn everything all over again. The pass protection part was real hard. I picked it up, picked it up. I worked on it every day after practice, two hours a night till those guys got tired. I worked at this. That's where it all started from, by workin, workin and whuppin, whuppin, whuppin.

When I walked on that field on Sunday and I looked at you, it wasn't *if* I was gonna whup your ass, it was *how bad* I was gonna whup your ass. *I* knew you wasn't gonna touch the quarterback, and *you* knew you wasn't. We just sit Johnny in the pocket, and for 11 years, didn't nobody touch him. The only time they touched him was against Chicago, when they give us 50 different defenses.

If it was the strong side, the tackle on that side would call the blockin. If it wasn't the strong side, anybody could call the blockin. So, that's the way we did it. I was the first offensive lineman to be selected into the Hall of Fame because of that system. They didn't change until '57, when the sportswriters in Chicago and the sportswriters in New York saw who was goin against Andy Robustelli, who was a great defensive ballplayer, and Sam Huff. They had these great defensive guys, and they wondered who was kickin their ass. They wondered, and they started noticin another football game on the field, other than the quarterback. They had to write about it.

We prided ourselves on protectin our quarterback. We didn't want the back of his ass dirty. We didn't want to see no grit on it. I remember in Chicago, my man Atkins just kicked the livin hell out of me and almost killed the quarterback. I looked at John. He was bleedin in the lip; lip was split from one end to the other. We were tryin to stop it from bleedin by pickin up handfuls of mud and packin it in it. His nose was bleedin. We was packin grit and mud in it, and it was still bleedin.

I said, 'John, I'm sorry.'

He said, 'Don't worry about it.'

What had happened, they had stunted. One guy went out, another guy came in. I tripped over Art Spinney, and just missed him, clean-cut missed him. I didn't have no excuses, and Johnny got 14 stitches in the lip, but we won the game. They didn't mention the 45 offensive plays we had when Atkins *didn't* get on the quarterback, but they raised a lot of hell about that one time he kicked my ass.

That's when I learned you don't let him kick your ass. If a defensive guy makes two tackles, then he had a great game, but an offensive lineman can have 45 good plays, but miss that one time, he had a bad game.

Shula come in the locker room raisin hell one day about the offensive line not doin the job, and Johnny was throwin the ball poorly that day. He yelled and screamed at us offensive linemen, and after we reviewed the films on Tuesday, he apologized. He said, 'John was throwin the ball poorly. You're doin a good job. It's not your fault.' He kicked John's ass right there in front of us, and that motivated the team.

WOODY WAS THE SAME WAY. He would call a spade a spade. But Woody did have favorites. I was one of his favorites. I'd always been, from '53 until the time he died. I knew it, but I never took advantage of that. I think he liked me because I was really honest with him.

He gimme his credit card, and I go down there and order two shirts and a pair of pants. I don't even charge $10 on his credit card. Anybody I know woulda taken that card, he woulda at least got $50, $60 dollars charged on it. And I didn't have anything at all to wear. All I had was a pair of brown pants, tennis shoes and those shirts we got from the Athletic Department with 'Football' on 'em or 'Athletic Department.' That was it.

Came time to travel, he said, 'Here, go get you some clothes.'

I had a job on campus. I cleaned the coaches' offices. Freshmen would do the work, and I'd oversee the work. I was a deputy sheriff in Columbus until the sheriff got fired, and then the new sheriff came in and told me I was still hired. Tug Wilson (Big Ten commissioner) came down, and Woody and said they was investigatin us for somethin. They sent me over to talk to Tug, and he said, 'You're an inspiration, boy. I wish we had more poor kids like you scufflin to stay in school.'

He talked Woody into givin him the names of the kids he gave aid to, and I was one of the first ones—Jim Parker. And I had to go back and face the man. I had told him what Woody told me to say.

When I walked in, he went, 'Ooooo, here comes the poor kid from Georgia.'

I almost died; you coulda bought me for 15 cents. He had asked me where was I gettin money from to stay in school, and I told him. I told him my aunts and uncles were helpin out, pinchin pennies here and there, and I did my own laundry. I told him just like they had rehearsed it, and I had to go back and face him.

I knew Woody was goin to give him the names, because Woody was too honest. Anything Woody did was honest. That's why he didn't die as the wealthy man that he should. Woody shoulda been a trillionaire for the speeches he gave for free and the donations he gave. He just never was a greedy person. He just didn't want that. Just like that car they gave him. He coulda demanded a car with an ashtray and a heater. That damn car he drove didn't have no ashtray, no heater, and some kind of artificial windshield wipers.

Woody was always askin questions: 'Let me see your grades. What kind of grades did you get? Why didn't you go to your psychology class?'

'Well, I didn't have to go.'

'Why didn't you?'

'It was called off.'

Bill Cummings had got a job in a buildin as a janitor, cleanin the offices. He could get the tests. He told me he could get me the tests, and I didn't worry about goin to class. Then, I think he gave me the wrong damned test. It was multiple choice, and I checked off everything wrong.

On Saturday mornins, we would go up to University Hall and be guinea pigs. You sit in a chair, and if you touch this button, you get a shock: *bzzzzzzz*. Then they'd give you a check, $3, $4, and that's how we ate on Saturday mornins.

They'd run these mice through a maze, and you'd be a part of it. Rat run across that and get an electrical shock. The mice run across it, their ass get barbecued. That's what we did.

We went to Wisconsin one time, and they had two airplanes, 'cause the airport was small on the other end and couldn't accept those big planes. I told Bill, 'I'll be damned if I'm gettin on that plane.'

I didn't like to fly anyway. You almost had to hypnotize me to get me on an airplane, even after I got into pro football. I took somethin to quiet me down before I got on the plane. So, what I did, I said, 'You watch Woody. If Woody get on this sonofabitch, I'm gettin on this one. If he get on *that* one, *I'm* gettin on that one.'

I USED TO BE A LITTLE EMBARRASSED about goin back. Sometimes, you just want to go back and see if they have your picture in the lobby. You spot yourself, you just punch yourself, knowin that nobody could recognize you 50 years older. You go back and see 90,000 people sittin in the stands watchin Ohio State football, when you could watch it better on TV, with the instant replay. When I went back the year before last, it was the same enthusiasm they had when I was there. The people you knew in '57, they look different, but they're the same old funny-ass people. It's a great feelin. In the pros, I had to motivate myself, because they don't motivate you like Woody. Woody would get the team so fired up when they run out of that locker room, and they're all singin that Ohio State battle cry—'Drive, drive on down the field'—you could out there and defeat Napoleon's army. Woody could take a guy with a wooden leg and make him run a 100-yard dash.

You come to professional ball, and everything changes. You're waitin for the fire and the brimstone, and it don't come. When I came here, you had players runnin the team. You had a seven-man, eight-man clique runnin the whole team. For some reason, they accepted me in the clique the first year. They gave me a job answerin their phone. See, the coaches' room was up here, and we had hooked up a phone down in the basement where they couldn't hear it or see it. Any time his phone rang, we picked it up to see who he was cuttin and who he was bringin in.

That was my job, to monitor the phone. Fuck, that was a big responsibility. If somebody like the commissioner was on the line, I called Marchetti to the phone, and he passed the word on to the rest of us. We listened in on every call Weeb made, every call. We knew who was gettin cut, who was gettin traded, who was comin and goin, what was goin on.

Marchetti was just like a big kid. Him and Donovan asked me to bring a half-gallon of vodka from the store one day, and I brought two half-gallons of vodka. I asked him what he was goin to do with it. He said, 'We're gonna pour it in the lemonade.' After practice, we had a big barrel of lemonade. We drank all we want, ice cold. They put the vodka in the lemonade, stirred it up, and put the top back on.

The players comin in after two hours of practice, they drank two or three glasses of lemonade, and all of a sudden, everybody start gettin drunk. They didn't know what was happenin to 'em.

I was gettin scared because Don Shinnick was a preacher. He never drank. Raymond Berry never drank, and he had drank about eight glasses of lemonade. These people had never drank before. After the evenin meal, everybody who came in the meetin was high as shit.

The coach got PO'd and called the meetin off, and the next day we came in after practice, and somebody had put a big old padlock on the lemonade barrel.

The thing that motivated me in pro ball was Art Donovan. Every game, about 10 minutes before the game, he'd start throwin up—*Uggghhh*. When he started throwin up, it just carried on like a chain. Everybody else started throwin up. Me and him in the shithouse throwin up, then everybody's runnin into the shithouse—*Ugghhh*—goin right through the chain. Then the coach says it's time for the team prayer. It happened 11 years just like that. That sonofabitch, he'd sit right there on that stool, and everybody got their eyes on him, waitin for him to throw up. He sit there lookin around, then *uggghhh*, he starts throwin up. Just about that time, you got 45 guys on the team, and about 40 of 'em are takin route to the toilet. Then we have the team prayer.

At Ohio State, Woody might give you an offensive play to start with. He might tell John Borton or Leggett to throw the ball down the field to let 'em know we got a passin attack. Everybody in the country knew we don't have a passin attack.

We used to just come to the line of scrimmage and look over at Iowa and tell Calvin Jones, 'We gonna kick your ass right in this hole.'

In college ball, Woody's offense was so basic that if he gave you that, you knew where it was comin, and you better move that guy three yards. If he's crawlin on the ground like a mole, you better dig him out of that hole and drive him back. It was a real simple offense, real simple. That's why I noticed that all the offensive people from Ohio State, even now, have it easy in professional football.

THE THING I HATED ABOUT WOODY the most was he worked his coaches from 8 o'clock in the mornin till 11 o'clock at night, and every one of them had a heart attack. The best coach I ever had—a guy nobody never gave no credit—was a guy named Harry Strobel. Harry hand-picked me, and he coached me at Ohio State for four years, him and Bill Hess. He put the chalk on the field and showed me how to pull. Everything he taught me came back to me in professional football—how to cheat to get in front of Lenny Moore. Bill Hess, my freshman coach, was good for me, too. He taught me the basic fundamentals of football, which I never knew. I was just a raw product, and he groomed me and filed me and taught me how to get down and get comfortable and get off the ball. When I watch a professional football team, the first thing I do is pick up a program to see how many Buckeyes are on the team.

The thing about Ohio State football is every team on the schedule puts Ohio State on a pedestal. If any team could beat Ohio State, that was a big deal for 'em. There was somethin about the Michigan game. Woody could create so much hate between Michigan and Ohio. I had two wins and one loss, so I got two pairs of them gold pants that they give you for winnin it. After the game, they have a gold pants banquet. If you win, you get little gold pants, like for a necklace. It looks just like a tooth. Guy came in my store one day, and he kept lookin at the pictures on the wall. I looked around his neck and saw these gold pants. He had two pair. I kept lookin.

I said, 'That sonofabitch, he either went to Michigan or he went to Ohio.' He kept lookin, he never ordered nothin.

I said, 'Hey, Bro, where'd you go to school?'

He said, 'Ohio State.'

I said, 'You beat Michigan twice, right?'

'Right.'

I said, 'I saw it on your neck.'

He wasn't no superstar. He was just on the team, but I don't give a damn how good you are, you get a pair of them. He was visitin a friend down back of the store, down on Forest Park. He told me he had seen my pictures at the school and he heard about me from Ohio State. He had two pair of gold pants, he damn sure had 'em.

THAT PARTICULAR GAME means more to an Ohio Stater than any other game. I think I'd rather lose every other game and win the Michigan game. One game, they were gettin ready to can Woody, and Woody stood up at that banquet and talked Dick Larkins out of firin him. He said, 'Do I have a job next year?' And Dick said, 'Yes, Woody.'

He had lost the Michigan game. He didn't have a bad season, but it wasn't no super season for Ohio State. He had a lot of people mad at him, people on campus, for puttin so much emphasis on football, which he didn't. He put more emphasis on studyin than he did on football, but, see, they was outsiders lookin in. He would kick the press out of practice. Only ones that could come in were Paul Hornung and Kaye Kessler and a few other of Woody's people who supported him. People from the Cleveland *Plain Dealer* and all over the state, he would kick 'em out. They got after him, too. Then, there was the campus man that didn't want us to go back to the Rose Bowl. Woody had to fight all of that, plus coach, plus he had to teach a course. He had to answer to the community, all over the state of Ohio, speeches here, speeches there. I just wonder sometimes how he did it. Woody didn't want no help. When he was older, he was crippled, and I tried to help him across the street. He told me to get the fuck off of him, he could do it himself.

Duke came up here and kicked our ass in '55. I'm tellin you they beat the dogshit out of us. We didn't get up for the game. We didn't do the job. The guy that played in front of me is a county executive here in my county. I can't remember his name right now. I ran into him one day and he told me, 'You know, I played against you when I was at Duke, and I just want to tell you, you were a gentleman on the field.'

I said, 'I don't think so. I remember you down on the field, and I almost spit on your head.'

That's the only question I ask myself, if I would give up a college life to play ball, but if Woody could come back to coach the team, I don't think it would even be a choice. If he'd come within a hundred miles of here, he would call. He'd call from Ohio. He'd be just sittin in his office and call.

When I came here, I had four children. I got a $1,500 bonus, all $1 bills again. I wasn't gonna sign. Same girl 'bout them ones, she kicked my foot under the table: 'Sign it, sign it, sign it.' I left Columbus and I went to the Hula Bowl. That's why I asked 'em for a two-year contract, which they gave me. That's why I was talkin all that shit my rookie year, because I knew I wasn't goin nowhere for two years.

BUT I NEVER TOOK IT FOR GRANTED. Twelve years, I never took no more than you can put in a bag. I never took a record player, I never took no extra nothin. Some of the players they cut, they had to get a U-Haul truck to carry all their stuff out of there. Man come up to me one night and say, 'Coach says come and bring your playbook,' all I had to do was throw my toothbrush, my hairbrush, my deodorant in my bag and I'm gone.

Gene Lipscomb, Big Daddy, they waited till he unloaded his car to tell him he was traded to Pittsburgh, which I thought was the wrong way of doin things. They shoulda told him before he unloaded his car.

One of the reporters asked me after my seventh year, he said, 'You're an All-Pro. You're not goin anywhere. Why do you live like this? You don't have no clothes here.'

I said, 'In case I get traded or cut, I can make it to the next city and make the next practice.'

I lived that way for 11 years with the Colts. I never carried no more to Westminster than I needed. I never took my ability for granted. The only good thing I knew about myself was I knew I was good enough to play somewhere. It didn't have to be here.

I played football for the Colts 11 years, and there never been but one player that really whupped my ass. He played for Atlanta, little linebacker from Texas, Tommy Nobis. That's who kicked my ass. I looked at him, saw him playin linebacker. I went back in the huddle and told John to give me this play. John called the play, and I said, 'I'm gonna kill this little sonofabitch.' I hit him, and he just stood there and drove my ass into the ground like a peg. My neck was out of my shoulder pads. I said, 'This can't happen to me.' I went back and to the huddle. I said, 'John give it to me again. Somethin musta happened that play.'

He gave it to me again. *Boom!*

Get back to the huddle, John says, 'Want me to call it again?'

I said, 'Hell no!'

He was killin me. Tommy Nobis, that's the only guy to hurt me in the 11 years I played football. Atkins, we hurt each other, but the guy who really, really stung me was Tommy Nobis. He was no taller than that. I saw him sittin back there at middle linebacker, I said, 'I'm gonna kill this little asshole. I'm gonna hit him like a truck hittin a Volkswagen,' and *POW!* That was it. We didn't stop runnin up the middle, but we changed some of our offensive plays for that game.

WOODY WAS AS GREAT AS HE WAS because he had real basic football. Just fire out. He had a seven-man sled, and he wanted all seven people comin at one time. We would work on that thing for hours, until we coordinated it like a dance. We had a little guy named Ernie Godfrey. He was the football coach that stood next to Woody on the sideline. Evidently, he must've been a pretty good linebacker in his day. He used to take 10 linebackers and line 'em up against me, and he used to have me knock them out, one at at time. I thought it was a cruel thing to do. I used to knock every one of 'em down, then they'd get back in line and take another turn. My arm, after practice, would be *that* big. I'd stick it in the tank to get the swellin out. That's the way he wanted it done, 'cause he enjoyed linebacker play. The next day, I put a piece of lead there under that pad.

When that whole thing happened with that guy from Clemson, I was afraid. I was scared he'd be fired before mornin come. I mentioned to members of my family he'd be fired. They said, 'You don't know what you're talkin about.' When I picked the paper up that mornin, he was fired. Woody could've saved his job if he had come out right away and apologized, but he was so bullheaded he would never apologize for somethin he thought he was right on.

After he hit the boy on the football field, I told myself, 'I'm gonna call him and talk to him about it, and I'm gonna ask him to apologize.' I got on the phone at the store, called, Anne answered the phone.

I said, 'Anne, this's Jim Parker. Can I talk to Woody?' I could hear him in the background.

Woody said, 'I don't give a damn who it is. I ain't talkin to nobody.'

I hung up. About four days later, he called me back, said, 'What'd you want to talk about?' 'Cause I been out of there 26 years, and there hadn't been a month that he wouldn't call here and ask me how am I doin, how much money I got in the bank, are you mistreatin anybody. He would ask me all these questions, but I would listen to him and answer him. So when he called back he said, 'C'mon down. I want to talk to you.'

And anytime he called and said he wanted to talk to me, I was on the highway in the next few hours goin towards Columbus. I wouldn't fly. If I couldn't drive, I'd catch a train or a bus.

The last time I talked to him, we went to the Holiday Inn. We had breakfast, lunch, and dinner. He gave me a thousand reasons why he shouldn't apologize. I was so highed up after I finished talkin to the man he had me believin he shoulda broke both of the guy's legs. Convinced, he had me. He said he would never apologize. If he think he's right, he would die and go to hell before he apologized.

We sit there all mornin, noon and evenin. We was bein interrupted for autographs by people comin through. He was tellin them who I was: 'This's Jim Parker, from the Baltimore Colts.'

We would sign autographs for a few people, then we would go back to the talk. I wanted to know why wouldn't he apologize, and he sit there and gave me one thousand, two thousand reasons he shouldn't apologize: all the students he helped through Ohio State; you know, 'On the field of battle, when you're fightin a team, and an accident might happen when you get over-emotional, you don't apologize for gettin over-emotional.'

I said, 'Do you apologize when you clip your opponent? Do you apologize when you steal a chicken from your neighbor?'

'Not if you need it. If you don't have any meat on the table, and you steal a chicken and don't get caught, you don't go over there and apologize.'

He just believed that he was right, and when he got finished with me, I believed he was right, too. You see, he just wasn't talkin to me. I knew what he had done for students. I knew that if a guy come up and needed a pair of shoes, or a guy come up and his dad got laid off and he needed some rent money, I knew it was illegal for him to do it, but he might just drop it on the ground and the guy might pick it up and it might be just enough for his rent. He might 'accidentally find it,' is the way he put it.

I didn't have no choice but to forgive him, because when I got up from that table, he had me so geared up. I went down there to kick his ass. That was my main purpose. I was talkin to myself when I got to Wheeling, West Virginia; I was talkin to myself when I got to the Ohio line. I was gonna whup it to him. *WHOP, WHOP.* And when I got there to the damn Holiday Inn, I sit down and we start talkin, and then he starts convincin me just a little bit more, convincin me, and by the time that evenin had came, he had thoroughly convinced me that what he did was right, and he shoulda broke both his arms. I felt that just smackin him wasn't enough; he shoulda broke both his arms.

I wanted to find out why didn't he do this, why didn't he do that, and I was scared to ask him when I was there. Things had been on my mind for years. I asked him, and he answered them for me, everything. I asked him why he had called Shula and asked him to move me to guard when it was none of his business. He said, 'Oh, to make room for Vogel, who was an excellent tackle but wasn't worth a damn at guard.'

And when he gave you a reason—when he explain it to you—you felt like that was the right decision. He talked to the coach, and they moved me that same day. Woody was gettin old and sorta slow then, and the week that he died, he had called my house and called for me to come down three times. I saw Stan White out here at a banquet that Wednesday night. I said, 'Stan, Woody called. I wonder what he wanted. When he calls me, he wants something, and I don't understand what he wants. I'm gonna have to get my ass to Ohio.'

Friday mornin, Stan called and said Woody was gone. I never got a chance to see him, and that's why I didn't go to the funeral. After Woody died, I said, 'I don't have no reason to go back to Columbus.'

Of all the people I been around, I think I would rather be around him more than anybody. I've been around presidents, three or four of them, I've been around priests, I've been around the Cardinal from New York, but I'd rather be around Woody, I mean of wordly figures. He left an ever-lastin impression upon me, and I'll never forget him.

He told me one time, he gave me my tuition, he gave me an ultimatum with it. He said, 'You see this boy right here.' It was Stevie, his boy; I think he was about 12 years old. He said, 'If he ever needs some money for an education, if he ever needs money to go to school and further his education, the only thing I'm askin you to do, if you have it, give it to him, and don't ask him to pay it back. That's all I ask.'

And that left a hell of an impression with me. I thought about that when I started playin pro ball. I thought, 'If Steve needs some tuition money, I have to send it to him.'

I never made no decent money with the Colts. I got $12,500 to start. I never had an agent. I had more money in the bank while I was playin for Ohio State than I did when I came here. I worked on campus, I worked all night long at the detention center, I worked for Woody at the stadium cleanin up the coaches' offices. When I came here in professional football with the Colts, the first year, I worked at the shipyards, I sold embalmin fluid and cemetery lots for two different companies, I sold whiskey for Schenley, and I played football. I just couldn't sit on my ass and live off a football check for twelve-five a year.

I went down there the first year I was here with Big Daddy Lipscomb to get unemployment. He put on a couple-hundred dollar suit and $200 shoes, and he got in line, and the line was from here to Ohio. At that particular time, nobody was workin. Rosenbloom got pissed off and called us in, but Big Daddy said, 'Fuck 'im. He ain't payin my salary in the off-season. I got to eat, too.'

RIGHT AFTER THE SEASON STARTED, Art Donovan got me a job with Schenley. That was one of the best things that ever happened to me, meetin the Kasoffs, Harvey Kasoff. His father was Mitch Kasoff. He gave me a job at Schenley, and I worked for him for eight years. He taught me the liquor business, inside and outside, then he told me to go out and find a store. It took me four or five years to find the store. This guy and me had went to settlement twice, and he backed out. The reason the guy finally sold me the store was a police officer was killed right in front of the door. He called me that night to come down to the store. I got down there, the blood was still on the front step.

He said, 'I just lost my best friend right out here in front of the door.' He said, 'I want to sell you this store. I can't work it no more.'

I said, 'Okay, I'll tell you what, I'll be down here in the mornin. I'll bring a check for $25,000, you bring one. If you back out, you forfeit the money to me. You talk to my attorney in the mornin. I'm not goin through this shit with you no more.'

He said, 'You don't need the lawyer,' and he came down and signed the papers.

In the meantime, I called Shula and asked him could I bring this police officer's kid to the stadium and could he come in the locker room, could he sit on the bench? I told him what had happened. He needed someone to lean on. So, I went all the way out and picked him up every Sunday mornin, and brought him to the stadium with me. I don't know what ever happened to the kid, but I went to the station one day for somethin and saw his father's badge number and plaque on the wall as a deceased officer.

Now, the whole family works there, all but one boy, and if they steal, they're stealin it from themselves, 'cause I'm gonna leave it to them anyhow. I been offered a million-five, just for the license.

I own the whole block now, and we're tryin to get some money from the government or from the banks to upgrade the whole block. All the buildins are rented out; we just want to fix it up. The people wasn't real receptive at first. There was no black folks here, and the people didn't know what was goin on. It was just like when I lived with Woody. The only black folks you saw up there where he was livin, in Upper Arlington, were the people goin to work. You didn't see no black folks comin out the house. I stayed in the house, then he brought me down campus and put me over there in a club in the stadium.

I WAS THE HAPPIEST MAN in the world, 'cause I could get out and do things, but he came over there and checked on me every day. He came in the room one night, he scared my roommate half to death. He knocked on the door. We said, 'Who is it? C'mon in.'

He wouldn't come in, just knocked on the door. My roommate, Bill, was sittin there smokin a cigar. The room was full of smoke.

Bill said, 'If you don't know how to open the door and walk in like a man, crawl your ass through the hole at the bottom,' and Woody opened the door, and Bill looked up and saw Woody. The last thing I seen was that cigar bein chewed up. I seen a big knot in his throat. He chewed that sonofabitch up and swallowed it.

The way I figure is like this. It all started in Georgia in 1934. I left Georgia to go to Toledo to join the army. I went to Ohio State. I got a chance to see some parts of the country I woulda never seen, California and everywhere we went. I woulda never been in Baltimore if it wasn't for Woody and the university, to wind up bein a first draft in '57. They drafted Lenny Moore, me and Leonard Lyles, three blacks in a row, which was somethin that wasn't heard of, because when I first came to this city here, we couldn't go downtown on Howard Street and see a movie. My mother came up for the championship game in '58, and I took her to downtown to get her a new coat, and she couldn't even try the coat on. Told her she had to go in the basement.

Things like that put a damper on it, but I'm not the kind of person who lives in the past. I try to teach my kids the positive things. You can get motivated from negative things, like when you go on the football field. You think about the guy that didn't sell you a ticket at the movie. He's sittin there in front of you, and here's your chance to get even with him. You can whup his ass and not worry about goin to jail. You can pretend he's anybody you want him to be, and the more you look at him, the more he looks like that person. Just whup his ass.

In the long run I'm satisfied with things. I'm satisfied with my efforts at Ohio State. I'm not satisfied with my grades, but I'm satisfied with my efforts toward my grades. I put a hundred percent into 'em. I didn't get my degree. I have about eight hours. I asked Dr. Hixson about waivin that, but he said I had to come back and get 'em. I never went back, and that's the only thing I regret about the whole thing.

When I came here, I didn't come to stay but three years. I figured three years would be enough for me, and after we got the store, we had paid that off in three years. Next year, I hope to get out, and make my son the chairman of the board. He can operate the store and oversee what we're doin here. I'll go back to Macon, Georgia, go cat-fishin—just from the dock, I'm not crazy about water. Gimme land, lotsa land, no swimmin. I can't swim a damn lick. It's a weird-ass thing—I went to State with all those great swimmers, and I had Mike Peppe, the greatest swimmin coach of all time, to teach me a swimmin course, and I fell in that deep end one day and ain't never been the same, the deep-ass end in that pool over by the stadium. My kids used to go down to Annapolis on the boat, and I used to drive down on the highway and meet 'em. The boat leave there, I meet 'em back at the Baltimore harbor.

Governor Rhodes called me a couple times since I been in Baltimore and told me I had a job with the state of Ohio if I ever wanted to come back. But without Woody and without Bill in Columbus, it would be difficult. I could live there, but knowin that I would never see Woody again, and never see Bill again, I couldn't. No, no. Two of the finest people that I ever met. ”

The Kid

"THE KID" IS pushing 60, but is still somehow boyish. Although his body has thickened since a sportswriter called him a "wasp-waisted sophomore," he bounces when he walks, as if barely able to contain his energy. His face is still cherubically round, his eyes mischievous, and Tom Matte still has his smile. It's a salesman's smile—equal parts affability and hanky-panky—and thus to be ignored. But Matte knows how infectious it is. Like Jay Gatsby, he can turn it on you, radiant as a flashlight beam, and make believe you're the only one who has ever seen its full warmth and sincerity. His smile is irresistible, and it's a wonder that Matte still possesses it.

Matte's father was a former professional hockey player who worked three jobs to support the family. A poor white kid who played hockey but spent most of his time with black pals, Matte grew up in a tough neighborhood in Cleveland. "We made zip guns in the seventh grade, and if you didn't have a push-button blade in your pocket, you were in trouble," he says.

The family eventually moved to the suburbs, and Matte realized that he was "behind the eight ball academically," that his parents couldn't afford college tuition and that football provided his best chance for a scholarship. However, in his first junior high school game, he injured a knee so badly that he underwent two operations. His father didn't speak to him for months because Matte played "that stoopid game of futball." By his senior year, Matte had become an outstanding basketball player, sprinter, and halfback. He was also the "class clown"—cocksure, glib, and freewheeling—who "thought you were supposed to have fun with the game." If Matte's athletic ability drew Woody Hayes to him, his nonchalance incited four turbulent years with the stern coach, who during a scrimmage once shouted at his squad, "You're too happy out there!"

"All I had ever heard about Woody was that he was a real hardass and tough to play for, and that was putting it mildly," Matte says.

A *Dispatch* photo taken after OSU defeated Purdue in 1959—Matte's junior year—shows Matte and Hayes strolling from the field. Its caption, "Coach and Friend," is a gross distortion of how the two men felt about each other by that time. Matte says he had come to Columbus "starry-eyed" but soon discovered "what girls and 3.2 beer were all about." His grades were so awful that Hayes threatened to take his scholarship.

Early in Matte's sophomore season, Hayes suddenly decided the promising halfback should switch positions. At halftime of a blowout over Indiana, Hayes sent Matte and a makeshift offense behind Ohio Stadium with an assistant coach under orders to turn Matte into a quarterback. "I've had it in the back of my mind for a long time," Hayes said. Matte, who had thrown three passes in his life, thought the coach was daft.

In 1959, Hayes was unable to decide on a quarterback: Matte, whom a writer called "a rootin', tootin', swingin', slingin' quarterback"; or Jerry Fields, a strapping, disciplined converted center. When Fields was hurt with five minutes left in the opener, Matte took the team on a long drive that included a fourth-down scoring pass to beat Duke by a point. Fields, however, started the next game, after which Hayes declared Matte to be first team. That week, Fields took almost every snap against Illinois. After the Purdue game, a newspaper headline said, "Matte

Moves to No.1 QB"; two days later, the headline was, "Fields, Matte Now 1-2 Punch." Named the starter against Michigan State, Matte threw three touchdown passes and earned UPI Midwest Back of the Week honors. The next Saturday, he tried but four passes in a 0–0 tie. Ohio State's 3-5-1 record was Hayes's worst. "It was war between Woody and me," Matte says of that season. "I ran rampant."

He was arrested, clad only in underwear, while leading a boozy rendition of "Script Ohio" during a snowstorm. Another newspaper photo shows Matte with Hayes and a half-dozen teammates about to board a plane. Matte's pinched expression is caused by his just having thrown up over the passenger ramp. He consistently referred to the coach as "Woody" in print and blithely told a reporter that standing around during practice watching Fields run plays might "give me a cold."

"He thought I was making a mockery of him," Matte says. "I really wasn't, but I just couldn't understand why he had done this to me."

Infuriated by Matte's clowning during practice one afternoon, Hayes chased him around the field until the coach was too winded to keep up the pursuit. Hayes wouldn't allow Matte to be included among the candidates for captain in 1960 and spoke ambivalently about him to the press. Finally, he gave Matte an ultimatum: He could either move into the Hayes home or live in a nearby fraternity house, but spend nearly every waking moment in the coach's company. Matte chose the frat house, but eventually, he claims, the running battle with Hayes gave him ulcers.

Primarily an offensive coach, Hayes saw his quarterback as an extension of his own ego. He once doffed hat and coat and ran the position during an impromptu scrimmage at halftime of a game. Hayes wanted his quarterback to hand off, run keepers, and, above all, avoid mistakes. Matte wanted to make it up as he went along. The public preferred Matte's daring improvisations, which only made Hayes resentful.

The mismatched pair finally made an uneasy truce. In 1960, the Buckeyes lost only two games, as Matte accounted for nearly half of the team's offense. Belatedly, almost apologetically, Hayes said, "He's the best quarterback I've seen in the Big Ten in 10 years. He's taught me some things about quarterbacking." Injured, bewildered by a sophisticated passing offense, miffed at sitting the bench behind Lenny Moore, Matte got off to a shaky start as Baltimore's first pick in 1961. However, he eventually found a home among the free-spirited Colts, who dubbed him "Kid." Able to play halfback, fullback, defensive back, tight end, or receiver, he gained nearly 4,700 yards, caught 250 passes, scored 57 touchdowns, and made All-Pro twice in 11 years.

He overcame crushed vertebrae that could've ended his career. He gulped medicine to soothe an ulcer so severe that after one game, he was rushed to a hospital to receive four pints of blood. In the 1966 title game, Matte tied an NFL record with three touchdowns, despite a bruised kidney. After the game, he sat before his locker in ashen-faced agony, unable to walk. Two weeks later, he set a Super Bowl record with a 58-yard run and gained 116 yards against the Jets.

Matte's most famous moment came when Johnny Unitas and his backup, Gary Cuozzo, were both hurt late in 1965. Encouraged to do so by Hayes, Shula made Matte his "Instant Quarterback." Matte led Baltimore to a win over Los Angeles, forced Green Bay into overtime in a brutal championship game ("He's a great athlete," Vince Lombardi said afterward), and threw three touchdown passes in the Colts' Playoff Bowl victory over Dallas. "He carried us through the last two games of the season on sheer nerve," Shula said. Matte will never make the Hall of Fame, but the wristband on which he scribbled plays to serve as a cribsheet for those three weeks is displayed in Canton.

As he reminisced, Matte scooped slices of pizza from a box, pausing to drink from a can of Coke, wipe at his mouth with a paper napkin or take a phone call. His smashed and crooked nose seemed incongruous with his pudgy cheeks and thick, shaggy hair, just as his casual manner was out of keeping with the large, austere office he occupies as a limited partner in Baltimore's CFL franchise. Twenty-two years later, he remains angry that he heard over the radio about the trade to San Diego that caused him to retire, rather than from Colt owner Robert Irsay ("the biggest jerk in the world"). Otherwise, Matte exudes bonhomie, if some of his stories have improved with the telling.

Before buying into the CFL team, he worked for years in computer sales and as a broadcaster. He has been married for over 30 years to the same girl he used to slip away on weekends to visit while he was at Ohio State and has raised two adopted children. He owns two companies, Tom Matte Sports Speakers and Tom Matte Marketing, and is active in charity work.

Matte has also long since made his peace with Woody Hayes, whom he says he appreciated more as time passed. The two men called and visited each other frequently, and Matte sought Hayes's advice on career and personal matters.

"We had our battles," he says. "But I've tried to put everything into perspective. He gave me my chance to be where I am right now."

Tom MATTE

"MY FATHER PLAYED HOCKEY for the old Pittsburgh Hornets. He ended up getting traded to Cleveland to play for the Barons, so I grew up in Cleveland. At that time, hockey players didn't make very much money, and I grew up in what was probably the number one crime district in Ohio, at 93rd and Huff. We made zip guns in the seventh grade, and if you didn't have a push-button blade in your pocket, you were in trouble as far as getting to school was concerned. It wasn't a racial issue in those days. It was school against school. I grew up in a black neighborhood, and some of my closest friends were black guys. I remember Clark Kellogg, the basketball player who went to Ohio State, when he was little. His father was one of my best friends. He and his brother, Shelby Kellogg, were two of the biggest monsters I've ever seen in my life, and they sort of took care of me. Clark, Sr. was a guard outside the gate for the Cleveland Browns when the Colts used to go there to play, so when Clark, Jr. was a young kid, I used to bring him in and introduce him to everyone. Who knew he was going to be an NBA player?

I never even picked up a football until the ninth grade. When I was in the eighth grade, I transferred from the inner city schools to East Cleveland. East Cleveland was kind of a white, Waspy neighborhood back at that time. The inner-city had gotten too tough. You couldn't walk the streets at night. It was tough on my parents, because they were trying to do the best they could. They just didn't have enough money.

I was lost in the new school. They were on subjects I'd never even heard of. They put my brother back a whole year in school, and they probably should've put me back. I bluffed my way through, but I never really did catch up until I got to Ohio State. It was a tough time for me.

I went out for football, even though I didn't know that much about it. The first game, I went down on a kickoff, and a kid clipped me. I ended up in the hospital. I had two knee operations. My father didn't speak to me for three months because I was playing 'that stoopid game of futball.' He thought football was a waste of time. He said I had a great career in hockey. I got hurt in the ninth grade, and then in the tenth grade, I went out for junior varsity. I made the team, but I was second string. My junior year, I was a second-team halfback. Finally, my senior year, I got my chance to play. That year, we got a great coach by the name of Leo Strang, who is now in the Hall of Fame in Ohio. He went from Shaw to Massillon to Kent State. He was one of the guys who was instrumental in making me a great athlete. He used to kick me in the butt all the time, just like Woody did. I needed that. I thought you were supposed to have fun with the game and not take it too serious. I'd always be out joking around, and once in a while, I'd get my butt kicked, and that would bring me into focus. He knew I had the ability to get the job done, and I was fortunate to play for him.

I sort of blossomed that year. I grew about four inches and filled out a bit. I got better speed. I could run the hundred in 9.9 in high school, I was running the quarter-mile in 47 flat, I was high-jumping 6' 2", 6' 3", I was pole-vaulting 12' 6" feet, I was running the 220 in 22-something. The thing I realized very young is that there is life after sports. That's a key lesson that Leo Strang and Woody Hayes taught me. You can play sports for a short amount of time, if you're lucky, and I never even thought I'd play in the pros. I knew I wanted to go to school, and I knew my parents wanted me to go to school, but they couldn't afford to send me. I saw my father finish playing and not have an education. It was always inbred in me—college, college. My dad realized he had made a mistake by turning pro, but he was such a great hockey player that he jumped at the chance to go into the pros. He was a very bright man, but that's what he decided to do. As a result, he told me, 'Hey, I want you to go to college. We'll sacrifice to make it happen.'

I was trying to play hockey and football, and it was hard to do both. I said, 'What am I going to get my scholarship from?' There were no hockey scholarships back then. I could get it in track, basketball, or football. Navy came up and saw one of our games, and I hit for 36 points. I could've had a scholarship to Navy for basketball. We had a great track team, the fastest mile relay team in the state, but there weren't a lot of track scholarships around. My senior year, I was second in the state in scoring. I'd been recruited by a lot of football schools all over the country. I was recruited by all the Big Ten schools, except for Michigan. I didn't have the grades for them. The first time I had ever been on an airplane was my senior year of high school, when I got recruited by Indiana. They sent me up there to see the Indianapolis 500, and I got sick as a dog on the airplane.

I HAD NO IDEA ABOUT WOODY HAYES when he started recruiting me. I wasn't an Ohio State fan. I wasn't much of a fan of anybody, except the Browns. All I had ever heard about Woody was that he was a real hardass and tough to play for, but Leo was the same way, and I liked that kind of coach. My parents convinced me to go to Ohio State. When Woody recruited me, he didn't really recruit me. He recruited my mom and dad. One of the key things he said was, 'Mrs. Matte, I will guarantee you your son will graduate from Ohio State.' That's all she had to hear.

I came to Columbus starry-eyed. Ohio State was a powerhouse. I looked around and said, 'What am I doing here?' But I had made a decision. I could've been a big fish in a little pond by going to a smaller school, but my dad said, 'Hey, you really want to take your risk factor, like I did. Go to the big school. If you make it big, okay. If you just make the team, you still get your degree.'

I thought I was in way over my head, but as things went along, I learned the system. Believe me, it wasn't too hard to learn. We had the belly series, and, Christ, that was it. At least I was playing defense back then, too, and that was a lot more fun than offense.

When I first came down to Ohio State, as a freshman, you couldn't play varsity. I came in there and, boy, I found out what girls and 3.2 beer were all about. After the first quarter, I had a 1.5 average. I didn't flunk anything, but I had a whole bunch of D's and a couple C's. I'm having a great time. Woody called me in.

He said, 'Tom, how'd you enjoy this fall?'

I said, 'Coach, it was wonderful. I just had a great time.'

He said, 'I'm looking at your grades here, and I really don't like these. What happened?'

I said, 'Well, I, ah....'

He said, 'I'm going to put this to you very clearly: Either you get your grades up, or your scholarship's gone.'

Now, if you want a real stark realization of where your future is, that's it. It was right in the palm of his hands.

I said, 'Well, I better start studying.'

He just laid it right on the line: 'Either you get your act together, or you're out of here.'

I got my act together, and I came back with a 3.3 the next quarter. He said, 'Now, that's the kind of quality boy I want.' He was always talking about 'quality boys.' He wanted his players to graduate.

MY SOPHOMORE YEAR, I played defensive back with Dick LeBeau and Don Clark and those guys, and we used to knock the hell out of anybody coming out of the backfield. I just liked to hit people, and we had a great defensive backfield. We didn't go all the way that year, but we had a winning season. All of a sudden, Woody decided he wanted me to play quarterback. I had never taken a snap from center in my whole life, but between my sophomore and junior years, he converted me from halfback to quarterback. We had a big battle about that, because I didn't want to play quarterback. I had real small hands, I had a hard time holding onto the ball and throwing the ball. I wasn't that great a thrower, which wasn't a big problem, because at Ohio State in those days, you didn't throw the ball that much. The quarterback just rolled out. If someone was absolutely, positively open, you threw the ball. If not, you ran it.

He tried me there during spring practice. We had two spring games that year. Spring games down there, they get 20,000–30,000 people. The first spring game, he puts me with the second string offense against the first string defense, and I go out there and we beat them up and down the field. The first defense is just dying. They're so upset it's unbelievable. We're marching up and down the field. I'm calling my own plays and having lots of fun, laughing and giggling. I threw five touchdown passes.

So the press grabs it: 'Ohio State finally has a running/throwing quarterback, blah, blah, blah.' The press was just hungry for somebody to throw the football, instead of that three yards and a cloud of dust that he had established. There's another spring game the next week. Well, what Woody does, he comes into the huddle and calls the play: 'Roll right option.' I'm going to come out right, set up, run or throw. Then he goes over and tells the defense what the play is and has the guys blitz from the outside. There's absolutely no surprise whatsoever. I throw three interceptions. I'm really upset about it. After the game, the defensive guys come up and say, 'Tommy, he'd call the play and come over in the defensive huddle and tell us what it was. You were set up to look bad.'

He did it because he didn't want to throw the ball, for one thing. He said, 'I don't want you to throw interceptions.' The other thing is he didn't like anybody getting lots of publicity. So he set it up that I would fail. It was unbelievable.

I figured, 'Okay, that's it, fine. I don't want to play quarterback anyway. They don't have to use me.'

We have one more practice that spring, because of a rain day. This's a true story. You can ask anyone who was there. I'm taking snaps from center, and I'm pulling my hands out early intentionally. I do this about six times. Bo Schembechler was there at the time, and he knows what I'm doing. Woody has no idea what's going on. And the poor center, Billy Joe Armstrong, he almost got castrated.

Woody's yelling at Billy Joe, 'You got to bring the ball up faster!'

He's bringing it up faster; I'm pulling my hands out; he's hitting himself right in the *cujones*. He'd go to his knees.

After six times, Woody looks at Bo and says, 'Bo! What're we gonna do? Goddamn you, Matte!'

He takes his left arm, gives me a left forearm shiver, knocks me backward ass-over-teacups. I'm laughing. Bo's holding back. Woody says, 'It's not goddamn funny, Matte.'

And with that, he hits himself in the temple with both fists and knocks himself out cold. He always wore that whistle, and that whistle comes up and lashes him in the eye. He's bleeding from the eye.

Bo looks at me and says, 'Matte, you better get your ass out of here, because if he wakes up, he's gonna kill you.'

THAT WAS MY QUARTERBACKING FOR THAT SPRING. We come to fall practice, and I don't even do anything at quarterback. There's no more discussion about playing quarterback. There's absolutely nothing going on at all. The first game, we're playing against Duke. I was playing offensive halfback, defensive halfback, I was the kickoff return guy, the punt return guy. I never came off the field. That's what I liked. We're behind 7–0 at the half. Jerry Fields was the quarterback, and he'd gotten bumped or roughed up or something. He wasn't playing at full strength.

At halftime, Woody says, 'I'm gonna put you in at quarterback. I want you to take some snaps from center.'

I said, 'I don't want to play quarterback. I don't even know how to call the plays.'

He says, 'Don't worry about it.' He grabs a couple centers and two fullbacks, and we go to the practice field at halftime. You got 90,000 people at the game. They're all looking to see where we're going. The whole team goes into the locker room. The coaches can't find Woody. They can't find me. No one knows what the hell's going on. I'm out there taking snaps. I thought he was nuts.

Halftime is over. There's no meeting of the team at all. I don't know what went on in the locker room. Right from the practice field, we come out to the second half. I go out and play halfback. Two minutes to go in the ballgame, we're losing 13–7. They kick off to us, and Woody says, 'You go in and play quarterback.'

I said, 'Coach, I don't know what I'm doing.'

He said, 'Roll right. If somebody's open, throw it. If not, you run the goddamned ball, you hear me?'

WE MARCH DOWN THE FIELD, 80 yards, in like a minute and 13 seconds, score a touchdown, beat Duke 14–13. One of the plays, I said, 'Roll right. Anybody's open, I'll hit you.' Everybody went right, student body right, like the old Green Bay Packers used to run. I was so tired, I got up to the line of scrimmage, and I thought I said 'roll left.' The whole team rolls right, I roll left. I go down the sidelines for 30, 40 yards.

He runs out on the field and says, 'Where'd you get that play at?'

I said, 'I saw everybody was following the pursuit. I just thought I'd go the other way on a naked reverse.'

He says, 'That's goin' in the offense! That's a good play!'

Christ, I get the headlines, the press. I said, 'Wow, this's a big deal.'

So, I come in the locker room Monday after class for practice, and at Ohio State, they had a bulletin board up there to show you the 10 teams. First-team offense, first-team defense, and on and on. I look up there for the first-team offense, and I'm not on there. First-string defense, I'm not there. I look under the second-team offense, and I'm not there. Second-team defense? I'm not there. I am now the third-string quarterback. I win the game, and Woody promotes me to third-team quarterback. I was first-string everything before the game. Needless to say, I'm a little upset. I'm ready to kill him.

I said, 'What the hell's going on here?'

Everybody thought it was funny but me. I'm really upset about all of this. I played four games at quarterback that year, and of those four games I played, we won three and tied one. I didn't play anyplace else.

I asked him about it, and he said, 'I want you to learn to play quarterback because you're going to be my quarterback next year.'

I said, 'I don't want to play quarterback.'

He said, 'You're gonna be the quarterback.'

I said, 'Let me play defense until then.'

He said, 'No, I don't want you to get hurt.'

From then on, it was a war between Woody and me. I was very bitter. I was sitting on the bench, watching us lose games that I thought I could help us win. It was a hard—a *really* hard—time. It was a lesson in humility, I can tell you that.

MY JUNIOR YEAR, I RAN RAMPANT. I didn't do anything in practice. I actually got arrested one night for writing 'Script Ohio' in my underwear. A whole bunch of us had a party, and we went out in our shorts and wrote 'Script Ohio' in the snow. One night, we went out and got hammered, and we were going up to Wisconsin to play. We were walking up the ramp to one of those old DC-3s, and someone took a picture of me throwing up over the side as I was getting on the airplane. It was in the paper.

One time, he called me in and said, 'You're worse than Bobo and Janowicz combined.'

I laughed. I said, 'God, that really puts me in a good class.'

He said, 'That's not funny.'

Bo Schembechler knew where I was coming from all the time. He tried to quiet me down. That's where I got ulcers. I was a worrier. I was so nervous about everything that Woody gave me ulcers. I was afraid of Woody, but he didn't know that. He thought I was making a mockery of him all the time. I really wasn't, because I really had a lot of respect for him. I just couldn't understand why he had done this to me. I could never comprehend it.

He was a monster for me. My junior year, I had been kicked out of about eight different apartments, so my senior year, he gave me the option of either moving in with him and Anne or going back to the fraternity house, where he knew I would be. I sure as hell wasn't going to move in with him, so I went to the fraternity house. He was going to try to control me.

The image of the Ohio State quarterback was always a straight-line guy, nice and quiet and conservative, the Frank Kremblases, just nice calm guys. I was bouncing off the walls. He followed me around everywhere. I had lunch with him every day, dinner with him every night. Later, he'd bring me milk and doughnuts, because I had started to develop the ulcers. He'd leave about 11:00, 11:15. He thought he was tucking me into bed. I'd just wait for him to get out the door, and I'd hit the streets. After the game, I was allowed to go out with my family and have dinner, then meet him back at the office at 10 o'clock and start watching film. That was it, baby. That was my life my senior year.

He must've done a good job, though, because I did get more serious my senior year. I knew that I had a responsibility to the team and to myself. I even learned a lot sitting on that bench. It helped me when I first came here to the Colts. I was sitting on the bench behind somebody who made the Hall of Fame, Lenny Moore, but it's still hard. Every once in a while, you say, 'Damn, I don't think he's doing a good job. I could do a *better* job.'

The thing that he did to me my senior year that really, really upset me happened when we voted on captains. The seniors were always captains, and I was a senior, I was the quarterback, the guys and I got along great. He came into the meeting and said, 'There's one guy who can't be captain, and that's Tom Matte.'

I said, 'Why?'

He said, 'You get enough publicity.'

That really hurt me. When he took away the captainship, which was a really prestigious thing at Ohio State, I was furious. It would really have been nice. I don't know whether I would've got it or not, but I thought I had a chance at it until he said that. This way, I didn't have any chance.

Jimmy Herbstreit, who is still a great friend, was offensive captain, and Jimmy Tyrer was the other captain, so maybe I wouldn't have gotten it, but I would sure have liked to have a chance. Hell, he could've made three captains. Who cares? It was a funny time.

Jimmy Herbstreit asked me a couple years ago if I would come back to an event they had for Jim Tyrer and represent the team as a captain. He said, 'Would you come back and be co-captain for one of the games?' I really, really wanted to get back for that, but I couldn't make it. I'd love to come back some time and finally get to be a co-captain at Ohio State.

Woody never pushed me for All-American. He never came out and gave me a nice article in the paper until after the voting was almost done, and I was, I think, fifth or sixth in the Heisman Trophy voting and up in the top in the nation in total offense generated. He finally came out just before the last game and said, 'I know I've been very hard on Tom, but I think he deserves to be a Heisman Trophy winner, because he can do everything.'

I asked him about it years later, and he knew I was a little bit of a hotdog. He thought the way to control me was the way he did it, and he did a pretty good job. My brother wouldn't go to Ohio State because of what Woody did to me. Woody wanted him, but Bo had left Ohio State and gone to Miami of Ohio. Bruce was going to come down to Columbus, but when Bo got the Miami job, he said, 'You want to end up like your brother? You saw what happened to your brother, how Woody treated him.'

Bruce said, 'Hell no.'

Bo said, 'Well, you come down here, and I'll take care of you.'

And Bo did take care of Bruce. My brother was an All-American down with Bo, and he got drafted by the Redskins and the Toronto Argonauts, because we had dual citizenship until we were 25, and by the New York Mets. But he also got drafted by the army and ended up in Vietnam, which completely screwed up his athletic career.

I RESPECTED WOODY, but I sure as hell didn't like him. I was a flamboyant type of guy, I'd do all kinds of crazy things, and he'd get mad at me. I always had the idea that sports were supposed to be fun. That made Woody mad. Don Shula was the same way as Woody was. I used to be the class clown. I'd screw around in practice. I'd put bees in a guy's helmet. You'd get a little bit of grass and twirl it in the ear hole, and it would sound just like bees in your helmet. Guys would rip their helmets off. I put a dead rabbit in John Mackey's locker one time, anything to liven things up, because everybody would get too serious, and then they started fighting and arguing. I just thought you could play the game and still have fun.

As I look back on it now, the reason I had the endurance and ability to do what I did in the pros is because of Woody Hayes. He made me think that I could do the job. I can't give him any more credit than that, and this is a guy that gave me ulcers in college.

I didn't finish my degree. I lacked six hours. I got three calls during the season from Woody Hayes that first year: 'Are you coming back? I've got your schedule arranged. I want you to get your degree.'

I went back, and I got my degree. I didn't think I was going to last in the pros very long, because I had gotten hurt. I felt like a real idiot in Baltimore, because the football was so much more sophisticated than we were used to. I just didn't think I could play very long. I went back in the winter quarter and finished my business degree, and I started taking some pre-law courses in the spring. I had a real light schedule, so I hooked up with Jack Nicklaus, and we started playing golf every day.

But when I got my sheepskin up there, as soon as I walked off the podium, Woody Hayes grabbed me. My parents couldn't come, because they both had to work.

Woody says, 'How do I get in touch with your mother?'

We went up to his office. He called my mother and said, 'Mrs. Matte, this's Coach Woody Hayes.'

My mom said, 'Yes, Woody. Is something wrong?'

'No, I just want to tell you that my obligation to you is finished. Your son just graduated from Ohio State.'

I graduated with good grades in my major—better than a three something—but he had to kick me in the butt every once in a while.

Our relationship grew after I was in the pros. We became such good friends that whenever he came to the East Coast, he'd come here and stay with me. Woody and I would stay up all night and talk. He'd talk about philosophy, about the game of professional football versus college football, what he was doing, how he was doing, how much you have to put back into the community, things that you should do as an athlete, responsibilities you have as a coach.

The guy was a classic. I had sort of the same relationship with Don Shula. I was better friends with him off the field than I was on the field. I'd goof off on the field, he'd get mad, and then we'd go have a couple of beers every once in a while.

When I was in Baltimore, and we lost Unitas and Cuozzo and didn't have a quarterback going into the playoffs, the first guy to call Don Shula was Woody. The game was nationally televised, and Woody called Shula on Monday morning.

He says, 'Listen, Don, if you need a quarterback, put Matte in there, and he'll get the job done.'

Never in my mind did I ever think I could become a professional. I got some letters in the mail towards the end of my senior season, saying, 'Would you be interested in playing pro football?' The usual stuff. I just didn't really think I was in that class. I didn't think I would even get drafted. Where would I get drafted? Why would I get drafted? I was amazed when I was drafted number one by Baltimore. They were coming off championships in '58 and '59 and just missed in '60. In '61, here I am getting drafted.

I thought, 'Where *is* Baltimore?' I didn't even know where Baltimore was.

MY ROOKIE YEAR, I SHOULD'VE BEEN CUT. I was so dumb as a rookie, *dumb*. It was very difficult for me to adjust from 'three yards and a cloud of dust' to the wide open game with John Unitas. I really didn't understand the philosophy of the game. A pass play for me was, 'Get open.' I didn't understand that I was supposed to clear out this zone for this other guy coming right behind me, and *he'll* catch the ball. I'd go out there and hook up, and this other guy would run right into me, and there's the interception. Unitas would go nuts. We had so many formations, so many plays in Baltimore, it was unbelievable.

Plus, I'm coming in with guys like Artie Donovan, Gino Marchetti, Weeb Ewbank, Jim Parker, Lenny Moore, Raymond Berry. These are all Hall-of-Famers. I'm in awe. The first day I went to training camp, I had just walked in from the College All-Star Game.

Someone said, 'Hey, there's Mr. Donovan.'

I walked over and said, 'Mr. Donovan, it's such a pleasure to meet you. I can't wait to play with your son.'

You don't think *that* endeared me to him? He'd been in World War II. This was toward the end of his career. He was *old*. But he was still a great player, 300 pounds, great quickness off the ball, could move laterally. Cripes, I still don't know how old Artie Donovan was.

I was very lucky. I came to a team that was a winning team, and back in those days, they were looking for versatility. They wanted someone who could do a lot of different things, and that's what kept me around. In high school, I was a good track man and a good basketball player and a good swimmer. I'm still a single-digit handicapper in golf. I wasn't great at anything, but I was good at everything. Even in college, I was a defensive back, an offensive back and, all of a sudden, a quarterback. By being versatile, by being the sixth or seventh defensive back, by being the third tight end, by being the second-string halfback behind Lenny Moore—which is no embarrassment—by being the third-string quarterback, by being the third-string fullback, being the sixth receiver, I stuck around.

In two years in the pros, I learned both sides of the ball. I finally understood the big picture. I could come out of the backfield and catch the football, and playing with John Unitas, if you couldn't catch the football, you were gone. I was smart enough to learn the defenses, to make the adjustments, to learn the terminology.

John would say, 'Hey, I know where you're going to be. If it's a zone defense, you're going to be *here*. If it's man-to-man, you're going to be *there*. I'll get you the ball.'

And he did.

The thing that made the Colts was the kind of people they were. They were really unselfish. Everybody was concerned about everyone else's family and children. I don't see that kind of camaraderie anymore in the pros. After weigh-ins on Friday, we'd have a team meeting, at least my wife always thought it was a 'team meeting.' We'd stop at the local bar and have a few pops, and if you left too early, Gino Marchetti would say, 'Where you goin', kid?'

You'd say, 'I have to go shopping with my wife.'

He'd say, 'This's a team meeting. Hey, give him another beer.'

I played quarterback three games in 1965, when Unitas and Cuozzo were hurt. No one touched me in the backfield. I was never hit in the backfield. That offensive line did such a great job for me it was unbelievable.

We went down and played the Dallas Cowboys that year in the 'Toilet Bowl,' which is what we called that runner-up bowl they used to play. Shula called the defense into the shower room for a private meeting.

He said, 'You guys might have to play a long time today.'

Bobby Boyd, the defensive captain, said, 'Why?'

Shula said, 'I'm gonna let Matte throw the football.'

Everybody started laughing. They all thought it was hilarious. And it did turn out to be pretty funny, because we went out and beat the Dallas Cowboys 35–3 in that game. We just kicked their ass, and I was the MVP. Don Meredith was the quarterback at that time. He said, 'You guys set us up.'

I said, 'No, we didn't set you up. Your mouths set you up.'

He had been bragging about how hard they were working and we weren't working hard and we weren't taking the game serious.

All I said was, 'Don't worry about it. When the bell rings, my team'll be here.'

TO THIS DAY, HE'S STILL MAD at me about kicking them so bad. It was a *team* effort, and that's one of the things I learned from Woody: There are no individual players; there is no coach who is good enough to coach a bunch of scrubs and win. You have to play as a team and it has to be a concerted effort by everybody to put it together. That's one thing that Woody Hayes could do, Don Shula could do, Weeb Ewbank could do, Don McCafferty could do. They were all well organized, they all surrounded themselves with great assistant coaches, and they all had players who were team players.

You never saw John Unitas pointing a finger when he got his butt knocked down. Now, when you got in the huddle, he might say, like to Danny Sullivan, 'Hey, Danny, you want to play quarterback today?'

Danny's tail would be between his legs: 'No, John.'

'Then you better block somebody, because I just got my ass knocked off.'

'Yeah, John, okay, okay.'

I'd come back in the huddle, and he'd say, 'What do you have, Tom?'

I'd tell him what I had, and he'd run it. Now, if you didn't have that, he'd be all over you. If you had it, he'd come back to you again later on in the game.

'What do you got?'

'Here's what I got. Last time, I took it inside; this time, I'm gonna go outside.'

We'd run the play, and, cripes, the ball was there. But you had to have his confidence. Remember Bill Brown—Minnesota Vikings, crewcut guy? He and I were talking, and I think we were the oldest running backs in the league for about five years. We were the last of the old white running backs. It was sort of crazy because everybody else was so much faster and quicker, but somehow we made that team.

Every year, the sports reporters would say, 'Matte's not big enough, he's not fast enough, he's not strong enough.' You'd look at this kid coming into camp, and he'd come in with a beautiful body on him, running 4.5, 4.4, something like that. Here's Matte running 4.6 or 4.7, more like 4.7, 4.8 at the end of the career. Everybody thought I was the slowest halfback in the world, but people don't realize, you can only run as fast as your offensive linemen. You get out there by yourself, you're naked. I'd always just get behind them, grab them by the pants and kind of steer them a little bit. You'd always see me grab those offensive linemen, especially my guards—Jim Parker, Alex Sandusky, Danny Sullivan—and push 'em and steer 'em, and I could break off on the blocks.

These kids would walk into camp and take one look at me and say, 'This's gonna be easy.' But after the last cut was made, I'd be saying to all these kids walking out, 'God, I hope you have good luck finding another team.'

Then, the sportswriters would look at the stats at the end of the year and say, 'How'd he do all that?'

I had the best game I ever had in my life against the Jets in Super Bowl III. Everybody says, 'Why didn't you win? You were 18-point favorites.'

I tell them, 'I played the best game of my life. My teammates let me down.'

Then I laugh. But you have to give credit where credit is due. To get to the Super Bowl, you have to be good. Nobody wanted to give any credit to the Jets around here, but Weeb Ewbank was the coach up there, and he had the same system that we had down here. It was two mirrored teams playing against each other, and on that day, Joe Namath picked our defense apart. We had a lot of mistakes—fumbles, balls popping up in the air, not seeing receivers open down the field. Everything that could go wrong went wrong on that given day. I'd've liked to played them two out of three.

Hell, I had to go to the Pro Bowl and answer to the other guys in the league. It was the first loss ever to an AFL team. They were all over me about it; you couldn't believe it. The following year, the same thing happened to Minnesota. The Minnesota guys came out to the Pro Bowl, and I said, 'Now I can give *you* guys some crap.'

We were the winningest team in all of football from '58 through '71. Nobody had a record like we did. We had a great organization, a great owner—until we got Robert Irsay, who was the biggest jerk in the world. That's when the team fell apart. Joe Thomas came here as general manager, and he tore down all the leadership, traded everybody away. The whole franchise fell apart, and that's why they left this city.

John and I both got traded to San Diego in the off-season of '72, and they didn't call us and tell us. I heard it on the radio. I spent 12 years with this team, and those bastards had the audacity to trade us without ever calling us and let us hear about it on the radio.

IN '73, MY ULCERS WERE SO BAD and I was bleeding so much that they had to operate on me. I went into the hospital in the spring of '73 weighing 236 pounds. Twenty-eight days later, I came out at 187. I almost died. I know I don't seem the type to have ulcers, but I kept everything inside. I was eating myself up inside. Nineteen sixty-four was my first bleed when I was in the pros here, and I had already had ulcers for part of that time. From then until '73, I had seven bleeds where I lost up to eight pints of blood. I had to have all of those transfusions. I mean, I was really bad.

In 1966, I played a whole game with a bleed. We were playing the Toilet Bowl, against Philadelphia, and I had told Shula that I wanted out. I wasn't happy with the way things were going. I wasn't playing as much as I thought I should. I was working my butt off and sitting on the bench.

Shula said, 'Tom, I'm gonna let you start and play the whole game.'

Before the game, I went into the bathroom, and I was passing blood. I told the doctor, 'I'm passing blood. Don't tell Shula, because I'm starting this game. I want to play.'

I played the whole game. They voted halfway through the third quarter for the most valuable player, and somebody from Philadelphia got it. I scored a touchdown in the last 30 seconds, and we won the game. I was MVP the year before against Dallas, and I would've gotten MVP that year, too, if they would've waited longer. Soon as the game was over, I took a shower and went to the hospital for four pints of blood.

We were dumb athletes, blinded by love of the game. I was so loyal to my teammates that I would do anything to get on that field. If somebody was in trouble on the homefront, or if their children were in trouble, everybody was there for them. Everybody thought about everybody else; they just didn't think of themselves. Now, half these guys grab their lawyers and their accountants, and they go in a corner and talk business.

When I entered the pros, I made a commitment to myself and to my wife. I said, 'The day I start playing for money is the day I quit.'

I played because I loved it.

I'm a limited partner with the CFL franchise here in Baltimore now. I guess I'd call myself second in command. I'm coordinating the marketing, I'm doing the broadcasting, I helped renovate the whole stadium. I'm back in my own element. I didn't get involved until I was sure we weren't going to get an NFL franchise. I did everything in my power to get a team here, and it just wasn't going to be.

These are all young kids. They're good kids, and they're hungry. They're not making 2, 3, 5 million dollars a year. They're making between $30,000 to $80,000 a year, if they're lucky. They want to show what they got. They want to be able to get a raise next year. They want to have off-season jobs, and I make sure that they're active in the community. It's like when I played. If I was hurt, I played hurt, because I knew if I sat on the bench, someone was gonna take my job, and I would never get back in there. These guys in the NFL now, cripes, they get a hangnail, and they're out. It's crazy. I was down at the Super Bowl this year, and it's not a game any more; it's a production. It's like you're going to a Las Vegas show or something. That's why I still like college football so much.

I've never liked corporations or bureaucracies. I've always been a team player. Everybody should be part of that team, part of a winning effort, whether it's the equipment manager or the business manager or the ticket sales person. If we're winning here in the organization as we have with the Baltimore CFL football club, it's everybody's effort. If anybody's here trying to achieve their own goals, I want them out of here. I don't want any hotdogs here; I've had enough hotdogs in my life.

TODAY IN THE PROS, it's difficult for players and coaches to communicate. Everybody thinks they're the big deals. Woody instilled in all of us that you have to put something back into the community. Athletes were given a talent. How many guys really make it in professional sports? It's such a minute number. The athlete has an obligation to the public, to his peers, to the kids who're looking up to him.

I remember a little kid named Jimmy Garret, when I was at Ohio State. He came from a broken home in Columbus. His father left him; his mother was a wonderful lady. This little kid was 10 or 11, and he sort of adopted me as his hero. One day in practice, he came out and gave me a $2 bill to send him a picture of myself. I still have the $2 bill. I got a bunch of crap about it. All the guys were ribbing me about taking money off little kids. Jimmy became my mascot, you might say. After every game, Jimmy Garret got my chin strap when I was running off the field. Now, they didn't have very much money. His mother was working in a restaurant or something. But he saved up his money, and after I scored my first touchdown, he gave me a beautiful trophy. He got one of my chin straps bronzed. It had M-A-T-T-E on it, and it said: 'Memories Are They That Electrify.' I'll tell you something, I still get choked up by it. Later on, he went into the Navy and got his act together, even though he had a tough time when he was young. You think you have an influence on them, but he had an influence on me just as much. I still have the trophy at home, and it's probably one of my most valuable trophies.

THERE'S A COUPLE THINGS I DID in the history of football that're still around. When I had to play quarterback in 1965, that's when they first came up with the wrist band for the quarterback, with all the plays on it; now, there all wearing wrist bands. I caused the NFL to raise the goal posts 10 feet higher and put an official on both sides of it, because they blew the call up in Green Bay, when they beat us in the sudden death game. Those're things I contributed to, and I'm still proud of them.

Pro football was an extended childhood for me. It lasted 12 years, then I was 35 years old and saying, 'What the hell am I going to do with myself *now*?' But I had that education to fall back on, and that's where Woody comes into the picture. He played such an integral part in my life in making me understand that there is life after sports.

I felt terrible for Woody the night that happened with the kid from Clemson, but they couldn't keep him after that, especially the way the camera isolated on him. Television has an innate ability of finding all those little things and blowing them way out of proportion. It was a sad way for him to end what was probably one of the all-time greatest careers in college football.

I'll tell you something, though, here's what lot of people don't know: The kid he hit was roommates with our owner here, Jim Speros, and Jim told me that Woody became very close with that kid's family, good friends. That was very impressive, because he was so intense that he probably didn't know that he did it.

After this all happened, some of the guys got together and decided to invite back players and coaches and have a little party for Woody. Everybody donated some money, and we bought him a jeep and fixed up his cabin. We raised about a quarter of a million dollars to do all this. I think we sent out something like 500 invitations, and 450 people came back, and the other 50 sent a donation. Not one guy that we invited didn't respond. At the end of the evening, we just sat down and talked. He was sad. I think if Woody would've had his druthers, he would've liked to have died on the battlefield. He would've like to have had a heart attack out there right in front of the 95,000 people.

He said, 'I really don't know why I did it. It was just an instinctive reaction.'

I said, 'I'm sorry for you, Coach.'

He said, 'I caused it myself.'

BUT WOODY CAME BACK FROM THAT. That's why I always like to have people who played sports work for me. You get knocked down, but you know how to get back up. That's the one thing that sports teaches you—how to handle situations in life.

Everybody has that bad image left in their mind about Woody hitting the kid. I'd like to know how many times he punched me. When you're an athlete and you're working for somebody as intense as Woody, every once in a while, you *need* a kick in the ass. That's what's wrong with our society now. We don't kick anybody in the ass anymore.

We don't say, 'You're wrong. This's the way to do it.'

You take Bobby Knight. I know Bobby; I like him. Woody Hayes was his mentor, and he has that same kind of philosophy. He'll fight for his players, he'll die for his players, but he'll also kick them in the ass when they do something wrong. Our society has become so complacent that everyone says, 'Oh, let's just take it easy.'

Bullshit. If you're wrong, you deserve a kick in the ass. You don't have to beat someone up or abuse them, but you'll learn a hell of a lot quicker with discipline. A good quick kick in the butt will get your attention.

I think that's what Woody did, and I appreciate what Woody did for me. You don't always have to like everybody when you work with them, but once you get away from those people who do have such an impression on you and you focus on what life is *really* like, you say, 'Hey, this guy knew what he was talking about.'

When I was growing up, I thought my parents were the dumbest people in the whole damned world. Then, all of a sudden when I became a parent, I said, 'Oh, man, they weren't so dumb.' That's what I had to go through with my parents, and with Woody, too.

I was really devastated when Woody died. I was out of town and couldn't get back there. I wrote Annie a long letter. I didn't want him to die. I really cherished those times when I had a chance to talk to him. I used to try to come down for one game every year, and I always went to his office. I'd bring my friends from Baltimore, and we'd just talk to him for about a half an hour.

He'd say, 'I'll see you next year.'

'Okay, Coach, I'll see you next year.'

It really upset me that I didn't get a chance to say goodbye. I think a lot of players felt like that—that they really didn't get a chance to say thank you and goodbye. I didn't get that chance. That's always been empty. I look back on it, and we had our battles. But I've tried to put everything into perspective. He gave me my education. He gave me my chance to be where I am right now. I know football as well as anyone in the country, and being back in football is where I belong. I've done all the other things. I have my real estate license and my insurance license. I was in the computer industry for many years, the leasing business. I've done it all, and I've come around full-circle. You ask yourself, 'What do you love the best?' The game calls you back.

I look back on my days at Ohio State, and they were some of the best years of my life. Jack Nicklaus was in my fraternity and taught me how to play golf. He and I remain great friends. I still go back and tailgate with some of the guys I played football with. I still have really good friends from college. I love to come back to Columbus. I wish I could get back more often. I walk into games, and people still yell, 'Hey, Matte, how you doin'?'

Which is really nice.

People say, 'Oh, that's bullshit' and all that, but I say, 'No, it's nice that people still remember you.'”

76
76

The Pastor *and the* Warrior

DESPITE NEARLY four decades of extraordinary similarities in their lives, the Pastor and the Warrior are both quick to indicate how unlike they are.

"It's interesting," the Rev. Daryl Sanders says of Bob Vogel, whom he met in 1958 when Woody Hayes recruited the two strapping young linemen. "Today, we're still quite different in our personalities, even how we do some things."

Three decades ago, Vogel and Sanders were paired at tackle on what Hayes called "a tremendously great offensive line," and Vogel was water-baptized by Sanders years later. Yet Vogel makes a point of saying, "Although Daryl and I have this relationship that we've had for a long time, we don't socialize."

They were reared in utterly different circumstances—Sanders as one of few white kids in several inner-city neighborhoods, Vogel in a series of small towns—but with the common bond of poverty. Neither's parents had graduated from high school or were able to afford college tuition; however, both boys were gifted athletes who saw football as a way to a better life. "I saw athletics as my way into society," says Sanders. "Open those doors—here I come."

They would both choose to play for the Buckeyes, but not for the same reasons. Whereas Sanders was "overwhelmed" by the excitement of attending an Ohio State-Michigan game and by Hayes's passionate salesmanship, Vogel's decision was far less emotional: "I don't know where I could go in the U.S. that had a better marketing program, and I don't know where I could go that was a better football program year-in and year-out, where my mom and dad could see me play. It was pragmatic."

Hayes was coming off his worst season ever, and left tackle was his biggest question mark in 1960. Vogel and Sanders were both 6' 5", both 223 pounds and both so well conditioned that in the annual mile run, they beat many of the running backs. Throughout the preseason, Hayes seemed hard-put to decide between them, declaring first one, then the other to be the starter. Vogel notes that he won the job, but he and Sanders played almost the same number of minutes that year.

"That's still the best way to play football—moving the ball on the ground," Hayes said in 1961, and with Sanders and Vogel at tackle and Bob Ferguson at fullback, he did just that, calling 522 runs in 621 plays. In Vogel and Sanders, Hayes had two big men who were fast enough to block downfield ("Those guys can really move," Hayes said) and who enjoyed brutal trenchwork. ("It was almost like boxing. It was a real personal match. I loved it," says Sanders.) That year, the Bucks tied TCU in the opener, then won eight straight, capturing the school's tenth Big Ten title and averaging almost 30 points in league games. They crushed Michigan 50–20, as Ferguson ran for 152 yards and Paul Warfield 122, and were named national champions by the Football Writers Association.

However, on the same day the U.S. shot Enos the chimp into space, thousands of students, many with their faces covered by bandanas, marched down High Street to protest the Faculty Council's vote to reject the Rose Bowl bid. The decision seems to have unnerved Hayes and contributed to an erratic 1962 season for Sanders and Vogel, who were among 19 seniors ("the best senior class we've ever had," according to Hayes) on a team that everyone expected to easily win the national title.

Ohio State lost its second game

of the season when fullback Dave Katterhenrich, running behind Sanders, was stopped three times from the UCLA one. The following week, OSU rushed for 517 yards at Illinois, a school record, but the team turned the ball over 16 times in its first seven games, lost to Northwestern in Ohio Stadium for the first time in 19 years, and finished in a tie for third in the league.

"I think there were some player problems, but I think there were some coaching problems," Sanders says. "Woody was only close to a couple of guys my senior year. He could never quite catch on to where the chemistry was on our team."

The frustrations were eased by the attention Vogel and Sanders received from the NFL. "Maybe they haven't got Ferguson," a scout said prior to the 1962 season, "but running behind that line, the fullback won't hit anything for five yards past the line of scrimmage anyway."

Hayes called them "the best blocking tackles in football," adding, "Those two tackles just block beautifully." Nonetheless, neither made All Big Ten or All-American, at least partly because one had become indistinguishable from the other. To Hayes, they were "our two tackles"; to the press, they were "the two mighty Buckeye tackles." Indeed, they even looked much alike: tall, sturdy and crewcut, with penetrating eyes and long arms and legs, long ears and noses. But photos reveal a hint of waywardness about Sanders that isn't present in the sober Vogel. Vogel's expression seems inordinately serious for so young a man, while Sanders appears to be suppressing a grin.

Hayes once remarked that Ohio State had so many great fullbacks because it had so many great linemen. Vogel and Sanders suspect that he might not've applied that belief to them when it came time to promote players for all-star teams. Neither felt any affection for the coach.

Vogel might well the only person ever to describe Hayes as "not a lot different than most coaches." He recalls that Hayes once instructed him to appear on a television show on the same day he was to take an important exam. Vogel skipped the TV session. "There wasn't much of a relationship before that, but there was almost no relationship after that," he says.

Sanders's natural disdain for authority ("a lifelong issue") didn't endear him to Hayes. "Your first year, you fear Woody; your second year, you respect him; but your third year, you begin to question him," he said.

Both felt more comfortable with offensive line coach Bo Schembechler ("a joy to play for," says Vogel) than with Hayes. During the team banquet his final year, Sanders, whose nickname was "Bo," delivered an impassioned tribute to Schembechler, while Vogel warned the freshman players that if they besmirched the Ohio State tradition, he would never forgive them. During the NFL draft, a representative of the Detroit Lions stashed the two players in a hotel and fed them steaks. Both first-round picks—Sanders by the Lions, Vogel by Baltimore—they missed out on the money available in the NFL/AFL bidding wars by immediately signing when league officials tossed two rolls of small bills on the floor in front of them. "Talk about country bumpkins. Daryl and I were the dumbest, biggest hicks," Vogel says.

Sanders was an immediate starter in Detroit; however, he seems to have been more influenced by Hayes than he realized. In four years, the Lions lost 29 games; like Hayes, Sanders found losing unbearable. ("I could never develop the losing mentality.") He'd also listened for years to Hayes's oft-repeated advice that football was a means to an end, not an end in itself. As soon as he arrived in Detroit, Sanders found a job with a sales/promotion company. When his boss left and the company offered him the lucrative position, Sanders walked away from the NFL.

In Baltimore, Vogel was a confused rookie starter in a huddle composed of future Hall-of-Famers: Raymond Berry, Lenny Moore, Jim Parker, Johnny Unitas. Undersized at 240 pounds and with little experience in a passing offense, he was humiliated in his first game by huge defensive end Doug Atkins (as Parker had been five years earlier). He worked every day after practice to learn the nuances of pass protection. ("It's like trying to hit a golf ball, except you're not running when you're trying to hit a golf ball and nobody's beating on your roof.")

Like Sanders, Vogel could not seem to escape Hayes's reach. Before Vogel's first camp in the pros, Hayes called Don Shula, Baltimore's new head coach, and suggested that Shula move Parker, a star tackle, to guard and put Vogel at Parker's former position. Shula made the move, and within two years, Vogel had become one of the league's outstanding players. He made All-Pro four times and played in two Super Bowls. As had Sanders, Vogel unexpectedly left the NFL, retiring after an All-Pro season in 1972 to become general manager of a cable television system. He went back only once to watch a Colt game. "Once I was done, that was it," he says.

Sanders quickly became a top executive, living a hectic life of "jets, Europe, parties and business" and, ultimately, being overcome by malaise. He went through a divorce, restlessly changed jobs. He'd been brought up a Lutheran, but hadn't even opened a Bible in years when his second wife, Barbara, took him to a church service. There, he found contentment: "We walk into this church, and I'm telling you, that's what I'm looking for. What I was really looking for was a meaningful relationship with God."

Likewise, Vogel "had an itch that wasn't getting scratched." Invited by several Baltimore teammates, Vogel and his wife, Andrea, attended a Fellowship of Christian Athletes conference, where he, too, underwent a spiritual transformation. On the last day of the conference, he and Andrea knelt and prayed, "Lord, we want to be your people. We don't know what that means, but we're committing ourselves to be your people."

Vogel and Sanders reunited 20 years ago when they purchased an automobile dealership in Columbus. "I just wanted to serve God and be a Cadillac dealer and make a lot of money," Sanders says, but he still felt unfulfilled.

He says that a vision of a church in northwest Columbus grew in him. When he was 44, a board of pastors agreed that Daryl Sanders had been "set aside" by God for the ministry. He began the Zion Christian Fellowship Church in a middle school with a congregation of 20; within 18 months, it had grown to over 100, including Vogel, an elder. In 1989, they moved into an impressive new church in Powell.

An ornate Lord's Prayer tapestry hung in a gilt frame beside Sanders as he spoke in his spacious office. He was dressed casually, in a raspberry-colored, heavy cotton shirt, starched and pressed jeans, and gleaming penny loafers. The bridge of his large nose is deeply scarred, as though someone had gouged it with a screwdriver. He's begun to grow a paunch, but he still has a thick shock of white hair. Energetic and gregarious, he laughed often, flashing a toothy smile.

Having finally learned to come under authority, Sanders seems at peace. "God will give you whatever it takes to know Him," he said in a sermon. "Knowing Him and doing His good pleasure is your and my brightest purpose. Let us quit asking why. Let us quit questioning."

Andrea Vogel answered the door to the couple's ranch home, which sits just off a lane cutting through miles of farmland and substantial houses on tree-studded lots. A set of shy, 19-month-old black twins clung to her neck, tiny legs gripping her waist and hips. She introduced the boys as Jordan and Jason, the 10th and 11th foster children—for the most part, children of drug-addicted mothers—the Vogels have taken in. "My heart doesn't see color; it sees babies," Vogel says. When Andrea took the twins to bed, Vogel kissed each in turn and said, "Good night, sweet boy."

No football memorabilia was displayed in the immaculate sunken livingroom. Bric-a-brac, family portraits, and snapshots of the foster children, many of whom still visit, decorated walls and shelves.

Vogel says that when he played, he was "a warrior" ("I'd do it again, because warriors like to battle"), and with his icy blue eyes, sandy hair swept off his broad forehead, and graying, russet beard, he does look like Jurgen Prochnow in *Das Boot*. His manner, however, is contemplative. He templed his fingers and pondered every word. He says he is at his high school playing weight, and the years have given him character, made him distinguished. He is a regional sales manager for one of the world's largest personnel firms and, like Sanders, content in his faith: "It's a commitment. It's excellence, and it's fulfilling my design. I was designed to fellowship with God."

Both Sanders and Vogel eventually came to view Hayes differently than they did 33 years ago. Sanders was watching TV during a skiing trip when he saw Hayes strike Charlie Bauman. He'd never been one of "Woody's boys," but Sanders felt that he had to rush to Hayes's side. He picked up Archie Griffin. They prayed together and then went to the Hayes home. Sanders and Griffin were the first people other than family members to speak with the distraught coach, who had secluded himself after the Gator Bowl. For the rest of Hayes's life, Sanders was his companion, business advisor, and confidant. Sanders was ordained in 1986. Hayes, though increasingly infirm, attended the ceremony. "When he died, I felt like I lost a friend," Sanders says.

Vogel still holds that the coach was not a dominate figure in his life ("My dad loved me, and I loved my dad, so I wasn't looking for dad"), but he now says that Hayes's intensity and lack of hypocrisy outweighed his shortcomings. Vogel regrets only that Hayes stayed trapped behind his own rigid idea of himself. "It broke my heart that he was unable, or unwilling, to ever receive Jesus, that he was never able to let that shield down and allow people to love him," Vogel says.

"That's eternal stuff—unlike football."

Daryl SANDERS

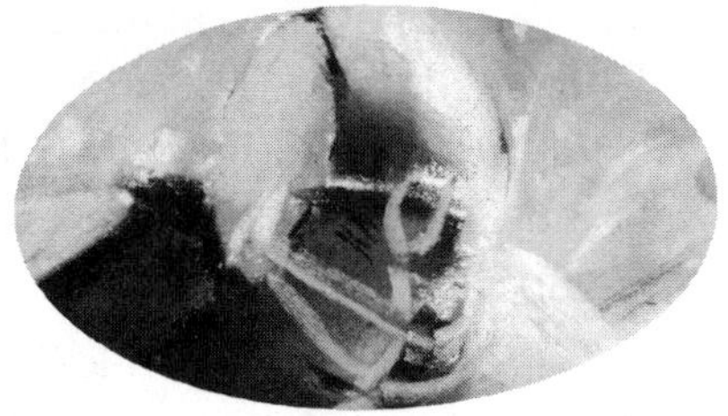

"WE MOVED OUT to the suburbs, to Mayfield Heights on the east side of Cleveland, the summer just before I was going into the ninth grade, and the first day in school people started asking me if I was going to go out for football. I was fairly large. I was about 5-10 in the ninth grade, weighed a little bit less than 150 pounds. I was larger than most. They started asking me, 'Are you gonna go out for football.'

It had never occurred to me. Since so many people were asking me about it, I just said, 'Sure.'

In those days, they had the face masks that kind of clung to your face. It was like a plastic hockey player's mask. The guys who had gone out the year before automatically got the uniforms. There were x-number of uniforms, and it got down to there were two of us with one uniform left. So the coach says, 'Well, whoever catches this ball gets the uniform.'

He throws the ball. So I catch it and fall down. And I got the last uniform. That was my auspicious beginning to organized football.

I was a fairly motivated kid. I don't know why. I just was. My father had only completed the eighth grade in school, but for some reason, it was written into my heart that I was going to college. I have no idea why, none at all. I just always felt that was what I was going to do.

I learned the game pretty quickly, and I got a lot of acceptance in the school. This was a new-found experience for me. I'd had a lot of rejection. Now, I had a lot of acceptance. It was just a real positive thing.

One time we had to do this tackling drill, and the equipment wasn't very good, especially when you get the last uniform. The helmet didn't quite fit, and the shoulderpads didn't fit. The first time I tackled somebody, man, it hurt. But the feedback motivated me. I remember consciously making the decision: 'Well, this's still such a good experience I'm just going to learn to live with the pain.' So that's what I did.

I found I had a lot of God-given abilities. I played basketball, track. I began excelling in all the sports and was getting recognition, not only in my own school, but in the community and in the city. I was pretty cocky. Pride's been kind of a life-long issue for me, particularly when part of the motivation to play—a coaching technique—is to feed off pride. You're told that pride's a good thing. When you pick up the Bible, the Bible says that pride comes before destruction. God hates the proud look. Right away, I was beginning to wrestle with an internal conflict. Football and my faith were placed in opposition to each other. I was raised to believe in humility and service and preferring the other person, and now I'm being told, 'No, you're *better* than the other person. *Beat* the other person.' I felt that conflict then, and I bought into it. I went the way of football.

I made conscious decisions to do what it took to become a great football player. It took focus. It took a willingness to pay the price, to work when others wouldn't work, to work longer than anybody would work, to out-work anybody. That ethic was built into me. Work is a healthy thing. I work hard in the ministry. I think you can do it without being so self-preoccupied. But I became self-centered. I was preoccupied with myself and what I wanted to do.

I BEGAN TO SEE FOOTBALL AS MY WAY OUT. I saw athletics as my way out into society. I was an offensive tackle, and my senior year I was the league's most valuable player. It probably hasn't happened before or since in that league that the most valuable player was an offensive tackle. I began to get that kind of recognition, and I was contacted by 40 or 50 schools.

I remember having to make the decision: Was I going to be a big fish in a little pond or a little fish in big pond? I remember having to come to grips with which way I wanted to go. I initially had the inclination to go to a small school, until I came to the Ohio State-Michigan game in 1958. It was the first college game I had ever been to. I walked into that stadium, and there were 83,000 people, and there was such a spirit in the place, I mean, it arrested me.

In those days, there were some schools offering you 15 or 20 bucks a week to play. First of all, 15 or 20 bucks wasn't all that tempting, even though I didn't have any money. I didn't even have a suit to wear. My first suit was given to me by one of the business people in my community my senior year of high school. But for some reason or another, I just came to the conclusion that if they were buying and selling for 15 or 20 bucks a week, who knows what you're getting into in that kind of situation? Who knows if those people will even be there?

I'm not sure that I knew what I was looking for in a school, but one thing for sure, I was overwhelmed walking into Ohio Stadium. Then, Thanksgiving weekend, Woody Hayes invited my father and I to come down and spend the weekend here. The Michigan game was before. There were maybe six or seven other guys down at that time, and they had already made the decision that they wanted to give me a scholarship. We were all over at Woody's house and had a cookout—hamburgers—and watched some football game on television. I think it was maybe the next day, my dad and I went over to Woody's office. Woody sat there, and the three of us talked for four hours, except my father didn't say a word and I said 'Yessir' about three times.

He talked about everything. Woody would always philosophize. Right then, he planted something in my heart that stayed in my heart. That was that football was a means to an end and not an end in itself. My four years of school, I constantly heard that phrase, and I took it very seriously. To me that meant, get an education.

WOODY WAS ONE OF THE GREAT SALESMEN. He was very endearing. I'd never been around anyone like him before. I'd never been around anyone with such passion, energy, and articulation. You were always ready to hit someone when you come out of his office. He was a pretty overwhelming guy for an 18-year-old inner-city kid. None of the other head coaches from other schools came close to him. He'd made up his mind that he really wanted me, for whatever reason, so he set out to get me. Nobody else had made quite the commitment to me that he did.

He would send postcards. It was pretty awesome to me. He would send them to the school. It was kind of an interesting strategy as I look back on it, because the office of the school would come and deliver a letter to me. Ohio State had that real plain stationary; it was like the White House—'The Ohio State University.' Woody would send you a note that he had traveled off some place and he was thinking about you. All my friends would see it, and it was a pretty big deal. It was nice.

Then I was faced with the 'big fish, little pond' issue. I decided to take the risk. I was willing to be a little fish in a big pond, with the opportunity to be a big fish. I believed I was going to have a fair opportunity. I wouldn't say that he treated everybody equally. I think he played favorites. In a very calculated way, he motivated people on an individual basis. I think he made decisions—very specific, individual decisions. There were about 25 guys in our class. I don't remember the ratio, and it was a lot more white than black, but we had a significant number of black athletes. He would bend over backwards for them. We used to feel that he preferred blacks over whites sometimes. As I look back now, he had sensitivities to the social pressures on the black athletes. No doubt about it—he was ahead of his time. In those days, there were no black athletes in the Southeastern Conference. My rookie year with the Detroit Lions, when I went into training camp, there was an athlete from the bayou country in Louisiana, and he just couldn't get over having black men in the shower with him. It was just overwhelming to him. It startled me that he would feel that way.

If Woody felt he needed to get something from an athlete or move a certain way with an athlete, he would. We had Bob Ferguson, who was a great athlete—two years All-American. Woody coached that guy every day. Other players, you coach periodically. Woody coached Bob every day. He gave him the attention he felt Bob needed, and it worked.

My sophomore year, I started some games on offense and some on defense. We played Illinois, and I didn't have a very good game. I just wasn't hitting anybody. So, we had a goal line drill that following week. It's one of those situations where the defense knows what you're doing, and the offense knows what you're doing, the same play over and over again. It's a goal line situation where everyone's jammed in the line, and we weren't getting across the goal line. Woody was getting madder and madder and madder.

We were bent over in the huddle. Woody bent over with us. He started to stand up, and we all started to back away. The temperature was over 20 degrees, so he was wearing just one tee-shirt—below 20 degrees, he wore two tee-shirts. He took his cap off. He tried to tear his cap, and he couldn't do it. He tried to do that ofen, but I never saw him able to tear up his cap. Suddenly, he started to punch himself in the head and started bleeding. He bent back over, called us back into the huddle, and called the same play. We still didn't score.

He came up to me and said, 'Well, you didn't hit anybody in the game last Saturday, and you're not hitting anybody here today.'

Then he punched me in the stomach. It didn't hurt me physically, but it was a real wake-up call. For me to play at this level and to succeed at this level, I was going to have to take my aggressiveness to another level. First, it hurt my ego. Then I reacted positively to it. I look back on it, that's probably what I needed.

I think Woody got the most out of me. That's what his goal was as a coach—to get the most out of people. While he varied his methods, he was a very passionate, hard-driving guy. Some people don't respond very well in that environment. But the guys who played for him did. Practices were very difficult. He worked with a half-line concept. So the pressure was always there to be able to get your block. You know the ball can only go one way, and that guy over you is trying to play, trying to get a job. And he doesn't have to see whether the ball's going the other way or not, so it's a whole different thing from a game situation.

FRESHMEN WEREN'T ALLOWED TO PLAY on the varsity then. We had our own locker room, but we were always out on the same general field as where the varsity was. We'd just be one field over, so you could kind of see and tell what things were going on over there. Then, sometimes, we would come over and run the opposing team's plays. Not in any live situation. I don't think we ever went live with the varsity. But when it came to spring, you pretty much knew what was going on.

That freshman rule was good for me. I wasn't ready to play. I think, even today, there are some kids who are ready to play, but there are some kids who aren't emotionally ready. I'm completely against what's going on in college football and basketball today. It's the most misused working class in America. They're abusing these guys. They're using the college athlete. It's five hours a day year-round. I mean, come on. And they're still getting the same four-year education that I got. It's ridiculous.

In the off-season, we were supposed to lift weights, but you only had to go down there a couple times a week. As long as you were working out and they knew you were staying in shape, you didn't even have to go down there. They just wanted to make sure that you were staying in shape over the winter quarter. And in the spring, you only had your 20 practices. That's all they expected of you. Woody's demands were completely fair—be ready to play.

The game was a lot faster than in high school. The contact was harder and faster. In the middle of my sophomore year, I began to acquire the techniques. In those days, I had an opponent. I wasn't playing a team. I didn't care what the team was doing. I had a guy over me, and I was playing against that guy. There was me and him, and by the end of the day, there was going to be a winner. Now they block areas and block two guys and three guys on a play, in those days it was, 'It's you and me, buddy, and we're going to see who wins.' There was a whole different psychology to the game for an offensive lineman in those days.

I LOVED IT. I LOVED TO HIT. In those days, we didn't block with our hands, we blocked with our heads. Stick the guy in the sternum. My goal was to hit my defensive end in the sternum every play and sting him. That's all there was to it. Just hit that guy. It was real personal, almost like boxing.

In those days, we ran the ball off-tackle, and I was a tackle. In one game, we ran off-tackle 47 times. Our fullback, Dave Francis, was running down field, and he just fell over on about the 15-yard line. His legs gave out. He couldn't help it, he had run so many off-tackle plays, and we're running down next to him, laughing at him because he just gave out. We'd go in the huddle, and Bob Vogel, who is an elder in the church, played on the other side. We'd say, 'We got 3 1/2 yards.'

He'd say, 'Oh, we got *four* yards.'

That's how we marked the game in those days. It was get out there on the field and wear that guy down and beat him up, so that by the end of the game, instead of three yards a carry you get four yards a carry. And every now and then, you'd break one away for a 10-yard gainer. In Bob Ferguson's junior and senior years, which were my sophomore and junior years, he was only stopped for a loss *once*. We had a great offensive line. We'd laugh even in the midst of that. If the other side got stopped, we'd joke with them. We had fun. I played football when it was fun.

Woody was always serious. He wouldn't laugh out on the field. I don't remember him doing much that was funny. During my freshman year, he chased out all the press. Kicked them all off the field. He got mad at them for some reason and threw them all out. That's the funniest thing I ever knew Woody to do.

One time, we're practicing and he's upset with us. There's no lights in those days. He made all the coaches go get their cars and pull them up on the track and turn the headlights on. We practiced under the headlights. We'd do those things, and we'd laugh about them. He'd be real serious. Our senior year in the locker rooms we'd just stand back there with our helmets on and laugh. It was amusing to us, his tirades and his energy, and sometimes not quite knowing what to do with it.

WHEN I CAME TO OHIO STATE, I quit going to church. My faith took a back seat. You can say, 'Well, I don't have time. I'm busy.' What was really going on was I had made choices about this duality. You can't live as a split personality. You start going one way or the other, and I started wanting to go my own way, not only in football, but in other things, and it was all born out of this self-centeredness. I became preoccupied with myself and what I had to do to get ahead. So, I chose to quit going to church. I didn't really go to church for 15 years.

I'm a pastor today, and you look back and say, 'What's the dynamics? What's that journey in life?' Certainly, the journey includes some guilt, but when you make a decision about God, you learn to justify that decision. If you want to decide God out of your life, you build up a rationale of either He doesn't exist, or He's a loving God, and He'll put up with whatever I do. So I made that decision, and during those 15 years I'll bet I didn't think about it a half a dozen times.

The rationale I developed was that the church was not relevant to me. That's a real common excuse used today to legislate God out of your life. I used His name in vain, but I wouldn't say, 'There's no God. There's no Jesus Christ.' But I wasn't inquiring, I didn't open my Bible. I can't tell you that I ever read my Bible during all those years. I was preoccupied with getting ahead, with making money, being well-known. That's what I set my focus on.

At Ohio State, you get well-known quickly, and we had an outstanding team. The fans here know people other than just your runningback and your quarterback, so I was pretty well-known. I took it for granted. It didn't surprise me. People would want to be around you. They would want to tell other people that they knew you or that they had been with you. So people would buy you lunch or buy you beer. I also saw the superficiality of it. I never got caught up in that. I never took myself so serious as a result of that, because I saw it as pretty shallow.

I had two dreams about Woody while I was in school, two dreams that were the same dream. The dream was that we were in the locker room at half time, and Woody lost it, and that men in white coats came and took him away. I mean, he was a piece of work at half time, a piece of work. My junior year, we had a great football team. We had five or six guys on that team who did great in the NFL: Tom Matte, Bob Vogel. One game, we scored on the first play from scrimmage and we laid down the rest of the half. We were winning, I think, 7–6 at half time, but after that first play—76-yard touchdown run—we didn't do anything the rest of the half, and at half time, Woody just literally went nuts.

The blackboard was one of those movable blackboards, and he threw a left jab; I mean, he hit that blackboard with a left and told us that we have to get out there and start hitting these guys. He swings on this blackboard, puts his fist through the blackboard, which we tried to duplicate the next day, and nobody could do it. He put his fist through the blackboard, and he couldn't get it out. You're sitting there watching this improbable scene. He's yelling at us and kicked us out of the locker room, I guess while he got his fist out of the blackboard. We went out and just killed them. It was against Oregon, and we beat them 22-12 or something like that.

WOODY WAS A PASSIONATE GUY. I remember—it was after I was out of school— the famous Michigan game. I was living in Detroit. It was the time when he kicked the yard markers and ran out on the field. I was sitting in the stands with a customer, and I saw Woody run across the field and right up, within one inch, of that official's face. I turned to the guy next to me and said, 'You have just seen one of the greatest acts, as in acting, as in movie-acting, that you're ever going to see. That's vintage Woody Hayes.'

While all the press said he was out of control, I say to you nobody can run 50 yards and into a man's face, within one inch, without touching him. Woody knew if he touched the official, he was gone, yet he ran 50 yards, and there was total control, and there was total plan and ploy of his, to demonstrate his passion for the moment. I always felt that Woody did those things on a very calculated basis. He knew he needed to intervene in that game, because it was going against him. Games have momentums; there are ebbs and flows. Since he couldn't play, he had to intervene, do something that would break the mood or the momentum or the lethargy.

Sometimes, you're playing a football game, and a lethargy sets in. You're just, 'Oh boy, we're losing, we're gonna lose.' You start buying into that kind of thinking, and you really need something to break it.

While I was in school, Woody and I were not great friends. We weren't enemies. I wasn't against him, and he wasn't against me, but we weren't great friends. A lot of players felt real close to him. I never felt that close to him when I was in school. I was much closer to Bo Schembechler. I really viewed Bo as my coach. He was the day-to-day guy for me, the guy that would relate to me and talk with me on a personal basis. So I viewed Bo as my coach and Woody as the boss. In Woody's last years we became very close, but while I was in school, we weren't very close. I wasn't in awe of him. I was interviewed one time by *Sports Illustrated* and made this reference: 'Woody Hayes is a lot like your father. The longer you're away from him, the smarter he gets.'

I DIDN'T THINK ABOUT PROFESSIONAL FOOTBALL until my senior year. I had some pro teams trying to contact me, and a couple of scouts came by. That's when I began to think about it. Pro football was never my goal. My senior year, when they started talking to me about it, draft day was a lot earlier. I think it was in December. This guy who was a former Ohio State player, from the Lions, Russ Thomas, flew into Columbus. He had prearranged to have Bob Vogel and I at a hotel. He ordered us a steak lunch, and he was listening to the draft on the telephone. It wasn't on the radio or television in those days. He said that they wanted to draft whichever one of us was there in the first round. So Bob was taken by Baltimore and I was taken by Detroit in the first round. He had a plane, and they flew us up to Chicago right away. They got us in a hotel to sign us. They dumped cash on the table. They took advantage of us. The AFL had just started, but it was before the big money. The AFL was in no way considered in the class of the NFL.

I tried to get some advice from Woody, but he just really stayed out of it. He just didn't relate to playing for money. It's a whole different dynamic. Here's the thing you have to think about with a guy like Woody: In our experience, in my senior year, we'd about had it with Woody. If I'd had to come back and play another year, forget it. I thought, 'I'm done with this. I've had enough of this.' I'm not sure that Woody's coaching style would work in the pros. You're turning over; every four years you've got a whole new set of people. In the pros, you've got to live with some of those guys 10 or 12 years; you've got to treat them differently. I don't think it would've worked. I think Woody was better off with that turnover, and I think his gift was for the college athlete. He was a great educator; he was a man preoccupied with education. That whole part of him just would'nt've had any place in professional football.

He stressed education all the time: 'Football's a means to an end, not an end in itself.' That's all he talked about. What it did to me, my first year with the Detroit Lions, part of my contract was that they were to get me a job. The only job they would give me was selling insurance. I don't know why—and there's nothing wrong with that; they guaranteed me good money—but I elected not to take that job. I found my own job in Detroit. My very first year, I immediately began to look for my job opportunity when I was through playing football. I attribute it to Woody talking to me my senior year in high school.

I look back and there were a lot of good things I learned from Woody. One of the biggest things that I learned from Woody was this: Woody had the greatest revelation concerning money of any man I've ever met or known, except for maybe Billy Graham. I mean, Woody Hayes never in his life ever did anything for money. Ever! I don't know anybody else who could make that statement, other than Billy Graham. Woody never did anything for money.

AT A VERY EARLY AGE, WOODY MADE UP HIS MIND to be the best that he could be. When he came to Ohio State, what he was going to do was not going to be dictated by others. He was going to live and die on his own abilities, and he was not going to be pressured by anybody. The time with him changed me. I think that I'm a better person for having been with Woody for four years. I look back on it now very fondly, and I'm glad that he was my coach. He taught me about education, about doing my best, and getting the most out of myself. I thought those were all positives. I also thought he was a little crazy. He was so extreme. He ate and slept football. You know, sleeping on the couch in his office. I thought he was crazy. I'm all for the work ethic, but there's a limit.

Yet I found out later, that was not all he did. I was quite unaware of how much he gave himself to other people. Which is also very Biblical. If you stand up in the marketplace and pound your chest and say, 'Look at what I'm giving,' the Bible says that's going to be your reward. Everybody's going to look at what you give, and that's it. But for the guy who comes in meekly and says, 'Oh, Lord, I don't deserve anything that you've given me. I'm just so grateful, and I come before you humbly and serve'—that man's going to have great rewards. So Woody did it not for the accolade of man. That's why he didn't play it up. He wasn't doing it so somebody else would think he was good. He was doing it out of a very unique genuiness of caring for people. It was a tremendous contradiction. He was a great paradox.

There was another part that crept into him, too, and you just don't know what part this plays: Woody always had a sugar problem. Well, at the beginning of the season—and I don't know much about this technically—his sugar is 80, 90. By the end of the season, it's 300 or 400. That affects you, too, and if you go back and look at his rages, they're all at the end of the season. For 28 years at Ohio State, his rages were all at the end of the season. That's always when his sugar would be high. He'd be so involved and preoccupied with football in our days he'd eat Fig Newtons. They'd be stashed in his drawer. He ate carelessly, because he's putting in all these hours. That was before Wendy's and McDonald's. So that could've had a big impact on his whole life.

THE BIGGEST ADJUSTMENT TO THE PROS was just as the game was faster and harder-hitting from high school to college, it was that much more from college to the pros. You have to step yourself up to that. I was surprised initially, but I got into it pretty quickly. I was a starter right away. They needed me, so I was an instant starter in the NFL. I was surprised over the enthusiasm the pros had. They wanted to win and play hard. I remember going to my first exhibition game. I mean, I was shocked. Guys were throwing up in the locker room. I thought they would treat it more like a job. But they weren't like that. I was pleasantly surprised by it.

I was there when Joe Don Looney was there. Joe Don Looney was a piece of work. He had a room next to me. He was a one-of-a-kind guy. Absolutely, totally eccentric. He locked himself in his room once for three days during training camp. Wouldn't come out. He'd just lift weights. An incredible physical specimen. He ate raw eggs and about 60 vitamins every day. He also ended up going to India and being an elephant tender.

I enjoyed professional football, but I didn't enjoy losing. I played in more losing games my rookie year than I did in college and high school put together, and I didn't like that. I was also working for a company in the off-season. It wasn't a question of *if* I would get out, it was a question of *when*. I was an assistant on the Chevrolet account for a sales/promotion company. It was the biggest account in the industry, and my boss left the company after I'd played for four years. They offered me the job if I would quit football. So I took about six or eight weeks of my fourth year to make that decision. I just decided to take the risk and go ahead and quit football because this job was the biggest opportunity in the industry, and I was only 25 years old. It was hard to walk away. I put things down on paper—pros and cons. The only reason I wanted to stay was because of the camaraderie in the locker room, and that wasn't a good enough reason to stay, because the job offered me all the opportunity for the future.

The Lions didn't take it too seriously, because it was the end of the season. They didn't know what would happen. There was some little negotiation, and they talked about giving me more money, but they made no real effort to sell me on staying. George Allen called me from the Rams. He got permission from Joe Schmidt, who became the coach—Joe was the one reason I would've wanted to stay.

I said, 'What's the money like, George?'

He said, 'What's it going to take?'

I said, 'It's going to take about 45 or 50,000 bucks.'

Of course, in those days, they were paying no lineman that kind of money. It surprised him. We're talking about 1967. He told me if I changed my mind to come out there and play. But he was the only person who called me. Word got around that I was priced out of the market.

I JUST MADE THE DECISION on the basis of a career path. I wasn't tired of football, I was tired of losing. It had a lot to do with my decision. And we were not staying up with the latest skills. As a team, we were not up to date in the training methods that were being developed. They were just starting in those days, these various muscle development techniques for certain methods of blocking. It wasn't being done in Detroit. Had I been with a winning team, I don't know whether I would've quit.

I loved working in advertising. I look back on it now and I say, 'My gosh, I was only 25 years old,' but I was cocky, I was confident, I strategized the whole thing. I took a $3 million account and made it a $9 million account my first year. I was the fair-haired boy. If I wanted the jet to go to New York, I got it. If I wanted to take a client to Hawaii, I did it. It was a real fast track. I was self-absorbed. I wasn't a very good friend to anybody. I wasn't a very good husband. I wasn't a very good father. But I was making a lot of money and having a good time. I did whatever I wanted to do. I was good at getting the business. For four years, I got all of GM's business. Every piece of business that Chevy or Cadillac did, I got it. Then they came to promote me. In a corporation of 5,000 employees, they jumped me up to number five or six, at the age of 28. I had a lot of passion, confidence.

Then I decided to go into the car business. We moved to Connecticut. We go up there, and my wife's family's from Detroit. She's away from her family. We're living on less. So, she finds a church, and we walk into this church, and I'm telling you, that's what I'm looking for. When I walk in and I sit down, what's going on there is what I've been looking for all my life. There were no emotional pleas or manipulations. It was like, 'Wow! This's it!' The previous 15 years, I was always looking for something. I thought it was recognition and All-American and All-Pro and first draft choice and more money. I thought it was jets, Europe, parties, and business, and it wasn't those things. What I was really looking for was a meaningful relationship with God.

Here was a group of people in Trumbull, Connecticut, they don't know who Woody Hayes is, they don't know who played where. These people just loved me. These people were the first people in my life that loved me without being able to run down and say they had a drink with Daryl. These are the first people that I had come across in my life who just took me and my family for who we were. It was awesome.

THAT WAS IN THE BEGINNING OF 1974. We stayed there for two years. We stayed real close into the church. God really touched our family, then a dealership opportunity opened up in Columbus, and Cadillac gave it to me. We came to Columbus in 1976 and thought I was going to be a Cadillac dealer for the rest of my life. I thought I had blown it to be called into the ministry, because I was divorced.

After I was in the business about four years, it just wasn't right. I knew that it wasn't right; I knew there was something else for me to do. A lot of circumstances came together, and I sold the business. I didn't come into the ministry until January of '85. I had the time and the money. I just really got myself ready to come into the ministry. A couple of events helped to solidify that decision. We were in a meeting in New Orleans in 1980, and this pastor was preaching. Just out of the clear blue while he was preaching, he said, 'Daryl and Barbara'—we had just met him that morning—'I was praying about you this morning, and God told me to tell you to go home and just stay there. Don't make anything happen. Your life-plan will unfold for you.'

We came home and waited, and about four months later, some men came to me and said, 'Will you teach a Bible study for us?' And that was the beginning. I taught that men's Bible study for 11 years. We were in a good church here, and the vision had grown in my heart about a church in the northwest part of Columbus. I shared it with my pastor. He said, 'I believe that you're supposed to do that.' That's how we got started.

WOODY WAS BROUGHT BACK INTO MY LIFE right in the midst of this. In 1979, I was with Dave Tingley and his wife. We were skiing in Seven Springs, in Pennsylvania. We're skiing there, the night of the Clemson game. And when he punches that guy, I mean, my stomach...I just knew; I knew that it was all going to fall apart. There was a real mystery going on for about three days there. They had fired him. Woody wouldn't talk to anybody. Everybody was wondering and worried.

I said to my wife, 'Honey, we've got to go back, because nobody will have the nerve to go see Woody. Nobody will have the guts to do it, and I've got to go do it.'

And we hadn't been that close. I just knew that I had to do it. So I came back, and I called Dan Heinlen, who's Alumni Director. He's a good friend of mine. I said, 'Dan, what's going on?' Because he would know what's going on on the inside.

He said, 'Well, we don't know. We don't know how he's taking it. He's not talking to anybody.'

I said, 'I feel like I should go see him.'

He said, 'Well, why don't we call Rex Kern in California?'

I said, 'Okay.' Because Rex was one of Woody's boys. I called Rex and said, 'What do you think?'

Rex said, 'I think you ought to get in and see him.'

He said, 'I'll tell you what. Take Archie with you. 'Cause if Archie goes, you'll have a black player and a white player, and Archie's one of his all-time favorites.'

I called Archie and I said, 'Archie, will you go?'

He said, 'Yeah.'

Archie and I met over at a parking lot on Lane Avenue. We prayed together and we went over and knocked on the door. This was the second day after the firing. We knocked on the door, and Woody came to the door. He looked at me and looked at Archie. I said, 'Hey, we're here to talk to you, Coach. How you doing?'

We sat there for seven hours without a glass of water, without anything. The old man just talked, just shared his heart. Talked about a lot of things. It got dark out. It was dark in the room. We sat there in the dark. He was real melancholy. It was a *real* catastrophe. It was a real shock. It was real unfair, the way they did it and what they did. Not that he shouldn't have been fired, just how it was done. He was glad we came, obviously, to sit there and talk for seven hours. We left and said we'd keep in touch. He was only answering a certain phone number.

So I go home thinking about it, and I go, 'The university? I don't know what they're going to do with him. They ought to give this guy an office. They ought to make him a professor emeritus. They need to do some things for him. Where is he on his retirement?' I knew he didn't know anything about any of that stuff. So I called him two days later, and I said, 'Woody, there's a few things you need to think about. Can I come over?' He still hasn't talked to the public.

I went over. I had written down some questions: 'What're you going to do about your retirement? What about health insurance? What do you want?'

So he called Anne in, and he said, 'Anne, listen to what he's saying here. I want you to hear it. I don't know anything about any of that stuff.'

I said, 'We need to do something, and we need to do something soon. We need to get this in order here—what you want done and how you want to do it.' I said, 'I'll help you. I'll do whatever I can do to help you here, but we gotta do it.'

He said, 'Okay, would you go talk to them?'

I said, 'Yeah.' So, I called Dan Heinlen. I said, 'We need to talk. I need to talk to the president.'

He calls the president. He calls me back and says, 'You need a letter from Woody that you're representing him.'

I took the letter in to the president. Woody hasn't said anything publicly yet. Of course, they're worried about what he's going to say. They started to cancel the meeting, because they heard I was bringing some attorneys with me. So, I ended up representing Woody with the university, and at the same time, some guy from Hollywood calls. It's an interesting deal. I look at it as kind of a blessing from God, because these guys called, and I happen to know some guy from New York who's an attorney with the entertainment industry. I call this guy and he says, 'Yeah, these guys are legit.' They come out. I end up negotiating a movie deal of Woody's life.

FOR THE NEXT SEVEN MONTHS, that's all he worked on. We flew out to LA together. It totally occupied his time and his mind. Woody and I, we were together every day, every single day. I saw him four days a week, and we talked the other three days, for months. He had fun. Of course, I'm sitting there, and my whole objective is not to have a good movie. My objective is to protect Woody. I'm kind of steering who's talking to who and who's doing what. It wasn't a very good movie, and it never got shot, but Woody got $100,000, which is more than he got from the university. It got his mind off the problems, and it gave him something to work on for almost a year.

Anyway, back in the president's office. They were paying Woody, at that time, $43,000, in 1979. By law, they could've paid Woody $59,000 as a state employee. So, he's making $16,000 a year less. So, I said, 'Mr. Enarson, if I or anybody else were representing Woody Hayes, how much would you pay him today?'

He said, 'We would've been paying him $59,000.'

He just said it right back to me, without thought.

I said, 'So, just because he wouldn't ask for it, you wouldn't give it to him?'

I said, 'I think we have a real problem here.'

I look back on it now, and I think he should've got a better package than he got. There were all kinds of rules about that. They had an annual contract. His contract was up June 30; they were paying him through till then, so they had no legal obligation. They did give him professor emeritus, and that was very important to Woody. They did give him an office and a secretary, and he needed those things.

I really saw a lot more of his human-ness in those days together and in the subsequent years until his death. I saw his real concern. Woody was always in favor of the disadvantaged guy. I mean, he cared for people with poor health. I look back on it now, and he always helped football players who needed extra help. He was always there to help the underdog. He was always concerned. I know, as a pastor, it takes a lot out of you to go visit somebody and try to cheer them up in the hospital; I'm not as good at it as Woody was, and I'm a pastor. This guy had an ability to go in and light up the room for someone who didn't feel good. He got many letters over the years, which have never been made public, about all of the things—seeing people if they're dying; what it meant to their families; seeing people that were going to be in wheelchairs for the rest of their lives. He's bought wheelchairs, he's given people money. It's incredible.

He would write a check, and Anne told me one time, she said, 'Daryl, I never know what he's going to do. I always try to make sure to keep enough money in his account. He has no idea of what he's got in his account. I've just got to be ready for whatever check he might write to give away to somebody.' That's how she had to live her life—never knowing who Woody was going to give thousands of dollars to. He paid off the house in 1957. They lived in that paid-off house for 30 years. She still lives there.

I remember Woody telling us, 'For those of you guys who're going to be coaches, don't you take any of this money from these equipment people. You take money for a helmet, now you've got to give your players this helmet. And what if somebody else has a better helmet next year? You're not going to give your player the best helmet because you've got a contract with this guy? Don't get involved with that stuff.'

He told us this back in the early '60s. Coaches in those days were happy to get an extra 5,000 bucks. Woody never did. Woody gave away his TV money to his assistant coaches. Woody never negotiated a contract. He didn't have anybody represent him. He just took whatever contract the TV station gave him for his show. He never held out; he never negotiated.

When he died, I felt like I had lost a friend. He wasn't my friend when I was a student here, but I don't think he was supposed to be. We had a coach-player relationship. But his last years, he was my friend. I loved Woody and spent a lot of time with him. I think we had a good relationship. I think he was happy for me.

I'm working with a ministry now. This guy's got a Christian tuition-free school. These kids, about half the time, the only meal they'll get in a day is at the school, and you ought to see these little kids. You'd have no idea they are in poverty. He has got them cleaned up. They come to school. There's some discipline. They're learning how to read and write and do arithmetic, and they're also getting some moral training and Christian teaching. He's got 46 kids. He can get no help, yet he's taken the kids from the worst possible conditions, and I'll tell you what, he's impacted those kids. And there's no government money, even though they've got zillions of dollars for this stuff.

My interest in the inner-city kids is borne out of my own childhood. I now see that it was planned for me to be raised in the inner city. I now see that it was God's plan. I see that it was God's plan to bring me to Ohio State, to this guy who had a sense of equality. To me, an African-American citizen is equal with me, and there's no separation. It's just been part of my own upbringing and what was reinforced here by Woody.

I HAVE LESS INTEREST IN THE GAME EVERY YEAR. I really feel that the game has lost its integrity with the players. I believe it's dishonest for the coaches to be millionaires. I feel there's a gross dishonesty at the very heart of it. This stuff is silly, what's going on about catching somebody buying somebody lunch and wanting to discipline them. I mean, it's the most two-faced, dumbest thing, when there's thousands of dollars going back and forth and you're nailing someone on a $5 lunch or a $60 dinner. The players are not even making minimum wage. If I wasn't a pastor and so involved with my faith, I'd start signing up junior high school players to a sports union. I really would. I'd mobilize them. They need a good old Walter Reuther, Jimmy Hoffa.

Let me ask you this: Why are they suddenly paying pro football players a million dollars a year? Only because the guys finally banded together and said, 'Nope. This's the way it's going to go.' And the owners have said, 'We can't hold up in court any more.' *That's* the only reason it's happened.

I walked past a football coach over here in Worthington about three years ago. I was going to a soccer game. These kids were six and seven years old, and this coach was grabbing a kid by his jersey, getting down in his face, screaming, 'I told you to hit that guy!' I don't know what we're creating.

I mean, yes, I have a passion for life, yes, I have a desire to excel, and yes, I learned a lot of these things playing football when it was fun. But that's not what's going on today. I'll tell you right now, guys are going to look back 10 years after playing football at a place like Ohio State and say, 'Man, it wasn't worth it. I was taken advantage of.' I'd rather see them either really restrict it or completely let it go. Let the kid make whatever money he can. Why can Carl Lewis make $100,000 for a race? He's an amateur athlete. These things are only what we call them. Why can't a fullback, tackle, somebody, say, 'Hey, I'm going to wear these shoes because they're going to give me $10,000 to wear these shoes.'? Why can't there be a free market?

What they say is, 'Well, there's no money in it.' That's what football owners in the NFL told us. Two years before I got to the NFL, they changed the schedule from 12 games to 14 games. All the contracts are signed. Joe Schmidt told me this story. The coach said, 'We're playing 14 games. There's going to be two more games at the end of the year.'

Somebody said, 'Yeah? Where's the money?'

'We don't have the money. There isn't any money.'

Night Train Lane was there. Train gets up and says, 'Am I under the consumption that there's no more money?'

You look back and say, 'Well, would you have done this different?' I'll tell you this: I'm glad I came to Ohio State, I'm glad Woody Hayes was my coach, I'm glad Bo Schembechler was my coach, I'm glad I played here, and I'm glad that I got an education here. It had its good moments and its bad moments. I had my good games and my not-so-good games. That's really all that life is here. That's why you've got to find a deeper meaning to life. That's where the spiritual side of a man needs to be cultivated.

I suppose the two sides of my personality have been reconciled in my own heart. Football was truly a means to an end and not an end in itself. It took me a while to catch up to the full truth of that statement. Now that I have, now that I see that there's a whole eternal side to life, and I have the opportunity and privilege to be able to touch the eternal part of people, now life is very satisfying to me. I have been blessed. ”

Daryl Sanders

Bob Vogel

Bob VOGEL

"I WAS THE FIRST FOUR-SPORT athlete in the history of Toronto, Ohio. Then in my senior year, I went to Massillon, and there'd never been anybody at Massillon who'd been allowed to play four sports. What was ironic was that the football season prior to that one, our season was over at Toronto, and the Steubenville Big Red was going to play Massillon. We had heard a lot about Massillon, so we went down there to watch them play. They dressed 99 guys. They came out and circled the entire field. We had 26 guys on our football team. We're sitting there watching Massillon, and it was just an awesome display—luminous tigers on their helmets, white Kangaroo shoes. So, these guys came down and said, 'Would you be interested in playing at Massillon?' I certainly was. They got my dad a job, and about two days before football practice started, we moved to Massillon.

That year was really a good experience for me, because where I had played before, I got by on just pure athletic ability and because I was bigger. I had to focus on technique, getting used to the pressure, and the crowd. Our freshman football team would play other varsities and beat them. Massillon junior high school had eight coaches.

My decision to go to Ohio State was pragmatic. My mom and dad loved to watch me play. They were people of extremely modest means. There was no way that they could have ever traveled any kind of distance on a regular basis to see me play. I had offers from something like 80 schools, and, when it came to the decision-making process, my analytical side says: 'What am I looking for?' I want a good education. I want to play in a good program. I want to go where my mom and dad could see me play. I wasn't burning to play at Ohio State. I just made some decisions.

You'd come home and get eight or ten letters every day. There wasn't a lot of home visits at that time, the way there is now, and you didn't have a lot of the phone calls. Of course, a good bit of the time when I was being recruited we couldn't afford a phone. My mother wanted with all her heart for me to go to Ohio State, but she never said anything. She stayed totally away from the process. I can remember as a child, on Saturday afternoons in the fall, the Ohio State game was on. She listened to it avidly. I don't think I ever heard my dad listen to a football game. So my going to Ohio State was really a pragmatic decision, no more than that.

I grew up in a very modest environment. I didn't have any expectations. I went to Ohio State, and I don't remember feeling in awe, because I didn't know anything about them. I just didn't follow them. I *played* sports. If the world was made up of people like me, the college stadiums would be empty. I loved the game. But sitting and watching has no appeal for me. If I thought they were going to do something that I'd never seen before, I'd go, but when you play for 22 years, the likelihood of that happening is not high. I take my wife and my two daughters, and the last time we went to a game, we were walking from the parking lot across the bridge, and these four young guys were really throwing out all of the four-letter words. I walked up to one of them and said, 'You see that bridge? You say one more word, and I'm going to throw you in the water. Shut your mouth.' You have all the booze in the crowd and all the people second-guessing the coaches. Who needs that?

WHEN I MET WOODY, I thought he was intense, driven. I have the same kind of intensity, and I respect that in people. It was hard to deal with him. You'd play a game, and you would have 85 offensive executions, and you'd have 82 'got men,' and for the other two or three you didn't get, the coaches would eat your lunch. He was not an encourager. You could spend yourself for him, and there was no acknowledgment of it. I wasn't looking for it, but it was just hard. You'd like to think that you could play well enough that someone would say, 'You did a nice job.'

I got the encouragement from Bo Schembechler, who was my position coach. Bo was a joy to play for. A good coach, great technician.

When I went into the NFL, I didn't know anything about pass protection, but there were veteran linemen who couldn't run block as well as I could. I'm not talking about overpowering guys. I'm talking about cutoff blocks, leverage, position, those kinds of things. I was just very well-schooled. Then John Sandusky was my line coach at Baltimore, and John helped me to become a technician. The success I had in the league was greater than my ability. I should not have succeeded or excelled to the point that I did, because I was only 240 pounds. I'd make a mistake and come to the sideline, and John'd say, 'Do you know what happened?'

I'd say, 'Well, it happened so quick.'

He'd say, 'Here's what *you* did. Here's what *he* did. Here's what you need to do.'

So Tuesday, Wednesday, and Thursday in practice, I'd stay out and work with him. I just refined all of those skills until I had the ability to play beyond myself. It was purely technique. I could only play technically. There's a part of me that would have loved to have been a dominate type, like Jim Parker, just steamroll people. The thing that I had to learn was that I had to harness my intensity. There were times before a game that I'd be up so much that there'd be tears coming down my cheeks, but my opponent could use that against me. I had to sit on that. I had to keep it contained.

On pass protection, I had to be very careful, because when I made a physical mistake, I wasn't strong enough to fight my way back in front, so it was frustrating to me. I would love to have played more aggressively, but I learned to look at a task and break it down and master the individual elements. I never deal with the whole in anything; I break it down into its pieces and master its pieces. I'm very focused. I'm very methodical. I do everything line upon line, precept upon precept. Although I was blessed with unusual athletic ability, my personal style is very conservative. I do things by the book. I think one of the great things that came out of my football experience is that I'm a technician in everything I do.

To give you an idea about Woody's style, I was up on the second floor, walking down, and he was standing at the bottom of the steps. When I got near him, he reached over and grabbed my arm and pulled me off to the side and said, 'What do you think about playing offensive tackle?'

I said, 'Not very much.'

I had been an All-American end in high school.

He said, 'You better start. You're a tackle.'

So walking down the steps, I'm an end; at the bottom of the steps, I'm a tackle.

I was brought up under authority, and he was in charge. I worked for him, and in retrospect, it was certainly the best thing that could have happened to me. I could have played as a tight end in college and been a good one, but I couldn't have played in the NFL. It was a good move. It wasn't a hard transition to make, because in high school, I didn't play on teams that were predominately passing teams, so I had to do a lot of blocking.

The first game I played my sophomore year was against SMU, and I can remember when we came out to warm up, there weren't a lot of people there. I was really kind of disappointed. I said, 'Whoa, what's going on here?' Then when we came out for the game, it was wall-to-wall people. The concentration that was required for me to play the game was so great that the crowd and the noise just disappeared. They would have been evident by their *absence*. Had they *not* been there, you would have been aware of it. But because you were focused, they just weren't there.

THE RELATIONSHIP I HAD WITH WOODY was purely professional. He was the coach, and I was a player. We had a major collision my junior year. We were getting ready to play Michigan, and we were supposed to go to the TV station to tape an interview, and I had a departmental exam for a major course. Woody told me to go, and I didn't go. I couldn't make up the exam. There wasn't much of a relationship before that, but there was almost no relationship after that. I'm probably one of the very few guys that he didn't punch. Never. He never yelled at me. I don't why. I don't have an inkling.

I guess some people would describe me as a loner. I'm solitary, and although I enjoyed the guys I played with, I didn't run with them. We didn't sit around and talk about, 'How are you doing with Woody?' I studied, read. I enjoyed classical music. I just did other things. There's a real clubbiness among athletes. Guys enjoy being with each other, and I enjoyed them. It's just that I wasn't a part of the group.

I did enjoy Ohio State, though. I was able to start three seasons. I remember when I was introduced as the Ohio State team captain. I remember playing against the McKeever brothers, Marlin and Mike. They came into Columbus with USC. Big reputations and everything, and we kicked their butts. My junior season, Iowa had a great team under Forest Evashevsky, and we dominated them. We beat Michigan three times. I have three pair of gold pants, and not many Ohio State guys beat Michigan three times.

I don't have many bad memories. I know my senior season was disappointing. We were national champions and undefeated my junior year. We came back my senior season hoping to have a really fine year and ended up something like 6-3. That was a real disappointment. We had the players. I don't know why we weren't as good as we thought we should be. I was just focused on my play. I guess a lot of people might take issue with that, but I had to be that focused. That's what allowed me to have what success I had. I didn't sit there in the films and say, 'If he had gotten that block or if he had just made that cut.' They did what they did, and I did what I did.

Bo Schembechler and I had an interesting conversation one time. He asked me, 'Do you play for the team?'

I said, 'No, I play for me.'

He got really upset, but I said, 'Wait a minute now. You're yelling at me, but think about it. If I play for the team, and we're behind by 25 points, I might give up because there doesn't appear to be any chance for the team to win. If I'm playing for me, I'm all-out the whole time.'

That kind of took him back.

I HAVE NO REGRETS ABOUT COMING TO OHIO STATE. I got an excellent education, played with some fine athletes, and playing for Woody was okay. I wouldn't assume that he's a lot different than most coaches. I wasn't looking for the guy to be fuzzy. I wasn't looking for the coach to be a father image. My dad loved me, and I loved my dad, so I wasn't looking for dad.

Woody was not at all a dominate figure in my life. It was a professional relationship. He was the coach, and I was a player. But if I had it to do all over again, I'd come back and play for him. He did what I wanted him to do. I wanted him to be a good coach, a symbol, and let me be a part of a good program. He did those things. It was pragmatic, it was practical. I got what I wanted. All my needs were met. I was part of a great program, a great coach, a great tradition. I wasn't lamenting it as I was going through it. It would have been nice if he had patted you on the back once in a while, but he didn't, and I accepted him. I respected what

Woody was as a person. I appreciated his integrity. His word was his bond, and whatever he told you, you could take to the bank. I admired that. I wasn't looking for the other things.

Woody was committed, and I respect commitment. That's one of the things that's attractive about following Jesus to me. It's a commitment. It is, in my opinion, the high road, it's excellence, it's fulfilling my design. To me, it's very simple. You read in the newspaper that someone was killed by a train. Well, no one is ever killed by a train. The crossings are well-lit, the gates are down, and the people are trying to drive around the gates, and they're run over by a train. The train didn't kill them; they killed themselves. There are godly principles that are just as obvious.

That doesn't mean that I've come close to approximating perfection, but the pursuit has been fulfilling. Having these 11 foster babies has been my greatest blessing, after my salvation and my relationship with Andrea. I can't even articulate what it means. Those babies have touched my life in a way that no adult has ever touched me. It began with Andrea praying. Our kids had all grown up and left home. What does she do with her time?

We took the first baby, and we had him for maybe eight weeks. When I had to say goodbye to him, it just killed me. I said, 'Andrea, if it's this way every time, I can't do it.' I was crying. It just tore me up. Every baby is that way, every one of them. Now, if we have an infant for eight days, I don't get that involved, but when we have them for six, seven, eight weeks, I'm gone. I think nine of them have been black. My heart doesn't see color; my heart sees babies.

ANDREA AND I MET IN 1961, on a blind date on New Year's Eve. She was a nursing student at Riverside Methodist Hospital. The girl I had a date with had an emergency appendectomy, so here I am without a date on New Year's Eve. I called this friend and said, 'I'm desperate and dateless.'

He said, 'I know someone. She has a nice personality.'

So then she begged me to marry her, and I did. I played my first year in the NFL, and I was going to be drafted into the army. The woman who ran the draft board here was married to a guy who used to play for the Green Bay Packers. I had already taken my physical. This woman says, 'Are you Bob Vogel?'

'Yes, ma'am.'

'The one who played for Ohio State?'

'Yes, ma'am.'

'The one who plays for the Baltimore Colts?'

'Yes, ma'am.'

'Are you giving any consideration to getting married?'

I said, 'Yes. In June.'

She said, 'If you can get married before December, I'll forget you're alive.'

This was September of my rookie year. I called Andrea in Columbus, from Baltimore, and said, 'How soon can we get married?'

She said, 'What's the urgency?'

I said, 'Well, my blue eyes will clash with that army green.'

After practice on Friday, I flew in here, had the rehearsal, got married on Saturday. We were both on the plane to Washington. I got off to play against the Redskins, and she went on to Baltimore. Apparently, it was in the Washington papers that I had gotten married, so on the first play of the game, I come out of the huddle and get down in my stance. Carl Kammerer is playing defensive end for the Redskins, and he goes, 'Uhmm, *uhmm*, uhmm, uhmm.' *That* kind of ruined my concentration.

MY FAMILY ALWAYS HAD A GREAT WORK ETHIC. I saw my dad out of work, and he and I went to apple orchards to pick apples to earn money. He and I would go around the neighborhood after storms, when there were lots of trees down, and clean up people's yards. Even at 18 and 19 and 20, I realized I had a great opportunity. No one in my family had ever gotten close to college, and I saw football as a tool. I had my best grades during football season, because it forced me to budget my time. It was tough. You frequently wouldn't get back to your room until, say, 7:30, after practice, and it was tough to put in three or four hours of studying after that. But you did what you had to do.

Woody emphasized education, and I never saw any sign of hypocrisy in him. I think the fact that I admired his integrity so much offset the rest of it. He was loyal, and I appreciated his loyalty. I think he liked his players. I'm not sure that Woody ever knew how to express that. I'd be surprised if he ever told his wife he loved her. I'd be astounded. You knew there were players who got into financial difficulty, and he helped them. You knew that he cared for players, but maybe his image of himself wouldn't allow him to be tender. He spent a lot of time in hospitals visiting sick kids and sick people, and no one ever knew about it. *I* didn't know about it.

I thought his bursts of temper were funny. We were playing against Iowa out in Iowa, and in the first half they were beating us something like 28–0. And the last thing Woody said going out for the second half was, 'If you guys play the second half like you did the first half, I'm going to be waiting at the top of the steps for you.' The second half was just about as bad as the first. Somebody said, 'I'm sure not going to be the first one in there. When he comes to whippin' me, he's going to be worn out from kickin' everybody else's butt.' I wasn't intimidated by that. That was funny to me.

His style of motivation was to throw a blanket over the group and motivate everybody the same way. I was offended by that. You didn't have to motivate me. Just coach me and point me and tell me where you want me to go and tell me what you want me to do, and I'll go do it. I was offended by some of his motivation techniques, his pep talks before games and things like that. I don't need a pep talk. Just let me get my chinstrap fastened, and I'm ready to go do it. But that was his style, and it worked for him.

I'M A WARRIOR. I'M A PLAYER. I don't want somebody to give me that sense that they've got to tweak me. A warrior doesn't want tweaked. Just give him a battle. I loved the physical challenge. If you hurt me, I'm more dangerous. If you hurt me, if you embarrass me, then you better watch out, because I'm coming to get your lunch. After they rung my bell, I was worse, because then I really wanted them. I always had that desire to excel and was embarrassed when I didn't excel. It wasn't so much that other people were seeing it; *I* saw it.

In the Super Bowl against the Jets, I went into the game with a broken arm, then got kicked in the thigh on the second play of the game. I was in incredible pain, but I went through the game and played hard and played well. I was so exhausted and my arm hurt so bad that I was sobbing. My arm was in a cast, and the official came up to me before the game and said, 'I'm going to be watching you carefully. I don't want to see you hit anybody with that cast.'

I said, 'Yeah, right, the last thing I want to do is hit anybody with that cast. I promise you I will not hit anybody with this arm.'

I remember being hurt and staying out one play, then going right back in. I couldn't stand somebody being in *my* position. That's *my* position. Stupid.

What's ironic is that this drive is appropriate and necessary, but as a person *out* of the athletic arena, it's totally inappropriate. You get accolades for making decisions in milliseconds as an athlete, then you make those kind of decisions off the field, and they're usually wrong. I had to unlearn a lot of my learned behavior as an athlete, because it was totally inappropriate off the field.

In spring practice at the end of my junior season, I thought I might have a chance to go on to the next level. Whenever scouts came on the field, Woody made them wear a red slipover on one arm, and with Daryl and I on the same team, there started to be a lot of them around. That's the first time I became aware of it.

The whole draft situation was kind of surreal. It was during the time when there was a war between the American Football League and the National Football League. Daryl and I got picked up by Russ Thomas, the general manager of the Detroit Lions. He hid us out in a motel someplace. We thought he just wanted to talk with us. Talk about country bumpkins. Daryl and I were the dumbest, biggest hicks. The draft started about noon and ran until 2 o'clock. We're sitting there talking and the phone rang. Russ got on the phone and said, 'Bob, there's no reason for you to stay here. Baltimore has taken you in the first round.'

Classic.

Detroit drafts Daryl, Baltimore drafts me. The draft was in Chicago. They sent a plane down to get Daryl and I, flew us up to Chicago. It was the first time in history that two first-round draft choices from the same school were negotiated with at the same time. They took us into a room and threw out two rolls of $5,000 in small bills. They were all over the floor. We thought we were millionaires. They had bumpkins, and they knew they had bumpkins.

WE DIDN'T HAVE AGENTS OR ANYTHING. We called Bo Schembechler. Woody never took a raise, so his coaches didn't get very much money. We said, 'Bo, they've offered us $18,000 and a $5,000 bonus.'

He says, 'That sounds like a lot of money to me.'

He was probably making $25,000. So we took it. Oh my, the innocence. I was really excited to be playing with John Unitas and Gino

Marchetti. When I was in the offensive huddle, Raymond Berry was on one side—Hall of Fame. Joe Perry was the fullback—Hall of Fame. John Unitas—Hall of Fame. Jim Parker—Hall of Fame. Lenny Moore—Hall of Fame. I was the only rookie who was starting. John Mackey didn't start until about the second or third game.

When I walked in, it was Don Shula's first year. They were just going to start me. They didn't like the guy who was there, Tom Gilburg. So they took me and stuck me in right away.

They said, 'We're going to sink or swim with you.'

Well, they did a lot of sinking for a while. The pass protection was the toughest technique I've ever mastered in any sport. Incredibly difficult, backing up at full speed, weighing 240 pounds, trying to stop a guy who's 290 pounds running straight ahead, trying to maintain all that balance, trying to keep their hands off of me, trying to make sure I stay on the balls of my feet, making sure that my knees are bent, my head's up, I'm breaking him away.

It's like trying to hit a golf ball, except you're not running when you're trying to hit a golf ball, and nobody's beating on your roof. Nothing I've ever tried to do comes close to trying to pass protect, and I played lots of sports and played them well. It drove me crazy trying to learn it.

Part of my problem was I was small, and being small exacerbated everything else. If I was 280 pounds, I could get by with mistakes. I couldn't make a mistake. I practiced and practiced and practiced. When practice was over, I practiced. I never came in. Ordell Braase stayed out with me, and he kicked my butt up and down the field week after week after week. Ordell Braase made me an All-Pro..

We played against the Chicago Bears in New Orleans when Doug Atkins was there, and he ate my lunch. He high-jumped his height, was a small college All-American basketball player. After the game was over, I came in, sat down at my locker, and passed out. I lost 23 pounds. No trace minerals in my system. I just went *splat*. He destroyed me.

That was the first time I ever questioned whether or not I could make it as an athlete, but then I got back into the technique part of it. It helped me to understand that there was a vast amount to do. As a college All-American and playing against some of the guys in the NFL who were not the great ones, I was doing okay, but when I got in against a great one, it was a learning experience. It redoubled my efforts as a technician. It made it even more clear that I couldn't survive trying to match strength. If I didn't have everything working perfectly, then I couldn't hope to play against someone like him.

Then in two years, I made All-Pro, and I could play him head-to-head. I still couldn't make a mistake, but when I did everything right, I could make him stop. When I had my knees bent, when I had everything right, he couldn't run over me. But when the game was over, even when we won, I'd come out of there in a terrible mood.

Andrea said, 'Didn't you look at the scoreboard? You guys *won*.'

I said, 'Yeah, but I can't turn off what I've been doing for the past four hours. I just can't go from this intense, focused person, come out and take a shower and change.'

I was more tired emotionally after a game than I was physically, and I was exhausted physically. I was just wiped out mentally. Focus, focus, focus, focus—it just wears you out.

PLAYING PROFESSIONAL FOOTBALL is a challenging way to make a living, but it is not as tough as what I do right now. Now, I've got to go to work every day. I don't have six months off, and I don't play only on Sundays. I've got to hit home runs every day. Football is single-dimensional; what I do for a living is multi-dimensional. That's far more demanding. From a marketing standpoint, the toughness of the NFL is overstated. You see some of the hard hits, but there's a generalization that it's that way all the time. You train, you're conditioned. There were games I went through I didn't come out with a bruise. People think that it's going in with a junkyard dog every time, and it's not.

I cherish the memories. I got to play in two Super Bowls, and we lost the one we should have won and won the one we should have lost. It was a gift from heaven to get that chance the second time. I remember Danny Sullivan, who played guard for us. We were sitting in training camp in the equipment room. Danny had the schedule, and he said, 'If we're ever going to do it, it's got to be this year.' It was prophetic.

That's the year Jim O'Brien kicked the field goal to beat Dallas. They were trying to block it on my side. They had about seven guys over there. I got buried. You heard a crowd reaction, but you were on neutral turf, so you don't know if he made it or didn't make it. They were stacked on me about three or four high, so it was some time after it was signaled good that I knew what had happened.

You really basked in the glow of it, particularly since we had lost it before. That made it even more rewarding. I was hurt so bad in the loss to the Jets that winning or losing was irrelevant. I was really in incredible pain: 'Do it! Shoot me! Just get it over with, get me out of here!'

That year, I was selected to play in the Pro Bowl. I called the guy who was heading up the Pro Bowl, and he thought I didn't want to come because we had lost the game.

I said, 'I can't walk, and I can't use my left arm. It's not that I don't want to. I *can't*. There's a half of a person here. What do you want from me?'

WHEN I RETIRED IN '72, just when Bob Irsay took over the Colts and Joe Thomas became the general manager, eight or nine guys retired. Joe Thomas came to me and said, 'You're the one I didn't want to lose.'

I said, 'Well then, you've got a funny way of showing it.'

About a third of the way through the season, I started praying. I said, 'Lord, should I come back and play the next season? If you want me to do something else, then show me.'

About two weeks after we started praying that, we got a phone call. We lived up in Hartford County, up north of Baltimore on the Susquehanna River. I got a phone call from a guy who was of some significance in the community.

He said, 'Bob, we're getting ready to start a cable television system here in the county, and we've been kicking around who we might like to be the general manager. Your name keeps coming up.'

I said, 'I don't know anything about cable television.'

I started meeting with them, and I just felt like that was really the Lord's answer, and I wasn't going to come back and play the 11th season. I went to Don Shula and John Sandusky, and I said, 'I need to tell you guys this. This's my last season, so if you want to start getting somebody ready, then go ahead and do it.'

People said, 'You're nuts. Just a year ago, you made the All-Pro team again. You're wonderfully healthy.'

I said, 'Yeah, but I'm done. It's over. I'm going to go do something else.'

I liked Don Shula. Our first baby was born with a serious birth defect, during the season, and when Don heard about it, he said, 'Your baby is more important than this football season. Go take care of your baby. Take care of your wife. When you're done, you come back here.'

I have a lot of respect for John Unitas, too. He was unimpressed with his celebrity, he was tenacious, he was dependable. When things weren't going well, he wasn't complaining about the blocking. I played with a lot of fine guys, people like Raymond Berry and Jimmy Orr and Earl Morrall.

We called Jim Parker 'Moobie Foobie.' He wasn't only strong, he had incredible balance and agility. He did things casually that other people were groaning and gritting their teeth to try to pull off. He was funny. He was terribly afraid of animals, and we did a lot of things to him. We were always out shooting groundhogs, and we were in two-a-day practices at Western Maryland College. We shot a groundhog and hung it on a hook in Jim's locker, then covered it up with his sweatshirt. Jim always smoked a pipe, and he was always humming. He came in there—*hummmmm, hummmmm*. We kind of gathered around.

He took his glasses off, pulled off his tee-shirt He's standing there—*hummmmm, hummmmm*. Picked up his shirt, saw that groundhog and slammed the door so hard, a whole section of lockers tipped over.

We were at Western Maryland when the locusts were coming out. Jim and I wore a kneepad in the tops of our helmets to make them fit better. I caught a locust and pulled the kneepad of his helmet back and stuck it up in there. We're out there practicing, going through drills. The locust starts to buzz. Jim snatched his helmet off and probably threw it 75 yards. If it were an Olympic event, he would hold the world record.

One day, he was sitting in the whirlpool, and Alex Sandusky, one of our guards, had been out rabbit hunting. Jim had his glasses down on his nose, reading the newspaper, humming away in the whirlpool, and Alex went by and just threw a dead rabbit in there. Jim levitated.

He was claustrophobic, couldn't stand being on an elevator, being pressed in. So we'd catch him on an elevator. A bunch of guys would walk on and pin him in a corner. He scream—*Ahhhh, ahhhh*. If you were smart, you weren't the one close to him when he was pinned. He'd wipe you out.

Great guys, quality guys. We loved each other. We were the first team in the NFL to have a team Bible study and a team chapel service. Andrea is the one who is responsible for the team Bible study. We went to a Fellowship of Christian Athletes conference, at Don Shinnick's and Raymond Berry's request. We got back from that, and Andrea said, 'What am I supposed to do now, just hang out here on my own?'

She called Raymond. She said, 'You're responsible. You nurture us.'

With her nagging him, we started the team Bible study. Then when Don and Raymond left, Andrea and I picked it up and ran it all the time we were in Baltimore. There was just something in me that recognized the importance of that relationship with the Lord. It's the Holy Spirit. The Holy Spirit woos us. It's God in there saying, 'I want to fill you. I want to add quality to your life. I designed you for fellowship with me.'

FOR THE LAST SIX YEARS, I've worked in a street ministry in the Short North of Columbus. That's the mean streets. That's the hookers, that's the addicts. We were encouraging the people in the congregation to go see where their money's going, go visit one of these ministries. We went down to Better Way Ministries, and the guy who heads that up is somebody that we've known for 12 years. We went down to observe, only for one night, and I got captured.

I was badly intimidated down there, but I was attracted by the alcoholics, the homeless. I remembered the comment: 'There but for the grace of God go I.'

I said, 'That's it. That could be me.' I said, 'I'll just go down next week and watch some more.'

Probably the biggest tension came one night when I was standing out in front of the center. There was a guy who was bigger than me standing there looking at me, sizing me up. He starts walking over to me. I said, 'Lord.' The adrenalin's starting to squirt around. He walks up, and his face gets that close to mine.

He says, 'I've got to ask you a question.'

I said, 'Yeah?'

He said, 'Is there anybody in there who can help me?'

I said, 'What's happening?'

He said, 'My mother just died. My heart's broken.'

When you come home and you get in your bed, you know that some of the guys you've just been with are sleeping in a cardboard box under a bridge. It makes you thankful. It's something that Andrea and I do together. None of these things are activities we started out looking to do. We've just recognized that we should be there and did it. By doing the fostering together, by doing the street ministry together, by doing some team counseling, we've really cemented our relationship. We're not passing each other in the dark.

As far as reconciling my faith with football, the Bible talks about being in the world but not of the world. I think it's possible to be in the situation but not of it. I didn't have to participate in all the things that were going on. I don't remember judging my teammates who did. They made some choices for lifestyle; I made some choices for lifestyle. I was not an exemplary enough person that I could point my finger at them and say, 'Shame on you.'

I WASN'T A MODEL. I just was working it out as it was revealed to me, trying to be the Lord's man. I didn't try to impose my system on my teammates, and they didn't try to impose theirs on me. They didn't put me down for what I was trying to do with my life, and I didn't put them down for what they were doing with theirs. We loved each other. The guys were like brothers, because of what you suffered together. You know what training camp is like. The great wins, the crushing defeats. That builds something. The relationship I had with guys in Baltimore was far deeper than in college, because you were with them more. Ten years, a longer season, exponentially more experiences. One year, we played six exhibition games, two full-scale intersquad games, 14 regular-season games, and three playoff games. My whole college career was 27 games.

I'll tell you a funny story that has to do with faith and forgiveness. One night while I was still playing for Baltimore, Andrea and I were sleeping. It was the middle of the summer, and we had a screened-in porch. I heard the porch door jiggling, but we had five dogs, and I thought it was just one of the dogs jumping against the door. Then I heard it again. I said, 'That's no dog.'

I got up, went out to the porch and flipped on the light, and a guy with a crowbar is standing there. He was trying to break in. I ran into the screen door, but it was locked, and I just bounced off the screen. The guy took off around the corner of the house. I got through the door and chased him, but he must have thought that I wasn't coming, because when I got around the corner, he was standing there.

He took off running, and I tackled him. While we're wrestling on the ground, he hit me in the head with the crowbar five times. By this time, Andrea is standing there. I told her to get my gun, call the police and bring me some clothes. I was stark naked.

After all of this, the guy looks up and says, 'Can I have a cup of coffee?'

Andrea was back with my gun, so I tell him, 'What you better do is stretch out your arms and put your cheek on the ground. If you move, you're dead.'

He left several golfball-sized eggs on my head, and the worst part was he used my own crowbar. Andrea was teaching Bible-study classes for kids in the neighborhood, and she had put a big welcome sign above the garage door. He took it literally, went in and took *my* crowbar to break into *my* house.

Andrea called the police, and they streamed into our driveway. When he finally got the story, one of them started laughing. I asked him what he thought was so amusing, and he said, 'What do you think that guy thought after he hit you five times in the head with a crowbar, and you didn't even blink? Why do you think you need a gun? He must've thought Godzilla had ahold of him.' I didn't even get a headache.

They loaded us both into the same ambulance, and while we were on our way to the hospital, the guy looked at me and said, very sincerely, 'I'm sorry.' I was really affected by that. When we got home, I told Andrea I wanted to talk to him. I went to the jail and talked to him through the glass, and he was really remorseful. His name was Major Bowling, and he turned out to be a famous cat burglar. There have been articles written about him. They still study his techniques in criminology courses. He was just a guy from a terrible background. We ended up sending him money, visiting him in prison, writing to him. He's spent three Christmases at our house. He sends Andrea a Mother's Day card every year.

Later on, I told him, 'Major, you represent an historic moment in my life. You're the first black guy I ever ran down.'

FOOTBALL WASN'T HARD TO GIVE UP, because it wasn't my life. I was into other things while I was playing. On Mondays after games, I worked. I worked at Allied Chemical Corporation, doing sales. It was part of the awareness that on one play, it's all over, and I didn't know when that was going to be. One of the unfortunate things I saw was that 98 percent of the guys I played with stayed too long—Unitas, Parker, Matte. They got bitter, they got benched, they got traded, they got cut.

I said, 'That's not going to happen to me.'

Jim Martin, who played for the Detroit Lions, got traded to us. We were going out to Los Angeles my rookie season. He came and sat down next to me.

He said, 'I'm going to give you some advice, even if you don't want it. You're a great one, and as long as you stay great and as long as you keep doing what you're doing, they're going to love you. But listen to me, boy, you lose a step, and they're going to throw you away like a pair of old socks.'

That's the way it is in college, too. It's a business. That was okay. Daryl and I—I remember this very clearly—we were down at the stadium one day, working out during the summer, and Daryl has an incredible aptitude for numbers. He said, 'I was recently calculating the value of our scholarship, and there are people in Mexico who are making more money per hour than we are.'

We were playing-slaves for the Athletic Department at Ohio State, but that was okay, too. We made the deal. We knew what it was like. We could not have afforded to go to college. We laughed about it. It was acceptable, just like dealing with Woody. Whatever his foibles were, they were okay. They were part of him. I bought into it. People have to buy into certain things with me, too.

Andrea said all during the time I was playing, she looked forward to when I retired so she could go to games with me, but I never went back. I went to one game. The Cowboys were in town, and I had a relationship with Tom Landry. I took my son. He was only about five years old. I took him just to take him to a game. I sat on the Cowboys' bench. That was funny. Baltimore's over *there*, and I'm over *here*.

WHEN I CAME BACK TO OHIO, I had developed a greater respect for Woody's integrity, because I had seen a lot more people, and I had seen how people who had celebrity got compromised. He never got compromised by it. At the same time, it broke my heart that he was unable, or unwilling, to let that shield down and allow people to love him and encourage him. I guess he thought it would be compromising to his personality. I would talk to him like I would talk to anyone; I wouldn't get down on my knees because it was Woody Hayes. What I said to him I said to him because I respected him and cared for him. I think he was a tragic character. A person who can't give and receive love is tragic. Visiting people in the hospital was his way of expressing love. It wasn't that he was devoid of love, but I don't think he was able to articulate it.

I haven't remained close to the program at all. There's a captain's breakfast every year, and I don't go. It's just another world. For the guys who want to do that, I don't say, 'Gee, why would you want to do that?' I know why they want to do it. It's a good thing. It's just not where I'm at. Daryl was really upset with me. We had the 30th reunion of our national championship team, and I didn't go. He was really upset with me, yanking me around. It's not an issue of wanting to be aloof, it's not that they're not good men. It's just that I'm not there.

For me to be the team captain and not be there, I'm sure that there were all sorts of reactions to that. I would say, 'Don't make anything that's not there. I'm not above you. I'm just not there.' It's not in any way saying it wasn't a valuable experience. It was a wonderful experience. It's just that it's over.

Surprisingly, people do remember me. Every once in a while, someone will give me one of my football cards to sign. I do a fair amount of speaking around town, and I spoke at a church a couple of Sundays ago, and there were a lot of people there who were at Ohio State when I was there or predated me, and they came up to reminisce. I like it when that happens. I do. I'm not without ego.

Daryl and I talked about this just a week or so ago: We didn't even make the Big Ten team. I was selected to the Kodak Coaches' All-American Team, but didn't make AP or UPI, and Daryl didn't either. Now, I played in the East-West Shrine Game, the Hula Bowl, the Coaches' All-American game, and the College All- Star game, and Daryl played in the Senior Bowl, the Blue-Gray, the Coaches' All-American game, and the College All-Star game. I don't know who the All-American tackles were in those games, but when Daryl and I showed up, we played. We didn't beat anybody out; the coaches just put us in there.

The bona-fide All-Americans at Ohio State have a tree and a hall of fame. Daryl and I will never make that. We find that very interesting. We had never talked about that, and I don't know what even started it. He laughed, the same as I did. We don't know if it was an issue with Woody or not. He was not always on Woody's Top Ten list either. During those years—and maybe it's true right now—if your coach was not supporting you, forget it. It's just a mystery when you see how things worked out after that. ”

The Once *and* Future King

HE WAS RECRUITED by almost every major college in the nation to play any of three sports. At 19, he was the most valuable player in a Rose Bowl game that drew the largest television audience in the history of college football and decided Ohio State's last national championship. He flew around the country making as many as three speeches a week. He gave the invocation at White House prayer breakfasts. He ignored plays Woody Hayes sent in and followed his instincts. ("Sometimes the plays from the bench ruin our momentum.") He darted out of crumbling pass pockets, flung himself into tacklers, and leaped up clapping. He won a National Football Foundation Hall of Fame scholarship. He married a Rose Bowl princess. He was a blend of narrow-eyed gall and grinning, red-haired boyishness. No one has ever bloomed with youth and promise quite like Rex Kern.

Kern came to OSU in 1967 as a member of what Hayes called "perhaps the best college team ever recruited." An assistant coach once said of Kern, "There is never any doubt in Rex's mind that he can do anything." His classmates were as audacious, asking as freshmen where they would room when they went to the following year's Rose Bowl.

Half of those freshmen would become NFL draft picks. They would win 27 of 29 varsity games. They would become so dominant that after Ohio State bludgeoned his team 62–7 in 1969, Wisconsin coach John Coatta said, "I was about to go over and see if all those Ohio State players had a big 'S' on their chests"; and Hayes would entertain the suggestion that his team ought to play in the Super Bowl.

In 1968, when 16 sophomores started games, even Hayes believed that his team was too callow. But from the moment Kern brusquely waved off the punter Hayes had sent in and scrambled for a first down on a broken play against SMU in the opener, the Buckeyes won with a panache uncommon in Columbus. Two weeks later, OSU defeated Purdue, the number one team in the country. (Before that game, someone chalked a nonchalant message on a blackboard: "Keep cool, baby, and run those fat tackles to death.") With Kern's clever ball handling, accurate throwing, and brassy freelancing, the Bucks continued to win.

They fell behind for the first time that season, 7–0 to Michigan, in the final game. All 85,371 in the record crowd at Ohio Stadium thought the young squad's improbable streak was about to end. However, the Bucks scored 29 points in the second half to win 50–14 and guarantee the school's first Rose Bowl appearance in 11 years. "That sophomore year was really a dream," Kern says. When he saw that celebrants had blocked off High Street and that the campus had become one huge party, Kern wondered, "Geez, what is this? This's Cinderella and Disneyland and fairy tales. Guys, what did we do?"

What they had done was become a national phenomenon. As Richard Nixon was the first television president and Vietnam the first television war, the 1968 Buckeyes were college football's first true television champions, winning the first Rose Bowl to feature the two top teams in America. That game was hyped as a showdown between Kern and USC's O.J. Simpson but was widely perceived as West Coast glitz versus Mid-American conservatism. To a nation riven by social turmoil, Kern and his teammates—scrubbed and well-spoken—embodied Hayes's lofty ideals about citizenship, scholarship, and dedication. "When somebody starts in with that bullshit about football players being dumb jocks and animals, I have just two words for them: Rex Kern," Hayes once said.

Kern would not be a consensus All-American, an All-Big Ten pick, or his team's MVP (indeed, he often split time with backup Ron Maciejowski), but he was OSU's most heralded player. Midway through his junior season, he was already the school's all-time total offense leader and had been dubbed by *Sports Illustrated* "King Rex or King Kern—your choice." Kern's fame was insitutionalized when after the Bucks walloped Purdue 42–14 in 1969, Nixon phoned Hayes and remarked that the quarterback was "a splendid little athlete."

"You don't think our kids are gonna let this slip away from them now, do you?" Hayes asked reporters after that game, his 22nd straight victory. A week later, the Bucks did just that. They had won eight games by a mean score of 46–9, although the first units rarely played after the third quarter, prompting the joke that Kern would probably win the Heisman Trophy but might not letter. However, Kern threw four interceptions and the flat Buckeyes—by a wide margin, the number one team in the country—lost to twice-beaten Michigan, 24–12. "The hardest loss I've ever had to experience," Kern says.

Before Kern's first game ("the most impressive rookie debut since Hopalong Cassady dazzled Indiana with three scores in 1962," the *Columbus Dispatch* wrote), Hayes surrendered control of his offense to the untested youngster, despite once swearing never to place his job in the hands of a teenager. Ohio State had lost 10 games in the three seasons prior, but with Kern checking plays and ad-libbing ("To a degree I played within Woody's confines, but then I improvised"), it won 18 consecutive times. The loss to Michigan, however, "made for a real ugly senior year for us," Kern says.

Hayes permitted his nervy star less freedom and reverted to off-tackle plunges from the T-formation. OSU struggled, trailing Northwestern and Illinois at halftime and beating Purdue by three points only because the defense stopped 17 third- or fourth-down plays. The media blamed Kern, who was said to be at the midst of a mysterious torpor threatening to keep the Bucks from the national title that, before the season, had been conceded to them. Kern had thrown for nearly 2,000 yards in two years, but in 1970, he passed for fewer than 500.

Kern gained a measure of revenge against Michigan, throwing a 26- yard touchdown pass to put his team ahead in the 20–9 victory. He was the game's leading rusher with 129 yards but completed only 4 of 13 passes in the 27–17 upset loss to Stanford in the 1971 Rose Bowl, Ohio

State's first Rose Bowl loss in 50 years.

His fitful senior season cost him the Heisman he'd been expected to win, but Kern says the trophy wasn't his goal: "My purpose was to win three national championships. I feel bad to this day that I didn't do that, because we were so close."

He had his first back surgery two months before summer camp in 1968 and has undergone four more back operations and a total hip replacement. He is unable to jog or play basketball, golf or tennis. "I'm paying for it now," he says. "I took a beating." He had trouble getting up from the booth to make a phone call. He put his knees together and turned both legs out from his seat, as if he were on a swivel chair. He braced his feet apart, pushed himself up with his arms, and walked stiffly.

Kern's physical condition is misleading, though. The illusion of youth has clung stubbornly to his trim frame, like a summer that has lasted deep into October. His sideburns are flecked with grey but are thick and long; wrinkles etch his pale face, but his clear hazel eyes are lively. He has the authoritative, disciplined manner of a youngish full colonel still rising through the officers corps.

On his way back to the table, Kern was stopped by a bubbly teenage waitress. "My father says you're the greatest player who ever lived," the girl said.

Deadpan, Kern replied, "Your father says?" The irony was lost on the girl, who expectantly held up an order pad and pencil. Kern signed several more autographs, then said being asked for his signature is "almost like an out-of-body experience." An undistinguished high school student who came to Ohio State in part because of the academic support the school promised, Kern is proud of the Ph.D. he earned there. After injuries forced him from professional football, he was president of the Nautilus franchise in California and Nevada for years, then went into banking and financial services, returning to Columbus in 1994.

Ohio State memorabilia had been hung around the restaurant's lunch counter. There were two photographs of Kern on the walls. One had been taken as he and Hayes debated a call just before halftime of a Michigan game. In the other, Kern crouches under center, staring calmly over the line of scrimmage as he shouts the snap count.

Earlier, Kern remarked that he felt as if he'd played his first Rose Bowl "in a daze." Now, he mused of the photographs, "I look and say, 'Was that really me?' Sometimes I think, 'Nah, that couldn't be me.'"

Rex KERN

"SOME OF THE FONDEST TIMES I had as a kid were in the winter. My brother and I would sleep with our clothes on at night so we could play basketball before school. We would go across to the grade school and shovel off a little place to play basketball. We'd cut off gloves so our fingertips would be free. We'd come home, get something to eat, then go off to school. It gave me a real adrenaline surge to make that basket or hit the ball or throw the pass, but it was the competition more than the winning.

I never liked losing, but I always felt that if you lost, you had to learn something. You know, 'Why'd you lose?' Sometimes there's no reason for losing other than you got beat. You were prepared. You did your best. But sometimes you have to face up to it and just go on from there.

I really didn't have a goal as a young kid, except playing major league baseball. I started playing baseball when I was five years old. I'd hang out with my brother and his team. Every once in a while, I might get to hit a few pitches at the end of practice, and that would spur me on. Football was not that prevalent on TV. We might get the Cleveland Browns every now and then, but the media exposure was not there for a kid, and in a way, I think that was good, because even if the game was on, my brother and my friends in the neighborhood and I would be out playing. Today, you can turn ESPN on and see almost any sporting event, any time of the day. I would rather go out and compete instead of sit and watch.

They had just started Pop Warner football in Lancaster when I was in the seventh grade. At that time, we had seventh, eighth, and ninth graders in the junior high school, and for the most part, on the seventh- and eighth-grade team, the eighth graders played and the seventh graders got beat up. They were cannon fodder all the time. Right before I went into junior high school, they started to talk about having this Pop Warner league. One day, I went to watch practice. A friend and I were standing around watching, and we started to throw the football. Apparently, I threw it farther than anyone else, and they wanted to know if I wanted to come out and play.

I said, 'Ahhh, let me think about this.'

I went home, and I'm not sure my dad was real excited about me playing football. But my mom was, so I said, 'Yeah, what the heck.'

So we went to Pop Warner rather than going the junior high route because we were entering seventh graders. My analysis at that time was, 'I'm probably not gonna get to play a whole lot and still get beat up a whole lot.' I thought I'd play on the new Pop Warner team and get a lot of experience, see if I like it, don't like it.

Again, it was the competition. It was your team pitting your ability against the other team. It was a lot like a checker game. They make a move, you make a counter move. It was just a matter of competition. That's what I really enjoyed—physically competing. It fit my personality. I had a little more aggressiveness than some kids. I used to have a temper when I was young.

Probably, being the younger one in the family—second-born, last-born—made me more aggressive. And being the smallest kid in the neighborhood. They beat up on you all the time. And probably having red hair; they always made fun of my hair. I think that tempers your personality: 'Wait a minute. I'm tired of this stuff.' If I got a chance to hit you, I hit you. If you can do that within the confines of an athletic contest, boy, that's great.

In a football game, which allows you that combative spirit, you could demonstrate—I don't want to say your 'anger,' but maybe your pent-up aggressions, be more aggressive in your play. Baseball, maybe you could do that when you slide into second or home. Maybe that's why I was a catcher. I caught for 10 years, and I loved catching. I had to be in the activity; I had to be in charge. Football allowed me to do more of that.

I've always enjoyed reading studies that people do on cybernetics and the psychology of winning. Was I successful at football right away? I thought I was, but that was in my own vision, in my own mind. I always felt like the old coach at Michigan State, Duffy Daugherty. Duffy never lost a football game; he just ran out of time. That's the attitude you have to have as an athlete. You live, dream, sweat, and toil with those images in your own mind. If you look at the truly great athletes and successful people, they're probably dreamers. You visualize something and you do it. I got a lot more strokes athletically than I did academically. I didn't really have an interest in working hard academically in high school. I didn't know how to do it. Athletics were easier for me than academics. Sports were where I could plug in.

IN LANCASTER, WE HAD GREAT fundamental coaches. There are things I was taught in high school that I still reverted back to when I was playing in the NFL. All my coaches were educators, sensitive people but driving people. They expected you to do your best, and anything less was not acceptable. We had good teams, and we had good players, and we were successful. But that's another perception. We were a great baseball town. If we were known for anything, it was a great baseball program. Our teams went to the state final four in baseball, and in football, we won our conference all three years. Going into our senior year of football, we had lost all of our upperclassmen. We started out with Upper Arlington, who was number one in the state that year, and they cleaned our clock. The next week, Columbus Watterson comes down, another number one team in the state, and they clean our clock. Then we go to Steubenville Central Catholic—here's the number five team in the state. Beaten again. I think we got a breather somewhere along the line, and our record entering conference play was 1-4. Our record said we were not a very good football team, but our football coach, Earl Jones, wouldn't allow us to believe that.

That's when I started to learn that it wasn't so important that you win the game; it's how you prepare for it each day. We ended up 4-1 in our conference. We lost our last football game. That's what I mean about perception. Did we really have a successful team? We did, but we ended up 5-5. You don't really say that's successful, but we were. We ended up winning our conference because we learned from our defeats.

I can't say I really knew that I might play in college until my junior year. But I didn't dwell on that. I tried to focus on going out to be the best every time I went out to compete. I would compete with myself. I'd say, 'Okay, I did this last week. I've got to raise it a little higher.' Therefore, I didn't say that I wanted to go to Ohio State or I wanted to go to Notre Dame or I wanted to go to USC or Alabama. I just wanted to compete. I guess maybe it was a natural progression that if you did well in high school, you'd go to that next level.

At the conclusion of my sophomore year, going into my junior year, colleges started to show interest. Fred Taylor showed an interest in me in my junior year, long before Woody and Ohio State football did. The one thing I really wanted to do was to come to Ohio State and play basketball. If I can say I had a goal, that was it. I could tell you more about Ohio State basketball than I could football. I grew up when Havlicek and Lucas and Seigfried and all those guys won a national championship. When my brother and I were playing with kids in the neighborhood, I was always Havlicek or Seigfried or Nowell or one of those guys. I wanted to be a number 3 or a number 21 or a number 5. Maybe that was the shining star—that I could play there.

I WALKED INTO THE LOCKER ROOM one day toward the conclusion of my senior basketball season, and my high school coach said, 'Kernsie, what's stopping you from going to Ohio State? Where would you really like to go to school?'

I said, 'Ohio State.'

He said, 'Well, why don't you tell them?'

I said, 'I don't know if they'll let me play football and basketball.'

He said, 'Is that the only reason?'

I said, 'That's the *only* reason.'

So he got on the phone and called Fred Taylor, and I think Fred and Woody said, 'Hey, if we want this kid to come here, we've got to agree to let him play both.'

I came to Ohio State primarily to play basketball. I finally decided when Fred and Woody said, 'Yes, you can play both.' I signed a football scholarship, but the agreement was that I could play both. So that was the end of it.

I did play both my freshman year, but, of course, freshmen weren't eligible at that time. Then, my sophomore year came, and we had to spend time at the Rose Bowl and win a national championship, and I had dislocated a shoulder, and basketball had sadly slipped away.

I had the opportunity to play all three sports in college. God blessed me with a lot of ability. I could've played basketball at Ohio State,

UCLA, North Carolina. I could've played football at Ohio State, at Notre Dame, throughout the country. I probably had had 125, 130 schools that were interested in me in one, two or all three sports.

Fred Taylor and Woody Hayes deciding I could play both sports convinced me to come to Ohio State. That was the kid inside of me, but there was also something else: Woody and Fred always talked about academic success. You might be fortunate enough to play in the NFL or the NBA, but that's a short time frame in your lifespan as opposed to what your college degree can do for you. They talked about that very seriously; they believed it; and they made me believe it. My senior year in high school, I was walking down the hall. It was during classes, and I don't know what I was doing, but I saw this big guy walking down the hall. The closer I got, I could see it was Woody.

I thought, 'Hah! This's cool!' I thought I'd go up and talk to him, and if anybody came around it would be: 'This's neat. Look what I'm doing. I'm talking to the head football coach at Ohio State.'

I started to approach him. I slowed down and said, 'Hello.'

He said, 'Hello,' and just kept walking.

That was it.

I thought, 'Wait a minute, wait a minute. Coach, I think I'm the reason you're here.'

Woody knew who I was, but he just kept walking right on by. He was polite, but he had been down to talk to our football staff, and he was on his way up to see our principal. If those two checked out, then he'd come talk to me. He wanted to find out what kind of football player I was, and then find out from the principal what kind of person I was.

I thought, 'Boy, he's not really interested in me. Well, I'll play basketball.'

I went home that night, and my dad said, 'You know what? I had a customer in the shop today. He was asking some things about where you wanted to go to school and what kind of degree you wanted to get. It was Coach Hayes.'

He was doing his spy work on me. Right after football season my senior year, we were playing Columbus Marion-Franklin in basketball. In high school, I was maybe six feet tall, but I jumped center. I went out at the beginning of the game and got ready to jump center. I looked over in the stands and saw Woody Hayes sitting there.

I went, 'Wow, this's great!'

Toward the end of the ball game, it's a close game, and I get fouled. I shot the front end of a one-and-one which would've tied the score, and I missed it. I was really down that we had lost the ball game and I had contributed to the loss. In the locker room after the game, I was sitting there thinking, 'Oh, geez, Coach Hayes is out there, and I'm going to have to go out and see him.'

I walked out, and no Woody Hayes. When I got home that night, my mom and dad said, 'Well, did you see Woody?'

I said, 'Yeah, I saw him in the stands, but I didn't see him after the game.'

They said, 'Yeah, he came up to us and said hello. He said, "I know how he feels. I don't much like losing either. He's probably not in a very good mood and doesn't want to talk to anybody."'

He didn't hang around to say hello, but I knew he was there.

Most coaches would've come up and said, 'Tough game, but you played great. We're looking forward to having you,' and tried to market their university. Hey, I *didn't* play great. I had an opportunity to bring us into a tie, and I didn't feel very good about it. Woody didn't even stick around. Woody went to the mom and dad. He was sincere; that's just the way Woody was. I really appreciated that, probably more than I knew. Intellectually, I didn't really understand what was going on at that point. As time goes by, I think, 'Hey, that was probably a pretty good move.'

I WAS PROBABLY IN AWE OF WOODY. I was in awe of Fred Taylor. That was something I wanted to be, to play for. Those guys were bigger than life, so I hung on every word. My first year in Columbus, freshmen weren't eligible, so I didn't spend a lot of time around Woody. But the first practice, we went out and walked on the field, and the varsity had already started practicing. They were having a scrimmage. Woody came up to Ron Maciejowski and I and said, 'Hey, when you two guys are finished, you're coming over with the varsity.'

Mace and I looked at each other and said, 'Oh my, what are we *doing* here?'

Woody's quarterbacks were all injured. Jerry Ehrsam had a pulled hamstring, Billy Long had a pulled hamstring. Kevin Rusnak was a quarterback at that time, and he was slightly injured. Woody was afraid that he could go down. Fortunately, neither one of us had to go in and play, but we were frightened.

My personal impressions of Woody and my impressions of him as a coach didn't match. You found Woody to be schizophrenic, in an admirable way. I saw a different personality in Woody. I saw a guy who was extremely intense: 'Hey, I want you to do it this way. I want you to lead with your right foot; you didn't lead with your right foot. You've got to have them 24 inches apart.'

He'd stop practice and say, 'By golly, I told you they have to be 24 inches apart!'

He'd get on his assistant coaches and say, 'Look! He doesn't have a wide enough split!'

The guy took so much time for detail. For me, that was good. My high school coaches did the same thing, but Woody brought a different level of intensity to that. At times, there was anger and a fit of rage, but that was only because he was trying to drive that kid to do a better job. Not to be perfect, but to search for perfection. He wanted to make sure that kid did it right. It didn't mesh with this personality that was patting you on the back and saying, 'We want you to come to Ohio State. We're going to take care of you.'

All of a sudden, you're saying, 'I don't know how this guy's going to take care of me. He might beat me to death.'

I THINK ANY TRUE COMPETITORS NEED THAT. From an historical perspective, Ohio State had been successful. Why? Is it because they had great athletes? Yeah, that's part of it, but what's the engine that drives the great athlete? I think you've got to say Woody was instrumental in that, like Fred was in basketball. I don't want to speak for other people, because Woody and I had a different relationship than with most quarterbacks. I'm probably one of the only quarterbacks I know of who Woody never physically beat on. I don't know why we had that relationship. I don't know how that relationship came about, but I do know that in the spring of my freshman year, when the freshmen had the opportunity to play with the varsity, it looked like there was going to be a lot of excitement that fall. The sophomores-to-be had stepped up—the Brockingtons, the Jan Whites, the Jankowskis, the Maciejowskis, the Zelinas, the Stillwagons, the Debevcs. Billy Long, who had been the quarterback, and Kevin Rusnak were both great baseball players, so that allowed Mace and I to come in and play.

But I was having a lot of pain in my lower back, really down my leg.

One day, I couldn't get out of bed. I called our trainer, and he said to come over. I ended up having my first back surgery at the end of June. Within 45 days, I was able to get up and run the mile and put on the uniform and be able to play. Woody sent some players down to bring some weight equipment to my house so I'd be ready for the season. I haven't had any contact, though. I'm relatively new out of surgery, and we're scrimmaging shortly before two-a-days are done. I always wore the gold jersey in practice, which meant you didn't hit me. Woody had this thing that if it was third and short or fourth and short, he'd always run me on the option, and I'd fall forward for the first down. That would really irritate the defense. One of those situations occurred, and I took off. I'm wearing the gold jersey; I'm not supposed to be hit. I come out on the option, and Stillwagon lays me out.

WOODY GOES BERSERK. Woody kicks him off the team, tells him to get out of practice: 'We're taking your scholarship! Get out of here!'

Wagon's looking around, saying, 'What'd I do?'

Woody's yelling, 'Get him off the field!'

Wagon's in showering, getting ready to leave. Bill Mallory was our defensive line coach, and he walks in and says, 'Jim, Jim, you did the right thing. You were supposed to do that.'

Wagon says, 'But I lost my scholarship! I'm out of here. I'm going to West Virginia. I'm not staying around here!'

Woody walks in and says, 'Jim, you did the right thing. How're your mom and dad doing? How would they feel if you left Ohio State?'

Well, geez. It was probably the best thing that could happen to me. The adhesions tore, and I started to heal quicker. We were getting ready to play Southern Methodist in the Horseshoe, and I distinctly remember Woody passing the authority to me.

He said, 'Rex, as long as you're on the field, you're in command, you're in control. There are times out there that you'll see things I don't see. You'll have a sense for the game.'

I'm only a sophomore. I think, 'Well, that's good.'

Anyway, it's before halftime, and we're moving the ball, but we're not moving it that well. It's almost like an engine missing. All of sudden, we come up and it's fourth and ten going into the closed end of the stadium, at about the 48, 49 yard line. I have great confidence in our defense.

They're playing a great football game. There's about two or three minutes to go in the first half. Everything was logically in line. Okay, we go for it; if we don't make it, our defense will stop them. I felt we were one play away from making something great happen.

Woody sent in Mike Sensibaugh to punt. My offensive team is looking to me and saying, 'What're we gonna do?' I waved the punter off the field, got into the huddle and called a play. Looking back on it, it was a horrible call. I went from the robust offense, which was a straight T, and we had a fullback delay, with Jim Otis sliding over the middle. He was our only receiver. On fourth and ten, you don't call a stupid play like that. Anyway, I did. Jim goes up, he stumbles at the line, and then he's covered. There's nobody to throw the football to.

They've got a fire game coming from the corner. The guy comes in and hits me about seven yards behind the line of scrimmage and knocks me up in the air. I do a 360 and land on my feet and run 16 yards for the first down. The crowd came unglued. They gave me a standing ovation, as a sophomore. They thought, 'This's great, man. Somebody defied the Old Man and made it work.'

PEOPLE ASK ME, 'HOW COULD YOU DO THAT?'

Well, if one understands the process, it's an easy decision to make. Woody had passed the command to me. I was in charge. I sensed something. I felt we were one play away from making a big play. I could see it in my teammates' eyes and their mannerisms. They wanted to be unleashed as much as I did. I went out for a play or two, came back in and threw a touchdown pass to Dave Brungard. We didn't do anything miraculous. We just did the everyday thing that was out of the ordinary at that time. Now, I was running for my life and my career when I took off. If I hadn't made it, you'd be talking to somebody else. Throughout that year, that kind of thing happened. Hugh Hindman was our offensive coordinator. They'd send in a play, and I'd check off at the line, because I saw a different defense and would counter their alignment.

That sophomore year was really a dream year. We come in as sophomores and win a national championship. Ohio State hadn't been to a Rose Bowl in years. They hadn't won a national championship in Columbus since '54. We just went out and played. As freshmen, we had been assigned a specific role. Our role was to get adjusted, athletically, academically and socially. Our sophomore year, it was, 'Geez, we get to go out and play.' We could play and have fun and be on the field without Woody in the huddle with us.

We had a wonderful blend of seniors who had great maturity, juniors who had experience, and we had the vitality of the sophomores. We hadn't been around very long. We just went out and played like heck all of the time. We felt a bond immediately as freshmen. We felt like we were special immediately, and Woody built that up. He talked about our class being the best class in the history of Ohio State. That's saying a lot. But there were 12 or 13 high school All-Americans in our class. I think everybody came in thinking, 'These are special people. This's a special football team.' We expected great things, and then we saw the guys do great things.

There was a tackling drill where the freshman running backs had to go down with the defensive backs, and they couldn't tackle us. We had Brockington, Timmy Anderson, Jack Tatum, Leophus Hayden, Maciejowski, myself. I remember the first day we went up against the varsity in a scrimmage in Ohio Stadium. We were helping them prepare for the opener. We're running the other team's plays, and we're beating them. The coaches had to tell the varsity what play was coming so they could be ready for it.

TO A DEGREE, I PLAYED within Woody's confines, but I started to stretch his confines after I gained his confidence. He'd call a play, and the play is supposed to work. If it doesn't, and the ball ends up in my hand, then what can I do to make something happen? Maybe he saw that and thought, 'Okay, if we screw it up, he'll still get us out of it. We're supposed to throw the ball down the field. It didn't work. The guy should take a loss, but he ends up jumping over people, running around and picking up a first down.'

Woody really couldn't coach that. He could control it, but when I improvised, I gave him a comfortable success ratio. He probably thought, 'Maybe it works. We're gonna call this play and we're gonna give him the Rip or the Liz formation, and when he comes out, he can get around the end and he can run it or he can throw it, and either one is good.'

We could have been overwhelmed by going to the Rose Bowl as sophomores, but this's where Woody's tenacity and ability to think ahead comes into play. Most of us had never been out of Ohio except on recruiting trips our senior year in high school. I didn't know what California was like. I knew they played great basketball out at UCLA, I knew they had palm trees, and I guessed that's where they had Disneyland. I couldn't identify with it, and I would venture to say that most of my teammates couldn't identify with it. But Woody had us so focused.

The newspaper people hated him on the West Coast, and Woody loved that. I really believe that the reason he did that was to take the pressure off the team and focus it on himself. They would write about this raving lunatic who is rude to the media and says all these stupid things. That was a great strategy. The Old Man wanted them to write about him; he didn't want them to write about us. When he got out there, he did his best to make them write about him. And they did. That allowed him to focus on us. He went right back to focusing on our splits: 'It's gotta be 24 inches. It's not 18 inches. Now, step with the right foot.'

He was so into detail and so into the process of getting you to the end result that you really didn't have time to think about extraneous matters. We went to Disneyland and here and there, and those were wonderful experiences. But we were so focused on what we had to do to play that we weren't caught up in all the festive activity.

You might go out there and play in front of millions on TV, and the game was shown overseas. But you don't really think about that when you're in the thick of things. Woody had us totally focused on that game. I don't think it was until years later when I moved out to California that it hit me. Then I thought, 'Hey, we won this thing.'

WOODY AND I NEVER REALLY GOT ANGRY with each other about calls. I was at a function the other day, and someone said, 'Rex, it looked like you and Woody argued a lot.'

He had seen pictures of him grabbing me and me pointing at him. Those times were very heated debates. He wanted to call something, and I'm saying, 'No, it won't work. We gotta do this.'

And he's saying, 'Are you sure it will work?'

'I guarantee you.'

Probably the one time I got angry with Woody and tensions got high was against Purdue our senior year. It was a close ball game, and we came back to kick a field goal to win 10–7. The field is muddy. It's raining all day long. I think Alex Agase was at Purdue at that time, and Alex left the tarp off the field all week long so that he could slow down our running game. For whatever reason, this day Woody wanted to pass the ball.

Every time I dropped back to pass, it looked like Purdue was in our huddle. We'd run this little delay over the middle, and they had four linebackers. They knew exactly who was coming, and they'd beat Larry Zelina to death coming across, then they'd wait for Jan White.

Normally, Woody runs fullback right, fullback left in a situation like this. I kind of took it on myself at that point to say, 'Hey, the Old Man's out of sync today. We need to run the football.'

He was sending in the plays with an underclassman. I'd step in the huddle and call a different play. All I was doing was running Brock up the middle, right or left, so he didn't have to cut a great deal. We took the ball and went right down the field and scored. I had changed off three or four plays that this underclassman had brought in, and I could see on the sidelines that he was getting the wrath of god. Woody was all over him, and I knew I would get my turn when I came out.

We scored our touchdown, and I came out, and Rudy Hubbard, our backfield coach, said, 'Hey, you're in hot water. The Old Man wants to see you right away.'

I kind of talked my way out of that one, but he did tell me, 'If you check me off anymore, you'll sit.'

THAT WAS THE FIRMEST, VERBALLY, that he got with me. His temper wasn't directed at me very often, and if it were, I'm not sure I would've responded positively to Woody's antics. Maybe he knew that about me. He didn't bat 1.000, but he did have a great insight into human nature. He could sense that what could motivate one person might not motivate another. I think all of your great coaches are like that. You've got 100-and-some different personalities on a team, and it's hard to distinguish between them. I think that's why he spent a lot of time with moms and dads, trying to find out what motivates their son, trying to pick something up that might help him later on. He was a master at pushing the right buttons on the players. He'd explode right now, then in the next couple of minutes, he'd ask how you were, how your parents are, how your classes are going. There was a sensitive part of Woody that he didn't want anybody to see. That would ruin his image.

Our junior year, we were beating teams so bad that the score was a foregone conclusion by the end of the second quarter. The starters didn't get to play a lot. I don't want to put us in the same category, but it's almost like the '49ers today. If the offense was having a bad day, I'd go up and talk to Tate or Stillwagon and say, 'Hey, guys, we need help. You've got to make a play for us. Sensibaugh, get us an interception.'

I just knew those guys would do it, because they had great athletic ability, they were smart, they were intense, they worked hard, they performed well. They would do the same thing with us. Tate would come up and say, 'Hey, Rex, you've got to run more plays. You're killing us. One play and a touchdown, and we're on the field all the time.'

We had that kind of synergy going on. We would win by three, four, five touchdowns, and we did that with the guys who played behind us. They could've started anywhere else in the country. We had tremendously skilled athletes at Ohio State. You're talking about Tatum, who could've been our starting fullback or a great track guy. Larry Zelina was a great baseball player. Dave Cheney was a great baseball player. Woody had never had a group of athletes this talented on one team before. He didn't have any idea what to do with them. George Chaump brought the I formation—we called it the 'Rip and Liz,' for right and left formations—from Harrisburg High School in Pennsylvania. We went into that our sophomore year. Had George not pushed Woody, we'd've sat in the full house. George got Woody to expand a little bit, but Woody wasn't comfortable with that.

OUR SENIOR YEAR, after we had lost to Michigan the year before, we went to a more conservative offense. I thought, 'Gee, we had been using an offense that won us every game but one. Woody's trying to find new offenses.' It's frustrating when you can't do what you know you can do. We had a great football team. I understood what he was doing. I didn't agree with it, but I was too young and not strong enough to say, 'Coach, we need to talk. We've got a problem here.' He was trying to find all the solutions to why we got beat by Michigan the year before, and in that he lost sight of what this team was.

The irony of it is that he handed me the controls as a sophomore; then as a junior, I got to call fewer plays; and by my senior year, I got to call fewer yet. Getting beat by Michigan made Woody revert back to his old style. Brockington and some of us were playing in an all-star game, and Alex Agase was there. He said, 'We were so afraid of your football team, but Woody shot himself in the foot. He took Cadillac material and made you guys run a Model T offense.'

That made for a real ugly senior year for us. Our senior year, we did not beat teams like we had the first two years. I remember times my senior year when we'd win in Ohio Stadium by only two, two and a half touchdowns, and we'd get booed. You say the teams scouted us and did a better job, but that loss at Michigan made Woody pull back. He'd lost confidence in us. He limited our offense. That's why we were in so many close games our senior year. We became predictable. We were tight. We were so concerned about not making a mistake. In spite of that, we still had the great football players to make it work. We went undefeated in the Big Ten, we beat Michigan.

WOODY WAS VERY AFRAID OF LOSING. That's why he probably didn't sleep much, why he worked harder than anybody else. He didn't think he was the smartest guy in the world, so he had to work harder than anybody else. He just didn't like to lose, especially to that team up north. You just didn't lose to those guys, and we did, and to a pupil of his on top of it. That was Bo Schembechler's first year at Michigan. That's the hardest loss I've ever had to experience. We just got beat. We had great football players. Michigan just beat us. They took it to us. They seemed like they knew what we were going to do on every play. They played their hearts out; we played our hearts out. We had a bad day, and Michigan made us have a bad day.

That loss was devastating. It was one of the most tragic losses in Ohio State history. I'm not sure we could've done anything differently that day. The only thing we could do was to come back and play them a better football game the next year, and that's what we did. We were able to get great satisfaction from that.

I think all the excitement about Michigan by-passed me my sophomore year. I knew it was different, but we were so focused on Michigan that the hoopla didn't set in. My focus was: 'They have a defensive alignment. How are we going to dissect this?' I had tunnel vision. When it really hit was after we beat them 50–14, and High Street was blocked off and there was a mass of students all over the campus. We're going to the Rose Bowl. 'Geez, what is this?' This's Cinderella and Disneyland and fairy tales. 'Guys, what did we do?'

Our senior year wasn't so much fun. It was so confining. At times, we were running new offenses that we had never run before. That didn't make sense to me. Here's a team that has lost one game—and, eventually, we would lose only two games in three years—and we're trying to fix something that really wasn't broken. The Stanford loss was very disappointing, but Stanford played a great game. Plunkett, Randy Vataha, and Bob Moore were outstanding. Offensively, Stanford neutralized Stillwagon by triple-teaming him. We didn't play a great game, and we came up short. Woody and I never did talk about that.

There was a lot of pressure, but I wasn't smart enough to know any different. I thought that was what you were supposed to do. That's when I began to develop ulcers. I internalized it. Physically, I started to deteriorate. I remember playing my senior year at maybe 173 pounds. Matte, Cornelius, and I all had ulcers. Woody would say, 'Hey, I'm a carrier. I don't have 'em.'

I'd say, 'Yeah, you get rid of all that stuff.'

The disappointing thing, the thing I missed, was that I didn't have a lot of time to spend with my teammates. I was jumping on a plane and going here and there, and I didn't have the opportunity to develop strong relationships with my teammates. I don't think anyone resented me for that. Our football team was a solid core of guys who worked for a common goal. You'd have to ask them if they ever resented me, but I never felt it at all. I hope I never contributed to any of that. I wasn't smart enough to think that what I did I did on my own. Even today, if anyone needed anything, everyone else would step up and help that guy out. We were really all out doing things individually, but when we came to play football, the group played as one.

Switching off with Mace didn't bother me. Ron Maciejowski was a great quarterback. Mace might've been thinking, 'Why did I come to Ohio State?' I never looked at it as something negative; I saw this switching off our senior year as positive. I knew that Mace could do some things that I couldn't do. Mace was great for the team. I just happened to be at the place and time where I had the opportunity to be the starting quarterback. I always feel uncomfortable talking about "the guy who played behind you." I always looked at it as Mace playing *with* me. Mace is probably my best friend from that football team. It was not only Mace. You could go right down the list. Dave Brungard. Here's a trivia question: Who's the only college football player to play for both Woody Hayes and Bear Bryant? Brunnie started as a sophomore, started as a junior, then Leo Hayden came in. Brunnie didn't feel that he was going to get a lot of playing time, so he transferred to Alabama and became their starting fullback, and I believe he was the captain of their football team.

We had so many great players that we needed to spread the football around to make everybody happy. You're not going to make everybody happy as it is. When you have talent on top of talent, how are you going to keep everybody going in the same direction? I'm sure if Woody had wanted to feature me more, I could've won the Heisman, but what would we have lost in that pursuit? We would've lost team camaraderie, we would've lost the national championship, we would've lost all of those great experiences that people sit today and talk about.

I remember when we were playing out at Illinois my sophomore year. We're close to the goal line in the first half, and we've scored on every possession that we've had. It's 24–0. Down at the goal line, normally the fullback or the quarterback would be the only ones to score a touchdown. We'd run fullback off-tackle or the belly series. Ray Gillian is our right halfback, and Ray's always blocking at the goal line. Jim Otis had gone out for a play or two, and Brock was in the game.

I GO INTO THE HUDDLE AND SAY, 'Okay, guys. It's first and goal. We have four chances, we have four players. Everybody gets a chance to score. Who wants to start off?'

It's first and goal at the nine. A play was sent in, but I called 'Robust 26' and gave the ball to Brock. He goes off tackle and picks up five, six yards. He's upset because he didn't score: 'Gimme the ball again.'

I said, 'It's Leo's turn.'

We call a play for Leo. Leo gets about two yards. It's third and goal from the one.

Leo says, 'Give it to me one more time. I score this time.'

I said, 'We're gonna pass this thing around. Ray, do you want to score?'

Ray had brought a play in. He said, 'No, here's the play.'

I made a play up in the huddle, just a straight dive play. I gave the ball to Ray, and he scored. I come off the field, and Rudy Hubbard got me again: 'Hey, you're in trouble. What play was that?'

I said, 'Hub, we made it up in the huddle.'

He said, 'You're lucky it worked.'

We had six, eight, ten running backs and wide receivers we could've given the ball to. That's a challenge for the quarterback, as well as for Woody. When you spread that all out, you develop closeness and you develop people who rely on other people. Everyone shared in the glory.

Winning a Heisman Trophy was not my purpose. It was not something I coveted. My purpose as quarterback and as leader of the team was to win three national championships. I didn't do that. I feel bad to this day that I didn't do that, because we were so close. We should've won; there's no question. That still bothers me. If my goal had been to win the Heisman Trophy—which it wasn't—then I'd probably sit here and be bitter and say, 'Woody didn't use me the way Archie Manning was at Ole Miss or Jim Plunkett was at Stanford.' We've got something that Archie Manning didn't have at Ole Miss, that Jim Plunkett didn't have at Stanford. We won a national championship, and how many teams can say they lost two football games in three years? Not many. Our purpose was to get better as a football team, and the way for us to do that was to give the ball to more people, so that they couldn't focus on one guy.

I WASN'T CERTAIN THAT I WAS GOING to go to the next level. My goal was to get an education. I wanted to get a degree from Ohio State University. Anything above and beyond that was great. I thought as a senior that I might go on and play. People were saying maybe as a wide receiver, maybe as a defensive back. I kind of wrote that off as not throwing the ball that much at Ohio State. There were questions in the NFL: 'Here's a kid who's probably a gutsy kid, a good kid, but he's not 6-4, he's not 210. He's been injured a lot in college.' Those are facts. 'Can he be an NFL quarterback?' They answered that and said, 'No, I don't think he can.' I remember the first day of the draft, a lot of my teammates were going off to Green Bay and Oakland and Buffalo and Minnesota. Reality started to set in, which was, 'Maybe you won't get that opportunity to play.'

The first day of the draft, you sit around and wait for the phone to ring. The phone rings, 'Oooo, maybe that's them.' That day came and went. The next day, I went down and had a photo session with the kids for the Easter Seals campaign. I still remember to this day that there were two little twins who were missing their legs since childbirth. They were like little footballs, one on one knee, one on the other. On the way back, we heard on the radio that I was drafted by the Baltimore Colts.

They had John Unitas and Earl Morrall. They said, 'Rex, if you're going to make our football team, you're going to have to do it on the other side of the ball.' I just looked at it as an opportunity to get me where I wanted to go in life. I knew that football would end some day—

not as soon as I thought, but we never think that's the case, and not the way I would've liked it to end. But's that's why you go to college, so that you have something to fall back on.

I probably shocked a lot of people that I made it as a defensive back. I hadn't played defensive back since high school. I ended up earning a starting position as a rookie, and we were still a good football team at the time. I got to start in the AFC championship game. I got to play in the wild card game in Cleveland against the Browns. We were one game away from the Super Bowl. That was all very exciting for me.

I liked the competition in the NFL, but the whole experience was more business-oriented. Playing under Woody, there was loyalty. I really didn't see that in the NFL. It was time to grow up: 'As long as you produce, we're going to keep you. But we might trade you if there's another commodity we need, and even though you've been a great player here, we can probably get two or three players for you, and that's going to help our team.' I sensed that there were more short-term rewards in the NFL. In college, you live together, you play together, and you develop more of a bond than in the NFL. It would probably be interesting to talk to the teams that have won a Super Bowl; they may have a better sense of community. Those guys probably experienced much the same thing in the NFL as we did in college, because a lot of what goes into making a national championship team also goes into making a Super Bowl team.

A COUPLE OF YEARS LATER, I had my second of five back surgeries, and I had to retire from the NFL. I went back to Ohio State and got my master's degree and my Ph.D. After a while, I thought academics was fun. Woody told me when he recruited me, 'Rex, you ought to get three things when you come to Ohio State University. Number one, you'll get the greatest education in the country. Number two, you'll get to play great football for a great football school. Number three, you'll have the opportunity to make lifetime friends. Those are the only things I can offer you at Ohio State. If you don't get an education, that's my responsibility.'

It wasn't hard to leave the game. I hadn't really had enough, but I was probably pretty close. I was with Buffalo at the time. I had become a player rep in Baltimore, and that wasn't very smart on my part. I had become a player rep to expand my administrative skills, but I got caught in the backlash. So I ended up in Buffalo. Anyway, I went in and talked to

Lou Saban. I said, 'Coach, I'd really like to stay in athletics. I'm working on my Ph.D. in athletic administration. Is there any place here in the organization for me?' Lou was great, but nothing worked out there. I had my academic credentials to fall back on. That's why I came to Ohio State.

I had gone to camp with the Buffalo Bills, and I flunked the physical. I could've gone on to another team and passed the physical, but the doctors said, 'Rex, if you play, you could end up in a wheelchair.' It doesn't take a rocket scientist to figure that one out. I decided, 'It's time for me to close this chapter and see what else is out there.' I remember there were two guys who'd been cut that day, and they had no clue what they were going to do. They weren't even close to graduation. These guys were talking about, 'I know a guy who knows a guy who may know a friend that I could maybe catch on as a free agent with some team.' I didn't need any more affirmation about the value of an education.

I CAME BACK TO OHIO STATE. I was working on my Ph.D. and I eventually got a job at the university as administrative assistant to the development director and administrative assistant to the athletic director. I worked in that position for about a year, and during that time I struck up a friendship with an Ohio State alumnus who was on the board of the development fund at Ohio State. He and his daughter purchased the Nautilus franchise for California and Nevada, and he came to me and wanted to know if I'd be interested in running that business for them. It just seemed like a great opportunity, so I took it.

We were successful out there. We wound it down two or three years ago and got into more financial-related products. I just returned to Columbus with my partners of about 20 years to continue our business relationship in banking and finance and financial services. It's like we never really left. Even though I was on the West Coast, I came back two, three, four times a year. My parents and brother were in Lancaster; I had business relationships here. I've always been involved with the university through the Alumni Association or the President's Club or the Athletic Department. Therefore, it wasn't like I was ever really gone.

It's gratifying to be remembered by people. It's an affirmation that you did something special. It's amazing to me that this town still remembers. I can walk into Bob Evans and have breakfast and see pictures of me and Woody and Jack Nicklaus. I think about it, and I get emotional. I'm part of Ohio State history. That's mind-boggling. It really is. I would call

Woody once every three or four months and talk with him and Anne. I still do with Anne. I would come back into town and stop and visit with Woody. I tried to stay as close as I could with him. We probably argued more after than when I played here. It was really over my health. Woody was in University Hospital. He went through surgery, they had left a sponge in him. Anyone else would've gone for a major settlement for a problem like that. I called to talk to Woody, and I didn't know if I could get through the switchboard, but I did. I was asking him how he was feeling. He said he was fine and getting better.

He said, 'Now, you've had another back surgery, haven't you?' I think that was number three or four.

I said, 'Yeah.'

He said, 'You need to get back here. We need to get you back here to the best doctors in the country, and they're right here in this hospital.'

I'm thinking, 'Here's a guy who loves the Ohio State University, and here's where there was a mistake made, and Woody does not say one derogatory comment about this institution or this hospital. He wants to bring me back to see the best doctors in the country.'

I said, 'Coach, I called to see how you're doing. I'm not asking you to talk about me.'

We're going on and on, and he says, 'Here, talk to Dr. Joe Ryan.'

Joe was his heart specialist. I asked him how Woody was doing.

He said, 'He must be doing all right. He's raising hell with you.'

WOODY AND I WOULD GO TO LUNCH OR DINNER. I remember when I earned my Ph.D., he hosted a lunch for me at the Jai Lai. He had a couple of my teammates there and my parents and my business associates. The day he died was probably one of the saddest days I've experienced. It still makes me very emotional. The guy conjures up those kinds of emotions. He didn't do everything right, and he would be the first to admit that he didn't do everything right. But, boy, I'll tell you, he almost did everything right. His heart was in the right place. He probably gave more than any human being I know. Woody could never give enough—to the community, to charities, to his players. It was a difficult day for me, and I'm sure for a whole lot of teammates.

I participated in the memorial service for Woody at the stadium with Bo, Earle Bruce, and Ed Jennings, our president at the time. On the way home to California, I wrote a letter to all my teammates. I said we needed to do something to demonstrate our affection. We needed to make a statement. I wrote a letter and said, 'Why don't we set up an endowed scholarship in Woody and Anne's names?'

I was thinking we'd raise something along the lines of $100,000 or so. Dave Foley suggest a deferred gift concept. We raised $1.3 million for Woody and Anne in the endowed scholarship fund. That's just from our national championship team. When I started this, a lot of people said I was nuts. They didn't believe we could do it. I know that Anne was being nice when I told her we were going to raise a million dollars. She said, 'Rex, that would be nice.'

WOODY MEANT MORE TO US than just a football coach. It's hard to say just how much effect he had on you. You don't know if you had a lot of these qualities before you got here and he brought them out. Woody taught me to value your education, to stand up and fight for something if you believe in it. He taught us you can't really pay back those people who have helped you; you have to pay forward by helping people.

There's probably nothing I do in my business that I haven't learned or experienced through athletics. Self-discipline, caring for your staff, not asking your staff to do something you wouldn't do. Woody wouldn't ask his players to do something he didn't do. Woody wouldn't say, 'Hey, why don't you guys go to the hospital tonight because I have to do a TV show.' Woody would do the TV show and go to the hospital before and after. This sounds hokey to most people. You hear, 'Football is like the game of life.' How can football be like life? Life isn't just a game. But it really is. Football and athletics teach values. The sport has all the elements, in and of itself, to teach values. Whether a coach elects to use that vehicle is his option.

Woody took college football and said, 'I'm going to teach values through football.' I think most people, including educators, say, 'You're all in it for the money or for winning.' I don't see it that way. Some of the values are fair play, sportsmanship. People say Woody wasn't a good sportsman. Woody might not've been a good sport, but he was a great sportsman. He believed in something and worked hard at it. He was relentless in his pursuit of excellence. I would love to see more people in their given profession be as relentless as he was, then I think we would have a far better community.

The value of sport still exists today as it did when Red Grange played the game, but it's not taken advantage of as it was in years gone by. It's shifted to, 'It's more important for me to come to go to X University so that I can get a big contract in the NFL than it is for me to come to college so I can get an education, be a productive citizen within my community, give back to my community, and enjoy my teammates.' The values are upside down.

Somebody might say, 'Oh, he's a little bit jealous because he didn't make that kind of money.' No, I didn't make that kind of money. That's not the reason I'm saying that. I'm saying it because we've got our priorities reversed. People should come to academic institutions to learn to become productive citizens for life. How many high school players ever go to college and go on to even have the opportunity to play in the NFL? And the number who actually play is a lot lower. Then, let's get a little crazier and ask how long that average life lasts for that person. The last number I saw was under five years. That gets you a pension of $800, $1,000 a month at age 65. What are you going to do for the balance of those productive years? Only a small percentage will make the multi-million-dollar contract. Even when you make the multi-million-dollar contract, you find out that you have a partner in the federal government, which is going to take a good portion of that. That's why I say it's out of whack. Sport teaches you discipline, it teaches you to get along with people, it teaches you to collectively make decisions. I don't think we're taking advantage of those values.

Many times, the academicians don't see that value, because they say, 'All you're worried about is winning.' Right, some coaches can distort that. But it was how you got there that was important to Woody. Woody would not do it by illegal recruiting or cheating or changing grades. He would not misrepresent the university in any way.

IT'S NOT JUST GO OUT AND WIN THE BALLGAME. How we win the ballgame is important. I don't want to sound like a Grantland Rice, but how did we get there? Did we do the right things? I still believe the good guy wears the white hat. Woody had the ability to go back to the person and coddle him, in his own way. He might not go up and apologize; Woody's way was to come up and ask you how you were doing in school, how your girlfriend or your family was. That's Woody's way of saying, 'Hey, I was pretty hard on you.' I'm not sure he was apologizing, but he was making you feel good. We were fortunate to play for a guy like that.

I wasn't surprised at all when they contacted me about the athletic director's position. I wouldn't say that I expected it to happen; I can only say that it happened before. When Hugh Hindman retired, I was contacted by the search committee. I wasn't waiting around this time to be contacted, but I wasn't surprised that I was. I had just come off of my fifth back surgery, though. In less than a year's time, I had my fifth back surgery, I had a total hip replacement, and I had an ear surgery. I also had the loyalties and the friendships I had developed with my business partners here. But it really came down to physical problems. I didn't feel it was fair to Ohio State, because there would maybe be some days when I would have to be down.

I met my wife, Nancy, at the Rose Bowl when I was a sophomore. She was a Rose Bowl Princess. When we landed, they used to greet the team with the queen and the court, and they divided up and rode in the cars that were provided. I saw Nancy, and I told one of my teammates, 'Hey, grab her and put her in the middle.' One thing led to another, and I convinced her to come back here to get her degree at Ohio State.

Over the years, I made it back for a lot of the Michigan games played here in Columbus, and for probably 20-some years, I hadn't seen the emotion and the enthusiasm from the crowd and the players that I saw this year. Even on the West Coast, if I couldn't come back for the Ohio State-Michigan game, I'd wake up the week of the Michigan game and know it was Michigan week. The internal clock was just ready to play.

Our team has remained close over the years. I think the reason for that is there's only one national champion a year. Our '68 team was selected by *Sports Illustrated* as the Team of the Decade for the '60s. Those guys are important people in my life, and I hope I'm important in their lives. It's the theme that bonds us. If I'm in Kansas City, I make contact with Bruce Jankowski. Tom Backhus is in Colorado, Randy Hart in Seattle The Stillwagons, the Maciejowskis, the Holloways, are here in Columbus. Of course, when Woody died, that allowed us to come back and see one another. It was unfortunate, but Woody would've loved seeing us all together. We're still close because we're still involved, and we're still involved because we saw Woody be involved. We have a lot to be thankful for. ”

An All-World Ass-Kicker

JIM STILLWAGON arrived at Ohio State on the cusp of monumental change in football. It was 1967, and a 215-pound middleguard willing to spend time in the weight room, learn the fieldcraft of his position, and hustle from sideline to sideline knocking ball carriers down could still captain a major college team, still be named a consensus All-American, still earn a place in the College Football Hall of Fame. Ten years later, and Jim Stillwagon wouldn't have had the chance.

Unfortunately, three decades ago, such undersized toughguys also assumed they would make a living in the National Football League. However, computer databases had begun to dictate the acceptable dimensions of those who would play the game. Stillwagon, who claims he is "6 foot or 5 foot 11 7/16 or whatever," quickly found that his accomplishments as a Buckeye meant far less to NFL scouts than his lack of height. They looked at him as an anachronism, a reminder of a quaint, scaled-down version of some executive subcommittee's concept of modern football—a development that infuriated him. Ten years later, and Jim Stillwagon wouldn't have been so naive.

"I was just unlucky," he says. "I really was. I always say I would've been a short basketball player if I'd been 6-4." He grew up in Mt. Vernon, Ohio, a self-described "hellion" whose father thought he should become a boxer. An enthusiastic athlete but indifferent student, Stillwagon followed his older brother to Augusta Military Academy in Virginia, where, his parents hoped, the discipline would tame their rambunctious son. Though but 15, he played against college freshman and post-graduate players who'd been stashed in military schools by Division I programs.

At Augusta, Stillwagon entertained offers from southern football powers and considered signing a professional baseball contract. But his father had lettered in baseball at Notre Dame, and Stillwagon dreamed of playing for the Fighting Irish. He spent an uneasy hour at South Bend with an assistant coach who ended the session abruptly by saying, "I've got to get going. I've got to recruit some good players today." Though Stillwagon had been an All-American prep school player, Ara Parsegian didn't even bother to speak to him. Thus rejected, Stillwagon signed with the Buckeyes because Woody Hayes "didn't bullshit me" and because his parents, who had been in a serious accident on the way to Augusta, wouldn't have to drive far to watch him play.

Stillwagon and the other "super sophs" of 1968 didn't wait long to establish their reputation. In the third game of the season, OSU faced top-ranked Purdue, which had humiliated Ohio State 41–6 the previous season. The Buckeye defense sacked quarterback Mike Phipps seven times, held star running back Leroy Keyes to 11 yards rushing, and shut Purdue out. Stillwagon set up the second touchdown of the 13–0 win with an interception at the Purdue 25.

Time and again, Stillwagon would make crucial plays to preserve wins. The Buckeyes won three consecutive Big Ten titles, a Rose Bowl, and a national championship. Stillwagon used quickness, flawless technique, strength (as a freshman, he could already bench press 150 pounds more than the next strongest Buckeye), and limitless determination to best offensive linemen, many of whom outweighed him by as much as 70 pounds.

"A technique I liked to use was to take the first three plays of the game and just, *bam*, hit that center with my helmet right there. I wanted to set the agenda for the day," he says.

Stillwagon became one of college football's famed players. He certainly had the name for it. Stillwagon: The name bespeaks old-fashioned, broad-shouldered Anglo-Saxon stolidness, while at the same time suggesting frontier independence, ruggedness, and daring. Sportswriters and spectators remembered it. The name helped, but Stillwagon was also what he would call "an all-world ass-kicker." Hobbled by a leg injury, he missed nearly the entire week of practice before the 1970 Northwestern game, then made eight individual tackles and two sacks and recovered a fumble against the Wildcats.

As a senior, he was his team's MVP and the first player to win the Outland and Lombardi awards in the same season. *Sports Illustrated* even created a new position for him: "Superguard." The College Football Writers gave Stillwagon the Outland Trophy, then in a memorable bit of damning by faint praise, said, "Some people make it on size, some on speed, some on desire. Jim Stillwagon made it on sheer athletic ability. He's probably the best defensive lineman in the country, if you don't take his size into consideration."

Woody Hayes had given him a leftover scholarship because Stillwagon had thin ankles and short hair, said "Yessir," and claimed to have read *Moby Dick*. The NFL would use somewhat different criteria in its draft. John Brockington, Leo Hayden, Jack Tatum, and Tim Anderson were all number one picks. Stillwagon was selected in the fifth round by the Green Bay Packers, who treated him so brusquely that he left in a huff for Toronto, where he helped the Argonauts to their first Grey Cup in 19 years and, in a final gesture of contempt, had a Canadian flag tattooed on his rear.

"Before the draft in 1971, that was the only time I ever wished I was taller and bigger, because the imbeciles, they were drafting basketball players before they'd draft football players," he says.

Twenty-two years later, a *Columbus Dispatch* article compared Stillwagon with Ohio State's next great defensive lineman, Dan "Big Daddy" Wilkinson. The piece serves as a primer on the differences in football between the two eras. Observed Wilkinson, who is six inches taller and 100 pounds heavier than Stillwagon, "It's like everything back then was shrunk. These days most players are bigger, and they're faster. Guys back then, I think, were playing in leather helmets. The game has changed."

In 1973, the Packers tried to lure Stillwagon to Green Bay, in what he must've found a satisfying act of contrition. He sold his home and business and moved to Kentucky. The Argonauts charged Green Bay with tampering, and Stillwagon became fed up with what he considered the Packers's mendacity and returned to Toronto. He would play only two more seasons, forced out of the game by injuries.

Stillwagon spent five years in sales, then started his own company, from which he does everything from peddle tee-shirts to promote inventions. Always opportunistic, he refers to himself as "a positioner." Outside Stillwagon Enterprises, his scarlet and grey Mercedes, its license plate bearing his jersey number, 68, sat behind his wife's Jaguar.

There remains something elemental about his prominent jaw and nose, thick brow, and deepset eyes, but maturity and an irreverent sense of humor have softened the overall effect of his face. As he talked, Stillwagon hooked one thumb in a leather suspender to support his right arm because the artificial shoulder he'd recently had implanted ached.

Without pausing for lunch, without having coffee, almost without taking a breath, Stillwagon talked for hours. He sounds like a kind of weird epic street-poet—Homer meets Dennis the Menace meets Sonny Crockett. He is impish, as if perpetually about to deliver one of his cynical punchlines, and his view of the world is strange enough that for him, the highlight of winning the Lombardi Award was meeting Red Adair at the ceremony. To Jim Stillwagon, it's all one grand joke, and that he's the butt of much of that joke only makes it funnier. He's still peeved over the direction his career took, but he accepts his fate as just another amusing irony.

"I always think, someday after I die, they'll go, 'Did he die? Yeah, I remember him. He played for fucking Minnesota, didn't he?'" he says.

His attitude toward football was always simple: "All I know is, there comes a day at 12 o'clock when the ball's in the air and all the bullshit's over with."

That is probably the best way to remember Jim Stillwagon: simply. A rugged little mug wearing castoff shoulder pads, a jersey on which a number has been scrawled in crayon, a helmet that once belonged to Notre Dame quarterback Ralph Guglielmi and four pair of wool hunting socks beneath the size 13 football shoes he borrowed just so he could wear low-cut cleats—at halftime of a Mt. Vernon High School game, rolling around with his pals in a puddle of grayish arclight on a chilly, dew-slicked field.

Jim STILLWAGON

"WHEN I WAS YOUNG, I started my own football team, the East End Rams. Some guy who owned a restaurant used to see us play up around the Mt. Vernon courthouse and sponsored us. Everyone showed up in their Hutch helmets or whatever helmets they had, decals on them, with wolves and skeletons. This one kid, Alfred Hutchinson, wore his mom's golf shoes. Nobody even knew what they were, but he wore them, and Dick Thorton came over to me and said, 'Man, I've got to get some of those football shoes Alfred is wearin', because they put holes in your hands.' That's how stupid we were then.

We used to play at halftime of the high school games, and I remember when low cuts first came out, this kid who played for St. Vincent-DePaul—his name was Jim Kelly—wore size 13. I went in at halftime and got his shoes, because I wanted to wear low cuts. Size 13, and I wore about four pair of hunting socks so I could wear 'em. I played without a facemask. I had a helmet from Notre Dame, because my dad went to Notre Dame. I had Ralph Guglielmi's helmet. Anyway, this guy who owned the restaurant saw us playing out on the courthouse lawn, and he said, 'What if I can get you some better equipment?'

I said, 'Yeah, sure.'

He ended up getting us rejected Mt.Vernon High School equipment. He knew the coach, and we got jerseys. We used to crayon things on them, and we had pants down to our ankles. That's how the East End Rams got started.

I played at my little Catholic school in ninth grade, then I played at Augusta Military. We didn't play high schools. When I was 15, I played against college freshman teams. There was a JV team, and they said I would be on the JV team, but I could get in shape with the varsity. I ended up being a center and a linebacker and a tight end. The first game, we played Frederick Military College, and the coach said we were gonna kick their ass: 'This team, they have a guy 300 pounds who's gonna kick the ball off. He's a tub.'

Well, that team took in I don't know how many guys from the University of Tennessee to get them juiced up a little bit. This 300-pound tub kicked the ball right through the uprights—on the kickoff. I remember thinking, 'He ain't a tub.' I ran down on the first kickoff, and this guy hit me so hard—I can still remember this—I looked up at the sun through my shoes and landed on my head. I said, 'This is a little different than high school football.'

Our fullback was 20 years old. He went to Oklahoma and got caught stealing, I guess. It was like the Dirty Dozen. I think we won the Virginia Military League that year. I remember waking up my first day and looking at the walls, and I didn't know where I was. They said, 'Get up. It's time to go to practice.' It was 6 o'clock in the morning, and I was in the barracks. I was looking up at this pea-green ceiling, going, 'What the hell did I do this for?'

MY SENIOR YEAR, I think there were something like 40 major scholarships given in the league. It was a real good league. Not too many people went to games, though. The corps was mandated to go to the first half, then after halftime, you'd look over and there'd be a guy and his dog watching the game. That's how military school was. It was a hellacious, physical game, and nobody really gave a shit.

Back in that era, you wore rubber suits and the coaches didn't allow you to drink water. It's amazing that a lot of people didn't die. Coach Siegler made us climb up this hill, and if you swore, you had to crawl up and down it on your hands and knees. I swear a lot; I don't know why, but I do. One time, the coach swore during practice, and he and I both were crawling up and down that hill after practice in the dark.

The mentality in those days was your coach always knows everything. If he said, 'Today, we jump off the bridge,' everybody'd be standing in line trying to beat the next guy to jump off and kill himself, because we thought he knew what the hell he was doing. Probably 85 percent of the coaches don't know what the hell they're doing.

Military school will either really screw your mind up or it will help you, because, basically, military schools are filled with people who'd had problems or they're rich and their parents don't want them around. Very few kids go because they just want to go to military school. I was voted the second-worst cadet in the school my first year. When he left, my brother was voted the number one cadet in all the school, and this guy, Colonel Gardner, called me in and said, 'Jim, I just want to know what happened. Your brother was voted the best cadet when he left, and we took a vote of the faculty yesterday, and you're the second worst.' This guy Truitt, who lived next to me, was voted the worst. But when I left Augusta after my third year, I was voted 10th—from the top. I about shit. It's called *Aspera ad astra.* It means 'To the Stars,' or somedamnthing. They had a graduation, and I was sitting there, and they said it was the first time in the history of Augusta Military they had a tie. The farthest thing from my mind was that I was ever going to be in the top 10 cadets, and they said this kid Gus Medina from some South American country—he was a yearbook guy and all that—and Jim Stillwagon. I about fell dead.

I think I set a record there. I think I had 14 letters. Anytime the bus was leaving, I was on it. I started getting recruited. West Virginia had an interest in me. Bear Bryant said he thought I was the kind of guy they needed because I professed the Christian qualities. I thought, 'Man, he doesn't know me from jackshit. I could be a rapist.' I remember Charlie Bradshaw: 'Son, you the kinda man, you put that Rydell on, and you'll break heads.' I never went down there. Then all the Big Ten started to get in touch with me. I liked Ohio State basketball—Jerry Lucas, and all that—but I just never liked Ohio State football because my dad was Notre Dame. I was always going to go to Notre Dame. They called me and said, 'Hey, would you come up to Ohio State?'

I'd do anything to get out of school again. So I flew up and met Woody Hayes and had a hell of a visit. I had civilians on, a short haircut. He came walking up to me and said, 'You must be the boy from Mt.Vernon that goes to military school.'

I said, 'Yessir.'

He said, 'Well, I like that.' He says, 'What's the last novel you read?' And I said *Moby Dick*. I never read a novel in my life. The last two books I had read were *Girls Upstairs* and *Martha the Lesbian*, or something like that. But I have a good memory, and I saw *Moby Dick* on TV. We're sitting there in his office for 45 minutes, and he's asking me all about *Moby Dick*, and I'm going, 'Man, this guy's something else.'

Woody's going, 'That's such a great American novel.'

He says, 'Would you mind if I looked at your ankles?'

I says, 'Why's that, Coach?'

He says, 'All great racehorses have thin ankles. They're quick. Are you quick?'

I say, 'Yeah,' and I take my pants down, and he says, 'Do you want to come to Ohio State? I can only promise you two things.'

I say, 'What's that?'

He says, 'If you're good enough, you'll make it, and if you're not, you won't.'

Yeah, ankles. Today, you'd probably be sued if you said, 'Let me see your ankles.'

I walked to the stadium, and the snow was blowing in it. I was an All-American prep school player, and I'll never forget, I went back to Mt.Vernon, and this guy said, 'I remember you being a hell of a football player. Do you still do that shit?'

I went, 'Fuck, I'm gonna go back to Ohio State and show these people.'

I LIKED WOODY HAYES, because he was a no-nonsense guy. He didn't bullshit me. They never even saw films on me. He just liked me. Woody has a record a mile long for doing impulse things, and I was one of his impulses. We bullshitted about *Moby Dick*. I say the only reason I was here was because I saw *Moby Dick* on TV.

Nothing against the south thing, but down south, there was a lot of bullshit. You know, 'You gonna make All-Pro, you gonna break Rydells, you gonna beat Bubba's record.' All that shit. I'm realistic, because I remember getting knocked on my ass and looking at the sun through my shoes.

So I went to Ohio State, and nobody had ever heard of military schools or me. I went into this room and saw the depth chart. I was third string.

I thought, 'Fuck, I never been third-string in my life.'

'I always admired you,' Brian Donovan said, 'because they had all these world-beaters, and no one had ever heard of you.'

I said, 'They're no different from us, just asses with shoes on.'

I was disappointed when I got there, to tell you the truth. I could bench press around 390, because in military school you don't do too many things but work out, and one of my friends was from York, Pennsylvania, big weightlifter. When I went to Ohio State, they asked me what I could bench press, and they all laughed. They thought I was lying. I asked them who the strongest guy on the team was. I forget who they told me it was.

I said, 'Well, what's he bench press?'

They said, 'Two-thirty or 250.'

I said, 'Shit, I do neck bridges with that.'

I had more weights than Ohio State had. I brought my weights over so they could use them. They had an old Universal weight machine that went to 220, and I used to have guys stand on it because you could never get enough weights on it. That's how far behind they were. They were good guys, but they didn't train. Some of the guys who played for Ohio State couldn't have played for Augusta Military Academy.

WHEN I FIRST WALKED IN, I knew what I could do. I was always in good shape, and I was strong. I started out as third-string center, and I could snap punts, because my brother was a hell of a center at Miami of Ohio. He was the best punt-snapper in America, the quickest, and we used to go in the backyard and snap through a tire. I could snap, and I used to go down and get tackles on the punts, and that's how they moved me to middle guard. They asked me if I could play middle guard, and I said yeah. I'd never played middle guard in my life.

Freshmen weren't eligible my first year. I remember we had to wake up a lot earlier than the varsity. We had to get on the first bus. We'd have meetings in the dark, get taped. I can still smell the Tuff-Skin. We'd get on the bus, and Tiger Ellison would say, 'Make sure you give 'em a good go today when we scrimmage against 'em.' You were just a commodity.

Our freshman team would give the varsity a hell of a go. We had a hell of a class: Doug Adams, John Brockington, Jack Tatum, Rex Kern, Bruce Jankowski, Jan White, Leo Hayden, Ron Maciejowsi, Mike Sensibaugh, Brian Donovan. I think, to this day, they had more guys drafted out of that class when they became seniors than any other one. We were the 'Super Frosh,' the sophomores who won the national championship. Sixteen of us started when we beat USC.

My first impression of Woody was that he was in charge. Woody

Hayes was a very primitive and non-innovative coach, but his theory was, 'Whatever I do best I'm going to do, because that's how I got to the dance.' He was very disciplined. His theory was, 'Little things make big things.' That's what I attribute a lot of our success to. We never got beat on fundamentals.

We got beat by Michigan my junior year because we got out-coached and out-played, and we didn't have the ability to adjust. We couldn't change our game plan. We sat back defensively. We had ball-control, but didn't score. We made a few mistakes and just couldn't catch up. Same thing against Stanford. We sat back defensively, we got behind, we had ball control for eight- or nine-minute drives, didn't score, and they came back and scored in two minutes. We beat ourselves. I always say if we play those teams nine more times, we kick their ass every time.

The trouble with Michigan-Ohio State, and Ohio State in Rose Bowl games was that Woody Hayes would out-coach himself. He'd sit and say, 'If we do this, they'll do that.' Pretty soon, we ended up going right and left. We threw our whole game plan away. He was a good coach, though. If he liked you, he was with you come hell or high water. If he disliked you, he told you, and you weren't around. I noticed that with a lot of great people I met. Nobody says, 'He likes me sometimes, sometimes he doesn't.' If he didn't like you, he'd tell you to hit the fuckin' road, and if he liked you, no matter what you did, he'd stick up for you.

HE WAS CONSISTENT. That's the best way I can describe him. People may not have really liked him, but they respected him because he was consistent. I loved him. As I reflect back, some of the things he did didn't make sense, but he never did it to be malicious. He did it because, I think, he was blinded to make it work. My senior year, we went to the Rose Bowl. He represented it like we were going to have it easy, but we had it 10 times harder. He took the spirit out of the team. When the Rose Bowl game was over and we got beat by Stanford, nobody even gave a shit. Most people just said, 'I'm glad this is over with.'

Some of the greatest games ever played at Ohio State were played on the practice field. Practice was brutal. Some guys were hanging by threads. Everybody who played us wanted to kick our ass. It was Homecoming every time we played. They said, 'Oh, you kicked the shit out of Northwestern,' and this and that. I don't care if I played Northwestern or the Green Bay Packers, I still was beat to shit. Everybody wanted to kick ass on you. To beat us was the ultimate high.

Then, they start beating the shit out of us at the Rose Bowl, and we were going to leave. We were going to have a mutiny on the Bounty. We had an agreement that these things weren't going to happen, but they still did. It was just bad management, but it was bad management because Woody didn't understand, he wanted to win so bad.

We used to spend 16 fucking days out there. We'd end up doing his lifestyle. We'd wake up and have breakfast. We'd have lunch. We'd go to bed at 10. Nobody did that shit. He beat us down physically, then he beat us down mentally. And then you go out and play somebody who just wants to kick your ass. There's a good opportunity that you ain't going to do too good.

WHEN I WENT TO THE HULA BOWL, I was living right next to Stanford coach John Ralston, at the Surfsider, or something, and he had Woody's *Hotline to Victory* in his hand.

I said, 'What're you carrying that for?'

He said, 'I fell asleep reading this. Every one of my coaches read it. That's how I beat you.'

Who was it, the Desert Fox, Rommel, that's how they beat him. Patton read his book, and I'm thinking, 'That's how the fuckin' guy got beat. They read his book.'

I told Woody. He said, 'He didn't say that.'

I said, 'You're fuckin-A right he did.'

He laughed. That's true. I can still remember that.

I used to say, 'Woody Hayes's strength is that he's consistent, and his weakness is that he's consistent.' You knew what he was going to do, and if you wanted to hit his red light, you knew how to do that, too.

What happened, I think, Lou McCullough did a hell of a thing. Woody had a theory that the best athletes always played on offense, and the rest of the shitheads played defense. Lou finally said, 'Well, we're gonna have a good team here. We're gonna have to have some good athletes go to defense.'

So they had a draft, I guess. Jack Tatum could've been one of the greatest running backs Ohio State ever had. He was an All-American from New Jersey who scored a friggin' zillion touchdowns. He was the hardest son-of-a-bitch I ever tackled in my life, when we scrimmaged. But they had Otis, Brockington, all these other guys, Leo Hayden, Reed Gillian. So

Jack Tatum got to be a monster man, which made him famous.

That theory was the right theory. You'd have some hellacious linebacker who played fullback at some high school someplace, and he was the fuckin' fourth-string fullback. He would've been a first-string linebacker, but Woody wanted all his shit on his side, so when he played against the defense in practice, he could kick their ass. He liked that because he could do that every day. One of my friends, John Bledsoe, who was one of the greatest fullbacks at Ohio State and never got his just dues—he was one of the greatest football players in Canada when I was up there—was telling me, he would make a good run against our first defense, and Woody would say, 'Bring it back and run it again.'

He'd go, 'Oh shit!'

Everybody but the ball boy was in the hole. He said, 'One time someone hit me so hard they spun me around and I was going the other way. Woody Hayes said, 'Get down! Get down! Get down!'

'I was lying on the ground, pointing the other way, and he made everybody at practice come and look at me, and he said, 'See the way he's pointing? He should be pointing the other way. He's pointing north. He should be pointing south. That's the wrong way to run the football. Now, everybody jump on him.' Everybody knew I was going in the hole. 'Run it again,' he said. Death City.

WE HAD A GOOD SPRING before my sophomore year. Our group started to move in. A lot of guys were upset, and I would've been upset, too, if I was one of those guys. But I was happy, because I was one of the guys getting moved in. Tiger Ellison said at our freshman banquet: 'It's like when you stand at the Grand Canyon, and you look out and say, "There's something great about this. There's a feeling about this team."' He was right, and I always remember that speech. We were supposed to get our asses kicked, but we'd win, and Woody would say, 'You guys should've never won. You played like shit.' The next game, we'd win: 'I don't know how we did it. You fucked up'; the next game, we'd win: 'You fucked up.' We'd be worn out and beat to shit. We'd think, 'Oh god.' Every week, we were fighting it.

After the Rose Bowl, my cousin came in from Vietnam. We were so worn out. He said, 'You're unhappy, aren't you? You don't think you did good. You did good.'

I said, 'I missed this play.'

When you're really into something, all those things people think are what you're thinking about, you're not. People ask, 'Did the crowd affect you?' I really never heard the crowd. The only game I ever heard the crowd was the Ohio State-Michigan game my senior year, when they were doing, 'O-H-I-O,' and I turned to this guy and said, 'Ain't this a bitch?' And I remember playing USC my senior year, and Brad Nielsen and I hit the USC quarterback. The center looked at me, his face all bloody, and said, 'You guys kicked the shit out of us today. You deserve to win.' And Ron Yary or somebody said, 'I'm gonna kick your ass if you ever say that again.' They started fighting amongst themselves.

We got a sack, made a big play, and they were fighting, and Brad Nielsen looked at me, and he said, 'We better get the hell out of here, because they might turn on us and kick the shit out of us.'

I said, 'Hey, Brad, look up. There's a million fucking people watching us do this shit.'

He said, 'Yeah, let's get the hell out of here.' That's the two times I remember looking up and thinking how many people were watching us.

ON GREAT TEAMS I'VE BEEN ON, each group thinks they can win the game. That's what makes great football teams. We felt on the defensive line that we could make the difference—Brad Neilsen, Bill Urbanik, Paul Schmidlin, Ralph Holloway, Rick Stottlemyer. Our team had a lot of big-play guys, which helped everybody else make big plays. If one guy didn't do it, another guy did. Jack Tatum was a great athlete, had great acceleration, would knock your ass off, but what made him famous was '53 Fire,' where he could go any time he wanted to. If he saw somebody wasn't sitting in, he'd knock your ass off. The reason he could do that was there were a lot of other guys doing a lot of other things. That let him take the green light. When they tried to dick with him, the other guy would kick your ass. That's what made a great team.

You think it's never going to end. You think you've done it all your life. A lot of kids get caught up in themselves. They think this is their fucking job for life, and I look at them and say, 'Don't do stupid things. You need to take advantage of this as much as you can, because it's real short. It's like a bug's life.'

A lot of guys have monumental things they want to do, like that Robert Smith kid at Ohio State. He's probably a good kid. But he's already a trivia question. Somebody probably blew in his ear and told him he was bigger than life, but nobody gives a shit. He pulled the brass ring too early, and instead of a whistle, he got hot air.

I always say our football teams weren't the best football team ever at Ohio State; the best team ever at Ohio State is the one playing the next game. They have to be, because that's who's going to play. Our team turned Ohio State around and started a great tradition. I feel it really saved Woody Hayes's job. I didn't know all the politics, but they really wanted his ass. But we turned it around. Each game, people would go and say, 'They won again. Holy shit!' It wasn't like they came to the games to see the gladiators kick ass on someone. They didn't expect it, and they all were a part of it.

MY SOPHOMORE YEAR, WE BEAT MICHIGAN. I couldn't believe how people acted that whole week. I had never been around that shit. Everybody was hyped. Then my junior year, I really found about how it was when we lost to Michigan. We went up there, and we were pretty worn out. At the Hula Bowl after my senior year, I got to know Dan Dierdorf, and I asked him about that game, 'What did Bo say at halftime?'

He said, 'It wasn't what he said at halftime. It was what he said before the game. He said, "Today's game is only 30 minutes long. If we're ahead at halftime, we'll win the game, because Woody Hayes will be predictable. You only have to play a half-hour today. Be ahead at half-time, and we'll win."' They were, and they did.

We sat back, and they knocked the shit out of us. We had three linemen, me and two tackles. Our ends were in the flats, the linebackers were going back. Jim Mandich had the day of his life, because he was catching 15-yard passes underneath in the no-man zone. At halftime, they said, 'What the hell's going on? We have to go after them.' We shut them off. They didn't score another point. We ran our stunts. We started kicking their ass. But then Woody went right and left, like Bo said. They jammed up the 27 and 26, so we were fucked.

Everybody was pissed off, because we should've beaten them. That was probably the most disappointing time. The crowd was spitting on us. That really pissed me off. I've never seen Ohio State people do that.

My dad used to say, 'See who's in the room with you after you lose, and they'll be your friends.' My junior year, we were the greatest team ever. People were breaking down the doors to give out trophies. After that Michigan game, Woody Hayes was sitting on a wooden chair. The room was empty. He was just sitting there. Every reporter in the world was over with Bo Schembechler, who had just kicked Woody Hayes's ass, kicked the Team of the Decade's ass.

I went over to Woody and said, 'Coach, we'll get 'em next year.'

He said, 'Yeah, we will. We will.'

I said, 'We'll kick their ass. Don't worry.'

He goes, 'Yeah, yeah.'

There he was, not one fucking person around the room. I thought, 'My dad was right.' One week later, though, there were 200 fucking guys, and they were all his brothers. But that's the way it is. I always understood that.

I call it the transition curve, when a lot of guys fall off the curve. My theory about athletes is they're like slaves. Who do you think the greatest athlete of all time was? Who did more for athletes than anybody? I think the greatest athlete of all time was Muhammed Ali. The athlete wasn't the fucking idiot anymore. He wasn't the jump-off-the-bridge guy anymore. He was an individual. He had something to say. He did things, and he didn't care. I remember people saying, 'That smartass nigger.' My dad used to say, 'Come here and watch this. When I was a kid, there was no TV. You ought to sit here and watch the best in the world do it how they do it. We could only read about it.' How many people mimicked his shit, took parts of it, cannibalized it? Athletes today say, 'Fuck 'em.' Before his time, it was, 'Get on the fucking bus or you're gonna be blackballed for the rest of your life.' He was a great fighter, but he did more for athletes, as a group, than anybody did. That's just my opinion.

WHEN ATHLETES PLAY SPORTS, people fucking take care of them. They say, 'You're going to eat at seven, get on the bus at 10, get dressed at 12. We're going to take you to the stadium, and everybody's going to cheer when you shit.' Then all of a sudden, that little sweet time ends. In business, when I make a sale, nobody goes, 'Ahhh, way to fucking go.' I'm sitting here with some fucking guy who goes, 'I want those baseball hats now.' You're wondering where the fucking cheers are.

A lot of guys never make the curve. They think if they fuck up, somebody will take care of it. I say, 'Hey, go over to the GM and see how many linebackers they're hiring because they need someone to make a tackle on some fucking guy at a dealership.' People want to meet you sometimes so they can see if you're dumb or smart. Then they can go back that night and say, 'Boy, I met the dumbest shit in the whole world. You know that guy who played for Ohio State. He's a fucking idiot, but he can do something for me.' They'll let you bullshit them one time, but there comes a time when Joe Blow has to have you make widgets, because that's how he gets paid. He don't give a fuck if you scored a touchdown in the Michigan game. He cares if you can make the widget for him, and it all gets down to that.

The kids are all thinking they're going to be Tyler, or Taylor, who's that fucking linebacker from New York, LT? That's good, but if you get there, you're lucky. The law of averages is against you.

A LOT OF FUNNY THINGS happened at Ohio State. I was one of the biggest linemen they had. We'd see the other team, and they looked like pros to us. Jack Tatum is 5 foot 9. Jack and I, one time, got called by the Dallas Cowboys. They said, 'Will you come down? We'll give you a couple hundred dollars to get timed.'

I said, 'Fucking A.'

I'll do that any time for pizza and beer. I went over to the facility, and I put cornplasters all over my feet and put a real thick pair of socks on. I came over to St. John's. This guy—some famous scout, Gil Brandt or Red somebody, their famous guy—he's going to measure me in the basketball area. He said, 'Oh, you have your socks on, but that's all right. Don't worry about it.'

I was six foot and a quarter. This guy got a boner on: 'Holy shit! This is great! Oooo, ahhh. You don't know what this means! You don't know what this means!' I'm going, 'Fuck, I should never have worked out. I should never have played one fucking football game. I should've just put corn plasters on my feet.'

This guy's going, 'This really means something! This really means something! You're over 6 feet. You don't know what this means!'

Then he goes to Jack—Jack's got a 'fro out to here—he goes, 'Jack, do you mind if I put a pencil through your hair?'

Jack doesn't give a shit. He says, 'Nah.'

Jack says he's 6 foot. The guy puts a pencil through his hair and says, 'Jack, you're only 5-9.'

Think what Jack Tatum did, only fivefuckingnine. I'm 6 foot and a quarter, and he's screaming, 'This's the greatest thing in the whole world!'

Doug Adams, who played for the Bengals, was a hell of an athlete. He ran for them, and he moved the fucking markers. At that time, Dallas was on the edge of the technology. You could have been All-World, but if you were a quarter inch short, you were nothing. A guy who was a basketball player would've been the greatest linebacker because he was over 6 foot.

This guy who was timing him had this horseshoe that said, 'Dallas Cowboys, World Champions.' He said, 'Heyah, son, you just get rat heyah. This's where you staht.'

He's marking 40 yards off, and when he turned his back, Doug picked that fucking horseshoe up and moved it up five yards. Doug blew by that fucker in like a 4.4, and this fucking guy's got a rod on. He's like, 'Doug, you faster than our whole team. You faster than Bob Hayes. This really means something to you, son.' I had cornplasters on, and that made me great, and Doug was great because he moved the markers.

We went to Illinois one time, and Woody started to talk about Lincoln. Woody Hayes loved Abraham Lincoln. Abraham Lincoln was the greatest fucking guy in the world, and Woody Hayes knew everything about him. We're kicking the shit out of Illinois up at Champagne. At halftime, Woody started talking about Lincoln. He said, 'Right down this river, that's where Abraham Lincoln stood on the banks and that's where Lincoln preached to this fucking guy, and some other fucking guy he was with. This whole thing with James Madison, Douglas, somegoddamnguy. They went down here.'

We went out, and Illinois about kicked our ass. The longest pass in football saved our ass with about 30 seconds left in the game. It was from Ron Maciejowski to Bruce Jankowski. It was called the longest pass in football. They said it was 'from Pole to Pole.' Larry Zelina made some great plays, and we beat them. But they about kicked the shit out of us. Everybody's going 'Jesus Christ.'

I go, 'Fuck, all this because of Abraham Lincoln.'

We went out to California one year. We were at East Los Angeles Teachers College practicing. Woody quit wearing a tie. We started calling him 'Woodstock.' That was his nickname. He wore a sport shirt with one of those Dickie things. We'd always say, 'Hey, Woodstock's lookin' good today.' He was like breakin' out a little bit. He was talking about scouting reports, and he called it 'WEFT.' He said, 'It's just like that guy from Ohio State during the war who developed the WEFT System.' It was a way of identifying aircraft: Wings, Engine, Fuselage, Tail—WEFT. He said, 'We called it Wrong Every Fucking Time. By the time you identified the wings, engine, fuselage, and tail, the fucker had bombed you.'

Another time, we were at Illinois, and we had our shake-out. It got over early, and we got on the bus. He said, 'It got over too early. We can't go back now. Let's go to class.'

Everybody's going, 'Go to class?'

He said, 'Pull the buses up here. Everybody's going to go to class.'

Everybody's going, 'Yeah, my ass. We're gettin' the fuck out of here.'

But he grabbed three or four of us and said, 'You come with me.'

Everybody else scooted off to the union. We just walked into a building up there. We walked into a chemistry class. It was some advanced friggin' thing. There was one of those things that went up on the board—staggered elevations or something. All the people in the class were older, graduate shit. This professor kept looking up; finally, he says, 'You're Woody Hayes, aren't you?'

Woody says, 'Yeah. What you're talking about there...do you care if I....'

He went down and started going on the board. The guy's going nuts. The fucking class got up and cheered him, and the professor said, 'That's unbelievable.' I didn't know what the fuck he was talking about. Only Woody Hayes could pull that shit off—talk to a chemistry class, and all the students got up and cheered him.

HIS BIGGEST PROBLEM was that he was diabetic. My daughter's a diabetic, and I really never understood before. You get low blood sugar, you get pissed off, you get irritable; you get too much, you get fucked up, too. They say that at Clemson, his blood sugar was like 450. I say he had some assistant coaches who weren't working in his best interest; he had totally lost control of that team from what I could see. We went back to a reunion, and these kids, they didn't even listen to him. What happened would be enough to fuck anyone up, but his assistants weren't doing the best for him. He had lost all the discipline. But they were still going to pull the game out—maybe—and this fucking kid intercepts the ball. Woody swung out at getting that chance to get it squared away again.

He wouldn't hit anybody to hurt them. I've seen him punch guys. He punched me, took my scholarship because I tackled Rex Kern and hurt him in a scrimmage when I was a freshman. He threw me off the fucking team, and I quit. Bill Mallory came in and said, 'You did the right thing.'

I said, 'Fuck it, I'm out of here.'

Woody told Mallory, 'You get him and get him the fuck out of here. I want him off of this fucking property.'

He threw me off the team. I was leaving. I said, 'Fuck this place.' I was taking a shower, and Woody came in. He said, 'You know what, you did do the right thing.'

I said, 'Coach, I was just playing football.'

A lot of that impulse shit was his diabetes. I don't know how he went on as long as he did. He was supposed to be on insulin, but I guess he never took it. I can't believe it, because if my daughter didn't take it, she'd be in deep shit. He managed to put up with all that shit while he was sick, too. That's what I told this guy who got smart with him in Houston. We were down there for the Lombardi Award dinner.

This guy said, 'Why'd you do that at Clemson?'

Woody said, 'I don't want to talk about that.'

The guy said, 'Well, why'd you do it?'

Woody says, 'Fuck you,' and left.

The reporter came over and said, 'Why would he be like that?'

I said, 'Do you have a grandfather?'

He said, 'Yeah.'

I said, 'Just think if your grandfather was really sick and someone started badgering him. How would you feel?'

When we traveled, we argued from the minute I picked him up. About how to get to the airport, where to sit, a whole series of shit.

He'd say, 'Go this way.'

I'd say, 'Coach, I'm gonna go this way.'

'Goddamn you, I've gone this way for 20 years.'

And he'd say, 'Okay, it's quicker, but it's a lot longer.'

Then he'd say, 'Goddamn it, I hate to carry my bag, that's what breaks me down. That's what breaks me down, carrying this fucking bag.'

I'd say, 'Okay, don't carry it,' and reach down, and he'd say, 'You touch my fucking bag, I'll punch you right in the mouth.

Then we'd get to Chicago or wherever and he'd say, 'You fucker, you made me carry this bag. That's what pisses me off, that's what pisses me off.'

We were in Chicago. We're going to some deal where I meet all these heavies. When they'd ask him, he'd insist on buying his own tickets. I didn't know it, but he bought my ticket, too, and when we got there, they'd changed a flight. They said, 'We don't have that flight anymore.'

Woody said, 'Then, how do we get there?'

Lady tells us and says, 'That'll be another $33 a ticket.'

He says, "Okay, I'll write you a check."

She goes, 'No, that will be a major credit card or cash.'

He goes, 'I said I'm writing a check.'

She says, 'Yes, sir, that will be a major credit card or cash.'

He goes, 'Goddamn it, didn't you hear what I said? I'm Woody Hayes. I know the president of the United States. My check's good. My Uncle Elmer, when he died, the last thing he did was look up and say, "Did you pay for my shoes that were on credit?" Now, goddamn it, I don't believe in credit cards and I'm going to write you a check.'

And the lady said, 'Yes, sir, that will be a major credit card or cash.'

That morning, before we left Columbus, he spoke down at a funeral directors' thing, and he said, 'Go get these books at my office,' and I had about eight cases of books. I was sweating like a sonofabitch. I got all these books up to the Sheraton downtown. I'm sitting there, and it was like a medicine show—$10 a pop; he's signing them. I had $3,000 in my pocket, cash.

I said, 'Here, Coach.'

He said, 'No. Keep it, because I'll lose it. I trust you, Jim. Just hold on to it.'

I have 3,000 bucks in my pocket, and he's saying, 'Listen, lady, I'm paying with a check. Who's the president of this airline? I'm calling him. What's your name?'

She goes, 'That will be a major credit card or cash.'

I pulled out this cash. He goes, 'Goddamn you. I'm going to kill you.'

He's screaming at me; all these people are watching. She just punched it up, did it, and we start walking away and he says, 'And this bag, this's another thing that breaks me down.'

I said, 'Gimme your bag. We'll put it over here in the locker.'

He said okay, and I put a quarter in it and put my bag in. He's over there, and I hear BANG, BANG. He's slamming this locker door. It sounds like a gun going off.

He says, 'This fucking thing....'

I go, 'Coach, you have to take the key out. You just do this.'

I showed him. He went, 'Goddamn you.'

Then he just looked at me. He says, 'You probably think I'm a crotchety old man down here. Let's go have lunch.'

We started laughing.

WOODY WAS FUNNY. He would say, 'Fuck'em all.' Ohio State will never, ever have another Woody Hayes. He was the people's choice. If Woody Hayes would go, 'Let's get rid of everybody at Ohio State,' the state of Ohio would go, 'Fucking-A right; let's do that.' That's why I say that Ohio State, administratively, will never—well, I don't want to say never—but for a while, they'll never have a strong coach. People say Lou Holtz. They don't want a Lou Holtz. Shit, Lou Holtz is too powerful. It would be like having Woody Hayes for 20 years. Woody Hayes would say 'Get fucked,' and you got fucked.

I'd go places with Woody and we'd sit and argue. He always wanted to buy lunch. One time, I said, 'Coach, I'm going to buy lunch.'

He said, 'If you touch that fucking bill, I'm going to smack you right in the fucking mouth, right here. I mean it, I mean it.'

The Houston Oilers wanted him to speak to the players one time, and we get on the plane. They see Woody Hayes, they automatically give him first class tickets. He's sitting there in first class. Eastern Airlines. Everybody's going to Florida. This flight's going to Atlanta, then we're going over to Houston.

They say, 'How about having a nice little Bloody Mary to open your eyes this morning?'

This lady says, 'Oh, that sounds great.'

Everybody's excited. It's the middle of winter. Everybody's going someplace warm. I'm going, 'Oh shit. This girl's going to hit him with a Bloody Mary, and she's going to catch shit.'

She goes, 'Coach Hayes, how are you doing? How about a Bloody Mary to open your...?'

'What? Nobody needs a drink! What's wrong with these people? Put that stuff away.'

You could see all these people cringing. We get down to Houston, and Larry Catuzzi, who played and coached at Ohio State says, 'Coach, the Houston Oilers would like you to say something to them.' He goes, 'I got to have my nap. I can't do that.' He was tired; he wasn't feeling well.

His hip was killing him. That's when that reporter jumped on his ass about the Clemson game.

Larry said, 'Well, Coach, they would just like you to come over. They have a big game.' They had this big gig. I think they were playing Pittsburgh. He finally goes, 'Okay, okay, I'll go over.'

We go over to the practice field. They all stopped, and there were a bunch of guys from Oklahoma on that team. They started, '*Ooooo*, the Buckeyes.'

Woody says, 'I don't take that shit from you.' Then he got up and talked about the underdog, and they all cheered him.

He used to make me sleep in the room with him. He'd go, 'This is for charity. That's stupid to waste another room. We can sleep in the same room.'

Oh, fuck, man, he never slept. You're sitting there, and you want to just relax. About four o'clock in the morning, you feel like somebody's watching you. You look up, and there's Woody.

'Jim, you up now?'

We'd get up, get dressed, and go down and talk to the night guard.

But I had my own room in Houston. We went through that whole episode with that reporter. I thought, 'At least tonight I can relax.' I went to my room, got cleaned up, had a little dinner, and went down to this cocktail thing. Everybody was wearing tuxedos. Real nice.

Guy comes up to me and says, 'Jim, we have a problem.'

I said, 'What the fuck is it now?'

'Coach Hayes isn't going to speak tonight, and he's the keynote speaker.'

I go, 'What?'

He says, 'After what happened today, he said fuck 'em. He's not even answering the door. If anybody can pull this off, it's you.'

I go, 'Why fucking me?'

I was sitting there having a drink. I go up, I say, 'Coach, it's Jim.'

He says, 'Oh, okay, okay.'

I say, 'Coach, you gotta speak. That one thing, that's just one incident. There's all these people. They can't wait to hear you speak.'

He goes, 'I know, but these sonsofbitches that do that....'

I go, 'I know, but that's just one guy.'

He goes, 'Okay, okay, but you sonofabitch, you didn't tell me to bring my tuxedo.'

I said, 'You got the same letter I did.'

This guy went down to the tuxedo place to get it. I'm helping him get dressed, and he's saying, 'You sonofabitch, it's your fault. You didn't tell me about this. I'm doing this for you. Goddamn it, I would never do this. Goddamn it, I'm telling you, when this thing's over with, you come to get me and take me to my room. I'm tired of this shit. I'm just doing this for you. That's the only reason. You hear me?' Then he didn't have any suspenders. 'You sonofabitch!'

'Here, Coach, take my fucking suspenders.'

He had to take his insulin shot, and I helped him. Then he went down and gave one of his greatest speeches.

WOODY, IN HIS LATER YEARS, either really nailed it or he really dragged it. This was one of the greatest speeches I ever heard the guy give. Everybody cheered. When it was over, I said, 'Coach, you ready to go?'

He said, 'No, no, I'm with all my friends. I'm going to have a few white wines with my friends, and I'm buying, but thanks a lot.'

I went, 'You fucker.'

It was the crowd. The guy was real sick and pissed off and tired, but man, when he got in the crowd, goddamn, that was it.

He gave me that picture there of him and Bo. I had it framed. It was sitting on his floor. I was up there talking to him. I said, 'Hey, Coach, man, I love this picture.'

He said, 'You want that? Some guy gave that to me.'

I just liked him. He always said, 'You never stay the same. You get better or you get worse.' He was a good man. He had a good heart. He did a lot of great things for people. When my mom died, she died unexpectedly. It shocked the shit out of me. I can't tell you how bad that was. We had just left our church. I was pallbearer with my brothers, and there was Woody in the church. He was crying. I thought, 'God, how'd he know?' Catholic mass on a Monday morning. Unbelievable.

My dad looked up at me and said, 'Jim, your mom got a special place in heaven today.'

I said, "What's that, Dad?"

'Oh,' he says, 'when your mom gets to heaven, all the sports fans are going to say, "Damn, Woody Hayes went to your funeral."'

He wrote my dad letters. He didn't have to do any of this shit. I don't know how he knew when my mother's funeral was, all the way from Columbus. He'd call my dad, and my dad and he would talk. He did things like that for people all the time. There's ten thousand stories.

A lot of guys were hosing him, but he never thought that way. At the end of his coaching, he always thought that people were giving a 110 percent. If you were with him, he'd go to the end with you. A lot of guys said, 'Fuck him, man, I'm going to get his job.' You can't believe how bad it was. He didn't even think there were drugs going on. There were the biggest drugheads in the world during the end. Woody would just say, 'That doesn't happen, not here.'

Someone would say, 'That guy's fuckin' you.'

'He wouldn't do that to me.'

He wouldn't even comprehend anybody not doing what he was supposed to do. It was really out of control. You could just see it. It was public. Guys were drugheads. He just couldn't fathom it.

I WENT TO COLLEGE BECAUSE I WAS GOOD in high school, and I went to the pros because I did okay in college. I sat down and looked at the pluses and minuses—Green Bay over here, Toronto over there. One was all pluses, the other was all minuses. I did what I had to do. I went to Toronto. A lot of nice guys, but the organization was fucked up. It was business. It was showtime. I didn't have too many options. I made the best of whatever I had. Green Bay told me, 'You'll either play for us, or you'll never play down here.'

We were at the Jai Lai in town. He threw the contract in my face and said, 'Here, sign this.'

I went crazy. I was from Ohio State; I had some self-respect. When I signed with Toronto, the guy from Green Bay called me up and told me, 'You made me look like an asshole.'

I said, 'That's what you are.'

He threw it right in my face. That was the big thing—everybody wanted to be a pro. Those guys were the bossmen. That was the way it was at the time. The athlete was just coming around, but you only have that little window, and you gotta go.

When I got in the CFL, I was the highest paid player. I couldn't go anywhere else, and I wanted to get out of there. You go anywhere else, and they tell you, 'Well, you gotta take a cut.' They wouldn't let you out.

Green Bay wanted me to sign for a $10,000 bonus and a $17,000 salary and $40,000 if I'm the first astronaut and some other shit. But it wasn't even that; it was the way they handled it: 'Here, I'm a busy man.' And he downgraded everyone, all the players who made them great, Ray Nitschke, Forrest Gregg. There wouldn't even *be* a Green Bay if it wasn't for football.

But in my second year in Canada, Dan Devine began to make contact with me. He said, 'We need you to come back. We're really fucked up.' I was All-Pro and all that.

I said, 'Yeah, I want the fuck out of here, too. Let's do it.'

He said, 'Good. Play your option out.'

I said, 'If I play my option out, I have to see some good faith money. I'm not going to do this like last time.'

He says, 'I'll send you $33,000 bucks today.'

I said, 'Send it on.'

So he calls me back in two hours and says, 'Jim, you can't believe what happened today. We just got filed with 11 charges of tampering with you and your contract. Man, we're in all kinds of shit.'

I guess Toronto got a whiff of what was going on. Who the fuck knows?

I couldn't go anywhere. Green Bay says, 'Well, if you don't play here, you're not going to play.' If I don't play in Toronto, I don't play anywhere. So, I'm trapped. Then I got hurt, and I had this fucking Packi guy fuck my arm up, kill 30 percent of the nerves in my arm. They said, 'Oh, we thought you had mono.' I was leading the CFL in sacks, and I hurt my hand, and all of a sudden I have mono. I went to see all these doctors. My arm was deteriorating. Just last year I had a whole new shoulder put in, stainless steel. My arm's still all fucked up.

Then Toronto traded me to Vancouver. It was a big thing in Toronto. The Vancouver general manager called me up. He said, 'It's so great to have you. We're going to build a whole team around you.'

I said, 'Do you know that I'm hurt? Do you know what happened?'

He said, 'No.'

I said, 'Do you know that I have a disability clause and if you sign me, you'll take on these liabilities?'

'No, don't fucking come out here. Let me make a phone call.'

And that was it. I quit football. I couldn't even lift weights. I lost 30 percent of the motion in my arm. My lawyer took action, but Canadians don't have to turn over records. To make a long story short, I got nothing. I suppose it's too bad it happened to me, but big deal. Things happen, so fuck it, you get on with it.

In Toronto, being captain of the football team, playing when I was hurt, playing when I was sick, doing everyfuckingthing, playing my ass off for them, when it came down to it, they said, 'Fuck him.' It was like a part that got nicked. I asked them to write me a letter so I could get my disability; they said, 'Fuck you. Good luck. Nothing's wrong with you.' I had a clause that said if I did get hurt there was a premium paid, and I did get my disability. It took a year.

I packed up the fucking pickup truck and the trailer and the dog and the kids and came home, man, and started all over again. I had some money, 80–90 grand in cash. The only reason I had that is I bought this fucking farm and sold it. Taxes up there will kick your ass. I don't know how anybody can make it.

NOW, I DO INCENTIVES AND PROMOTIONS. I have what I call the Lost Cause Syndrome. I listen to people's stories. If someone walked in here with a three-legged dog and told me this fucker could race, I'd get him ready. We have different innovative products. We have a company called Starlock Systems, which has a proprietary latch and a locking system. We have our Gary Guard, a barrier guard for highways. It's a highway maintenance tool. I'm a positioner. I put things together.

Kathy, my wife, works right here with me. She handles a couple of the companies and does the books and all that other shit. I like the hunt, and I like to make money, because in this society, you have to have money to do things. If you have a lot of money, you're a frigging genius. It's funny how smart people get when they get a lot of money.

I'm the guy who goes out and kills something and brings it back, and a lot of people feed on it. I say, 'You would never have eaten this if I hadn't been here.' I like the hunt and I like to make the money, but it's all relative. I've been around people who have millions and people who don't have fuck, and they all have the same $3 odd problems—you know, people don't like them. Their kids don't love them.

I say, 'Fuck, buddy, you have 30 million.'

'Yeah, but they don't love me.'

The next guy says, 'My kids love me, but I don't have any fucking money.'

At least when I fucking die, they're going to look in my casket and say, 'This motherfucker did a lot of shit. I don't know if he did it right, but he sure tried doing something.' I can adapt to anything; I'm an adaptable sonofabitch. I remember driving down to where I get some work done on the car. There's an intersection in Columbus where some people who haven't been so fortunate live. I'm sitting there smoking a cigar in my car, dressed in a $500 suit, in my Benz. There's a guy there sitting on a fucking couch. He had a bag of potato chips, family size, had a fucking liter bottle of Pepsi, smoking a cigarette, baseball hat on. Couch is out in the middle of his yard. Door was blown off the fucking house, windows were knocked out, kids running over the top of the couch, dogs running around. I'm sitting there, thinking, 'Look at that poor bastard.'

He's sitting there smoking his cigarette, looking at me, I'm looking at him, and I just started laughing. I thought, 'This motherfucker is thinking, "Look at *that* poor motherfucker. He's fucking working. I got my chips, cigarette, my Pepsi. Kids don't even have to open the door. Fuck, I have air-conditioning."'

I'm sitting there hoping I can pay for this shit, and he's saying, 'Fucking-A, man, I got me a Pepsi.'

I CAN REMEMBER WHEN I HAD 10 BUCKS to get a beer and a pizza in college, had an old junker car. You go to Ohio State now and it looks like the Los Angeles Rams training camp. Sometimes you wonder why you do things. You do things because of your family. You do things because you want to go somewhere. When you think nobody else can do your job but you, you're fucked up. Joe Blow fucking dies, and I say, 'Hmm, Joe Blow.' I always think, someday after I die, they'll go, 'Did he die? Yeah, I remember him. He played for fucking Minnesota, didn't he?'

That's what I tried to tell that Green Bay guy: 'I worked all my life for this, and I only have this fleeting moment. Give me a break.'

'You're one of my better dogs in the kennel, motherfucker. Get in your fucking cage, and you're lucky I'm going to feed you tonight.' The owner in Toronto used to bring his girlfriend around and go, 'This is my fast fucking dog; this is my strong dog.' I said, 'You asshole.' And he's saying, 'I'm the mean dog, motherfucker. You're all my fucking property.' And he was right. When the World fucking League crashed, this guy came from the Hawaiian Stars or something, or he played for the New York Fuckers or whatever. I can't remember his name, but he said, 'You know, I haven't been paid for two years.'

I said, 'What the fuck are you doing?'

He said, 'I love it. I played for New York and they fucked me, then I played for Hawaii and they fucked me.'

This is a goal line stand, and he's going, 'Hey, Jim, are we really going to get paid after this game? Do you think they'll really pay us?'

I said, 'Shut the fuck up. Here they come.'

He said, 'I just want to know. Will we really get paid?'

The team's coming to the line, and he's going, 'Will they really pay me? I really need the money.'

He's asking me if we're really going to get paid. 'Just shut the fuck up, we're gonna get paid. You just play.'

He said, 'Okay, good.'

Amazing.

FOOTBALL NEVER REALLY GOT TO THE POINT where it was fun, because I never got over the hump. I got knocked off before I got over. Some guys sign one contract and they're set for life, then they can sit back and philosophise. The majority of guys never get over the hump.

College was different. I had some really good laughs, but to tell the truth, the atmosphere was never that kind around here. I don't think I ever got a chance to take a breath and say, 'Wow, that was fun.' You did things, and you achieved, but it was like you were still attacking, still trying to gain ground.

College football is coaching and management; pro football is personnel management, because you're buying the fastest and the strongest. It's different now. How many years is it, 20 years or so? It's a big market now. The athlete has an unbelievable opportunity today to really do well—if you can get to that pinnacle of play, which very few do. You get the high school kid with all the chains hanging off his jacket. At Ohio State, I saw all the Johnnys come in, all East-West-fucking-Northern Ohio, and they get blown away. There're casualties all the way up the tree. Johnny doesn't make it, then he goes back home where Johnny was the greatest and it's, 'Oh, Johnny was never that fucking good.' He's fucked up for the rest of his life.

The worst ones to play against were the walk-ons. I used watch and think, 'Those are some mean motherfuckers.' They're happy just to be there. This fucking guy just comes out here for the fuck of it. Now it's all like I dreamed it.

People say, 'You look good enough that you could suit up tomorrow.'

I say, 'Man, there's not enough fucking tape.'

I always want to see Ohio State win. I want to see Michigan win when they don't play Ohio State. I always want to see the Big Ten do well, because I think the Big Ten is the most honest conference. I don't do that much for the program, because you can't do that much any more. They bring kids in, and I go to lunch with them, bullshit with their parents. I always tell them if you're from Ohio and can go to Ohio State, go to Ohio State, because the after-life is a much better life than being the guy from Ohio who went to Alabama. If you're the guy from Ohio who went to Alabama, they said, 'What the fuck happened to him?'

I can honestly say that I never saw Ohio State cheat. When I was there, the last guy and the first guy got treated the same. Everybody got the same fucking jockstrap. I belong to the President's Club. I donate to the Woody Hayes Foundation. My second daughter is going to go Ohio State now, too. It's a great school. I just hope it keeps its tradition.

You know what's great about football? Football happens in an hour. You get in a business deal, it takes 10 years, and it still doesn't happen. You can't grab somebody and beat the fuck out of them. The clock doesn't run out. In football, in one hour, your shit is either right or it's wrong. In business, they go, 'In three months, I'm going to look at that. Right now, we don't have the budget. Maybe next year. We really appreciate what you did, but we're going to go with the other guy because he was Jerry's friend when he was over at HPD.'

My dream is to wear a tee-shirt, shorts, and thongs, and to ride my bike down to my boat in the Keys, and to look up and go, 'I wonder how those motherfuckers are doing today, going crazy fucking each other?' When I first got into business, I had to dress up in this costume. I said, 'This is a costume. This is theatrics. That's all this is.' If I never met you, I can walk in and say, 'I'm a brain surgeon.' And if I talk the right shit, you say, 'This guy's a brain surgeon.' Act like you're successful, and you'll be successful. People say the best teacher is having things not go the best, but the best teacher is success. I say give people success and they'll know how to act. ”

And
Still Champ

PERHAPS THE MOST poignant image in the history of football at Ohio State University is captured in a photograph on the first sports page of the *Columbus Dispatch*, September 23, 1973, the day after the Buckeyes defeated Texas Christian 37–3 for their second win of the young season. Captioned "Henson Hurt," the disquieting photo shows Harold "Champ" Henson, Ohio State's elementally powerful junior fullback, being gingerly guided from the field. Left knee ruined, toe of his left cleat scraping the turf of Ohio Stadium, the 6' 4" Henson appears to dangle between a doctor and a trainer. Henson's long arms are draped over the shoulders of the two much smaller men. His head lolls. His chin has fallen between the 3 and the 8 on his mesh jersey. A frieze of stunned spectators forms a mute backdrop.

Barely a year earlier, Henson, the huge, grinning, fresh-faced son of an Ashville farmer, made his impressive debut as Ohio State's starting fullback, the definitive position in Woody Hayes's conservative offense. Henson's 79 yards and two touchdowns against Iowa that day helped to put Hayes in an unusually jovial mood at the post-game press conference and prompted *Dispatch* sports editor Paul Hornung to compose an open memo to the coach, immediately elevating Henson into the pantheon of legendary Ohio State fullbacks.

Henson proved that first game to be no anomaly. He gained 772 yards as a sophomore, only 21 fewer than Archie Griffin. His school-record 20 touchdowns were the most scored in the nation in 1972. Henson was the very personification of raw strength, battering the congested midst of defenses for scores and short-yardage first downs. He once earned two oak leaves—the OSU equivalent of the Silver Star—for hauling six and seven Wisconsin tacklers with him on respective plays, and he once carried the ball 21 times *after* suffering a broken nose.

When he was a boy, playing fullback at Ohio State seemed a dream to Champ Henson, "like winning the lottery or becoming president." Just as he began to live that dream, he was awakened by a blindside tackle, a torn medial ligament, and reconstructive surgery in Riverside Hospital. The *Dispatch* photo is a stark depiction of power rendered impotent by happenstance, of potential greatness destroyed by a millisecond's unfortunate collision of masses and velocities.

Harold Henson came to Columbus from rural Teays Valley High School as a gawky, uncertain tailback who'd nearly been overlooked by the one program for which he yearned to play. After Buckeye recruiters cast only a cursory glance at him, Henson, indignant, decided to enroll at Michigan. He was dissuaded only by an 11th-hour visit from a somewhat contrite Hayes. He arrived with the remarkable agility he'd acquired from playing basketball all night in local haybarns, a frame capable of easily carrying an additional 40 pounds, and the perfect nickname. Family tradition holds that he received the appellation at almost the moment of birth. His father, Harold Raymond Henson Jr., hitchhiked home from Ft. Eustis to see his new son, and, after a difficult trip, viewed the 11-pound boy and proclaimed, "After all this, he has got to be a champion."

By the mid-point of his sophomore season, Henson had become a hero every bit as lionized as Griffin. Yet if Champ Henson's ascent had been dizzying, his fall from grace was no less precipitous. He scored three times in the opening game of his junior season, moving Minnesota coach Cal Stoll to remark, "They're no longer three yards and a cloud of dust. Now they're 12 yards and a mass of humanity." When he was injured on the final play of the first quarter against TCU, Henson had already gained 26 yards and scored a touchdown. He was as astounded by the injury as he'd been by his meteoric rise: "Just like I believed the other thing wasn't happenin', right when I'm believin' it is, I ain't believin' this either." Though the knee was terribly damaged, Henson thought he could rehabilitate it through the force of his own will. He was wrong.

Bruce Elia, a converted line-backer, held the fullback spot as a temporary for most of 1973, scoring 14 touchdowns. Soon, however, another large, uncommonly swift young man, Pete Johnson, would inherit the mantle and score 26 touchdowns in 1975. Johnson would go on to gain over 5,500 yards and score 82 touchdowns in eight pro seasons, while Henson, in an abortive attempt to make the NFL, tried vainly to regain his speed and power. Finally, after leasing oil and gas rights from farmers for several years, Henson bought a piece of property near Ashville and began farming. He lives in a home he built himself, with his wife, Karen, and the couple's three beautiful towheaded children.

Henson still has the broad, off-kilter smile, the calcimine white teeth, the scrubbed wheatfield face, the clear, intelligent eyes, and thatch of sandy hair that had helped to make him a favorite at Ohio State. And he's still as big as the outsized whitetail buck he loves to hunt in the fields and woodlots around his home. Hulking, strong, but also bright and sensitive, he speaks fondly of his time as a Buckeye, with a fine dry comic timing and an entertaining sense of irony, utterly lacking any suppressed fury over losing his chance at superstardom. Always the pragmatic farmboy, he remains curious about just how good he could"ve become, but says, "There ain't nobody holdin' a gun to your head, man. It's your own volition, part of the deal."

He has ended up where he once said he'd never be—back on the farm—and now can't imagine being any-where else, particularly if it meant being away from the kids for an entire day. He farms his own land and, through lease arrangements, some other plots near his home, and sells produce to food chains and at his farm market on Route 23. And if it seems a cruel irony, given how things turned out, that Harold Henson should have to be called "Champ" for the rest of his life, perhaps the nickname is appropriate after all.

Champ HENSON

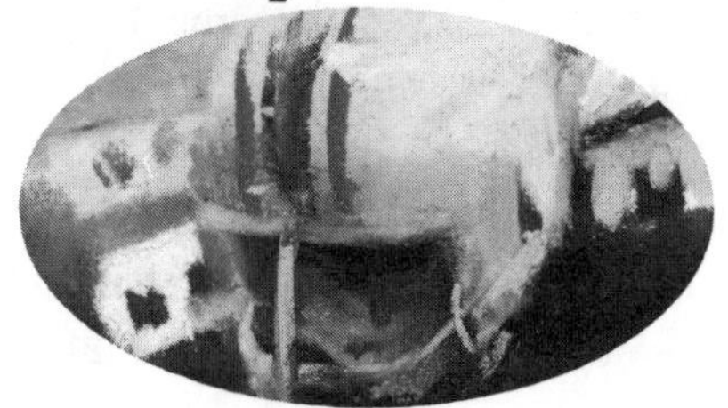

"I'M THE THIRD GENERATION to grow up in this part of the country. My family has always been farmers. My grandfather grew up on a small hill farm and moved to Columbus to work on the railroad, along with a lot of other guys back in the '20s and '30s. His dream was to own a farm, and that was the farm where my father was raised, and my mom and dad live there today.

I went to—which I'm really proud of—a three-room school that had six grades. Best teachers I ever had, including four years at the university. A little township school, mostly farm kids. Football wasn't that big in this area. We had just got a new high school. Before that, everyone played six-man football, and I just missed that by a few years. We had a lot of tough kids. Some guys went to school a few places, but we were really kind of unexposed. When I got recruited, I really wanted to go to Ohio State. Every kid at that time did. 'Course, you're talking about '68, '69 and '70, and here we are 20 miles from downtown Columbus, and, I mean, Ohio State never recruited me. Everybody else in the country was recruitin' me.

This was Sark's area to recruit, and for one reason or another, he sent one of the graduate assistants down. I remember when they came to practice. They got there late, didn't stay around, they left. Dick Walker told Woody, 'We've got a kid 20 miles from here who's going to go to Michigan.'

So Woody said, 'Well, get a couple films. We'll look at him.'

This was gettin' late in the year, almost national intent day. So they get a couple films, and I guess Woody watched about five minutes of one and just flipped the projector over. He said, 'If he goes to Michigan, you're all fired.'

Then Woody came down himself. My grandmother was at the house. Of course, she lived just right across the yard.

My dad said, 'Mom, you know Coach Hayes. You've probably seen him on television.'

She said, 'Has he been here before?'

Dad said, 'No.'

She said, 'Well, it's so hard. There's been so many here.'

Of course, Woody always lands on his feet. He said, 'Yes, way too many, but the right coach's here now.'

He came to the high school. It was a big thing. Of course, all these other coaches just looked like everyone else. Around here, Woody was like Elvis. You know, there was no mistake: 'That's Woody Hayes.' All the other coaches looked like insurance salesmen, but Woody's Woody.

When I found out he was coming down to see me, I was really like, 'So what? The only reason he wants me is because I'm goin' to go to Michigan.' I was a little bit ticked off, and I told him and my dad told him.

And Woody said, 'Well, we made a mistake. I'm not going to lie to you. I apologize. I'll be back. Don't make a decision. Think about it.'

The next time he came to see me, he picked me up at school and drove me home. He took his time on back-country roads. He said he understood how I felt but, he said, 'You should never let your pride stand in the way of making the best decision.'

I said, 'You're right.'

We shook hands, and that was the deal.

IT'S HARD TO FIGURE OUT just what I thought of him. I was young, and they had just won the national championship, and for you to be considered was kind of humbling. He was big as life, bigger. I didn't really think that I'd get to a place like that. I always thought that that was something that would be like hittin' the lottery, be like bein' president. You know, 'That's too far out of reach for me. I'll never achieve that.' I thought maybe I'd go to a small college—Denison, maybe Miami, Ohio U at the tops.

You hear the story of how my dad used to take me up to Ohio Stadium all the time, but I think he took me up there once. I used to go up to the dental clinic all the time, because you could get your teeth fixed for $5. I remember, when I was small, waitin' on my turn in the chair, I'd walk over there. You could see it from the dental clinic. I'd walk over and look around. I remember tellin' the guy who worked on my teeth that I was going to play there some day. He laughed. 'Sure kid,' he said. 'Open wide.'

But you got to dream. You have to strive for something. How many kids in this state that was their dream? You never thought about playin' for the Browns or somebody. It was, 'I'm going to go to Ohio State.'

When you play ball, 'I'm the Buckeyes. You're Michigan.'

'No, no, I want to be Ohio State.'

It was a dream come true, really. I had a good career in high school, but I never really thought I was that good at the time. I was a gawky, clumsy kid for a running back. I was 6' 4" and weighed 185, 190 pounds. You read in the paper about these guys from the big schools—Lancaster, Canton, Massillon—who gained 2,000 yards, how fast they were. I never considered myself in that category, and at that time, I wasn't. I was not in that class.

But I think the best thing for me, at that time, was freshmen not being eligible. They took a lot more kids on their potential then, instead of right now, a kid who's going to play next year. My freshman year, I learned so much. They'd just put you into the breach in practice and beat the hell out of you.

When I got there, I was just amazed. I had just started gettin' my taste of this, visitin' these other schools, everyone tellin' you how great you are and all this. I came from a small school, lived way out in the country. Things like that were just amazing to me, gettin' on airplanes and flyin' out to all these places to look at these schools. It was really mind-boggling.

SO WOODY BROUGHT ME IN, introduced me. I think he always did have somethin' special for me because of my background. He always had a thing for people who worked hard. Anyway, he brought me into this coaches meeting, and he introduced me.

Woody says, 'Pull down your pants.'

I'm going, 'Excuse me?'

Meanwhile, these graduate assistants are lookin' around like, 'The old man's finally flipped.'

He's going, 'Now, just pull down your pants. I want them to look at your legs.'

'Well, whatever you say, Coach.'

I pull down my pants.

He goes, 'Look at that pair of legs. Did you lift weights?'

'No, I run a lot. I run every day.'

He was just amazed: 'Look at those quadriceps. Look at those hamstrings.'

And those coaches: 'Umm hmm, umm hmm.'

It was like General Motors, you know: 'What do you think of the new fenders?'

'Ahh, great, boss. Whatever you say.'

'Pull your pants up.'

Some of those guys who were graduate assistants in that meeting I really got to be good friends with. They couldn't believe it: 'Woody had you pull down your pants, man.'

IT WAS HILARIOUS, but Woody always was different. The way he did everything was different. Some things he didn't care a bit about. Like, most of the coaches played golf and all that. He wouldn't be caught dead playing golf. He worked all the time. There was no off-season. He was always connivin', chiselin', workin'. Woody would say, 'Meet me 6 o'clock in the morning. There's something I want to talk over with you.'

I'm like, 'Oh no, I've got to eat.'

The dining hall didn't open until quarter to seven.

He'd say, 'That's all right. I'll bring breakfast.'

So you'd hike over to his office, and he'd be there all bright and ready to go to work, and you'd go, 'Hey, Coach, what about breakfast?'

He reaches in his pocket and pulls out a napkin with like three pieces of cold toast in it that he took off his plate when he ate at 4 o'clock that morning: 'Oh, yeah, here.'

He might get you over there to make you study, or just to get you up and get you going, to see what was making you tick at that time. He'd ask you what you observed on your walk over. So many times you couldn't tell where he was going; you didn't know what to answer. You had no idea what he was gettin' at.

'How you getting along in your English class? What do you think of this new play I have? How's the food?'

One thing Woody did—and at the time, you said, 'Ahh, man, you're nuts'—is every road game, you had a different roommate. He would spend hours over, 'Well, who's going to be with who this week? Should we put this guy with this guy? Maybe they'll talk about this.' Like when we'd go to the Rose Bowl. Every week, we'd have to change roommates. 'Ahhh, man, I just moved my stuff in. I don't even know this guy.'

What he was doin' was makin' everybody live with everybody and find out about each other. When you look back, it was the greatest thing I could think of anybody doin'. Even as close as we were, certain guys hung out with certain guys, and the guys you lived with, you were goin' to stay with them on the road. But no, uh-uh, 'You're stayin' with him.' Now that you look back on it, it brought us even closer. You learned about the other guy. At the time, we never thought about that. Of course, he never mentioned it. It was his idea and, 'That's the way it is. Shut up. You're stayin' here.'

They said he would take hours doin' that: 'Maybe I should put...'

And the coaches would be like, 'Just put 'em together.'

'No, we're not doin' it that way. Now, what about these two guys?'

He thought over everything: when you were going to eat, what you were going to eat, how much you were going to eat, when you were going to bed. He used to do this thing when we traveled to the West Coast: 'Well, it's 8 o'clock our time. That means it's 5 o'clock here. So that means....'

He's got these itineraries, and everybody's going, 'What?'

It's, 'Now, turn your watch back to Ohio time.'

It was everything, everything. It wasn't just the plays or the games or practice. His itinerary for practice was just everything, down to the minute. If you made mistakes, everybody would just turn their watches back. 'Coaches, turn your watches back.' We'd even go right back to calisthenics sometimes: 'I got nowhere to go. All my friends are dead. You guys want to get out, I know, I know, yeah, but we're not doin' it. Just turn your watches back.'

The players called it 'Woody Time.'

It was hard to handle at first. I looked at the plays and said, 'I will never, ever get this.' Of course, when you look back on it, it was so simple, but we had such intricate line play. We had line play that I don't see much of today. Of course, we had the best players. We had great line coaches. No matter what anybody did, it was, 'Okay, we're doin' this. When they do this, we do this, and then, when they do this, we do this.' You had one play, but you could block it 15 different ways. A lot of it, you didn't know how you were going to block it until you saw what the defense was goin' to do. If they'd run a stunt, it was totally different, and you had to read that and know where the hole was going to be. I don't know how I did it, but all of a sudden, through repetition and practice, you start hittin' the seam every time, every time.

A lot of schools recruited me to play defense. I played some defense on the freshman team but, mostly, I played running back, and we went against the number one defense every day, every day, every day. A couple of times, we beat them, and Woody would flip out.

I WANTED TO GO HOME. I said, 'This's nuts. It's just wild.' They beat you up every day. Here I am 200 pounds, and they're beatin' the hell out of me. They just keep stickin' you in. Woody's kickin' you in the ass, yellin' at you. Woody would cuss at you like a storm trooper, man. I mean, this guy had a vocabulary. He'd come up, smack you in the head, smack you in the belly. He'd smack you in the stomach, and if you'd tense up so he wouldn't hurt you, he'd like wait 20 minutes, sneak up behind you, get you: 'I got you now.'

I'm goin', 'This guy's nuts, man. He's flipped.'

But you learned to live with it. The only salvation was, he did it to everybody. He treated everybody the same. Now, when I look back on it, I can hardly remember any of the games. I remember a lot more of the practices, because they were mostly harder than the games. The game, when you look back on it, wasn't even secondary. It might've even been third or fourth, and I think Woody knew that, too. But his feeling was, 'We're gonna play the game, we're gonna play it right, we're gonna play as hard as we can.' 'Course, anything you do, I think you should do that. But he knew the real thing.

He told us, 'You guys, this's one of the greatest times in your lives. Not because of the games, but look around you. You're gonna be friends forever. You're gonna go through a lot of things that a lot of people are never, ever gonna get to experience.' And I really do think that really, deep down, that was his ultimate goal.

When I was a freshman, the team went 6-4. Northwestern beat 'em up here, and Woody just went crazy. They started the 'Goodbye, Woody' stuff, and he's too old and all that. Of course, he knew the team that he had comin' up—'Just wait,' you know, 'until I unleash these guys on you.' From my freshman class, I think 17 were drafted. We had a franchise. Our sophomore year, we started to come along. We were number one in the country, but we were by no means the best team. Michigan State beat us, then we went to the Rose Bowl and USC beat us bad. Of course, they had Lynn Swann and that crew—Anthony Davis, Sam Cunningham. They were loaded. I remember standing in the huddle, and Steve Myers says, 'Man, these guys are really good.'

We were battle-hardened then. The next year, physically, no one was our match. Before the first game my sophomore year, Woody came to my room and said, 'Well, we're gonna start you tomorrow.'

I remember callin' home. It was like winnin' the lottery, to be the starting fullback at Ohio State, after Jim Otis, John Brockington. All through the years, Woody Hayes's fullbacks were his weapons of destruction, and all of a sudden, it's you: 'This's not happenin'.

MY FIRST GAME WAS AGAINST IOWA. The first time I carried the ball, I fumbled: 'Ahh, man, what did I do? This is it. I ruined it all.' I came off the field, and, I mean, Woody was glaring at me, oh man, like I just killed his dog. Luckily, the next play, they fumbled, and we recovered. We just went back the other way. What a stroke; I may've never played again. I don't know if he had enough faith in me, or it's just the way circumstances happened. I just ran back out on the field, and I carried the ball three or four more times. I never fumbled the ball after that, never. Three hundred and whatever some carries, and I never fumbled again.

I scored 20 touchdowns that year, and Archie and I gained the same amount of yardage. We both had 700 and some yards that year, which is not bad out of one backfield, especially for a freshman and a sophomore. We ran it inside the tackles. We were pretty conservative with the fullback. I would've liked to've done some more things I think would've put some more pressure on the defense. Whenever he'd get mad or get mad at the crowd or someone would throw a snowball and hit him or something, he'd come in at halftime and say, 'All right, we're just gonna grind meat. We'll show 'em who's boss.' I'd get ready: 'We're gonna grind meat.'

I carried 44 times in one game, against Northwestern. Real muddy day, terrible day. Woody said, 'Forget it. Give the big dumbass the ball.

Tighten up your chinstrap. We're gonna grind meat.'

I carried 44 times, not countin' the ones called back by penalties. I scored four touchdowns; I scored every touchdown. We always scored when we were down in close. You know Woody: 'Get rid of the field goal kicker, and we'll score a touchdown every time.' Don't even think about the field goal; we're gonna score the touchdown. I can't remember ever gettin' stopped inside the 20 yard line. The only time I can remember is at Michigan State when they didn't count the touchdown and we lost the national championship. That was my senior year, best game I ever had. They beat us by three, and we were so much better than anybody in the country. Then we lost to USC in the Rose Bowl by one point.

I was completely worn out by the time we went to the Rose Bowl. We were spent. You've got another six weeks' practice with Woody—scrimmage, scrimmage, scrimmage, half-line, inside-outside. 'Christ, we've been at this for six months, Coach, not countin' spring ball.' And we had to be out there for like three weeks while these USC guys are sittin' at home. We're livin' in a hotel, just goin' nuts every night, goin' out and havin' a blast.

Everything we did was a joke to us. Most of the players were never as serious as Woody was. Woody made this comment to John Bizick, 'cause they were really very close. Wherever you go, the equipment man knows everything; they're always the first to know, and I think they know more about what's going on than anybody else. And he used to tell Bozik, 'You know, John, I just can't control these guys, but God can they play football.' I think Woody kind of took us over the edge a little bit. I mean, Woody made us so close that we became somewhat defiant.

IN 1972, WE WENT ON STRIKE. We had a little altercation with Woody; he got mad at one of the guys on the team, put a padlock on his locker and said he's off the team, forget it. This's when I was a sophomore, about the third game of the season. Woody said, 'You're off the team. Get the hell out of here.'

I don't know what he was trying to achieve, he was just so ticked off. We got in a room, and our captains—Rick Galbos was one; George Hasenohrl was the other, and George was the meanest, toughest guy, another guy who was not the greatest athlete but a guy who made up for it out of brute strength, determination, and self-motivation; he was just a bull, could bend your facemask with his hands, about 260, about 6 feet tall, from the old school. He said, 'You know, guys, I don't like what's going on, but we're gonna vote on it. Here's your choices: Cave in to the old man, or we can tell him how we feel. We either go to practice and cave in to him, or we just go on strike and see what happens. It ain't gonna be pretty, but I'm telling you what, when we vote, it's one thing, but whatever we decide to do as a team, we're all gonna do. If we vote not to go to practice, and Woody comes in and starts to put pressure on us, ain't nobody going out the door. We're in it together.'

So they went and talked to Woody in Woody's office, and, oh man, the stuff was smashing into the walls. Woody was gonna hit George, and George said, 'Uh-uh, Coach, no. Don't start that.' Then it was every foul word you could think of going back and forth.

Woody said, 'This is an insurrection.'

So, finally, Woody came in, said he wanted to talk, sat down and said, 'Guys, I have to admit, you stuck together. Let's go practice.'

The guy wound up back on the team.

After that, we started to get more out of control all the time, 'cause we did everything together. We'd go down to High Street to have a few beers, and there'd be 20 starters out of 22 all doing the same stupid thing. What's he gonna do, kick us all out? That was just what it kind of evolved to. It brought us so close together we actually revolted a little bit.

But we played hard and we practiced hard, practiced harder than we played. He killed you in practice, in every way. We hardly ever had to run windsprints after practice—the backs didn't—because we ran the whole time, back and forth, back and forth. You ran the plays, you ran back to the huddle. Everything was 25 seconds, 25 seconds. Everything was that way. We had officials at every practice: 'Too much time for that play.' They'd throw the flag. He'd argue with the officials in practice, especially when we'd scrimmage. Even in scrimmage, you played to win. He'd tell the other coaches: 'You got this team, I got this team.'

ONE TIME, HE FIRED AN OFFICIAL during a scrimmage: 'You're fired. Get out. That was interference.' He hires the guy to officiate practice, then fires him because he didn't call it right.

'Get out.'

The guy's like 'What? I've been doing this for 22....'

'Get out!'

When we played, we more or less won by forfeit: 'Let's go in for a couple quarters, beat the hell out of 'em and let the other guys play. Let's get out of here. Let's go to work and get it over with.' By the third quarter, they're done. They're bleeding. First quarter, it'd be 7–0; second quarter, maybe 14–7; third quarter, 21–7. By the end of the game, it's 56–7. Woody called it 'the accumulative effect.' You just keep taking your toll. When you're in better shape and had as much talent as we did, you're always one step above 'em. You're getting four and five yards, then it's 10, then it's 15, then it's totally out of control. They're helpless. As many weapons as we had, the whole idea was to pound them with the fullback, then run the option to stretch 'em out, then pound 'em, come back with the counter play, then a couple short passes, then it's like, you know, they don't know what to do. Woody used the military term: 'Attack on a broad front.' You're hitting with everything. They didn't know what to do. Finally, it's just gaping holes, and 'C'mon, Coach, let the other guys play. C'mon, man, they're done. Forget it.' We'd go hang out on the sidelines and B.S.

MY SOPHOMORE YEAR, I think we ended up about fifth in the country. We lost a game to Michigan State and then got beat in the Rose Bowl. We should've never lost to Michigan State that year. Duffy announced his retirement that day, before the game, and they came out—they were nuts. It was getting toward the end of the season, and we came out and had a bad day, and they just had one hell of a day. A lot of times on game days, Woody would get a little too uptight, too conservative, I thought. If he'd've let George Chaump call a few more plays, nobody would've come close to even being on the same field as us. He had a good football mind. I think as far as managing the game, and knowing how offenses work, and how you react to the defense and what you do when they react to you, the only guy I've been associated with who might have an edge on George Chaump was Bill Walsh, when I was at Cincinnati.

I came back my junior year expecting big things. By that time, I'm weighing 235, 238, was in great shape. I was really just starting to mature. I was just growing up. I had worked out all summer, worked for a paving contractor. I came back early, and we didn't run a mile anymore. We ran a series of windsprints with 25 seconds in between. It was the greatest thing. It made a lot more sense than running the mile. I was running 4.59 40s. I thought I was invincible. My attitude was that I didn't think there was anybody in the country who could take me one-on-one.

The first game of the season, we played—who the hell did we play? I can't remember. Anyhow, we just physically abused 'em. Archie was magnificent that day. There were gaping holes, and I could get up a head of steam. It was just nothing but off-tackle for me. We never broke stride. Get the ball under your arm, get up a head of steam and drop your shoulder and just hammer 'em. I could whip myself into a pretty good frenzy. Make 'em pay, just hammer 'em, just hammer 'em.

Woody said, 'The running back's not gonna block anybody, the quarterback's not gonna block anybody, so it's 11 against nine. For somebody to go all the way, two guys have gotta make two blocks or you have to break two tackles yourself.' Guys would be coming from nowhere. You know how when you play defense, your team swarms to the ball? Our offense swarmed to the ball. It was wild. And then I learned that if you'd give 'em a little time to make blocks, things went a hell of a lot better. Instead of going like a madman, just use your head, man, just be patient, be patient—and at the time, one second seems like an eternity—'Be patient, be patient, the big boy's coming.' That's hard to learn. During repetitions, you just have to keep harping at it, as far as teaching is concerned. And that's what separates a lot of great ones. I played with Walter Payton for a little bit before I got hurt. Here was a guy who had patience. He would just stay back and stay back, but of course, when he's going 85 percent of his full speed, he's as fast as everybody else. And then, boy, he could just turn it on, and he's gone. He was a big guy, 220, 225, and with that kind of speed, he could inflict a lot of damage.

I think the first game of my junior year, I had just shy of 100 yards, scored three touchdowns, only played like two quarters. I forget who we were playing. We just blew 'em out. The next game was Texas Christian, and we were, again, just out of control. Every time we touched the ball, it was like 15, 20 yards, then Archie'd go 40, then it was 15, 20 yards. We were just beating these guys up. It was just a few plays after the second quarter, I got hurt. Like I say, at the time, I thought nobody could hurt me. We were down near the goal line, and I carried off left tackle or left guard, and, I don't know, I think I got the first down, and I'm trying to go eight or nine more yards for the touchdown, just trying to get that extra yardage, and I'm spinning out of one guy, and he had one leg, and I had planted my other foot, and a guy came in from the side, and my knee was—you know—just gone.

I didn't believe it: 'Ahh, tape me up. I'll be all right. I ain't hurt.

You don't know what you're doing.'

'You're bad. Look here. Look at your leg. You're bad.'

'Tape it up. I don't care. Get away from me. You've lost your mind. There's nothing wrong with my knee.'

I had total reconstruction. Lost a ligament, I mean totally, just snapped off. They operated the next day. I still couldn't believe it: 'This ain't happening.' Just like I didn't believe the other thing wasn't happening. Right when I'm believin' that it is, this happens, and I ain't believin' this, either. That's part of the deal, you know. After they did the reconstruction, I said, 'I'm gonna play in the Rose Bowl.'

They said, 'That's 12 weeks away. Nobody can do that.'

AND I DID. At that time, rehabilitation was really in its infancy, too. The weight program really hadn't started, and I just read books on rehab. Even in the cast, I did all kind of flexing exercises. It just worked, and Dr. Murphy says, 'Amazing recovery. I can't believe it. Nobody has ever done it, before or after.'

I never played in the game. They thought it might hurt my redshirt, but I could've. I practiced with the team. Could've played. Pete could've got hurt, and I'd've played. Went out there, went through all the two-a-day practices on the West Coast. I was back. I mean, I was a little shaky, but I still felt that me at 85 percent was better than anybody else at 100. Sure, I lost a step, but I figured I was still the best man for the job.

I came back for my senior year, and I don't know what happened at that point. Woody'd play one guy one week, or he'd play a quarter and I'd play a quarter. I think I could've came to grips with it if he would've just said, 'I'm gonna play Pete.'

I'd've said, 'Let me play linebacker, coach. Let me play end.'

I don't know what his rationale was. My senior year, we played up at Michigan State. We got beat. Woody said, 'Think you can get in there?'

He puts me in there, and I had the best game I ever had—three quarters, just shy of 100 yards, scored a touchdown, at the end of the game, scored a touchdown they didn't count, and we got beat. I felt if I'd've carried the ball 35 times in that game, we would've beat 'em. But that's only a personal opinion.

Of course, I was upset by switching off with Pete. I would really motivate myself. When I knew I was gonna play, man, I'd start the process. Come game time, 'We're going to work. We gotta job. Go do it.'

Come right up to it and, 'You're not playing today.'

'What?'

It's hard to come to grips with. You know, for me, it's not something you turn off and on like a light switch. As far as me and Pete, we got along great. Pete's a likable guy. He's jovial. I don't know why Woody chose to do it that way, and nobody else could figure it out. I know Pete didn't like it for the same reasons. We talked about it. After that Michigan State game, Woody had me on his show, and he said, 'I think this's the best game you've ever played. Even though we lost, I want you to know that I really appreciate how well you played and how much you put into it.' He says, 'We switched you around a lot all year long, and I want you to know right now, you're the fullback from now on.'

I felt great. I felt that I finally recovered from my injury. We played Iowa, and I think I was Back of the Week in the Big Ten that week—I really can't remember—and then the next week, minutes before the Michigan game, he told me I wasn't playing. After he told me all that and I practiced with the first team all week long. One game, Woody said, 'I don't know who I'm gonna play today. Pick a number between 1 and 10.'

Don't beat me up like this. Either I'm in or I'm out. I wanna play, but at least let me know. Don't put me through this mental anguish. I had another year of eligibility left, and I said, 'Ahh, I'm not coming back. I'll just go in the NFL and play.' I just couldn't take the up-and-downs, you know, the rollercoaster ride. If he'd've just said, 'I'm not playing you, I'm playing the other guy, play defense'; or, 'You're gonna be second team fullback'; or something like that, I think that would've been easier to swallow. I just couldn't take that emotional up and down all the time.

AFTER MY SENIOR YEAR, I played in the College All-Star Game. We played the Pittsburgh Steelers. John McKay was the coach, and some of the Southern Cal assistant coaches wondered why Woody didn't play Pete and me both with Archie.

They said, 'We were scared to death that you guys were gonna whip something like that on us.' Power-I, T-formation, whatever. He said, 'He coulda switched you two guys back and forth from fullback to blocking halfback.'

Hell, that would've been fun. The two best fullbacks in the country in the same backfield.

I went to Minnesota, the first player in the fourth round. Bud Grant was the coach, and that was right in the middle of their glory years. It was right at the end of the old-time NFL—you know, Fran Tarkenton, Dave Osborn, Chuck Foreman, Carl Eller, Alan Page, Ron Yary was playing tackle, Ed White, Mick Tinglehoff. They were wild; they were fun. They were old-time NFL tough guys. At that time, the roster limit was 41. That's pretty slim. They had a lot of injuries. They'd lost, I think, three wide receivers, and they wanted to keep 'em on injured reserve. Then, Ray Gilliam came back from the World Football League when it folded, and the day before the first game, they cut me to make room for him. It was just a numbers game, and, man, I was crushed.

Cincinnati picked me up, and I played a year down there. It was totally different from Minnesota. We had a good team there, too. We made the playoffs. I hurt my knee, and, man, it felt really bad. And I was really coming on. I was getting to the point where I was gonna play. I hurt my knee, and it felt terrible, worse than I hurt it before.

The doctors down there were saying, 'Oh, you tore some scar tissue. You're all right.' They were givin' me shots. It'd feel good for a while. I'd play some special teams, then I'd make a cut on it, and the pain was unbearable: 'Aww, same thing. We'll give you a coupla shots. You tore some scar tissue from the old surgery.'

January, we were playing basketball, barnstorming around. Man, my knee popped out again. I said, 'Oh, this's terrible. I gotta do something about it.' You know, they want you to go to team doctors all the time. I went to the doctor from OSU who operated on me before. I was in this man's office five minutes: 'Get up on the table. Let me look at your leg.' Do this, do that, gave me all the tests. He goes, 'Oh, man, you tore a cartilage. Doing anything Friday? Meet me at the hospital Friday. I'll take it out for you.'

These guys'd been shooting me up. For what, man? Wanting to keep me going so they could trade me? They traded me to Chicago. They never even told me. I saw it on TV. I went up there, and I really hated Chicago. No personality, no anything. They were so impersonal.

I said, 'Man, I gotta get outta here.'

I got hammered up there, man. Doug Plank, a guy I played with at Ohio State. We're in a no-contact drill, got shoulderpads, shorts on, helmets. I just happened to be cutting, you know, and he comes out of the blue like a madman, hits me. I went down.

I said, 'Jeezus Christ, what was that?'

I go in, and they're like, 'Your knee's really not so bad.'

Man, they run the needle in me, drain it. It's blood, fluid, all this stuff. It's the same thing again: 'We're going to inject you with some enzymes here. We don't think there's anything really the matter with you. You have all your range of motion.'

Well, man, they're draining my knee every day. I went through like 10 two-a-days, and I finally got to the point where I couldn't do the drills and stuff. And they're going, you know, 'You gotta play with pain.'

So, finally, it's, 'Bring your playbook.'

I DRIVE HOME. Got a message when I get home. Seattle Seahawks, Jack Paterra, from up at Minnesota, was the coach. Great guy. Oh, I'd love to play for Jack, man. I fly out there, doctor gives me the physical, gets to my knee, and he's just, 'Jesus Christ, how'd you get in here? Did you walk in here?'

I'm like, 'Sure, man. What's the matter?'

He says, 'How can you take the pain?'

I say, 'It hurts quite a bit, but I just tore some scar tissue.'

He goes, 'Oh, man, no. You've lost two, maybe three ligaments. I can't pass you for a physical, obviously, but, more importantly, you've got to get your knee fixed so you can go through life. It's really bad. I'm sorry to have to tell you this.'

So, I fly home. I get home, got a message. It's the New York Jets. I fly out there the next day. I'm like, 'What the hell's going on?'

I talked to my dad.

He says, 'Well, at least you'll get another honest opinion.'

When Joe Namath's doctor won't pass you for a bad knee, you know how bad you have to be?

He says, 'Oh, you're wrecked. Sorry, man, you've got to get this fixed.'

So, I went back to Chicago. I've got seven medical reports, and I had to fight tooth and nail to get any money out of 'em. The players association went to bat for me, and we finally got our money. It took two or three years. Money for my surgery and all that. And that was it. Flunked the old physical the next year, and it was coming to reality again.

I liked the NFL, but I found it was pretty impersonal. I was probably out of it five years before I figured out what their angles were. It was all money, and that was really hard after coming out of Ohio State. It's a whole new world, all of a sudden. I'm used to doing stuff for people because I like 'em or because I want to.

WHAT YOU GET OUT OF IT GOES BACK FAR, all the way to how you were raised. You see these people—and, boy, I really feel strong about this—who talk about these sports heroes and people you look up to. People say, 'Oh, you're a bad role model for my kids.'

You know, 'Why don't you be a role model for your own kids?'

You should try and do the right thing, but you can't be a role model to every kid. You want to talk about heroes, there's a couple old guys around here, guys who went away in 1941, didn't come home until 1946. Four or five Christmases away from home. Come home, work like dogs all their life. Never hear 'em complain. You know, those are heroes. Some guy, because he scores a few touchdowns or hits a few home runs, I'm supposed to look up to him? As far as being a role model for what's right and what's wrong, it has no correlation at all.

It's like my wife's grandfather. I never met the man. He's long been gone. But Karen's grandmother told me that in World War I, he told her this story, something that touched him more than anything. Christmas Eve, 1917, they were shootin' at each other back and forth in the trenches, midnight, Christmas Eve. They stopped shootin' when they heard the Germans singing 'Silent Night' in German, and they started singing 'Silent Night' in English. When it was over, they just loaded up and started shootin' at each other again. These guys are real heroes, did a terrible job that had to be done, for very little pay.

Those are the kinda things I think about. I don't watch football now. I don't think I've ever watched a Super Bowl all the way through. I like to go and watch a high school game. My son Clayton has athletic ability, but doesn't have much love for it yet. I think he'll play sports some day, and I think when he gets ready, he'll do it right. But as far as making him good—I make 'em go to school and brush their teeth, you know, use their manners, respect their mom and dad and their grandparents. Other'n that, I'm not gonna badger 'em to play sports and all that. They should play because they want to.

It was really hard the first few years away from football. You feel like you're an outcast. You almost become a recluse. You don't want people to know who you are. You feel like you're some kind of failure, but 99 percent of the people never get a chance to do what I did. You all have a common goal. When that's gone, it's kind of hard to adjust to everyday life, where you're out chiselin' against everybody else.

AFTER WOODY GOT SICK, I spent some time with him. I'd stop by and see him at his house, or he'd come by and see me. He liked comin' out in the country, particularly after he had his stroke. One time, he came down to the farm market. We had just gotten in from the field, and I saw Mrs. Hayes.

She said, 'Woody's out back.'

I went out, and I was talking to him. He was real feeble right after that stroke. He was walking with a cane. Of course, what do you say to the guy, right?

'Hey, Coach, how you doing?'

'Oh, okay, I'm getting around.'

Mrs. Hayes says, 'Why don't you help him a little bit so he doesn't fall down.'

I'm thinkin', 'This's Woody. Woody doesn't fall down.'

I don't know why I said it, but I said, 'Boy, Coach, you'd have a hard time kicking me in the ass now.'

He was on a cane. He laughed.

He said, 'Yeah, I'd just have to make an assistant do it.'

I could just see him: 'Hey, go kick him in the ass. I can't do it. *You* go kick him.'

I don't know why I said that, but I think he liked it.

He came down quite a bit. They would come down and get sweet corn and melons and stuff. Woody liked melons real well. They'd get 'em and give it all away. They'd get a whole pickup truck full and give 'em all to people who had done something for them. That was their favor back.

That went on for a few years. We had some good talks. He was different about some things, but he was the same about others. I don't think he liked the directions the program was goin', especially when they started buildin' all those mausoleums, that new training facility and all that. I don't think he liked that. You know, Woody believed 'first to feast, last to fight.' If you ever go up there, have 'em show you his old office. About as big as my bathroom. He had a desk; he had a projector on the desk. He had a little screen there at the end. He had a chair.

Nothing else but books and papers just stacked to the ceiling. I see the coach's office now, and it looks like you're in General Motors.

Woody, man, he'd go in there, watch films, stay in there all night, live in there. Come in the next morning, he'd be asleep, projector just goin' around and around and around.

'Hey, Coach.'

'Oh, I was just resting my eyes. You know, I think I noticed something here.'

He always said, 'I might get out-coached, but they'll never out-work me, uh-huh. That's one thing you have control over, uh-huh.'

He'd chuckle. He'd say, 'I know they're asleep right now in their beds, but I'm awake, and I'm working, uh-huh, and I found something... uh-huh.'

It was always that 'uh-huh' thing, like he was reassuring himself.

'We're gonna exploit this. They think they're safe in their beds, but they don't know we're working.'

The facilities that they have, with all the carpet and the music. We had to fight like hell to get carpet in the locker room. You ever see the old locker room up there? It's just a square room, lockers all the way around it, a bench in front of the lockers in a square. Woody designed it, and that's just the way it was, and they had a vinyl floor in there.

We said, 'Coach, everybody's gettin' their locker rooms carpeted.'

Woody says, 'Everybody but us. Carpet the visitors' locker room. We'll make 'em soft.'

I have some small regrets. You make some decisions, you look back, they were wrong, but at the time, they were right. You can't dwell on that. If you do, you'll go crazy. Like not playing my fifth year. I kinda wish I would've done that, but the way it turned out, my knee—it seemed like it was ready to go. I probably would've gotten hurt my senior year again and probably wouldn't've ever got a taste of the NFL, which I thought was a great experience in my life. I wish I hadn't gotten hurt. I really would like to've seen how good I could've been.

I mean, I'll always wonder how good I could've been. But you never know, man, maybe if you would've turned left instead of right you wouldn't've got killed the next minute in a car wreck. Who knows? ”

Family Man

KURT SCHUMACHER remembers weekend trips to visit his mother in Turney Road Hospital, an old mental institution of big, dilapidated sandstone buildings. At first, the boy went inside with his father. After his mother's condition worsened, he waited outside.

His sisters and brother, all much older, had moved away. Schumacher was frequently left alone because his harried father, a millwright, worked overtime, as well as cooked, cleaned, washed clothes, and drove to Turney Road on Mondays, Wednesdays, Fridays, and twice on Saturdays and Sundays. Schumacher signed his own report cards, receiving mostly passing grades in exchange for behaving himself.

On New Year's Eve, just after his 14th birthday, Schumacher and his father were on their way home from

Turney Road. They stopped for gas. Schumacher's dad walked into the station, paid, and talked to friends about the car he'd just bought. He came back out, started the car, and died of a massive heart attack, the boy sitting next to him.

Three months later, Schumacher's mother, who, he says, had completely lost touch with reality, also died. (Years afterward, Schumacher would realize that though she had yet to turn 60, his mother had developed Alzheimer's. Her memory lapses and hallucinations were diagnosed as madness. The cause of her death was listed as arteriosclerosis.)

Taken in by his sister and her husband, the boy wondered why he had been singled out for such misfortune. He felt guilty over having failed to show interest when his father, a skilled mechanic, wanted him to hold a safety light or hand him tools. Life seems to have given him every opportunity to fail, yet Schumacher now says, "If my dad hadn't died, I don't know what course my life might've taken, because there was a lot of unsupervised time, there wasn't much emphasis on education. Anybody can choose to make bad decisions, and, fortunately, I didn't. But I can't take full credit for that. There were a lot of people around me, encouraging me to make the right choices."

Living with his sister and brother-in-law in Lorain, Ohio, Schumacher was required to do homework and encouraged to participate in athletics. The football coach at Southview High School lived next door, and he took a particular interest in the big teenager. Schumacher was a 6' 3", 235-pound junior at Southview when recruiters came to see a teammate, Ray Felton, one of the state's outstanding offensive linemen. Coaches noticed Schumacher in game films. The next year, he visited Michigan, Purdue, Indiana, Kentucky, and Ohio State, but Schumacher couldn't decide where he wanted to go.

He had been dating a girl who was a student at OSU, and she called one day to ask Schumacher if he would ride back to campus with her and her mother. Without telling anyone where he was going, Schumacher left as soon as wrestling practice was over. Carrying the girl's suitcase, he walked into her dormitory. Woody Hayes was sitting in the lobby. ("Now that he's dead, I'll never know the answer to the question, but I truly don't know how he knew I was going to be there.")

Hayes asked if he were ready to commit to Ohio State. Schumacher put him off, saying he had to talk with his sister and brother-in-law. Hayes hurried to a nearby telephone booth, dialed a number, handed Schumacher the phone, and said, "Here you go."

Cornered, Schumacher became a Buckeye. Hayes took him, his girlfriend, and her mother to dinner at the Faculty Club. Before they were seated, a newspaper photographer had snapped a picture of the coach shaking hands with his newest recruit. Hayes had closed the sale.

Two years later, Schumacher believed he'd made a mistake. At offensive tackle, he was one of a crowd of fine players, including future Outland Trophy winner John Hicks, and he spent most of 1972 on the bench. He asked to move to defense and considered transferring until, as a conciliatory gesture, his coach, Ralph Staub, sent him into the Rose Bowl for a handful of snaps.

A football adage declares the lord to be on the side of the team with the best tackles. In 1973, with Hicks, Doug France, Scott Dannelley and Schumacher, who had grown to 6' 4", 248 pounds, Staub would claim to have four tackles capable of starting at any school. OSU ran for 3,588 yards, while gaining fewer than 450 by the pass. They set a school record with 84 runs against Illinois. When USC packed nine men on the line in the Rose Bowl, the Bucks rushed for 323 yards and six touchdowns and won by 21 points.

As a junior, Schumacher made All-Big Ten but was overshadowed by Hicks, who finished second in the Heisman balloting. The following season, Hayes was calling Schumacher "a great tackle," and the consensus of the staff was that Schumacher had become Hicks's equal.

He was named the team's outstanding offensive linemen when the Bucks rushed for a school-record 517 yards against Illinois—Hayes's 200th win and Archie Griffin's NCAA-record 18th straight 100-yard game. Schumacher, who started 20 of Griffin's 31 100-yard games, says the streak meant far more to the line than to Griffin: "This may sound corny, but when the stat sheets came out, you would get run over by the offensive linemen because we wanted to see how many yards Archie got. Archie could've cared less."

Schumacher and Doug France joined Daryl Sanders and Bob Vogel and Dave Foley and Rufus Mayes as the third pair of Hayes's tackles to be first-round draft picks in the same season. Selected by New Orleans, the league's worst franchise over the previous decade, he was disappointed by pro football, as were so many Bucks.

Schumacher was astounded to learn that the Saints had no system for calling audibles, whereas at Ohio State, any play could be called from the line. New Orleans changed coaches three times in three seasons. Schumacher played his final year at Tampa Bay, where he reinjured the knee that caused him to miss the 16–

13 upset loss to Michigan State in 1974, the memory of which still gnaws at him. Unable even to turn upfield and throw a block on a dummy, he left football.

The phone rang often in the well-appointed study as recruiters called to speak with Schumacher's son, Tim, a tackle at Avon Lake (Ohio) High. ("Tim was kidding earlier in the year that, because of some of the press coverage he was getting, he was going to officially change his middle name to 'Son of Kurt.'") The copy of Hayes's *Hotline to Victory* that the coach signed for him when Schumacher was in high school sat on a book shelf. Above a polished desk hung a photograph of Schumacher at a Rose Bowl dinner, adorned with muttonchops and a thick Fu Manchu; a painting (ubiquitous among the Bucks) of Hayes surrounded by his All-Americans, and an action shot of Schumacher driving off the line against Michigan as Cornelius Greene pitches on an option. Schumacher's wife, Jackie, was working second-shift as a delivery room nurse. Before sitting down to talk, he fixed lasagna for Tim and Betsy, his daughter, and made sure that Tim's calculus study group was underway.

A meticulous man who says that he viewed himself as a "solid and dependable" football player, he planned his future 20 years ago. He and Jackie married when he was a junior, and he said before he graduated that becoming an All American would be nice because he could tell his kids about it and that he hoped he could make enough money in the NFL to send his children to college.

Schumacher is polite, articulate and balding; he looks like a larger, younger, healthier Peter Boyle. He was working for a company that specializes in motivational programs. Schumacher's soft voice sounds incongruous when he speaks gleefully of blindsiding free safeties as Brian Baschnagel cut back against the pursuit. As he talks about his childhood, he sometimes seems unnaturally detached, but Schumacher's dispassion is borne out of the pragmatism that was forced on him at such an early age. (Woody Hayes said that Schumacher had been an adult since he was 15, but the boy had actually been forced to grow up much earlier.)

Schumacher says, "While I would dearly have loved my mom and dad to have met my wife and seen their grandchildren grow up and those kinds of things—I mean, neither one of them ever saw me play football or basketball or anything else—in a lot of respects, my life is better now. Their deaths changed things, long term, in my life, but there's still obviously a lot of things I wish they were around to see. Things have turned out pretty well for their youngest kid."

Kurt SCHUMACHER

"I WAS FORTUNATE in that I was really never seriously hurt playing football. You blow a knee out early in your career, and you think, 'Oh, maybe I should be carrying the tuba.' I had bumps and bruises and sprains and twists, but nothing serious. I played basketball my freshman year in high school, and then it was kind of a mutual decision between the basketball coach and myself that my fortunes were not on the basketball floor. I wrestled varsity my junior and senior years, and in that period of time, I lost five matches. I was third in the state in the discus. So I had success in different areas. We had some real physical football teams at Lorain. We had a talented but very small tailback, fellow by the name of Ron Fields, and we had enough big people that they didn't need a 6' 3", 235-pounder at tackle, so they moved me to fullback. I was primarily a blocker. We were going to feature the tailback, but the tailback got banged up and was hobbled that whole year. I played fullback, and on defense we played a Notre Dame 4-4, and I played the strongside inside linebacker. Notre Dame, Kentucky, and Indiana recruited me as a linebacker. Ohio State and Michigan recruited me as an offensive lineman.

We were 7-3 my junior year and, I think, 6-4 my senior year. We had some bizarre finishes. Sandusky beat us two years in a row when we had the ball, fumbled, ball bounces up, same kid scoops it up and goes the opposite way for a touchdown. We went down to Findlay. I think we had them down 21–0 at halftime and lost 26–27. We played Parma-Valley Forge, and I thought I was going to have a heart attack. They fired a cannon when they scored, and I wasn't quite prepared for that. That thing went off, and I was like, 'Oh, whoa, not only did they score, but now they're going to shoot us.' We beat everybody up; we just didn't outscore them.

I didn't have any problem with playing offensive line after having been a fullback in high school. I was a fullback in name only. This will give you an idea of what kind of fullback I was: My senior year, Southview Lorain had a fellow by the name of Chawanski, who was their safety. Our tailback, the wingback, and me, the fullback, were sitting together, and our coach walked up, pointed to the other two guys and said: 'If you guys break in the open, find the end zone.' He pointed at me and said, 'If you break in the open, find Chawanski.' That was the name of the game. I never had any misconceptions about being a fullback.

I was recruited as a linebacker, and there were times, particularly during my sophomore year at Ohio State, when I thought, 'Gee, maybe I should be a linebacker.' I may be biased, but I've always been a big believer that what are normally referred to as skill positions are really not. They're talent positions. Skill positions are the places where you have to learn your task, and there's no more skilled position than offensive line, because of the intricacies that are involved in it. Nobody taught Archie Griffin to run like Archie Griffin ran. With many of the great offensive linemen, it's technique that makes a big difference.

Nobody in my family had ever gone to college. One of the coaches on our staff, Chuck Bryant, played at Ohio State. I remember when the recruiting process was in full swing, I went to Chuck and asked him, 'You played there. Do you think I can play there?' Because I wanted to go somewhere where I had a chance to play.

He said, 'You can play anyplace that you want to.'

I VIVIDLY REMEMBER THE FIRST TIME I saw Coach Hayes. He was at the high school. I was taking trig and analytical geometry and a note came up that they wanted me to come down to the office. That was a little bit unusual because I was a pretty good kid and didn't get called to the office very often. I came down the steps—a big wide set of steps right in the center of the school—and made a lefthand turn, and Woody was standing out in the hallway. I said, '*Whoa.*'

I was pretty much in awe that he would come up to see me. I really didn't have any preconceived notions of him. He was a nationally known figure. He was coaching a team that was one of the best in the country. In Ohio, I dare say, not even the governor was better known than Woody Hayes. It was just a real honor to have him come and pay special attention to you, a high school kid.

I didn't see much of Woody my first year. My freshman year was the last year that freshmen were not eligible. Being an offensive player, we really got to know the defensive coaches quite well. We referred to it as the 'Card Offense.' Day in and day out, the freshman offensive team would be down with the Bucks and the Bombers, the first- and second-team defensive units, and the coach would hold an 8 1/2 by 11 card up, and on that card would be drawn the defense they were supposed to be in and the play that we were supposed to run against them. We'd break the huddle and run it.

If anything made me a better football player, it was a guy by the name of George Hasenohrl, the defensive tackle that I played over day in and day out. Nobody in my four years at Ohio State or my five years in the NFL ever hit like George Hasenrohrl. He was the prototype defensive tackle. He was 6' 1", 270, and hit like a ton of bricks. My sophomore year, we played N.C. State, and they had an offensive guard they were touting as an All-American. They were dangling red meat in front of George to get him ready for that game. I was running second team, and during pregame, the second-team offensive unit would fire out into the first-team defensive unit to get loosened up. Dick Mack was the guard who played next to me. We broke the huddle and fired off, and I came back to the huddle. Dick said, 'Are you okay?'

I said, 'Yeah, why?'

He said, 'Because the whole side of your face is red.'

Well, George beat on this kid so badly—not dirty football, just hard, physical football—that the kid didn't finish the game. That was the last you heard of him in terms of any All-American status, or anything else. George just beat him to a pulp.

Going against him in practice made our three games pretty easy. Practice was a lot tougher than the games. You gained a lot of experience. You felt good when you held your own against those guys. That was the group whose picture was on the cover of *Sports Illustrated* with the big goal line stand that beat Michigan that year. We helped them be as good as they were. We were a damn fine freshman group. If you look at our class when we were seniors, the tight end, both tackles, the right guard, and the center were all in my class. We gave them a good look at what they were going to see that week. When you play against people who are good, you're either going to get beat or you're going to get better. Most people who go to a school like Ohio State are of the ilk that's going to get better.

There was a time at Ohio State that I gave serious thought to transferring because I wasn't playing. Everybody who goes to school at a place like Ohio State was a star in high school, and you get down there, and you realize: 'Hey, there's 120 stars down here.' And now, all of sudden, you're playing and I'm not, and I'm thinking I'm every bit as good, maybe even better. That's a tough act. At the end of my sophomore year, I actually went in and talked to George Hill, who was the defensive coordinator. I said, 'Could you get me moved to defense? And what's involved in a transfer?'

I had lettered as a sophomore, but I hadn't played very much. I wasn't real sure what my future was. George reassured me that I was very well thought of, and the defensive coaches thought I was a player, and I should really just stick it out and good things would happen. That spring, I was the starting left tackle. I sprained my foot during the Parents' Day scrimmage and missed that last week. You don't know: 'Did I lose my spot? How is this whole thing going to shake out?' But I came back to camp that year, was the starting left tackle, and played that spot for the next two years. The only time I sat down was when we were well ahead, or a couple of times when I was hurt.

I would not make the statement that Woody was a second father or a surrogate father to me. He was not. I truly never felt that close to Coach Hayes. A lot of guys probably did. There were some great life lessons that he helped teach. I'd never known anybody who had the work ethic that he did. He had a single-mindedness about him that was truly amazing. He also cared more about the person than he did about the football player.

WOODY PROMISED ME—and I assume he promised everybody the same thing—that he would do everything he could to make sure that I got my degree and that I would get a fair chance to play. He also told me that if someone promises you more than that, they're lying. He said if they promise you you're going to start, the program is probably so bad you don't want to be there anyway. He was true to his word. I had a fair amount of success and I can tell you that what I received was exactly what

I was supposed to have received in terms of my scholarship—room, board, books, tuition, tutors if you needed them. There was never anything else. That's how it was supposed to be, and that's how it was.

Woody would tell us at the beginning of camp, 'If you've got a problem, air it here, but leave it here.' The balancing act of being able to take 120 kids who were all great high school football players and bring them together on a team that only starts 22 says something about the organization, not just Woody but the other coaches as well. It was a good environment.

I would never describe anything that Woody did as abusive. At times, he would cause you great embarrassment. I don't think there's anyone who's ever played for him that he didn't get angry with at least once. The tough part was going back to the huddle after Woody kicked you in the ass. As a freshman, you weren't really around him very much. As a sophomore, your first exposure is that spring on the practice field, and it was incredibly intimidating. He'd start to yell and scream. He'd come up and hit a player, but he'd hit him with the flat of his hand on the breastplate of the shoulderpad. He was not intending to hurt you. He just wanted to make real sure that he had your undivided attention. He never, ever did anything that physically hurt anybody, that I saw.

Did he try to intimidate or perhaps anger in an effort to get you to do better? Sure. There's nothing wrong with that. I think the kid glove approach that many college athletes want is a joke. Ralph Staub, our tackle and tight end coach, was very much the antithesis of Woody. Ralph would come up and talk to you. My hearing was fine. He didn't have to yell at me. I was a serious enough athlete that I would listen to him and try to do what he asked me to do. But I can also tell you that some of the best moments I had on the practice field came right after I'd been reamed by Woody and I was mad. It was, 'I'll show this so and so.' And he's standing back there, going, 'Hah, I got him.'

WOODY LOVED GREAT GENERALS and great battles. I think he loved the end of the season, because the weather would turn ugly, and we didn't have an indoor palace to play in. We practiced outside or we went to French Field House, to the artificial track, which nobody liked to do. I probably should know whose quote this was, but just when America was getting into World War II, they were producing war ships and doing the shakedown cruises in the Caribbean, and one of the admirals said, 'By God, if we're going to fight in the North Atlantic, we're going to train in the North Atlantic.' Woody used that one a lot. As the weather turned ugly, he'd say, 'You know, you're right, it might rain and it might snow out there Saturday. Therefore, if we're going to have to play in it, we might as well practice in it.'

I don't know where we were, but we were playing an away game. Coach Hubbard had the unenviable job of selecting the movies that the team would go to see the night before the game. There was a movie starring James Caan, called *The Gambler*. If it weren't for this incident, it's not a particularly memorable movie. In an early scene, James Caan is a professor in a classroom. The camera was positioned in the class, and James Caan was talking about how many courageous people did things out of cowardice as opposed to doing them out of bravery. He was building this point and referring to people like George Washington and Patton, and you hear this, 'Bullshit.' Well, the camera's in the classroom, and it could be somebody in the class. He goes on a little bit further, and you hear a little bit louder: 'Bullshit.' At that point, you realize it's somebody in the audience. It goes on a little bit longer, and Woody stands up and gives out another '*Bullshit!*.'

We're all going, 'Oh, man, Rudy's going to catch it for this one.'

When we got back after the movie, he apologized for subjecting the team to that. In his eyes, it was inappropriate. It was wrong, and he just wanted to make sure that everybody understood what his position was on that. That was Woody.

AFTER THE INCIDENT with the Clemson player, as I heard it, Hugh Hindman asked for Woody's resignation. What I've been told is that Woody's comment was, 'If you want my job, you fire me. I'm not going to quit.' Whether he said that or not I don't know, but it is exactly how I would picture Woody's position. Woody could've just packed his tent and faded off into the sunset, but he wasn't done. He continued to be an influence in a lot of people's lives, right up until the end.

He believed that discipline is the machinery that drives great accomplishments. If I were to be critical of anything during my association with Coach Hayes, it was that he actually allowed discipline to slip a little bit. I think my senior year we could've been a better football team had there been a little more discipline, but it was at a time—we're talking about the mid-'70s—when there was a tremendous transition in everything from hairstyles to peoples' mindset. Woody was reacting to that. He was trying to keep the program somewhat in step with the times, and I'm not so sure that was the thing to do. The other side of that is if you stay mired in the same rigid beliefs, maybe you run people off. I don't know what the right answer is.

Woody used to tell us, 'An honest guy doesn't have a chance with a thief, because the honest guy is expecting the truth, and the liar or the thief is never going to give it to him.' Woody was a very honest man. We were out at the Rose Bowl my senior year. Those of us who were married were allowed to take our wives with us. Bed check was 11:30 or 12 o'clock, and a couple of the guys had made mention of the fact that, 'Geez, you're waking us up when you come around for bedcheck.' Woody said, 'Well, fine. We'll put a blackboard outside my room and you can sign in. If you sign in, we won't have to hit your room for bedcheck.'

Certainly, those of us who had our wives out there were in once we were signed in. But there were any number of guys who took the opportunity to sign in and then leave, or have someone else sign in for them, since they were already gone. Those were some of the little things that began to happen. When Rex Kern was out there as a sophomore, he probably didn't have that option. It wasn't part of the deal.

AS YOU GOT OLDER, some of his actions that as a freshman just scared you to death, became less intimidating, and as a senior, you kind of looked at it and said, 'Glad it wasn't me.' Coaching my youngsters in soccer, I gained some tiny insight into what it must've been like for Woody. We never went into a game unprepared. Nobody ever threw anything at us that we hadn't seen a dozen times before in practice. But, occasionally, you'd blow an assignment or you'd jump offside or you'd hold, and my little insight into that as a soccer coach is that you quickly realize how frustrating it can be. You look at them and say, 'Little Johnny, I told him to stay closer to that sideline, but he didn't, even though he knew he was supposed to.' And if you'd go, 'Johnny, where're you supposed to be?' He'd go, 'Oops,' and run over to the sideline.

Well, here's Woody with these people who are getting to be adults, who are good athletes, and who are still doing stupid things. As a player, you screw up, and you have an opportunity on the next play to make it better. You at least have an opportunity to vent the frustration that is generated when you made an error. The coach doesn't. The coach just sees one thing after another on the sidelines, and at some point, he goes, 'I either have to let off some steam or I'm going to blow an artery.' Woody was not big on blowing arteries, so he was going to let off some steam.

There are some classic Woody Hayes comments. One of the greatest was after he was fired. He was going through an interview, and the interviewer asked him, 'Has your competitiveness caused you problems?' He said, 'That desire to win took an average guy from a little farm and turned him into a pretty damn fine football coach.'

Woody's desire to succeed overrode everything else that he brought to the party. He conveyed that to his teams. If you were not competitive, you wouldn't play, although there were certainly guys that I went to Ohio State with who found their niche, and it was not as a starter. I know how I would've dealt with that, because when I was not a starter, I was one real unhappy kid, to the point of thinking about leaving. He fostered that, and the environment he created was one in which only competitive people rose to the level of a regular player. There were too many good athletes. If you didn't have that desire to succeed and the willingness to do a little bit more, there were too many good players there for you to be a success.

There were only two or three times a year when we were genuinely tested. Most games, we played the first series of the second half and then we'd sit. Some of the records that were established—Archie's career rushing totals and things like that—were done in just parts of games. Tony Dorsett, who came out after Archie and broke some of Archie's records—if Archie had played the minutes that Dorsett played, had the carries that Dorsett had, he would've set records that Dorsett wouldn't've sniffed.

BY AND LARGE, MOST OF THE GAMES were easier than practice. The exceptions would be the Michigan games, and the three consecutive Rose Bowls, which were physical and hard-fought. We went out to Washington my senior year. I don't know if we played Washington or Washington State. I think we touched the football five times, five or six, and whichever it was, we had five touchdowns and were driving for the sixth, or four and were driving for the fifth. Our defense would grade films on Sunday morning. The defensive battle cry was, 'Three and out.' Our battle cry was, 'Three and three and three and three.' Literally, a half of film for us would not go on a roll. We had so many plays the film would just barely fit on the roll. We'd be finishing grading the first half, and the defense would be done. They continually gave us the ball, and we would continually hold it for long periods of time.

My junior year, which is the best team that I played on, had nine first-round draft picks. I wonder how many seconds and thirds there were. My junior year, three of the top five vote-getters for the Heisman were on our football team. You just don't do that. We absolutely never stepped on the football field when we didn't expect to win. It wasn't very often that we had to come from behind, but we just always figured that somehow, some way, things would go right. We had great players to make them go right. Give the ball to Archie 25 times, he's probably going to put it in the end zone two or three. Pete Cusick, who's a very good friend of mine, talked about Corny Greene in spring practice. He said, 'Trying to tackle Corny Greene is like trying to tackle a fart.'

You'd watch Corny run the option, and you'd think what it would be like to play defensive back. You have a guy who's just as quick as can be at quarterback, and if you take the quarterback, who does he pitch it to? Make a choice. You have guys like Henson and Elia and Johnson who're just going to pound on you up the middle. Baschnagel could hurt you. Morris Bradshaw was not good enough to play tailback at Ohio State, but played for the Raiders for six or seven years. Take Steve Luke. Steve Myers was our starting center as a sophomore. Myers took ill out at the Rose Bowl. I mean, seriously ill. At one point, they thought he might die. He had some kind of viral infection. They flew his mom out. He was one sick pup. Steve Luke started and played every snap at center as a sophomore in the Rose Bowl. When Henson went down, they moved Bruce Elia from linebacker to fullback, and he led the Big Ten in scoring, and he ended up making it with the San Francisco '49ers. Doug Plank was never a regular starter at Ohio State and was a terror in the NFL. It was an incredible array of athletes.

LAST YEAR WHEN WE WENT DOWN to one of the football games, I was looking at the program, and there's a section that lists All-Big Ten, All-American by year. My junior year, All-Big Ten, first team: Archie; on the offensive line, both of the tackles, Hicks and myself, and the left guard, Kregel. My senior year the All-Big Ten guard, center, and tackle are all from the same team. You just don't have that. There are too many good players. When Hicks and I were selected All-Big Ten, I'd say the last time that that happened was also at Ohio State, with a pair of tackles named Foley and Mayes.

My junior year, we should have been national champions. We tied Michigan 10–10 in Ann Arbor. It was, ironically, the last year that the final polls were taken prior to the bowl games being played. Notre Dame ended up as national champion that year, and they got waxed by Alabama in the bowl game. That was the last year Ohio State won the Rose Bowl. We beat USC 42–21. Had the polls been taken after the bowl games, we still may have ended up national champions. I truly believe there was not a better football team in the country.

Look at the Michigan teams over that time period. In three years, they lost two games and tied one, and those kids never played in a bowl. When we went into that game, we were one and they were either two or three in the country. We had just thumped everybody we played, and so had they.

The low point for me was the 10–10 tie at Michigan. I remember walking through the tunnel back up to the locker room. We felt that we had to win the game to go to the Rose Bowl, because we had been there the year before, and in case of a tie, it was our understanding that the team that had gone most recently would be eliminated. It was a very emotional time for us. We were heads down on our way back to the locker room, and the Michigan guys were celebrating. Then we were informed while we were airborne that the decision had been made to send us. Initially, we didn't believe it, because everybody was so resigned to the fact that we weren't going to go. It was a reprieve; it gave us a chance to play one more game. That Rose Bowl was the best game I was every involved with. I don't know where it ranks in Ohio State annals, but USC was a fine team with a lot of talent, and we ripped them.

Michigan was always the best team that we played. It was assumed that it was going to come down to that game. It was a very emotional game. Those games were physical, fight for every yard you can get. Archie took a tremendous beating in those games. You'd make a block, and the next play, you'd get beat. Very equally matched football teams, and you played hard for 48 minutes. They were great games. We could've played better in that 10–10 tie. After the game, Woody—I wouldn't say he apologized to the team—said he consciously buttoned up the offense. He didn't think they could score on our defense; therefore, if we didn't make any critical errors, they couldn't beat us. As it turned out, he was basically right. They couldn't beat us, but they did tie us.

I always viewed myself as solid and dependable. I didn't make many mental mistakes. I didn't always get it done physically, but I was always mentally prepared to do what we had to do. It was a fairly interactive offense. The tackles were responsible for making many of the blocking calls. Depending on the defense and where the guys were aligned, you would block the same play different ways. The guys who played on the other side of the line would argue for points: 'I called this.'

'No you didn't.'

You're like, 'Just let the film run. It doesn't make that much difference. The game's over, and we won.'

We had a vested interest in how the backs did. Without fail, when the stat sheets came out, you would get run over by the offensive linemen, because we wanted to see how many yards Archie got. Archie could not have cared less. It was just not part of his focus. We liked him, and we realized that he was the horse. Archie was so much of a team player that everyone wanted to see him do well, and it was our moment in the sunshine. I don't know how many consecutive 100-yard games he ended up with, but that was something that we took a lot of pride in as an offensive line. If you stayed on your man, Archie would find a place to run. The same was true of Corny. The fullbacks were going to run over people, but give Archie a seam and watch him make the defensive backs miss.

ONE OF THE NICE THINGS about being an offensive lineman is that nobody knows who you are. I rarely wore my letter jacket. I chose not to wear the letter jacket because I was down there as a student more than I was down there for anything else. The old stories about football players getting preferential treatment certainly didn't apply. I had two cases where things were made more difficult and none where things were made easier in my four years. Micro-economics—you walk into a lecture hall, and you see three or four people you know, and you sit with them. It doesn't matter if you're a football player or not. You just do that. This female professor walked in, and there were three or four football players sitting together. She put her books down at her desk, and she looked up at us and said, 'I just want you guys to know that I flunked one of your teammates last year because I caught him cheating.' Well, if he'd just been a regular student, would you have passed him if you caught him cheating?

I took an astronomy class and genuinely loved it. I went in and talked to the professor to see what was involved in majoring in astronomy, because he was the most captivating professor that I had in my four years down there. He dissuaded me from doing that because he said there was no money in it. But I was one point away from an A. I thought I had enough points for the A, then the grades came, and I got the B. I went down and asked him about it. He said, 'Well, you were real close.' It had been a big lecture class—150, 200 kids—and some of the other guys who were in the class had caused a little bit of difficulty, and he was sort of punishing the football players, and I was one of them. That part of it wasn't a plus.

John Hicks was the starting right tackle my junior year; I was the starting left tackle. John was all-everything his senior year—Outland Trophy winner, Lombardi Award, second or third player picked in the draft. If you go back and look at films, we were not a right-hand dominated football team. We ran effectively to both sides of the ball. Playing well as a junior and being selected by the coaches as a first-team All-Big Ten player, I felt that there was a pretty good chance of going on to the pros. The Rose Bowl that we won, I had a real good game against the defensive tackle I was playing against. I figured I'd get a good look.

THE OPPORTUNITY TO COME INTO THE LEAGUE as a first-round draft pick was exciting. The money, while it's fractional to what it is today, was pretty darn good. I was the 12th player drafted in 1975, and my signing bonus was $100,000. Even by today's standards, it's a lot of money. Back in '75, it was a whole boatload of money.

It was unfortunate that I ended up with the Saints, because they were not a particularly good football team. It wasn't until the front office changed that the program changed. In three years, I was under four head coaches. My rookie year, I started about half of the games and played reasonably well. I was selected as offensive player of the game against the Giants. Things looked pretty good. Then Hank Stram came in, and Hank brought in with him a strength and conditioning coach. We moved back to New Orleans in late June, and I was just under 280 pounds. But it was a solid 280 pounds. I met Alvin Roy, who was the strength and conditioning coach for the very first time. I walked into the locker room. Alvin walked up and said, 'Let's hop up on the scales.'

It went to like 279. He stepped back and said, 'You don't look that heavy.'

To me, that was a compliment. In the next breath, he said, 'You ought to play at 245.'

So I was given an assigned weight for training camp to report at 245. There was also a procedure where you weighed in on Tuesday. If you didn't make weight, for every pound you were overweight, it cost you $100. You continued to weigh in until you made weight. Every time you weighed in and you were over, it was $100 a pound. Starting off as a math major, I figured it was a good idea to give myself a little cushion in case I had that extra ice cream sundae or something. I report to camp at 242. Keep in mind, my senior year in high school, I played fullback and linebacker at 235.

Hank ran us through three-a-days all training camp: Monday, Tuesday, Wednesday, three practices; two practices on Thursday; one on Friday; play on Saturday; off on Sunday. I went from 242 to 229. We played Buffalo in our last preseason ballgame. I was 229 pounds before the game, as an offensive guard. I got killed, in a very real sense. Confidence is a funny thing. If you have it, it's great. If you don't, it's tough to get it. When you lose it, it's tough to get back. It was humiliating enough that I gave serious thought to not going back to training camp my third year. I felt that much out of place, and things were never the same after that.

WHEN I ENDED UP IN TAMPA BAY, I got hurt. It was a pass play. We were just kind of winding things down in the Kansas City game. I had jammed the tackle pretty squarely at the line of scrimmage, and the defensive left end had a stunt. Our tackle drove him down the line of scrimmage, and the two of them hit me as they were coming down. That ended that season. I came back that next year. Again, I had worked out hard. I took pride in the fact that I was in good shape and ready to play. I came back, and the knee that I had hurt at Ohio State—I had displaced the knee cap on my left knee—swelled. They put me on some anti-inflammatory medication, and I'd be off for a day or two and the swelling would go down. I'd go back out to practice, and the swelling would come back. It swelled to the point that I couldn't extend it and I couldn't bend it all the way. I couldn't run. The team doctor, who was not an orthopedic surgeon, was going to drain my knee. He was discussing with the trainer exactly what part of the knee he thought should be drained. I went, 'Whoa! If you're not sure that's the pre-patella bursar sac or not, you are not putting a needle in my knee.' I went to see the orthopedic surgeon.

I'm laying on the table, and he says, 'What's the problem?'

I said, 'I've got this grating in my knee, and it's swollen.'

He said, 'Let me hear what you're talking about.'

I lifted my leg and bent my knee, and he grimaced and said, 'Oh, that's sick.'

He examined me and said, 'You shouldn't be playing on this.'

At that point, I came back, went into the trainer and said, 'That's a wrap.'

I packed up my stuff, and I came home. The hard part was getting a job afterward. I think someone in human resources wrote a book, and part of the book said if an individual is going to make less money in the new job, compared to what they made in the previous job, they won't be happy. That may well be true, but when you are changing professions, and particularly when you are getting out of one that is notoriously short-term and notoriously well-paid, it's different. I don't think I interviewed with anybody that made as much money as I had made that previous year, and I interviewed for a wide array of jobs. That first bridge—not from a psychological standpoint, but just trying to get somebody to say they'll hire you—is tough to cross. I remember one interviewer asking me: 'When do you think, in adjusted dollars, that you will make as much money as you made last year?'

My answer was, 'Never.'

IN '75, I MADE $75,000. I don't know what that would equate to now, but, clearly, it's more than I'm making now. People just seemed to have a hard time grasping: 'I'm not changing jobs, I'm changing professions. The career that I was in is no longer available to me, and I've got to find something else.'

Psychologically, it wasn't hard to get away from football. I think if the experience had continued as the Ohio State experience had gone, then it might have been more difficult to leave. But it was a very tenuous, at times somewhat ugly, situation, at New Orleans and at Tampa. Very little consistency in the players. Constant turn.

There are some significant differences between the NFL and Ohio State. For one thing, not many NFL franchises at that period of time were as successful as Ohio State's teams. Nobody likes to lose, and everybody likes to win. If you're on a team that loses more than it wins, you're not going to be as happy. The other thing is that at Ohio State, while there was intense competition—to the point that I almost transferred because I was not happy because I was not playing—if people didn't play, they didn't lose their scholarship. If I was the third-team offense tackle and never, ever stepped on the field during my four years, I still received my books and my tuition and my room and board. That's not the way it was in the NFL. There were no third-team offensive tackles in the NFL. If you were not a starter, you'd better be able to play both sides, and maybe guard, if you wanted to have a reasonable assurance of making the ballclub. It was a cut-throat business. Forty-eight people were going to make a living, as opposed to 120 on scholarship.

The downside was if you got cut, particularly if you were with a team like New Orleans, the other teams weren't scouring the wavier list for guys New Orleans didn't want. If you didn't make it there, you probably weren't going to make it anyplace. If you want to talk about organization and equipment, there probably weren't many NFL teams that took care of their players—not financially, of course—as well as Ohio State did. We always had the best. I've still got football shoes from there. Most of us wore Pumas with all leather uppers, and to cut down on the traction of the football field, Woody had the grounds crew water the artificial turf before practice to cut down on the bite. You wear leather shoes and go out and run around and get them wet, they stretch. You just walk by the equipment window. John Bozick would be back there.

'BOZ, NEED ANOTHER PAIR OF SHOES.'

'What size?'

'Twelve and a half.'

'Here you go.'

We had separate game equipment from our practice equipment. During preseason, we wore the game equipment for a couple of days just to break it in. That was it. You go to an away game, you go into the locker room, your stuff was hung and ready to go. Your headgear and shoulder pads were the best there was. That was not necessarily the case in the NFL. Ohio State had organization and consistency. When I was there, Woody celebrated his 25th year. How many NFL coaches stay in one place for 25 years? It just doesn't happen.

I saw Woody very infrequently after I left. I did not feel terribly close to Coach Hayes. I had a tremendous amount of respect for him, even when I was upset that I wasn't playing. He was always up-front with what was going on. When the Clemson incident happened, I thought it got blown out of all proportion. Clearly, it was the wrong thing for him to do, but it was an emotional response. He shouldn't have hit the kid, but, clearly, when you look at it, the kid's helmet is bobbing up and down, which means he was running his mouth. What he was saying I don't know, but he was clearly standing there running his mouth at the Ohio State bench. Not at Woody, because he was standing almost side-by-side with Coach Hayes, but he probably said something in a very emotional period, and Woody reacted and popped him one.

Did he hurt the kid? No. I don't know if Woody ever apologized to the kid. Maybe that would've been a more appropriate response, but it just blew up out of all proportion. From another perspective, it may have also been time. It might have been the right time for Woody to step down and do something a little bit different with the rest of his life. As I said, a lesser man could have been bitter and spiteful. Woody kind of went, 'Hey, I'll do something else that's worthwhile.' And he did.

The unfortunate part of that whole incident is that people are too often remembered for the last thing that they do, and most people didn't have a clue about him. They knew very little about Woody Hayes. It was almost criminal that so many people end up asking, 'Were you down there when he punched the kid?' No, but I was there when he won three consecutive Big Ten championships and when he would go out of his way to stop and talk to a kid on campus who didn't play football but who just wanted to talk to him, or when he went to the hospital to see somebody who was ill or when he went out of his way to help a former player with an interview or a letter of recommendation.

I'M GLAD I PLAYED FOR HIM. You look at the tough times and you look at the good times, and my memories of Columbus are not spotlessly beautiful, but I had a wonderful time going to school at Ohio State. I played in the *Chicago Tribune* All-Star Game, I played in the Hula Bowl, and there was not an offensive lineman that I came across in those games that was better coached than I was. I played on a team that was one point away from being one of the best teams Ohio State has ever fielded. The life lessons—things that I only hope to be able to convey to my kids and other people's youngsters I come in contact with, the corny stuff: hard work, dedication—Woody didn't teach me all of them, but he surely reinforced them

To the best of my knowledge, Woody never did anything intentionally to harm anybody. When we didn't play well, he took full responsibility. Fortunately, that wasn't all that often, but there was never any finger-pointing. When we got beat, he got out-coached, even if *we* got beat. When we played well, it was because *we* did it. There's not a lot of that left anymore, in major college or in the NFL. He had a strong enough ego that the only people who he cared what they thought about him was a fairly finite circle of about 130 people. He didn't care what the press thought; he didn't care what other coaches thought. I don't think he cared what the administration of the school thought. What he cared about was the coaches, the players, the people who were a part of that program. There were probably 90 kids who were pissed off that they weren't playing, but he kept the family knit. You didn't see the sophomore tackle go storming off to *The Lantern* or one of the Columbus papers or the TV stations and say, 'The Old Man's playing favorites.' It didn't happen.

I have no regrets. The fellow who recruited me for Notre Dame is now coaching at Ohio State. I was playing in the Buckeye Booster golf outing two years ago, and he came up and reintroduced himself. He said, 'I just wanted to tell you that I followed your career. I'm sorry as hell that you didn't come up to Notre Dame, but you made the right choice.'

I didn't need him to reaffirm that for me. It would be incredibly greedy for me to have had the success that I've had and played on the teams I played on at Ohio State and look back and say, 'Oh, but if only.'

When we go down to the games, we usually park by the Student Union up on High Street, grab a bite to eat and walk down to the stadium. Walking across the oval, down past University Hall, the Bus Stop. I think, 'Yeah, I used to go in there and get a Little Debby's cake and heat it up in the microwave for a couple of seconds and eat it on the way to football practice.' The stupid little things that you think about that were all part of going to school.

I think that one of the prettiest areas on campus is right around Mirror Lake. Jackie used to work at the student health center. All through our four years, she worked nights, until 11 or 12 o'clock, and I used to go over and walk her back to her dorm. Walking through there, holding hands with the lady that you're in love with is like the beer commercial: 'It doesn't get any better than this.' Somebody else is paying the bills. All you have to worry about is money for pizza and pop. There's nothing I'd do different. That's for sure. ”

True Believer

AFTER PAUL Hornung died, a fellow sportswriter said of him, "He was obviously very loyal to his beat and the people he covered. He never created any kind of chaos. He didn't stir up controversy, never looked for a bad story."

Intended to eulogize a worthy, longtime competitor, the remark nonetheless cuts two ways. Hornung wrote about Ohio State football for 43 years, 23 of them as sports editor of the *Columbus Dispatch*. But in that time, he became more well known as an intimate of Woody Hayes and an unwavering supporter of the Buckeyes than as an incisive analyst, tenacious reporter, or deft stylist.

Hornung relished the fraternal distinction of being one of "Woody's guys," not just admitting to close friendship with the subject of so much of his coverage but taking pride in their relationship. In flowery prose spattered with chummy asides and purple riffs of adulation, Hornung regularly defended Hayes, cheered the Buckeyes, and exalted what he called "the Ohio State phenomenon."

Skeptical colleagues might've thought him a gullible hanger-on who'd been duped—or bullied—into shilling for Hayes, but Hornung claimed that he knew precisely what he was about. "I believed in what I was doing and never regretted it and never have since," he said. "I gave the people who read the *Dispatch* the best that I could possibly do, and I gave them the best under my philosophy."

That philosophy was more than a little jingoistic, as if Columbus were encircled by armies bent on invading "the Hallowed Horseshoe" and seizing the town's rightful title (bestowed upon it by Hornung) as "College Football, USA." He often referred to the team as, simply, "Ohio," affirming his notion that it represented not just a university but an entire state. He gently chided opponents for their sparse crowds and declared Columbus the logical site for the National Football Foundation Hall of Fame. For 30 years, he was the "Chief Quarterback" of the booster club. His perspective was limited, as could be expected of a self-described "hayseed" who grew up in a town with a population of barely a hundred, who attended a one-room school, and whose only trip outside of Henry County before he enrolled at Ohio State was a visit to an uncle in Cleveland.

Like many sportswriters, Hornung was an unsuccessful athlete who seems to have been a little flustered in the presence of ballplayers, his unease taking the form of gushy deference. Cut from the Holgate High School basketball team, he became its statistician and wrote up games for a local weekly. He began with the *Dispatch* by covering football and basketball practices part-time, and throughout his career, he enjoyed frequenting locker rooms. He chatted with whomever was around and relayed his findings in quasi-technical jock talk ("On passing downs, Ohio used a loose 4-4-3 defense, with the linebackers playing three yards back of the line in a semi-zone pass defense.")

Hornung covered the "Blizzard Bowl" of 1950—played in high winds, ankle-deep snow, and 10-degree temperatures—from the sidelines, wearing cleats, socks, sweat suit, and cape borrowed from the OSU equipment manager. "Who said I wasn't an athlete?" he asked readers. During one of Hornung's annual tours of Big Ten training camps, Michigan State coach Duffy Daugherty invited him to ride a blocking sled. "They really jolt that sled—and I've got the stiff neck to prove it," he wrote, as if pointing out a battle wound.

Paul Hornung had made the traveling squad after all, and he repaid with loyalty those who had accepted him. After wins, he dispensed praise broadly (one of his columns was entitled "Fans Love Backfield, All Bucks"); after losses, he dwelled on individual excellence. While the rest of the media harped on Rex Kern, who struggled during his senior season, Hornung let readers know how well "Mace" (back-up quarter-back Ron Maciejowski) was playing.

He wrote about "the warm, happy feeling" at a team Christmas party and called the Senior Tackle "inherently lump-in-the-old-esophagus material." He admonished fans for booing and assiduously avoided offending anyone, which younger colleagues saw as cowardice in the face of the enemy, but which he thought of as simple good manners.

If Hornung often sounded star-struck, many of his pieces also have the quality of a proud uncle idly boasting about gifted nephews. His own marriage childless, Hornung spent his life watching the children of others accomplish great things.

With each new season, however, he could choose among splendid young men, selecting the cleanest of limb, the sharpest of mind, the most decent of nature on whom to dote. Hornung never had to experience the disappointment of having his own flesh fail to live up to his expectations.

Jack Armstrong hyperbole peppered his stories, but Hornung's idolatry was based, in part, on his understanding the importance of maintaining Hayes's favor. Mercurial in his dealings with the press, Hayes could be entertaining and forthright as well as suspicious and boorish ("I've never known a newspaperman to win a game for us"). Should the coach have taken exception to Hornung, the *Dispatch*'s sports section would've consisted of little more than accounts of Jack Nicklaus's latest victory, updates on John Galbreath's race-horses, and warmed over press releases from OSU's sports information office.

When Hayes was hired in 1951, Hornung found him emotional, unorganized, and testy, and the paper's coverage of the Bucks that first spring was marked by its restraint ("The Bucks bobbled the ball, missed assignments and generally had their rough spots," he wrote after Hayes's first practice) and paucity. Even a photo of Don Apache, Jr., a Chihua-hua appearing at the Central Ohio Kennel Club Show, received more prominent display than football practice. Eventually, though, Hornung "threw in" with "the Bossman." He constantly noted Hayes's moods, dutifully recounted his every off-hand utterance and wandering digression, and kept the coach's more indiscreet comments safely off the record.

"He talked to me because he knew I wouldn't put everything in the paper," Hornung said. "He'd get it out and then he'd be all right."

Always faithful to Hayes, Hornung called him "a towering figure on the right and good side of sports, education and life" in the last of his four books, *Woody Hayes: A Reflection*.

Paul Hornung was unlike the stereotypical reporter. He didn't smoke, he didn't curse, and the most potent beverage he drank was Faygo Redpop. He also had none of Roger Kahn's literary pretensions, none of Jim Murray's often strained sense of humor, none of the acerbic cynicism of Jimmy Cannon, none of Paul Zimmerman's smug presumption of technical knowledge, none of the harebrained sociology of Robert Lipsyte. Certainly, his work is more notable for its abundance than for its excellence, but Hornung, an unaffected and egoless man, took the approach favored by such writers as Arthur Daley: Write about your friends and ignore your enemies.

He once called Woody Hayes "a throwback," but Hornung himself was a reminder of older age. His style was rooted in the florid exaggeration of Grantland Rice, Ring Lardner, and Damon Runyon, who wrote when players were mythical figures and the sports pages a cycle of legends. Eventually, Hornung's breezy sidebars about the band's patriotic halftime shows, his heartwarming tidbits about "team spirit," his endless analyses of opponents, his recitations of the number of buckeye leaves earned each week, his cliches and jargon began to sound dated.

Competition with television forced sports sections to move away from agate play-by-plays and conspicuous boosterism to eye-catching graphics, investigative reports, and uncompromising opinion pieces. Not unaware of the drift, Hornung replaced the benign, smiling photo at the top of his column, "In the Press Box," with one more stern, as if he were attempting to appear hard-edged. He saw 326 consecutive Buckeye games, the string broken in 1975 when he covered the Reds in the World Series.

Hornung's last piece was a recap of the 1993 Memorial Golf Tournament for the event's press book. Paul Azinger, the winner, had contracted lymphoma. Afflicted with the same disease, Hornung was admitted to Riverside Hospital in November of 1993 and died the following spring, shortly after being presented with an honorary varsity "O."

Someone once described Grantland Rice as "a relatively innocent man in a relatively innocent era." The same could've been said of Paul Hornung, and he probably wouldn't have disagreed.

Paul HORNUNG

"I CAME FROM A LITTLE TOWN up in the northwestern part of the state, called New Bavaria. But I wasn't good enough to be an athlete. I couldn't make the basketball team. I became the statistician and the scorekeeper, and the local paper wanted somebody to report the Holgate High School basketball games, so I did that. I came to Ohio State with the idea of going into journalism. To show you how naive I was, I had gone with my parents to visit an uncle in Cleveland one time, and that's the only time I had ever been out of Henry County. I came down here a real babe-in-the-woods. I took a room at the YMCA, which is seven miles from campus. I didn't know how to ride streetcars; I didn't have enough nerve to get on one. I walked from the YMCA to campus and from the campus back to the YMCA. After about a week of that, I got smart enough to *move* to the campus.

Francis Schmidt was the football coach at the time. He didn't get along with any of the downtown sportswriters, much less a campus sports writer. He was very gruff, very self-absorbed. He was constantly thinking football. He'd go somewhere to eat, and he'd draw plays on the tablecloth. Schmidt's last year was 1940. We got beat by Michigan, 40–0. Tom Harmon scored three touchdowns, kicked the extra points, and punted for a 40-yard average. He had an unbelievable day, and Schmidt was fired after that game. Paul Brown came in the spring of 1941.

He was king of the hill, right from the start. He had that phenomenal record, 80-1, when he came from Massillon. He took the place by storm. A lot of people thought he was fairly cold and aloof, but he really wasn't. He was a private man in a public profession. He accepted the spotlight, and he did a good job in the spotlight, but he was more at home out of it. He was easily embarrassed by praise and wasn't really at ease in high-pressure situations. He was a private person who had to be public. He was the most organized man I ever knew. That was one of the secrets of his success—his organization. He was the complete antithesis of Francis Schmidt. Francis was rough, very profane, very obscene. Paul was very gentlemanly, never raised his voice. The thing he loved most about football was the contest on the sidelines. He loved matching wits with the guy across the field.

In Massillon, he ran his own show, and when he came here, it was with the understanding that he would have free rein. He came in and completely organized everything. He even picked the uniforms, the equipment, the shoes. He did everything. He was 32 years old; he'd never coached in college. I think he rubbed some people the wrong way. He wouldn't let anybody or anything stand in his way. He insisted on running his own show, and they had not been used to that here, so he had some critics.

With the public, he was ace-high. With the players, he was a hard taskmaster, but they loved him. I've had guys tell me, 'If he told me to run through the stadium wall, I'd do it.' They believed in the discipline. The first year he was here—I think it was after the second game of the season—he found out one of the guys was breaking the training rules, and even though it was one of his Massillon players who was on his way to being All-American, he kicked him off the team. Just like that. There was no recourse: 'He broke the rules. He didn't live by my rules. So, he's no longer on the team.'

Boy, that woke up a bunch of guys. That cemented his relationship with the players, because they knew he meant business. They either did it his way or they just weren't here. He was like Woody a lot, because some guys didn't appreciate it at the time. Some guys resented it, but once they became seniors or got out of school, they realized the benefits it had for them. His first year, he inherited a very rundown football team, but they still went 6-1-1. They lost to Northwestern 14-7, I think, and they tied Michigan 20–20, when Michigan was a two or three-touchdown favorite, playing in Ann Arbor. If there were any questions before that, they were removed. The next year, with a lot of sophomores he had recruited, they went 9-1 and won OSU's first national championship.

What happened when Ohio State was looking for a coach in 1940 was the high school coaches in the state all got together and told Ohio State, essentially, 'We want you to hire our man.' The inference was, 'If you hire our man, we're 100 percent behind you.' So when Paul came to Ohio State, he was a good recruiter, *and* he had all of those high school coaches behind him. In 1942, he had one of the greatest freshman teams Ohio State ever had. The only better one, I think, was Woody's recruiting class of 1967—Jack Tatum, Rex Kern, John Brockington and those guys. In '42, Brown only had three seniors on the team—so the next year, he would've had all of those guys coming back from the national championship team and the great freshman team. It would've been a dynasty. Who knows how long it would've gone on?

But in early 1944, he went into the navy, and Carroll Widdoes, one of his assistants, took over. Carroll didn't want the job as head coach. He was a very retiring guy. He didn't like public speaking or anything to do with that. He loved coaching, but he didn't like the other part. He went undefeated in 1944 with Horvath and Bill Willis, Bill Hackett, and those guys, but Mr. St. John, who was elderly and reaching retirement, didn't make enough of an effort to keep Paul. In the meantime, Mickey McBride started the Cleveland franchise in the old All-American Conference. Mickey McBride had a lot of money but he didn't know anything about football. He offered Paul about four or five times more money than he was making at OSU. He gave him carte blanche as far as organizing a football team.

My wife and I were at Great Lakes when Paul got a letter from Mr. St. John, who said, essentially, 'You know Carroll Widdoes has been doing a fine job in your absence. Now, if you want to return, the job will be yours, and I feel that I can assure you that I can get the Athletic Board to pay you $9,000 a year.' Well, he'd been offered at least $75,000 a year to coach in the professionals. I think, despite everything else, if they had given him the impression they wanted him and they were anxious to have him back, that they were going to pay him more, he would have come back. But it was a lukewarm reception.

The hullaballoo around here was incredible. Losing Paul Brown was more than people could stand. Poor old Mr. St. John. He brought Ohio State athletics out of the cornfields and gave it a national name. Unfortunately, he was elderly and not in great health, and he was just badly advised by some of the people on the campus who were not wholeheartedly behind Paul anyway. And the poor fellow—they had a day for him at one football game, and they rode him around the track in an open car, and he was booed.

Wes Fesler resigned after the Rose Bowl game in 1950. He had been an All-American football player here at Ohio State, extremely popular guy. He'd been a basketball player for three years, a baseball player. He played golf and went out and shot a 79 the first time. He was one of the great natural athletes ever here. But I was never convinced that he really liked to coach. He liked working with the players on the field, and he liked the notoriety, but he detested recruiting and he didn't like all the things a coach has to do to be successful. There was a lot of criticism.

Vic Janowicz came here as one of the most highly recruited players ever at Ohio State. He was nationally publicized before he ever played, and everybody in the world knew he should be the starting tailback, but Fesler played him on defense. It infuriated people that Fesler didn't play him on offense. A lot of the alumni were unhappy and the Ohio State officials were in Chicago for the Big Ten meetings in 1949, and Wes had dinner with the president and the athletic director, and he told them he was resigning. He caught everybody by surprise. He just said he didn't want to coach anymore. He didn't like the criticism, so he didn't want to be involved.

IT PERPETUATED OHIO STATE'S reputation as the 'Graveyard of Coaches.' Everybody thought when Schmidt came to Ohio State that he was the answer to their prayers. They had fired a fellow named Sam Willaman who had been successful but whose personality seemed to clash with everybody. They hired Schmidt, who came in with great fanfare, had success for the first few years, but then he resigned under fire. Carroll Widdoes had the undefeated team in 1944, but then the next year, things didn't go as well. He was a devoutly religious man, very family-oriented and resented the time he had to give to coaching and recruiting and public speaking and everything else. He voluntarily stepped down, and Paul Bixler, who was one of his assistants and a very popular guy around here, became head coach. The job was just too much for Paul. He got beat 58–6 by Michigan in 1946—the last game. It capped off a disastrous season. He had an opportunity to go back to Cornell, where he had been, so he decided to go back. That brought Fesler in, and then Fesler quit, and then we had Woody, for 28 years.

I think Paul Brown would've come back. The Browns were in the All-American Conference, which was sort of a second league to the NFL. The Browns had dominated the AAC, but some of the teams were not very stable. Competition wasn't great. I don't think Paul was getting satisfaction out of what he was doing. He had a great warm spot in his heart for Ohio State. He still said right up until a couple of weeks before he died—I talked to him about it—he said, 'Those were the happiest days of my life, the happiest days of my coaching career, at Ohio State.' He always loved the college atmosphere.

But there were people on the campus who were determined that he would never come back, primarily because he left Ohio State, and when you left Ohio State, you automatically became an alien. That was one thing, and also, the alumni secretary here was a very outspoken guy named Jack Fullen. I've always felt that he expected to move up to either a university vice president or maybe even the presidency. When Paul came here, Jack jumped on Paul's bandwagon with both feet. He was riding Paul's wave of popularity with alumni and the legislature which doles out the money and people in general. Paul was a great meal ticket, and when he left, he left Jack high and dry. I can't document that, or anything of the sort. It's just what I've always felt.

Jack wrote in the alumni monthly and said things like Ohio State is lucky to be rid of Paul Brown, and he was disliked in the Big Ten. Well, if they disliked him, there was one reason: He was going to dominate the league for the rest of the century. So it became sort of a vendetta with Jack, and, unfortunately, Mr. St. John was elderly, and he had been through a lot of wars, was not in good health, and he allowed Jack to manipulate him into joining this thing. The result was that it split the camp. Dick Larkins, who was the athletic director, made the statement that Brown would come back over his dead body. It wasn't as much against Paul as it was about the fact that Dick felt it would split the university, split the Ohio State followers. I guess the way he phrased it was that Brown had became controversial, so he wasn't about to use his influence to bring Paul back and start all that controversy over.

Woody had a tough time the first couple of years. He was not the most popular candidate that ever came on the campus. The players had been used to Wes Fesler and a whole heck of a lot looser discipline. Woody was go-go and a lot of his players took a dim view of him. His only coaching experience in college had been at Denison and Miami, and some of the players didn't think he was aware of the Big Ten and what they did in the Big Ten. He had his rough times.

Going into the '54 season, everybody felt that the first four games were so tough, that by the end of them, he wouldn't be around. What they didn't count on was that, now, he had all of his own players. The '54 seniors had been his first recruiting class. He had by then convinced people what kind of guy he was, he had picked up a lot of support among alumni and former players, he was pretty solid with the athletic administration, and he had a good football team. He did a good job of coaching all the way around, and he won the national championship. The next year, he lost virtually everybody from the national championship team, but the team came back strong and won the Big Ten championship. Woody was on his way.

I HAVE TO ADMIT that there were times when I didn't think he was going to make it. I thought he was in a little over his head, to be honest. I wasn't sure that he was going to really, really win. I admired the work ethic that he had, and I admired, especially, that he was willing to learn. He came in with a chip on his shoulder, and he was going to show everybody he could do the job. But he sort of backed off a little bit, which I thought was admirable.

It's a big jump, from Miami to Ohio State. Miami was still a small community, and now, all of a sudden, you have the whole state of Ohio and the whole city of Columbus—a lot of things he didn't have to deal with before. It's a big jump. But he adjusted and he picked up things and he improved. He proved he was big enough for the job. In fact, he became *bigger* than the job. I've done maybe 25 book signings in this area, and it's amazing how people still love that guy, and respect him and admire him. Just the things people said to me when I was signing books. A lot of them wanted to talk, you know: 'I still love Woody'; 'There's nobody like Woody.' John Cooper's probably suffering from that. Earle Bruce did, there's no question about that. I felt sorry for Earle in that respect, because everybody, me maybe most of all, was always making the comparison. What you have is an extraordinary human being and then you bring in a mere mortal. Earle Bruce was an outstanding football coach. As far as Xs and Os, Earle was at least as good, or better, than Woody.

Earle had the advantage of having been here as an assistant coach, and he had been successful where he had been before. I liked him, and I thought he was a good choice. He was an Ohio Stater. People had always been looking for Ohio Staters. I thought he had an awful lot going for him, but I knew that he was going to be constantly compared. I knew he was going to have trouble living up to that.

Charisma is such a buzzword that I hate to use it. But if anybody ever had charisma, Woody had it. All he had to do was stand up in front of a group and start to speak, and he had everyone in his pocket. Earle did all right, but he was your average football coach speaking. I give him credit for not trying to be another Woody Hayes, which is something he would not have been comfortable doing. I give him credit for being himself. He was doing a good job in what he was doing.

One night a couple of years ago, an old gentleman in the Quarterback Club was telling me that on his birthday, he opened the door about 7 o'clock that night, and there's Woody. Woody said, 'I came to wish you a happy birthday.' I don't even know what the old guy did. I think he worked in one of the factories here. Just an ordinary Joe, but he was at the Quarterback Club meetings all the time, and he'd see Woody there, maybe sometimes he'd walk up and say hello after a meeting. But not a friend really. He said Woody came in and talked to him and his wife and his son and daughter-in-law. Spent a half-hour there. And he said he'd just come back from Indianapolis. This fellow, he's telling me this story, and his chin's trembling, and he's getting misty-eyed. He said, 'My son called him and told him that it was my birthday, and he wondered if there was any chance Woody could just stop by and say hello. And he came out to my house and stayed for a half-hour and talked to my wife and I and my kids. Can you imagine that?' It was things like that that put Woody so far out of the realm of the average coach. Who else would do that? No one.

I used to go to the Faculty Club with Woody a lot, and we'd sit at that big long table, and there'd be professors there, and Ed Jennings, the president, would come in and sit down, the deans. It was an interesting group all the time, and a number of times, someone would say, 'How's come Earle Bruce never comes over here?' See, Woody used to half-live at the Faculty Club, and he loved to mingle with the people he felt were on a level above him.

It was not public relations at all. Oh, he made good contacts with people on the faculty. He knew that, and I knew that; you can't separate the two. But 98 percent of it was genuine interest. He loved to talk to them about their fields and their specialities, completely away from football. Earle liked to go to pal around with his buddies. That's what he enjoyed. Woody was a personality, and he was so far beyond just a football coach. The comparison was unfair, and it was damaging. Whenever things came up, you know: 'Well, Woody would've anticipated that.' If you heard that once, you heard it a thousand times. I kept it to myself primarily, but you'd hear so many people say, 'Well, if *Woody* would've been here....'

When Earle got fired, so many people said, 'If Woody had been here, they'd never had been able to fire Earle.' But Woody *wasn't* here. There's no use living in the past. It's all over. But you just can't help but think what kind of a thing we had here for 28 years.

I THINK I'M VERY MUCH LUCKIER than anyone deserves to be. I was close personal friends with Paul Brown, who I consider to be one of the greatest people in the history of sports. I was close personal friends with Jack Nicklaus and his family, and I think he was the greatest golfer of all times. Then I came along with Woody, who has to be one of the most extraordinary men ever in sports. And to be in a job where I did something that I loved so much. It never occurred to me that I was working 60, 80 hours. I worked the same schedule that Woody did. He never followed the clock, and I didn't either.

He had that energy, that stamina. He believed in what he was doing, and he loved what he was doing. If it was going somewhere and making a speech, he loved that, and he believed in what he was saying. He didn't go there for public relations; he went there to try to give those people a message. He used to do a lot of commercial things, a lot of inspirational-type things for business meetings, where he really thought he was doing some good. He was doing it not for the money involved, but because he thought he was doing something for somebody. He thought he actually had something to tell them they could use.

People think that I supported him because I was stupid or that I didn't know any better, or never thought about what I was doing. But I always felt, and I justified myself, if I had to, that I was the sports editor of the biggest newspaper in town, and Ohio State University football was the biggest thing, by far, in Columbus in the way of sports, and it was wholesome, it was clean, it was uplifting, it was connected to education, it was providing great examples to young people, it was providing a wholesome outlet for the community, so, therefore, why should I not be what some people derogatorily called 'a cheerleader'?

Why shouldn't I want Ohio State to win? Why shouldn't I want Ohio State to be good athletically? Why shouldn't I want Ohio State to be known around the country? Why shouldn't I want to tell people what a great man Woody Hayes was, and what he stood for, and what his philosophy was? Why shouldn't I write enthusiastically about him? Maybe it grated on some people, and maybe it got to be old, but if it did, it was worth it. I felt I was rendering in my own small way and with the *Dispatch* a great service by doing my best to encourage and help bring to other people what I knew and thought about Ohio State football.

That's a personal thing, I guess, and I'm not justifying myself. I know I've been criticized. I was a little struck one time when I read in our own *Dispatch* that the cheerleaders have disappeared from the press box, and I felt that was a slap at me. I've seen references in other papers about my being a cheerleader for Ohio State football and for Woody, and it's usually used in a context of criticism. I never felt offended for it, because I wouldn't change it for anything. I gave the people who read the *Dispatch* the best that I could possibly do, and I gave them the best under my philosophy.

Woody absolutely did not insist that I print or not print certain stories. The only time he ever, in his 28 years, called and asked me to print something was when prior to an Ohio State appreciation banquet, they had a squad meeting. Some of the players had gone out and spent part of the afternoon in a tavern, and they came into the squad meeting where they elect captains or something, and most of the guys knew well enough not to say anything, but one of the guys shot off his mouth. Woody called me up the next morning and said, 'I'm kicking him off the squad and I want you to print it.'

It was a legitimate story, and the purpose was obvious. He was going to tell those other guys, 'I knew about you guys, but you were smart enough not to shoot off your mouth and make an ass of yourself in front of the squad.' He wanted to send that message to the whole squad. I used the story because it was news. I talked to the kid and got his side. He was very contrite. He took his punishment. I wrote a couple of columns about him, and he was accepted back, and he played. That was the only time Woody ever actually called me up and asked me to write something.

A hundred times, he told me, 'If you print that, I'll deny it.' It was always something that was complimentary to him. I was in there one night, and he got a call from a town in another state about a boys-girls club fundraiser banquet. They wanted to pay him $1,000 to come up and make a speech. It was during spring practice, and he said, 'There's no way in the world I can come up during spring practice, but I'll tell you what I'll do, if you send an airplane down to pick me up after practice, I'll come up and speak at your banquet.' He said, 'I won't take any money. You shouldn't be paying anybody that kind of money. You should be saving that money for your club. Send a plane down to pick me up and bring me back, and I'll come up and make a speech.' I was sitting there, and he said, 'Now, if you print that, I'll deny it. Don't you dare print that.'

He felt that if anybody knew about it, other than the people involved, then he was doing it for publicity, and he didn't do it for publicity. He wanted it to be strictly as he did so many things: just between the people. Nobody ever knew. I've run into a lot of examples since I wrote the book (*Woody Hayes: A Reflection*). People have called me up and said, 'I just have to tell you what Woody did for me...'; or, 'I'll tell you what I know about what Woody did for somebody.' Some of the letters I got actually choked me up. I knew he did some of the things, but I didn't know all of what he did.

HE WAS IMPATIENT, more impatient with himself than he was with anyone else. He just couldn't stand for people to make mistakes. I used to go to all the practices, and if things had been going badly, afterward he'd go into his room, close his door. Maybe I'd hang around a little while, talk to the players, hang around the training room. If things were bad, he'd come out and go directly into the shower, so I'd just go on home. I knew he didn't want to talk.

When he was in a talkative mood, he used to enthrall people. Writers used to come in here from out of town, and when he was in a good mood, which he usually was, guys would tell us, 'You have the best thing in the world. Covering a guy like this is the best thing in the world.' But there were times when he was mad and said things that he didn't really mean, and I never quoted him on those things. He talked to me because he knew I wouldn't put everything he said in the paper. He'd get it out and then he would be all right.

I always wished his public outbursts hadn't happened, but I understood why they did. He was so intense, and he had put so much effort and time into those things, and he just couldn't accept it. It was part of Woody's makeup. He didn't do those things with malice aforethought. They just *happened.* He was so intense, and he was so involved, and he would want so much, and the officials would call something against him, and he couldn't stand it. He'd put all that work into it.

When he threw the yardmarkers up at Michigan, he knew what he was doing when he went out on the field. He said if they would've allowed Michigan to keep the interception, then the game was over. So the 15 yards didn't mean a thing. The game was over anyway. He claimed that the guy who was holding the yardmarkers had made a smart remark. Michigan claimed no such thing happened. He may have thought they did, or somebody else did. Throwing the markers onto the field was part of his protest of the whole thing. He just went way farther than he should have.

JACKSONVILLE WAS JUST TRAGIC. He said he wanted to retire in August of that year, and he said his coaches talked him out of it. Well, I can understand why. He would come in a lot of nights, and he would just sit there. He wouldn't even take off his shoes. He was beat. He'd been in it too long. He kept saying, just between us, when we'd be sitting in there, 'Coaching after 50 is really tough. You get farther away from the kids, and they look at you as more their father than their coach.' It was a combination of a lot of things. Then in the last game of the 1978 season, they got beat 14–3 by Michigan. In the second half, Michigan just ran them off the field.

Woody wasn't excited about going to the Gator Bowl, but he made up his mind that 'We're not going to end this season with that 14–3 loss by Michigan. We're going to salvage something out of this season.' He really worked hard on the game, and he worked the squad hard in Jacksonville. The conditions were awful down there. They worked out at a high school field. It was raining, it was muddy. It was a bad experience, even before the game.

So they start a drive in the fourth quarter, and it looked like they were going to pull it out. Then Charlie Bauman was in a place where he should've never been. He intercepted, and the game was over. Woody claimed at the time—insisted—that Bauman got up and waved the ball, an 'in your face' type of thing. It was just the cumulation of everything. He lost control. Writing about it was the hardest thing I ever had to do. I'd written about a lot of losses, but nothing like that, because I knew it was all over. I sat with him for more than a half an hour after everybody was gone. We didn't say a whole lot to each other. We talked some, mostly just sat there. He was still so frustrated and so mad. He was so frustrated that he was beside himself. He had a diabetic problem, and he was supposed to take medicine, and he'd get so wrapped up in things that he'd forget to take it, and I've been told his blood sugar was out of whack—wild—that night. He wasn't feeling well, and he was dead tired. He went over the edge.

My tape recorder ran through almost that whole 30 minutes, and I didn't even know it. I've only listened to it once. It was a guy just beside himself with frustration and disappointment. He also knew it was over. The only criticism I had of Ohio State was that I felt he deserved something better than they gave him. They hurriedly called a press conference, at 9 o'clock the next morning, and fired him. In the meantime, he had called me and told me he was retiring. So our noon edition came out with a retirement story, for which we were roundly criticized by some people. But it was an honest thing. In later editions, we ran both things: his calling me to say he had retired, and their announcement that he was being fired. I thought they could've waited until everybody came home and the dust settled, and then they could've been decent about it. They could've said 'We regret the incident but we understand it, and Coach Hayes has voluntarily retired. We thank him for his 28 years, and we apologize if he has offended anybody.' It could've been done humanely and with some class.

HE NEVER SAID ONE BAD THING about the university. He did what he could to encourage the kids he had recruited to still come to Ohio State. He praised the university every time he could. He continued to go to alumni meetings. You know, Earle called him up and invited him to come over and talk to the squad, and he went. He went over there and gave one of the most inspirational speeches you ever could hear to Earle's squad, when Earle thought that he needed help. That was when Woody showed what kind of a man he really was. I don't know how many people could've treated it like that. I would have been so bitter that I wouldn't've gone near the place.

In 43 years of being around those kids, I got to know them as people, not just as football players. That's why it would've gone against the grain for me, to have criticized. To really criticize those kids in the paper, I couldn't have done it, because I knew too much about who they were. When they made mistakes, they didn't do it because they wanted to, and I knew how bad they felt, because I've been in too many locker rooms. If that is a weakness, it was a weakness I was willing to risk. If I honestly felt that it I was hurting the paper, I might have changed. I wouldn't have liked it, but I could have changed. I never did, because nobody ever asked me to, and I never believed that I should.

One of the greatest things about covering Ohio State football is seeing the kids come in as freshmen and see them develop and mature. I always remember Paul Warfield. He had good grades in school, but he was so shy and withdrawn that you'd ask him a question, and he would look at the ground and bite his lower lip. He'd shake his head, or he might say, 'Uh-huh, yeah.' It was painful to try and interview him. A couple years later, Woody had him back for an Ohio State coaches clinic, and that guy stood up there—he was with the Miami Dolphins at the time—and he delivered a speech that a professor would have been proud to deliver. I had the privilege and the enjoyment of seeing this kid go from the shyest backward kid that you could imagine into a guy who stood up with perfect command of English.

It's been a great life, and I don't want to say it's over, because I keep trying to do things. I do the *Varsity O News*, which is an eight-page newsletter on Ohio State athletics. We come out four times a year. It doesn't seem like much, but it keeps me involved in all of the Ohio State sports. Occasionally, people ask me to do something about Ohio State football or about the Memorial Tournament or about Jack. I've written four books since I've retired. I still go to practice once in a while. I go to basketball games. I wouldn't trade what happened to me for anything in the world. I can't think of anything that I would prefer to have had at the time I had it. Nobody could've been so lucky. ”

Little Big Man

AT CANTON-Glenwood High School, Tim Fox earned 10 varsity letters. He scored five touchdowns in a single game and ran a 9.9 hundred meters. He averaged in double figures as a 5' 10" basketball center. He played on the tennis team and was a gymnast. He high-jumped 6' 3" and long-jumped 22' 11". None of those achievements convinced Fox that he was good enough to play major college football. "I had an inferiority complex," he says. "I always felt that I wasn't good enough to play the game." Though four inches shorter and 20 pounds lighter, Fox had himself listed in the basketball program as 6' 2", 195. The University of Pittsburgh called, but lost interest as soon as coaches saw how small Fox was. After a ruptured kidney and torn knee cartilage kept him out of his last three games and off all-star teams, Fox resigned himself to playing at a small school. Even his father, a high school coach, believed he should attend Bowling Green or Kent State. Certain that Ohio State wouldn't recruit him, Fox claimed not to be interested in the school, saying that he just didn't care to play for Woody Hayes. An alumnus hectored the Buckeye staff into looking at film of Fox's high school games, but Earle Bruce, an assistant at the time, decided Fox was too small to be a tailback in the Big Ten.

Only after Ohio State had lost a number of recruits to other schools was Fox grudgingly offered the last scholarship in what was thought a weak recruiting class. He still doubted his ability ("I knew I wanted to come, but I wasn't sure I could play at that level"), but Fox accepted, figuring that once he had it, the scholarship couldn't be taken away.

On picture day, he was one of two players wearing the same jersey number, and the freshman coach had no idea who Fox was. When he learned that Archie Griffin, Brian Baschnagel, and Woodrow Roach would compete for the tailback spot, Fox became a defensive back. Sent to the scout squad, he faced a choice: spend a season as a compliant blocking dummy or attack the varsity in hopes of getting a chance to play. 'Oh, what the hell? I'm gonna go crush 'em,' he thought. He'd been such an enthusiastic hitter in Pop Warner ball that he'd nearly been thrown out of the league, and Fox turned that aggressiveness on the starters. He disrupted scrimmages with big hits, one of which left both Fox and Morris Bradshaw, the starting tailback, unconscious. He earned a place on special teams. In his first game, he lined up on a punt return opposite a huge Minnesota tackle. The tackle nonchalantly came across the line and was flattened by Fox, who sprinted downfield and made a second block. "You just do what you do best, and what I did best was hit people," he says. By the third game of 1972, he was playing on passing downs; by the eighth game, Hayes was calling him one of the team's outstanding freshmen.

During preseason practice in 1973, secondary coach Dick Walker called Fox "a natural safetyman," but a week before the opener, Walker switched Fox to cornerback, though he doubted the little player was strong enough to fight off blockers. Still fretting ("I got to thinking what it would be like to go into a game expecting—and being expected—to win. I thought it would be a lot of pressure, and I didn't know if I could handle it"), Fox beat out Doug Plank, who had started in the Rose Bowl. Against Minnesota, he repeatedly caught swift halfback Rick Upchurch on sweeps, making 11 tackles and prompting defensive coordinator

George Hill to call him "a very important addition to our defense."

Soon, coaches were comparing Fox with consensus All-American and NFL All-Pro Jack Tatum. "He's as quick as any kid we've had there," said Walker. "He has the same type of quickness of Jack Tatum. He's as fast as anyone we've got, he's got great hands and he's got great ball sense."

Fox combined with Neal Colzie to give OSU a pair of speedy, opportunistic cornerbacks and punt returners. He blocked a punt and returned it for a touchdown against Northwestern in 1973, a game in which he earned 5 1/2 buckeye leaves. He and Randy Gradishar led the team in tackles in the 1974 Rose Bowl, although Fox played only three quarters, and he blocked another punt in the 1975 Rose Bowl.

Against Wisconsin in 1975, Fox executed for the first time what would become his trademark act. He returned a punt 73 yards for a touchdown, waved off teammates who were gathering to congratulate him and did an extraordinary no-hands backward flip in the endzone—an exclamation point that emphasized how far he had come in four years. Fox expected the stunt to irk Hayes, but the coach seemed as amazed as everyone else at the athletic ability the feat required.

He was a team captain, an All-Big Ten pick and an All-American and had kept Plank, a fierce hitter who became a rookie starter for the Chicago Bears, on the bench. Yet Fox still seemed uncertain. When an NFL scout came to time him, he crept up several steps while the man's back was turned and was credited with a 4.39 40-yard dash.

While the country waited to learn which NFL team would select Griffin, Fox became the first of 11 Bucks to be drafted in 1976. In New England, he joined a moribund team that had won three games the previous year. With Fox and fellow number one pick Mike Haynes shoring up the worst secondary in the league, New England led the NFL in takeaways, finished 11-3, and made the playoffs for the first time.

Fox became a solid professional (he made All-Pro in 1982 with San Diego), but he was forced to spend extra time in the weight room, which he despised, and to play with numerous injuries. "I applied the same work ethic I had in college," he says. That ethic left him little time to prepare for a career after football. He took some law courses, trying to keep a promise to Hayes, but most of Fox's off-season was dedicated to preparing for the next training camp.

Remarkably for a defensive back of his size, he lasted a dozen seasons—almost four times longer than the average career of an NFL player. He went to the NFL championship game with the Rams in 1985, but a year later asked to be released when coaches told him he would no longer start. As if incapable of giving up what he had worked so hard for, he caught on with Cleveland, as a free agent, after coach Marty Schottenheimer convinced Fox that he could still play. "It got to be an ego thing," Fox admits. Finally, an injury forced him out of football. "At 22, I could play with broken ribs," he says. "At 35, I just couldn't do it."

He'd graduated college with a dual major—communications and psychology—but Fox was at loose ends. Searching for a new career, he resorted to a head-hunting firm that put him together with a financial publishing corporation. In the sales and service ends of the business, he works an average of 80 hours a week, as well as doing radio and television broadcasts for the Patriots and spending time with charities.

Fox lives in a large, prosperous, wooded subdivision not far, coincidentally, from Canton, Massachusetts. His deck overlooks Foxboro Stadium. A Mercedes coupe sat in the driveway of the split-level home.

At Ohio State, Fox was darkly handsome, as if part Indian, with long, black, wavy hair and a cobweb of a mustache (for which Hayes chided him), and he retains a strong jawline and high cheekbones. He looks like anything but an NFL defensive back, however. Face lined, shoulders narrow, hint of paunch beneath jogging pants and tee-shirt, he looks like an itinerant tennis pro or a enterprising lawyer about to make full partner.

Fox gulped orange juice and popped vitamin C to combat a severe flu. He was haggard, but a core of toughness and intensity were evident beneath Fox's wan countenance. As he speaks about his career, he sounds bemused, almost incredulous that so much could have happened in what seems so short a time.

Well-off and recognized in the community ("I'm on a quasi-celebrity list for people who want to have people come to events"), Fox says that it was Hayes who finally cured him of self-doubt. "He was a great confidence builder," Fox says. "If anyone got rid of my inferiority complex, it was Woody. He taught that if you work hard enough, you'll be successful. It doesn't really make a difference what you do."

Tim FOX

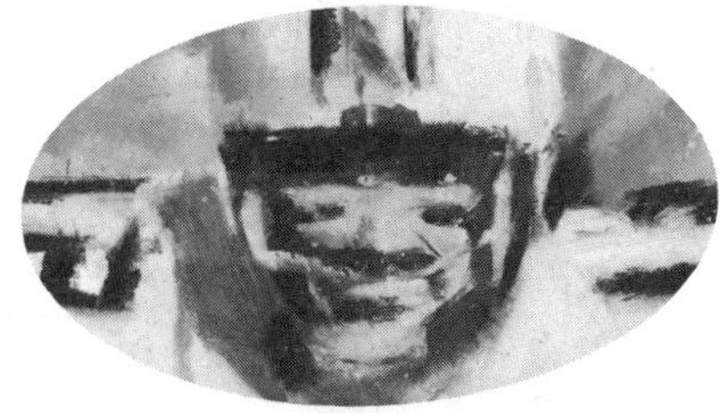

"I WAS RAISED IN CANTON, Ohio, which is probably *the* hotbed of high school football in the country. In Canton, if you're physically fit, and can walk and chew gum at the same time, and you don't play football, everyone looks at you funny: If you didn't at least try to play football and get cut or sit the bench, people would say, 'What's wrong with that kid?' There was a *serious* emphasis put on football.

Canton had a smalltown mentality, but it wasn't that small. There were a couple hundred thousand people there, but everything revolved around high school athletics. If you opened up the *Canton Repository*, you opened it to the sports pages, and high school sports were always on the first sports page. Always. Ohio State and collegiate athletics got the second page, and the NFL and the pros got the back page. Around here, everybody reads the *Boston Globe*, and it's exactly the opposite.

When I was 12, I played at a different intensity level than a lot of the kids. I wasn't a big kid, but there was talk around the midget league of having me thrown out because I was hitting people a little bit harder than the other kids, even though it was well within the rules. We went undefeated and played some other team for the championship. I ended breaking my arm in that game. I went to give a guy a stiff-arm, and he knocked my legs out from under me. I had a compound fracture, but I had it set, and I've been playing ever since.

I don't know what I attribute that intensity to, to be honest with you. It's just that my whole career, I was always trying to keep up with the bigger guys. My philosophy was you had to go 100 percent, or 120 percent, every time you try to hit someone. I always did that. I did it in midget league. I did it when I was in college. I did it when I was in the pros. It was just the way you did it. I liked the contact. It's one of the few legal forms of taking your frustrations out on other people.

When I was in high school, I was always being asked where I wanted to go to college. When you grew up in Ohio, the way it was then and I think the way it should be now, is that your goal would be to go to Ohio State. I didn't think I was good enough to go to Ohio State, so when people asked me where I wanted to go to college, I'd name off some schools. They'd say, 'Well, what about Ohio State?'

I'd say, 'Oh, I don't want to go to Ohio State as long as Woody's there.' It just seemed like an easy out.

People would say, 'Oh, yeah, I know what you mean.'

That was back in the very early '70s, after he had some of his fiascos—breaking the yardsticks at the Michigan game and those things. He'd had his fair share of indiscretions and temper tantrums, and when I told people that, it was always, 'Yeah, that makes sense.'

In reality, it was because I didn't think they wanted me. I was probably 5' 11", 175 pounds, and I didn't have that great a high school career, either. My girlfriend at the time, who is my wife now, was working at a little breakfast place in Canton, called Juicy's. There was a businessman who worked across the street, guy by the name of Harry Myers, an Ohio State alum. He used to come in and have breakfast, and my wife would wait on him every morning. They'd shoot the breeze, and at one point, he asked Deb if she was dating anyone, and my name came up. He asked what colleges I was thinking about going to, and she told him. She was a year older than me; she was already going to Ohio State. She had mentioned to Harry, 'Boy, it would be nice if he could go to Ohio State.'

Harry said, 'Why don't we see if we can get him in one of the Mid-American schools.'

She said, 'You should really come and see him play.'

So Harry got a chance to see me play a couple games my senior year. He saw me play basketball. Well, he was a friend of Woody's, and at one point, he approached Woody with the idea of me going to Ohio State. He said, 'There's a kid up here in Canton who had some problems his senior year, so not a lot of teams are looking at him. But he's a real competitor, and I think maybe you should take a look at him.'

We sent him some films down from my junior and senior years, and when you're able to take films out and show them specific things, I think it made me look a little better than I really was. They looked at the films, and I don't know what finally got them off the dime, but towards the end of basketball season, they finally sent Earle Bruce up. Earle wasn't that interested. He said, 'Oh, well, you're a little small.' They never said yea or nay or anything else. There was a lull for a while because Earle left, and then George Hill came on as defensive coordinator, and he was in charge of that part of the country. By that time, I think they'd realized that they were going to have a real small freshman class.

At one point, we saw a list of priorities for scholarships, and of 13, I was 13th. I think they ended up coming after me because they knew they had a weak recruiting class. They had lost a lot of players they really wanted to get, and Harry caught their attention, and they finally agreed to say, 'Yeah, okay, we'll take you.'

WHEN I WAS IN SCHOOL, WOODY used to say all the time that he had personally visited with every player's parents who ever played for him. That's a little bit of a stretch, because he never came to my house. I was kind of a last-minute decision. George Hill had been there, but not Woody. He had never even been to the school to visit me.

They invited me to a visit at Ohio State, and that's the first time I met him. We went to a game, and, obviously, I was impressed by the Horseshoe, and I think they won that game. They had my parents come down to a game. They invited them to a brunch out at the golf course, which was really nice. That was the first time that Woody realized my father was a coach. He really liked coaches' kids. My parents were going through the buffet line, and my mother was trying to carry her purse, so Woody came up behind her and grabbed her purse and said, 'Here, let me carry your purse for you.' She thought that was the greatest thing in the world, that Woody had carried her purse through the buffet line.

I was a little unsure whether or not I wanted to come. I knew I wanted to come, but I wasn't sure that I could play at that level. My father was unsure, as well. I think my father's choice would've been for me to go to Kent. He said, 'Do you want to be a big fish in the little pond or the little fish in the big pond?'

I finally got to the point where I said, 'Hey, it's a legitimate opportunity. They want to give me the scholarship, and they can't take it away from me once I get down there. If I don't play, I don't play.'

I wound up being a big fish in a big pond. It can happen, I guess.

Before I met Woody, I thought he was a maniac. My only exposure to him was what I read. I found out that his only concern was winning football games and what his players thought about him. He could care less what anyone else thought of him. A lot of people say that, but I honestly believe that he's the only person I've ever known who actually meant it.

I was absolutely nervous about going to play for him. I didn't know what to expect. I'd heard all kinds of things, and they were coming off of a horrible year. I don't know what their record was, but I think they were around .500 that year. I was very much concerned about playing for him, but it was just one of those things where you said, 'That's it, I'm going. That's where I want to go.' I put my game face on and went down to play at Ohio State.

THE FIRST DAY OF PRACTICE was picture day. Finally, they get around to the freshmen. They said, 'Let's have all the freshman offensive backs.' I didn't even know what they had recruited me to play. No one had really talked about it. John Mummey was supposed to be the freshman coach if we had a freshman team that year, so I went up to Mummey and said, 'Coach, they're asking for offensive backs and defensive backs. I played both ways in high school. Where do you want me to go?'

He looked at me and said, 'Ahh, what's your name, son?'

I said, 'Tim Fox.'

He said, 'You say you played both in high school? Just go wherever you want.'

So they already had the offensive backs over there. We ran an I-formation, and there's really only one position for a guy my size. There were probably five freshmen who looked to be tailback size, all vying for the same position. One of them was Archie, one of them was Woody Roach, another one was Brian Baschnagel. These were guys I knew about before I even got there because they had set all these records in the state.

I said, 'Man, I don't have a chance to beat those guys out.'

Then they called for the defensive backs. There were four positions, and the only guy who went over there was Craig Cassady. I'm thinking, 'One guy going for four, or five guys going for one?' That's how I became a DB; I was a defensive back from that point forward.

I started out on the scout team. All you did was take plays against the offense. There were some freshmen there, but there were also some guys who were kind of disenfranchised with the game because they knew they weren't going to get the chance to play. They're over there going through the motions, because they didn't want to get Woody pissed off by screwing up the offense. The more pissed off you got him, the longer you'd be out there.

THAT WAS WITH THE EXCEPTION OF ED TREPANIER. Ed was a defensive tackle, a tremendously strong guy. I'll tell you what Ed's mentality was: He had a tattoo of an army tank on his arm. He'd flex, and it looked like the tank was shooting a bullet. He was either a sophomore or a junior. He had something like the national record in the bench press, but he had terrible knees. He couldn't run. He couldn't get to the perimeter, but if you ran at him, he could stuff a double-team all day long. He'd just push them off and make the play. Woody loved to run that half-line scrimmage, where you have just those three guys on the offensive line to one side. He'd put Ed in there at tackle and have the tight end double down on him with the offensive tackle. Ed would stuff it every time. You could run around him all night, you could trap him all night, you could sweep him, but you couldn't run at him, and that was Woody's favorite play. He expected to be able to run that play in half-line.

I remember lining up as a freshman over there, and after the first couple of days, Ed got a little cocky, and he started with the mouth. Ed was probably pumped up with steroids at the time, because no one thought anything was wrong with steroids back then, and he had this real high voice. He'd taunt Woody from the other side of the line: 'Woody! Woody! You can't run over here, Woody!'

Woody would start getting mad. He'd pull his hat and everything. He'd go back and call the play, Ed would stuff it:

'Hey, Woody! Hey, Woody! You old cocksucker, you can't run over here.'

He'd call Woody every name in the book. You see, Woody was such a competitor he didn't care what you called him. The only thing he wanted to do was run that play at Ed. Ed could say anything. What concerned Woody was that he was making the play.

This went on for a couple of weeks. Woody ripped his hat, ripped his jacket, his shirt. Ed finally got under Woody's skin, and Woody came up and confronted him. Woody is like a midget compared to Ed, and he came up and shivered Ed right in the facemask. He just couldn't take it anymore. He shoved Ed up underneath the facemask and started to say something and Ed just went *boom!* He shivered Woody right in the chest. Woody did a couple of back somersaults and ended up with his legs spread around one of those water bottles with all the hoses coming out of it. Ed just turned around and walked off the field.

We're thinking, 'Ohhh, man.'

Woody was pissed. He had the wind knocked out of him. He's on the ground. He gets up, straightens out his hat. He looks around. Ed's walking off the field.

We figure, 'That's it. Ed's history.'

The next day, we come to practice, and Ed's back. He gets dressed like nothing happened, goes out like nothing happened, goes through warm-ups like nothing happened. First thing, half-line. Ed lines up, off-tackle. Ed stuffs the play.

'Hey, Woody! Hey, Woody! You can't run over here!'

It went on for the rest of the year. Woody never said a word to him. He never played him another down, but Woody didn't say a word. And Ed stuffed him every time he ran at him.

THE THING WAS, ON SCOUT TEAM, a lot of guys were just going through the motions. I figured if Ed could do that, I could go ahead and play, try to get their attention. Woody'd have a monster back down there, so the guys could cut 'em and pull and do all that stuff. I played hard. I came up and tackled guys on varsity. I'd disrupt their whole practice. I thought Woody hated me for it, but I did it anyway. I just thought, 'Hey, I'm not playing anyway. I'm gonna knock people out.'

The defensive coaches got mad. They said, 'Hey, Woody's gonna be pissed. C'mon, just go through the motions. Do what they want you to do.'

I thought, 'Oh, what the hell, I'm gonna go crush 'em.'

The varsity backs were pissed off, too. That's how I really got into some trouble. Morris Bradshaw was the starting tailback that year. He came around the corner, and he and I hit helmets and knocked each other out. Then I was really getting some shit, because he was the starting guy. They wanted me to back off, but that caught Woody's attention. The next thing you know, I got moved off the scout team. I'm third team, second team, and then somebody got hurt. It's the third game of the season, and he throws me on the field.

It was against Minnesota. All I knew was when they hand off the ball, I run and make the tackle. You just do what you do best, and what I did best was hit people. I was scared to death. That was the year Rick Upchurch was a sophomore. He was supposed to be the all-around great player. I played most of the game at free safety, and my job was to tackle Upchurch, whether he had the ball or didn't have the ball. In their option scheme, the free safety was unaccounted for. The idea was to let the quarterback run the ball, but if they still pitched to Upchurch, I had to go make the play, from one side of the field to the other. I had a good game. They could've passed on me all day long, but they chose not to. I wouldn't've known what to do with the pass. I was just running to the ball. It was a perfect setup for me. All I had to do was beat Upchurch to the perimeter, and I was able to do it. I'd get him on the cutback, and Woody thought it was great. From that day forward, he had me playing.

I WASN'T REALLY SURPRISED BY ANYTHING at Ohio State. I expected to be in over my head, particularly as a freshman. The skill level of the players was just about what I expected. The exception is the first time I played in a varsity game. I was in on a kickoff. I'm running along, you know, and I expected it to be the same level as high school athletics. I'm running down there, and the next thing you know, I got hit harder than I'd ever been hit in my life, and I never even saw it coming. I never had anything ever happen to me like that in high school. Man, *that* woke me up. I said, 'This game is moving at a different pace than anything I've ever been used to.'

It only took one hit, and my head was on a swivel and my eyes were open from that point forward. I was surprised by the level of intensity. I'd never been hit like that before.

I was very surprised by the amount of time we spent in meetings, the amount of time we spent with Woody, and the time spent talking about things other than football. He'd go on and on and on about all these different things having absolutely nothing to do with football. As a freshman being away from home for the first time and trying to manage an academic schedule, trying to manage a social life, trying to manage the time that you need to put in to play that type of football, I don't think you could have a better coach. He got you centered and concentrated on what you needed to do. When all is said and done about Woody, I don't know that Woody was that great a coach. He knew what his teams could do well, and he would to it over and over and over again. He was not an imaginative coach who would bring a lot of new things to the game, but his greatest asset was the fact that he was an incredible motivator. He had very high expectations of his players. It was very difficult to meet his expectations, but when you did—and it wasn't very often—he'd tell you. He would have his teams ready to play, and a lot of that didn't have anything to do with football. It had to do with character-building.

Geez, he'd talk about the Vietnam War, the gas shortage, student unrest, Richard Nixon, Watergate. One of the worst days of Woody's life, if I remember correctly, was the day Spiro Agnew resigned. I mean, that just killed him. He just had a horrible day that day. Woody was the original Rush Limbaugh. There were no ifs, ands, or buts; he was right-wing for God and country. He was proud to be an American, and he instilled that in his players. We were always afraid that if Woody ever snapped, we weren't concerned about him hitting a player or something like that; we were afraid he might go up to the top of the university tower with a gun or something and start shooting at Japanese students. He had a real dislike for the Japanese that carried over from World War II. He was still fighting that war.

He used to get pissed when guys would drive Japanese cars. Well, first, he'd get pissed when we drove our cars over to the north facilities: 'Goddammit, you're wasting gas. People, there's a gas shortage out there. There's no reason for you to be driving. Take a bus. Walk over. You don't need to be driving over here.' But time was precious; everybody drove over. Then, if you drove over in a foreign car, it was like, 'Goddammit, what do you have to drive that foreign car for? Jesus Christ!'

At one point, Toyota or Datsun or one of those Japanese car manufacturers had a promotion going where if you test-drove a car, they would plant a tree in a national forest. That just drove him up a wall. I mean, he just went on for an entire meeting: 'And now, those goddamned Japanese, it's not bad enough they're taking all of our fuckin' money, they're coming in, they're running over the goddamned country. Now if you drive one of their goddamned cars, they'll plant a goddamned tree in a goddamned national forest! What's that all about?!'

It was almost surreal, because you almost couldn't believe that what he was saying was real, that *he* even believed it. But he did. As a freshman, this was all new to you. You'd sit back there, eyes wide, ears wide. You'd hear these things, and you'd just be amazed. 'What were the seven aircraft carriers in the Pacific during World War II?' Well, geez, you better know 'em. I don't know *why* you should know 'em, but you better. I don't know them now, and I'm almost embarrassed.

HE HAD THIS ONE SAYING that he had said for years and years and years. He said it when I was a freshman, and he said it again when I was a sophomore. It had something to do with the Battle of the Bulge because he always likened football games to war. I can't remember exactly what it was, but it had something to do with the Germans coming around behind the lines in the Battle of the Bulge, sealing off the Allies and putting together an ambush. I think it had something to do with the Maginot line or something, I don't know. I'm almost embarrassed that I don't remember exactly, but he would tell the story, and every time he would tell the story, he'd say, 'We're not gonna let those Heinie bastards sneak up behind us and hit us over the back of the head with a sock of sheeiitt!'

As a freshman and a sophomore class, we knew what that thing meant. We knew why he was saying that. But then, when we were juniors and seniors, he never told the story again, just the punchline. We'd be playing Minnesota or something, a team that we were favored against that he was afraid we were going to take lightly, and all of a sudden, he'd get up there, and he'd be hammering the table, and he'd say, 'We're not gonna let those Heinie bastards sneak up behind us and hit us over the back of the head with a sock of sheeiitt!'

We all knew what he meant, but the freshmen and sophomores are going, 'What the hell did *that* mean?' They didn't have a clue.

I don't know how many years he went on with that line, but when we were seniors, he was saying it. We kind of passed it down: 'Well, it has something to do with the Battle of the Bulge and the war, and the guys got around behind them.' But I'm sure that it got to the point, after so many years of saying that, that the guys never knew what it meant. It became an unknown; nobody knew the origin of that line.

Those were some interesting meetings. We heard about values, we heard about the war, we heard about dating women. He had some theories on *that* you couldn't put into a book. He'd go off on tangents. That was just at the beginning of when the pill became prominent on campus. He'd say, 'Hey, some girl tells you she's on the pill, goddammit, don't believe her. She's a goddamned liar. Don't believe her! Don't believe her! You better know what they make in Akron!' He'd go on and on and on. Every year, we'd get the sex education lecture: 'Can't trust 'em, can't trust 'em.'

Then we'd get to talk about the alumni. He'd always say, 'I don't really want you to do this, but you know what, you guys think you're pretty good winning all these games. You've got the alumni coming up to you and telling you how great you are. When you get that old lady coming up to you about the age of your grandmother, and she tells you how great you are, you know what you really should do? You should kick her right in the goddamned shins and tell her she's making you soft, goddammit. She's making you soft, because you're not that goddamned good!' Yeah, kick old ladies in the shins.

When we had the Arab oil embargo, that drove him nuts, the fact that the Arabs could bring a country like ours to its knees over the cost of oil. From that point forward, he walked to work every day; he wouldn't drive: 'Goddammit, I'm not going to use any goddamn A-rab oil! They're not getting a dime out of me. Goddammit, you guys should walk over to the facility. If I can walk, you can walk.'

We'd be on buses. That's when they dropped the speed limit back down to 55. Woody would be sitting up in the front of the bus. As soon as the bus driver got up over 55: 'Goddammit, you're going too goddamn fast! There's no goddamn reason to be going over 55 miles an hour. You're wasting gas. You're helping the goddamned A-rabs wasting gas. We've got plenty of time. There's no reason to be going over the speed limit!'

The worst thing that could ever happen to you was you would be driving your car down the outer belt around Columbus and to have Woody pull up next to you when you were going too fast. He'd be gesturing at you: 'Slow it down! Slow it down!'

There was right and there was wrong and there was no gray area. But that wasn't hard to deal with, because as much as he lectured and as much as he tried to instill those values in us, once you were off the football field, he did not try to control your lives. He was a firm believer in that he did not want the athletes to be living in their own dorm. He wanted them to be living in the student population. He didn't want there to be like an Animal House. He wanted the athletes to be student-athletes, and wanted them to mix with other students.

I grew up with my father as a coach, and I had to wear short hair all my life. Any time I wanted to grow my hair long, my dad would be all over me: 'You don't look like an All-American, son. You don't look like an All-American.' When I got in college, Woody hated long hair, he hated mustaches, he hated beards, but he wouldn't tell you you couldn't do it. He would just harp on you, harp on you, with the idea that eventually you wouldn't do it. That never worked on me. I had a big old Afro and a mustache that looked like a basketball game, with five hairs on each side. It was horrible. I remember him pulling me off into the hallway one time. He said, 'Your hair looks like hell. The hair's bad enough, but why in the world do you have to have that mustache?

I said, 'I don't know, Coach.

'I just can't imagine why anyone would want to cultivate something around their mouth that grows naturally around their asshole.'

But he never told me to cut it.

In my junior or senior year, platform shoes came in. They used to drive him crazy. He came in at bed-check. I had this pair of black ones that had *this* much heel and *that* much of a sole. He just went, 'Goddammit, if you fall off of those things and twist your ankle, I'm gonna be up your ass like a hemorrhoid! There'll be no excuse for you falling off those shoes.'

'Don't worry, Coach. I'll be all right.'

'I'm just telling you. I'm telling you if you fall off those shoes, your ass is grass.'

But he'd never tell you you couldn't do it.

HE WAS FUNNY, BUT YOU ALWAYS FEARED HIM. He was a master psychologist when he came to using his anger as motivation. You didn't want to get him mad. You can't get away with it now—you can't get away with a lot of things you used to get away with—but he used to hit guys on the field. People think that's ridiculous and shouldn't happen, but when you stop and think about it: All right, you have a bunch of kids 18 to 21 years of age in full pads and a guy who's 63 years old in no pads coming out and hitting you on the pads. It gets your attention. I never had a problem with that, but you still didn't want to get hit.

Once, Doug Plank was playing the strong safety position, I was playing the free safety position, and it was Neal Colzie and Steve Luke playing the corners. Teams used to have this play called the counter-option, down-the-line throwback. The quarterback would take the ball. He would start to the strong side of the formation. The fullback would dive. The quarterback starting that way would draw the strong safety up to force. The free safety would go to the post. But as soon as he faked to the fullback, the quarterback would turn and go back down the line the other way. He'd have the tailback behind him, and he'd either pitch it or he'd drop back to pass. Well, as soon as the quarterback went down the line and dropped back, the free safety and the strong safety had to switch responsibilities. Well, you could run that play 100 times in practice, and you could get Doug Plank with it 98 times. Doug was a very physical player and went on to have a great career with the Bears. Doug loved to hit, and when he saw the ball coming his way, he would come. You were supposed to take reminder steps, little back-up steps, in case the quarterback decided to go back the other way, so you could get to the post. Well, while Doug's coming up, the wingback's shooting back to the post. It's there every time.

THEY BEAT US ABOUT THREE TIMES IN A ROW during spring practice. Woody storms out. He decides he's going to attack every player in the defensive secondary. He's going to hit every one of us. He comes out, and everybody kind of gathers around, and I'm right behind him. He goes up to Doug, and he shivers Doug right in the facemask. He gets Neal; he says, 'You should be telling him! You should be talking to him! It's your responsibility to play as a team!'

He's spinning around in circles, and I'm staying right behind him. I'm right behind him the whole time. He gets Doug, he gets Neal, he gets Steve. He knows he has one more guy to go, but he's so worked up he isn't sure which group he had in there anyway. He wasn't sure who was playing free safety. I knew if he saw me, he'd know he should've hit me, but I stayed right behind him the whole time. He spun around about three times, then he just gave up. He pulled Doug out, put somebody else in, and we just went ahead and practiced. So, yeah, you were afraid of him. You didn't want to draw his wrath. You didn't want to be the object of his affection, at least in that regard.

I think a lot of his outbursts were calculated. He knew exactly what he was doing. I think it was during summer camp before my sophomore or junior year, some writer from *Sports Illustrated* or someplace talked Woody into letting him do a story about the program. And he didn't like to talk to the press; he didn't even want us talking to the press. He didn't trust them, but this guy convinced Woody that the story was going to be all positive, just the positive things about the program. Woody agreed, but when the article came out, it was completely negative. The guy hadn't done his homework. He hadn't checked all of his sources. He didn't look beneath the surface. He just went with all the sensational stuff he had heard.

Woody was just devastated by that. It broke his heart. The day the article came out, we were in the dining hall, on the bottom floor. Woody called a meeting for the dining hall on the top floor, and he was getting everything set up there. He was up by the podium, and he told one of the managers to bring him one of those trays of glasses. He said it very calmly, very matter-of-factly, 'Oh, and bring one of those trays of glasses over here and put it on the table. Yeah, that's it, one of those trays full of glasses. Just bring it right over here and put it down.'

He started the meeting, and he read from this article to us, and he came to some part he didn't like. He reached over, grabbed one of those glasses, and smashed it against the wall. He went through the whole article like that. Every time he came to something that made him mad, he threw another glass against the wall. The whole article, and it was *long*. Eighteen glasses later, he was finished.

It was all calculated to get to us, just like cutting the strings on his hat or cutting the seams on his shirt. He'd get mad and grab his hat and tear it to pieces, and we'd wonder how this old guy could be so strong. Well, he took a razor blade and cut the seams first so he could rip it apart. Or he'd take an old pair of glasses or an old watch and throw it down and stomp on it. He was a master at that kind of thing. He knew just what he was doing.

WOODY WAS VERY, VERY SERIOUS about academics. He would see everybody's grades. Obviously, if you were threatening to be ineligible for some particular reason, he'd be all over you. But even if you were a good student and you were having trouble—if you were an A/B student and all of a sudden he sees you got a C—he'd call you in: 'All right, what's the problem?'

'Oh, I just had a bad test.'

'You need any help?'

'No, no.'

They made tutors available, but if you said no, if you chose not to take a tutor, and your grades didn't come up, he would tutor you. He would call you in, and you would have to sit in his office. He'd sit at his desk, and you'd sit across from him: 'All right, goddammit, where are we here? What chapter are we on?'

He'd take the book, and he'd read it. You'd sit there and listen, and he wasn't that great a reader anyway. You'd have to sit there and listen to him read. The idea there was to avoid that, because your time could be better spent doing it on your own. You didn't want to have Woody read to you.

What was an interesting thing to me was that it didn't make any difference whether you were becoming ineligible or whether you just were not performing up to your ability. His concern was that you get a good education. He always said, 'When you come here, we make a deal. You come here and play football for me, and in exchange for that, I give you an education. If I don't give you that education, then I haven't lived up to my end of the bargain.' I think he truly believed that.

I HAD NEVER HAD ANY ASPIRATIONS whatsoever of playing professional football until I was a senior, never even dreamed I would play. The guys I played with as a junior were Doug Plank, Steve Luke, and Neal Colzie. They were all pretty good, but none of them were superstars, at least in my eyes. I thought I was an equivalent player to those guys. I was the only guy coming back my senior year, and all of a sudden, halfway through our season, all three of those guys are starting in the NFL. Doug Plank, I think, was 12th-round but ended up starting as a rookie. For the first time in my life, I said, 'Damn, maybe I'm going to play professional football.' I had never even thought of it. I didn't know what I was going to do, but I told Woody I was thinking about going to law school.

From that point forward, he harassed me about it. I made the mistake at one point of saying, 'Well, Coach, I'll tell you, I would never have thought this before, but, you know, I'm looking at the guys I played with last year, and they're all playing professional football. I'm looking at going and playing professional football.'

'Goddammit! You don't want to be playing that goddamn game. That goddamn game will ruin you. Go to law school!'

He wanted Brian Baschnagel to be a Rhodes Scholar. He got it in his mind, and that's the way it was going to be. I remember I went back at one point after I was done playing, and he asked me if I was in law school.

I said, 'No, I'm not.'

One hundred and eighty degrees; he turned the other way and wouldn't speak to me. End of conversation; that was it. He was pissed I wasn't going to law school. It got to the point where I was up here playing, I was established, I started going to law school part-time. It was after I had graduated. He had been in the hospital for something, some surgery where they left the sponge in him. I think I was in a contract dispute at the time, between playing in New England and San Diego. I went to visit him in the hospital on a Sunday, and as soon as I walked in, he turned the football game off. It was Sunday, so he had to be watching a professional football game. It was a preseason game. I said, 'Oh, Coach, you watching an NFL game here?'

'No, no, no, no. It was just on. I wasn't watching it. Are you in law school?'

I said, 'Yeah, Coach.'

'Great, great. Sit down.'

I DON'T THINK HE REALLY HAD ANYTHING against professional football. What he didn't like was that guys would come to Ohio State with the aspiration of playing professional football and then not get an education. That was just the way his mind worked. If he endorsed professional football, then he couldn't encourage people to graduate.

I'm sure he was disappointed to see guys go in and out of professional ball as quickly as they were. I know when Pete Johnson came into Ohio State, you asked Pete what he wanted to do, he said, 'I want to play professional football.' That drove Woody nuts, to the point where he had a graduate assistant whose sole duty, other than standing on the field and taking notes and stuff, was get Pete and walk him to every class. He didn't take tests for him or anything, but that was just Woody's way of making sure that Pete got to class. There were people on campus who said it was wrong for some kid to have somebody to take him to every class, but Woody did everything he could do to make sure that he went to class and that he got an education.

We had a tiny, tiny class. I don't think there was ever that small a class—13 scholarships. When you look at the teams we were competing with at that time—Oklahoma, Nebraska, Notre Dame, Alabama—they're giving 40, 50 scholarships a year. At the end of four years, they'll have 200 guys on scholarship. We gave 13 to my class. The fact that we were able to compete was a real tribute to Woody.

Unfortunately, when I look back on our career, I don't remember a high point, but a low point, and that's losing the national championship in the Rose Bowl in '76, when we lost to UCLA, a team that we had already demolished in the regular season on their home field. When I look back on my college career, that kind of overshadows everything. We were in position to have the storybook ending to a four-year career. We were number one all year, and the fact that we went out and blew that chance really bugs me.

We didn't play real well, I can tell you that. Corny Greene didn't play too well, I didn't play too well, and I don't think the coaches coached too well. We never lost a game at home; we never lost to Michigan. When we went out there for the fourth time in a row, we had seen it and done it three times beforehand. In the past, where it had always been mandatory to do this and that, all of a sudden, it was *not* mandatory. The bedchecks were relaxed. One time he came around and said, 'Well, guys, it seems like when I come around and check, I'm waking you up. I don't want to do that. So, if you're going to bed early, I'm going to leave a board outside my room. Just sign your name, and I won't come in and wake you up.'

OH, GEEZ, YOU CAN'T TELL a bunch of kids from Ohio who are out visiting California that they can sign a board and not be held accountable for their time. That wasn't real good. For years and years and years, you stayed at a monastery the night before the Rose Bowl. He'd take you up in the hills someplace to some kind of monastery. He'd bring in a movie—a very physical movie with a lot of killing; Charles Bronson movies were always great for that. That was before video tape. Now, it's a simple thing, but back then, it was a big deal to try to get a feature-length motion picture in for your own use. You'd have your movie, and they'd bring the hot chocolate and apples and cookies around. They'd put you in a room up in the hills, and all that was in that room was a bed, a desk with a Bible on it and a crucifix on the wall. A lot of these guys from Ohio, the inner-city kids, they'd put them in this monastery, and as soon as they'd lay down, they'd start to hear the coyotes out in the hills. Those coyotes would be yipping and howling. The brothers were scared to death. They thought they were in a middle of a horror movie or something. We always did that, but for some reason, that year, we didn't do it. He let us stay right in the hotel.

Just little things in preparation going up to the game led to us taking the team a little bit lighter than we should've. All the way down to the game plan. We just trashed them the first time we played them, and when we looked back at that game, the only play they hurt us with the whole game was a pop pass to the tight end. They hit it like four times. But rather than prepare the way we prepared for the first game—prepare against their strengths, the things they had done up to the point—we prepared for that play. They didn't hit the pop pass on us, but they hit all the things they had done all year long. It was just one of those games where, geez, we just couldn't get things going. It was absolutely heart-breaking. Woody set off across the field with about 30 seconds left in the game, while the clock was still ticking. I mean, there was time for another play, but he went across the field to shake Dick Vermeil's hand. We got Vermeil his job with the Eagles, because that game catapulted him to the NFL. Woody took it hard.

FOR ME, IT WAS A LITTLE BIT MASKED, because I left from the game to go straight to the Hula Bowl, then left straight from the Hula Bowl to go straight to the Japan Bowl, then came from the Japan Bowl to Hawaii for another five days, then went back to Columbus. I was away from it all, having a good time. I missed half of that winter quarter. I had other things going, but that's the one thing I look back on now and say, 'That would've been the perfect ending to four years. We had it in our hands, and we should've done it, but we just didn't do it.'

I don't think guys were taking advantage of him, no more than any college kid would of anyone else in that situation. It's just that there was just such stark contrast between when we started as freshmen and when we finished as seniors. He had evolved a long way. Of course, he had the heart attack in there. I think the heart attack changed him, and he was on medication, too, and that medication can really affect your personality. You take somebody who's already tempestuous, and the medicine can exaggerate that. Depending upon what medication he was on, we could see his personality go up and down.

People ask me a lot about his last play, when he hit the kid on the sidelines, and I remember watching that game on TV. I could've said it was going to happen, given the scenario where he was playing in a bowl game that was not the Rose Bowl. He was a firm believer in that there should only be one bowl—you should only be in the Rose Bowl; if you didn't win the Big Ten championship, you shouldn't go to a bowl. Other bowls lessened the value of the Rose Bowl. He's playing in a bowl he didn't want to play in, that he didn't think his team deserved to play in, and they weren't playing very well. Towards the end of the game, they come back. They had a chance to win the game, a game they should've won easily. How does he lose? He loses on a *pass*. He hates the pass anyway. His famous saying was that three things happen on a pass, and two of them are bad.

The guy comes over. He gets tackled on the sidelines, and I think Woody even gets knocked down. There's a big pile up. The kid jumps up. Now, whenever Woody gets hit, he thinks he's in the game. He pops up ready to go. The kid takes the ball, and he holds it in Woody's face. At that point, I said, 'That's it.' There was no doubt in my mind that he was going to hit that kid when he put that ball in his face. I could see it happening. I'm not saying it should've happened. But I can understand how it happened.

I FELT BAD FOR HIM. Knowing him as I did, I didn't think it was enough to say that he should no longer coach. But it's that same thing—he didn't care what other people thought of him. It came full circle on him. It came back to haunt him in that nobody heard about the good things that he did for the players and the good things that he did off of the field. So at that point, the tide of opinion went against him.

I didn't talk to him after that. I would've been scared to death to call him. You wouldn't want to bring that up. Maybe I should've. Woody was probably the perfect coach for me. He got the most out of me. I can't think of anyone else I would've rather played for. Not only did he make me into a good football player, but he gave me something that I could take away from the game—the tools to be successful later. Whether guys liked him or disliked him, played or didn't play, they all left with the same tools. It would be a tough survey to take, but it would be interesting to see the guys that Woody coached and see how they've done now that they've gotten away from the game, when they have to provide for a family. Even the radicals, the guys who couldn't stand Woody, the Nick

Buonamicis, it would be really interesting to see how much of Woody is still in them 20 years later. I'll bet there's a lot of him. Even the guys who didn't like him, man, when the whistle blew, they were ready to play football.

I started doing that flip in the end zone after Corny did his little touchdown dance. Woody didn't like that. He got on Corny a little bit. I said, 'If I'm going to do something after I score a touchdown, I want to do something better than that.' I just didn't know what it was going to be. I knew I could do this flip. I just said I was going to do it, and I did it. I really didn't know how Woody was going to react. We were in this press conference somewhere, and somebody put the words in Woody's mouth. They asked him what he thought of it. He hesitated, and somebody else said, 'You have to admit, at least it's quite an athletic feat.'

He said, 'Yeah, goddammit, yeah, yeah. I like it. It takes a real athlete to do that.'

As long as I was doing something that no one else could do, as long as it was something of an athletic feat, it was okay. When I did it, I wasn't worried about him. Woody didn't care what you did off the field, or even on the field, for that matter, as long as you did well. Hey, you score a touchdown, he's not going to be pissed. My only concern was whether or not I was going to make it. You don't want to try to do something like that then not do it.

I told you that my dad talked all the time about getting my hair cut and all that: 'You don't look like the All-American.' Finally, when I made All-American, I went back to him and said, 'Hey, Dad, look. This is what the All-American looks like.' I was an asshole.

I REALLY HAD NO IDEA WHERE I WOULD GO in the draft. Some people were saying, potentially, that I would be drafted in the first round. Draft day came around, and I remember that all three of the local TV stations were set up over at Archie's house, waiting for him to be drafted. That was the big question: When would Archie be drafted? The assumption was, obviously, that he would go high in the first round. As it turned out, I was the 21st player picked, and think Archie was the 28th player. I was shocked.

I didn't see the same difference I saw from high school to college. As a kid growing up, you have this natural assumption that as you go through the different levels, things would continue to get bigger and better. From high school to college, you get bigger crowds, better equipment, better medical staff, better everything. Then when you go from Ohio State into the pros, the assumption is the same thing's going to happen. Well, when I came in to the Patriots, it was a step down. We had some superior coaches, but the medical staff wasn't as good, the equipment wasn't as good.

We should've won the Super Bowl my rookie year. The Raiders ended up winning it, and we were the only team that beat them during the regular season. They beat us with 12 seconds to go in the first playoff game. The game was just taken away from us by the officials. It was kind of back-to-back disappointments, the national championship and the Super Bowl in one year.

Chuck Fairbanks was here for three years, then went to Colorado. Ron Erhardt came in for three years, then he got fired and I got traded. I spent three years in San Diego. We had an owner change out there, and I ended up with the Rams for the next three years, playing for John Robinson. I liked John Robinson a lot. He was a player's coach. He reminded me a lot of Woody. He was a very basic, Xs and Os type of guy. Very vanilla offense and defense. He got guys ready to play.

I enjoyed professional football. Not many people get to play a game and get paid for it. A lot of it is just being in the right place at the right time. I got 12 years in, which puts me in the 99.9th percentile, I guess. I had to do a lot of work in order to stay at the level I wanted to be. I wasn't very big, so I had to spend a lot of time in the off-season. I hated every weight I ever lifted, but if you want to play the game, you have to do it. A lot of people hate practice; I liked going to practice. I can't say I liked summer camp, but during the season, I liked practice. Football, boy, it looms for you in the middle of July, and it ruins your entire summer. You can't enjoy June because you're getting ready for July. You can run and run all you like, but until that ball's in the air, you don't give it that extra effort. But as long as I was preparing for a specific event and the event was within reach, practice was enjoyable. I guess anything is what you make of it. I took the 12 years I had and applied the same work ethic I had in college.

They made the decision to get out of football for me. Actually, John Robinson kind of made the decision for me. We'd had an agreement when I went to play there that if I wasn't going to be given an opportunity to start, then I wasn't going to sit on the bench. In 1986, I had torn a muscle in my leg, and I played through it. In 1987, he called me up and said, 'Listen, Tim, I appreciate the way you've played with the pain that you had. You continued to hang in there, didn't dog it. You really helped us out, but I've got to tell you—you're 35 years old, you're going into your 13th year. You're not going to have an opportunity to start. I can't give you that shot. If you want to come and try out, we'd like to have you on the team, but I've got to tell you you're probably not going to play. Do you want to come back under those conditions?'

I said, 'No.'

I HAD RETIRED, BUT THE RAMS had not officially released me. They officially released me about three months later. Then I get a call from Marty Schottenheimer. He said, 'Geez, I saw you play last year, and I saw some tapes on you. I think you can still play. What do you think?'

I said, 'I think I can still play. That was not my reason for retiring. It wasn't the fact that I didn't think I could play. It was that John didn't feel like his future was with me, and I didn't want to sit the bench.'

He said, 'We've got a situation here with our free safety.' It was the kid Rodgers, who died of a cocaine overdose. He said, 'I need a veteran in the secondary. I need someone who can play. I think you could be the guy.'

I said, 'I'll tell you the same thing I told him. If you promise me an honest opportunity to start, I'll come play for you.'

He said, 'Absolutely.'

I went into training camp with the rookies. I did very well, was starting at free safety. Right before the first preseason game, we were in a goal line thing, and a guy put a helmet in my side and broke two of my ribs. I was basically screwed. At 22, I could play with broken ribs; at 35, I couldn't. I went out and tried to play through it, like I had done with the Rams, but I just couldn't play up to the level that I wanted to play at.

I tried to play in one preseason game, and I asked to be taken out because it was just too painful. The next game, I had them shoot it up. I went in and played. The injection didn't help.

After the first two preseason games, I went to him and said, 'Marty, you and I made the agreement that I was going to be given the opportunity to start, and I just don't see how, with these broken ribs, that you're going to give me that shot. I'm going to be out of commission for probably another four weeks before I can play at a level where I can compete and be your starting free safety. I don't think you want to wait that long for me to get ready. If I were you, I wouldn't want to wait that long. I'm ready to go home right now, and let's just call it even.'

'Oh, no, no, no, no. I still stick by what I said. I still think you can play. I want you to hang in there. Let's not play you this whole week. We'll rest you this week. The trainers tell me when they x-ray that thing, they can hardly see it any more. Let's give it another week and see how you do next week. We'll go week to week with it. I want to give you that chance.'

I said, 'Okay, fine.'

He sat me out the next week. We broke training camp, went to the hotel. That Tuesday, I get the call to come and see the general manager. They cut me. I looked at the general manager and said, 'You're releasing me?'

He said, 'Yeah, it's a numbers game. We've got to make room on the roster.' Blah, blah, blah.

I said, 'Wait a minute. A week and a half ago, I went to Marty and said you can release me right now if you want to. I was willing to walk with no strings attached, and now you're telling me that you're going to release me after he said we were going to do it on a week-to-week basis.'

He said, 'Oh, we talked to the medical staff, and we think you're healed.'

I said, 'What are you talking about you think I'm healed? There's no question that I have broken ribs.'

'Well, we think you're healed well enough to go,' he said. 'You want to talk to the head coach?'

I said, 'Was he involved in this decision?'

'Yeah.'

'Then no, I've got nothing to say to him.'

I left there and went to the Cleveland Clinic and had an x-ray done on my ribs, which were still broken. I came home, filed a grievance with the union and, three years later, collected my salary. They drug it out and drug it out, and, finally, they couldn't put it off any longer, and I got paid for the year. A lot of guys have that kind of problem, but not many guys win. It's a good excuse to get out of the game. But my case was as clear as could be. The x-rays were there. What really irritated me was that I gave him the opportunity, and he didn't take it. It amazes me. It gives you an idea of the disregard that teams have for players at that level. They knew they were wrong, but they didn't care. The majority of players would either not file a grievance or not follow through with the steps to collect the money. Or they would've settled. They did that with me. They offered me $20,000 or something out of my workman's comp to settle.

I said, 'Screw you. I'm not settling. What's workman's comp have to do with this? You released me when I had broken ribs.'

It took four years to do it, but we ended up winning. That's how I retired.

ACTUALLY, THE WAY I ENDED MY CAREER was I went down to Baton Rouge, Louisiana, for about three weeks and filmed a movie called *Everybody's All-American*. Dennis Quaid starred in it. Lou Erber, who was a coach with the Rams when I was there, was the technical consultant for the movie, and he went and got a bunch of guys that he knew to be in this movie. Guys like Cliff Branch, Clarence Davis, Raymond Chester, Jimmy Laughlin, who is from Ohio State. Taylor Hackford was the director, and he put a real emphasis on having this look like a real football movie.

They had this highlight film of hits that they wanted to emulate throughout the movie. They tried to spread the hitting around to all the guys, but I was the only guy who had just walked out of an NFL training camp, and I was in better shape than any of the guys. They had some poor kid who played baseball for LSU who was Quaid's double. What it came down to was that almost every hit that was staged in the movie was me hitting him. When you watch the movie, it's me doing all the hitting. I ended up breaking Quaid's collarbone. It cost the movie $1.3 million.

Quaid didn't take any hits, because he was a non-athlete. As much as he tried to think he was an athlete, he just wasn't. Lou would work with him and try to get him to run and do things. He just couldn't. It came to the place that they were trying to emulate this stick that Ron Kramer takes for the Detroit Lions a few years back. He's trying to get a first down, and he's trying to reach for the first down marker with his feet, and a guy comes and hits him and knocks his helmet off. It had to be Quaid, because his helmet gets knocked off. They wanted to see his helmet come off, so they rigged his helmet and chinstrap so it would come off. We did it on a Thursday, and we were supposed to finish filming on Saturday.

Lou is describing the scene, and I *know* that Dennis Quaid is done. He's *not* going to want to take this hit.

I said, 'Taylor, do you really want this thing in here?'

He said, 'Let me tell you. I know what you know: Once you hit him, he ain't comin' back. One time. Hit him as hard as you can. Let's get it in one shot so we don't have to do it again.'

'Okay. You sure?'

'I'm sure.'

We do it. Quaid comes running out, catches the ball. He drops his shoulder. I hit him right here, just snaps his collarbone in half. He goes down; his helmet comes off. They were supposed to do that in a second shot, another scene with him on the ground in pain, but they just kept filming, because he was on the ground, he was writhing, he was in some serious pain. That was the end of it. They had to cancel shooting.

I have it on a home video. A buddy was filming it. It was hilarious, because Quaid was full of bravado before the scene. He was all dressed up in his pads, and either Siskel or Ebert—I don't know which one is which—was there doing an interview with Dennis and me before the shot. The whole thing is that Dennis is doing his own stunts, which we know he's *not* doing his own stunts. He's only doing this one because he has to do it.

The guys asks him, 'Well, are you at all concerned about being hit here?'

'Ah no. I've got the pads on. I've been an athlete all my life.' He goes on and on.

Then he asks me, 'Do you think Quaid can stand up to an NFL-type of hit?'

'I've got to be honest with you, I don't know,' I said. 'It's one thing being an athlete. It's another thing playing at this level. I guess we'll find out in a minute, won't we?'

Wouldn't you know it, *bam!* He's down. He's out.

The bad thing is Quaid's down, and none of the players liked him, because he was always trotting around and being kind of a jerk. After it happened, on the tape, you see Clarence Davis and Raymond Chester go over to check on him. Raymond Chester comes walking back to the camera. He's going, 'He's done! He's done! That's it. He's not gettin' up.'

That was the last hit of my career, and I broke Dennis Quaid's collarbone.

It was hard to leave the game. What's hardest about it is despite all your best efforts, it has to end. Everybody knows they're going to die eventually, but people don't always make the best arrangements for it. Football's the same thing. You know you're going to have to leave the game at some point, but you just don't know when and what the circumstances are going to be. You get used to a certain lifestyle, and, ideally, you'd like to stay at that standard. Every day you go to bed, it's on your mind, you're worried about that. That's common throughout the game: What am I going to do when I grow up?

I WENT TO LAW SCHOOL FOR A WHILE. I was a stock broker for a couple of years, until I got traded to San Diego. I was involved in a couple of different businesses while I was playing, but when I got out, I was looking for something to do. I have to be honest, the guy who originally hired me hired me because I played pro football. I went to a head-hunter, and I talked to this guy who was placing people. He said, 'Hey, I've got somebody who might be interested in you.' It was just kind of a blind thing. I went and talked to the guy, and he hired me. I want to say he hired me because I did a great job selling myself, but the idea was I might have some name recognition in the area.

I work for R.R. Donnelley. Donnelley is the largest commercial printer in the world, something like 45,000 employees. Sales is a lot like athletics, it's very, very competitive. It's hard work. Five o'clock rolls around, and there's always somebody else you can call: 'Okay, do you want to call them now, or do you want to call them tomorrow?' I'm doing about 80 hours a week. I'm finally to the point where I'm making more money at this than I made in football; of course, I wasn't making that much money when I played football. It wasn't like it is now.

I work pretty hard at trying to keep my name in front of people. It's almost a job just to do that. I do the pregame and postgame shows for the Patriots on their flagship station. Steve Grogan and I broadcast the preseason games on TV. That's about as much as I can do right now. The good thing about my career in the league is that the average person can relate to me better than to a big football player. They see me and say, 'Geez, he's no bigger than I am.' It's come full-circle. Lack of size is finally a benefit to me. ”

Flam 7

WOODY HAYES must've known immediately that he'd found the solution to his perennial dilemma. Frustrated by the monotony of watching Ohio State fullbacks slog through the line, fans and reporters had assailed Hayes with the same question for two decades: When were the Buckeyes going to start throwing the ball? Hayes remained obstinate. Almost without exception, he chose his quarterbacks from a succession of strapping farmboys who could as well have been linebackers.

The answer finally arrived in 1972, in an unusual form—a quiet, sensitive kid from a Washington, D.C., ghetto who wore a wispy goatee and a huge Afro, who'd played only three years of organized football, and who'd never had a white teammate. Hayes is unlikely to have paid much attention to Cornelius Greene's color, but he would surely have been enthralled with the willowy youngster's speed, quickness, and instincts.

Though clearly gifted, Greene was unpolished. He'd literally diagramed plays on the ground at Dunbar High School, where as a senior, he threw 23 touchdown passes. His dazzling broken-field runs during scrimmages were offset by numerous interceptions, which infuriated Hayes and kept the uneasy freshman on the scout squad.

"I got by in high school on just sheer athletic talent. I could run around, scramble, do whatever," he says. "I just didn't have any technique. I looked out of place."

Greene lifted weights, passed to anyone who would catch with him, worked on the basics of dropping back and setting up, carrying out playfakes, reading defenses. Most important, he learned to deal with the pressures Hayes exerted on his quarterbacks. Greene developed ulcers, but he was the only offensive back to make every session of spring practice—allaying Hayes's fears that Greene was so frail that he'd be seriously injured—and challenged Greg Hare, the senior captain who'd led OSU to the Rose Bowl the previous year, for the starting job.

In 1972, Hayes predicted that Hare, a 6' 3" redhead, was "going to be one of the truly great quarterbacks in college football." A year later, he said that Greene was being given "serious consideration" for the position. The situation was rife for Hayes to vacillate between two quarterbacks, as he'd done often, but he went with Greene although Hare was the better passer.

Ohio State would begin the 1973 season with a new red, block "O" at midfield, new scarlet and grey seats, and the school's first black quarterback. On opening day, Greene took the Bucks to five touchdowns in their first seven possessions. He ran for the second score himself after his fake pitch to Archie Griffin froze defenders. Greene held the ball aloft and did an incongruous mincing shuffle of pure joy in the end zone. Everyone who saw it expected the dance to provoke Hayes, but the coach ignored it.

By Greene's fourth game, opposing coaches were complaining that they couldn't find anyone athletic enough to emulate him during drills. Greene became the most versatile and exciting quarterback in college football. He brought to football the skills and flare of basketball (he'd been a three-sport All-American in high school): deft ball handling, creative, instantaneous decision-making, balletic footwork. A teammate, frustrated by chasing Greene in practice, groused, "It's like trying to tackle a fart."

He, rather than Griffin, was

named the team's outstanding sophomore on offense in 1973. He led the Big Ten in total offense in 1974, setting a school record with 1,636 yards and making the all-conference team. Griffin won his second Heisman in 1975, but Greene was Ohio State's MVP (each voted for the other) and the first Buckeye quarterback to win a Silver Football as the league's most valuable player. Greene accounted for more touchdowns and gained more yards than any OSU quarterback before him, never lost to Michigan, and led his team to three straight Rose Bowls.

Hayes had discovered the means by which he could both silence his critics and do with his offense what he wanted to for so long: Attack, to borrow an expression from Sherman, across a broad front. Ohio State struck flanks with Griffin's sweeps, charged interiors with bullish fullbacks Pete Johnson and Champ Henson, tricked opponents with reverses to wingback Brian Baschnagel, and baffled them with Greene's daring options. Hayes's dull offense had become a fastbreak.

"I believe Ohio State's backfield could be the greatest in the history of college football," said Illinois coach Bob Blackmon in 1975. That year, a newspaper contest to name the backfield drew over a thousand entries; the winner, derivative but accurate, was "The Fabulous Foursome." In Ohio, Greene and his mates were as famous as the Beatles.

Greene also learned to throw effectively. His career is framed by games in which the pass figured prominently. Before the 1974 Rose Bowl, Hayes intimated that his quarterback would throw the ball often against USC. The hint was treated as a joke, compounded when the Big Ten's float in the parade depicted Greene in the act of passing. However, before a television audience estimated at 50 million, Greene outplayed Trojan star Pat Haden, completing six of eight passes for 129 yards, scoring the go-ahead touchdown in the 42–21 victory, and being named MVP. Against Michigan in 1975, OSU was losing by a touchdown with seven minutes to play. Greene entered the huddle on his own 20 and muttered a prayer. ("I have found that being a quarterback under Woody Hayes, you need all the faith you can get.") He then hit three passes for 49 yards in the drive that tied the game and carried Ohio State to a 21–14 win. He had become, according to Hayes, "almost a great passer."

The Bucks entered the 1976 Rose Bowl undefeated, ranked number one and matched against a team—UCLA—they had beaten by three touchdowns earlier in the season. The rematch was no such triumph. Greene completed just seven of 18 passes, with two interceptions, and Ohio State lost the national title, 23–10.

After the quarterback's first pass of the 1974 Rose Bowl was intercepted, Hayes told him to forget the error and keep throwing. His final pass against UCLA was also picked off, deep in Bruin territory, with the Bucks down by six points. The next day, an anonymous assistant coach fixed responsibility for the loss on Greene's having called an audible, which resulted in the interception. "We automaticed ourselves right out of the game. When you teach your kids to do that, what can you expect?" the coach said to a reporter, apparently forgetting that Greene had called four audibles that went for touchdowns against Wisconsin in 1974.

Cornelius Greene's graduation from fame to obscurity had begun. The Dallas Cowboys chose Greene in the waning rounds of the draft—as a receiver, not a quarterback—but released him in training camp. Cut off from what had been such a vital part of his life, Greene was devastated. "Reality came knocking on that door," he says. While his friends played in Super Bowls, Greene worked in the world of pinstripes and wingtips as an account rep for Xerox Corporation, eventually becoming the top advertising salesman for a television news channel.

Twenty years ago, he had his high school number retired, received congratulatory telegrams from senators, appeared on the *Tonight Show*, was given the key to the city of Washington, D.C. Now, his joys are more private: knowing that by earning a college degree, he achieved the goal his Aunt Jenny, whom he has always called "Mom," set for him; watching his young son; savoring his long friendship with Griffin.

His colorful wardrobe and dashing style of play—the touchdown shuffle, the cleats taped into spats, the small towel fluttering at his waist—once earned for Greene the nickname "Flam" (for *flamboyant*). The license plate on his Grand Prix bore the legend "Flam 7." He still plays softball and basketball year-round, but there is little flamboyant about Greene today. His hair was neatly cut. He wore a blue Pony windsuit and basketball sneakers, as if he were on his way to the YMCA for a pick-up game. Still at his playing weight—170 pounds—he looked fit and lithe. The whirl of time has left him serious, almost pensive. Indeed, he says the image was never accurate, that he was always "just a real timid kind of person."

The memories don't come easily—not because they are so painful, but because they are so splendid.

Cornelius GREENE

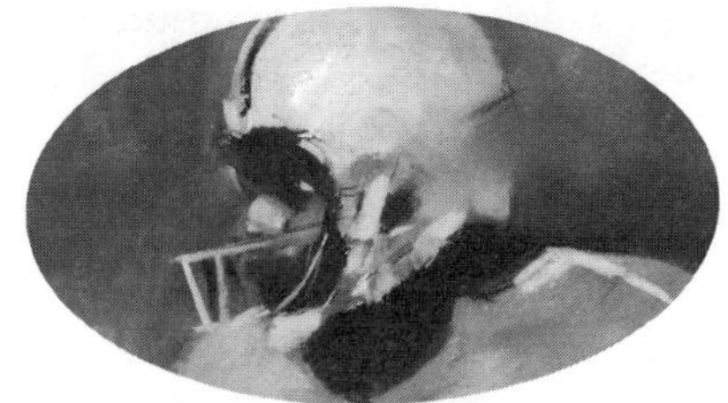

"I GREW UP IN WASHINGTON, D.C., only about six blocks from the capitol building. It's a very prominent neighborhood now, but back in that day, it was a tough neighborhood to grow up in. I had three brothers and three sisters, but I didn't have the opportunity to be raised with them. My father's older sister and her husband raised me. They were really my aunt and uncle, but I called them my 'Mom' and 'Dad,' and I still consider them my mom and dad. Ever since I was five years old, it was always like a little game: 'What was I going to do in life?' And I always knew to say I wanted to go to college. That was pushed upon me at a very early age.

The average families in the neighborhood probably had about seven kids. I was like the only child growing up out of my home, and I had to learn how to protect myself. You know, a lot of times, you beat one kid, and he had a brother a year or two older than him, and there was another one a year or two older than *him*. So, I did a good job getting along with folks because, obviously, I didn't have any brothers at home to protect me.

My uncle got me interested in sports. He took me to my first Washington Senators baseball game when I was five years old. From there, it kind of mushroomed and spread over to football. My idol was Willie Wood, a Hall of Fame defensive back for the Green Bay Packers. He grew up down the street from me. He was one of the main reasons that made me want to pursue football.

But I was pushed academically, too. I had awards in junior high and high school for not missing a day of school. I went to Dunbar High

School, a very prominent, traditional high school in the Washington area. I would say during my era, it was about 97 percent black, an inner-city school. Back in the early '50s, a lot of lawyers and doctors graduated from Dunbar. I started at free safety the second game of my tenth grade year, and the third game, I was starting quarterback. I got banged up quite a bit, but we had a record of 5-4. My junior year, we lost in the playoffs. My senior year, we went to the championship. We lost, but I had a good senior year. I threw 28 touchdown passes.

We threw the ball a lot, and a lot of people didn't believe me when I told them I wanted to go to Ohio State. But my memories of Ohio State in high school was Rex Kern scrambling. I didn't realize that Rex didn't have the opportunity to throw that much, either. I really didn't know a lot about Ohio State at the time, then I started hearing about 'three yards and a cloud of dust' and wondered what that meant. I didn't know that it meant the fullback carried the ball all the time.

Rudy Hubbard, who became the head football coach at Florida A&M, recruited me. He was a running back at Ohio State. He sold me to go there. My main fear was that I would to go Ohio State and they would switch me. I wanted somewhat of a guarantee they wouldn't change my position. You know, even if I wasn't at the starting level, I still wanted to quarterback. You hear so many old stories—you go to a school, and they switch your position. But Coach Hayes sold me, too, when I met him. He said if I was good enough, I was going to play, and if I wasn't, I wasn't going to. What you hear from all the other schools is, 'You're a great athlete. You're going to start for us.' I thought Coach Hayes had insulted me at first by just saying if I wasn't good enough, I wasn't going to play.

You get promises, under-the-table offers, scholarships for your girlfriends—all kinds of things. I had to sit down and talk to my mom—my aunt—and she couldn't recommend a school, because she just had an eighth-grade education herself. She had to leave a lot up to me, but she said, you know, 'Look, out of all the schools, who told you the truth?' I had to sit back and say, 'Coach Hayes said, if you're good enough, you're going to play. If you're not, you won't play.' Simple as that. And the weekend I was there, 80 percent of the weekend was, 'What you want to be in life?' I said I wanted to major in business. He introduced me to a professor in the business college, and I went over there and talked to the professors. No other school did that.

When I first met Coach Hayes, I thought he was a real nice gentleman. I didn't know he was as fiery as he was. I just followed along with the rest of the Ohio State quarterbacks. My freshman year, I had stomach aches every night. The next thing you know, I was getting ulcers like the rest of the Ohio State quarterbacks. I said, 'I thought this was an old man's disease. You can't have an ulcer. You got to be like like 40, 50 years old to have an ulcer.' The Rex Kerns, the Tom Mattes—it was just traditional for an Ohio State quarterback to feel that way. The pressure that Woods put on a quarterback, I mean, it was very easy to go out there and play in front of 90,000 people versus having him on your back.

He might've done anything, from grab me and shake me up a little bit to belittle me, make me feel like I wasn't bigger than an ant. He'd tear your ego down to shreds and make you feel like you're not worth two cents. He hated mistakes. When we were running pass plays in a skeleton drill, when you're not throwing to wide receivers who're covered by defensive backs, with Woods, you better be hitting 10 out of 10 passes. He doesn't think the ball should hit the ground. You practice under that kind of pressure, and on game day, it was easy to go out there and produce.

WHEN I FIRST GOT TO OHIO STATE, I thought I had made a mistake. In high school, I had one pair of shoes, and I had to make sure that those shoes were in good shape Friday before the game. At Ohio State, I had about five or six pairs of shoes. The school was just so big. We had over 100 ballplayers, and I was like fifth or sixth quarterback. I didn't have any confidence in myself. I didn't have any technique. I didn't look polished. I looked out of place. I got by in high school on just sheer athletic talent. I could run around, scramble, do whatever. Here, everybody had a responsibility. You got to carry out the fake; you can't get the ball and just look around, wait for someone else, to see what they're doing. You had *responsibilities*.

Coach George Chaump was the guy that took the extra time to develop my talent. I had a summer job, and he would work me out at 6:30 in the morning, then we would practice again at, like, 7:30, 8 at night. I didn't like it a lot, but, you know, as the summer went on, my arm was getting stronger, I was progressing, my confidence was coming back. It took me a long time to grasp the system. I came from a real easy, simple system—the guard to your right is '2,' the tackle is '4,' then '6,' then '8.' Those numbers didn't mean anything at Ohio State. Everything was just totally different, the format, the passing routes, *everything*. It was difficult for me, then all of a sudden, a light went on in my head, and everything started coming together. Once you get the system down, you got to start producing. I wasn't producing once I got the system down. It took me until the spring of my freshman year to really feel comfortable.

My focus at first was just trying to get the ball to whomever I was supposed to give it to, but I didn't have any knowledge of what defense they were in. I mean, I was looking at it, but I didn't have any idea what they were doing. I was just trying to learn offensive strategies in the beginning of my freshman year, my sophomore year, too. I had a great sophomore year, but overall, in terms of reading defenses and things like that, that didn't come until my junior year.

The spring game was the big game that we had my freshman year. It was the third-string backs and the first-string line, against first-string backs and second-string line. We had to play Archie and those guys, and what ended up happening was we beat them 42–21, and I threw two touchdowns and scored two.

That really kind of brought me back, 'cause that summer before my sophomore year, Greg Hare and I were tied as quarterbacks. Greg was the captain, going into his third year starting, and for me to be tied with him—it couldn't get any bigger than that. I looked up to Greg. Greg had taught me a lot about quarterbacking, how to be poised. Greg was a typical NFL quarterback: 6' 3", 220, strong arm, hell of a leader, but he didn't have the opportunity to play his senior year. I kind of felt for him. I wanted to play bad myself; unfortunately, those kind of things happened. I think I was a better runner than Greg. I think the style of football that Coach Hayes wanted to play was running options and having that kind of attack.

I presented a lot of problems for a defense. I had great running skills. I didn't have a big body, only weighed 175 pounds, but I was very durable. I had proved that in spring practice, because I was the only back that made all 20 practices. They gave me the Iron Man Award. At that point, I think Woods felt comfortable with me quarterbacking. I think he was a little afraid to play me at my size. He thought my neck wasn't strong enough, and I might get seriously injured out there, but I proved to him over spring football that I was durable enough.

You know, I grew up in a tough neighborhood. I thought I was tough as nails. Woody made me soft inside, then he eventually got me tough mentally by me being able to handle him. A lot of the antics he pulled on me the first two years didn't bother me anymore. I had to block him out, because it was tough having him on your back in addition to trying to be prepared mentally for the kind of big football games we played. That's enough pressure: knowing your assignments, knowing the audibles, what types of plays you want to run. When you got to call an audible, you got about six plays. Out of that six that's going to work for you, which play do you call first ? Those are the kind of things I started concentrating on. In practice, the weeks before the big games, you just had to tune him out.

YOU HAD TO TAKE SCHOOL seriously, too, because we had to average 45 hours, 15 hours a quarter. We only had three semesters to average 45 hours, unless it was summer school. I knew if I went to summer school, then I didn't have an opportunity to work. So I took it very seriously. One thing I didn't want was for the coaches to have any kind of concerns that I wasn't going to be there academically. In high school, I graduated in the top 10 percent of my class, which I was very proud of. I had like a 2.8 average, which probably doesn't sound great, but I won nine letters in school. I started baseball, basketball, and football my sophomore, junior, and senior years. You go from sport to sport to sport three straight years and still come up on a 'B' average, you know, I was proud of that.

I had to have some tutors when I first got to Ohio State, because a lot of the classes I was taking weren't offered in my high school—political science, economics, accounting—things I hadn't had the opportunity to study. A lot of the kids went to prep schools and strong academic schools which prepared them. I had to have some tutors to help me until I learned how to get into study habits.

Our freshman year, it was mandatory that you had study hall for the whole year, right after dinner. Study hall started at 7 o'clock, and if you finished dinner at quarter to 7, and you didn't have the opportunity to go back to the dorm, that was just too bad. You were in that study hall from 7 to like 9 every night. I thought that was good. If you screw up that first quarter, it's very hard getting that grade-point average up. I got off to a pretty good start academically.

I came in with four or five other quarterbacks. Gary McCutcheon ended up being a wide receiver. Jim Cramer ended up being a linebacker and transferring to Pittsburgh and was on that national championship team with Tony Dorsett. The other guys, that were all-everything in high school, ended up playing behind me. I knew those other quarterbacks, if they were playing, Ohio State would've still won with them. I knew that I wasn't so good that Ohio State wouldn't win without me. That mentality keeps your head together; plus, me and other quarterbacks were good friends. The competition destroys the friendships a lot of times, but it really didn't destroy our friendships, which was unheard of.

You know, me and Archie Griffin and Woodrow Roach—we were the only three black freshmen out of 17, so we were very close. Here's Woodrow Roach averaging 5.2 yards a carry at Ohio State, and he's playing behind Archie, and, you know, all three of us was best friends. Woodrow had to play behind Archie four years in a row, but the bond all three of us had, and him and Archie had, was just unbreakable.

IT WAS TOUGH FOR ME AT FIRST. I had never had the opportunity to play with whites on any ballclub. Let alone *live* with them. I remember Woodrow and I were going to be roommates. He was from the Washington area, too. I'll never forget the day his dad dropped us off. We arrived in Columbus about 10:30 at night, and I thought his dad was going to stay around for a while. He turned around and left about an hour after he had dropped us off. I remember Woodrow and I ran out onto the street and watched the taillights disappear. Then they assigned our rooms. I was by myself in my room, and Woodrow was in another room. I told Coach Hubbard we were supposed to be roommates. The next day, I'm out walking, just trying to learn High Street. I come back, here's this guy in my room. It was Brian Baschnagel. Brian's from an all-white background, and here I am from an all-black background. We're in the same room with one another. Me and Brian ended up being the best of friends. We just accepted one another for who we were. We had a lot of differences. We liked different music. My music was on when he came in, he never told me to turn it off. His music was on when I came in, same thing. We started learning each other's cultures, accepting one other.

That was a very rich experience for me. I wouldn't trade that for the world. You can't pay for that kind of experience. I thought all whites were as one, then you learn that Jewish background is a little different from German background and all kinds of things, and I'm sure Brian probably learned a lot about Afro-Americans. Which makes you grow up. You treat people for who they are instead of trying to stereotype somebody for how they look.

I treasure that experience, and it's something I want my son to be able to experience. I have him in a mixed background, and he's only five. I wish I would've had that earlier. His name is Jason. He's Jason Howard and I'm Cornelius Howard. I didn't really want to name him after me. I kind of watched Archie. He didn't name any of his kids after him. You have a boy, it seems like the kid should be named after you. It's something I always wanted. Archie had his first son, and it took a lot not to name him after him. I know it took a lot for me not to name my son after me. But, you know, if he participates in sports later on in life, he doesn't have to live in my shadow. He's Jason Greene. He'll be his own man, and I hope he'll grow up to be a productive citizen. If he plays football or not, that doesn't bother me. I see myself in him because he favors me, but he doesn't have to live my life.

When I started the first game of my sophomore year, I was very apprehensive. Adrenalin was just flowing. You know, you're just on a high. Woody didn't tell me I was starting. I found out I was starting in the paper. We were going to play Minnesota and I read in the paper that I was starting. That made me want to go in the bathroom and throw up. Greg and I were neck-and-neck that whole time. He was the starter in the morning practice, and I was the starter in the afternoon practice. He pulled a muscle, and for about five days leading up to the season, I was number one morning and afternoon because he was injured. Then all of a sudden, Woods put in the paper that I was starting.

THE FIRST DRIVE AGAINST MINNESOTA, we took the ball on about an 80-yard drive, and I scored the first touchdown of the season. I did this little celebration dance in the end zone. It was really a mistake. It was just nervous energy. Everybody was telling me about this dance, and I really had to watch on the films, because I would've bet all I had that I didn't dance. I didn't even realize I had danced. People didn't believe it, because we're so conservative. Something like that you might could be benched for, if you didn't score the touchdown. But Woods kind of relaxed on us. From my dance, it spread to Tim Fox doing the no-hands flip. Some guys started doing a lot of little celebrations in the end zone. I think Woods started to loosen up somewhat—as long as you got in the end zone. But Woods was the kind of guy, too, that you might make an 80-yard run and someone might trip you up on the two, and he wouldn't even look at you. We knew we had to do spectacular things to get a big pat on the back from Woods.

Many days, I might've went home mad at him. You're just not going to have great practices all the time, I don't care what's going on. Our second team that we had to practice against was probably better than some first teams that we played against. People like Doug Plank, who played defensive back for the Chicago Bears, never started for us. I had to play against him every day, and we had many people of Doug Plank's caliber. It was tough. Unfortunately, when things don't go as well as planned, we just get chastized by Woods. His favorite move was to slam his hat and stomp it, then he'd get up and rip the hat apart. I remember our equipment manager triple-stitched the hat one day, and Woods didn't know it. He throws the hat down and stomps it. He picks the hat up. He takes it, and he can't tear that hat for nothin'. He's just rippin' at it. He can't tear that hat, so he just throws it down and stomps on it some more. We're in the back row just laughing at that. That's about the only way we could get back at him. That was fun for us, because we knew the big move was to rip the hat.

THE PRESSURE WAS TERRIBLE. You're playing at Ohio State during that era, and you're following that Rex Kern tradition, and a lot of people are looking for that excellence from our ballclub. A loss early in the season could've just been devastating. You know, we're looking at going undefeated and being national champions. That's all we had on our minds. To play under that kind of pressure daily is tough on young kids like we were. But at that time, we thought we were tougher than nails, so we took it. God, I look at it nowadays, and that's an awful lot of pressure to put on kids, really an awful lot of pressure to play under. People expected these unbelievable things from you. You know, they expected Archie to get 100 yards; they expected us to win by 20 a game. I mean, point spreads in some of our games were 30-some points. It was nerve-wracking, but *everything* was nerve-wracking.

I was the first black starting quarterback, which was played up real big when I was there, but I tried to tone it down as much as I could. It was something to be proud of, too, but I didn't want to ruffle any feathers, thinking it was really bigger than it was or talking out about it. I kind of attribute that to my parents. They weren't the kind of people who won a lot of accolades or anything like that. I saw them work hard; hard work had put me in that type of situation. I just wanted to be recognized to be a person that worked hard, a person that kept his nose clean. You wasn't going to read about me coming out of a bar being trashed or slandering Ohio State in any manner. That just wasn't my style.

Now, I wasn't an Archie Griffin by no means, either, when I say that. Archie is the epitome of every kid that wants to emulate an athlete. I always used to say, 'Be like Archie,' because he was truly a genuine All-American person. The first time I met him, it was really funny, because in high school, our guards were maybe 195, 200, and Archie was real muscular from the waist up, and I saw him run the 40-yard dash. I'd say I ran about a 4.5. Woodrow Roach, he ran a 4.5. I still hadn't met Archie, actually. This was the first day we were out there with all the freshmen together. We were in shorts, tee-shirts, football shoes, and helmets, and Archie ran a 4.5. I went over to Woodrow and said, 'They're not kidding. When you go to college, the linemen are as fast as the backs.' I thought Archie was a guard. I said, 'Goodness, the *guards* here are running 4.5.'

Archie and I ended up being roommates three years in a row, and we had a lot of memorable experiences. We learned a lot from one another. We joined the Fellowship of Christian Athletes at the same time. We both were very spiritual people. On a Sunday, after going through six straight days of practice, Archie still had the determination to get up at 7, take a shower, and go to 8 o'clock mass. After maybe two Sundays in a row, I'm still in the bed, and he gets up. I couldn't let him outdo me, so the next thing I know, I'm taking that shower and going on to church. He was special, and you knew special things were going to happen to him. Our whole team did, and that's why none of us was upset because our offense was built around him. We molded our goals into team goals, and for Archie to be the one who got the two Heismans, nobody even had a second thought about it.

Archie's father's vacation was to get off so he could see his kids play on Fridays or maybe to travel to see his sons play in college. You just couldn't help to look up to a man like that. You could just tell the drive that Archie and his family had. His father was a hell of a man. He dedicated his life to work three jobs, around the clock, to provide his family with a better life. I think watching that made me a better person.

We never would boast or brag or anything like that. We had a lot of Bible classes, that kind of thing. I think we turned a lot of the younger guys coming in. They could see us in a different light. Even though they saw us on television, they could see that we wasn't afraid to stand up and say, 'Hey, we love the Lord. This is why we've reached the kind of success we're reaching. We're not taking the credit personally. We're given this opportunity because of Him.' I think that made it much better to stress to them the difference, because you didn't egotistically state that the reason why you were successful was because of yourself. You always gave the credit to your line. You always kept the pressure off of yourself. That was the main experience in life that I received from associating with Archie.

One good thing that's embedded in you from Woody is not to believe everything people are telling you. When I was in high school, I kind of began to believe that I was this person that I was reading about. At Ohio State, I separated myself from the articles that were written about me. I truly knew who I was versus what was read about me. You could see other people reading about you and thinking that you were this person that they just read about and finding out that you're nothing like him. That in itself is one good thing that Woods did. No way that we could get so big-headed that we thought that we were that individual that was talked about in the articles.

IN COLLEGE, THEY CALLED ME FLAMBOYANT. I was a pretty spirited dresser, and during that time period, a lot of loud colors were acceptable, people wearing Afros. I had a car with my nickname on the tag. I think my outside appearance made me look egotistical, but I was really very shy. But the position I was put into—I had to talk a lot being the quarterback. Archie and I were very similar. We both were subdued. We both liked to sit in the back of the room. Neither one of us would raise our hand first. We would observe the situation first. I probably got the out-going image, the selfish image, the partier, but I really wasn't like that. Anybody that really knew me behind the scenes knew I was the kind of person who would take my shirt off and give it to somebody that needed something. I'd go out of my way to make somebody happy.

I would do whatever it took to be successful, too, yes, but even when Rod Gerald came up and was my heir-apparent, I took him out every day and made sure he knew the plays, even though I had to compete against him. It wasn't like, 'Well, I'm not going to teach him anything because he's competing for my job.' I looked beyond that. Here's a guy who's going to play for Ohio State, and if I can pull him to the side and give him a lot of my knowledge, then he's going to be a better person. No one did that for me. I was isolated and didn't have someone to kind of put his arm around me and pull me in, nor did Archie. When we came there, it was tough. We kind of gave back in a different way. The younger guys coming in, we'd give them extra attention. Our house was always open to them. We never thought we were so big we couldn't socialize with them. We always had a lot of freshmen over at our house.

Once I beat Greg Hare out, our relationship changed. When I wasn't a starter, I kind of trailed Greg to see what he was doing. Now, I'm out in the forefront, but I always went to Greg if I didn't understand a few things, and Greg would always come up and tell me different things a defense was doing. The relationship changed because I had to take a step forward and grow up. I wasn't a follower anymore. I was in a leader's position, and I had to act like a leader. My first year, it was very easy to be a follower, being in the background when the scrimmages were going on. I had to take that leap. You're going 10-0-1, and there's a lot of big, big games. Going up to Michigan my sophomore year, there were 110,000 people at the game, so you had to step up. I'll always be indebted to Greg, because he was married and had a kid, and I know he had ambitions of playing pro ball. And to have that cut short and not being in there his senior year—and we elected him the captain of the team—you have to applaud him.

THAT SOPHOMORE SEASON, I ended up having about 800 yards rushing. Every game was a different experience. We played in Wisconsin, and I got shook up. I hit my head on the turf pretty hard. It was an option play, and the hit really scared me. It was the first time I was shook to the point that I might want to come out of the game. I got totally racked up and came to the sideline.

I told the doctor, 'My head's hurting. I don't know if I want to get back out there.'

My heart was troubled. I was scared. He told me to go and talk to Coach Hayes. Coach Hayes asked me what class I have at 11 o'clock. I told him. Then he asked me another question about a class. I told him what time it was.

He said, 'You're all right. Get back out there.'

I always think, what would've happened if he had told me to come out of the game? Any time when the goin' got tough, would I have wanted to come out of the game? By him putting me back out there, he tested my manhood. If you're an athlete, when your will is tested, when a guy done clobbers you one good time and you have to go up against the guy for the rest of the day, are you going to let him clobber you for the rest of the day or are you going to stand up like a man? I was willing to take the backseat for an instant, until I was pushed back out there again.

After every game, I was physically destroyed. I played a lot of basketball and ran a lot. If I was in better shape in the fourth quarter than most of those linemen, then I was going to be the better man. Then it began to be psychological. Even though I got pounded, I would get up first and grab the big linebackers by the hand and help them up. Psychologically, the linebacker says, 'Wait a minute. I just gave this guy my best shot, and he's helping *me* up.' People respected you. The next thing, you saw where guys were helping you up. They might could've got a good lick at you and they didn't give it to you because they respected you.

WOODS AND I DISAGREED. Sometimes, you'd see a pass play open when you're up by 20-some points, and I'd call a pass audible that went for a touchdown when Woody probably wanted me to run the ball. But all I saw was the open play. I didn't look beyond embarrassing the other coach at that time. You see that now that you're older, but I'm out there, all I see is winning. If you win big, you win big; if you don't, you don't. But if the play was open and I had to call it for us to score a touchdown, I did. I used to get hammered for that, but then again, I didn't really see what he was talking about at that time. You're in the Big Ten, you have a lot of coaches that have been around for a while. Obviously, those coaches have good friendships. You don't want to see a guy being embarrassed even more than he has to be. It was almost like a gentleman's honor to keep the score down.

I never really understood Woody. He was difficult to study, difficult to understand. You didn't really know what his antics were for. He was a difficult man on himself. He was very hard-driven. My only disappointment is that we weren't national champions in all those four years. Every year, we were right there, but something always happened. The last two games of the season always haunted us. There would be a Rose Bowl loss, or something down the road. As good as we were, we could've been national champions all four years. There's no doubt about that. We still felt like we were one of the best teams Woody ever had, but I you can't say that without us being the national champions.

We scored more points than any other team, gained more yards than any of his teams, our defense gave up less yardage than any of his teams, we gave up less points than any of his teams. In our four years, we had a Heisman trophy winner two of the four years, four straight Rose Bowls. It was winner take all, and all four years, we were able to pull it out. I think if Ohio State was playing under that type of pressure now, they wouldn't have played in any of the bowl games. It would've been an insult for us to be considered for the Gator or the Liberty Bowls. The Rose Bowl was the bowl, and there wasn't a second bowl. Win the Big Ten, win the Rose Bowl, be national champions. That's all there was.

When I was a freshman, we beat Michigan 14–11. I didn't play in that game, but that was the most intense game I ever saw. The first Michigan game I played in was probably two times more intense than the game I watched. There's nothing like a Michigan game. The hitting's two times harder. The strategy, the pressure. Whenever you got inside Michigan's 30, you had to score. There was no turning back. It was just everything. We practiced for Michigan in the spring, the summer, the fall. I remember we played Indiana one year, and we practiced for Michigan Monday, Tuesday, and Wednesday, and we practiced for Indiana on Thursday and Friday. Every time we played Michigan, we were both undefeated, and it came down to whoever won that game was going to the Rose Bowl.

I feel good because I never lost to Michigan. I was 3–0–1 in my four years, and I can put that record up against any other Ohio State quarterback. That's probably one of the biggest things I'm proud of. Not many people in Ohio State history can say they never lost to Bo Schembechler or to Michigan. Archie and I and the rest of the '72 team can hold our heads up and say, 'Hey, no matter what, we never lost to a Michigan team.' That probably holds up more than going to four Rose Bowls.

When we went to the Rose Bowl the first time, I was floored knowing my mom was finally going to see me on national TV. All the people back in this area would get to see me. They had seen me against Michigan, and we tied them 10–10, but I had chipped bones in my thumb. My thumb was so badly swollen I couldn't throw. I only attempted one pass in that game, so a lot of people were saying I couldn't pass. You don't want to share your dreams of all these great things you're going to do, in the hotel before the game, because you say there's no way they're going to come true. The phenomenal game I had and ending up being MVP was unbelievable. Then to come back here to the D.C. area and get the key to the city, my high school retired my jersey, the mayor proclaimed it 'Cornelius Greene Day' and gave me the city's flag, the highest honor you can win. Hubert Humphrey, the representative from Minnesota, sent me a personal telegram. It was too much for any human, too much.

At 19, to receive all that and still try to be a regular person, to say, 'Hey, I received all this. Now, I still have to go to school. I still have to be one of many,' was difficult. I attribute that to Coach Hayes again. So much happened to me between 18 and 22, it's tough for me to go on in life and say, 'Hey, I'm not going to be nowhere near as big for the rest of my life as I was between that time period.' Yeah, everybody across the country knows who I am; I'm a household word. Now, I'm 38, and I know for the rest of my life, I'm never going to reach a pinnacle like that. I don't try to set goals in my life now that I know are not achievable. I would love to be nationally known, have a business where I'm out selling all over the country. I never thought I would ever get to California. Just to go to California—that was my aunt and uncle's dream. They knew it would never come true for them. They knew they would never have enough money just to go to California and vacation.

THEN I GET DRAFTED BY DALLAS. I went in the 11th round, but I didn't get drafted until the second day. The first day, all my friends came over to my place and were waiting on me to get drafted. It was going to be a celebration kind of thing. And I didn't get a call that day. I remember leaving my friends, going in my room and closing my door. I stayed in my room about two hours when I had all this company in the house. I was devastated. I really was.

I got three calls: 'We're going to call you back.' Never call you back. One call was for another ballplayer—Randy Cross, who was a great lineman for the '49ers for all those years. We had played in the Hula Bowl together. Randy Cross, they called my house and asked for Randy Cross. I'll never forget that. Ask for Randy Cross, and I just knew that was it. Every phone ring, you just know that's the call. It was always a friend: 'No, no, didn't nobody call yet.' Then I got a call: 'San Francisco '49ers calling for Randy Cross.' I'm like, God, 'No, this's not Randy. This's *my* number.'

The next day, I woke up at about 8:15, and 8:30, it's the Cowboys calling. Before I could even brush my teeth, I was drafted. There was just this big relief. I was just relieved that I was drafted. It really didn't matter that it was the 11th round. I was drafted, but, I don't know, it seemed like the night before meant so much to me. Everybody felt so bad for me. I didn't say goodbye to half the people that left. Reality knocking on that door.

You hear so many guys say, 'Hey, you better take your education seriously. What do you want to become in life?' It's like, 'Well, not me. I'm still experiencing a lot of success so far. I'm looking third, fourth round. Everybody pretty much told me they were going to draft me that high.' Then a guy from the '49ers talked to me, and he said, 'The rumor about you is that you're going to go to Canada because the pros are not looking at you seriously as a quarterback. The rumor is out that if you're not drafted as a quarterback, you don't want to play in the NFL. That's why no one has touched you.'

I didn't say that by any means. It was really disappointing that something like would get out about me during the most important time of my life. Draft Day—it's something you look forward to for your whole four years. You're seeing your friends, your classmates, your teammates are getting drafted before you. I'm putting my talents up and comparing. I knew I was close to them. I never was a big guy, and in pro ball, they really look at size. But for a rumor to destroy your whole career.

I went to Dallas, and they had two third-round picks, Duke Ferguson and Butch Johnson, and I had to compete against those guys. I was ahead of them until I hurt my finger. They told me at first I was going to play quarterback, but when I got there, Danny White was in his rookie year. He had a no-cut contract. They had Clint Longley and Roger. They only had room for three guys; you didn't have to be a rocket scientist to know there wasn't going to be room for four. The only way for me to make the team was for them to make me a wide receiver. Then I hurt my hand, and that did me in. You have six weeks in a cast, you can't get in any of the passing drills, you can't play in any of the scrimmages. Butch and Duke were given opportunities, and they made the best of them. Both of them were great athletes, as well, but I knew I was right in there, too. But being in the right place at the right time was the key, and I obviously wasn't in the right place at the right time.

Dallas released me, and by the time I got home to Columbus, I had a flight going out to Seattle. Seattle was an expansion team, the first year they were in the league. It was between me and Steve Largent. Jerry

Rhome, Largent's college coach, was there, and they elected to go with Steve Largent. If there had been a George Chaump there, they might have went with me, knowing what I was capable of doing. But I don't feel bad saying that Largent beat me out. The guy ended up being the all-time leading wide receiver in NFL history.

I'M OUT IN THE COLD, and it's hard to deal with because I know I still have the athletic ability. I know I should be playing, but for some reason, I'm not playing. I can't put my finger on it, but I don't have the perseverance to keep trying out year after year. A lot of other teams contacted me after that, but the fire was gone. Some guys, they might try eight teams, then, *boom,* they finally get a team they can stick with. I didn't have that in me anymore. The disappointments took their toll. It was just too much for me. I'm saying, 'If I try out for two more teams and, boy, I get let down....' Why put myself in that kind of situation again? Even though it could've been 50-50 that it might've turned out right for me, I just couldn't chance that disappointment any more. It was too devastating.

When I came back to Columbus, my first job was a youth manager for the National Alliance of Businesses. I'll never forget it—you know, my first real job. I was going back to school in addition to working. I was saying, 'Boy, this's really what I *don't* want in life. I don't want this kind of job.' But I couldn't put my finger on what I really wanted to do. More than 75 percent of my life had been football, or some form of sports, and here I am giving it up totally. Archie's with the Bengals, Pete's set with the Bengals, Brian's in Chicago, Tim Fox is in New England. All the guys I played with, they're still playing. I'm trying to hang up my shoes. It was tough to go see Archie and them play, meet them after the games, knowing I've got the capability of being out there, being a little envious, looking at a lot of wide receivers out there and saying, 'Man, I know I'm as good as this guy.' But on the other hand, I knew I had to come to grips with reality: 'Hey, you're *not* out there, and this's what you are doing, so let's start enjoying this new life of yours. You best put a gameplan together.'

I came back here and I got hired by Xerox as an account rep, and I was very successful with Xerox Corporation. I kept an athletic attitude, and I stood on my own two feet and made some things happen. For some reason, people like to associate themselves with athletes and kind of give you a lift along the way. I was glad to see I had the motivation within myself to go out and be successful with a major corporation, of showing that I know more than Xs and Os, that I can go out and present myself and do well.

I did spend a couple years playing semi-pro ball, but I couldn't help that. I mean, football was in my blood. I thought it was good for me, because I proved to myself that I could be a great wide receiver. I was averaging over 20 yards a catch and leading the team in scoring. That rebuilt the inner confidence I always had in myself that the NFL had knocked out of me. A lot of people who saw me play semi-pro ball said, 'Man, you should go back in and give it another shot.' I had played in front of 100,000 people. Now, 5,000 was a big crowd. In Columbus, we might get eight. On the road, we might get two or three. The small crowds weren't a big letdown. Even at Ohio State, you really don't see the crowds. You're just into the game.

I think now when I look at Ohio State, two individual accomplishments stand out. I was most valuable player my senior year on the team, which led me to be the MVP in the Big Ten. I only won by one vote. Archie voted for me, and I voted for him, which is funny, because if he had voted for himself, he'd've been the MVP. Just for the team to recognize you as the MVP, when you have a guy who won his second Heisman Trophy on the same squad. I mean, that's a trivia question: 'What guy won a Heisman who wasn't the MVP of his own team?' That's unheard of. That has to rank as one of the highest things I've accomplished. But, then again, Archie was involved in that, and that shows the kind of person he was. He could have easily put his name down, but he voted for me.

When I was at Ohio State not long ago, I was looking at the things I had contributed, and to be my size and score 29 touchdowns in my career, I'm still ranked up there with the big guys in all-time career touchdowns. I'm not too far behind the Pete Johnsons and those kind of people. I didn't realize I had scored that many touchdowns. I averaged almost 10 touchdowns a year. Those two things stand out in my mind.

One of the saddest days was when we were 11-0 my senior year, and we lost the Rose Bowl. We had beat UCLA previously—41–20, I think the score was—and then we got knocked off by them in the Rose Bowl. I didn't have a great game. Archie broke his wrist. It was one of those days that nothing seemed to go right. We should have beat them handily, and that was our last chance to be national champions. To this day, it haunts me. There weren't too many sad days, but that game and my junior year, we were winning 17–10 in the Rose Bowl, and USC scored in the last minute and a half to beat us 18–17 and went on to be national champs. My junior and senior year Rose Bowl games were devastating.

I LOOK BACK NOW, I'm still the last winning Rose Bowl quarterback, and it'll be 20 years next year. The '73 team that went into the '74 Rose Bowl was the last Ohio State team to win a Rose Bowl. Whoever thought it would be 19 years before Ohio State ever won another Rose Bowl?

I stayed around Columbus for a while, but I wanted to separate myself from the university. I wasn't involved in the recruiting or anything like that. I always said, 'If you need something call,' but I wasn't the kind to see a guy and then go after him and call the university. I separated myself for a number of years—intentionally. I wanted to find out who I really was, find out what I really liked in life, instead of what Woody told me. For so many years, my whole life was kind of scripted out. I didn't have any say-so in my own life, because I was on this schedule all the time. It was always, 'Be here this time. Do this. Do that.' It was nice to be my own man.

Back here in the Washington area, people know my name but they really don't know my face. I think I'll always be a celebrity in Columbus, but I'm inconspicuous when I go back there. My hair is short, now. I had long hair back in those days. I think a lot of people don't recognize me who haven't seen me for the last 20 years. I go back for reunions. They had a reunion last year. They introduced the whole '75 team at halftime, so you got that roar of the crowd again when your name was introduced. I had my son with me, and it was touching. I was teary-eyed. You say, 'Wow, this was every down you'd get that roar.' I hadn't had that roar for 15 years. It felt good. I took it for granted so much before when I played. I cherished that roar because I hadn't had it for a while.

Twenty years ago the 20th of this month, I left for Ohio State. It blows me away. Twenty years went by so fast. But I'm still at game weight. I'm still very active. I play softball, I play basketball. I get back, and I see a lot of running backs who look like linemen now, put on a lot of pounds.

Things have turned out all right. I'm really happy with where I am in my life. I'm not trying to achieve goals that are unachievable. Even though I'm in sales, which can be intense, too, I'm able to keep everything in its right perspective. I'm able to keep my job where it is, instead of bringing it home. I'm an account exec for a new cable news television station. I'm the number one direct sales rep. I always keep a football attitude. You're going to get knocked down out there, and the person that's able to get up and brush himself off and get back in there is going to be the successful one.

I'd go to Ohio State again, no doubt about that. I couldn't have been featured more or respected more. I was glad to be a team player versus an individual player having everything built around me like my high school program was. The pressure was more so on Archie every game to get 100 yards. But then, all of a sudden, I'm well known. Then they got to stop us both, and the pressure's back on. But it wasn't as intense as it was on Archie. His string of 100-yard games started mounting, and everyone wanted to be the one to stop him. He was under a bigger microscope than I was. Then again, we both went into a ballgame with an extreme amount of pressure. That kind of pressure, I wouldn't put that on any young kid in today's time. I could see why the ulcers were coming for me. Playing for Woody and playing for a program as big as Ohio State was tough. You had to be a special kind of person to be willing to go through that kind of thing and look forward to it.

I want to try to guide my son as much as I can to be sound academically. If he wants to participate in athletics, it's just a hobby for him to do versus, 'Boy, this's the only thing he can do.' If he doesn't have the grades, he can't participate in any extracurricular activity. I really stress that. He has a good mom. She's very strict, and he should come up being successful in some type of profession, even if it's not athletics. He's going to have to make his own decisions.

I want to know I did all I could, but I'm not pushing athletics. He's only five right now, and, obviously, he has a long way to go. At one point, you couldn't get out the door without him crying. Now, it's 'Bye, see you later.' It's not going to be long before you're not going to be able to get him to go with you to do anything. They get on their own little schedules; life takes its turns. I'm not really looking forward to that day, but I know it's going to come.”

The Importance *of* Being Archie

THE BEGINNING was like a legend concocted by Grantland Rice from a tale by Horatio Alger. He was "Butterball," a chubby kid from the poor side of town who hung around the stadium before games, hoping someone would give him a ticket. He matured, grew leaner, and became a Buckeye, but on that day—the day of his annunciation—he was a scout-squad tailback, a fifth-team squire who fumbled on his one previous carry and thus thought he'd spend the season watching others do battle. After all, Coach Hayes (he still calls him "Coach Hayes") had gone through the depth chart with reporters earlier in the week and hadn't even mentioned his name. He'd prayed on his knees for a second chance. He'd read and reread scripture—"knock and it will be opened unto you."

Midway through the first

quarter that day, when Hayes called for him to go into the game, he didn't move, thinking the coach had made a mistake. He remembers someone in the huddle telling him to run as he never had. He says he was "in a daze." Two quarters later, he had gained 239 yards, 10 more than the school record.

"I just ran. That's all," he said.

He called the day "a miracle," said his setting the record was "truly a mystery." Hayes bestowed upon him six buckeye leaves; no one had ever been granted more than three for a single game.

"I didn't know anything about him at all," said Bill Dooley, the coach whose North Carolina team was beaten that day in Ohio Stadium. "So he's a freshman? Well, he's one hell of a freshman. Where's he from? A hometown boy? Well, we didn't know one thing about him."

It was as if Archie Griffin, garbed in scarlet number 45, praising teammates, thanking God for the privilege of running for the greater glory of Ohio State, had sprung directly from Woody Hayes's atavistic imagination—which in some ways, he had. His youth is the stuff of modern myth. A junior high school teacher called Griffin the most single-minded student he'd ever known. That fabled desire was bequeathed to Griffin by his father, a former 120-pound All-State lineman raised in a grim West Virginia coal camp.

For 23 years, James Griffin, determined that all eight of his children would attend college, worked two full-time jobs during the week, and cleaned schools on weekends, yet never missed one of his sons' games. "You got to do things for yourself," James told the children. "You got to work and keep on working."

As he would later do with Hayes, Griffin absorbed his father's every word. In midget ball, he was a pudgy guard too heavy to make the weight limit. He stripped away adolescent fat by turning the family bathroom into a sauna and doing calisthenics while swathed in plastic cleaning bags. He lifted two cases of beer that he filled with dirt and attached to a mop handle. At Eastmoor High, he carried for 304 yards in one game, was the Ohio High School Back of the Year, and came to the attention of Woody Hayes.

They seem an odd pair—Hayes and Griffin. One was nearly 60, white and reared in the country, the other a black inner-city teenager; one was tempestuous, the other unflappable; one was virulently outspoken, the other laconic. Indeed, with 150 scholarship offers before him, Griffin almost didn't come to Ohio State. Unconvinced that Hayes truly wanted him, he planned to attend the Naval Academy or Northwestern. Despite their innate differences, however, Griffin found in Woody Hayes a like spirit, someone just as committed as he.

After that incredible first game, Griffin wouldn't miss another start at Ohio State. Quick, infinitely courageous, economical in his movements, he ran with bullish persistence, always driving forward, always attacking. "If you want to know why coaches get ulcers, sit around and think about Archie Griffin carrying the football for three more years," said Illinois coach Bob Blackmon in 1972, after Griffin ripped his team for 192 yards on 27 carries.

His career took on a wondrous statistical symmetry. The 1,577 yards he gained as a sophomore were the most in Big Ten history. He became the league's only sophomore MVP in 50 years and only the second player to win the honor twice. He set NCAA records for rushing yards and all-purpose yards. He was the first player since Doak Walker—a quarter of a century earlier—to be named a first-team UPI All-American three straight years. His teams won 40 of 46 games and four consecutive Big 10 titles. He is the only player to win two Heisman trophies. Most remarkably, he gained at least 100 yards in 31 straight regular-season games, despite spending much of each week recuperating from the pounding he took from successive legions of titans who had vowed that his streak wouldn't last another Saturday. His years at Ohio State were as unsullied as they were unequaled.

Said Hayes, "Archie Griffin is the greatest back I've ever seen or coached. He's also the most popular player we've ever had, by far. In fact, we value Archie's attitude more than his football ability, which is saying something, because he can do everything."

He lived by "The Three D's" that made up his speeches to school children: Desire, Dedication, and Determination. He made his bed in hotels, refused to hang around bars, admonished teammates for missing class, dragged himself to church every Sunday no matter how battered he might be, cast the deciding vote for Cornelius Greene as team MVP in 1975. Hayes wanted him to attend law school, then enter politics, predicting that Griffin could become the first black president. The national press called him "a divine presence in a facemask," "some kind of seraph in scarlet and gray," and "the sainted Archie Griffin."

By the time he graduated ahead of his class with a degree in industrial relations, the two images of Archie Griffin were fixed in our consciousness. Archie in Motion: an efficient wind-up machine, a coil of slithering, pounding cables, heavy-thighed, helmet festooned with badges of honor, slashing, twisting, ricocheting through defenses. Archie at Rest: arm slung casually around a Heisman statue, unabashedly happy, gap-toothed smile generously inviting us to share his joy.

After winning his second Heisman, Griffin said that he was pleased that he could "make a myth of the Heisman jinx." He didn't realize that in doing so he had become his own myth. Hayes once said that he didn't know how his young hero ran so singularly well, that Griffin wasn't big but ran over tacklers, that he wasn't fast but no one caught him. (Griffin said the Lord was the source of his ability, and it could therefore be taken away from him at any time.) Hayes meant his statement as praise, but it could also have been taken as dire prophecy.

As fierce as his desire was, professional scouts thought Griffin undersized, an indifferent receiver, and an unproven blocker. Five backs were drafted before him. A teammate, Tim Fox, was picked three players sooner. Griffin was not even the first selection of the team that chose him—the Cincinnati Bengals. He endured two coaching changes and suffered a torn Achilles tendon. After four years, he asked to be traded. By the time Cincinnati was preparing for the 1981 playoffs, he had returned to the scout squad and would remark that watching a television special about the Heisman Trophy moved him to tears.

"I'll just hang loose on the sidelines and be prepared to do whatever has to be done," he said before the 1982 Super Bowl. Griffin's seven years in the NFL weren't nearly the catastrophe he has frequently heard them described as. "I did what I was asked to," he says. "I felt good about what I did at Cincinnati."

Our unreal expectations, however, made the nearly 3,000 yards he gained and his average of over four yards a carry seem inconsequential. He left the Bengals, briefly attempted to catch on in the USFL, and returned to Ohio State when Hayes arranged for him to be hired as an assistant athletic director. Now, he is where he seems most comfortable, in St. John Arena, just up the concrete stairs from the glass case that holds his Heismans.

At first, he looks surprisingly small, but his depth of chest, breadth of shoulder, and narrowness of hip aren't immediately apparent. He is trim, compact, neat, and composed. His fitted, white Oxford shirt was monogrammed at the waist. In his tiny office, surrounded by a Leroy Neiman print of himself, an aerial photo of the band forming "Script Ohio," and a charcoal of Hayes, Les Horvath, Vic Janowicz, and himself, Griffin often thumped his extended fingers on the desk for emphasis.

He won't be fenced with, the cloak of his image always drawn around him. He sounds earnest—if sometimes corny—as he acknowledges the debt he owes to teammates, discusses the profundity of Hayes's teachings, and pays homage to the epic grandeur of Ohio State football. And if he's not one to ponder the nuances of his life and career, that trait only makes him like the rest of us, most of whom try to live up to some notion we have of ourselves.

Except that Archie Griffin's idea of himself is ennumerated in statistics, writ large in headlines, and held in a frozen memory of cheers like a butterfly encased in amber. To this day, the only stains on his image are a painful divorce and a bankrupt chain of shoe stores that he owned with his brother Ray—small blemishes by any standard but his...and Hayes's. Remarried, he is still involved with charities ranging from the Little Sisters of the Poor to Canine Companions for Independence, still a familiar spokesman for car dealerships and grocery store chains, still extolling to school children the virtues of the three D's.

If ever the idol were to reveal feet of clay, it would've happened when, after nine years as an assistant, Griffin sought the athletic director's job and didn't win it. During the search, letters to the *Dispatch* had promoted him for the position as if invoking his name would serve as an incantation, instantly transporting the Buckeyes back to the glorious age when Griffin started in four straight Rose Bowls. The university unexpectedly courted another demigod, Rex Kern, for the job, despite Kern's having little experience as an athletic administrator, and a revolution on Olympus seemed imminent.

Stories had Griffin leaving for the University of Cincinnati. However, Kern withdrew from the fray, Andy Geiger was named director of athletics, and Griffin accepted a promotion that placed him in charge of the football program. Archie Griffin remained a Buckeye, and all was right with the world. That is how it should be. Griffin is unselfconciously committed to the broader significance of his image. He is Archie, and it is important that he remain Archie—important for him, for Ohio State, and, as the case of O.J. Simpson demonstrates, for us.

As the old newspaper editor advises at the end of *The Man Who Shot Liberty Valance*, "When truth becomes legend, print the legend."

Archie GRIFFIN

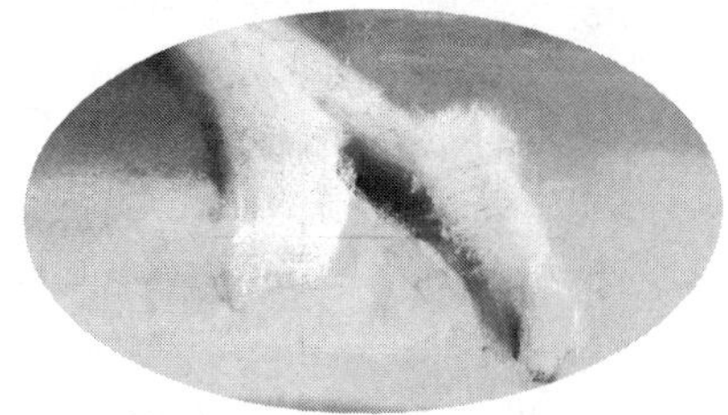

"ALL MY LIFE I'VE BEEN HERE. The only time I've been outside of Columbus is when I played at Cincinnati. I grew up dreaming of playing at Ohio State but that's exactly what it was—a dream. I just didn't think it would happen. You didn't hear of many Columbus players playing at Ohio State at the time. I just didn't think Coach Hayes would recruit me, to be honest with you. But it happened. Coach Hayes recruited me. When I was coming out of high school, there were a few schools I was interested in: Northwestern, Michigan, the Naval Academy, and Ohio State.

My first impression of Coach Hayes was that I was pleased to have the opportunity to talk to him. I was in awe. We had dinner, and I was a little bit disappointed because during our whole dinner, he never talked to me at all about football. I thought maybe he looked at me and saw I wasn't big enough. I remember going home that night and telling my father that I didn't think he wanted me to play football for him, because he didn't talk football to me.

And my dad asked me, 'What did he talk about?'

I said, 'Education.'

And my father looked at me and said, 'Well, don't you think he's concerned about other things, not just you running up and down a football field?'

One of the strong points about Coach Hayes was that he didn't only recruit the player, he recruited the family. He spent a lot of time with my mother and father when he was recruiting me. I remember when I was getting ready to make my visit to Northwestern, my father was home that evening, and he didn't flat out come out and say it—'We want you to go to Ohio State'—but what he did say was, 'You know, we'd like to be able to see you play every game.' It was as simple as that. They wanted me to play here. I was used to my folks being at every game, and I'm sure that they wouldn't've been able to make every game in the Chicago area.

I've got six brothers and a sister. All of us went to college on athletic scholarships, all the boys on football scholarships and my sister on a track scholarship. My father was a remarkable man. He was certainly one of the most important people in my life. I didn't know that at the time, but when I look back now, I can see that we really didn't have much at all. My dad worked three jobs. He worked for the Columbus Sanitation Department, he worked for Ohio Malleable Steel Casting Company, and he worked some janitorial jobs on the side. And one of the things that impressed me most about him was that he would still always be there when we played our games. He would take vacation days on Friday nights when we were in high school just to watch us play our games, and that would be his vacation. That left a lasting impression—the hard work ethic. He was a big inspiration of mine.

I had heard all of the things that you'd hear in the press about Coach Hayes—that he was tough, that he would work you to death. But that didn't bother me, because I always felt that's what a coach was supposed to do. I played for a guy named Bob Rand in little league football. I played guard and noseguard. I wasn't a starter. But I used to think Bob Rand was one of the hardest coaches who ever could be living. He would work our tails to death. He would make us run one lap around Maryland Park, where we practiced. Every day, we'd have to run that one lap. And I always finished in last place. All of a sudden, he said, 'Whoever finishes last has to take an extra lap.' I ran as hard as I could but still finished last, so I had to take the extra lap. Talk about punishment! To me, that was punishment. Even though it was only about 800 yards, it seemed like it was about two miles.

I was only nine years old then, but the guys I played with were 12 to 15, and the reason I had to play with them was because I was pretty fat. The weight limit was 135 pounds, and I was close to that, and I couldn't play with the guys my age, because their weight limit was 110 pounds, so I had to play with the older guys, and that was punishing. So, my whole life, I've been around coaches who were tough.

It was a challenge, just the fact that I was the first in my family to be recruited by Ohio State. That meant a lot to me. To play in Columbus—I didn't know that I would ever have the chance to do it. It was a dream, and I never thought it would come true. But it happened. It happened in a good way, being in the right place at the right time with the right people.

You really want to know the moment I thought I was in over my head? It was when we got a letter from Coach Hayes before our freshman year, and in that letter they told us what we were going to be expected to do once we reported to camp. Now, this's going to sound weird to you, but it's the honest to goodness truth. In that letter, it gave each position the time they needed to run in the one-mile run. And I was never a distance runner, as you can tell by my experience as a nine-year-old. It had never been my big suit. And I got that thing, and it said that the halfbacks had to either run a 5:45 or a 5:30 mile. And so I went out and tried to train to do that. Well, every time I tried to run that mile, I'd be over six minutes. I'm saying, 'Man, maybe I'm not in the right place, maybe I am over my head here.' And I tried and tried it, but when I tried to practice that thing, I could never run it under six minutes. A lot of times I'd be by myself, and I could never get under six minutes. I even had my high school coach come out and time me once, and I was right at six minutes. I'm saying, 'Man, how am I ever going to make 5:45?' So I was really scared. If you're 15 seconds behind on anything, you're way back there. But we got to camp, and we ran it, and I did it in like 5:25, and it was amazing to me. Maybe it was because I was running with my teammates and my adrenaline was flowing and I was trying to psych myself up

I FUMBLED THE FIRST TIME I GOT THE BALL in a game, against Iowa. Got in the game, and the first play called was an 18, a pitchout, and I got a little excited. I was looking ahead of myself. Guys had opened up a nice hole and my eyes were on the hole instead of watching the pitch come in. The pitch hit me in the hands, and I fumbled it and went out of the game. Coach Hayes didn't really react. When I left the field, I kind of went away from him, so I didn't get that reaction, to be honest with you.

But I knew he didn't like fumblers. In practice, you'd fumble, and he'd really get on your case. He wanted to make the fewest mistakes possible. Fumbling was a 'game-killer.' You could be going in to score, and you fumble and lose it, and the other team gets some momentum, drives down and scores. It could just ruin a whole game for you. I thought I would probably never get the opportunity to play again that year.

I'm sure Coach Hayes knew my ability. There's no question in my mind about that, because I don't think he would've put me in the game if he didn't. But also, Rudy Hubbard, our backfield coach, was a guy who was really pushing for me to get into the football game. Coach Hayes used to call it 'pounding the table,' and Rudy Hubbard pounded the table for him to put me in. In coaches' meetings with Coach Hayes, if a coach had a point to make, and Coach Hayes was not sold on that point, the coach had to pound the table.

I count that as a miracle in my life, because there was no way I was supposed to get in that second football game, the North Carolina game. Even the night before, the team was at the hotel, and we freshmen and reserves were in the dormitory—everybody was dressing at home games—I remember praying and asking the good Lord to give me a chance to play. So, to me, it was a miracle. And all along, I found out that Rudy Hubbard was pounding the table for me, and certainly Coach Hayes knew I had some ability or no matter how hard Rudy pounded the table, he wouldn't've put me in the game.

I was shocked a bit that day, but I didn't know the magnitude of it. You have to remember, I was just out of high school, and in high school I'd rushed for 240, 250 yards in games. That just used to happen. That game, rushing for 239 yards, I was really happy about it—I don't want to say, 'No big deal'—but I was used to it. It was still a miracle to me, because I just didn't think I'd have the opportunity to play. Getting that rushing record? I guess I just thought I was doing my job.

I've got to tell you, though, that I was in a daze the whole time. Coach Hayes liked to have bench-discipline, so you had your space on the bench where you were supposed to sit. I was sitting back on the bench when he called my name, and I hesitated. I figured he was making a mistake. I finally went up to him and he told me to go in the game. It was truly a mystery to me. I was in shock, but at the same time, I felt I could run with the football. I believed in myself. Man, I'm sitting in the huddle, my eyes were *this* big. All I can remember is lineman saying, 'Archie, run like you never ran before.' They were opening up holes and I'm just running. I was in a daze the whole time. In all the football I played, that was my most exciting moment.

And it's probably better that he handled it that way. I think, in his planning, he may have thought, 'We'll put Griffin in the game.' He didn't put me in after the four other backs in front of me. He skipped over a few other people. He put me in after Morris Bradshaw. Morris Bradshaw played a little bit, and then I was put in the game. Morris moved out to wide receiver after that and played some wingback, and he went on to have a fine career in professional football with Oakland and New England. He was very fast and very smooth.

It was satisfying winning two Heisman Trophies, but winning the Heisman was a team award for us. When I won the Heisman, it was as if *we* won the Heisman, our whole team. I'll never forget one of the games I played against Michigan. It was my junior year. They had two brothers, their name was Banks, and they said they'd rather die than see me get 100 yards, and the offensive line, they took it more personally than I did. They were going to make sure that I was going to get 100 yards. They'd come up to me, pound me on my helmet and say, 'We're gonna get you this 100 yards. We're gonna run right over these guys.' To a man, all of them said that. That really got me pumped up, seeing guys want to work that hard to get 100 yards for me. That's the kind of team we had.

COACH HAYES WAS SOMETHING SPECIAL, because of his leadership, the way he helped people. He wanted you for your ability on the football field, but he also felt he had something to contribute to you as a person, something that might help you later on. When he recruited me, I didn't think he wanted me to play for him. I thought he may have looked at me and said, 'This guy's not very big. We run three yards and a cloud of dust, and he's not going to be able to pound it up in there.' But he was interested in me. Not only was he interested in me playing football for him, but he was interested in my future, and that impressed me.

That was the strange thing about Coach Hayes. He didn't want people to know that on Thursday nights he'd go into Children's Hospital and talk to the kids, and he'd even pull us along with him sometimes. But he didn't want the public to know that. I think he kind of felt that people might look at him as being soft. But he was a man who had a big heart.

You knew that Coach Hayes just wasn't paying lip service to caring about his players, because he had each one of his coaches know the player's schedule, know where that player was going to be. If a player was having trouble making his eight o'clock class, Coach Hayes was there before eight o'clock to get that guy out of bed.

You might have a practice that was real bad and Coach Hayes might really be on your case. You'd feel down, go in the locker room, get showered up, leave the locker room, and you'd have to walk by his office. And he was always standing out there. You'd get ready to go by, your head down, and he calls you in and tells you why he got on your case, and you come out feeling better. He could bring you down, he could get on your case, but at the same time, he knew how to bring you back up and make you feel good about yourself.

THE MICHIGAN GAMES were the best ones for pre-game talks. I lived in Columbus, and I knew how big the Michigan game was, but, still, once I got here, it was much bigger than I ever thought. I'll never forget my first Michigan game. The first day of practice, it was a Monday, and Coach Hayes used to bring in former players to talk to the team about Michigan experiences, and he brought in Dave Whitfield. Dave Whitfield got to going, and all of a sudden, tears came out of his eyes and he ended up saying, 'This's not a game; this's war.' And I looked around the room, and I saw tears coming out of everyone's eyes, and I asked myself, 'Oh, my goodness, what did I get myself into? This's *serious*.'

I played with some great ones. John Hicks was big, fast, quick, powerful, very confident. He went into a game believing he was going to beat anybody in front of him. Sometimes, he even told them, 'The play's coming our way.' Cornelius Greene was probably the best all-around athlete on our football team. I think he made all-state in football, basketball and baseball back in D.C. He was probably one of the smoothest option runners I've seen. He was so good throwing that ball out there, making people think he was pitching it and taking it up the field, making people miss him. He was not big. He probably played at 165, 170 pounds, but he was so quick, so smooth. We roomed together for three years, and we were great friends.

Pete Johnson, for his size, was extremely fast, and he was extremely strong. He despised weights, to be honest with you. But he was extremely strong, very hard to tackle, very confident, one of the hardest runners I've ever seen. I used to see guys shy away from him, especially when we got in the pros. I used to see Pete run by guys and they would jump on his back. And I don't blame them, because, I'll tell you, you hit him head on, and you have some work to do.

People say sometimes how Coach Hayes talked about me, but I can remember fumbling in practice a couple times when he just ripped me. I remember a game my freshman year—Michigan State, I think it was—and I fumbled about three times. I think I carried the ball the next game, against Northwestern, once or twice. Our fullback carried the ball about 44 times. He let you know that he didn't like the fumbler.

Coach Hayes used to say, 'I'm not the smartest person in the world, but I'll be damned if anybody will out-work me.' I always remembered that. I look at myself. I know I'm not going to be the smartest person in the world, the smartest person in the Athletic Department, but I'm going to work hard. That's just something that really stuck out in my mind about Coach Hayes. And he would work. I mean, he would work nights, early in the morning. He wouldn't let anybody out-work him.

Most people thought of him as a really tough, no-nonsense guy, a guy who really didn't smile a lot or crack jokes. But he wasn't like that. It was tough, but he made it fun. I think that's the way you have to play the game. You have to laugh about some things. There're going to be tough situations, but you still have to be able to laugh. You have to laugh at yourself, and he made you do that.

THE GAME I REMEMBER MOST is the game against North Carolina my freshman year. That's my most memorable game in all of football. But after that, I remember our win over Southern California in the Rose Bowl, my sophomore year. The reason I remember that so much is that we tied for the Big Ten championship with Michigan. We played them to a 10–10 tie at Michigan, and the athletic directors voted to see who would go to the Rose Bowl. We ended up getting the vote, and a lot of people said that Michigan should've gotten it because Ohio State had gone the year before and got killed by Southern California—they beat us 42–17. And we went out there that year with all this on our minds, and we beat them by pretty much the same score they had beaten us the year before, 42–21. We went through that whole season undefeated but we had that one tie, and I think we finished number two. That one tie kept us from being number one.

I was always glad we played Michigan at the end of the year. I can think of at least three of those games that if we had to play the next week, I probably wouldn't have been able to play. The hitting was just that hard. After being the Heisman Trophy winner, I was even more of a target. Once you get that trophy, it doesn't get any easier. Believe me. I'd get hit and guys would give me that little extra; they'd make their comments, all the things that go on on the football field. Somebody get a good hit on you, and they're certainly going to say something about it. I looked at it as fun, and I'm going to get my chance the next time. I really don't think anybody went after me cheap. I believe all along, at least in college ball, everything was just good hard football.

I'd come right at it; I'd drop a shoulder on you, then sometimes I'd make you miss, make a move, something like that. At the same time, to keep you guessing, I'd try to run over you. Sometimes it would work; sometimes it wouldn't. I took some hits, and not only that, you get three and four people falling on you at a time, that's when you take the pounding. You don't really take the pounding on the first hits. I remember my freshman year playing Michigan State, I ran a kickoff back. Guy came through untouched, and I got maybe five steps and *pow!* I mean, this guy just splattered me. I didn't see him coming. It was the hit of the week. It didn't knock me out but it was impressive. But I never missed a game in college. I missed a couple in the pros, but not in college. Coach Hayes knew the pulse of his team. He knew the players he could maybe let take a couple of days to rest their bodies, and he used to do that with me sometimes. He'd tell me to come out and just catch the ball. He knew how to bring people back.

He allowed people to have fresh legs when he did that, and I thought that was important. So many times you see teams out there that are in condition but they don't have any spring in their legs. They can't do the things they want to do; they just can't uncoil. I believe in that fresh legs theory to this day. I believe if you have fresh legs, that you can do more in a game.

I REALLY DIDN'T THINK I would win the Heisman Trophy my junior year. I thought Anthony Davis would win it. I knew I was in the running, because in my sophomore year, I think I finished fifth, and just to give you an idea of the kind of players we had on our team, we had three players from Ohio State that year in the top six. John Hicks finished second, Randy Gradishar finished sixth, and I think I finished fifth. So I knew I would be in the running, but I didn't think I would win it. It wasn't something I really wanted bad my junior year, but after winning it, I wanted it my senior year. Coach Hayes used to say, 'You're getting better or you're getting worse. You're never at the same level.' Being young, I thought at the time, 'Maybe I need to go ahead and win that Heisman Trophy again.'

I have them sitting on my bookcases, at the top, so every time I want to get one down, I have to climb a ladder to get it. It's a great feeling to be in with that group of people who have won the Heisman, and I'm honored to be the only one to win two, but it's still a team award for me.

In football, you go to little league, you go to high school, you go to college, you go to professional football, and at every level, it's different. It was different in the pros than it was in college. College was certainly a great time, but I enjoyed pro football, too. I enjoyed my years in Cincinnati. My first year was the year after Paul Brown had given up coaching and was the general manager. I played for Tiger Johnson, Homer Rice, and Forrest Gregg, and we had some tough times. There were a couple of seasons we went four and twelve, one season we went six and ten, and then we went to a Super Bowl.

SOME PEOPLE SAY I didn't do much in the pros. I listen to that all the time, and I guess I kind of chuckle when I hear that. You go into the game with certain expectations, and my goals were high. I wanted to gain 1,000 yards a season. Well, it just happened to be that Cincinnati at the time was not a running football team. We were a passing football team. I figured to gain 1,000 yards, I'd have to carry the ball 225 times. My average per carry ended up being over 4.0, and I felt I could've gained 1,000 yards in professional football, if I would've had the carries, and I just didn't have them. I averaged somewhere around eight carries a game during my career, and on eight carries, you can't get it done. So, I made my goal then to average five yards a carry, which is outstanding in professional football. I adjusted my goal. But people don't look at the yards-per-carry, they look at the 1,000 yards.

I got hurt in the '83 season, the last pre-season game, against Detroit. I had what you call a rectus abdominus tear and an adductor tear at the same time. It's one of those injuries you think that it's not going to keep you out all that long. I thought after four weeks I'd be ready to play again, and after eight weeks, I started practicing. The first day, I did okay, but that second day, I stretched to catch a pass, and it ripped all over again, and it ended up keeping me out the rest of the season. It's just one of those things. I've seen some kids in our program get that rectus abdominus muscle torn, and they're thinking that they're going to come back. In my mind, I'm saying, 'It's a lot worse than it seems.' I couldn't move or anything, because it's just excruciating pain. I hate it that it happened that year—1983—because I had worked hard, and everything looked like it was going to fall into place for me.

I went to the USFL, and Mike Rozier used to call me 'Grandpa.' I said, 'Dang, these guys are *young*.' That was after that injury. I sat out a whole year, but I wanted to give it a shot and see if I still had it. Tim Sullivan, a reporter with the *Cincinnati Enquirer*, had mentioned to me that Lindy Infante would be interested in me playing for him. I was here working here at Ohio State at the time, and I thought about it, and I said, 'Well, I wonder if I can still get out there and do it.' We all wonder that. I went out there and did the best I could possible do, but it's hard to sit out of that game, once you reach a certain age, and try to come back and do it the way you used to do it. I knew what I wanted to do, but everything wouldn't get there when it was supposed to get there. I wanted to see if that was the time, and it wasn't. I had to put it behind me.

It's hard to put football completely out of your life, particularly if it's been an important part of your life. I don't think it's hard to not play it. It doesn't bother me that I don't play it. People ask me all the time, 'Do you want to be out there?' I can flat-out tell you, 'No.' I've had my go at it. I love the game, but I don't want to be out there. Sometimes, I look at it now and say, 'Man, you mean to tell me I was takin' those kind of licks?'

I NEVER REALLY HAD A STRONG DESIRE TO COACH. I thought I'd be working for a corporation at this time, something to do with personnel, industrial relations of some sort. I thought about it, and I said, 'No, I like the administration end of it.' I've been approached by politicians, wanting me to get into politics, but that's nothing I really want to do. Some things that Coach Hayes said made me seem like I'm perfect, but I'm not perfect by any means. I've made mistakes. I've had some tough times. But I have to tell you, I enjoyed playing the game of football with the people I played it with and certainly enjoyed playing under that man.

One of the things he used to say is, 'When you get knocked down, you got to get back up.' You're going to have your tough times. When my shoe business went bad, that was a tough time in my life. I had to get back up. You can't sit down and sulk about things that went bad. And it certainly helped me, that experience in football. I wasn't going to lay there. I was going to get back up and get things going again.

I knew when I was in junior high school that I wanted to go to college. I wasn't thinking about pro football. It wasn't really a goal of mine. It was something I dreamed about doing, but I didn't think I'd have the opportunity. My goal coming out of high school was to get a scholarship, get an education, and football was going to be the vehicle to get me there.

When I got out of football, I was working as assistant director of staff employment here at the university, and we were going through a fund-raising phase. Rick Bay was our athletic director and he asked me to come over and help out in athletics. I came to find out that Coach Hayes was the guy who kind of pushed that deal along. He thought that I could help athletics, and he wanted to see me over here.

I've been here ever since, and I've loved it. My responsibilities are in fund-raising, marketing, and promotions. I get involved with advertising sales on our radio network and our scoreboards. We're involved in external affairs, pretty much everything outside the running of the actual programs. We have a huge budget, and our area plays a big role in helping to meet that budget. I still sign a lot of autographs. I get all kind of stuff in here to sign. I try to sign it all and get it back, and answer all the letters that come in.

AS FAR AS FOOTBALL'S CONCERNED, the 31 straight 100-yard games are my greatest accomplishment. You talk about a pounding. It took a lot of pounding to get that done. I'm not insulted by people who say, 'The system made him.' I'll be the first to tell you that I had some outstanding blockers, but not anybody can gain 100 yards in 31 straight games. If you have your team working for you and everyone's doing their jobs, those kind of things happen. But I think you'll see there were times when I had to break a few tackles, I had to make people miss me. Everybody had a role to play, and I had to do some things. I'm not insulted by that at all. I'm thankful. I'm thankful for the system.

It had been a fullback-oriented offense until I came. My freshman year, Champ Henson was our main fullback; Champ ran the ball most of the time. Our fullback would always lead the country in scoring, because when we got close, our fullback was going to put it in. We'd get in that robust-T and our halfbacks would do the blocking for our fullback to put it in. That never really changed under Coach Hayes. Then Champ got his knee hurt in my sophomore year, and that's when I really started carrying the ball. It was a shame. Champ was talented, big and strong. He led the country in scoring; he'd bowl right over you.

Coach Hayes was what I liked in a coach. I knew his goal was to make the team the best we could possibly be, and make sure everybody was doing the very best they possibly could do. That was his whole thing, and that's what I wanted in a coach. The extra was the fact that he cared about people. Other people may say his football showed that he wasn't very versatile, but he was so versatile that he could talk about anything with anybody. He could be with anybody and make them feel comfortable.

I have two boys, Anthony and Andre. Anthony is 13 and Andre is 12, and I'd want my own boys to play for someone like that. Anthony, the oldest, doesn't play football. His sports are basketball and baseball. Andre loves football. He's probably like I was. He probably likes it too much. That was in my first marriage. They live in Cleveland. My wife now is expecting a child on Michigan day this year. I hope it's not Michigan day, because I'd like to go to the game. If she has the baby on Michigan day and I'm in Michigan, I think I'm in deep trouble.

I liked sports, but education was important to me. In junior high, I used to talk about my older brother playing football at Muskingum College, and I told my teacher I wanted to do that some day. I said, 'I'm gonna do that. I'm gonna get an education.' In junior high school, my mind was made up. I was going to go to college and I was going to get it through football, because my older brother did it through football. I knew it back then. I was going to work hard. And I was going to enjoy the heck out of it in college. I really didn't think about playing pro football until after making All-American here as a sophomore. People said, 'Hey, you have a chance to play pro football.' And it worked out.

I would just like to be remembered as a person who in every situation did the very best that he could possibly do, a person who gave it his best shot. I think I've lived up to that. ”

Of Toads *and* Kuhndogs

WOODY HAYES scoffed at questions about "the role of football in a changing society and all that junk." Nonetheless, after Haight-Ashbury, Woodstock, and Kent State (and the campus riots that brought the National Guard to Columbus in 1970), football would never be the same. Thirty years ago, the highest praise a coach could give a player was, "If you told that boy to go move the stadium, he'd kill himself trying to do it." By the time Ken Kuhn came to OSU in 1972, skepticism had begun to replace blind obedience—even in football, which Hayes still regarded as America's last haven of order and discipline.

As plump youngster growing up in Louisville, Ohio, Kuhn was derisively nicknamed "Toad." Every fall, he was embarrassed at having to buy his school clothes in the "husky" section of Sears. A diet doctor prescribed a regimen of vitamins and Dexedrine for him. He put on a rubber suit and sat in the hot crawl space above the family's garage. He also became the neighborhood clown. "I was always trying to be funny. I would make up for being made fun of," he says.

Kuhn outgrew his chubbiness and turned to sports, like his older brother, Dick, to whom he was constantly compared. Both Dick and Mark Stier, who married Kuhn's sister, played for Ohio State's 1968 national champions. Kuhn remembers watching the Rose Bowl on television, afraid that he would never be good enough to play in such an important game. He was good enough: Named All-Ohio and All-American, he turned down other scholarships to play for Hayes, who, he says, was "like a god." With a freshly shaved head and a new nickname—"Kuhndog"—he arrived in Columbus just as the first Watergate burglars were indicted.

Kuhn says he never doubted that he'd become a starting linebacker, but he found himself behind juniors Randy Gradishar, Rick Middleton, and Vic Koegel, all of whom would play in the NFL. However, Gradishar was injured in the fifth game, and Kuhn came in to make seven tackles and earn his first buckeye leaf. The following week, he led the team with 18 tackles against Wisconsin. He made 14 tackles and intercepted a Minnesota pass inside the OSU 10 to preserve a one-point lead in the Homecoming game. ("One of the big plays of the year," Hayes said.) Along with Archie Griffin and Brian Baschnagel, Kuhn was called by reporters "one of Ohio State's brilliant freshmen."

Kuhn's early accomplishments made his next three seasons all the more frustrating. "I had the misfortune of coming between Gradishar and Cousineau," he says, but Kuhn's "bad luck" goes beyond having to compete for the spotlight. For the rest of his career, Kuhn alternated fine, gutsy performances and games on the bench because of injuries ranging from severe ankle sprains to shoulder separations.

He also became embroiled in a long-running conflict with defensive coordinator George Hill. Kuhn won't mention Hill by name, but claims "my coach" had little regard for him. Sensitive, bright, a loner, Kuhn had come to Columbus scarred from a childhood of ridicule. He chafed under authority, refusing to quietly back down when he thought he'd been treated unjustly by Hill, who called Kuhn a "coach-killer." "Maybe he felt that way because I was anti-establishment," Kuhn says. "I always try to be myself. I wasn't their nice little guy. I voiced my opinion."

Inevitably, Kuhn's outspokenness led him to clash with Hayes, who once said, "In football, you learn when a coach calls play 26, you run play 26. You don't say, 'Ah, maybe he shouldn't have called that.' You're goddamned dead if you do that." Kuhn was elected a captain in 1975, but only after teammates insisted that he be placed on the ballot in defiance of Hayes's decision to exclude him.

Hayes and Kuhn approached football—and life—from fundamentally different angles. "You don't win when you're too damn happy, and I like to win," Hayes once said. By contrast, Kuhn explained to a reporter, "I just like to enjoy life. That's what life is all about. Too many people are tied up in things and don't enjoy life." Yet the two men were also similarly headstrong, impulsive, and willing to live with the consequences of their actions. Indeed, those who know both say that though Hayes could be exasperated by Kuhn, he also had a soft spot for the rugged linebacker.

During the violent unrest of 1970, Hayes roamed the campus, making passionate speeches about traditional values. Autocratic and in his 60s, Hayes agonized over how to deal with players who talked about "needs" and "hang-ups" and "individual freedom." "I guess he thought it was still 1958," Kuhn says. "He just couldn't deal with the changes in players." (Later in his career, Hayes said that a coach should retire at 50, because after that age, he can no longer relate to players.)

In that confusing time, the gulf between football's paramilitary structure and the tumult in society widened, exerting new pressures on players as well as coaches. Intellectually, Kuhn was able to manage the contradictions; he is, for example, the only Ohio State linebacker ever to make the Academic All-Big Ten team twice. Emotionally, he was baffled by instructions to act like a madman on the field and a gentleman off it—neither of which attitude was consistent with the behavior he observed around campus.

Hayes insisted that his players live with the student body rather than in athletes' dorms, thus broadening the perspective of his charges. The practice had results the coach didn't anticipate, though. "I came to Ohio State, and it's a whole different world," Kuhn says. "All of a sudden, you're thrust into a society within a society." And that society included an active counterculture to which Kuhn—naturally curious and alienated by a distant relationship with his old-fashioned, blue collar father—was drawn.

Shortly after UCLA upset Ohio State in the 1976 Rose Bowl, Kuhn and junior defensive tackle Nick Buonamici showed up at a team meeting after having been to a tavern. Infuriated, Hayes denied Buonamici, a second-team All-American, the opportunity to be a captain. When Buonamici asked for an explanation, Hayes threw him off the squad "for disciplinary reasons." Kuhn took the battle to the student newspaper. In a document unique in the annals of Buckeye football, he called Buonamici's dismissal "a disgrace to Ohio State University and its football staff."

"Let us do our own thing as long as we produce," Kuhn told the *Lantern*. "Why must we minimize our free spirit when he himself is free-spirited? Hayes is a great man and an excellent coach, but he must begin to realize the needs of his players, both on and off the field, as individuals and as human beings."

Kuhn was drafted by Cincinnati, but a knee injury ended his professional stint after only two seasons, and he became deeply depressed. Ironically, Kuhn found solace in the very conventional verities that Hayes advocated: Teammates, hard work as a carpenter, marriage, a new career in sales, two young sons, a new home, community service, being involved with the university.

A reporter once called Kuhn "one of the most engaging young athletes on the Buckeye squad," and he remains extremely personable. He seems eager to please, odd for one who so often did what important figures in his life didn't want him to do.

He's still self-concious about his weight (though he's no more out of shape than most other 40-year-old former athletes) and tends to wear baggy sweat clothes. He has a salt-and-pepper beard and a receding hairline. His shoulders are broad, his hips surprisingly narrow, his forearms thick and powerful. He looks like a long-haul truck driver or a stevedore, until you notice his intelligent, melancholy, deep-set eyes.

Sentimental, he is sometimes moved to tears as he speaks, but he just as frequently laughs heartily. He maintains that he would rather have played for a coach with whom he could have talked more openly, but Kuhn is also quick to take responsibility for contributing to his own troubles. "I don't have a halo over my head, obviously," he says.

He has also concluded that he was frequently influenced by what others expected of him: "A lot of people think linebackers are supposed to be wild, crazy people. I never was a wild, crazy person. I acted like that when I really wasn't."

Although he was tormented for years by how things might've gone, Kuhn says that he's finally come to terms with it all: "I look back on it now, and the fond memories outweigh the negative memories, but for a long time, the negative memories outweighed the positive ones."

Ken KUHN

"I WAS A FAT LITTLE KID. I was nicknamed Toad. What a name to grow up with. There was a big swimming pool there in Louisville, Ohio. I used to wear a sweatshirt when I went swimming because I was self-conscious about my weight. I had these fins and goggles, and I would swim around under water and mess with the girls' trunks or whatever. One day, I came walking out of the pool. My brother and his buddies were sitting up there on the grassy area shooting the bull. I come walking out with my goggles on, and one of my brother's buddies says, 'Hey, Kuhn, your brother looks like a toad.' So I grew up as The Toad.

When I was a little kid, I was always the last one to catch people playing tag, but we had this game called British Bulldog, which I was great at. I don't know if you know what British Bulldog was, but you have two lines of kids. One line would run, and one guy would be 'it.' One guy would be in charge of tackling, and you'd tackle one guy, and he'd be on your team. You gradually tackled everybody until the final guy was tackled. I was always the final guy tackled, because as big as I was, I was always carrying four or five kids.

I wanted to be accepted. There was a lot of hurt inside of me when I was a kid, from being made fun of. I think, to this day, that I was learning to become a salesman when I was The Toad. I was learning how to deal with people, to get beyond that facade. As a child, the first six, seven, eight years of your life, you develop what affects you the rest of your life—

the love, understanding, what's right and wrong. When you're a fat little kid and made fun of all the time, that affects you the rest of your life.

I tried to lose weight. We had this crawl space over our garage. I'd go out and jog and wear this rubber suit, and when I got done jogging, I'd climb up the ladder into this crawl space in the summer and just sit up there to try to sweat the weight off of me. I think that period of time, growing up and being made fun of and being compared, is what made me work harder my whole life. My brother and I would play basketball, throw the baseball, and the other kids my age who weren't heavy could do things better than me. They said, 'You'll never be as good as your brother. Look at your brother. Look how good he is. Toad, fat boy.' I've gotten over it now, but for a long time, it hurt. I think it made me work a lot harder. I don't know if it made me more aggressive. A lot of people think linebackers are supposed to be wild, crazy people. I never was a wild, crazy person. I think later on, I acted like that when I really wasn't. I'm like a puppy dog. I need the spoken word of love and affection.

My father's father was a drinker, abused the kids. My father never knew how to express love, so when we were growing up, he would try to get my brother and me mad at him. He would try to get us mad to go out and play good sports. I know it helped me, but now there's not a day that goes by that I don't grab my kids and hug them and kiss them and tell them I love them. Every time they do something good, I always give them positive reinforcement. I guess I'm making up for what I didn't have.

I LIKED FOOTBALL because it reminded me of British Bulldog, the one thing that I did well as a kid. I couldn't play tag on the playground because I couldn't catch kids. I wasn't fast enough, but I was great at British Bulldog. I remember this one teacher watching us play on the playground and saying, 'How could you carry all those kids on your back?' This was one thing I could do and do well, and I was proud of that. I guess that's what made me like football. I guess what I liked most about it was the camaraderie. The guys I ended up playing with in high school were the guys who made fun of me when I was younger. All of a sudden The Toad started getting all the glory. My senior year, we were undefeated, and we were a tightknit group. A lot of those guys were talented, but they didn't have the size, the physique, or the total skills I had. There was a lot of resentment that I got all these offers to go to college. There again, I was alone. I had a lot of hurt inside of me because a lot of guys I thought were my buddies weren't my buddies anymore, for whatever reason, whether it was jealously or envy or disgust about their career not going on like mine did.

I was first-team All-Ohio, first-team high school All-American, Scholastic All-American, Stark County MVP. That's pretty strong when you consider Massillon and Canton-McKinley were there, and I was from little Louisville, Ohio. That one trophy over there in that case is the Stark County MVP trophy from my senior year. There was a running back out of Massillon named Willie Spencer who was a senior at the same time, and we competed to be the leading scorer in the county. I punted, I kicked off, I kicked field goals, extra points; I was a fullback and a linebacker. I never left the field. That gave me a sense of accomplishment, but it still didn't fill that void. I had one girlfriend I dated all through high school, Mary, and she was more my best friend than any of the players I played with.

My senior year at Louisville, Mondays were kind of slow. We had a great team, and on Mondays, the coaches let us play touch football. While the other guys were playing touch football, I was out jogging a couple of miles. They're over there having fun, but they never invited me to come play with them. I was out there by myself, jogging, getting that endurance, that extra little edge. I was beat up and sore, but I was still out there pumping out a couple of miles. Instead of being over there with the boys, I was running around the big practice field. I knew I needed to go that extra mile if I wanted to be as good as I hoped to be. That drive came from when I was a kid, The Toad.

My brother went to Ohio State and played on that '68 national championship team. I remember watching them play in the Rose Bowl against USC and O.J. Simpson and wondering if I'd ever be good enough to play on a team like that. I never thought I'd be that good. In little league football, if you're a big kid, they make you play center or line. As a freshman, they decided, 'Kenny looks like he could be a running back.' That's when I first became a fullback. As a sophomore, I started varsity. I was a three-year letterman in football, a three-year letterman in basketball, still hold the high school shot record. But as a freshman, watching that Rose Bowl, there was still that doubt inside of me.

I don't remember envying my brother. I remember being afraid that I wouldn't be that good. I can remember to this day worrying about what the people back in the hometown were going to think or worrying about what the old man was going to say. No matter how good a game I had, there would be a critique. Michigan wanted me pretty bad, and a rumor got out that I told some people I was going to go to Michigan. At the time, my brother was a graduate assistant coach at Ohio State. Woody found out that I was thinking about going to Michigan, and he called my brother into his office and threatened to fire him if I didn't come to Ohio State.

Woody spoke at my high school football banquet my senior year and the auditorium was packed. He was like a god. I had just won Stark County MVP. I was All-American, All-State. I had everything in the world going for me. Woody Hayes in little Louisville, Ohio.

In Louisville, that wasn't as strong as if Ara Parsegian had been there, though. Louisville is a Notre Dame town, always has been, always will be. Between me, my brother, and my brother-in-law, we played in six Rose Bowls. But that don't cut no ice in Louisville. If that would've been Notre Dame, there'd be statues in Louisville of us. They didn't give a crap about Ohio State in Louisville. I don't want to sound prejudiced, but it was a Catholic town, and we were Baptists.

MY BROTHER NEVER TOLD ME much about Ohio State or Woody Hayes. All Dick ever told me was, 'Hey, they know you're a great athlete. They want you really bad. I know how good you are. You can come here and play.' That's all I needed to hear. I didn't know what was going on in Columbus.

I didn't smoke, I didn't drink, I was a born-again Christian, straight-laced. When I came to Ohio State, it seemed like almost everybody was doing Quaaludes and drinking. I wasn't accepted. Lou Pietrini was my roommate, a *Scholastic* All-American from Milford, Connecticut, a defensive tackle. He got a knee injury, got mononucleosis, had a terrible freshman year. He went back to Connecticut that summer, and we talked to each other a couple of times. He never said he wasn't coming back. We reported back to camp our sophomore year, and Lou never showed up. I'm lost, because Lou and I did everything together. I called up there, and he told me, 'I'm not coming back.'

I said, 'Why?'

He said, 'I just don't want to come back.'

He said he was going to become a plumbing apprentice or maybe go to college up there. We reported on a Saturday, and we had a team breakfast and a team meeting on Sunday. I was lonely again, without Lou. I wrote this personal letter to Woody, slipped it under his door, and jumped in my car. I took off for Milford, Connecticut. In the letter, I more or less said, 'Coach, I had a great year as a freshman. I might've become kind of arrogant, and I wasn't accepted by some of my peers. Lou Pietrini was my best friend in the world, and I love Lou Pietrini. I think he's given up on his career, and I think he's doing the wrong thing. I'm lost without him. So I may be doing the wrong thing for my career and my future, and maybe I'm not doing the right thing for the team, but I'm leaving here today, and I'm not coming back without him.'

I did that from my heart, and I put it under his door. Woody stayed in the dormitories with us, and we all knew where his room was. That Sunday morning, I slid it under the door, and I just took off. I had just turned 19 years old. I had never driven out of the state of Ohio. I was scared to death. I had started as a freshman. I knew I had the ability to be great. I don't want to sound egotistical, but I knew I had the talent. Randy Gradishar was a great player, but one on one, I'd eat his lunch. You check out a run isolation play, I could handle it. I was the best. Randy's skill was pass coverage and pursuit. Randy would make 22 tackles a game, but a lot of them were five or six yards down field. I'd make the tackle, and it'd be at the line or in the backfield.

Anyway, I put that letter under Woody's door, and I took off for Connecticut. It was real wild, and I'll tell you what Ohio State's coaches did. Once they got that letter, they called Lou's parents in Connecticut and told them, 'We sent Kenny up to get Lou.' It was the defensive tackle coach, Chuck Clausen. Woody had him call, because he recruited Lou.

I stopped at a gas station somewhere in Pennsylvania and got a map of the northeastern United States. When I got to Milford, I got off and went into some fast food store that was just closing, and one of the girls there said, 'I don't know where he lives, but I know his uncle owns a restaurant.'

I went down there and knocked on the door. They had already closed. It was about 3 o'clock in the morning. I finally found Lou. We went back to his house, and the next morning, we got up, and I said, 'I don't know what the hell I did.'

We got packed up, got back in my car, and drove back, 10, 12, 13 hours, however long it took. When we got back to Columbus, it was in the middle of the night, too. The dorms were locked. We looked around;

there was one window open on the lower level. It was a hot summer, and at that time, Woody wouldn't let us stay in a dorm that had air conditioning. We crawled through a window and went up to our room and went to bed.

The next morning, we came down, and every morning at breakfast, Woody would sit right there at the door. You had to say 'Good morning, Coach Hayes.' If you didn't, he'd chew you out. Lou and I come walking in, and everybody's, 'Hey, Lou, how you doin'? Lou, you're back.'

I'm thinking, 'What the hell's going to happen? Is he going to kick me off the team or what?'

We come walking in, and there's Woody sitting there. He looks up at us and just kind of gives us this mean look. He didn't say a word.

I go, 'Oh, here we go.'

We sat down. They got up and made their announcements. He says, 'Okay, everybody's dismissed except Kuhn and Pietrini.'

Everybody shuffles out. Lou and I are sitting there. Woody looks up, calls us over. He says, 'Kenny Kuhn, I don't agree with what you did, but, goddammit, that's the finest thing a man ever did for his buddy. Goddamn, that's a fine thing to do for a teammate.'

He said, 'I don't condone it, but I want your permission to publish that letter you wrote to me. I want to give it to Paul Hornung to put in the paper.'

The next day, there it was, right there on the front page of the sports section: 'Kuhn Goes Long Way To Help Friend.' It goes back to being a lonely kid, and here was the one buddy who helped me get through that freshman year. I think it was more selfish on my behalf. It came out looking like I went to help my friend, but I went because I needed Lou. He was my buddy, my friend. He helped me get through that freshman year. Lou ended up coming back, and he finally got to play. He ended up starting as an offensive tackle his redshirted senior year. I talk to Lou as much as possible. He's probably my best friend in the world, to this day.

I STARTED AS A FRESHMAN, after Gradishar went down with a knee injury. It was the second, third, fourth game of the season, I don't remember. By that time, I had been there long enough to know the system. My coach put me in. I was 18 years old. Woody made a big deal out of this at a team meeting. He got me up in front of the team and said, 'Kenny Kuhn, how old are you?'

'Eighteen, Coach.'

'How many tackles did you have?'

'Eighteen, Coach.'

It was a big deal. I led the team in tackles. I'd be lying if I said I wasn't scared when he put me in, but during the heat of a game, you don't hear the crowd. You're concerned too much about what you have to do. There's too much going on. I was more worried about not being in the right place at the right time. Against Minnesota, right before the half, we were losing, and they threw a pass, and I intercepted it on the one yard line and almost ran it all the way back for a touchdown. From then on, all the fears went away.

But my sophomore year, I had to be satisfied sitting on the bench, backing up all three linebackers. As a sophomore, I was plagued with injuries because I was on all the speciality teams—hip pointers, twisted ankles. I wanted to play, and I played. Any time they needed to spell somebody, I went in. Here's two linebackers who end up being first-round draft choices, Randy Gradishar and Rick Middleton. They're seniors, and I'm a sophomore. My coach is not going to pull them out and put me in. But I played enough to letter.

During my sophomore year, I got introduced to drugs. I don't know how much I want to say about that stuff. There's a book inside of me—*Four Roses and a Crown of Thorns*. That's my life. I've always known that my life went the way it did for a reason, and I'd really like to tell the honest, true story about what it was like to have grown up at that time. When I left Louisville, I had everything going for me. I came to Ohio State, and it's a whole different world. All of a sudden, you're thrust into a society within a society. That campus was a city within a city. What it's like growing up in Stark County, the mecca of high school football, and being The Toad and learning all those pains and aches. It's tough enough being a kid in the world, but when you've got some kind of burden, physical or emotional, some kind of a handicap, it's worse. I want it to be a book that a dad can give his son and say, 'Here's a guy who's done it all. He had it all. He went through a change in society, experienced those changes. He learned from his mistakes. He realized that partying is fun, but it can ruin your life. It almost ruined his. Here's what he did after he realized that.' That kind of a book.

Here comes my junior year, and I'm the most senior linebacker. I have the most experience. It's the second or third week of the season, and we're playing Wisconsin, and I make a tackle. I've got the picture somewhere. It shows me tackling him, and we're falling, and all of his weight and all of my weight hit right here, and my shoulder popped out. Well, I had such a muscle mass in my upper body that the doctors and trainers said I didn't separate it, I just bruised it. Yet I could lay on my back in bed and take my collarbone and wiggle it. So, inevitably, what happened was they needed me to play, so they made this big fiberglass pad that dispersed the blow everywhere except right there. They bolted it to my shoulderpads and shot me up so I could play.

Starting off my junior year, I was picked as a possible All-Big Ten, All-American linebacker, but because of that injury, it didn't happen. I played with that all year, and they're shooting me with cortisone and novacaine. By this time, I've become a substance abuser, doing it all. I'm thinking to myself, 'What's the double standard there? They're saying drugs are bad for you, but it's good enough for them to shoot me up with cortisone and novacaine. They just want me to play. If I feel I need to take an upper or downer or whatever to play, then I'm doing it.'

A LOT OF IT WAS ABOUT BEING ACCEPTED, back to when I was The Toad. They put you in dormitories with regular students: 'Oh, you're a jock, a square jock.' Well, that was right in the heart of the early '70s, and it seemed everybody was partying. I had this idea that I wanted to be a football player, but I wanted to prove I just wasn't another dumb jock. I wanted to play football and party, too, but now I know that partying like that wears and tears on the body. You just can't speed for games and party all night and expect the body to keep maintaining. That's why I had two shoulder operations and two knee operations.

During that time, my father had a series of heart attacks and almost died. One time, he was here in Columbus visiting my sister. I showed up at the hospital when they brought him out of the wagon. My mom said, 'Your dad told me it was your fault he had the heart attack.'

I have no one to talk to about all this stuff I'm going through with. Coaches don't care. How many coaches have you ever played for who really took you aside and wanted to be your friend, find out really what makes Ken Kuhn tick? As a matter of fact, I found out later, my linebacker coach called me a 'coach-killer.' I was always a thorn in his side. I was never the kind of guy to not say what I felt.

I remember playing against USC my junior year. I separated my shoulder in the first half of the Rose Bowl. I went in at halftime, and they shot me up so I could play the second half. They finally decided that my shoulder was separated. The day we got back from the Rose Bowl, they operated on me. While I'm in the hospital, Woody calls a team meeting to pick the captains for the next year. I found out about the team meeting, and I went ahead and checked myself out of the hospital. Didn't even tell the hospital or anybody. I just got on my outfit, walked out the door in a sling, popped a pain killer, and went to the meeting. We had gotten beat by USC. I played against Bill Bain, who was a 6' 6", 260-pound All-American. I'm playing against him with one arm, protecting this shoulder. I come down to the meeting. I sat there sweating, in pain, and you know how Woody was after a loss, very bitter.

He said, 'Okay, we're picking team captains. On offense, we've got Archie and Brian Baschnagel, because they've been starters for three years. On defense, we've got Tim Fox.'

He didn't even mention my name. I had played all year in pain, with a separated shoulder. One of my teammates, Pat Curto, stood up and said, 'What about Kenny Kuhn? He deserves to be a co-captain.'

Woody says, 'Bullshit. He didn't contribute enough this year.'

I'm sitting right there, in pain, and it goes right back to when I was a kid. Here's a guy who's cutting down on me in one way or another. He doesn't feel that I contributed enough, yet I played with a separated shoulder. They shot me up so I could play, and he feels that I don't deserve to be captain.

One by one, my teammates got up and said, 'Kenny Kuhn deserves to be on the ballot.'

It was the happiest feeling I ever had in my life. It was like that movie *Rudy*, when all the players come in and drop their jerseys on the coach's desk and say, 'I want Rudy to wear this jersey.' When I saw that movie, I cried. If I recall correctly, I ended up getting the most votes. I'll never forget that. When my teammates stood up, it was like all that hard work, playing with the shoulder and everything, had paid off. What greater accolade could I have than my teammates doing that for me?

After that meeting, my coach took me in his office and said, 'Kenny Kuhn, you're a no good son-of-a-bitch. All you are is a drunk.'

I didn't fit the mold of what Woody or my coach or any of them wanted me to be. I always wanted to be my own self. If a player on that team had a problem, he came to me, Kuhndog. Here it is, right here on my shoulder—the Kuhndog. I got the Kuhndog tattoo when I was a sophomore, then I got the four roses put on after I played in four Rose Bowls. It used to be bigger when I was lifting weights. It's the Marine bulldog.

You ought to have seen Woody's face when he first saw that tattoo. There was a little tattoo shop in town, guy by the name of Stoney, little crippled guy who had a tattoo parlor right there on High Street, in the Short North. Steve, Ed, Lou, myself, and Pete all got tattoos. These guys were our idols. These guys were wild, crazy, body-building, partying, butt-kicking men. The tattoos became a tradition. Cousineau has that shark on his leg. Ed Trepanier had these arms that were almost 25 inches, and he had this little tank with a bullet coming out of it and a puff of smoke. We weren't blasted drunk or anything when we did it. We knew what we were doing. I just wasn't sure what dog I wanted to get. I didn't want some goofy looking dog, so I walked in, and there was the Marine bulldog. I said, 'Yeah.' A linebacker, the Marine bulldog.

We never thought about losing. Some of us would go out Thursday nights, party, get drunk, get psyched up for the games. We'd've probably done it Friday night, but they had us locked up in hotel rooms. We had this inner belief in ourselves, and we were just going to go out and beat people. You'd look at Woody and see this old dictator out on the football field getting fired up and punching people. We loved him, and we hated him. Yelling and screaming didn't go very far with me personally. It might've with some of the kids, and it might've worked well for him in the '50s and '60s, but by the time the '70s rolled around, it was a different world. I think we were more aware of ourselves; we were more aware of what was going on in society. That old brow-beating tradition didn't go very far anymore, but it was successful for him for years. The guys who played for him during those years...you hear some of these guys talk about him, and he was like God to them. There's no doubt about it. But, I think, as his age came on, he didn't adapt, he didn't change. He was like Nixon. They were tight buddies.

His tantrums were funny. It was almost embarrassing sometimes to see this old man who's supposed to be this great idol in Ohio, this man who's made men, punching kids and kicking them in the butt, and verbally abusing them. I wasn't intimidated by him. I'm 6' 2", 250 pounds. How am I going to be threatened by an old man? Maybe a very introverted type might be affected, but I was never intimidated by Woody. I guarantee you there are a lot of guys who'd say they weren't intimidated by Woody. Anyway, he wasn't trying to hurt anyone. I mean, how is a 60-year-old man going to hurt you, especially if you're wearing a helmet and shoulder pads? It's not like he was always smacking someone, and when he did, I think it was for the psychological effect more than anything else.

My freshman year, Toyota came out with this plan to plant a tree for every car you buy. He said, 'Those goddamned communist Japanese. They bombed Pearl Harbor, and now they're trying to take over America by planting trees, the sonsabitches.' Some of us would be high in meetings. We'd be laughing our asses off. He'd talk about smoking marijuana: 'Yeah, guys who smoke marijuana go over and piss in the corner.'

HE WAS NOT IN TOUCH with what was going on with his players. He thought that because we were Ohio State football players, we were somehow supposed to build barriers between ourselves and real life. They put us in a dormitory room—me and Lou and this heavyweight wrestler. We were in a triple, a corner room. Right next to us were these three hippies dealing pot out of their room. You walk out of our room, and their door is right there. The smell. The first time I got high, they came over and got us high in our room.

How are you supposed to keep yourself from the society itself, especially when you're a voracious young man, a linebacker who'll do anything one time? They're right next to us, black lights, Pink Floyd. How're you supposed to keep yourself separate from that, unless you have that discipline in yourself to do that? I wanted to be accepted. I didn't want to be the dumb jock, especially when you're trying to have a good time.

I guess Woody thought it was still 1958, and it's not like everyone on the team partied like some of us did. A lot of guys were clean-cut, All-American boys. He just couldn't deal with the changes in players, and that's what ultimately cost him his job. I was not shocked when I saw him punch that kid on national TV, because we saw it happen every day in practice. As soon as I saw that kid run over there on the sideline and start waving that ball, I said, 'Oh, oh, something's going to happen.'

What surprised me was that an assistant let him do it. When I was there, John Mummey was the coach who was always with Woody. Whenever he saw Woody getting steamed, he was always there to block it off.

Somebody should've been right with Woody that day to keep him from punching that kid. He did it out of frustration, and he was just getting old. He got to the point that he felt he was so powerful that he could do anything. He was like a dictator. The whole staff was afraid of him. Hell, all the reporters in town were afraid of him. He had a select few reporters who got all the interviews nobody else did. He had total control. When he didn't have control, that's when he'd lose it. It went back to his naval days. He was the commander, and everything on that ship was under his control. He ran the team like he ran a ship.

I was sad when I saw that happen, because I knew that was the end of Woody as a coach. I knew there was going to be some serious retribution. I didn't know if they would fire him. I thought that's what probably should have happened, but I didn't know if that was going to happen. I felt no sense of satisfaction at all. I was saddened by it. All things said and done, I still loved Woody Hayes, and I respected him, but I wondered about some of his methods, too.

Everybody who came to Ohio State was a great player somewhere or another. A lot of guys came and never played. I saw him form opinions about players, and if he didn't like them, they weren't going to play—no way. In my case, he might not've liked me, but he had to play me because I was the best he had at that position. He made a statement to my brother after my career was over. He said, 'You know, Dick, the other day I met a man who was an English professor. He told me something that kind of shocked me at first, but once I thought about it, it made a lot of sense. He told me that one of the most intelligent students he'd ever taught at Ohio State was your brother Kenny. After I thought about that, it made a lot of sense. He was *too* damn smart. If I had it to do over again, I'd've handled your brother, instead of letting his coach handle it.'

After Dick told me that, I sat and reflected: 'Thank God he finally realized that I wasn't as bad as he thought I was.'

My coach was the linebacker coach and defensive coordinator, and he screwed my head up big time. When I came in as a freshman and played and started in big-time college football, he and I just butted heads. We never hit it off. It got so bad that once I entertained the thought of getting one of those little CO_2 cylinders for a pellet gun and dropping it in his radiator. He'd be driving down the road, and the motor would blow up in his face. I never really seriously considered doing it, but I was so frustrated and angry that the thought did cross my mind.

What hurt me most was that I was the first linebacker that he had from a freshman through a senior. He actually came to my home, sat in front of my parents, told them, 'I'll take care of your son.' I envied some of the other players. Ralph Staub and George Chaump were great coaches. They got along with their players. My coach had his nose stuck so far up Woody Hayes's butt I don't know how he breathed. He wanted that head coaching job bad. That's why he called me a 'coach-killer.' That's why I was always coming up in discussions: 'Kuhn's this, Kuhn's that.' I never did get along with him. As a matter of fact, my mother said, 'I don't trust that man, because he can't look you straight in the eye.' Even when he was recruiting me, he never looked me in the eye. He was always looking over your head somewhere.

I NEVER CONSIDERED TRANSFERRING, because I loved Ohio State. I loved my teammates. That's the best memories I have, the times I had with those guys. How can you not have good memories when you won? We rarely lost. The bad memories I have, the worst memories, are my brother and my brother-in-law both have national championship rings. I don't have one. To this day, I don't wear my rings, because they don't mean that much to me. They're not national championship rings. I know guys who would give their left arm for a Big Ten ring or a Rose Bowl ring. Hell, I had four Rose Bowl watches and four Big Ten rings. They don't mean that much because we didn't win it all. I had it inside of me that I would maybe someday have a Super Bowl ring.

A lot of what came on me, I caused myself. I could've not tried to revolt as much. Cousineau came in, and I knew he was going to be a great linebacker. I showed him how to be a linebacker for the defensive coach. Cousineau liked to party, like a lot of us did, but I told him, 'Don't be as stupid as I was. This's how our coach is, and here's how to deal with him.' And he did. The guy loved him. When they needed me, I was there. I filled the shoes. I did what I was supposed to do. As a freshman, come in and lead the team in tackles? That's pretty strong. But that also tells you how our defense was geared. The linebackers were supposed to make the tackles. It wasn't that great a thing for a Randy Gradishar or a Rick Middleton or a Ken Kuhn to have 20 tackles a game. The way our slant defense was, scraping linebackers—backside, weakside linebackers—filling gaps were supposed to make the tackles. That's the way the defense was set up. If you didn't make the tackles, then you shouldn't be in there.

It was all like a chain of disappointments—being The Toad, the loneliness, the unfulfilled dreams. Another things is, I didn't graduate. I could kick myself. I was Academic All-Big Ten my sophomore and junior years. After we lost the Rose Bowl my senior year, they kicked Nick off the team, and I just kind of dropped out. I said, 'The hell with it.' I didn't think I was going to get drafted. My coach wouldn't even talk to me to tell me when the scouts were coming to watch. I heard through the grapevine that the Senior Bowl called and wanted Lenny Willis and me to come, but the coaching staff told them they didn't know how to get in touch with us. How bad is that?

They gave me grief, yet I played for them the whole year before with so much pain. Then he tells me I don't deserve to be captain, but my teammates tell me I do. We go the whole senior year. He calls me a no-good alcoholic son-of-a-bitch and says I've been nothing but grief to him. I don't care. I'm a 20-year-old kid, still trying to figure out what I am, where I want to go, what I want to be.

Then for Woody to come out and tell my brother after my career was over that he should've handled me, not let my coach do it, that was like, 'Great, now you realize it, Woody. Thanks.'

There again, though, I caused a lot of my own grief. We went to the Rose Bowl my senior year, and a girl I dated in high school had a relative, a lady who was divorced, living out there, a good-looking lady. I talked on the phone with her a few times before we went out. I don't have a steady girlfriend. We get out there, and she comes to the hotel and meets me. She was a good-looking lady in her mid-20s, late-20s, had an ex-husband that abused her and her gorgeous little kid. Well, Woody would always give us no curfew Christmas Eve. All you had to do was be back for breakfast the next morning. I spent Christmas Eve day with her and her kid. We went out and got a Christmas tree, decorated the tree. Nick and Lou came over, and she cooked dinner for all of us. When it came time to leave, Lou said, 'C'mon, let's go. It's time to leave.'

I said, 'Go ahead and go. I'm not going. I'm staying here. I want to be here tomorrow morning and open up gifts with them.'

I stayed there. We had a great morning. She finally brought me back to the hotel. I knew all hell was going to break loose, but I didn't care. I don't know why I would do it. Maybe some of that deep-seated need to be accepted, needing to be loved, more than anything. That's what made me make those wild decisions without worrying about the consequences.

It was probably a stupid decision, but I lived with it. My mom once said, 'Kenny, you never hurt anybody except yourself.' I agree, but I've lived with the consequences.

When I got back, they were looking for me. When I wasn't there for breakfast, the word was out: 'Find Kuhn.' They went to Lou. Poor Lou, he got drug into a lot of stuff because he was my roommate. Lou's not going to say, 'He's with this chick.'

He said, 'Oh, I haven't seen him since yesterday.'

So I got my neck in trouble because I didn't show up for breakfast that next morning. I mean, we're at the Rose Bowl, and I didn't show up for breakfast. I'm sure my coach got crap from Woody for that. I got chewed out; I was confined to my room. I'm surprised they didn't send me home. Well, I'm not surprised. They didn't send me home because they needed me.

There was Ken Kuhn making a decision, just like when I took off to get Lou Pietrini. It meant more to me to be with this woman and that little boy on Christmas day, because this was the fourth year in a row I was away from my family on Christmas.

I know, when we lost that game, he blamed it on me. I thought we were going to win, and it wasn't going to matter. I didn't know that interception would end the game. We were on a drive. Craig Cassady had just intercepted a pass, and he says that he has a picture of me throwing a block for him, knocking out two guys to get him free. We run down to their 35, 40 yard line, and there's enough time for us to score. Woody sends in a play. Corny audibles. I see the look on Woody's face. He's going, 'No. No.' Still, in my mind, I see Corny throw the ball right to this guy. Not that it was Corny's fault that we lost that game; we were all to blame for that one. Woody, tears just came from his eyes. That was it. It was over. That was my chance to have a ring like my brother and brother-in-law.

I know he blamed that loss on me not coming back for breakfast. He didn't come out and say it, but I know he felt it. I can bitch and complain about the coaches, but I caused a lot of my own grief. Everything that came after that game I deserved, I guess. They disowned me. They wouldn't tell me when the scouts were coming to check me out. The team banquet after that game, Nick and I show up drunk, and I'm so depressed and pissed off, I don't care anymore. We're in a team meeting, and they're picking captains, and Nick, by his performance, in my opinion, deserved to be considered, just like I was. He wasn't the type of guy Woody thought should be team captain, so they didn't even include him on the ballot. So, right in that team meeting, right before the banquet, Woody kicked Nick off the team. Woody's up at the podium, and when Nick doesn't get captain, he starts getting real loud. He's sitting right next to me: 'They're screwing me! What's going on here!'

Woody points out at Nick and says, 'You're no good. You don't deserve anything. You're off this team.'

He says, 'You, too, Ken Kuhn. You've been a no-good son-of-a-bitch the whole four years you've been here.'

NICK GOT KICKED OFF THE TEAM. We went into the banquet. All the captains got up and said something. I got up—and I'll never forget this—my parents are out in the crowd, and I said, 'I didn't get all the awards my teammates got. I wasn't an All-American or anything, but I know this, all these guys up here know me and love me, and that's the best award you can have.' I was fighting tears, especially since Nick just got kicked off the team.

Then I got my butt in trouble because Nick was my roommate, and the national press is trying to find out why Nick Buonamici got kicked off the team. They're all calling my apartment, and I'm trying to be the go-between, because I don't want to see him screw up his career like what happened to me. To make a long story short, he and Woody came back together, and Nick had a great season, intercepting passes, All-American. But if I wouldn't have been fielding all these calls from the press, he would've probably gotten his butt in more trouble.

I hope most of the players who played with me or were younger than me would smile and say something positive: 'He was wild, but he was a good guy. He would do anything for you.' I would hope that's what they would say. If so, then I've gotten what I want out of life. A lot of guys aren't going to talk about what went on there. I guarantee you, there weren't many guys as wild and crazy as Ken Kuhn and Nick Buonamici, but we're all different now. We've all mellowed. I'm amazed I'm still alive to talk about it.

I loved the guys I played with. I loved Nick Buonamici, I loved Champ Henson, I loved Lou Pietrini. Those are things that coaches or politics can't take away. I loved Woody Hayes, but I resented him, too, because he didn't have the ability to try and understand us. He couldn't accept the fact that he couldn't understand us. There was a guy by the name of Billy Joe Armstrong. Billy Joe was like Woody's second son. He was a great center for Ohio State, and he was president of Worthington Industries for a long time. Billy and I became real good buddies and he gave me my first sales job. He said, 'You know, Kenny, when you guys were playing, I got a call from Woody. Woody told me, "Goddammit, Bill, I don't know what to do with these guys. They're crazy. They've got long hair, beards, but goddammit, they sure can play football."'

That was true. We were part of those times. We reflected those times—the looks, the sideburns, the hair. Somebody asked me not too long ago, 'Whatever happened to Ohio State's success?'

I jokingly said, 'The advent of urinalysis.'

But that's not just true for Ohio State. When I went to the Bengals, there were guys there from Texas A&M, Nebraska, Oklahoma, Penn State. It was the same thing everywhere.

I owe a lot to Ohio State football. Even to this day, being a co-captain, playing in four Rose Bowls, I'm amazed how many people will hear my name and remember. If you're a four-year player and a co-captain at that level of competition, people have got to remember you. I'll be at a local pub or something and I'll hear someone say, 'That's Ken Kuhn over there.' Some little old guy will come over to you and say, 'Let me shake your hand. I remember that game where you stuck this guy.' It makes you feel good. That and 75 cents will get me a cup of coffee. It opens doors. That's all it does, open doors. You still have to do the job.

I DIDN'T THINK I WAS GOING TO THE PROS. I thought I'd be black-balled. I finally did get drafted in the seventh round. It was a surprise. I never went and ran for any of these scouts. After what happened at the Rose Bowl, I guarantee you that my coach said, 'You don't want Ken Kuhn, because he's a coach-killer. He's not the kind of player you want on your team.' I had this hope inside of me that if they went by my abilities, I should be drafted in the first wave. At that time, they did seven rounds on the first day, then came back and did the rest on the second day.

That day, we had a big blowout party at my apartment, waiting for the call. Well, the call never came. It came early the next morning. I had gotten drafted in the seventh round, which was late that night. I got a call from the linebacker coach, who said they drafted me in the seventh round and they were surprised because they thought I would be gone in the first three rounds, which I should've been just knowing what I know about my ability compared to the other players who were drafted in the first three rounds. My coach and the things I pulled cost me a good sum of money.

Two short years, a knee injury ended it all. But by that time, it didn't matter. My head was messed up. I was pissed off. I was partying like a madman to cover the pain. Pro football was a step down from Ohio State. It was shocking how much of a business it was. The Bengals' facilities were a joke compared to Ohio State. Spinney Field, what a joke. I signed for meager money, compared to what it is now, went down and had a great rookie camp, came back to Columbus, was working out. I was keyed. This was my chance to come back and prove them wrong. I lived in an apartment complex, had a couple of Buckeyes living in an apartment down below me. Their refrigerator went out, and the maintenance guys got the old one out and were trying to get the new one in. I went down there, and there's these three guys sitting there with their girlfriends, jamming and partying. This maintenance guy can't get the refrigerator back in where it should be, so I get down and start pushing it, and when I went to get up, I lost my balance and twisted, popped my knee, tore the cartilage. I kept hoping it would go away. I had been through rookie camp. They were real happy. They said, 'We're looking for you to step in at middle linebacker.' They had only drafted myself and Reggie Williams. And I hurt my knee. Here we go again.

Finally, I had my agent call them and tell them I hurt my knee. I went down and had their doctor look at it. It was a buckle-handle cartilage, where the cartilage gets bent over, and you can't straighten it out, you can't bend your knee because of the pain. They let me come back and have Ohio State's team doctor do the surgery. They put me on the injury reserve list. They almost activated me, but they never did. I didn't even get the full money of my first-year contract.

I go back my second year, and I'm gung-ho, I'm in great shape, I'm on speciality teams. The next to the last preseason game, a guy blows my knee out totally, cartilage, ligaments, everything. It was a punt. I looked over at this guy, and he's got these wild eyes. I said, 'This guy's on something. He's probably trying to make the team.' They all went to the gap, and I went to the gap to block him, and these guys over here all collapsed down on me. I remember getting up. Natural instinct—get up and run. I'm running, and I'm feeling my leg kind of blowing in the wind behind me. I come off the field. The team doctors come over and look at it. They moved it sideways. They said, 'Oh, you're not playing any more today.'

We get back to Cincinnati, and the team doctors say, 'We're going to wait and see how it responds.'

I got the word: 'Kenny Kuhn, Mike Brown wants to see you. Bring your playbook.'

I go down to Mike Brown's office. He says, 'Well, Kenny, the doctors have decided there's nothing wrong with your knee.'

This's after they said they were going to operate on it. Mike said, 'We're going to put you on waivers. The only thing is, we need you to sign this paper that says there's nothing wrong with you so we can put you on waivers, or they won't pick you up.'

At that time, in '77, we had virtually no players' union. That same chain of events is happening to me. I'm fighting tears. I said, 'Mike, you know my knee is messed up. I can't sign that paper.'

He said, 'I'll give you $500 if you sign it.'

I said, 'Mike, I don't know what you're trying to do. My knee's screwed up. I can't sign that paper.'

He said, 'If you don't sign that paper, you're not going to be picked up by anybody.'

I'll never forget limping out of that stadium. I had been in a car accident. My car was screwed up. I had no car. I walked out of Riverfront Stadium with a satchel with my personal belongs in it, stuck my thumb out, and hitchhiked to Columbus.

AFTER WHAT I HAD BEEN THROUGH at Ohio State, I wasn't psychologically equipped to continue a career, now that I look back at it. In fact, if I hadn't have gotten my knee injured, I might've ended up being a statistic, being a coke freak, got killed in a car accident or something. That could easily have happened. Until drug testing came around, they didn't care. As long as you were playing and performing, that's all they cared about. I almost went off of the deep end. I didn't talk to anybody. I went and stayed with Champ Henson in his apartment. I went into hiding. I didn't call my parents. All of a sudden, everything the coaches said about me, that I was a no good son-of-a-bitch, was coming true. I almost ended my life. I just really didn't want to live any more.

Fortunately, by the will of the good Lord, I was able to come out of it. I guess there was a little light there deep inside of me that never went out, and it came back. For a three-day period, though, I was in total depression. Almost any player will tell you that that's what they go through when they're finally cut. But Champ was there, and he had gone through something very similar with the Bengals. Champ and I were good friends. Heart as big as the world. Just having him there as a friend and knowing he had been through something similar helped me get out of that.

I had to sue the Bengals, and for a whole year I couldn't get a job. You should get workman's comp or something, but I didn't get anything. Finally, a year and a half later, it came to an arbitrator, and I knew I was in trouble when I met the attorney for the NFLPA. We're in this hotel room in Cincinnati, and here comes the arbitrator walking in with his arm around Paul Brown. You could see where the doctors and trainers had actually changed their entries into their log—the descriptions of my knee injury. I think they owed me 40 grand that year for my contract. They ended up deciding they would pay me so much for every game I played in the preseason. I think the arbitrator said I deserved something like $7,000. After taxes and fees and everything, I think I got a check for something like $3,200 bucks, and they didn't fix my knee. That's the way it ended.

It took me a long time to fight back from that. For a long time, I didn't believe in myself. I almost gave up. If I had a gun, I'd've probably done myself in, because I didn't like myself any more. All along, I knew that I am a pretty good guy, that I am a good player. I do things sometimes that are stupid, but I try to help my friends. When that happened, it was like, 'Maybe they're right.' I didn't do a whole lot for a long time. I did a lot of thinking. My knee was a mess. I couldn't even get a job loading a truck. If I worked, they would say I wasn't hurt. So for almost a year, I lived with my brother, had no income. I tried to go back to school, but my head wasn't into that. My head wasn't into anything. It's probably the toughest time I ever went through in my life.

I prayed a lot, dug deep down inside, went back to the days when I was playing British Bulldog, tried to get back in touch with what made me go then. I told myself, 'Kenny, either give up or go, one or the other. Do it or don't. Do yourself in or get on with it.'

There were a couple of days, if I would've had a gun, I would've been a statistic. It was by the grace of the good Lord that I came out of it. I got a job as a carpenter. I always enjoyed carpentry work, and that's what got me started back. It was almost like starting over as The Toad again.

I worked about four years as a carpenter. That was the best therapy for me, pounding nails. Pound nails, throw studs around, build a wall. There was something I built myself. It showed I was worth something. I could see that as a result of my efforts, the wall was there, and it was going to stay there for a while. Plus, there was once a man who didn't do anything wrong and was crucified for his beliefs. He was a carpenter, too, so it's not a bad trade to get into.

I WENT OUT TO SAN DIEGO. I needed to get out of this area, where people knew me. Everybody was wanting to talk to me about how my career ended. That just made it worse. Out in California, the only thing they remembered about Ohio State was Woody Hayes punching that kid from Clemson. They didn't know who Ken Kuhn was. I just took off like I did when I went to Milford, Connecticut. I had a couple of high school buddies who were living out in San Diego. I took my hand tools with me, my pouch and stuff. I just went through the ads in the paper and got a job as a carpenter. For a long time, I couldn't even watch a football game. To this day, I don't even watch football. Part of that came because it hurt me so bad to watch guys on there who I knew I was better than. I kicked their can in games, but they were playing, and I wasn't. I missed it. I used to tell people, 'When I had a bad day, at least I could go out and beat up on someone.' If I had a bad day, I could take it out on a big tackle. How can I do that now? I'm not the kind of guy who beats up on his wife and kids and shoots the dog.

I lived out there for about a year and and a half, came back to Ohio. I went into a car dealership on the north side. I wanted to lease a car, and the guy talked me into selling cars for him. That was my first sales job. From there, I went into the steel industry, sold steel for a while. I was in the trucking industry. I've been in sales ever since. I currently run the Columbus warehouse for the Extendit Company. We sell asphalt sealer and asphalt crack filler. I'm the general manager/sales manager. I don't make anywhere near the money I would've made playing football, but between me and my wife, we make a pretty decent living. I don't need to make a lot of money to be happy. I'm happy with myself. The good Lord's blessed me. I have two gorgeous, healthy little boys. I've got a lot of good memories, and, finally, a lot of bad memories are leaving.

I met my wife through a girl I was dating in college. I stopped dating this other girl, and I ran into my wife in a bar one night, shortly after my

Bengal career ended. We danced a couple of times, went out for a while, and finally got married. We've made it 10 years. Susie O'Grady, a redhead, a great lady. Anyone who would marry me would have to be understanding. After all these years, the university is coming out with a program that's designed to help all the athletes who might have some kind of abuse problem, alcohol, drugs, whatever. Former athletes come back and get involved and help out. As soon as they said that, I said, 'Yeah, I'll jump on that wagon.' I wish they would've had it when I was there. It might've changed my life.

I WOULD SEE WOODY OCCASIONALLY, but I knew he still blamed me for missing that breakfast and us losing that game. He was cold to me, especially after what happened with Nick. It was like Kenny Kuhn was never there, Kenny Kuhn never played four years, Kenny Kuhn was never a co-captain. The whole administration treated me like a nobody. The thing about Woody saying that he should've handled me instead of my coach. That happened right in that period when I was going through that stuff with the Bengals. That was the low time of my life, and my brother came back and told me what Woody had said. It was like, 'That's great. Look at me now, and here's Woody telling you he should've handled me differently. What good's that do me now?'

You would think I would've resented him for all that, but I don't. I could've changed a lot of things that happened to me by not doing a lot of stupid things. But then, when you're 25 years old, you think a lot differently than you did when you were 19, 20 years old. And you think a lot more differently when you're 39 and have a wife and two little boys. I learned a hell of a lot from Woody. I learned discipline, learned there's nothing wrong with getting pissed off. I learned that verbalizing your emotions is not bad for you.

There was another side of Woody that he kept quiet. He was always going to Children's Hospital, helping people. If I really had a problem, I could have gone to Woody and asked him for help. In fact, even after all of that happened, I went to Woody after I went to California and came back and was selling cars. I went to him and said, 'Coach Hayes, I made a lot of mistakes. I haven't graduated. I'm in sales. Coach, I need your help to find a better job.' He picked up the phone and called Billy Joe Armstrong. Woody helped me get that first job.

It was hard for me to go see him for help, but it wasn't like I was going to someone who didn't know anything about Ken Kuhn. It wasn't like I hadn't paid my dues. I played four years for him, helped him go to four Rose Bowls. I felt like he might've owed me something. Anyway, my middle name is Wayne, and you know what Woody Hayes's birthday is? Valentine's Day, the same as my mother. Once he found that out, every year, my mother got a birthday card from Woody.

All he wanted to talk about was me getting my butt in gear and going back and getting my degree. If I had it all to do over again, I'd still play for Woody. I just wish I would've had a different coach, someone other than the defensive coordinator. You know what was something, and I never thought I would ever react this way? The day they announced that Woody died, I was going on a sales call, and I had to pull over and stop because I got real emotional over it. It shocked me that I got that emotional when I heard it; I never thought I would. I didn't go to his funeral. I thought, 'There's going to be so many people there.' I stayed away, but he was in my thoughts and in my prayers. I didn't need to prove that Ken Kuhn had showed up at his funeral. That night, I grabbed my knee, wished him well and told the good Lord to take care of him.

For a long time now, I've wanted to bury some of the negative feelings for my individual coach I had at OSU. I had the chance not too long ago at a giant fund-raiser, an 80th birthday party for Anne Hayes. A lot of former players and coaches were there, including my old linebacker coach. I hadn't talked to him in almost 15 years, and I wondered what I would say or do when I saw him. Well, he was there, in the private VIP area before the banquet. I took a deep breath, walked up to him and extended my hand. It was a sort of a white flag of peace. He looked at me with this very blank glare. He had a drink in both hands, and he seemed like he didn't want to put them down to shake my hand. I flashed right back to 1975. I felt this great well of animosity grow up from my toes, through my stomach, to my eyes. Then, without any big tumultuous confrontation, the animosity left me. I felt satisfied. I felt like I had buried the hatchet, and I think I'm a better person for the attempt. ”

A Fan's Notes

YOU WONDER how many guys like Don Hurley are out there: Guys who every Saturday afternoon of autumn sit in their favorite taverns, cradle sweating mugs of beer that have been half-full since the middle of the first quarter, tilt their stools forward until their sternums press against bartops and peer up at television sets bolted to small platforms above cash registers...guys who pace their living rooms alone (wife and kids having gone shopping because what's the use being home when the Buckeyes are on?), fling themselves onto couches in despair over fumbles and leap up in paroxysms of glee over long pass completions (tipping over coffee tables, splattering French onion dip on carpets that were vacuumed just that morning)...guys who grudgingly smear paint on garage walls or hack at rows of hedges, muttering to themselves like madmen as they listen to the game through headphones.

Guys who grew up on farms, maybe, who went to college for a year or maybe two, to Ohio State, maybe, or maybe not at all. Guys who played some ball, maybe, and who worked hard and raised families and had heart attacks (maybe) and scraped together enough money over 30 years to build a little cabin on a little piece of property beside a little lake. Guys who bedeck their dens with pennants and posters, who host or attend Michigan parties, who can't imagine missing a Buckeye game on TV or the radio. ("Most exciting time of my life is when Ohio State is playin' football," Don Hurley says.) Guys among whose fondest memories are shaking hands with Woody Hayes or chatting for a minute or two—awestruck—with Archie Griffin or Tom Cousineau at a benefit auction or an auto dealership's Big! Big! Labor Day Extravaganza!

Guys who don't have the heavy money or the heavy connections to get season tickets, who've dreamed all their lives of going to a Rose Bowl (but they'll never be able to afford it), who scalp tickets a couple times a season or—if they're lucky—get calls from buddies who have extras and go up to the stadium and grill some burgers and stand up during "Script Ohio" and chant "O!-H!-I!-O!" and come home and tell everyone about the trip until no one wants to listen anymore. ("To be able to walk into that stadium was just so unbelievable. The bigness of it, that huge monster building, the Horseshoe. God, when we went in and looked down on that field, it was just so pretty and everything. Players in colored uniforms and green field with white stripes. Man, I thought it was tremendous.")

They might've listened, as boys, to cheap transistor radios propped against barndoors...breathless announcers calling Vic Janowicz's twisting runs as the milking cows shuffled their hooves and the static crackled. They studied the long antiquity of child princes, mythical figures who seem to merge and become ageless...a procession in which Ferguson becomes Otis becomes Brockington becomes Henson becomes Johnson and Matte becomes Kern becomes Greene and on and on. They raised hell with Woody for refusing to throw the ball and with Earle for gambling on fourth down and with Cooper for going for the tie instead of the win. They were made bitter and jealous by losses and joyous by victories.

To them, an Ohio State game is not an opportunity to stroke potential clients amid an immense *kraal* of lumbering recreational vehicles or to flaunt their wealth through the size and succulence of the pregame buffets they set out. To them, it is not a huge, boozy frat party or a seething outdoor rock concert or an occasion to boast about their substantial contributions to the athletic program.

To them, an Ohio State game is a readymade connection to tradition and so to their own youths. To them, it is a tribal celebration of tens and hundreds of thousands wearing like garb and displaying like talismans and seeking like rewards, an acceptable means of joining a collective consciousness in a society that pits everyone against his neighbor for a share of the spoils. To them, it is a chance to toss off cynicism and fear, to escape distant wars and famines in a blissful ritual that has hardly changed over the decades, that regenerates itself every September, and that at least thus far, hasn't been corrupted.

And despite what their exasperated and disdainful critics might think, all but the most rabid among them understand that football is of no great consequence in this world and that deep down, it's all a business. It's just that their blood can't but be stirred by "Hang on, Sloopy" and "Carmen, Ohio" and by the epic martial spectacle of The Best Damned Band in the Land sweeping across the field as cheerleaders wave huge battle standards or turn somersaults like royal acrobats performing at court, and the Horseshoe swells with cheers.

"I call Ohio State 'my team,'" Don Hurley says. "I don't have a thing to do with 'em, but I still consider 'em my team. It's still important to me, far back as I can remember. I guess I'll do that for the rest of my life."

For guys like Don Hurley, it is all so wonderfully innocent.

Don HURLEY

"I WAS BORN DOWN IN Pickaway County. Raised on a farm. We didn't have TV when I grew up. There was TV out at the time, but we didn't have TV. So, you had to go to the movies if you wanted to see the pictures or anything. I listened to the radio a lot. That was a big thing. Sports, I loved sports. I played basketball. I was one of the leading players on our team in Walnut Township High School the last couple of years. I loved basketball, and I played baseball some. We didn't have football, so I couldn't play football. Not enough kids to play football. I don't know why I ever loved sports so much.

I loved listening to sports on the radio, especially Ohio State football. I started that, probably, about 1948. I started listenin' to it, and it just grew on me and grew on me. It was the most important thing in my life. Ohio State football was my bread and butter; that was what I really liked. I wouldn't miss an Ohio State ball game. I bet I haven't missed three or four ballgames in all those early years, and none in the last 25 years. I started listenin' to it, so my dad started getting interested. He would listen some of the time, not always, but some of the big ones, like the Michigan game. We'd listen together. He knew somethin' about football. I don't know where he learned it, because he never went to any games that I knew of, but he knew what was goin' on.

Wes Fesler was coachin' when I first started listenin'. I listened to Vic Janowicz when he first started, and, boy, I'll tell you, there was a ballplayer. He was the first great superstar that I ever heard of. Best, I think, there ever was in college. Boy, you just figured every time he got the ball, he was gonna do somethin' with it. He was gonna make some kind of a play and do somethin' good.

I had my own little radio. I got that little radio for my birthday when I was about 10 or 11 years old. I'd listen to the games maybe in my room, or out in the barn. We had electric in the barn at the time. I mean, when you didn't have TV or telephone or nothin' like that, you had to have somethin'.

Not too many friends were into Ohio State football then. I mostly listened to it myself. Kinda a loner. I'd take off Saturday afternoons to listen to the ballgames when I was workin' in the fields. Sometimes, my grandfather didn't like that. I'd leave the fields to come in and listen to the ballgames, and he'd say, 'Oh, you ain't never goin' to amount to anything.'

You know how the oldtimers felt. If you didn't work all the time, there was something wrong with you. They talk about 'the good old days,' but I'll take today. It's a much nicer world to live in today. I worked hard, but I wasn't goin' to miss a football game, I'll tell you that right now.

I remember listening to the Cleveland Browns a little bit when they had Jimmy Brown. I followed the Bengals a little later. I'll probably get stronger on the Bengals now that they got some Ohio State players down there. They got Tovar and Big Daddy and Cochran, so I'll start followin' the Bengals a little bit. But I can take or leave the game in the pros. I just never had that tingling feeling about the pros like I do about Ohio State. I can miss a game, and it doesn't even bother me. Miss an Ohio State game? No.

WHEN I FIRST STARTED LISTENIN' TO FOOTBALL on the radio, I had never really seen a football game. I never went to see an Ohio State football game. It was too far away, and I just wasn't in the class to get tickets, either. None of my family had ever went to college. Nobody that I knew of personally went to Ohio State. I would listen to it on the radio and imagine what was goin' on.

Back then, when I listened to *Superman* and all that, it was all on radio, so you had to imagine what was goin' on. You had to have this in your own mind. You had to think of what they was doin'. I had never seen a football game, and would listen to them every week without really knowin' exactly what it was like. I had seen a high school football stadium. I knew what it was, and from the radio announcers, I knew the rules of football. But I had to imagine all that was goin' on. I first saw Ohio State on TV. I was probably 16, 17 years old.

It was a neighbor's little black and white TV. I tell you what, it was pretty close to what I imagined. It wasn't that far off. There was a few differences from what I imagined. I really thought that the stadium was not so big. I thought it was more of a compact area. When I seen it on TV, I saw all this vast space out there—and that big stadium; that was a big place. I just looked at all the vastness of it, and said, 'Boy, that was *big*.'

I first came up, it was my last year of high school. I come up and seen that football game. Oh, my god. If I remember right, they were student tickets, and my buddy bought them off of a student, and I went with him. They weren't winnin' real big at the time. It was after Cassady, when they hit a lull there. It was a preseason game, before they played the Big Ten. To be able to walk into that stadium was just unbelievable. The bigness of it, that monster building, the Horseshoe. God, when we went in and looked down on that field, it was just so pretty and everything. Players in colored uniforms and green field with white stripes. Really big and really pretty. Listenin' to it on the radio and imaginin' and then comin' in and seein' it like that is just two different things.

The game, when it unfolded, you could see everything that was goin' on—the players comin' in and out—and I was really intrigued at that. I have to admit, that first game at Ohio Stadium was one of the very big highlights of my life.

IN '56, I WENT TO SCHOOL AT OHIO STATE. I just got to go to college for part of one year. I was goin' to major in engineering. I wanted to go to Ohio State. Everybody talked about it, it was a big school, they had the football up there. Back then, you had to have money to go to college, and we didn't have that kind of money. I run out of money, and I couldn't go any longer. I had to work to make my own money to go to college. I got tickets, and I got to go to every home game that year. I didn't miss one home game, and I wasn't goin' to sell my tickets, either. I *used* my tickets.

I was very disappointed when I had to leave school. No money, no scholarships. You couldn't get the scholarships unless you made real good grades, and I didn't make that gooda grades at the time.

I had never heard of Woody Hayes when they hired him. I was about 12, 13 years old. I knew a lot about Ohio State, but I didn't know who Woody Hayes was. I was listening to Wes Fesler, and they said they was gonna hire this Woody Hayes. He was comin' out of Miami. I said, 'I never even heard of 'im. Who's he?' I said, 'Well, he's got Janowicz back, and I'll guarantee you, you don't have to be too good a coach if you have Vic Janowicz comin' back.'

After Janowicz, Woody would just run, run, run. He never would throw a pass. He didn't know what a forward pass was. Then they got that tremendous team in '54, '55, when Hopalong Cassady come along, almost all runnin', you know. He just come on the scene as a freshman, then they got Hubert Bobo in front of him, and, boy, that was great, 'cause old Bobo was a tremendous blocker. He run in front of Cassady, and he was just clippin' 'em off, and Woody got some real tough linemen, too. They couldn't stop 'em for a couple years. For two or three years there, Ohio State was on the top again. Boy, they was really tough.

Woody stayed that way until Cassady graduated, then Ohio State kinda slipped down a little bit. But he was still winnin' a lot of ball games, up until 1964 through '67. I think he only won four or five ballgames one year, and at that time, the alumni wanted to get rid of Woody. Aww, it was a big thing.

I WANTED TO KEEP WOODY. I thought Woody was just in a lull. I told 'em all. I said, 'You watch and see. This Woody Hayes is good. He'll come out of it. He'll have a great team again, and it ain't gonna be too far down the line. Maybe he'll learn to pass once in a while.'

A lot of people says, 'Oh, no. He's done. He's out.'

I said, 'Nope, you watch and see. Woody's gonna come back. I stick with Woody.'

The only thing I didn't like about Woody was he wouldn't pass, but later on, he got so he passed some, too. Remember the interception in the bowl game? People said you got to have a coach that'll throw the forward pass. That's the reason why they wanted to get rid of him in the '60s.

I said, 'Woody'll adapt. He's a student of the game. He knows the game.' He adapted. He got Rex Kern. Kern could throw the ball, and he could run, too. He was a tremendous quarterback. The best there's ever been at Ohio State, I think, is Rex Kern.

Then Woody came along and he got Archie Griffin, one of the

superstars. Man! You could never find a better running back than Archie Griffin. He had a line in front of him that just would not stop, and Archie was good at hittin' them holes. He was little, too, and they couldn't see him too well behind them big linemen.

We had great defenses. I can never remember Woody Hayes not having a good defensive team. Always some of the great linebackers. Randy Gradishar, Kenny Kuhn, Cousineau, Stillwagon. Linemen, good ones. Woody had tremendous power. That's what his pride and joy was.

One time I got to shake his hand, just one time. It was when I was goin' to college, at a practice or somethin'. I went up to him, and I said, 'I'm a student here at the school, and I just want to shake your hand. I'm out of Pickaway County. Farm boy. I never played football or anything like that. I'm just interested in Ohio State football.'

I never did think Woody Hayes was a god. He was just a good guy and a good coach. But he was just one of a kind the way he did things. The way he recruited. Go into the people's homes and recruit the parents. He'd go in there and get to talkin' about history and everything else, and he'd let 'em know how good Ohio State's educational program was, and pretty soon, the parents would be on his side, and most of the athletes would listen to their parents and come to Ohio State.

WOODY HAYES PROBABLY INFLUENCED a lot more people in this area than any other coach or player has. He just had a way about him to influence people. He influenced me. He knew about other things, not just football, but a lot of things. He was just an all-around person. You'd think, 'Well, hell, he's just a coach. He don't know nothin' about anything else.' But Woody Hayes was smart on about any subject you could get on. I talked to players who said, God, they just wouldn't never get in a conversation and think they could back Woody down. He just knew.

There was a lot of times I didn't think he called the right plays. I raised hell with Woody a few times. I said, 'Daggonnit, Woody, you got the player out there too late and cost us a five-yard penalty'; or, 'Woody, you called the wrong play.' All of us fans give 'im hell, but, you know, we was talkin' to a TV. We wasn't talkin' to his face. You can give a TV a lotta hell.

You tell me there's one coach out there that you think calls the right plays all the time, I gotta see 'im. I think Woody Hayes called a lot of wrong plays. I seen 'im get beat by Michigan one time and he shouldn'ta gotten beat, because he called the wrong plays. I raised hell with Cooper, too, but I still like 'im as a coach and wanna keep 'im. But that's just my opinion. Shoot, you take another armchair quarterback over here, and he'll give you another opinion.

I was kind of sick to the stomach when Woody hit that kid in the bowl game, 'cause I knew it was the end. I was watchin' the game, and my son was there.

He said, 'He punched that guy.'

I said, 'No, Woody wouldn't do that.'

He said, 'He did. He punched that guy.'

I couldn't believe it. I hated to see him go out that way. Woody deserved to go out better. Had he not done that, I think Woody woulda left that year and not come back. Just one of those things. I felt bad about that. The guy kinda asked for it to some degree, comin' up there and tauntin' Woody with the football, but you just can't get by with that, not on national TV anyway. Woody just got too enthused.

Woody had a habit of doin' those kind of things. He just got too deep into it. It didn't bother me too much, and probably not the player for Clemson, but a coach just can't do that during the game. That's just the temperament of Woody. You gotta know his temperament. Would I do that? No. Do I think it's good for a coach to do that? No, it ain't good. Everybody's got their own thing, though. It's just Woody. It didn't detract from his coachin', just because he tore up the yard markers at Michigan or hit that cameraman in the eye out there at the Rose Bowl. Those antics didn't detract me from the respect I had for him as a coach. He's one of the great coaches and one of the great human beings. He just needed to pack it in a little bit.

WHEN WOODY LEFT, EARLE BRUCE COME IN. Earle Bruce was what I call a good coach, but he wasn't a very good recruiter. He recruited one guy who I thought was one of the greatest players ever at Ohio State. That was Chris Spielman. Earle Bruce got him, but I think he had some help. His recruiting fell off from there. Earle Bruce could coach football, but I was glad when he left. I thought that he didn't get the talent. We needed better talent. He had a player here and there, like Spielman, but he didn't have overall consistent talent. I was really glad to see him leave.

I didn't have as strong a feel for Ohio State during the years of Earle Bruce. They were still my team, but they kind of went down, down, down. Cooper, I didn't know about him at all. I knew he had just got through beatin' Michigan in the Rose Bowl, and I heard he was coach of the year from Arizona State, but I didn't know much about him.

I said, 'Well, he must be good, because he beat Michigan.'

My opinion is that John Cooper is as good as Woody Hayes at recruitin'. He gets the talent. I think Cooper is going to make Ohio State a good team. I'm a Cooper fan. He's a gentleman. He's what you call 'the coach's coach.' I think he's got a bad rap right now. I've got in arguments with people over sayin' that, but they know I'm a true Ohio State fan. People are fickle. Let Cooper beat Michigan a couple times and be in the top 10 for a few years, and you can bet your bottom dollar everybody'll be on Cooper's bandwagon. He'll last. He'll be up there just as long as he wants to, I imagine. They been tryin' to run him outta here for three or four years. Awful lot of people been on Cooper tight. Jimmy Crum just poured it on 'im, and I didn't think too highly of Jimmy Crum for doin' that. Me, I stick with 'em unless things are really bad over a period of time. I don't jump on a guy 'cause he loses one ballgame, even if it was Michigan.

IT'S LIKE WHEN EVERYBODY wanted to get rid of Woody. I said, 'Hey, give the guy a chance.' In '68, you couldn't find anybody who didn't like Woody. When Cooper first took over, he didn't have much talent. He was really hurtin'. He had good players, but it wasn't the superstars he's gettin' up there now. I think Cooper's got the talent comin' on.

You ask anybody, when Ohio State's playin', there ain't a bigger fan around than I am. I don't want to miss a play. I still get excited when football season is startin' up. I sure do. Most exciting time of my life is when Ohio State is playin' football. I was so worked up last year. I wanted to go to the Rose Bowl so bad. If the Buckeye's woulda went last year, I woulda went to the Rose Bowl. That tie at Wisconsin really hurt. That woulda been one of my great things in life.

When the season's gettin' ready to start, I start readin' up on all the players, see every little thing I can get ahold of, read about how they're doin', listen to the talk shows. I seem to have more inside information than most when it comes to what Ohio State's doin'. A lot of people ask me questions about 'em, even people who went to school there. I follow 'em real close, all the injured players, the recruits. I always have a list of the recruits. I know exactly where they came from, what they did, how good they were. Even some of the recruits that didn't make it. I follow 'em all the way through. I can tell you what happened and what caused it.

People say, 'Who's this new guy who just went in?'

I can tell you where he came from, what he did there.

MY WIFE DON'T LIKE FOOTBALL AT ALL. I don't talk to her about football. She don't wanna hear it. That's not her game, man. She don't want nothin' to do with football. My son, my brother, and I talk about football a lot. It was a highlight of my life to take my son to the Ohio State football games when he was growin' up. I made sure I could get him to at least one of the ballgames every year, while he was in high school. I just had the one son, no girls.

He was a great football player in high school. He was all-league as a defensive end. At Pickerington, they won 20 games and lost none when he was down there his last two years of high school. He was a heck of a ballplayer. I hoped for a while that Woody would recruit 'im, but he didn't. The first place I wanted him to go was Ohio State. He did get two letters, one from Penn State and one from Alabama. Joe Paterno and Bear Bryant wanted him to walk on. They said he come from such a small school that really he didn't get the publicity, and they didn't know him. He didn't get the shot at it. He ended up going to a small college, Muskingum, for a year, then went in the air force. He came back and went to Franklin University in computer science and graduated *summa cum laude*.

He's a real avid fan, too. He and I watch 'em every game, root for 'em. The Michigan game, we've got a regular group that gets together. My son, my brother, and about five or six of us who worked together have a big party. I've got a big rec room, about 1,500 square feet down in the basement, with all Ohio State stuff in it. I have two or three TVs sittin' around so we can all see the ballgame.

I had several favorite years. I think when Vic Janowicz was a junior and he won the Heisman Trophy, that was one of my very first most favorite years. Then I liked Hopalong Cassady when he won his Heisman Trophy. I really was heavy over that one. Then, of course, the year of '68. That was a top one. And the years of Archie Griffin.

Of the quarterbacks, I'd pick Rex Kern number one and Schlichter number two, and you could say Corny Greene's in there somewhere later. The greatest player of all time was Vic Janowicz. Cassady and Griffin, Tim Spencer were some of the great running backs. Jack Tatum was unbelievable. They had many great linemen, but Ward or Hicks in front of Archie was hard to beat. Foley and Mayes weren't bad. Big Jim Parker, one of the best who ever came out of there.

My last years, I worked on the cellular line out at AT&T. I had a really great job. No complaints. I've been retired a couple of years now. The company come along and offered us early retirement. I think they was wantin' to get the younger guys in there. I took it, thinkin' I was gonna go try somethin' else. Never once dreamin' that I would have a heart attack, though. The work you do today isn't the real tiring work. It's more stressful, though. I think that was one of the causes of my heart attack, all the stress I put on myself out there at AT&T.

I HAD A VERY SERIOUS HEART ATTACK. It was the stress that I had, it was not just the company that did it. I put it on myself, trying to get so much done, trying to make sure we done it just right, trying to please the company, please the boss. A person ought to try to do the best they can, but don't kill yourself doin' it.

The doctor said I was legally dead for 15 minutes. He said, 'It's a miracle you're alive.'

That's why I had to start takin' them pills. I take four dollars worth of pills every day. I exercise almost every day. I try to eat right, too. It's just important to me to wake up every morning and look around and know I'm still alive. Doctor said that ten years ago, I would never had made it. Said if I woulda been a little bit later gettin' into the operating room, I woulda been dead. He thought I was dead as it was.

You look around and say, 'Daggone, life is awful short.'

I never thought about it. I said, 'Heck, I'm gonna be around until I'm 80, anyway.' I was goin' to do somethin' else, maybe not full-time, work part-time maybe. Now, I just don't think about those things anymore. I just enjoy life so much anymore. Sometimes when I'm drivin' down to Circleville to visit my mother and take care of the place, I just stop and look around, especially in the mornin' when the sun's shinin'. I just look around at the hills and trees and land. Sometimes you miss all that when you're in the rush-rush world. All the beautiful things in life, you just don't see 'em. I was in the rush-rush mode. I was just workin' all the time.

Every week, I go down my mother's and look around her old homeplace and try to get a few things done down there when needed. I just try to enjoy life. But I am an Ohio State football fan. That's my number one thing in life that I look forward to. When they get beat, I feel bad. I mean, it's just natural. When they got beat by Michigan this last year, I felt bad. You don't know what to do. You don't say nothin'. You just kinda try to take it in stride. Used to be when they lost, I'd feel bad for three or four days. We'd talk about it. We'd say, 'Daggone, why didn't Woody call the right play?' Or Cooper when he had the fourth down and nine inches to go late in the game, and he let Greg Frey run the ball. I mean, if you're gonna let somebody run it, you're sure not gonna let Greg Frey run it. Fourth down on the 20 yard line, and we was tied with Michigan. Well, they got the ball and kicked a field goal and won the game. I mean, gee whiz! I didn't blame him for goin' for it; he just shouldn'ta let Greg Frey run it.

A lot of people've told me how much I look like Woody Hayes. Matter of fact, they got a nickname for me around here in a lot of the places I go. They call me 'the Coach.' 'Cause I look like Woody Hayes. When I got up to Ohio State there, I put my Woody Hayes cap and my jacket on and my glasses on, people think I look just like Woody Hayes. Kenny Kuhn played for him for four years, and he tells me, 'You know what? You look like Woody, but you don't have the temperament of Woody.'

I call Ohio State 'my team.' I know I don't have a thing to do with 'em, but I still consider 'em my team. It's still important to me, far back as I can remember. I guess I'll do that for the rest of my life. 'Til I die, I'll still feel that feelin' that it's great to walk into that tremendous stadium they got up there. The memories, the tradition behind it, the football greats and everything. I just like to go in there.

If you don't know about Ohio State football around here, you musta had your ears closed and your eyes closed for a long time. It's just a way of life around here. You say Ohio State won or lost around here, they know what you're talkin' about, buddy. ”

32

Loving *the* Gulag

PLAYING ON THE scout squad is like serving a term on Devil's Island. Whether you're called the scrubs, the card team, the look squad, the Green Weenies, or the Gungas (two old Ohio State expressions), on the scout squad you are, in effect, a sparring partner: During drills and scrimmages, you imitate that week's opponent and thus exist to be blocked and tackled by players who will actually take the field on Saturday afternoon.

The scout squad is a test site for raw young talent, a forced labor camp in which those too slow or too small earn their scholarships, a holding pen for the lame, a penal colony for players who've run afoul of the coaching staff, a proving ground for wild-eyed walk-ons who are determined the make the varsity or are just in love with the game. ("The worst ones to play against were the walk-ons," Jim Stillwagon says. "I used to think, 'Those are some mean motherfuckers. This guy comes out just for the fuck of it.'") Regardless of why you're sentenced to it, if you're on the scout squad, you are set up like a large target in an arcade gallery and then knocked down time and again.

(One spring when I was playing ball in college, a guy showed up at the table we players sat around during lunch. He was plump, his face perpetually flushed. He told us his first name—Floyd—and was immediately nicknamed Pink Floyd. He said he was a marine just back from 'Nam. He claimed to have been an all-state center in high school and loudly announced that he would certainly be a starter by the end of spring practice. As he bragged about his prowess, I could see in the hard eyes of my teammates that Pink Floyd's first day in full pads was going to be difficult.

Pink Floyd was made a scout squad center, and from the first snap in the first half-line scrimmage, the defensive players attacked him. Ignoring ball carriers, they threw forearms into his fleshy chin, launched helmets at his ribs, drove knees into his back. Behind the bars of his helmet, Pink Floyd's cheeks blazed. Cornered by his own foolish boasting, he looked like a desperate animal. After 45 minutes or so of punishment, Pink Floyd staggered off, collapsed in a copse of trees near the field, and lay there moaning. We practiced until dusk; as we trotted off, I could still hear in the gathering dark Pink Floyd's whimpers. He didn't come back.)

Scout squadders are instructed to behave just as their varsity alter egos at Michigan or Wisconsin or Indiana do. They are not so much dehumanized (although I've seen frustrated starters kick or fling aside a scout squadder as if the scrub were merely a blocking dummy) as constantly rehumanized, transformed from Buckeyes into Spartans one week, Hawkeyes the next. The ultimate mixed blessed is to be made to portray an opposing star. To wear the jersey number and affect the peculiarities of dress of a Mike Adamle or a Ron Johnson is to become the object of particular violence from the starting defense.

Even calling the scout squad a "team" is a misnomer. Everyone on it—even the coaches who run it—is trying to get off the scout squad. That lack of unity makes each offensive play run by the scout squad no better than a ragged approximation of the real thing. A successful play is an intricate mosaic of timing requiring weeks of repetition. On the scout squad, a coach stands in the huddle holding up a file folder on which the opposing team's plays have been drawn in magic marker. You are expected to get it right immediately, as if running a play were some violent exercise from a grammar school primer.

As a scout squad running back, you line up knowing you have a better chance of finding a rope of pearls in the chewed up turf than of getting a series of crisp blocks from the line in front of you. You're caught between conflicting demands. Coaches insist you "give 'em a good look"—that you run every play with the proper hustle. However, run the plays aggressively and you risk being alienated by the starters, who just naturally don't want to endure a brawl every afternoon. A starter who lets you off easy does so at his own peril. Failure to deliver a blow on a scout squadder is regarded as a high crime committed only by a slacker or a coward.

(I was coaching years later when a freshman tailback named Stevie came to summer camp. One of the top running backs in the state, Stevie had been recruited by major colleges until a shoulder injury cost him most of his senior year. Only 5' 6", Stevie weighed more than 200 pounds—a sculpture of bulging pectorals, wide lats, and biceps as thick as roasting chickens. The mouthy former high school star irritated coaches and players alike. Shunted off to the scout squad, Stevie ran every play with ebullient abandon. He careened through scrimmages, bouncing off varsity tacklers like a musclebound billiard ball. The starters vowed to beat the cockiness out of him. Pads cracked like sharp peals of thunder. They tackled Stevie and piled on in angry waves. Giggling, he would claw his way up through tangles of limbs and torsos, race back to the huddle, and demand to carry the ball again. He taunted the varsity, flipping the ball at their helmets and asking if they could hit no harder. After every brutal practice, he sat in front of his locker, grinning and chattering and hooting at the varsity, his muscular body wrapped in a serape of blue contusions and carmine welts. Stevie endured four months of pounding and eventually became a captain and an All-American. I still think he was crazy.)

There is no good time to be on the scout squad. By the second practice of the 10th day of August camp, dust blooms up around you; the soles of your feet are raw with oozing blisters; bruises tattoo your arms and shoulders with ugly splotches of burst capillaries; your head still rings from the morning's collisions. In mid-November, frigid wind turns your flesh into brittle porcelain and you believe the next solid hit will shatter your frozen sternum. All you have to look forward to is being named "Scout Team Player of the Week"—a dubious honor that wins you a tee-shirt and a seat at training table and, perhaps, the right to dress for a game.

You suppress your ego as the

guy who lockers next to you is featured in *Sports Illustrated.* You realize that no matter if you run the play well or poorly, some coach will be screaming—at you or at the starters. You play with pain because you know that to be injured is to lose whatever chance you have of escaping purgatory. Out of pride or optimism or stubbornness or the desire to say you played at Ohio State, you resist the urge to transfer out and be a star at a smaller school. You wait for Tuesdays and Wednesdays—scrimmage days—and the inevitable command: "Buckle up, men. This's live."

(David was an earnest young man who, unfortunately, was too small for defensive tackle and too slow for linebacker. He never missed a practice, weightlifting session, or meeting, and David never played, except on the scout squad. Forbidden to put him into a game, I nonetheless slipped David into the fourth quarter of a 40-point win, hoping the defensive coordinator wouldn't notice. However, several minutes of David's haplessness resulted in his being yanked from the field and my receiving a tongue-lashing.

As a senior, David was still a scout squadder. In the midst of a lugubrious "front drill"—scout defensive linemen and linebackers vs. varsity line and backs—someone rolled up David's right leg. His knee splayed out at a sickening angle. David plopped down and gripped the joint with both hands, rocking and breathing in small, explosive grunts. Someone took his place. Trainers hauled David off to the stadium in a golf cart. He seemed to have received an honorable discharge. Half an hour later, David hobbled back on the field, his knee encased in a massive hinged brace, and took his turn in the next drill.)

In 1971, Dave Mazeroski was all-state at Cadiz High School. Playing fullback in an all-star game, he separated his shoulder on his first carry. At OSU, a second shoulder separation, stretched foot ligaments, mononucleosis, and the presence of Champ Henson and Pete Johnson kept Mazeroski on the scout squad for four years. Before his last game, he went onto the field, in mufti, and greeted his classmates as they ran out, bathed in cheers. Near the end of the afternoon, Mazeroski's classmates received an ovation that stopped the game for almost 10 minutes. In four seasons, they had lost only two regular-season games while Mazeroski played rarely, instead carrying in scrimmages against some of the best defensive players in the country.

As if he's just returned from a stretch in a Soviet gulag and can't wait to tell everyone just how lovely Siberia is in January, Mazeroski says of those four years on the scout squad, "I loved it."

Dave MAZEROSKI

"I SPENT THE FIRST EIGHT years of my life in a coal-mining community, Unionvale, which is about four or five miles out in the boondocks from Cadiz, Ohio. All the roads were paved, but there was a total population of only 200 or so, I guess. That's where all the Mazeroskis came to live when they arrived from Europe. Clark Gable was born there and grew up in Hopedale, just another five miles down the road. We also had the world's largest earth-moving machines operating in and around Cadiz for decades. One scoop from one of those giants could pick up your whole dining room. I never apologized for being from a small town. I guess no matter where you come from, it's where you're going that counts.

My dad worked at the Y&O, Nelm's #1 mine. He was a welder and maintenance man. He went to work at 11 o'clock at night, got home at 7. He was a hard worker. But whether it was Little League baseball or high school football, he and my mother made sure they came to all of my games, always made sure I had decent grades on my report cards.

My dad groomed me for sports from the time I was able to walk. Throw a ball, catch it, confirm that it's a good thing. He was a pretty good player himself. Out in California, he was running back on the division football team. My dad was very aggressive: 'Go get 'em, beat 'em, win.' My mom, on the other hand, would tell me to let the other kids win sometimes. I pitched Little League, and when I was 12 years old I could throw pretty good. We'd win, and I'd come home and my mom would ask me why I had to throw so *hard* to those little kids. If I was playing Monopoly with my cousin Ron, who was three years younger, she would say, 'Why don't you let him win once in a while?'

I had another cousin, Bill Mazeroski, who played for the Pirates for 17 years. He grew up in the Ohio Valley along with the likes of Lou Groza, John Havlicek, Bob Jeter, and Phil and Joe Neikro. Bill was a terrific baseball player and basketball player. When he played high school ball, it was nothing for him to pitch a doubleheader.

We used to go to Forbes Field three or four times a year to watch Bill play. Sometimes he'd get us tickets, and sometimes we'd just show up and go over and sit on the third base side. Bill was responsible for the world being able to pronounce our last name, particularly after the home run against the Yankees in the '60 World Series. After that, I was no longer 'David' in school; I was 'Maz.' The only time people called me 'Mazeroski' was when they were mad at me. Of course, there was a certain jealousy. People couldn't believe that I was related to *Bill Mazeroski*. That died down, and then my dad coached Little League. Where did he put me? Second base: 'Hey, there's Bill Mazeroski. Ha! Ha! Ha!'

IN LITTLE LEAGUE, WHEN I WAS 11, I hit a home run probably once every six at-bats, and when I was 12, it was probably every three at bats. We played down in the middle of the horsetrack, at the fairgrounds, and the fields were together, back to back. The fences for the two fields were close to each other. And when I took batting practice before games, people who were standing there watching the other field would get out of the way, because I was going to hit five or six out. I had my share of strikeouts, too, because I was *swinging*.

We had biddy league football in Cadiz in fifth grade, and my cousin, Bob Richards, was the coach. He was 6' 4", over 200 pounds. He had been a quarterback in high school. Most of my cousins were big. Another cousin, Ben Mazeroski, was about 6' 3", 220. Ben scored three touchdowns in the first half of a game his sophomore year, and he came into the locker room singing 'They Call Me Mr. Touchdown.' So in the second half, no one blocked for him. He got the message pretty quick. Ben got his knee hurt when he was a junior in high school. Before that, he just ran over everybody. His father was also blown up in the coal mine. My grandmother told me that Ben's dad was the best-built man she'd ever seen in her life. He had about a 32-inch waist, but when he came through a door, his shoulders were so wide he had to turn sideways.

Ben was my hero, because he was a fullback, and that's what I wanted to play. He didn't get to play his senior year because his knees got worse and worse, and they couldn't fix them like they do now. So he played basketball. His senior year, he averaged 30 rebounds a game. When he told me this, I said, 'I don't believe that. That's crazy.'

He said, 'Hey, I'll send you the sheets. They're in a big box upstairs.'

He sent me the original, 30-some-year-old, blue, mimeographed stat sheets on all the guys who played that year. They still smelled like mimeograph.

I said, 'How could you do that? When I played basketball, if I got 14 rebounds in a game, that was a fantastic night.'

He says, 'I don't know. I guess I was just frustrated because I couldn't play football anymore.'

I asked my dad about it, and he said, 'When he'd go up for a rebound, everybody would just bounce off.'

Organized football was easy compared to the way I had been playing. I was always the one who ended up getting hurt and crying, because I was the youngest kid, playing with kids two or three years older than me. Now, I was able to play with kids my own age, with equipment. In tenth grade, we had a poor program. I played, but I was a lineman. In small schools, if you're big, you're automatically made a lineman. Things were so bad that we only had 23 kids on the whole varsity. Guys were stealing their helmets and jerseys at the end of the season so that they'd make sure that they had them the next year. I was so discouraged I didn't take anything. I figured, 'I'll just concentrate on basketball and baseball.'

Luckily, they fired that coaching staff and brought in some new guys who were just night and day different—quality, class, knowledgeable—and they started to build a program.

When the new coach came in, he made me a fullback. I had some speed, but I just ran straight forward. But you have to know how to juke, fake, use your head, stiff-arm, see out of the corner of your eye to know where the flow's coming from. There's so many things. My junior year was frustrating. I think we ended up 3-7. A couple times I shouldn't've gotten tackled, but I did. I'd see on the films the field was wide open, but somebody would stick out a hand or an arm and catch one of my feet, which were size 13 1/2 at the time. Instead of going 60 yards for a touchdown, I'd go down.

My senior year, we only lost one game. I got a lot of post-season honors and cards and letters from colleges all over the country. Drawers full of them, expounding on why I should go there, wanting to schedule visits. I liked the attention, but I was kind of embarrassed about it. My senior year, I even had coaches come and watch me play basketball. Usually, I didn't find out until after a basketball game that such and such coach was in the stands watching. I was embarrassed by it if I was told this in front of any other players. It put me on the spot.

I HAD ALWAYS WANTED TO GO TO OHIO STATE. I remember the excitement of listening to the 1968 team on the radio. I remember how excited I was when it was on TV maybe once or twice a year. I listened to the games from start to finish, by myself, in my room. I didn't want anyone to interrupt me or even say anything to me. I might miss something. It was like an indoctrination.

I never in a million years thought that I'd get the chance to play for Ohio State. Inside, you feel like you're pretty good, but you think, 'I couldn't play there. Those guys play on TV, for goodness sake. I couldn't possibly play there.' Never seeing a player up close, you don't know that they're not these eight-foot, 400-pound Cyclops.

I thought, 'Well, I might be able to make it in the MAC.' I guess I just thought, 'They're not on TV, so I can probably play there.'

I had seen the campus because my sister, Donna, went to the Columbus Business University, so when we went to pick her up or drop her off, we used to drive right by Ohio State. I'd see the sign on High Street—'Established 1870,' in red and gray metal letters—and that thrilled me no end: 'Hey, there's Ohio State.' That's all I knew. It was Ohio's team.

I made my first official visit to Ohio State, it must have been January of my senior year. I had already visited a couple of other places. Dick Mack, who was a terrific offensive guard, and Tom Swank, his roommate, were my hosts. We went to a basketball game to watch Ohio State play Indiana. I couldn't get over how loud it was in there, and I couldn't get over how Swank and Mack were cheering. They were yelling, 'C'mon! C'mon!' every time Ohio State brought the ball down the floor. They were excited. I thought, 'This's great.' I got excited, too.

When the game was over, we went upstairs to talk to Woody. He'd do a lot of the talking, ask you a question and kind of answer it for you, too. He'd make a statement, then say, 'You agree with that? Yeah, yeah, I know you do. You're that kind of person.'

He said, 'When are you going to make a decision?'

I said, 'I've already decided I want to come here, but I've got some places that still think I'm good, and what the heck, I might as well go see them.'

'No,' he says, 'don't do that. Don't waste their time. I wouldn't want you wasting my time. If you already know where you're going to go, call them and tell them. Otherwise, you're wasting their time, and you're wasting your time. The sooner you make a decision, the better for you, the better for everybody.' What he said made sense: Don't take advantage of these people. Don't spend their money if you really don't have any intention of pursuing it. I agreed, and when I went back, I canceled my other visits.

I MADE THE ALL-OHIO FOOTBALL TEAM as a linebacker. I went both ways like most kids in high school used to. Back then, we only had three classes—Class A, Class AA and Class AAA—so it was a lot harder to make All-State. A couple of running backs from Central Catholic High in Steubenville were ahead of me. I think they averaged like 52 points a game and went undefeated. Since their fullback made first-team All-State fullback, I made first-team All-State linebacker, as a consolation, I guess.

I played in an Ohio-West Virginia all-star game the summer after my senior year. On the first carry of the game, I broke through the line, went for about eight or ten yards, and some defensive back came up and took my legs out from under me. I came down on my right shoulder and separated it. First carry. It hurt. It hurt bad. But I didn't come out. Finally, I could hardly lift my arm up anymore it hurt so bad. I partially tore a rotator cuff, too, I found out later. Here I am—injured. I didn't tell anybody. Luckily, I didn't have to go both ways.

The other team got the ball and drove down to our five-yard line. The defense stopped them. Coach says, 'Maz, go in, tell the quarterback to run the triple option, but don't run the option. We can't afford a fumble in the end zone. Tell the quarterback to just give it to you.'

Tom King was a master at fakery. He put the ball in my belly and left it there. I just kept on going. The other team had a linebacker who weighed about 240. He hit me so hard that my helmet came unsnapped, and the facemask went over to the side of my head. For a couple of seconds, I was looking out through the air hole, he hit me so hard. But he didn't think I had the ball, the quarterback had faked so well. He let me go and took off in search of the pitch man. I just cut left and went 95 yards. From there, nobody touched me. To my knowledge, that's still the longest run in that game's history. I was running, and the helmet I had on was too big for me, because my own helmet had gotten split open in practice. The helmet was shaking all over my head while I was running.

I remember trying to get my jersey off at the end of the game, and I was just in terrible pain. Two weeks later, I go to Ohio State with a separated shoulder. Here I am, already injured, and my college career is off to a rocky start. I'm very discouraged.

I was pretty much held out of practice after the first week, because it kept getting worse. I couldn't really go through the drills.

'Okay, fullback, take out the end with your right shoulder.'

Well, I couldn't do that. I had to put my helmet into the guy, and then Woody would scream at me because I didn't use my shoulder.

Rudy Hubbard, the backfield coach, told him, 'Coach, he can't use that shoulder. He's injured.'

He says, 'Well, get him out of there.'

So I did all kinds of therapy, the wheel, and this thing and that thing. They finally gave me an injection, but only because I begged for it. They weren't in the practice of shooting people up. After the shot, it was like, 'Wow, this's the first time I haven't had pain in two months.'

I hadn't been able to practice very much, so I was out of shape, and they were two months advanced from where we started, and that's a long time. Consequently, I was kicked into the last row before I ever got into the classroom.

When I got there, there was a senior fullback named John Bledsoe, but it wasn't long into summer practice that he got pushed back and Champ Henson got put in. As a sophomore, Champ was 6' 4", 230, and ran the 40-yard dash in 4.5. Not bad for a white farmboy from Ashville. He was a specimen, and I still say to this day, if a few things could've been different, he could've been another Larry Csonka. When Csonka broke into the open field, he looked for a defensive back to run over. Maybe Champ would've been better than Csonka, because Champ also had the speed. God, he was powerful. Big bones, big legs. When he broke into the open field, he'd just run away from tacklers. And they'd be glad.

Everybody knows how great Pete Johnson was, but I don't know who would've played more if Champ hadn't gotten hurt. Champ might've been the better overall fullback, but Champ wasn't quite the blocker that Pete was, because Pete was built close to the ground. He was 6' 1", 250, a human bowling ball, and no one wanted to get in his way. The greatest thing that ever happened to Archie was he had two of the greatest blocking fullbacks in the history of Ohio State football on the same team, blocking for him. It was a match made in heaven.

When I was a sophomore, Bruce Elia, a junior, played fullback. Champ was hurt that year, and Pete wasn't quite ready yet, and they brought Elia over from linebacker, and he did well at fullback, too. My shoulder had been hurting me so bad I couldn't lift weights, and you have to keep your strength up to play football. If you can't lift weights, you can't get strong; if you can't get strong, you can't play. I also got a case of mono. I went from 215 pounds to around 190. I played spring ball my freshman year, but I was out of shape and breathing like a racehorse.

I WAS EXASPERATED, but I'm not the only guy this ever happened to. Hundreds of guys who played college football have had the same thing happen to them—bad luck, injuries, great players in front of them. I had all three. My sophomore year, in spite of all that, I built myself back up to about 220 pounds or so. I was having a pretty good August practice. We were having a scrimmage, and I broke through the line, went about 15 yards, and I got tackled. It was the worse thing that ever happened to me, worse than the shoulder. When I was going down, my foot was straight up and down, and somebody fell on it. My toes were bent back. It just ripped all of the ligaments out of my foot. I never had pain like that, ever. It sounded like you took a bunch of sticks and just broke them.

Someone said, 'C'mon, Maz, get up.'

I said, 'Don't touch my foot! It's killing me!'

They took me to the hospital. The foot was all discolored and everything.

I said, 'When's the surgery?'

They said, 'We can't do surgery.'

I said, 'Why?'

They said, 'Nothing's ripped. It's just stretched.'

It was like taking a rubber band that's supposed to be three inches long and making it eight. They gave me some special shoe to wear, like something they wear in Holland. It was a wooden, flat shoe. My toes were totally exposed, and it had no heel. When I walked, it went *clonk, clonk, clonk, clonk*. The guys on the team would follow along behind me and duplicate my walk and laugh. I'd look behind me, and they'd all be behind me, doing the *Gunsmoke* Chester walk. They called it 'The Maz Shuffle.'

So, my sophomore season was blown. Again, the coaches had to play who was going to help them. After that, I was more or less out of the picture. The rest of my sophomore year, I'd go to practice, but I couldn't do anything. Woody, I think, didn't fully believe that I was actually that hurt. If a ball would hit around him, he'd say, 'Hey, Mazeroski, go get that ball over there for me.'

I'd hobble over and get it. I guess he wanted to see if I was still limping. That's all I could do—hobble. That foot didn't heal for a year. It took me probably five months before I could even walk normally on it.

Here I am now with a bum foot and a bum shoulder and feeling low. After having experienced nothing but success, here I am with a broken body and can't do anything about it. Finally, I started building my shoulder up little by little. I healed up. I got timed in the 40 at 4.65, but, heck, here's Pete Johnson. Champ's still there. I'm on the scout team. But I figured, 'Hey, what the heck? I'm going to practice, and I'm not going to be the punishee. I'm going to be the punisher.

My junior year was probably my best year, as far as I'm concerned. I was able to lift weights, so I added some strength and weight. I was pretty healthy. Everything was fine. I used to enjoy the heck out of running against Kenny Kuhn, when he was at linebacker. He was a punishing linebacker. He'd hurt you if he could. We had some spirited practices running against those guys. They'd be cussing at us, and we'd be cussing at them. We'd tell George Hill, the defensive coordinator, to kiss our behinds. He didn't care, because we had some great practices. We were told that we made that defense what they were, and they all knew it.

You had to get up for those practices. Number one, to survive. Number two, that was *our* game, that was *our* Saturday. Our Saturday afternoon game was Tuesday and Wednesday practices, and to a man, we all believed that. My dream was to have a head start, about six yards of space to run and ram somebody and get through the line. As a fullback, you get about two steps, and either you're hit or there's a hole. When you're a tailback, at least you can pick a place to run or have a chance to pick up steam and maybe hurt somebody if they want to tackle you.

I also got a different color jersey each week. If we were playing Iowa, it was black and gold; if it was Indiana, it was red. I had a drawer full of jerseys. That was our pay. Guys wanted to buy them from you. You'd sell it to them for a couple of pitchers of beer. I still have a couple of those jerseys at home for posterity.

You had to give the defense 'the look.' If you gave them a bad read, you were in trouble. I remember one time I was running a quick pitch. I got hammered three times in a row. Somebody made a mistake, so now, they wanted to run it the fourth time. By that time, the line's not even going to block, and the whole defense knows where it's going.

I said, 'Aw, geez.'

I took the pitch and went up like I was going to pass. George Hill and Dick Walker, the defensive backfield coach, went berserk. If they'd've had a gun, they'd've pulled it out and shot me: 'That's not in there! What the hell kind of play is that? Goddamn, Mazeroski, run the plays on the card!'

I said, 'Hell, why don't you run it five times in a row and let them tear my head off? Why can't we at least run it to the other side? Why don't I just stand in the middle and let 40 guys tackle me?'

THE NEXT DAY, THEY PUT IT IN. They said, 'Maz, run that play you ran yesterday. You know, it was like a quick pitch and you pretended you were going to pass?'

I said, 'Yeah.'

They said, 'Well, pass it this time.'

I said, 'You're kidding.'

All I was doing was trying to keep from getting killed for the fourth time in a row. The words most feared by any scout team running back are: 'All right, run that play again.'

You'd hear guys, 'Hey, ah, trade me places this time. *You* take the ball this time.'

'No, man, *you're* in there.'

You *know* you're going to get hammered. The first guy who comes at you, either give him a forearm or get on the ground. To save yourself, you had to be like Csonka—run and deliver forearms. He'd dare people to tackle him. If someone was going to hammer you, especially if it was a defensive back, you had to get a forearm on them or stiff-arm them. We'd put the ball on the 10 yard line. They dared us to score; we dared them to stop us. And if we'd score on them, we'd laugh at them, we'd taunt them. They'd get so mad they'd turn green over there, and George Hill would go berserk. Bruce Elia got real mad one time because we scored, and as I started to get up to come back to the huddle, he started kicking me. I'm trying to get up and get at him, and a couple of other guys jump in and start kicking me. Everybody's yelling. I didn't even run the ball. We ran an isolation play, and I blocked him and knocked him down. He didn't like that, of course, but, hey, that's too bad. I was pissed off about that. I thought about it and thought about it. The next day before practice, about 1:30, I went over to the football office and asked to see George Hill.

HE SAID, 'YEAH, MAZ, what can I do for you?'

I said, 'Can I speak to you privately?'

He said, 'Yeah, come on in.'

I said, 'Coach, being on the scout team is a pretty thankless job. We don't get a whole lot of recognition, we don't get to play on Saturday, but we're doing the best we can, and I think we give you a pretty good look.'

He says, 'You're damn right you do, and we appreciate it.'

I said, 'Well, if you appreciate it, you better tell your defensive guys that the next time they kick me or do anything dirty to any of us, I'm taking out their knees. Elia's first, and anyone else who does it is next. I'm not going to put up with it.'

He said, 'Hey! Wait a minute! We don't want you hurting our guys.'

I said, 'Fine. I don't want to be hurt either. We're doing the best we can, trying to give you the best look we can. What are we, ranked number three in the country in defense? There must be a reason for that.'

He says, 'I know. I agree with you. We're not going to have that anymore. I'm sorry. I apologize. I guarantee you it won't happen again. As a matter of fact, I'm going to tell those guys that when they see you at practice today, they better apologize to you.'

I just let it hang out. I was mad, and, besides, the scout team was doing well. We were giving them a better game than they got on Saturday. We had more talent in our scout team than, probably, all but four teams we played that year—Michigan State, Penn State, UCLA and Michigan. The other teams were a cake walk.

Anyway, I went over to the training room, and I was in the whirlpool, as I always was, because I got beat up every day. You figure, you had some of the best players in the country tackling you, hitting you, knocking you down, and you've got to get up and go. Elia came over and apologized to me. He explained that it was after the Michigan State game that we lost 19–12.

He said, 'You knocked me down on that play, and I didn't want to get knocked down. We just lost to Michigan State, and we're getting shit over that, and I just broke loose. It's just that I took it out on you, and I'm sorry.'

Yeah, the defense would get mad when we went too hard against them, but I'll tell you what, when the eye was in the sky—when the camera was rolling—it was *hell* out there. They knew they were getting evaluated, and they're playing like they did on Saturday. You'd come in after practice and say, 'Man, Kuhndog, you were *something* out there today. What was going on?'

'Hey, man, you got to do it for the eye in the sky.'

The eye in the sky is that extra edge. Look out!

WOODY WAS ALWAYS DOWN on the other end of the field with the offense. The defense had their own domain. My buddy Don Coburn was a middle guard. He was another guy who, if not for a few bad breaks, would've played. He played two years with a broken neck and didn't know it. His neck was always hurting, always sore. They x-rayed it several times but couldn't find anything. Finally, they had a new procedure and a different angle, and they found a hairline crack in one of his vertebrae. He comes back from the doctor to where we were living. Someone says, 'Hey, Cobes, what'd you find out today?'

He says, 'I've got a broken neck. No wonder my head hurts.'

'Well, what's *that* mean? You going to be able to play or what?'

He says, 'Yeah, it was broke two years ago, which means for the past two years, one false move, and I wouldn't've been able to wipe my own ass.'

One day in practice, Rick Applegate, who played a real fine center for us, missed his block on Don. And Cobes put a hard hit on Archie. Woody immediately goes nuts. 'All right, now goddammit! Who missed that block?' After a few awkward moments, he says the much-feared words: 'OK! Run it again!'

Archie's helmet needs adjustment, so Woodrow Roach is at tailback. Well, Cobes clobbers Roach this time, and Woody comes unglued.

'Jesus Christ! Can't we block that son of a bitch!'

As Coburn is getting up from the ground, Woody grabs Cobes by the facemask and says, 'Who's supposed to be blocking you?'

Cobes doesn't want to get Apple in trouble so he acts dumb and says he doesn't know. He saves Apple, but Woody is just more frustrated and mad. He still has Cobes by the facemask, and while he's telling everybody they've got to block better, he's twisting the facemask around. Then he's hitting Cobes in the head and kicking him, like it's *his* fault that they're not blocking. He's not mad at Cobes; he's just *mad*. He's hitting Cobes on the helmet, saying, 'You've got to block this son of a bitch!'

MY SENIOR YEAR, the week before the Michigan game, we're back on keel, everything's going well, we're on the goal line again. I ran the ball, and I got hit so many times on one play that the last guy who hit me split my helmet. I still have a scar on my temple. It's great—you get that adrenalin going, you don't realize you're hurt. I get back to the huddle. I see there's blood all over my hands, there's blood on my pants, blood on my practice shirt. I'm looking around, trying to see which one over there on defense is bleeding.

I said to someone in the huddle, 'Someone over there's bleeding. We got one of them.'

After about three or four more plays, someone comes up to me and says, 'Maz, get out. You're bleeding.'

I said, 'No, I'm not. Someone over there is.'

He said, 'No, *you* are.'

I said, 'It can't be *me*.'

He said, 'Put your hand on your face.'

I went like this.

He said, 'No, put it up inside your helmet.'

Blood was everywhere, so I went over to the sideline, and they put a couple of butterfly bandages on it. I went back in, and it started hurting by this time. The helmet was split and jagged. It was cutting me even more. I had to come out and get sewed up.

I went to the doctor's office there inside the training room, and Dr. Murphy says, 'Okay, Maz, we're going to put a couple stitches in there.'

I said, 'How many do you think it's going to take?'

He said, 'Oh, it looks like it's less than an inch, about three quarters of an inch. We might be able to do it with two.'

I said, 'Fine. Do it with no novacaine.'

He says, 'Are you sure?'

I said, 'Yeah.'

He said, 'It's going to pinch.'

I said, 'I saw Arnie Jones do it one day. If he can do it, I'm going to try it.'

It's two stitches. I figure I can stand it. He put five in there.

'Ooooo, aaaaa! How many you have in there?'

'Two, but you don't want a scar there, do you?'

'No.'

'Well, we better put a couple more in there.'

My eyes are watering, my face is red, I'm clenching my fists as hard as I could, my teeth are like this. By this time, I had a little crowd watching me: 'Hey, Maz is in there getting stitches with no novacaine.'

I remember watching Arnie do that. The blood was trickling down as it was done. He didn't look like he was totally relaxed either, but he did it. So I thought, 'Hey, I'm going to try that.'

Biggest mistake I ever made.

IF I HADN'T GOTTEN MY SHOULDER HURT, if I hadn't got my toes hurt, who's to say what would have happened? There was no doubt in my mind that I could play at Ohio State. The first indication came from playing in that all-star game. There were some much bigger guys there, as big as you could find anywhere else, and there was speed, and there was a lot of other talent, and I was able to excel. And I can't help but believe that if I didn't have those injuries, I would've been able to do something. Maybe I wouldn't've started and been a star, because let's face it, I was there during the best four years they ever had at Ohio State. And although I was essentially on the scout team for four years, I would rather have been on the scout team for those four years than to have been there for any other four years they've had.

At Ohio State, everybody is pretty much equivalent in talent. The ones who get to play are the ones who stay healthy and get better, but if you're not healthy, you can't get better. You can't practice, you can't learn, you can't be coached. You're standing on the sidelines with an arm in a sling or on crutches. It's not your fault. Most injuries are accidents. It happens to thousands of guys every year, but of course you don't think that way when you're 18 years old. You feel like you're in a glass house and everyone's looking at you. You lose confidence. You think, 'Geez, did I make a mistake coming here? Do I belong here?' Sometimes I thought I'd made a mistake, but only for a few minutes at a time, and only because I was frustrated that I was hurt. I can't play, I can't practice, I can't get stronger, I can't lift, I can't run, I can't do all the things I need to do to play. I'd look at guys like Champ Henson and Pete Johnson and say, 'Hey, those guys are terrific athletes. To even be on the same field with them is a terrific accomplishment.' If I was healthy, could I have beaten them out? Chances are I wouldn't have, because they were better. They had more speed, and they had more size. I don't think I ever weighed more than 225. Not small, but here's Champ at 240, Pete is 250, and they're faster than I am. While I was recovering from my injuries, they were getting the experience. You have to do what the politician does. You concede. You concede that that's the way it is.

One time, I felt like throwing up my hands and leaving. I was a freshman, in summer ball. I'm in pain with my shoulder, frustrated, not getting a look, because I'm hurt. I'm down there with the freshman backs. Sark, who was the best defensive end coach ever, is there. We had to pull and kick out defensive ends for 30 minutes of every practice. I never had such a headache and stiff neck and sore shoulder in my life. It's hot. Hundred and ten degrees. 'What am I doing here? What am I out here for?' But a few days later, two-a-days were over, and those thoughts went away. Now, I was only getting beat up once a day.

Sometimes, you got your shots in, too. I know he probably won't like me saying this, but my senior year, we were running scout team offense and Bruce Ruhl was the cornerback. My job was to kick him out. I hit him so hard he flew through the air and landed on the track. He may not want to remember it, but I still remember John Mummey said, '*Woooo*, Maz, you were the hit-*ter* and he was definitely the hit-*tee*.'

THE MOST FEARED GUY I ever played against was Walter Douglas Plank, 'Mr. Missile' himself. He knocked me out three times in three years. We'd run sweeps against the Buck defense, and when I'd get down in my stance, I had to look and see where he was, because if I didn't, he'd take my head off. I didn't care about anyone else. His job was to take down the fullback on the sweep and let someone else make the tackle. *Geez*. He knocked me into next week three times. And he'd always say he was sorry. He'd knock his own players down and say he was sorry. He'd knock the referees down and say he was sorry. He loved it.

I don't want to use the term 'Jekyll and Hyde,' but it was like he had an on-off switch. He'd walk on the field and turn into this Mad Max guy. The one time he knocked me out, I went down on my back, and my hands were up in the air and my feet were up in the air, and as I started to come around, it's like I was underwater. I hear these sounds like I'm underwater. I can still see my feet up in the air. It was like I was saying, 'Get down. Get down,' but they wouldn't come down. My hands were up like this. One of the coaches came over; the trainers came over. They're asking me questions. I heard someone say, 'Okay, move it over here.'

Plank comes over and says, 'Maz, you okay?'

I couldn't even say anything. Next thing I knew, they had me on the training table with smelling salts, trying to bring me around, and he comes over and apologizes again. Here I was 225 pounds, and he's 195. You wouldn't think that was much of a challenge, but he'd launch himself like a Titan rocket. He would elongate himself like a frozen rope and use his helmet as a battering ram and put it on the side of your helmet. *BOOM!*

On kickoffs, he'd pick out the biggest guy he could find and just see if he could knock him out. One time against California, he knocked himself *and* this other guy out. I remember Dick Walker saying in films, 'Plank, where the hell were you on this play?'

He said, 'Aw, coach, I got knocked out the play before that. I was on the sidelines.'

Walker said, 'Well, as long as you weren't somewhere else beating the hell out of someone.'

When Doug was in the pros, his teammate Gary Fencik got a lot more publicity, probably because they ran away from Plank. No one in the NFL would run a crossing pattern against the Bears because of Plank. He was a madman.

I WORE LINEMEN'S ARM PROTECTORS, because my arms would turn purple from getting hit so much. After awhile those facemasks *hurt* on bare muscle. I don't care how much muscle you had. When you just do it over and over and over again, running against the best there was, and getting hit so much, your body takes a beating. I went to the equipment guy, John Bozick, and said, 'Can I have some of those things?'

He said, 'Well, hell, Maz, you're a running back.'

I said, 'I know, but I can't even move my arms.'

So I'd wear those things, and sometimes on my right arm, I'd wear another pad, because I had to keep putting my forearm on somebody's facemask. Now, Champ never wore any pads. But if it was up to him, he wouldn't even have worn shoulder pads.

It's a bit disappointing that I didn't get to be a household name on Saturday afternoons. I'm sure my dad was disappointed, but he knew I gave it the best shot I had and that I had some bad luck. One of the people I tried for, of course, was him. It's not that I told myself that or said it out loud. Just like any other dad, he would rather his son played and started and gone off to the NFL. At the same time, I contributed, and I contributed on teams that went to the Rose Bowl four years in a row.

IN FOUR YEARS, we lost just two games in the regular season. I cannot imagine being on any college team today and having a losing record. I can't imagine what it would be like losing three, four, and five games, and then going out to practice. We *expected* to win. There was no doubt that we *were* going to win.

By my senior year, I knew the handwriting was on the wall. I knew that Pete was the man, without a doubt, although it was entirely possible that I could've been second team. But it wasn't to happen. By this time, my other shoulder had gone out on me. It happened on the last week of the previous season. Same problem. Left shoulder separation, partially torn rotator cuff. Now, I had two bad ones. Consequently, I couldn't lift again, no benches, no militaries. I had a right shoulder injured three and a half years earlier, a freshly-injured left shoulder, my foot still hurts. Matter of fact, it hurts *now*. I was the beat up grizzly bear.

It's a crapshoot. You don't know if you're going to be healthy or not. It's luck, it's preparation, it's all kinds of things. Who's to say? If I could've stayed healthy the whole time, I think I could've been a real good second team player. I wouldn't've beaten out Pete Johnson, because he was a world-class talent. But if he had gotten injured, who knows what might've happened to *him*? We might never have heard of him. It's like what happened to Champ. He got hurt, and he was never quite the same again.

What I'm telling you now is one of the few times I've ever acknowledged all of this. The question of how good they could've been is very, very meaningful to some other guys. Champ and Kenny Kuhn, for example. If not for a couple of things, those guys would've had tremendous NFL careers. They had the talent, the ability. Then all at once, everything changed. Before you get hurt, you're going to set the world on fire. Then when you get hurt, it knocks you down a couple of notches. You get hurt again, and it knocks you down again. Pretty soon, you say: 'Well, if I can get over this, I'm going to try to come back, but I think it's probably not going to happen.' And you can't be all-consumed with that, so you have to say, 'Hey, I understand. This is not to be my destiny.'

A few guys came close, like I did, then stepped over the edge. Maybe they had problems at home or their grades went down. I think my class ended up with 13 guys. I just realized that due to circumstances, namely the injuries, that I wasn't going to be a star. Believe me, I was frustrated and self-concious. I didn't travel with the team much. When we'd be playing an away game and I wasn't on the traveling squad, someone would say, 'Hey, I thought you guys had a game at Iowa tomorrow.'

I'd say, 'Yeah, but I'm not traveling this week.'

'Oh.'

It was like these preseason banquets with the Quarterback Club and the Touchdown Club and this and that. They'd have these rows and rows of tables, interspersed with players and the members of these clubs. People would sit down with these big smiles on their face and stick out their hands: 'Hi, my name is Joe Blow, and your name is?'

You'd tell them, and they'd go 'Oh.'

You weren't a star, and they wanted to sit across from someone with a *name*. You're a third-teamer. Here they are, their whole night's been blown because they have to sit across from someone who's probably not going to play. They can't go home and tell their wife and kids they sat across from so-and-so who everybody's heard of.

Then you'd come around to thinking, 'Hey, you know what, I'm *not* a star. I'm not going to start Saturday, but I'm here, and you ain't. We're going to the Rose Bowl this year and you're not.' If anyone took issue with that, we might counter with, 'Oh, you're starting for who? Oh, I see. Where're you going post-season? Oh, the Cabbage Bowl. Well, we're going to the Rose Bowl. The third year in a row. No, I take that back. This's our *fourth* year in a row, and I get to go again.' *That* made it worthwhile.

I played in some games, but, of course, I was the late third quarter or fourth quarter—usually fourth quarter—type of guy. I didn't carry the ball much. I think my longest gain was eight yards. It was another one of those deals where it was an off-tackle play, and I cut it back to the middle, and there was nothing but grass—I should say astroturf—ahead of me. I was going for 80 yards or whatever it was. There was nothing there, but then somebody got a hold of my big foot. It would've been nice to get that one touchdown or even go for a decent gain. There was *nothing* in my way.

When I got in a game, in the third or fourth quarter, it was like playing against high school kids. These guys on the other team were nothing to block. When they tackled you, they pulled you down, but it didn't hurt you. Even if they put their head into you, you didn't feel it. The only reason we didn't score points on those guys was that we weren't used to running our own plays. We'd been running everybody *else's* plays. If we were used to running our own plays, we could've scored as many points as we wanted to.

MY FIRST PRIVATE CONTACT with Woody, except for the recruiting interview, was when he had his heart attack in 1973. That was a pretty dark time for everybody, but after a few days, everybody thought he'd be fine. He had these postcards made and mailed out to us. The card started, roughly, 'As you know, I've had a heart attack.' But he pooh-poohed that immediately and said, 'Get your butts ready to play some football when you get back here, because I'll be there.'

He lived at 1711 Cardiff Road. I'll never forget that. I thought it was important for me to go by and visit him. He was about in the middle stages of his recovery. I knocked on the door. Annie answered. She said, 'Hi! What can I do for you, Dave?'

I said, 'I just came by to visit Coach.'

She said, 'He's had so many visitors today. He should really be sleeping. I can't get him to take it easy. Visitor, visitor, visitor, and people all stay too long.'

I said, 'Mrs. Hayes, I guarantee you I'll talk with him for five minutes, and I'll be gone. I just want to tell him I'm here, I care about him, and that's it.'

She said, 'Well, okay.'

I go in. As soon as he sees me: 'Dave Mazeroski, glad to see you. Are you getting ready for the season?'

He starts talking, asking questions. He's always got to be in control, you know. After he's done asking me questions, I said, 'Coach, let me ask you something. Are you feeling better? Are *you* going to be ready for the season?'

He smiled. He said, 'Don't believe all that other crap that's out there. I'm going to be fine.'

I said, 'That's all I wanted to know. I'll see you in a couple of months.'

On my way out the door, Annie said, 'Hey, Maz, you can come back here any time you want. You're the first person who said he was going to stay for five minutes and stayed for five minutes.'

Woody could get mad as heck at you. Like, you'd go over to the football building, and you'd pass him in the hallway. The hallways were about 15 feet wide in there. If you walked down one side, and he was coming the other way, and you didn't speak to him, he would chew you out right there in the hallway: 'Goddammit, you speak to me. Don't just walk past me!'

'Good morning, Coach.'

'That's better.'

Then he'd give you a lecture. He'd say, 'I know, sometimes I might be walking with my head down, thinking about something, but, goddammit, you speak to me. I'll speak back to you. Goddammit, we spent all this time together; of course I want to speak to you.'

I DON'T THINK THERE'S any one particularly rewarding moment from that time. It's a compilation of things: being recruited there, going there, knowing the guys who became famous—you shared a locker with these guys. You knew them under the most humbling of situations. I can't imagine anyone saying it wasn't the greatest four years of their lives. Just like everybody else, I thought I was ready for it to be over: 'Aha, only one more week of practice!' Then you miss it. I remember when spring practice was over, heading into our senior year: 'Well, that's the last spring practice we'll ever have. No more of those.' Then, a little while later, you think, 'Oh, I'll never do that again. I had three of them, and I'll never do it again.'

It's a milestone, like reaching the age of 30 or 40, and you wonder where all the years went. You really don't miss the hard work, you don't miss the sweat, but you miss the camaraderie, the sense of belonging. You miss being cared for, catered to, you even miss being told what to do. You have to do it yourself now. For four years, you've had these rigorous guidelines, and now there's no more guidelines. That's hard for a lot of guys.

In 1981, my wife and I moved to Louisiana. We were there until February of 1990. We thought it would be terrific to live in the South. One of my most fond memories from that time was Ohio State played LSU at Baton Rouge. Our neighbors were also originally from Ohio. About 12 of us got together and rented a Winnebago and drove over to Baton Rouge. I fixed Craig Cassady up with a van from one of the rental places down there, and he brought another six people with him.

There's one thing I'll always be grateful to Craig Cassady for. In Cadiz, we didn't have any fast food restaurants or any fancy restaurants. I'd never eaten shrimp before in my life, and when I got down to Ohio State, we had shrimp during summer ball every now and then. I didn't know how to eat them. I looked around and watched these guys: 'Oh, just dip it in the sauce and eat them.' I was eating them up. It was great. Fried shrimp, all you wanted. Craig says, 'Hey, Maz, you don't have to eat the tails.'

I said, 'What?'

He says, 'You don't have to eat the tails.' He was embarrassed for me.

I said, 'What do you mean, the tails?'

He said, 'This part right here. Just hold onto that and bite it off and discard that.'

I said, 'Oh.' I was embarrassed, too. Heck, I thought they were pretty good, nice and crispy, kind of reminded me of bacon a little bit. Every once in a while, I'd sneak one when he wasn't looking.

ANYWAY, WE WENT OVER and watched Ohio State and LSU battle to a 13–13 tie. I won enough off of that to not have to chip in for the Winnebago rental. The first thing I thought when I moved back here was, 'I'll be able to use my Ohio State tickets again.' I had kept them for all those years. My parents used them while I was in Louisiana. Whenever I'd send in money for tickets, I'd send a contribution to the athletic department. That way, I thought they'd remember me a little better.

I was always extremely proud of my teammates in the pros. I never begrudged them anything. I wanted them to play 20 years if they could. I was extremely happy about that, because the more players that went to the pros just confirmed how good our teams were during those years. The last several years there haven't seen as many players drafted as there used to be. As a matter of fact, at our 15th reunion in 1990, I stood next to Sark when we went out on the field. Each of us was assigned a hash mark.

Sark said in that guttural voice of his, 'Hey, you can tell a lot about a team by the number of guys who go to the pros. There hasn't been that many lately, has there?'

There's about two minutes left in the half, and the Buckeye defensive players are coming back off the field. I'm standing behind the OSU bench with Jim Savoca. Some big defensive tackle comes off the field—I don't know who it was—he's looking us over like, 'Who the hell are you?'

Savoca says, 'What're you looking at? I'll go one on one with you right now and kick your ass.'

We all burst out laughing. He probably would've, too.

I felt completely at home down there, but because I never made it to the starting lineup, I won't ever be held in as high esteem as some other guys who contributed on the field on Saturdays. I realize I can't discuss all the same things that these guys can talk about. I can't discuss with Archie how I made the block that sprung him on this 40-yard touchdown run, like Pete or Champ can. I can't discuss with Corny Greene how I saved his ass because I went up and caught a pass that could have been an interception, like Brian Baschnagel can.

But I feel comfortable because I feel comfortable with myself, that I did make a contribution. In my heart, I feel that way. What's rewarding is to hear guys say you helped by being on the scout team, guys who were All-Americans, guys I feel privileged to be associated with. It's been told to me that it was guys like me who helped them sharpen their skills so they could do that stuff. The last guy to tell me was Van DeCree, who was a great defensive end.

At one of the reunions, I said to Van, 'You were one of the best.'

He said, 'You made me that way. If it wasn't for guys like you, I wouldn't have been good.'

I can't tell you the number of guys who've said that, and it makes me feel like a million bucks. It confirms just how much it was all worth. ”

33

Manchild *in the* Promised Land

PETE JOHNSON is so different from his public image that, after talking with him only briefly, one begins to feel like the victim of a juvenile prank. In four seasons at Ohio State and eight in the NFL, Johnson acquired a reputation as a gifted manchild whose cavalier disregard for everything from his physical condition to his personal life fell somewhere between crass and foolish. An acquaintance once explained that Johnson's idea of being punctual is to arrive within 48 hours of an appointed time.

At Max and Erma's, Johnson was early. In a heavy cotton sweatsuit, he slouched on a bench in the foyer, one hightop basketball shoe resting on the other, fingers laced over the ample midsection that received as much attention as the nearly 7,000 yards Johnson accounted for as a professional fullback. Prompted by newfound maturity or humility brought on by 10 years out of the spotlight, or a desire to set straight an incorrect perception, Johnson mulled over his life and career for hours.

"You put up a ladder and say, 'No one can climb that ladder,' I'll do it," Johnson says. "You make it a little taller and say no one can do it, I'm going to do it. It's not that I was lazy. I was just doing the best I had to do."

The promptness, the seriousness, the worldly insight were enough to make a listener suspect Johnson of having sent an impostor. After all, he rushed for 112 yards, including a 57-yard sprint, one afternoon for the Cincinnati Bengals, then weighed in at 262 pounds and said, "That wasn't me out on the field. Fat men can't run that fast."

Johnson has always been difficult to pin down. Born Willie Hammock to a 13-year-old mother in rural Georgia, he changed his name for obscure reasons, most likely because he began playing varsity football when he was 12, against the wishes of the great-grandparents who reared him. He later registered at Ohio State as Hammock but played as Johnson and signed his academic work either way. He decided on the latter name after Woody Hayes made him choose.

The striking difference between his appearance and his ability further demonstrates his contradictions. He was recruited out of the band to play football, and with his pleasant, round face and round body, he still looks like a jovial tuba player. During his career, he weighed as much as 279 pounds ("A refrigerator with feet," Bengal coach Forrest Gregg said), but he ran a 9.9 hundred and friends say he can still dunk a basketball. He was such a physiological anomaly (his thighs measured 29 inches) that Johnson's coaches became obsessed with his weight and conditioning. Players, coaches, and trainers crowded around to watch Johnson weigh himself. To make him feel less conspicuous, Hayes even climbed on the scale first. The coach wanted Johnson to play at 240, but after practice and some extra laps one sultry August day, he had gone from 255 to 256. Hayes surrendered, calling Johnson "the ideal blend of speed and power."

That Johnson was a special athlete quickly became apparent. After his first practice on the scout squad, coaches chattered about Johnson's explosive blocks on the varsity linebackers. He seemed the natural choice to step in after Champ Henson was injured in the second game of 1973. But Johnson was homesick and sulking over the decision to make linebacker Bruce Elia a fullback. Hayes's believed he was simply loafing. "I guess it was like the same thing all my coaches thought of me," Johnson says. "They didn't think I applied myself. I think it took Woody the longest to know that I was just being me."

Johnson got his shot in the last game of the season. He scored the team's only touchdown in a 10–10 tie with Michigan, crashing in from the five with three Wolverines clinging to him. As OSU trounced Southern Cal in the 1974 Rose Bowl, Johnson gained 94 yards in 21 carries and scored three touchdowns.

Henson returned in 1974, and Hayes announced that the two players ("484 pounds of well-directed, devastation-dedicated football power," according to the *Columbus Dispatch*) would share the position. "We'll run Champ Henson to the left and Pete Johnson to the right," the coach said. But by the sixth game, when they combined for only four rushes, the fullbacks had virtually disappeared from the offense. Torn between two talented, congenial farm kids of whom he was equally fond, Hayes flipped a coin to determine who would start. The coach eventually admitted he'd made a mistake. "We wound up with no fullback," he said.

In his junior year, Johnson became a star. He carried seven times in a fourth-quarter scoring drive to seal a 17–9 win over Penn State, knocking a defensive back senseless along the way. He scored a school-record 30 points against North Carolina. Against Illinois, he broke Henson's Big Ten record by scoring his 21st touchdown of the year, and he scored all three touchdowns against Michigan in a seven-point victory. He was the national scoring champion, and he, Cornelius Greene, and Archie Griffin made up the all-league backfield. Johnson and Griffin remain the only Buckeyes to gain 1,000 yards in the same season.

"Their offense is the simplest thing to defense on the board," said Minnesota coach Cal Stoll. "But try and go out there and do it on the field. You got to stop the buffalo, and then Corny or Archie will make the big play."

Johnson claimed he wanted his senior year to be his best; rumor even had him watching film for the first time. His records for points and touchdowns in a game, a season, and a career still stand. But by the Orange Bowl, two lingering ankle sprains had relegated him to the short yardage offense in favor of the quicker Ron Springs and Jeff Logan. It was, for Johnson, "an unfortunate season," according to Hayes.

The first player chosen in the second round, Johnson led the Bengals in rushing for seven straight years. He set team records with 1,077 yards and 16 touchdowns in 1981 and with 5,421 yards in his career. He was so powerful and so fast as to make tackling him a complex—and potentially dangerous—matter of physics. "I used to see Pete run by guys and they used to jump on his back. And I didn't blame them, because you hit him head on, and you have some work to do," says Griffin, Johnson's teammate in Cincinnati as well as at OSU.

Johnson, who'd come to Ohio State to play linebacker, was as aggressive as he was strong, saying he went "into a trance" when he carried the ball. "If someone's going to bother to tackle me, I want him to feel it more than I do. I want him to pay," he said. Though he speaks with relish of punishing tacklers to gain their respect, there's also a great gentleness to Johnson. He is soft-spoken, his smile warm and playful.

In Cincinnati, he became known for spending more time in "The Cisco Kid," his plush van, than in the weightroom. ("I did just enough to win. I've seen a lot of people hurt because they're doing more than that.") Just a year after helping the Bengals to the Super Bowl, Johnson was suspended for cocaine use. He appealed the suspension and still claims that the case was one of "guilt by association." Traded away, he played one more season—a lackluster one in Miami—then simply never went back. He says he didn't enjoy professional ball anyway and now would much rather tailgate than watch a game.

Johnson swore he'd never return to Columbus, but as with so many former Buckeyes, he was drawn back to the place of his first fame. Indeed, while he was suspended, Johnson met Hayes every morning to work out—at the coach's insistence.

During the long afternoon at the restaurant, Johnson had been chatting up waitresses and bartenders, as if to demonstrate his contention that "I'm just me all the time, and everyone's crazy about me." Judging by the response to his good-natured banter, he is right.

Johnson was selling cars and promoting a system to convert diesel-powered vehicles to natural gas. He had also been visiting prisons to speak about the importance of family and had become a familiar figure at charity events. ("I have three kids of my own, and I like to work with schools.")

"If anybody has something to bitch about, this's the guy that does," he says. "But I don't, because I don't have time to bitch. I have to go on. That's what Woody was about. I'd do it over in a minute."

He'd consumed enough cold draft beer—his enormous hand obscuring the mug—and rich fern-bar food to engorge a lion, but Pete Johnson was suddenly in a hurry. More nimbly than seemed possible, he scurried through the parking lot to another expensive customized van and hopped in. He didn't want to be late for his racquetball game.

Pete JOHNSON

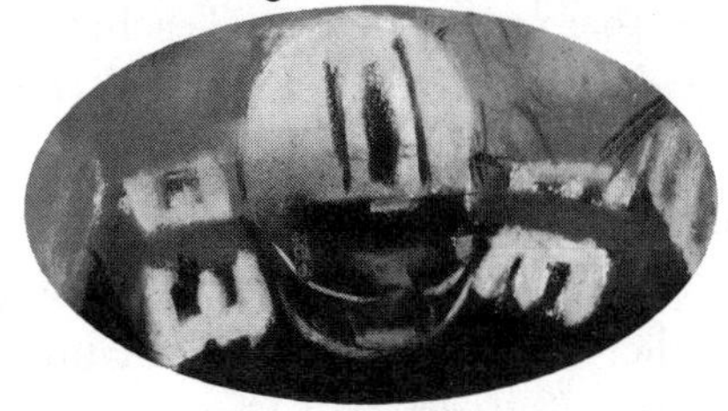

"MY MOTHER WAS 13 when she had me. I was raised on a big farm in Peach County, Georgia, by my great-grandparents. They always wanted a boy and they got a perfect opportunity, so they raised me. The summer I had just turned six, they finally sold the farm and moved to the city so I could go to school. Before I went to school, I was listening to my aunts, and they were talking about this one teacher who would get mad at them and stick their heads between her legs and spank them. Man, I used to have nightmares. When it was time to go to school, my great-grandfather walked me there, because Peach County Elementary was right across the street. He walked me to school, and when he got home, I was sitting on the steps waiting for him. I beat him back. He said, 'Okay, you don't want to go to school, you're going to work.'

We got in the truck and drove over to the farm. It was pruning season for the peach trees. They had to cut and pile the branches up. Six years old, I drove a tractor up and down the aisles. I'd drive it to the end, I'd hit the lever to stop, he'd turn it around down the next aisle, and I'd do it again. By the time that school year was over, I was *praying* to go to school. I just didn't want that fat lady sticking my head between her legs.

A lot of my friends were white, but we didn't go to school together until 10th grade. We shopped at the same stores, and I tell the kids I remember when they had the signs on the bathroom doors, COLORED and WHITE. I was the renegade when they integrated the schools. I'd be walking down the hall, and teachers would be pulling kids into the rooms and saying, 'Here comes that uppity nigger.' Teachers! I was ornery as hell. But they never made me mad. You lose then. Any time you try to get even, you lose.

My great-grandmother was the most prejudiced woman I ever met. There were certain people I couldn't bring to my house. I think my great-grandmother was prejudiced against everybody, mainly whites, light-skinned blacks. My great-grandfather just loved everybody. Then he got sick. He had this little sore on his foot, and it kept getting bigger and bigger. They were all from the old school and they took him to what they called a 'fixer,' someone who believed in roots and potions, and I'm like, 'Take my dad to the doctor.' I finally took him to the doctor, but it was gangrene and it ended up taking his whole leg.

I used to watch *Perry Mason*, and that's when I made up my mind that I was going to play pro football or pro basketball, because I heard someone on that show saying that you could make a lot of money. I was going to make a lot of money to buy him a wheelchair and buy him a house that had those little rails you can put a wheelchair on and slide up and down the steps. I made up my mind I was going to do that, but I never got the chance. He talked me into going to live with my mom, and about midway through my senior year of high school, he passed away, not long after I left. He just didn't want me to see him die. We had to bathe him, we had to pick him up and put him in that wheelchair, we had to clean him. That killed him more so than his leg, not being able to do things for himself.

I made the high school team in the seventh grade. I was on my way to band practice and this guy came up to me and said, 'You look big. You should play football.' It was the high school football coach. He didn't know I was in seventh grade. All he knew was he saw some big kid walking down the hall. The first practice I went to, I didn't even know what a jockstrap was. The guy who gave them out said, 'Here, go ahead, put this on.' I just watched the other guys and did what they did. I got dressed and went out, and the coach said, 'What position you playing?'

I says, 'Anything.'

He said, 'What position you want to play?'

I looked around. I said, 'What position is the best?'

He didn't say anything, so I said, 'Okay, what position gets most of the girls?'

He said, 'Quarterback.'

I said, 'That's good. I want to be a quarterback.'

He said, 'You're too big to be a quarterback.'

He put me at defensive end and offensive guard, then moved me to offensive tackle. They put a tackle-eligible pass in for me. I don't think I ever missed one. I played varsity in the seventh grade. After I started playing in seventh grade, the mayor, Paul Reeling, had a radio program, and I was on his radio program every Saturday morning. By midway through the season, I was always the player of the week, and the black and the white player of the week got to be on his show. Seventh grade, I'd be driving the car, and I'd get stopped. The policeman would just say, 'You be careful now. How you guys gonna do?' It was great.

IN 10TH GRADE, I played middle linebacker and offensive tackle. I was All-State middle linebacker. I always had the tackle-eligible pass. Any time they got the ball to me, I scored. In Georgia then, there was a Football Jamboree in the spring. You had spring training, and you had this Jamboree where a bunch of high schools got together and played against each other. Everybody gets a quarter, and the winner goes on to play someone else, and that's when they introduced me to running back. We had this little quarterback—I can't remember this little white kid's name, but he would hand the ball off to me and he would get stuck on me, and I was carrying him *and* the ball 15, 20 yards down the field. He'd give me the ball, and all I would see was the goal line.

By my senior year, I was 225 and ran a 9.9 hundred. People would say, you did this and you did that, and I didn't remember any of it. I did just enough to win. Every coach I ever had said that about me. I did just what it took. I've seen a lot of people hurt because they're doing more than that. Instead of doing just what it takes, they try to do more, and they hurt themselves. It's like a great racehorse. You try to make him do too much, you're going to end up with nothing. I made it seem easy.

I was All-State as a sophomore, a junior, and a senior. The real fun was at linebacker, that's what I loved. If you watched me play, that's what I played fullback like. I used to look for people to hit. There was a lot of times I could've gotten another five or six yards going around a man, but uh-uh. That's what Woody always said, 'Make them respect you.' You can't make anybody respect you running around him. You run *over* him. You let him know what's going to happen if he gets in your way.

I finished high school at Long Beach High School in New York. It was a lot better in New York. There was more to do than down south. You didn't have to say 'Yessir' and 'Nosir' all the time, which I did, because I'd always been respectful because of the way I was brought up. It was just different; it was like being in a new world: the people, the ideas. I used to sneak to the city and just stand on the street and watch people walk by. I used to go into stores just to listen to people talk. Chinese, I'd never been around. You've got so many people who look different and their voices are totally different. One of the big things for us to do was to sit around and just listen to people. To this day, I study people. And all the time, you're getting to know yourself.

When I first went there, we lived right off Park Avenue. Then we lived in Oceanside, another little town right around there. My mom always had about four or five jobs. When I went to the Bengals, the first thing I did, I moved my mom from New York. I got her off welfare. I bought her a house. And she still works just as hard. She's 13 years older than me, and I look older than my mom. She runs the kitchen at the Holiday Inn out at the airport. She's been there now since back in '77.

I had a great senior year. Every year, I wanted to get better than the year before. I did that my whole career. You look back at my career and you see that, every year, I was better than I was the year before. I had 250 letters, a lot of them with airline tickets in them, and scholarships, and I had 35 in basketball. Every school—every junior college, every Big Ten, Pac 8—all of them recruited me out of high school. I went with Woody because of Woody. As a matter of fact, I had signed a letter of intent with West Virginia University, and Woody sent a guy named Chuck Clausen to recruit me. He was such a nice guy that even though I had signed with West Virginia, I still let him come visit me.

NOW, I HAD NEVER HEARD OF WOODY HAYES. I'd never heard of Archie Griffin. I went to football practice or basketball practice, then we went to Geno's Pizza, and I was on the beach. I didn't know who Woody Hayes was. My gym teacher went to Ohio State, and it was like every second, she was telling me, Woody Hayes is this, Woody Hayes is that. I started inquiring about Woody Hayes. People said he was a maniac. You know, he does what he wants to do, he turns pay raises down. *Hmm*, I thought, sounds like a dedicated man to me. He came to the school three times. He never mentioned football. He talked about school, education, and he was smart, he got me talking about my great-grandfather. I told him everything about my great-grandfather, and that's when he got me. That's when I told him I was going to the University of West Virginia. He said, 'That's like choosing a Ford over a Cadillac.'

He said, 'I want you to know, the only thing I promise you at Ohio State is a great education, one national championship, four Big Ten championships and, probably, four Rose Bowls. That's it. I can't give you any money or anything.'

He said, 'I want to let you know something about these schools that're giving you money—you'll get suspended, you won't be seen on national TV, and TV is what gets you in the pros.' That's what he said. You could get out of a letter of intent then, because there wasn't any Big Ten letter involved. I wondered if I made the right decision. I remember taking the airplane out. We're driving in from the airport, and then, it was all woods along the way, just one little building. And New York had got into me. I thought, 'What the hell am I doing here?'

A lot of things were going through my mind. I remembered Woody talking about these 86,000 screaming people. The first game came around, I went out without my shoulderpads on, and I looked around, and I had more people at my high school games. Everybody should be here now, I thought. I've been lied to, and that's one thing you don't do, you don't lie to me. I don't forget a lie. Right away, I'm feeling down. I'm ready to leave. I've been lied to. So we go in and put our shoulderpads on, and I'll never forget when they opened that door, and the roar of the crowd hit me like someone took an electric socket and stuck it to me. It was a scary feeling. Right there, you look at all those people, and they look like a disturbed ant bed. You ever find an ant bed and just kick it? Well, that's the way it looked. I'll never forget looking at all these people.

They put me in, and the people just took to me. After the game, people are coming up to me for my autograph, and this and that, and I'm like, 'Thank you, Lord. You guided me to the right place.'

BEFORE GAMES, WOODY used to have guys crying. I thought it took away your energy. I got far away from those guys. I thought they were nuts. Oh, man. I used to tell Archie, 'Man, don't you ever cry again, long's I know you. I'm goin' to kick your butt if you cry, 'cause you one ugly person when you cry.' Michigan games, he'd have these guys crying like they just lost their best friend before they went out on the field. I'm looking at 'em like—*man*.

He'd say, 'Archie, they think they have a pretty good running back, but we think we have a damn good running back and All-American in you. Now, why don't you get up and tell the team what they gotta do.'

He'd get up there crying, 'Oh, ah, oh, ah....'

He'd go through the whole team. He got to the point with me that he wanted to do me last and just get it over with. He had to do it because of the team concept. John Hicks and all of them are crying, and here's me. He says, 'Okay, son, they think they have a pretty good fullback, but we think we have the best fullback in the country. Why don't you tell the team what they gotta do.'

'Coach, I'm ready to go out there and kick their ass.'

'Goddammit, son, do you ever get excited about anything?'

Before every game, I played it a million times in my head. I think Woody did the same thing. After a while, he could see what I was doing. It wasn't that I wasn't into the game. I was thinking about what I had to do. I wanted to remember the plays. I didn't want to make a mistake, because I didn't want to have to wear a helmet around campus with a football under my arm. That's what they told me you had to do if you made a mistake. Archie and them said they saw guys, when they fumble, he made guys do that. I was petrified at first.

Woody was famous for putting these last-minute plays in, and he always would name them something that had to do with Archie: 'We're going to put in Nathan 8. You know why I call it that, don't you? Because that's Archie's middle name.'

HE PUT IN THIS ONE PLAY. It was me, Archie, Brian Baschnagel and Cornelius Greene. He sent this play in, and we're all in the huddle, and I don't even think Brian knew what to do, even though he was going to get the ball. But after all the repetition, the mind just automatically knows what to do. We're all looking at each other, and I say, 'Cornelius, what do we do on this play?' He ignored us, looking to the sideline like he's getting the call, when it was sent in. He's hoping to change the play. But he calls it. We go to the line, and Archie and me are both screaming, 'What do we do? What do we do?'

He turned around and said, 'Shit, do what you been doing.'

I fake left, Archie fakes right, he hands off to Brian—20 yards for a touchdown.

The first training camp, the first practice, when we went into pads, they put me down on the scout team. But I was on the regular team that evening. I think I was on the scout team one day. The morning, I knocked Randy Gradishar out, and the evening, I knocked Rick Middleton out. I wanted to play linebacker, and those guys were the guys I needed to take out. I was on the scout team as a fullback, but when I went there, I wanted to play linebacker. I figure, they're the starting linebackers. I get them out of the game, then I got a shot. They used to fake the ball to me, and those guys come in there to tackle me, and I'd just open up.

CHAMP GOT HURT, and they wasn't sure I was ready, so they took Bruce Elia—he was a linebacker, too—and made him a fullback. I'm real pissed off about this. I *know* I'm ready, but it was getting to know how to deal with people. 'Yessir' and 'Nosir' I'd got out of saying, and that was one thing about Woody, he demanded respect. You were going to say that to Coach Hayes, or you weren't going to play for Ohio State. That was about the only thing you had to say to him; you're good enough, you're going to play. They kind of felt I was a renegade, because I spoke my words. When I felt like speaking, I spoke.

I ended up doing real well academically, but I had to apply myself, and a lot of it was Woody. Up until sixth grade, I was an excellent student, but with football, if you have anything to do with football, the school seems to let you go. My senior year, I got lucky. My English teacher there, buddy, she didn't let me off the hook about anything, and I thank her for that. It was Woody and my English teacher my senior year who made me a good student. As a matter of fact, she made me go to summer school. The principal told her that I had to be excused to see recruiters. She said, 'No. No recruiter or anything is going to come before my class.' There were recruiters camped out in the washrooms. From the time I got to homeroom, you'd hear, 'Ah, could you send Pete Johnson to the office, please?' All day long, except for her class.

It was kind of a lonely feeling, being recruited. After football season, every 30 seconds there was a recruiter there. I kind of enjoyed being recruited, but what I really enjoyed was the happiness I brought to everybody else. I liked seeing people happy. Coach Finkel, my high school coach—he was a little short Jewish guy—you never saw anybody so happy. Everybody at that school was happy. Everybody in the town was rooting for me. It felt good. Some of the recruiters were so full of shit. They would say stuff like, I know you're from a poor this or poor that, when I always had everything I wanted. The lines of bullshit they gave me. I'd think, 'Yeah, I'll fly on your plane, and I'll spend your little $50, and I'll have fun at your school, but I'm not going there.'

Woody was just real. You could see it; you could feel it. There was nothing phony about that man. Woody would knock on your door at 7 o'clock if you had an 8 o'clock class. He'd tutor you if you needed it. He used to always tell the guys who liked girls, 'You guys are missing the boat. I got one of the nicest women you could ever date, and I married her. You know where I met her? At the library. The best looking women are always over there at the library.' He just forgot one thing. They're a lot different than when he went to school. That's where all the sleazy women were, at the library, buddy, because they were wanting to catch on to a doctor or a lawyer to marry them. Shoot, that was pick-up heaven, so I picked them up. I figured, he ain't never lied to me. So I just went to the library, and, boy, all the women *were* there.

When I speak in the prisons or whatever, I tell people you have to take advantage of all your resources, and that's what I did. We had tutors. They could call the teacher and say, 'Now, what are you having next week?' And the teacher would tell them, and we would go over it. I'll tell you what, it's a lot more comfortable knowing what's going to happen in a classroom when you're going in. Some teachers seemed like they wanted to surprise the students. Why? Tell them what you're going to do, and do it. That way, you create the self-esteem, the confidence. I thought, 'We ain't playing *Jeopardy*.' That's why I used tutors. I tell kids, 'You use all your resources.'

There's many a-time I thought I was in the wrong place. When Champ came back, Woody would flip a coin to see who started. Everyone on that team knew who should start. But Woody knew the type guy I was and he knew the type guy Champ was. He was praying I won that coin toss—I guarantee he was—but you know what that does to a kid? You know how embarrassing that is, in front of your team, for a coach to flip a coin to see who starts? I think he did that because it was something Champ needed. I don't think Champ could handle that total rejection. Woody knew me. He knew it was just going to piss me off and make me play harder when I got in there. He was smart; that man was smart.

One time he made me so mad, because the only reason we lost to Michigan State that time was he put Champ in there. Me and Archie are in, I'm averaging five yards per carry, and he takes me out and puts Champ in. We figured we had the game under control. We never realized we were going to have a breakdown and Levi Jackson was going to run 60 yards for a touchdown, and that momentum built up. Woody, though, he loved people. He figured you win with people, and his football players were his main people. Champ was real down in the dumps, and there's no telling what direction a kid will take. He was worried about what was going to happen to Champ in the future. It pissed me off. I cussed him out on the sidelines. In mean I ripped him. Oh, God, I don't even want to use the words.

But he was mad, too. He got on *The Woody Hayes Show* that night, and he had Champ Henson on. The people who saw that show probably forgot about it. But he said, 'Champ, you're my starting fullback from now on.' Everybody on the ninth floor of Siebert Hall was crying. That was a girl's dorm, and I was like the mascot of that floor. They were all crying. He was wrong, but you just don't tell a coach he's wrong. It cost us a game and a national championship by putting him in.

I REMEMBER LOSING. I remember the fights in the locker room after the game. I remember Woody telling us, 'They think they kicked our ass on the football field. They're only across the hall. Let's go over there and kick their asses.' And Steve Luke: 'Yeah, Coach, let's kick their goddammed asses.' And I remember Neal Colzie saying, 'Y'all better sit your goddammed asses down. We'll be in trouble out there, all those Michigan people out there.'

I remember that, and I remember that next week of practice, when I wasn't included in the offense—at all. I could have easily quit. Matter of fact, I was going to quit, and Diane Stuckey, this girl in the academic advisement office, said, 'Let me tell you something, that isn't the Pete I know. You always fought.' I was ready to go home, but Woody was gambling that I wouldn't. He was gambling on me doing just exactly what I did. And the reason that I know is he told me. It was the heat of the moment. He understood why I was mad. He knew I had a right to be mad. He was mad about the same thing. But that's why he was the head coach. The head coach makes the decisions; whether they're right or wrong, he's the head coach. There were other times he did things in my favor that probably pissed other people off, too.

I'll never forget, we go the whole practice. I'm not even on the field.

I'm not even on the scout team. I'm just a body. I dressed myself, got my ankles taped, go on out to practice. I stood on the sideline, and I say, 'Humpf, nah, I got to do something.' So I just start running laps. When they're practicing, I run laps. When they stop practicing, I stop running laps. They totally ignored me. He wouldn't even say my name.

Then we go to play Iowa, and they're just about to kick our butts. And he puts me in the game. The first play, I run 35 yards, and the next play, I run 20 yards for a touchdown. After the game, he's pissed, the first time I ever saw him mad at Archie. He's mad at everyone. He says, 'Archie, you couldn't do nothing. Champ, you played like some duck waddling.' He went down the line. I still was 'that other guy.'

'I put that other guy in and he did better than all of you.'

Then, the next week, we started to practice. He called me in his office and said, 'Now, we're playing Michigan. That man I watched this past week, that's the man I want to show up this week.'

I'm looking away.

He says, 'Goddammit, son, look at me. That man I saw last week, that's the man I want to see.'

I didn't have to be told, I just did it, and that's what he was trying to bring out in me. I guess he had listened to his coaches, and his coaches said I need to be watched, I need to be guided, I need to be told what to do. But he wanted to see, because he was planning on starting me that Michigan game.

I WAS TRYING TO HURT SOMEBODY when I ran the football. Every time I ran the ball, I was trying to hurt somebody. I wanted respect; I wanted to make them respect me. It's another thing Woody drilled into me. He said, 'You go to a place and it's going to be loud, people clapping their hands and yelling—you make them respect you, and you'll have them sitting on their hands.' I wanted that respect.

You get in my way when I'm trying to score, I'm going to hurt you. A lot of times, I could get an extra five yards, but then I can't get your respect. I got to make you feel the pain first before I can do the rest of my job. My next move, someone gets in front of me, I hit 'em, and they know how it's going to feel. Just to get 'em thinking about it. Then I can run around them, I can run through them, I can do whatever I want to do.

We were playing North Carolina and I had 140 yards and five touchdowns. On Friday, we had our dinner there and on Sunday, we had brunch at the golf course. Woody had this thing where he called you, and you knew, if you sat with Woody, you were going to have to say grace. He made you feel like a little kid, say grace and stuff. So, I had to say grace that Friday. That was a wild weekend after that game. I think I ended up with some girl under a pool table.

Sunday brunch, I walked in, Bill Conley says, 'Pete, Coach Hayes wants you to sit with him.' I'm shittin' bricks. I'm like, 'Oh no, someone cover for me.' I didn't know how he knew, because the only people down there were some of the players and some girls. 'Damn, I'm in trouble.' We sit there, and we're eating. I didn't say grace, so I know I'm in trouble. Coach Hayes looked over at me. He had his chair pulled up; he wanted me to sit by him.

He said, 'You look at the paper this morning.'

'Yessir.'

'They had a lot of good things to say about you, didn't they?'

'Yessir.'

He reached over and grabbed me by the collar and pulled me to him and said, 'If you were smart, you'd find that reporter and you'd kick him dead in his ass. Son, good things make you weak, but it's not going to make you weak, is it?'

Now, that's what I remember the most.

IT'S ALWAYS GOOD TO SEE MY TEAMMATES. I walked out of my office yesterday, and there's Garth Cox standing on the showroom floor. I look at him, and I think of Woody right away. I remember, I think it was my freshman year, and I scored the only touchdown against Michigan, and the Big Ten voted whether Michigan or Ohio State would go to the Rose Bowl. Garth Cox was in my freshman class, and he was sick. He had some kind of virus. Woody had let us vote among ourselves who we wanted to go. And someone said, 'Coach, what about Garth? Are you going to take him?'

And he said, 'You don't think I'd go to California with my Cox out, do you?'

I was sick when all that stuff happened with Woody. By knowing him, I noticed that the last two times we went to the Rose Bowl, the papers had started guiding him. You know, they'd have an article 'Ohio State Will Have to Pass to Beat USC,' than all of a sudden, we're trying to pass. I watched, and a lot of times, he'd get mad, and he'd just start hitting himself or biting himself. Then, that kid comes up and puts the ball in his face, and you don't know, he could've been trying to hit Art. Truthfully, he could've been trying to punch Art. Art Schlichter was standing right there behind that kid. All this stuff was going through my mind.

The average person gets in their mind to do what this man did, how long would it take before they crack? I thought about the time he called me in his office because he was going to help me with some history. I get to practice early, and that's when Bear Bryant had retired. I thought of the look in Woody's eyes, when he said, 'Pete, that man's not going to live long. Once you quit what you love, there's not but one thing left—to die.'

Then I think of my great-grandfather when his legs were amputated, and he couldn't work, and it's almost like when Woody said this, my great-grandfather had said it to me. He reminded me a lot of my great-grandfather in the way he said and did things. I got all these other guys sending me literature about their universities, clothing store catalogues, you know, just enticing me, and Woody sent me a book, *You Win With People*. It was words the plain man could read. You could read that book with a third-grade education, but it was true. I would've loved to meet Woody Hayes's dad. I'll bet his dad was a lot like my great-grandfather.

THE PROS WEREN'T EVEN CLOSE to as much fun as college; not even close. I was the first pick in the second round. I just knew I was going to get a million dollars. Guys mislead you. Some of the guys from Ohio State go to the pros, they come back, tell you about all this money they're making. They were lying. I got a $30,000 bonus and $30,000 a year. After the end of seven years with the Bengals, you know the most money I made? $100,000. Everybody told me I was making $500,000, $600,000. I told them what I was making, no one believed me. Kenny Anderson, in '83, Kenny made $500,000. He was the highest paid.

They'd tell me, 'We only drafted you for short yardage.'

I said, 'I've been your leading rusher and scorer every year I played.'

'Hey, you did extra, that's your business. We drafted you for short yardage.'

I remember one time I went in there after I fired the agent, and I wanted a new contract. They're like, 'Who do you think you are, Earl Campbell?'

'He can't do half the shit I do.'

'Well, I suppose you want as much money as Franco Harris.'

'Matter of fact, yeah, I want more than Franco Harris. I make the game exciting for the fans. I don't run out of bounds. My boundary is the goal line.'

'We don't know what to tell you. No one else needs a fullback.'

Tiger Johnson was the head coach when I went there, then we had Homer Rice, the philosopher, then we had Forrest Gregg. I put him second in all the coaches I had. I put him right up there with Woody Hayes. Homer cracked me up. He reminded me of Sam Wyche towards the end there. Sam started looking like Homer to me, that's when I knew he was gone. We were playing Buffalo. Buffalo beats us 51–2, or something, and after the game, Homer tells us, 'There's something positive in this, men. Let's put it in the right perspective.' Oops, I thought, Homer's gone.

I had some good times in pro football, but it wasn't like I lived it. It was a job. When you're out on the field and you're playing, and you come off the field and you check out the fans and they're going, 'Pete! Pete! Pete!' It's a rush. The fans made it good, the owners didn't. It was all political. The owners are going to ruin the game. They're trying to take the excitement out of the game for some strange reason. What's with the players celebrating? I saw a guy score a touchdown in a playoff game the other day and they threw a flag because he was excited. Archie got fined about five or six times for having his socks down and his tee-shirt out. It's just not a go-to-the-office type job.

I LOVED FORREST, THOUGH. A great coach. The Bengals made a big mistake when they tried to tell him how to run his team. That's why he quit. They were at every practice. The coaching staff and I were real close; Forrest and I were real close. Some days I'd get to practice on Tuesday after our day off, and he'd say, 'What the hell's going on? They told us to look for some reason to bench you.'

Information like that made me beat the Browns. I kicked their booties. In every aspect. I left the Bengals the leading rusher, and I quit. They didn't cut me, they didn't fire me, I'm the one who quit. They figured no one could say goodbye to football. I made it because I always had another job. I sent my brothers and sisters all through college. And that damn sure wasn't from what I made playing for the Bengals.

A lotta things have happened, but they just make you stronger. I'm just like a rechargable battery; the worse things get, the better I am. The only thing that ever happened to me that really cost me money was there was a guy here in town, a guy I know, and no one ever liked him. But because you don't like someone, if they never did anything to me, then they're okay with me. I never knew what he did. He claimed to have invented some solution to clean contacts. I got indicted. He said I fronted him $3 billion in cocaine to free the hostages in Iran, that he was working on a $3 billion oil deal in Saudia Arabia, and he was going to use the money to free the hostages in Iran. He said he came to borrow the money from me, and I gave him $3 billion for cocaine—*$3 billion*. He said I owned all these shopping centers and malls and all this. It's public record; go down and get the transcripts; you wouldn't believe it.

I THOUGHT I'D NEVER COME BACK to Columbus again. But it wasn't the people of Columbus, it was just a few assholes. It was a new D.A. who wanted to make a name for himself, and this guy sold them. I'm not as friendly as I used to be, but then again, I have to be me. Now, no one rides in my car. They have to be immediate family to ride in my car. That's just some rules I thought up. I feel as though someone took a part of my life away. People still love me, though. I get a 1,000 fan letters a month. People still think I play. You have to make one hell of an impact for that to happen.

I remember when Ross Browner and I got suspended. It was that new rule in the NFL: Guilty by Association. The guy that they claimed was a drug dealer wasn't even a drug dealer. He was my plumber at the club. I think about what Woody said about that, about the time he called me into his office. He never said anything about it. He said, 'Are you working out? You know you have to work out, because when you go back down there and have a bad game, everybody's going to call you a druggie.'

I said, 'I know that.'

'What're you doing?'

So then, I got to lie: 'Well, Coach, I play racquetball all day, then I run two miles in the morning.'

'Well, that's not enough. Now, what time do you work out, son?'

Now, I know what's coming, so I say I work out at seven every morning.

'Whereabouts?'

'At the stadium.'

'Okay, I'll be there at seven.'

I figure to myself that I'm going to get there at 6:30. That way, I can work up a little sweat and tell him I already have my workout halfway done. I gets there at 6:30, and you know who's sitting there? Yeah. He's waiting on me. He's laughing. 'Son, I know you. I know you better than you know yourself. We have to get you ready to go back on that field. I could've told you 50 years ago that Paul Brown was a sonofabitch. What we have to do is when we get you back on that field, and those people are going, "Pete! Pete! Pete!," by golly, he'll give you that money you need.'

So after we work out, I said, 'Coach, how's come you never said anything about this to me?'

He said, 'Son, you'd no more do drugs than the man in the moon. Anything that happened, you're protecting somebody, you're trying to help somebody. We never had a problem with you that way. That's my least worry. What we have to do is we have to make sure the fans are still behind you. Only way we can do that is to get you ready. That first game will be on *Monday Night Football*.' He'd already done his research. I had no idea that game was going to be on *Monday Night Football*. I hadn't even thought about it. But Woody did, and he probably knew I had never thought about it.

We'd be working out, and just the glow in his face. He's like coaching again. Here's an old man, retired, he showed up every morning, seven in the morning. He's handing the ball to me, running down the field. I was running 20–30 yards, and by the time I get there and get turned around and lined up, he's right there to hand the ball off to me. He didn't have to do that. That man did that because he cared. He cared about Pete Johnson. I was one of his players. And he didn't want anything to happen to his players. ”

Harpo

AFTER ALL HE'S been through, only someone as relentlessly, ebulliently optimistic as Tom Skladany could say, "Every time something happens to me, it happens for the best. I'm never down, because no matter how bad it is, something's gonna work out. Nothing can happen that's so bad that you can't keep going on."

A halfback, receiver, and cornerback in high school, Skladany was too slow to play those positions at a major college. It was his skill as a kicker that attracted Notre Dame, Michigan, Penn State, and, reluctantly, Ohio State to western Pennsylvania. Woody Hayes, to whom past practice was sacred, had never given a scholarship to a kicker. He selected his punters and placekickers through informal competitions among walk-ons and athletes who played other positions. Only intense lobbying by assistant coach George Chaump got Skladany a belated scholarship offer.

Unaccustomed to kicking on artificial turf and feeling like a rare specimen collected for a lab experiment, Skladany was incapable of hitting the tight, 40-yard spirals that had been standard for him in high school. Players who received no financial aid punted 10 yards farther than he. Teammates advised him to "go back to Pennsyltucky." Reporters and fans whispered that his scholarship had been wasted.

His tumbling, 35-yard kicks humiliated Skladany, but he found that he was doing exactly what Hayes wanted. Gary Lago had led the Big Ten in 1972 with a 42.1 average but two of his punts were blocked and he often out-kicked coverage, allowing long returns. To Skladany's surprise, Hayes told the jittery young punter to average 35 yards a kick and the two would be friends for life. Skladany suspected that he'd been made the punter and kickoff man only because the staff was trying to save face. More out of poor technique than compliance ("I'd rather get a 40-yard average and keep it high"), Skladany averaged 35.6 a punt, the league's lowest. Worse, in the second quarter of the Michigan game, a clip left him writhing on the turf with a fractured ankle. When Mike Keeton averaged 41 yards in the Rose Bowl, Skladany feared his career might be over. ("Here I am, the worst punter in the NCAA, and, now, I can't walk.")

However, he insists that dragging a hip-high cast around made his leg stronger than before the injury. He convinced Hayes to let him kick the ball deep (to "jam," in his personal lingo). Skladany led the nation with a 45.6 average and made All-American. His long, high punts and kickoffs gave the Bucks a tremendous advantage in field position. When Tom Klaban kicked four field goals and Skladany averaged 42 yards a punt, including a 63-yarder, in a 12–10 win over Michigan, Hayes gave both players game balls. The *Columbus Dispatch's* headline read, "OSU Wins by 2 Feet, Klaban and Skladany."

Skladany also gained the acceptance of teammates. Distant, brooding, not made to do exhausting scutwork during practice, kickers are rarely viewed as "athletes." Skladany jumped into drills to imitate opposing players, jogged with the injured, ran patterns for idle quarterbacks, and said his dream was to catch a pass in a game. He was also eager to make tackles on special teams. "A lot of guys kick and run off the field or hang back, but this guy is a part of our defense. He's a participator," said defensive coordinator George Hill. After Skladany set a Big Ten record with a 59-yard field goal against Illinois in 1975, Hayes, who regarded most kickers as prima donnas, said he was "glad to see a real football player get the record."

When unoccupied during practice, the restless kicker devised ways to entertain himself and his pals, who called him "Harpo" because of his large, unruly tangle of curls. He practiced until he could throw a golfball from the block "O" at midfield completely out of Ohio Stadium and fling a baseball from one end zone to the other. He performed card tricks, organized kicking contests, talked backwards, and was such an accomplished accordion player that NBC expressed interest in having him on *The Tonight Show*. "I should've paid Ohio State," he says. "I had more fun than anyone could possibly have." He left Ohio State as one of only six three-time All-Americans in school history and as the only specialist to be named a team captain or have a tree planted in his honor in the Buckeye Grove.

Skladany's carefree days soon ended, however. Drafted by Cleveland in the second round, he refused to sign. The Browns promised he'd never play in the NFL. The team portrayed Skladany as everything from his agent's pawn to a spoiled brat of the type who was ruining professional sports. The public wondered how a nice little ethnic kid from Pennsylvania could be so greedy and how a mere kicker dared to be so presumptuous. Skladany became the first NFL player to sit out a whole year and become a free agent. "It was a lot of stupidity, or balls," he says.

Skladany was imprisoned by the so-called "Rozelle Rule." NFL commissioner Pete Rozelle decided the compensation a team would receive for losing a free agent, and Rozelle was duty-bound to discourage players from leaving the teams that had drafted them. Shortly after the 1976 season, Skladany got his break. The league and the players signed an agreement establishing a formula by which teams would be given draft choices in exchange for free agents.

Under that arrangement, which came to be known as "the Skladany Rule," the kicker was dealt to the Lions. Rescued from the mud and cold of Cleveland Stadium, Skladany took advantage of the Silverdome, leading the NFL in punting with a 42.5 average. After the season, he sent Browns' owner Art Modell a thank you note.

That same season, he had hit a punt against Atlanta. He was defenseless—right leg extended, left foot off the turf—when two Falcons crashed into him from opposite directions. He played the rest of his rookie year, but the ruptured disc forced him to miss nearly all of 1979. Fearing the worst, he bought a print shop in Columbus. "I can't punt. I figure I'm gonna be out of football," he says. He wasn't. After surgery and arduous rehabilitation, he made the Pro Bowl in 1981, again leading the league in punting. Two years later on *Monday Night Football*, he made a head-to-head tackle against a punt returner 30 pounds heavier. Skladany never played again.

He now owns a second, larger printing house and a company that produces trading cards featuring All-Americans from many of the country's top athletic programs. As manic as a fox squirrel, he spends his days making rapid-fire deals over a telephone headset.

A photo of Hayes on the sidelines hangs in Skladany's office. The kicker is reflected in the coach's glasses. The picture is inscribed, "To Tom Skladany. I've got my eyes on you. Your Old Coach."

Unlike those who had less time to savor his antics and more reason to fear his wrath, Skladany was consistently amused by Hayes, with whom he remained close. "The guy was hilarious," he says. "He's the most honest, straightforward, intense, hardworking guy there could ever be. He had a hell of an effect on my life."

Skladany is bigger than one expects of a kicker. His broad shoulders and thick neck seem more suited to a strong safety. He is handsome, with a long nose and wide, prominent cheekbones. His expression is puckish, as if he's barely able to contain his enormous energy. He is cheerful and given to quick familiarity, his torrential speech interrupted by frequent splashes of giggle. Skladany lives in an impressive home overlooking the 16th hole of Highlands Lake Country Club. He plays golf, attends charity events, and dashes among his four daughters' baseball, softball, and soccer games. "I work hard, I play hard, I sleep good," he says.

He is ever on the lookout for an opportunity. One afternoon, he went to a lawn party at which an Elvis impersonator, Mike Albert, performed. Impressed, Skladany wanted to book Albert to entertain some clients. He asked the performer for his manager's number. When Albert said he had no management, Skladany offered to represent him. Albert had been earning a few hundred dollars for birthday bashes and wedding receptions. Skladany soon had him booked into large halls and performing with the Jordanaires, Presley's back-up group.

He must do 150 situps every morning to keep his back strong enough for golf, but the roller coaster of his life has left Skladany otherwise unscathed. Indeed, he looks a decade younger than his 40 years. He says his one regret is that he can't do it all again: "I was the goof-off, but that's how I got through it. If I could only bring it back. It was the best four years you could ask for."

Tom SKLADANY

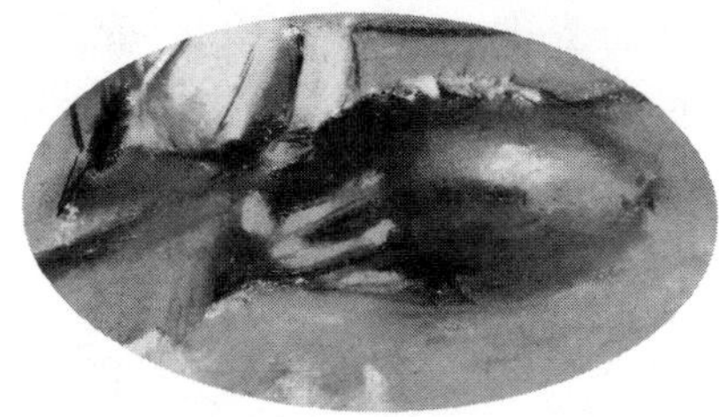

"THE SKLADANYS ARE A strong family. My father was Tom, and he played for Temple as a fullback and a punter, and then he went to the Giants. His brother Andy, my uncle, played for Temple and went to the Rams. Leo played at Pitt, and then went to the Eagles. He was a rookie on the championship '49 Eagles team. Leo blocked Bobby Waterfield's punt in the championship game against the Rams. 'Muggsy' was the best one of them all. He was a two-time All-American end at Pitt, under Jock Sutherland, then played with the Steelers. That's four brothers all in the NFL. The fifth one, Ed, played baseball for the White Sox. An unbelievably strong family from Larksville, Pennsylvania, and the coal mines. Their father and mother died early. The father died of the black lung, and the wife died two days later of a heart attack. Five brothers and five sisters, ten of them. Five brothers in the pros.

Here's something that was key in my development. My father wasn't encouragin'. He was *deflatin'*. I remember when I'd be in a baseball game, 10-11 years old, and my father would be umpirin'. The count would be 3-0, and I'd just be waitin' for the next one to be a ball. And the ball would be two feet down in the dirt.

Striiieek.

I'd look back, and he'd be fixin' his mask, and I'd say, 'Why don't you get in the game?'

The next one, I'd swing and miss, and now there's a full count. The thing is, he put the pressure on, which was good. I'd get out of a baseball game, and I'd be three for four—double, triple, single, long line drive or fly out. We'd win the game, and I'd be sittin' there waitin' to hear him on the way home. I'd say, 'How'd we do?'

He'd say, 'Oh, pretty good. You went three-for-four. Why weren't you four-for-four?'

Never the positive, always the negative. It pissed me off. Same with football. I'd average 44 yards per punt. On the way home, I'd be just waitin' for him to say something, 'cause in high school, that's a big average, and I was bangin' 'em.

He'd say, 'Hey, good game, nice runnin', got two touchdowns. Now, your punts. You averaged about 44 is what I got it at, but once again, you could've averaged 46 and a half, but you gotta hit one 37 and bring your average down.'

Now, I'm all shook up. I'd say, 'I just didn't hit it.'

He'd say, 'Yeah, but you gotta hit it.'

It was constant, all my years of growin' up, same thing with all my brothers. Never happy. It pissed me off, but it pushed me straight through all the sports in high school, and I ended up gettin' a scholarship for puntin', from Ohio State.

In high school, I was a wideout and a defensive back. I was a pitcher and a shortstop. Basketball, I was a guard. I played golf. But I knew football was the only way I was goin' to get to college, because no one was comin' around for full rides in the other sports. It was either go to a smaller school and play, or go to a big school and punt.

So, I figured, a full ride at Ohio State, and once you start jammin' there, with Woody behind you, then the pros might come.

I HAD HEARD THE STORIES—crazy maniac—but, see, I was from Pennsylvania and I didn't even know where Ohio State was. I didn't even know they *had* a football team. I was a nerd with a crewcut in high school. I swear to God. My friends would tell me, 'Hey, you're goin' up to Ohio State.' All I knew was Pitt football, Notre Dame, because you saw it on Sundays. What's a Buckeye? Then I took the visit. Eighty-eight thousand fans. *Wow!*

Woody didn't even want me to come. There was a guy by the name of Dennis Franks, who was also from Bethel Park, and Woody came down in the summer to recruit him, and everybody was goin' crazy: 'Woody is comin' to Bethel Park!' He goes in there, sees some films, offers him a four-year scholarship. Franks says, 'I'm comin'.' Then Franks goes to Michigan.

Woody was pissed. Next year, George Chaump says, 'Hey, we got a punter down at Bethel Park. He's kickin' the shit out of the ball.'

Woody says, 'Where's this punter?'

'Bethel Park.'

'I'm not goin' down there again. No character, no character to those people down there.'

Chaump comes down: 'Woody doesn't want you. *I* want you, but they don't want to give you a scholarship, because there's never been a scholarship given to a punter at Ohio State.'

Chaump saw that I was averaging 40 yards a punt, something like that, in high school, in the mud. We played all of our games in drivin' rainstorms. He thought if I could do that in the mud, put me on astroturf, and I could bang 'em. So, he comes down. Everybody says, 'Hey, Ohio State's comin' down today. Where's Woody? Oh, you're not gettin' Woody, huh?'

I come to OSU for my visit, and Woody says, 'Now, you know why I didn't come down there. You got that Dennis Franks we played against, and the guy has no character. He's not honest.'

I said, 'Yeah, Coach.'

He said, 'Now, we're probably not goin' to give you a scholarship. But I hear you kick pretty good, and if you come up here and if you do what Coach Chaump says you can do, you may end up gettin' a scholarship in the next couple of years.'

SO I GO BACK. Notre Dame, Michigan, Penn State offer me full rides. I talk to my father, I ask him where I should go. He says, 'I don't know. That's your decision.'

Chaump says, 'You comin' up?'

I say, 'Nah, I got full scholarships. I'd like to come, but I have full scholarships offered.'

He starts lobbyin' for me. Woody says, 'If you think he can do it, then go ahead, give him our last scholarship.'

I was lookin' at the four top schools. All they wanted me for was puntin'. I was too slow to be a receiver.

Woody calls up and says, 'Ah, son, we're goin' to give you a scholarship. Now, are you comin' or not?'

I said, 'Well, I have one more visit left, to Penn State.'

He said, 'I want to know if you're comin' here.'

I said, 'Well, I have to go there first.'

He said, 'You don't want to come here, son? Now, you better make up your mind.'

That's how he treated you. It scared you. You're in awe of the guy. I had a great visit to all the schools, but Woody caught me face-to-face. He'd look you right in the face, and he'd never talk football. He was honest. It was the same reason I almost went to Penn State, because Paterno was honest.

I said, 'Who punted last year?'

Woody said, 'A walk-on that's punted the last two years.'

I said, 'Who you got in the hopper?'

He said, 'I don't know. We have about 15 of 'em out there. We're always runnin' them in and out. Whoever's doing the best before the first game, we let him kick.'

I said, 'Well, what if I go out there and kick their ass in summer ball?'

He said, 'Then, you'll play. But you're the only one who has a scholarship.'

I said, 'Hey, at least I have a chance to play at OSU as a freshman.'

I END UP SIGNIN' THE SCHOLARSHIP here, and I was the first kicker ever to get a scholarship, but when I went out on that field for the first practice, there were seven punters and eight kickers. All walk-ons. Now, I'm thinkin', 'Shit. What did I get myself into?'

The first guy I met up here was Ken Kuhn. I'm gettin' recruited. I'm sittin' there at this big bar on campus, and they said, 'That guy over there at the bar's our captain.'

I said, 'What position?'

They said, 'Linebacker. I'll introduce you. Hey, Kuhndog, come over here. This's Tom Skladany from Pennsylvania. He's a punter.'

Kuhn reached over. I thought he was goin' to take my hand, but he took my glass of beer. He drained it, bit it, and chewed the glass. Blood was comin' out of his mouth. He went back over to the bar. That's my first impression of Ohio State. I swear to God. He *ate* glass.

I come up, and I'm gettin' my ass handed to me out on the field, because I'm just a scared kid from Pittsburgh. Here I am, first scholarship punter, and these junior and senior walk-ons are poundin' the ball past me.

People are toyin' with me the whole time. The players, the fans. 'Ah, come on, what do you mean, a scholarship for a punter?' That's what they're tellin' me: 'Go on, get the hell out of here. Go back to Pennsyltucky.'

I was tryin' my hardest, but I was completely wiped out mentally. I knew I could punt, but it's a different thing puntin' in front of Woody Hayes, Randy Gradishar, and John Hicks. Institutions, you know. The press, they start talkin' about this punter they got: 'He's green.' I'd go home at night and just sit there. I didn't want to go out. I had the scholarship, but these guys deserved it.

It went down to the final week of camp, and Woody named me the startin' punter, as a freshman. These two other guys were killin' me. I said, 'Oh, man, they're just tryin' to make themselves look good for givin' me a scholarship.' I went to the junior punter. He's looking at me sideways. I said, 'Hey, don't look at me like that. You're kickin' my ass. *They're* puttin' me in.'

So I go out there for the first punt, 88,000 people in the Horseshoe, and I get a 41-yard fair catch. I came off that field, I was numb. Eighty-eight thousand people. I played in front of 10,000 at Bethel Park.

They're goin': 'Enterin' the game, freshman Tom Skladany, number one, Bethel Park, Pennsylvania.'

BUT I BANGED IT OUT THERE. People are just jammin.' So, I start to get confidence. I ended up that year with 35 punts, 35 yards returned, and averaged 35 yards. Everything was 35. Woody told everybody at the banquets: 'My punter takes his coachin' well. The only time we get hurt is when we get a long punt and they return it on us. So I told him I want the ball 35 yards and high, with hangtime.'

Well, hell, that's all the farther I could kick it under pressure.

Everybody says, 'Oh, that's good, we only had 35 yards in returns all year.'

That's because they were all so short. I was last in the NCAA, last in the Big Ten, and on top of that, I break my leg in the Michigan game. I got clipped. I led the team in tackles on kick-offs my freshman year. I was a defensive back at Bethel Park; I loved to hit. So I led the team in runnin' down on tackles. When I didn't bomb it out of the end zone, I made the tackles. In the Michigan game, it was the year where it meant the Big Ten championship and a Rose Bowl berth. So they just sent a guy after me.

Clipped my ass from behind, broke my leg, and dislocated my ankle completely out of the joint. The first kickoff. So, I'm layin' on the ground, and the thing is, it never hurt. From day one, I never felt any pain from that injury. The pain's so bad, your body shuts it out.

I tried to get up, and they said, 'Stay there, man. You broke your ankle.' All these guys are pullin' me up. I looked down. I said, 'Oh, man, that's bad.' But I didn't feel it.

Woody comes up and says, 'Well, how is he?'

'Coach, it's bad.'

He says, 'Well, check him out over there.'

Here I am, the worst punter in the NCAA, and, now, I'm walkin' around campus with a cast up to my hip for two and a half months while my buddy Mike Keeton's down there averagin' 43 in the Rose Bowl. Isn't that beautiful? He's averagin' 43, and he's comin' back for another year. So you're talkin' scholarship, worst punter, can't walk, doctor says I have a 40 percent chance of walkin' without a limp.

THAT SUMMER, I WORKED MY ASS OFF. That break made my career. I'm walkin' around campus with that cast for two and a half months, and this thigh that I was draggin' around with me grew an inch and three-quarters. My pants don't fit to this day. That was from draggin' it around campus. That's what did it. There's no question in my mind. I'm tellin' you, my leg got hard as a rock.

The next year, I lead the nation—46.7 yards per punt. That's what did it. Well, not all of it. I worked my ass off because I was so embarrassed. Every time I went out to practice that summer, I had to tape my ankle up, because it would sprain itself. I went out every night but Sunday in the summer. My buddies would say, 'What're you doin' tonight?'

'Well, let's go kick it first.'

'Ah, let's go golfin'.'

'I'm gonna kick it first.'

I'd get home from work—I worked a construction job—and I'd change into my punting shoes, and I'd take about five or six guys and eight balls out and kick it for two, two and a half hours every single night. When it got dark, we'd come home and jump into the pool, then we'd go out and party. I just kept bangin' and gettin' that rhythm, and I could just see myself being able to smack the ball higher and farther.

I told Chaump, I said, 'I'm not averagin' no 35 this year. That's bullshit. Everybody's makin' fun of me back in P. A.'

He says, 'Well, what do you want to do?'

I said, 'I'm gonna bang 'em.'

He said, 'No, we'll get it returned.'

I said, 'I'm gonna bang 'em *and* keep 'em high.'

He said, 'No, you can't do it.'

I said, 'Well, that's what I'm doin'.'

He went and talked to Woody. Woody comes to me: 'Keep 'em high and short.'

'Coach, I'm gonna kick 'em.'

'You're worried about yourself instead of the team. What about the returns?'

'Coach, I'm hittin' 'em.'

He says, 'You have to prove it to me in practice.'

I get out there, I'm smackin' that ball, summer camp, end-over-end, wobbly, 40, 45 yards. Guys're runnin' 'em back. I got my steps wrong with my ankle. Keeton was bombin' high spirals, and I'm sayin' to myself, 'What the hell is goin' on?' I can't believe it.

So here goes Skladany in the first game. I hit this one ball off the side of my foot, but I hit it pretty good, so it hit and it rolled, and it ended up 61 yards. So, now, I'm leadin' the nation after my first punt. Sixty-one yards. Lord knows how it got there. I come back out, and that very next punt—I'll never forget it—was a 55-yard spiral, fair catch. You tell me how or why. God? Who? I don't know. All of a sudden, now, I'm at 58 yards, leadin' the nation.

AND FROM THEN ON—I don't know if it was mental, my father, practice, Woody, my leg—I've been hittin' spirals the rest of my life. I lead the nation. I went from worst to first in one year. Made All-American as a sophomore, 46-yard average. Here I am on top of the world, and they're sayin', 'Oh, we knew he was good.' And it's just luck.

At Ohio State, at the end of each practice, you kick five punts. The linemen run down and cover 'em and get winded, after they just got done runnin'. I remember I hit four straight spirals—46, 48, 45, 47. This's the week before my first game, when he told me I was the main guy. Now, all of a sudden, he's startin' to say, 'This son-of-a-bitch can punt.' This's pressure. The fifth punt, I didn't catch a spiral. It went about 38 yards, not like the other ones.

Woody says, 'Now, dammit, punter, if you can kick four, you can kick five.'

I thought he was kiddin'. I started joggin' off.

He goes, 'PUNTER! GET BACK HERE!'

He didn't even call me by my name. I didn't get called by my name until I made All-American. You get called by your position until you make All-American. 'Punter.' Then it was 'Tom.' I came back there. Now everybody's attention is on me. I hit the next one 38 yards, end-over-end. He says, 'Dammit, punter, I brought you here to kick five out of five. You kick four, you can kick five. Now, you don't kick the next one, I'm gonna kick *you*.'

Well, shit, I missed it, and he kicked me right in the ass. You talk about embarrassing. *That's* embarrassing.

MY BEST GAME EVER, he never said anything to me. I had a 59-yard field goal, which was a Big Ten record, and I averaged 56 yards a punt, and Woody never said nothin' to me. He didn't say anything about my 46-yard average games, and it was startin' to come back to me about my father. I went up to Chaump. I said, 'Is Woody pissed at me?'

He said, 'Why?'

I said, 'He never talks to me, unless he's yellin' at me.' I said, 'Did I have a good game last week?'

He said, 'Tom, Woody knows you can punt. That's why he gave you a scholarship. He *expects* you to make All-American. You gotta understand that. If you don't hear from him, you're kickin' ass.'

I said, 'Here we go again.'

Three straight years, he never once came up to me, not once. I made All-American three years in a row, led the nation twice, and not once did he say, 'Great game.' I started lovin' it, because that's the way my father was. That's what pushed me, because you know what it does to you? It makes you say, 'What if I do something and he *does* come up to me?' It makes you reach for the things you thought you could never do.

But you know what he *did* do? He put it in the paper. When he talked to the press, he said, 'Boy, that Archie Griffin is the best running back in the history of college football'; 'I've never seen a man who couldn't be brought down by two men, and that's Pete Johnson'; or, 'That Skladany—you won't find a better punter.' He'll say it to the press, but he won't tell you, because he didn't want you to get fat-headed.

Did anybody ever tell you what his favorite sayin' was—'If anybody ever gives you a compliment, kick 'em in the shins, unless it's a lady over 80, because they're tryin' to soften you.' You know, the press would come up after eight straight wins: 'Oh, you guys are the best. You're the greatest.' *Bing*, someone beats you. He said, 'If someone gives you a compliment, smack 'em, because they're hurtin' you.' It was beautiful. He wouldn't say anything good about you, but he'd tell the press.

When you really got to know him close was after you're done. Then, he'd tell you—in front of other people, too. You'd take recruits out to dinner, and he'd say, 'This guy sittin' next to you was the greatest.' But not when you're playin' for him. He'd make an average player a good player. He'd make a good player great. And he'd make a great player an All-American. Oh, he could get inside you.

WE WERE AT MICHIGAN, AWAY, IN '75. We're sittin' there at the lunch room in the hotel, and it's so quiet you couldn't hear anything. You couldn't even hear the forks clickin'. It was just dead silence. Shit, your stomach's up in your throat. You're playin' Michigan. Everyone's nervous—national TV, Big Ten championship. All of a sudden, Woody hits his glass with his fork. Any time he hits his glass, you sit up.

'Maitre d', maitre d',' he's yellin' at the top of his lungs.

I said to someone sittin' next to me, 'What's he doin'?'

He goes, 'I want all of the cooks out of the back to come out here and serve my men, and I want these co-eds who were planted here by Bo to go in the back.' And, I mean, these girls who were waitin' on us were beautiful. Then he said, 'Men, Bo infiltrated our lunchroom today. He put these girls in here to get your mind off the game, but I caught it. I just want to let you know the kind of guy you're playin' against tomorrow.'

I was laughin' so hard at him—inside, because you can't laugh outside. He was *serious*. You should've seen the freshmen and the sophomores who didn't know about him. Next thing you know, there's chatter. Guys're talkin'. He took the pressure off. He got everybody pissed, we beat the shit out of 'em, 21–14. You believe that? That's what he did. He sensed the tenseness. Then from then on, everybody was talkin': 'That son-of-a-bitch. He sent those girls in here to take our mind off the game.' He turned the whole lunch around, and we went out there and kicked ass the next day. Tactical warfare. That was him. He was captain of the ship. That's vintage Woody.

At the Rose Bowl one year, we're sittin' there, and you talk about tense—this was for the national championship. We're there, four hours before the game, you eat your spaghetti and steak, to get your carbohydrates. Same thing. It was dead quiet, nothin'. There goes that glass. I said, 'Oh, shit, he can't use the same one. These people are gonna think he's nuts.' But Woody's yellin' at the maitre d' again. I said, 'Oh, man, he's gonna do it.'

Maitre d' comes out, and Woody goes, 'Sir, I want your cooks to come out here and cut four ounces off of every steak you see on my men's plates.'

Guy says, 'What?'

Woody says, 'Gentlemen, you know we have six-ounce steaks. USC has 10 ounces in here, makin' us sluggish and slow for the game today. I'm glad we caught it.'

He sat back down.

I swear to God, here they come, cuttin' four ounces of steak off. Son of a bitch. That's just the way he thought, and everybody got pissed again. He would get the pressure away from you, and get you to think about something else.

PENN STATE GAME, '75. Woody says, 'I'm out at midfield in warm-ups, and Joe Paterno comes over and says, "How's your health?"' Woody had just had a heart attack, four months prior. 'He said, "How's my health?" "My health's good," I told him. He says, "You've got to cut back on your schedule now. You're gettin' a little older. You have to watch your heart." You know what I told him? I said, "----my heart!"' That's what he told us right before the game. He said, 'I had a notion to slap the son-of-a-bitch.'

The guy was hilarious. Here's what I always tell people: You were afraid of him as a freshman, you hated him as a sophomore, liked him as a junior, and loved him as a senior. He took you on an emotional roller coaster because of the way he was. When you're a freshman, you're standin' there at practice, and you see someone fumble, and Woody bites his hand until it bleeds. You know what I'm sayin'—*bleedin'*. That freaks you out. Then, someone throws an interception, and he starts beatin' himself in the face. Black and blue, fat lip. You're sayin', 'This guy's *committed*.' You realize how bad the guy wants to win, and you want to help him win so he doesn't hurt himself.

He'd take those glasses and snap 'em; he'd rip his shirt down to his belly. He smacked that turf until his hands bled. Now, you saw how intense he was; how you gonna practice now? The guy was awesome. But you knew some of it was an act, and once you got to know the man and see how much he wanted it, you got used to it.

You'd go in for practice in summer ball, and you'd be there at 7 a.m., and he'd still be on his couch from fallin' asleep at night with the projector on. He'd burn out three or four projectors a year. He'd still have the same clothes on. And we'd walk in and he'd say, 'Mornin', men.' Slept on the couch with the projector goin'. God only knows what time he was up. 'I'm gonna get a shower.' He'd come back out ready for work.

THAT'S WHAT ENDED UP KILLIN' THE WOODS—16-, 18-hour days. He was relentless. He wouldn't let anyone out-work him. He just wouldn't let it happen. He'd get up and say, 'You guys are All-Americans, and you're the best athletes in the country. Otherwise, you wouldn't be here, because that's all I select. And I am not the best coach in the world. There's Bear Bryant, there's Paterno, but I'll tell you no one's gonna out-work me, and if I get the best athletes and no one's gonna out-work me, then we're gonna win.'

To this day, I still don't know if he realized he was bein' funny. As a senior, I made captain, and we were at the Orange Bowl. He had a midnight curfew five days before the game. All the players were pissed. They wanted to have one more night of 2 a.m. I said, 'Don't make me go in there.' But as captain, you have to relay all the messages. I said, 'Coach, I have to talk to you about the players. They're not real happy.'

'Ahh, what's wrong with them? They're down here goin' to Disney Land. We've got a game to play.'

'Now, I don't want to stay out. I'm just lettin' you know what the team wants to do. They want to stay out until two tonight. This's five days before the game, and you said midnight, and they're all pissed.'

'We're not doin' that,' he says. 'I'll bring it up tonight in the meeting. I may go to one, but I doubt it. We're here to win a football game.'

We're eatin' the team dinner. He makes his announcements after the dinner. He gets up there to make his speech: 'We're a week away from the game. Good practices. Everyone's doin' good.' He goes, 'Hey, ah, your captain came to me tonight. I thought we were doin' good in practice. Now, maybe I'm wrong, because everybody's worried about stayin' out. Oh, you guys want to stay up until two tonight? You guys want to have a little fun out there with the girlies instead of worryin' about the Colorado Buffaloes? I'm gonna tell you what we're gonna do: I'm not gonna give you two o'clock. I'm gonna give you one. One o'clock.'

Everybody's whistlin', clappin', cheerin'.

Then he says, 'One condition: No beer.'

The whole team died. Coaches are spittin' up their food. He was serious. He got pissed when we laughed at him. How the hell no beer? You're in a bar all night already, and to stay out to one, you're not gonna have a *beer*? Everyone laughed, and they just left. He sat up there, and he was fumin'. The assistant coaches came up to him and said, 'Don't you realize what you said?' And he couldn't understand why they were laughin' at him, but to him, that was a compromise: 'All right, I'll let you out, but you can't drink any beer.'

On the same trip—I think at this point, he was just being Woody—he's sittin' in the room watchin' film of the Colorado Buffaloes. We're out tannin', because we had practice already and he let us go to the beach. Now, I knew the manager real good, and I'm walkin' down the hall to go in to dinner, and the manager gestures for me. I go into the office room.

There must've been, I would say, a pile five, six feet wide, and three, four feet high, of film, projector film, spaghetti.

I said, 'What happened?'

He said, 'Look at this shit.'

It was a note. It said, 'Mark, I found I could view a lot more film if I didn't have to rewind it on a take-up reel.' He just ran it right off onto the ground and had Mark put it back together again. He was gettin' more work done. Is that beautiful? He didn't use a take-up reel, 'cause he was goin' crazy while he was rewindin' it, thinkin' he could be watchin' more film. That's how obsessed he was.

One night, my buddy Jim Pacenta had a recruit, and Woody came to pick them up at the dorm in his car. It's snowin', a little blizzard action, they're drivin' right down by St. John's, and Woody takes a left to go to the Jai Lai. He's goin' down a one-way street. Jim's not gonna say anything. This kid's sittin' next to him in the middle, thinkin': 'Woody. Columbus. Maybe it's all right.' All of a sudden, here comes some lights.

Woody said, 'Oh, oh, this's not good. This's *not* good.'

Jim said, 'What do you mean, Coach?'

He says, 'I believe we're in the wrong lane.'

And he jumped that median, screwed up his muffler and everything on the bottom, and went straight, like it was nothin' wrong. He just went straight. He said, 'Now, this's better.' He said, 'This is good.'

He'll *hurt* himself to prove a point. That's when you got that sick feelin' in your stomach that you were makin' him hurt himself. That's how he coached. That's what he drilled people with. Which is weird in the beginnin', but then you grew to say, 'Hey, let's try to get it right without Woody punchin' himself. No offsides, no fumbles, no interceptions.' Because you grew to love him, and you didn't want him to hurt himself.

He'd have a fat lip, and you'd see him on TV that night, and someone would ask, 'Coach, what happened?'

'Well, I got too close to the action today on the sidelines.'

BEFORE MY JUNIOR YEAR, everybody was saying that the sophomore All-American, leadin' the nation in punting was a fluke. That pissed me off—hard. Here I am, a sophomore, walkin' around with an All-American trophy and leadin' the nation, and everybody says, 'Ah, he's just lucky.' So I went home, and I punted around South Park Golf Course, nine holes. This's something I thought up. I remembered when I walked around the first year with that cast on, my thigh was rock-hard. That next year I didn't break my leg, so I punted from the side of the number one tee. I would jog, pick up the ball, stop, punt it again. I'd punt to the green, and as soon as I got to the green, I'd pick it up and jog to the next tee. Four or five punts a hole, if they're really deep, 'cause I can only kick the ball fifty yards. Three hundred yards, and you have six punts just to get there and runnin' in between. This leg would be so sore after six holes, seven holes, I just kept sayin', 'Go for it.' I didn't know whether I was damagin' myself or not. I tried to do it just before dark, when there weren't that many people around. Then I'd go home and ice it.

The next day, my leg would be black, blue, red, green, yellow, because you break everything. Then when it healed, it strengthened. It would just kill your leg, but when your muscle repairs itself, it's stronger.

I went back and did it again as a junior, and everyone stopped talkin'. Then the pros came around, but I still said, 'Man, the pros are so far above me, and now you have guys who run 4.3 comin' at you off the corner, and you have to be a lot quicker.' I just didn't think I could be a pro punter.

But the Browns drafted me, first punter taken in the draft, second-round pick. I get drafted by the Browns, and I don't sign. I go up there. I'm all excited. And Modell says, 'Who's your agent?'

'Howard Slusher.'

And he dropped, on this three-inch thick Persian rug, a coffee cup. Coffee all over the place. On purpose, to prove a point to his general manager, Peter Hadhazy. I went to get it. He said, 'That's all right, they'll clean it up.'

I said, 'What happened?'

He said, 'Oh, an inside joke. Pete knows Howard.'

I came up for rookie camp. I was kickin' off over the goal posts. I had the whole city shook up. The adrenalin's flowin', the wind was behind my back, I was just rippin' 'em. I was bangin' these high-hangers; I mean, I was on for rookie camp. I had 'em sweatin'.

They said, 'Let's get this contract done.'

I said, 'I just have to call Howard.'

We negotiated the whole year. They wanted me to sign a seven-year deal with an option, and we wanted three. We fought for a whole year, and I just ended up missing the season. The first guy ever to get drafted and not sign a contract. Howard had six second-rounders that year, and all of them were being signed for $50,000 more on the bonus and about $30, $40 grand more a year. He had four or five fifth-rounders, and his fifth-rounders were getting more money than me, so I called Modell.

'Why are you givin' me fifth-round money when I'm a second-round player?'

'Well, you're a punter.'

I said, 'Well, if I'm a punter, why didn't you take me in the fifth round? All I want is second-round money.'

He said, 'Well, you're not gettin' second-round money. You're goin' to be punting for 20 years, like Blanda, and you'll have a chance to do three or four contracts, and these other guys are goin' to break their knees and legs and be out in four years.'

I said, 'Okay, I'm not gonna sign.'

He said, 'Oh, they all say that. You'll be smellin' this locker room when it comes to be August. Just like everybody else, you'll drop your agent and come in.'

He told me that right to my face. I said, 'I'm tellin' you straight up: If you can't get together on a contract, I won't be here.'

He slapped me on the back and said, 'Yeah, Tom, I hear you.'

That pissed me off. Sixth-rounders gettin' more money than me, and second-rounders blowin' my salary away. I said, 'Howard, if you're tellin' me I'm gettin' screwed, I don't want to play here anyway. Worst kickin' conditions in the NFL. You got the wind comin' off of Erie, and you got the mud. I don't want to be here to punt. The team's no good, so if I can't get a good contract, then I'm not doin' this.'

IT WAS THE WORST YEAR OF MY LIFE. I worked for Ted Stepien, Nationwide Advertising Services. He owned the Cavs. He paid me good money. I sold advertisin'. I was three blocks away from Modell's office. Oh, were they killin' me. Every night in the paper: Snotty, arrogant, Ohio State Skladany, pampered by Woody all his life, gettin' taken advantage of by a high-powered attorney from L.A.

Howard said, 'Don't talk to the press; they'll turn it around.' So I couldn't even get my story out. He said, 'If you're that adamant, go ahead and sit out. It's your choice.' Keep in mind, if I sit out, he doesn't get any money, right? If I don't sign, Howard doesn't get paid. But he needs money like I need another broken leg. It was a thin line between bein' stubborn or just standin' up for what you believe in.

I said, 'Listen, if I'm gettin' screwed—and I need you to tell me that, because I don't know what's out there—I don't want to play here anyway, so get me the hell out of here.'

He said, 'They won't trade you. They're goin' to sit on you.'

So, Modell called Stepien. I was bangin' these accounts left and right out there, because everyone took my calls. They were readin' the papers.

'Hello, Mr. Williams.'

'Who's calling?'

'Tom Skladany. Let's go to lunch.'

'Go to lunch? Why don't you sign? How's Woody Hayes?'

'Wait a minute. Let's do a little business here.'

Now, I'm gettin' all this leverage with this job, and Stepien goes goofy on me. He says, 'Man, you'd be great here in the off-season. You could really help our company. I want you to hurry up and sign.'

He calls up Modell and says, 'How far are you guys apart?'

Modell says, 'What's it to you?'

He goes, 'He's workin' for me. I'll put the money up.'

Modell says, 'We're $30,000 apart.'

He says, 'Sign him! I can make that up in business over the years.'

So here come the Browns. They call me up and say, 'Hey, Tom, we're gonna go ahead and do the deal. We'll put the $30,000 in there.'

I said, 'Okay. We're at $220,000 like we're supposed to be, instead of $190,000?'

'Yeah, come over and sign it.'

That's $220,000 over three years. It wasn't big money then.

He says, 'The only thing we want you to do is say that you dropped your attorney, Slusher, and we'll give you that money.'

I said, 'Why?'

'We want people to think we won the negotiations so that you don't give credence to all these other people.'

THIS WAS EIGHT GAMES INTO THE SEASON. They're tied with the Steelers, 5 and 2. It's when they played 14 games. They're still tryin' to sign me. It's Halloween.

I called Howard up. He says, 'What's happenin'?'

I said, 'They want to do our deal.'

He says, 'Do it.'

I said, 'They have one condition—I drop you. Publicly, in the paper, I have to admit it.'

He said, 'So what?'

I said, 'Isn't that going to hurt you?'

He said, 'I don't give a shit. I'll take the heat. I got you your money.'

I could call him right now and he'd help me with anything. To this day, we go out and stay in his mansion in Palm Springs, right down from President Ford and Sinatra. He's not even there. He just gives us the key. He's a straight-hitter, man. He's the best.

He goes, 'Tom, say what you want. Did we beat 'em? Go get your money, man. It's a great deal. I just appreciate you thinkin' about doin' it. What am I goin' to do, stand up on my pride and ego or your money and your career? Tell them you think I'm an asshole and you dropped me. Just be careful. When you get over there, make sure all his columns add up, and call me from the office.'

I go over there, and those bastards put the money in incentives, and it wasn't even their money. Is that stupid? That's *stupid*.

I say, 'Wait a minute! I thought it was $220,000 for three years.'

They said, 'Well, it is.'

I said, 'Yeah, and I've got to be All-World.'

I gotta lead the NFL in net, lead the NFL in gross, as a rookie. I gotta make all these teams. I gotta average 45. And it's not even their money. But I didn't know it wasn't their money.

I said, 'No, we're not doin' that. We don't have a deal.'

Modell said, 'Don't leave this office, or we won't sign you ever.'

I said, 'I can't believe you would tell me on the phone it was done, and I come over here and it's incentives. We already *had* incentives.'

Modell said—I'll never forget these words: 'I am appalled and flabbergasted at your decision. I wish you well, but I'm going to bite the bullet on this one. You won't play.'

He tried to blackball me. I go back to the office and call Howard: 'Slush, what's happenin'?'

'Did you get the money?'

'No, there's some other stuff goin' on.' And this's when it really hit home that Slush and I were straight up. I said, 'It was in incentives.'

He says, 'You gotta be shittin' me.'

I said, 'No, it's incentives.'

He says, 'Well, why would he do that?'

I said, 'I don't know.'

He said, 'Well, you didn't sign it.'

I said, 'No, I didn't sign it. You tell them never to call me again. Don't ever contact me again, just to contact you.'

IT WAS LIKE A BURDEN WAS OFF. They tried to screw me for the last time. Five minutes passed, and Stepien calls me in his office. I go up there. He says, 'I heard you were over there tryin' to sign with the Browns today.'

I said, 'Yeah.'

He said, 'Why didn't you sign? Are you an idiot?'

I said, 'How'd you know about this?'

'You asshole. That's *my* money. I want you here.'

'Wait a minute. *You* put up $30,000 for me?'

He says, 'Yeah, I want you here in the off-season for the next 20 years. You'll run the office one day.'

I said, 'You need to call Modell up. He didn't even put the money in the contract.'

He says, 'Who cares if it's in incentives? You're supposed to be so damn good. You think you're such a great punter, you should win it.'

I'm right out of college, and he's talkin' to me like this, and he's payin' me five grand a month to work for him. I looked at him. I said, 'Wait a minute. Why are you gettin' so upset?'

He said, 'That's *my* money. You're screwin' with the wrong guy, now. You get back over there and sign it right now. You think you're worth so much money, you're goin' to win all these awards anyway, or you're fired.'

I said, 'I'll take the fire!'

He fired my ass! He did. He fired me, makin' five grand a month out of college. That's big money in '77. This guy fires me. Now, it's in the paper. They just leaked it. It made me look like an idiot.

So, I go back, and I'm livin' at my girlfriend's house. I get drafted to her home city and tell 'em to go to hell, I'm not playin'. I go back and I call Howard. I said, 'Man, I just got fired.'

He said, 'He can't fire you.'

I said, 'Why?'

He said, 'We had a contract with him.'

I said, 'Well, do what you gotta do.'

I go home, call Howard, and say, 'Howard, this's stupid sittin' here in the winter when you're out there in California.'

He said, 'Get your ass out here.'

So I flew out to California and stayed a month and a half with Brudzinski, my college buddy. He was with the Rams. I punted every day. Every single day, it was 75 degrees. Rode the bike about 8 or 10 miles. I'd punt, and when I got done punting, I'd throw to Brudzinski.

When I was out there, we were doin' our strategy. Never in the history of the draft has anyone been drafted and not signed. Modell wasted a second-round pick, and he wouldn't trade me, so he's tryin' to blackball me in the league. We're in a right-to-work state. So Howard called Rozelle. He said, 'If he doesn't trade him, we're gonna sue.'

So Rozelle calls Modell, and Modell says, 'I'm not wastin' a second-round pick over that idiot.'

Rozelle says, 'We don't want a lawsuit, so either trade him or he's goin' back in the draft.'

So, now, the Browns have to call me up: 'Where do you want to go?'

I say, 'Oh, I have Howard for this.' Now, the leverage came back to us.

I said, 'Number one, I want to go to a Super Bowl team. Second, I want to go to a play-off team. Third, I want to go to good weather. Fourth, astroturf and a dome.'

To make themselves look good in the paper, they picked the Rams first, which was a Super Bowl team, good weather and everything. I had 48 hours to sign, because this was right before the draft. They had two days to sign me. They fly me out. I'm pumped for the Rams. They say, 'Here's your contract.' The same offer as the Browns.

I said, 'Wait a minute. Why would I sign this, if I didn't sign it for a year?'

'Well, TV, commercials, movies, endorsements, play-off team, weather.'

I said, 'Yeah, but the cost of livin' out here, compared to Cleveland. You guys think I'm stupid.'

Now, *they're* pissed.

MODELL SAVED FACE, THOUGH. He puts in the paper, 'See, the Rams couldn't even sign him. It's not just us.' They got the public on their side, then they came back and said, 'All right, where do you want to go?'

I said, 'I already told you. Fly me somewhere else this week. Fly me up to the Lions.'

Which was not a good team, but they had astroturf and a dome. We go up there and negotiate. Their punter was last in the NFL. *They're* tryin' to get us cheap, and *we* have all the leverage. They gave up a third and a fifth to the Browns, if I sign. They say, 'We want to see if you can still punt.'

Like I forgot. We go out there and bang it in the dome. You talk about just poundin' some bombs. The dome, no air. They give me 25 punts from the goal line out, and they recorded the distance and hang. I was averagin' 48 yards a punt with about a 4.6 hang. *Bang, bang, bang.* Then they gave me 25 punts from midfield out of bounds. Eighteen were out inside the 10. So I just blew their minds. We signed the contract. I ended up making about $165,000 for missin' that year.

Halfway through the season, I hurt my back and still led the thing. I was always in pain. I had to get surgery, and I missed my whole next year. I got every game check, though. They pay you when you're hurt. Sittin' up in the press box, drinkin' beer and eatin' hotdogs, and every game, I got a check. To this day, I do 150 situps a day, or I wouldn't be able to golf. The next year, I come back, and I end up fourth in the league. Then I win it again the next year and end up goin' to the Pro Bowl in '81. Every time something bad happens to me, I bounce back unbelievable. That's one of the things my father told me early on, and I never believed him. And now, that's how I've been livin' my life. That's why I'm never down. He told me in high school, 'Whatever happens to you, happens for the best.' That sounds like a cliche, but it's not. I broke my leg in college, and the next year, I lead the nation. I break my back. I can't punt. I figure I'm going to be out of football. So I bought this print shop, and now this place is really makin' it. If something really bad happens, I always say, 'A year from now, look at the calendar and see where you are.'

IN MY COLLEGE DAYS, I should've paid Ohio State. Once I made All-American, I went and talked to Woody: 'Two-and-a-half-hour-long practices. I can't stand for 2 1/2 hours, Coach. If you kick all 2 1/2 hours, then you can't kick at the end of practice, because you kick your leg out. I stand all practice and my legs are dead-tired. The rules are you gotta stand. My legs won't be limber Saturday.'

'Oh, we can't have that. I think you need to have a seat.'

So I went and sat in the bleachers. The other punters had to stand. That's a long practice, 2 1/2 hours, so you know what I did? I studied. And in the winter, I took my crew—seven punters and eight kickers—into the locker room, and we had hot chocolate and jelly doughnuts durin' practices. 'Cause they didn't need us until the last 15 minutes.

One day, it's 15 degrees, and they're out there practicin'. We're eatin' doughnuts and drinkin' hot chocolate. I always had my scouts, the younger guys, because dependin' on how practice was goin', we usually kicked about 5:10, 5:20. So I always had them go out a little early, because they might be runnin' a little late or a little early. Don't forget, I was in there since three, playin' cards, gamblin' and eatin'. This one day, it was about 4 o'clock. It wasn't even halfway through practice. We're jammin', eatin' doughnuts, and playin' cards. All of a sudden, this trainer comes in, 'SKLADANY! SKLADANY!'

I'm like, '*What?*'

'THEY'RE PUNTIN'!'

I said, 'It's 4 o'clock.'

'WOODY CAN'T FIND YOU.'

Whooosh. I'm on a dead run. I had to go 140 yards, and I'm runnin' as fast as I can. I hear Woody: 'Where the hell's our punter?' I get there, jelly all over my face.

'Where were you!'

'We were puntin', Coach!'

He kicked me right in the ass for bein' late. All the coaches are sayin', 'What the hell's goin' on?' This is Woody, right. They were practicin' the runnin' game. They fumbled three times, it was so cold.

He said, 'To hell with this! We can't run, we'll pass.'

Nobody was catchin' it. Freezin' hands.

He said, 'Damn, we can't even pass. I know one thing we can do, we can punt the ball. Where's Skladany?'

And they can't even punt, because I'm in the locker room. And everybody was laughin' because they saw me with jelly doughnut all over my mouth. I just stayed out after that. I had more fun than anyone could possibly have, because not only did I get to punt for the top team in the country, but I got to play in front of a huge crowd. We were always on national television. What a place to be in your life.

I THREW GOLF BALLS OUT OF THE STADIUM. I could go from the sideline and throw a golf ball across the field, across the other sideline and into C Deck of Ohio Stadium—in my prime. I threw all during practice, because I didn't do anything. So, after practice, I'd take off my shoulderpads. We'd wait 'til Woody started leavin', and all these guys are hangin' around, and I'd bet five bucks a man. I'd have 15, 20 bucks ridin'. I'd get all warmed up, put one in there, and take the cash.

Another thing I could do, I could throw a golf ball from the block 'O' in the middle of the field right out of the stadium. All these guys thought, 'Oh, it must not be that hard.' But no one did it in four years.

Doug Plank and all these guys said, 'Oh, we can do it, too. Gimme my five bucks back.'

No one did it. You really gotta rip. Another thing I used to make money on—this was before practice, because Woody didn't get there yet—I could stand with my left foot on the goal line and throw a baseball five yards deep in the other end zone. I could always throw. So I screwed around. For four years during practice, I didn't do anything.

Woody used to get real worried with the wind, on the kickin' game. I used to worry too, but I punted so many times that I kicked real tight spirals. So, anytime I got a wind into my face, 10 or 12 miles per hour, I liked it, because the deep guy would come up, thinkin' the wind was against me. Well, you could drive it over his head with a nice, tight spiral. So Woody, would come to me on game day and say, 'Tom, what kind of wind is it? Pretty stiff wind?'

'Yeah.'

'Which way is it blowin'?'

You look up there in C Deck, and there's flags blowin' like this, but you look down in the open end, it's goin' like *this*. So, I'd say, 'Coach, it looks like you got a swirlin' wind over here about the 20. Down here, it's goin' dead out of the stadium.'

I was just makin' it up, and Coach Chaump was standin' there, ready to beat the shit out of me. I was screwin' with Chaump. I needed something to get excited about, because I'd only punt once. Some games, I didn't punt at all. So what I always wanted to do was make sure the wind was at my back for kickoffs, so I could hit one through the goal posts. I'd give him the information, and I'd stand there, and Woody would go over to Chaump, because Chaump was the offensive coordinator. He'd say, 'Tom says the wind's blowin' this way. We're goin' to have to pass. We better take the wind in the third quarter.'

Chaump would say, 'The wind's not blowin' that way.'

Woody says, 'I just talked to Tom. He knows.'

I'd go over to Chaump and say, 'Don't worry, Coach. We don't pass anyway.'

And he'd always relay my weather report to the offensive coaches, and I'd laugh the rest of the game.

But I should've paid. I absolutely should've paid. When I sat in the stands durin' practice, the other players couldn't see me. Because there were injured players, and they couldn't sit. They had to stand there on crutches. That was the rule. Woody would say, 'Hey, look over and see our punter sittin'. We have to keep his legs fresh.'

The coaches said, 'How the hell can he say that?' They knew what I was doin'. I could've stood. But I didn't want to. I wanted to *sit*. The only thing that could backfire is if I didn't hit them on Saturdays.

That era—'72, 3, 4, 5—that was the best football. If only I could bring it back. It was the best four years you could ask for. Forty victories, five losses and a tie, I think. I went to three Rose Bowls, the Orange Bowl, the Japan Bowl, and the Hula Bowl. I went to six bowls. I've got six rings and six watches. And I didn't even know there was a school called Ohio State.

I was never satisfied with my performance—ever. Even my best game ever. It was at Illinois, when I had a 59-yard field goal, and I averaged 56 yards a punt on eight punts. I could've averaged 62. One punt brought me down. I was always the guy lookin' for that perfect game that never happened.

MY BACK STOPPED MY CAREER. I had surgery, and I came back and played for four years after surgery, then I fell on it. I know exactly what play, too. It was *Monday Night Football* at the Dome, playin' against the Jets. Bruce Harper was bringin' back a punt. He's 220, and I'm at 195, and I hit him and stood him straight up, and he fell on me, and I jammed this hip into the ground, and it torqued the operation. To this day, I have to go to the chiropractor every two weeks or so. It goes out. My left hip is 17 millimeters higher on the left than on the right. If I play too much golf, I get a pinch, and he's got to go push it off the nerve.

I stayed pretty close to the program for a while, but they had me speak at the Senior Tackle a couple years ago, and I felt like I was talkin' to some people that weren't there. Our Senior Tackle, when they brought back somebody, you were like, *'Wow!'* Today, it's different. It's a pampered athlete today, and it's an athlete that really doesn't have to stick to his commitment: Everything's too easy, and I firmly believe that our team—'73, 4, 5—could beat any team since then. And I still say it would be a hell of a game goin' back with any team.

We had a party for Woody a year after he was fired. He got pissed at that. He didn't want it, but *we* wanted it. Everybody put up 50 bucks, and we had a little banquet, party, drinkin', dinner. Guys came in from California, Kansas, Texas. Woody got up and talked. Bo came back and talked. We showed some old clips, and Woody said, 'Rex, I don't like the idea that you're spendin' money flyin' all the way from California for this party.'

Rex Kern said, 'Woody, just be quiet.'

Woody was always worried about his guys—the economy, money, not wastin' it. Behind his back, we raised the money and fixed his cabin up for him. For $20,000, we remodeled it. He got pissed at that. He always got pissed. We didn't care. You couldn't do anything for him.

After I got out, four or five of us would take him to lunch every four or five months. We had to give him an answer on everyone he asked about. He said, 'Don't be callin' me if you don't know what's happenin' with all my guys.' We'd go down to the Jai Lai. And you know what? We could never pay. He wouldn't let us pay. He would call ahead and tell them it was on his account, which pissed us off. But what're you gonna do? He just wanted it that way.

HE NEVER TOOK A RAISE. That's why he lost all his assistant coaches. How can you give an assistant coach more than a head coach? Money meant nothing to him. Did you know that when he died, his wife found in his pockets $14,000 in checks that were not cashed? They were in his coats. He forgot to give them to the charities. When he spoke, the checks weren't written out to him. They were written out to the charities. Money was insignificant. He never made a decision on money. Anything materialistic was meaningless.

He'd say, 'Did you say you were gonna do it, or did you do it?'

That's what he wanted to know.

'Did you study hard enough to make the B?'

That's the Woods.

One time, he was working late up at St. John's, and he was goin' home. He went down, and he forgot his keys. This's vintage Woody. He goes back to get his keys so he can get in his car, but the door locked behind him. This's like two in the morning. He can't even get back in St. John's to get in his office. So he takes out the firehose hatchet and breaks the door, goes in and gets his keys and leaves.

The next morning, he's walkin' in, and the maintenance man goes, 'Woody, Woody, we got ripped off. I don't know what they stole, but somebody broke in last night.'

Woody goes, 'You're kiddin' me.'

He says, 'No, look. The door was broken with this ax right here.'

Woody goes, 'Are you the first one here?'

The guy says, 'Yeah.'

Woody says, 'Well, just get it fixed. I locked my keys in there and had to get back in here to get my keys.'

The guy about died. He told the coaches, and they were laughin' so hard you couldn't bring it up. That's how intense he was: 'I'll just break the door down.' That's Woody.

He got pissed off at these people handin' out credit cards from other schools, gas cards, allowances, clothes. He played straight. He knew that if he had a great athlete that worked hard, he'd win. He didn't have to cheat. He hated when people gave you stuff, because it didn't have any value in it. He hated lotteries. If someone gave you something and you didn't work for it, he said it hurt you because you wouldn't take care of it. All the old values, man.

He had a hell of an effect on my life. It was hard, in your mind, to see a guy 67 years beat the hell out of himself. That affects you. And then you understand why. He wants to win. He instills the will to win in you through the way he acts. There's no coach like that today.

There's another image I have of him. He was on his coach's show, *The Woody Hayes Show.* An assistant coach comes and says, 'Hey, Woody wants you to be on the show tonight. You did good and he wants you to be on.' And the image I have of him is passed out between a Pepsi machine and a Coke machine down in the lobby. I mean, with his tongue out, droolin' right on his tie. You know why? He was absolutely beat. He was beat from the week. He was sleepin'. They had to wake him up five minutes before the show. He wouldn't stop. He wouldn't relax.

I work hard durin' the day, and I play hard, fishin', golfin', but I can cool out. I know some guys who can't cool out, and that was Woody. He always thought he could get an extra edge on somebody if he went back and looked at one more reel of film. You couldn't change him.

A week before he died, they had An Evening with Woody and Earle. They were raisin' money for the Buckeye Fund. Woody was in a wheelchair, and he was back in this room, and there was a line of people 30-deep. I said, 'Man, I'm not gettin' in that line. I can see the Woods any time.' People came from all across the country. They were sayin' hi to him, but really they were sayin' goodbye. He died a week later.

I guess you can work your body and your heart too much. He was that driven, a driven man. He made you a different person just by bein' around him, just by the way he looked at you and the way he held himself. We knew when we were there we were playin' for a legend. Not after. We knew right then and there. ”

The Unnatural

MEETING TOM Cousineau is like being ushered before the gracious heir to an immense blueblood fortune: pleasant, but also somehow unnerving. Cousineau seems wholly aware of both his station in life—gifted, celebrated, wealthy former athlete—and the obligation that station creates for him to be kindly to those not so fortunate. Avidly courted high school star, two-time All-American linebacker, overall first pick in the NFL draft, beneficiary of an expensive bidding war between two leagues, possessed of a charisma reminiscent of Joe Namath, Cousineau is at ease with his renown. However, he behaves with a chumminess that appears slightly forced, unless, of course, it's just that the very talented are indeed different from the rest of us.

He was to the manner born. Tom, Sr., was a semi-pro lineman who became a high school football and wrestling coach, and the former Marine Corps heavyweight wrestler immediately began preparing his namesake to become a football player. By age 10, Cousineau was assiduously following the workout regimen developed for him by Fred Hoffmeister, a pioneer in weight training for athletes, and could bench press 100 pounds 10 times. Tom, Sr., put his eager young son into matches and scrimmages with varsity athletes. Father and son grappled at home, crushing furniture and upsetting Cousineau's mother. One of his most vivid memories is of wrestling an Olympic medalist, a pal of his father, on the living room floor.

Lest his son be tainted, the elder Cousineau moved the family from basketball-crazed Indiana to Cleveland, where football still unquestionably dominated high school sports. The careful, difficult grooming paid off handsomely. At St. Edward High School, Cousineau became one of the most sought-after scholastic players in America. He was big, fast, and so dedicated to the game that even his father thought he might be too driven. He was the second-ranked heavyweight wrestler in the state, though he hated the sport, and graduated among the top 10 of his class.

Cousineau paid an hilarious, obligatory visit to Indiana and deigned to drop in on several of the nation's most august programs; however, he carried a recruiting letter from Ohio State with him as if it were gold leaf inscribed on vellum. "I wanted to be part of that tradition, part of that program," he says.

Cousineau says that "being a linebacker is about participation," and he participated as well as any OSU linebacker ever had. Not big enough at 6' 3", 220 to overpower blockers or make a reputation as a feared hitter, he used speed, quickness, and intelligence to, in his words, "make something happen." He was the first sophomore in school history to lead the Buckeyes in tackles. He set records for solo, assisted and total tackles in a game, tackles in a season and tackles in a career. He was an All-American in 1977 and 1978.

If his four seasons at OSU weren't notable enough, what Cousineau would do next certainly was. Rated by many teams the best athlete in the 1979 draft, he was the first Buckeye ever to be the overall number one pick and the first linebacker to earn that distinction since Tommy Nobis more than a dozen years before. He informed Buffalo coach Chuck Knox that the team "was making a wise choice." He giddily claimed that he felt like the first kid chosen in a sandlot game. He then signed a three-year, $850,000 contract with the Montreal Alouettes.

Cousineau's audacity and the

sum of his contract—harbingers of a new order in professional football—made NFL owners cringe. Playing in Canada was "a business decision," Cousineau says now, but not one either Woody Hayes or Tom, Sr., understood. Feeling jilted, Buffalo fans burned him in effigy. He called them "simple-minded asses" and went north to become the highest paid linebacker in CFL history, the Alouettes' rookie of the year, and MVP in the 1979 Grey Cup game.

Cousineau's decision to be the first top draft pick in two decades to spurn the NFL should've come less as a surprise than as a public indication of his freewheeling unpredictability. He had, after all, grown up around his father's beer-swilling, brawling Continental League teammates. He refused to play center for St. Edward because he found the offensive line "too constraining." He once dived, in mid-winter, 50 feet from a lighthouse into Lake Erie. Twice, he has leaped from speeding ski boats just to see what it is like to be a stone skipping over water. He has called himself "just a little loose," a condition befitting someone whose only sports hero is Ion Tiriac, the volatile Rumanian tennis guru and entrepreneur whom Cousineau admires for his worldliness, commitment, fiery nature, and command of languages.

Cousineau arrived at Ohio State with six inches of hair dangling beneath his helmet, unintentionally inciting a low grade war of nerves with Hayes. The young linebacker's habit of grinning enigmatically while chasing down ball carriers baffled Hayes, who once gave a preseason lecture about the need for his squad to smile less. That so free a spirit could thrive under Hayes's straitlaced rule is remarkable, but Cousineau expresses only unbounded respect and deep affection for the coach, just as he fondly recalls the time he spent at St. Edward clad in blazer, shirt, and tie, just as his father remains his closest friend in spite of the demands Tom, Sr., placed on his son. As mercurial as he can be, Cousineau speaks earnestly of the satisfaction he derives from being a part of football history, of the responsibilities inherent in tradition, of the benefits of strict discipline. Several years ago, he felt compelled to repay Ohio State by serving as unpaid assistant coach.

Four years in Canada, where hockey, basketball, and soccer are much more popular than football, made him feel like "a yard dog." After complex negotiations, during which rumor had it he was being offered oil wells by Houston, Cousineau came home to play for the Browns, rolling into training camp in a white Corvette, wearing sunglasses and a neck bandana and declaring, "I want to play with the big boys."

His oddly dignified bearing

wavers only when he hears the frequent claim that he was a flop in the NFL, that he wasn't, as expected, the one player Cleveland needed to win a Super Bowl, that head coach Sam Rutigliano was preposterously mistaken when he said after Cousineau's first game as a Brown, "I had to sell my home and give up two of my kids, but he was worth it."

"I did what I could to hold up my end of the bargain, and that's good enough for me," Cousineau says.

Seven years after niggling injuries ended his career, Cousineau looks as if he would be perfectly capable of playing next Sunday. With his thatch of wiry hair, arched brows, deep-set, ironic eyes, and hawk nose, he looks like the actor John Tuturro might if Tuturro were to take numerous cycles of a potent steroid and spend some serious time in the weight room. He wears on the inside of his right calf a tattoo of a shark, a storm cloud, and a setting sun ("I wanted to make sure I have a little sunshine in my life every day"), as his father, whom he strikingly resembles, has an eagle emblazoned on his left calf.

He spent his youth so consumed with football that he had little time for anything else. Now, well off from his professional career and married to a physician, he has the time to do whatever he pleases. He has said he would like to paddle a canoe across Erie, skydive, learn to bullride, become a commercial pilot or physical therapist, or attend law school.

"People have the capacity to do so much more than they do," he once remarked. "The things they dream about never get done. That's sad. I won't do that. Not ever." He said, as he sat on the porch of the trailer he keeps parked along the Ohio River, that he planned to open a highway sign and paving marker business in Columbus. At the time, though, Cousineau seemed more concerned with an ongoing guerrilla conflict between the small community of serious water-skiers to which he and his wife belong and a flotilla of bass fishermen—"bassholes," he called them—who compete for the same stretch of water.

As a younger man, he tended toward the ostentatious: powerful motorcycles, expensive sports cars, diamond earrings, and bandanas under his helmet. He says now that his years in Canada taught him patience and humility, and though still impulsive and restless, he is also unfailingly polite and thoughtful, as if some of those thoughts come from a place he alone inhabits. Tom Cousineau is above all else a thoroughbred, and thoroughbreds are entitled to their eccentricities.

Tom COUSINEAU

"MY DAD HAD A BRIEF STINT with the Raiders and then played in the old Continental League. It was guys just playing for 25 bucks and all the beer you could drink, barnstorming across the Midwest, where trades happen when they send a guy to another team for a bag of doughnuts. From a young age, I was always around a kind of renegade group of football players, people who played just because they loved to play. I used to be the ballboy, and they'd send me up to try to get the timekeeper to run the clock off when they were ahead: 'Here, take a hotdog up to that guy and try to get him to run a few seconds off the clock.'

I grew up with my dad as a high school coach all around Indianapolis, because that's where we ended up through when I was in grade school. He used to take me to practice all the time. It horrified my mother because he'd throw me in with the freshmen, JVs, varsity, it didn't matter. I used to wrestle with them, and it was like a baby with men. The age difference was big, but I learned very quickly about toughness. There was no way a sixth-grader was going to beat a junior or senior in high school. They didn't take it easy on me, either. If they did, my dad would get really mad.

He was a tough guy, an ex-Marine. A lot of people thought he was unreasonable, but he was very loving and he challenged me at a very young age because he felt that was the way to get me an advantage among my peers. Sometimes, we bit off a little bit more than we could chew, or my *dad* bit more off for me than I could chew, but in the long run, it helped. Sometimes it was painful, but he never endangered me. I learned some great lessons. He had a friend who had won a bronze in the Olympics, I think. I was probably a seventh-grader. My dad pushed all the furniture out of the living room, and we wrestled. This guy had my arm barred behind my back, and he was pushing my face into the carpet. He peeled the skin off of my face. I was sniffling, and my dad said, 'Goddammit! Get up!' Let's just say it was a good character-building experience.

We moved to Ohio when I was in seventh grade. He grew up in Euclid, outside of Cleveland. It drove him nuts that basketball—not football—was king in Indiana. He was afraid I was going to grow up and play basketball, I think. I'm really mad at him now, the way I feel. I'm falling apart.

When we moved back, he was offered a coaching position at Lakewood High School. I went to junior high, then I had a choice. I could've gone to Lakewood, but my mother would not allow me to play for my father. She wanted me to experience another coach. It was a good choice. I had an opportunity to go to a private school, St. Edward; otherwise, I would probably have played for my dad.

I played some center, some fullback, some tight end before I got into high school, so I dabbled around. But linebacker was my favorite. There wasn't much glamour as a center. When I went to St. Ed, they liked me as a center. I said, 'If you put me at center, I'm going to Lakewood, where my dad is. He'll let me play linebacker.' They said, 'Oh, okay.' Being a linebacker certainly isn't as glamorous as being a quarterback but, defensively, it's pretty visible. Plus, the offensive side was, to me, more disciplined, constraining. You couldn't use your hands; you didn't have the same freedom. Too many rules.

We were undefeated as freshmen and sophomores. We lost two games my junior year and one my senior year. We had some pretty darn good players. Our defensive end, Joe Hornik, accompanied me down to Ohio State. Mark Angelo ended up being a darn good player for Miami of Ohio as a wide receiver. We had eight or nine guys out of my senior class play college football. I was just thinking about getting my college paid for.

I loved Ohio State. From a young age, I followed what they did. That was the ultimate for an Ohio kid. In '69, they played USC with O.J. Simpson. When I was a senior, I played in the Hula Bowl, and Lou Holtz was the coach of the West. Coach Hayes had just been removed as the coach, and Lou Holtz's name was number one on the list. Lou asked me to go to dinner one evening out there in Hawaii. He was OSU's defensive backfield coach at the time, and they had held O.J. to virtually nothing the first half. But it's a matter of time; The Juice'd eventually get you. The Juice broke off about a 70-yard touchdown run, and Lou said he immediately looked for Coach Hayes, because there were a lot of missed tackles. Here's Coach Hayes running directly at him.

He said Woody grabbed him by the throat and said, 'Why'd you let him go 68 goddamn yards for a touchdown, Lou?'

And Lou said, 'Because that's all he needed to score, Coach. If he'd needed more, he'd have got more.'

Lou was an interesting guy. He was asking me about the state of affairs at OSU, just some general questions, but as a kid, I wasn't privy to all the inside information. He seemed like he wanted to make that move. I think, at that time, he was the highest paid coach in the country, at Arkansas, and the pay scale at Ohio State was severely retarded. That's the way Coach Hayes was. He declined any pay raise for years and years and years. That's not what he was about. In fact, he was like anti-pay raise, so he was one of the lowest paid coaches in the Big Ten, by choice.

It was like he didn't need currency. As a senior, one of my duties was to drive him around, drive him to practice. We'd be out of gas. He'd say, 'Oops, better get some gas,' and he couldn't pay for anything. Everybody knew who he was. They loved Coach Hayes. That's the way it was in Ohio: 'Whatever we can do for you, we're happy to do it.'

He loved what he was doing, and he had enough. His life revolved around coaching kids. He spent hours and hours in the filmroom. He didn't go home for days. You'd see the lights on in the office at two in the morning. His car's still there. We'd be coming home from partying. We weren't quite as dedicated as he was. The mind will only absorb what the seat will tolerate, and his seat could tolerate a lot more than ours.

I REMEMBER WHEN I GOT MY FIRST LETTER from Ohio State. God, I carried it around I was so excited. They said, 'We'll be stopping in at the school. We'd like to meet you and chat a little bit.' I knew that Coach Hayes would be there at some point during the day, but I didn't know when. When I walked in through the front doors of the school, the whole lobby was full. The whole student body was down there. I got to the door, and everybody made a little aisle for me. They had him surrounded, cornered. Nobody went to class. He was just talking. That was Coach Hayes at his best; he was just holding court.

I felt compelled to look at other schools, but my uneducated opinion prior to recruiting was that Ohio State was the place I wanted to go. I liked the proximity to home. My parents could watch me play, and that was important to me. I also visited Michigan, Notre Dame, Penn State, and Indiana. I visited Indiana because I felt a little bit obligated since my dad had gone there. There was a lot of pressure to get me there for a visit.

I got picked up at the airport by an old teammate of my father's, and we get in his car—big old Cadillac—and he looks over at me and says, 'Tom, you ever drink beer?'

I said, 'Well, yeah, a couple times.'

He reaches in the back seat. There's a couple cases of beer on ice. The next thing I know, we're smashed. We stop at this bar where he and my dad got into this barroom brawl, and he's telling me all about it: 'Right here, da, da, da.' And I know we're late. He's calling, and I can tell something's wrong. He's got a look on his face when he's coming back from the phone. He says, 'We gotta get out of here. We're really late.'

We pull out of there, and Lee Corso had every coach from every varsity program lined up, including Bobby Knight, to meet me, and I'm smashed. I mean *smashed.* I open up the car door, and beer cans fall out, rolling down the road. Howard Brown, who had coached my father and was the freshman coach, runs up to me, throws his arms around me and says, 'Welcome home, Tom!'

I was trying to breathe through my nose. It was embarrassing.

Almost every major program in the country requested that I visit. There's a lot of sought-after high school players, and I suppose I was one of them. Those were the days when coaches had unlimited visits, too. Woody camped at St. Edward. He was there once a week. When he wanted you in his program, he was relentless. He did that with a lot of guys; I wasn't the only one. He spent his whole day—*boom, boom, boom*—always moving, from one school to another. He was bigger than life when I first met him, so I wasn't able to digest what he was talking to me about. I was in awe. But as he spent more time I got to know him. That's the problem today. A coach cannot get to know a kid and a kid cannot feel comfortable with a coach in two visits. I'm going to be at Ohio State for four years, every day, with this man and with the program that he has established. I'm going to play within those constraints. It's like dating.

Coach Hayes wanted you to fully understand the program you were getting involved in—what Ohio State could do for you and what you could do for Ohio State. At the time, there was a lot of cheating going on, and there were a lot of things offered to me. He said right off the bat that it wasn't going to be that way at OSU, and it was a great relief to me. He was notorious for his political/social comment. He'd talk about everything—the environment, just anything—and you'd just listen. He was trying to bring you out. He'd talk about your school. As I got to know him, he started to talk about where I'd fit in. We'd get into Xs and Os: 'This's what we want to do. This's how we do it.'

He never talked about me starting immediately. Quite frankly, if you've got a lot of freshmen starting, something's wrong with your program. He told me I had a chance to compete for that position, but, quite frankly, that there were some pretty proven people there. You know: 'We'll try to work you in. You'll have every opportunity in the world to try to prove yourself. We think you can do it. We hope you think you can do it. Do you think you can do it?'

I WASN'T AFRAID OF COMPETITION. And it wasn't imperative to me that I start as a freshman. I wanted to be part of that tradition, and I thought it was worth waiting for. And when I got there, I really understood it. For instance, Pat Curto, our shortside end, played his ass off, and he had to wait three years to be recognized as a starter. He was so immensely proud of it, and he played his ass off with a vengeance, because he'd waited so goddamned long to play. But I think if you'd talk to a guy like Pat, he'd do it again.

The other thing is, people go down in football, and Coach Hayes talked about that: 'You've got to be ready. We've got 11 guys here, but as the season goes on, we'll need others.' He called them the Young Turks. You know, 'The Young Turks have got to be ready to step in and do it Don't fall asleep on me here. You've got to be ready to do it.'

And sure as shit, man, things happened. That's actually how I got in there. I didn't start initially, but for the first few games, they got me in. I ended up playing our second game my freshman year, against Penn State. Huge game. Kenny Kuhn, senior captain, went down. *Boom*, 'You're in! You're in!'—in a very big, nationally televised game. I think I put my mouthpiece in bassackwards and upside down. It was on my bottom teeth. In fact, I may have swallowed it. I don't know. 'Who? *Me*?'

There's no time to think. When you're in, you're in. You're throwing your body around. It was a pretty tight game, but, luckily, I didn't make any bad mistakes. I made a few tackles, and I ended up playing the rest of the year. It was terrific. I led in tackles my freshman year while I was in there. This's a great example of how Coach Hayes is. I play all year. Kenny gets healthy, and we go to the Rose Bowl. He deserves to be in there. Coach Hayes sat me down and said, 'Tom, you've played really hard. We couldn't be happier with what you've done, but Kenny's back, he's paid the price, and he deserves to be in there.'

I understood it absolutely. It was refreshing to know that if that happened to me, I'd have the same consideration. He was really good at communicating that. I don't know that it had so much to do with me as it did his ability to make people understand where he was coming from. It told me, 'When you get to that point, I'm going to do the same for you. I owe it to him.' Kenny was a great player, too. It wasn't like they were taking me off the field and putting somebody out there who shouldn't be. He was probably a better choice—more experienced, captain. That's the way it should've worked.

WHEN I GOT DOWN TO COLUMBUS, it scared the shit out of me. The first week, I lined up across from a guy named Ted Smith, who was an All-American guard—huge, fast, explosive. I think it was the second day of practice. He cracked my helmet. *Whack!* He just knocked the shit out of me. I got another one; same thing happens. Chris Ward, All-American tackle, comes down on me, breaks my shoulderpads. Now, I've gone through two helmets and a set of shoulderpads in the first week of practice. I'm so sore I can't move, and the pace is so much faster. We're the scout team. We're cannon fodder. I was miserable, sore, and they were just beating on us. I called my dad and said, 'Hey, maybe I made the wrong choice here. This's really, really different.'

Dad told me to be patient. He said, 'You'll learn the speed. It's happening really fast, but just listen to what everyone's saying, and it'll come to you.'

Then Coach Hayes threw me off the field. It was probably our third week of practice. Pete Johnson was a great player, but he was a telegrapher. You could tell where he was going by his body language. If he got real forward, you knew isolation was coming; he'd be looking right at you. So I said the heck with it one day, and at the snap of the ball, I just took off. I hit Pete when he was just coming out of his stance. I went through him and got to Archie's legs, and the play was over for about a four-yard loss. Coach Hayes went crazy. He was pissed, screaming and yelling, pushing people around: 'Get in the goddamned huddle!'

His thought process is, 'We're gonna run the same goddamned play here.' Well, here comes Pete. He sets up the same way, and I do the exact same thing. He threw me off the field. He was so damned mad. I was making them look bad, and it was irritating him, so he threw me off the field. That was the last time I played on scout squad. George Hill, who was our defensive coordinator, said, 'Great job. Don't worry about it. You're doin' good. Just keep it up.'

The next thing I knew, I was working on the right side of the ball. I was off the scout squad. That's how it works.

It took about two weeks to feel good with the pace, but I had a lot to learn. That's not like saying I had a grasp, because I didn't. There was just so much to learn. Scraping off a tackle's slant down tight enough. There's always something, you know? When will I quit biting on the underneath throw and having a 20-yard curl thrown behind me? You talk about it, you talk about it, then you go out and do the same thing over again. That's what was hard for me, because I'm very hard on myself. Sometimes, George Hill would pull me aside because I'd get so goddammed mad at myself. A couple of times, my sophomore year, he used to tell me, 'You've got to stop it. Your mind's preoccupied with the mistake you made three plays ago, and it's affecting how you're playing *now*.'

I FINALLY LEARNED. Coach Hayes used to say, 'It's not about getting knocked down; it's about getting up.' The ball might be snapped, you might get knocked on your ass, but get your ass up and chase the ball down with a vengeance. Or if you got beat that play, if you got totally taken out, make up for it the next play. That's a part of maturing. Until the day I left football, I never played a perfect game. I don't know anybody who ever has.

Woody was great on the field. He'd be standing there right in the middle of the huddle, just ready to start talking, and he'd just fart: *pop, pop, pop, pop*. 'Course, you want him *outside* the huddle if he's going to do that. We're hot, sweaty, and we're trying not to laugh, because he'd really get really pissed off: 'Goddammit, it's not funny.'

He had a great affection for pretty girls. People would come and watch practice, and he would literally stop practice to have his picture taken with a pretty girl. So unbeknownst to him, we used to have girls come down all the time—ringers. We knew they could get his attention, give us a little break.

He was a very vociferous guy. He would carry on. I think Coach Hayes should've had stock in Timex, he broke so many watches. God, he'd smash them to bits, jump up and down on them, throw them. Once, he got so mad, he tried to rip his whistle off. He couldn't do it, so he tried to rip his shirt off. He had it up over his head, fell over backwards, and did a perfect somersault. We were like: '*Whoa!* Pretty athletic move for the Old Man.'

BUT A LOT OF IT WAS FOR SHOW. He was mad; there's no question about that. But he felt that was a way to get us refocused. You know, 'Goddammit! You guys are capable of being so much better!' I remember he'd get mad and punch a hole through the chalkboard, and in the same instant, he'd literally be crying: 'You guys are so much better than this! You're selling yourselves short out there! I know you can do *better*!'

He'd have us looking inward so hard. He was unbelievable. He felt it so much. There's a thing about being mad and just yelling, because you're irritated and grumpy. That's not how he was. He was hurt, for us and for the effort and for himself, as well, because he put so much into it. That was his life. Here's a guy who prepared so thoroughly for every possible occurrence on the field. He was in his office at three o'clock in the morning, trying to figure out an angle. That's what hurt him so bad. He was trying to make us know that we had paid such a price that we ought to give the best effort. And it usually worked.

The reason, I believe, that he got so much out of his players is that everyone understood that he was willing to pay the price himself. He took it very, very seriously, and we all understood. It was a responsibility to live up to that tradition. We all made a choice in the program, and it's what you got to do: 'This's the level you've got to play at, and this's what's expected.' He was the best at making people feel that pride and be willing to take on that responsibility.

We were definitely aware of a sophomore team, led by Rex Kern, who goes out and wins the Rose Bowl and the national title. A team of *sophomores*; nobody thought they could do shit, and they end up winning it all. Coach Hayes would try to make you understand that. We weren't living in the past, but he was showing us that we were associated, and find comparisons. If they could do it, we could do it, too: 'We've seen it done. History bears out that we can accomplish this.'

He was very serious about football, but he also got us to think, if only for a moment, about more philosophical issues, about what's happening after football, grades. Academics were very important to him, and he sure talked about going to class a lot, and he sure got mad if you didn't go to class. And everybody knew that he was mad because he'd bring it up. He didn't want to lose anybody. But he was genuinely concerned about life after football, and he talked about that. You know, 'Football's big, big time here. Everybody wants to play pro football, but the reality is that very few of you are going to play pro football. So, let's keep our eyes on taking care of our own here and making sure that we do okay after these four years are up.' He harped on it all the time.

If you had a propensity not to go to class and he found out about it, he'd show up at your apartment and escort you there. So if you weren't going to go to class, you needed to hide. Another thing he did was he made you feel like you were away but still at home. He always knew your parents' names, your brothers' and sisters' names, your girlfriend's name. I've never met anybody who was that way. And he would ask about them—by name—and know things about them. It's unbelievable. That's the mark of somebody who's concerned. He wasn't calling people 'Hey.' He didn't refer to me as number 36. He *knew* me. That takes work.

THE FIRST TIME I RAN OUT ON THE FIELD at home, against Penn State, was something, man. That scarlet swarm just keeps coming. That was the most violent part of the game. You got the shit beat out of you. I just got away from that after a while. Christ o' mighty. I'll never forget when I coached there a couple of years ago with John Cooper—I was a volunteer coach and the NCAA has since eliminated that position—and Derek Isaman was so pumped up, he grabbed ahold of me and head-butted me a couple of times—*boomp, boomp, boomp, boomp*. I don't know what he was thinking. He had a helmet on. He just knocked me cold. I felt my legs go, and I grabbed him and held myself up. Split my head open. Blood's running down the back of my head. Fred Pagac looks at me and says, 'What the hell happened to you?'

I said, 'Derek, don't ever do that again, my man.' Big knot on my head.

We played in a major bowl game every year. There are very few programs that provide that kind of consistent high-level notoriety. Ohio State was always on the spot. Everybody wants to beat you. It's a lot of pressure on a kid, but that's good, I think. You can overdo pressure, but you have to feel some sense of obligation to be serious, to be good, to be committed. That's where the reward comes from. The pressure was there. It helped me. And I loved it.

Football's a difficult game to master. It really is. Even the great running back—hand him the ball, and he's a natural—still has to understand blocking schemes. If there's a position on the field that you don't want to over-coach and squelch someone's natural ability to find his way, running back might be the only one. But everybody else needs help—to make a counter work the right way, or an option, or pass-reads. In my case it was great preparation for the professional ranks.

Playing at home was the best, because they embraced us so completely. Everything about it was like playing professional football, in many respects better. Everything we did was first class. They do things right there. You get treated very, very well. They take care of you, the facilities are great, the doctors, everybody. It was terrific, not an unkind word from the hometown people, even when we screwed up. Professionally, it's, 'You bum! Get the asshole out of there!'

WOODY USED TO SAY, 'Perfect preparation prevents piss-poor performance.' He used to get so goddamned mad because, he said, 'Guys, mistakes will kill you! They'll kill you, and we cannot afford them!' Mistakes would drive him absolutely nuts, and he'd go into a tantrum.

But he knew when to be lighthearted. He'd step into the huddle, he'd fart, he'd tell a joke. He knew when to poke fun. I think he knew when he was being funny, and I think there's great humor in acting like you're not funny. I mean, when you're telling a joke, you're telling a joke, but there were times when he was very subtle.

I thought he was honest with us, and that's one of the ways you command respect. Start lying, and kids sense it. He was very good about that. Was he strict? Yeah. He did things that were unpopular. We'd get out to a bowl game, and did we have curfews? Yes. Were we expected to do things that we didn't want to? Yes. Did we always make curfew? No. I broke curfew. The trick is not getting caught.

We were sitting in a place in New Orleans, Pat O'Brien's. We were down there for the Sugar Bowl. We were sitting in this place drinking Hurricanes. Coach Hayes walked in. There must've been 15 of us around this big round table. He'd given us a day off, so this was during the day. We were partaking in the festivities, for sure. He walks in, and before we knew it, he was at our table. We're sitting with our head coach, and we're all smashed. He thinks—and this is how Coach Hayes was—that this's a no-no, and it would never occur to him that we would be in there drinking alcohol. We were all drinking punch in this big fancy glass, this pink drink. So nothing's happening. He's visiting with us, and we're talking. It doesn't even occur to him that we could be drunk, because we're drinking punch. He's sure of it. We'd been talking for a while—20 minutes or so, 25 minutes—and he reaches over. He wants a sip of punch. He's dry. Well, it's chock full of five different alcohols. Man, did the shit hit the fan. He cleared the table. He started knocking all the drinks off. 'Jesus Christ!' I got on my hands and knees, under the table, through it, and got up and ran like hell. He's grabbing faces to remember who was there.

The best curfew story was—and it happened totally by accident—I was with the Browns, and we were down in Houston playing. This cab driver must've been new, because he got all fucked up. I went with Bob Golic to some country and western bar and restaurant. We had a nice dinner. It's time to go. Jump in the cab. Well, we're an hour late. Bob gets in. I'm walking down the hall. Elevator opens up. I look down the hall; it's clear. I'm halfway down the hall; I think I'm there. Marty Schottenheimer turns the corner, and I close my eyes and put my hands out in front of me. I'm sleepwalking, right? I've got my eyes just barely open so I can see. He doesn't say anything. He walks past me. He doesn't say anything until he's behind me, then he goes, 'Tom, when you wake up, this'll cost you $500.' He was very cool about it. That's how they solve that problem professionally. Hit you in the pocketbook. They don't take it personally.

I HAD IMMENSE RESPECT FOR COACH HAYES. My freshman year, shit, we were undefeated, and people talked about him losing it. A couple of incidents happened, then we lost a few games. We had prepared for the Clemson game very well. We were in a position to win the game, and Art Schlichter was told, point blank, 'This's what we want to run. This's where we think it's going to be open. We're close enough to kick a field goal, but we'd like to get closer. If it's not there, don't throw it. If there's any question, sit down, and we'll kick a field goal. Don't force the ball.'

Well, that was a tough position for Art to be in, but the ball was forced. Woody was very explicit about what he wanted done, and that's what I'm telling you about how he used to go off about mistakes. He just snapped, briefly; he just got mad.

Everybody was mad, disappointed, and nobody more than Art. It's a tough position for a young kid to be in. He had every intention of sticking that ball in there, and he thought he could do it. He did it plenty at Ohio State. That's part of the game. If you don't have balls big enough to take a chance, then you shouldn't be there in the first place. I have no problem with that. You've got to try to make things happen.

EVERYTHING HAPPENED SO FAST. When Charlie was forced out of bounds, Coach was right there, and if you watch, it was a frustration blow. He didn't take a vicious swing. He actually hit him with his forearm, you know? It was an exasperation thing: 'Goddammit!' It wasn't anything against Charlie; it wasn't anything against Clemson. It wasn't personally directed. It was a frustration thing. But, ultimately, you can't do that. Well, players can, coaches can't. Eventually, he was held accountable for that, and he never ducked it.

It didn't even faze Charlie; it didn't knock him back a bit. The man was 65 years old. He couldn't hurt anybody, not even if he wanted to, especially somebody in full gear. But the point is, if you really watch it, it was a frustration thing. It was really like a push. It was the wrong thing, and quite honestly, I've only seen the clip isolated. I don't know how it was commented on by the network. The press gets ahold of it, and it gets overblown. Is it wrong? Yes. Is it what Coach Hayes should be remembered for? Not even close, not even close. It became so skewed and unfair, and I think the people who know about football, really know about it and care about it, know the difference. That broke my heart. It broke everybody's heart. He didn't deserve that.

He'd go from practice to the hospital. He'd go to the training table, make sure everybody was eating, talk to players a little bit over dinner, then, 'I need to go.' University Hospital was right there. He'd have film work to do, and he'd be at it until two, three in the morning, but before he'd get into that, he'd get over to University Hospital. Or somebody would call in and say, 'Can you stop over and see so and so?' He was always very diligent about that. He'd take a football over or a team picture or something.

People say, 'Well, there was a series of incidents.' Kicking the yard-line marker, pushing an official, whatever. Was it always right? Maybe not. But nobody's hurt. Is it a bad example? If you really dissect it, I suppose it is, if you overly emphasize it. But we were proud to stand up next to him, with him, any time.

The day he passed away, I was with him earlier in the day. I had been calling his office talking to his secretary. He had been out of town. I wanted to come in and see him. His secretary promised me that she would call me when he was available. I went over and picked him up and took him to a freshman group of ROTC students, where he spoke for that period. Then we went back to his office, and we must've talked for about two hours. I told him, 'Coach, I want you to know that coming to Ohio State is one of the best things that happened to me in my life, and I want to thank you from the bottom of my heart for giving me the opportunity.' He really liked that.

I took over this big picture of him that I'd had since leaving Ohio State. I brought it with me and asked him to sign it, and, of course, he did. Toward the end of our conversation, he was tired. He didn't look good. His secretary took him home, and the next day I realized that he was gone. So I felt really satisfied that I'd had the opportunity to visit with him and tell him how I felt about the whole thing, and that was enough.

I miss him. I really do. I thought the world of him. He was very concerned about me, and he did right by me. That's all I know. Athletes are ambitious, and they have big egos. Do they all want to play? Yes. Can everybody play? No. All in all, I think he did a terrific job of managing a great number of kids at a major institution where it's very big-time and trying to satisfy everyone's needs, keeping them all involved in the program even though they may not be starting or playing as much as they want. He had a great ability to do that. He kept us all on the same page.

COLUMBUS IS A WONDERFUL PLACE to play football. There's no place better to play. They treat you in the community like you're very special, and that can give a youngster a skewed view of the world. It's like, 'I can do this or that because I happen to be a good football player'; 'Or I can perhaps treat somebody with less dignity than they deserve and get away with it, because I'm a good football player.'

That can happen very easily, if you're not screwed in properly. That can get to your head a little bit. It certainly can challenge a youngster.

The thing he was really good at was he didn't allow it to happen. Today, you see it in some college programs, and it's even different at Ohio State today. Take, for instance, the Robert Smith incident. Coach would've never, ever let it come to that. Everybody played, but Coach Hayes was the man. No one player was bigger than the program, and he talked about that every day, harped on it: 'Goddammit, don't anybody be dumb enough to say anything that can hurt us or hurt somebody's feelings. Circle the wagons and stay tight, stay loyal. When you have a bitch, talk to me and we'll get it handled. Whatever it takes.'

Coach Hayes always had top billing. That's the way it was. He kept his players kind of quiet. In fact, when I was drafted as the number one pick in the entire NFL, there were people who went: 'Who's he?' Because he didn't allow us to do interviews. He shielded us from that. He thought it was in the best interests of the team. He would do the talking, and we would do the playing. That's how it was.

My freshman year, when I was tossed in there and ended up playing pretty well, I thought I might have a chance in the pros. Again, you say, 'Well, I played against this guy, and he got drafted. He's now playing in the NFL. He couldn't block me, and he's not going to block me four years from now'; or, 'I was able to tackle this guy.' I watched linebackers. You're comparing yourself against others at your position all over the country. I'm seeing guys who are playing at the same level who are going on and doing it. I said, 'Man, I'm gonna be a pro.'

There was too much to do. I was too consumed—everybody was—with getting better. It was nice to dream about but he kept you so busy that you had to focus on what was going on. I never felt like I had enough control, or mastery of my game, that I could sit back.

MY GAME WAS A RUNNING GAME. I chased the ball down. I played undersized my whole career, so I'm not what you call a huge hitter. I'd find a way to drag you down. I didn't miss tackles. I didn't make mistakes. I was able to direct people. I understand defense pretty well, and I could take responsibility for getting people lined up properly, making sure everybody knew where the hell they needed to go. And if you'd leave me in there long enough, I'd make something happen. Being a linebacker is about participation, being around the ball. Wherever the ball is, you need to be there. Find a way to get the ball out; claw it out. Or come up with an interception. Whatever. I didn't have the size to be a real physical player. I was more inclined to use speed, finesse, quickness. We played small, too. If you looked across our front that was around when I was at OSU, we weren't big at all. We did a lot of moving, a lot of angling and slanting, trying to spring people free and make something happen.

In college, everything about the Michigan game was such a level above the rest of the year. Clearly. Even my fourth year—the fourth time I played—I was amazed at how we could pick up the pace that much. Not that we weren't playing before, but it was just a nasty-ass game. I played my freshman year, but I don't believe I started. That's when they brought Kenny back. But I played, and we won. It was big time. Once you realize what it's like, you can't wait to do it again. You want to play it again the next week.

Beating Michigan would be right at the top of my memories of Ohio State. Unfortunately, we didn't have great bowl success. We went out and blew the national title against UCLA my freshman year. My junior year, we didn't play very well against Alabama in the Sugar Bowl. That was disappointing. Not prevailing there in the end in the Gator Bowl. But we went down and won the Orange Bowl my sophomore year against a very highly ranked Colorado team. We beat the shit out of them, and I was player of the game.

I GREW UP SEEING BOB HOPE and his All-American team, and to go there and stand next to him on his television show was kind of a proud moment, I guess. Being able to speak, my senior year, to the student body before the Michigan game was great. I forget what I said. '*Rrrrghh, rrrrghh, rrrrghh.*' People are yelling. I had a shirt and tie on. I pulled the tie off and ripped my shirt off. I had 'Fuck Michigan' on my tee-shirt. That went over pretty big. Just the opportunity to play in some of the nationally televised games. The respect that going to Ohio State and being a good player there commanded at places like the Hula Bowl with the best college players in the land. I went from there to the Japan Bowl. We took basically the same team from the Hula Bowl to Japan, and when they introduced players—we played at Olympic Stadium there in Tokyo—only two players got standing ovations: Joe Montana from Notre Dame and me. Ohio State was very recognized at the time.

When Buffalo drafted me, I really wasn't prepared for it, because, as I said, Coach Hayes kept us sequestered from the press. He had no use for the press. He said they pat you on the back, looking for a soft spot to put the knife in. He totally mistrusted them, so, consequently, the less we dealt with them, the better, in his mind. So when that whole thing happened, they pulled me into a press conference in New York, at the Waldorf-Astoria. The world press is there, about 70 microphones in front of my face, standing up in front of national television. Whoa! I just wasn't quite ready for that.

I made a business decision, and it broke my heart. Coach Hayes never understood it, because money was not important to him. He wasn't sure how it could get so out of control that it would be that monumental that I would have to go to Canada. There was a huge difference in the money. A lot of people didn't understand. My own father didn't understand. But it got to the point that it was so drastically different that it just made no sense to go to Buffalo.

I would've loved to have played there. Chuck Knox was a fabulous coach, a lot like Coach Hayes. He was very excited about having me in the program. Chuck is a kind of salt-of-the-earth guy, hard-nosed, a players' coach. I would've loved to have played for him, but that wasn't to be, and it broke my heart. Coach Hayes always told us that playing at Ohio State would be the best days of our lives, and football would be the best at that level. For the guys who went on, it would never be the same. And he was right. It wasn't that he disliked professional football; he just didn't get involved on a personal level. He said to me, 'I can't imagine that money could be that big in the issue.' He said he was sorry that I had to go to Canada, that I belonged in the NFL.

IN MANY RESPECTS, I'M GLAD I WENT. All things being equal, I would never have gone to Canada, but I had some great experiences up there. I played in Montreal, and Sam Berger and the Berger family, the people who owned the team, were very gracious, kind, and they paid me very well. That was it. My pals were playing in the NFL. They'd call me and bust my balls about playing up there. I'd turn the games on and go, 'Oh god.' It's hard for somebody who can play.

My choice when I left Montreal was Houston. The Cleveland thing took me by surprise. I had no idea. Buffalo was not prepared to meet Houston's offer, but if they let me go, they got nothing in return. I was a member of the Buffalo Bills for maybe 30 seconds, and they had made a deal with Cleveland, so I became a Brown. It's not like recruiting. You can't choose where you want to go.

It's tough to play at home, though, because on the professional level, there's less positive things that go on. I'm not crying, because I made my bed. They paid me a lot of money, and we had a pretty good team, but we weren't in the Super Bowl. I played nine years, and when I was on the field, I led in the major categories that a linebacker should lead in. I was a good team player.

I played for Sam Rutigliano. Marty Schottenheimer was the defensive coordinator, then became head coach, and I played for him for two years. Both good coaches. I liked Sam a lot. He's a hell of a human being, beyond his ability to coach football. He had immense consideration for his players' personal lives. In the end, it got him. Owners are not really interested in that. Sam started a drug rehabilitation program before the NFL ever required that. Before they ever acknowledged the problem, Sam did and was trying to help people very privately. Slowly, when he saw what it was accomplishing, he became more and more focused on it. Not that he wasn't paying attention to what was happening on the field, but I think it wore some people out. They wanted to quit hearing about it. They were interested more in football. He's in a position and place now, at Liberty University, where he can be genuinely concerned with people's lives as well as with football. Good man. I'm lucky to have had the chance to play for him.

The premium in professional football is on youth, and I started to get hurt, some little nagging stuff. I just couldn't keep myself healthy. Unfortunately, I lost some of my most productive years in Canada. Some people say, 'Well, you didn't make quite the impact in the NFL that you should've.' Well, I played very well up there. If I hadn't dominated up there, I wouldn't have gotten the contract I did when I came back.

I GOT TO THE POINT where it was getting harder and harder to stay healthy. I played undersized my whole career. I mean, I was playing at 212. That's small for an inside guy. On the outside, you can survive a little bit longer. The premium is on young, healthy bodies, and if you can't stay productive, there are people who can. That's the hard reality of it. Sundays have never been quite as exciting since then, but on Mondays, I always feel much better. That's all I can tell you.

I didn't really prepare a lot of things to do after football. The catch-22 is if you spend a bunch of time preparing *not* to play, then you're not preparing *to* play. It's that competitive. It's hard to do both. Some folks develop a post-football career during the off-seasons, but not very many. It's a fun ride while it lasts. I regret very little, if anything, really. I know that I played as hard as I was capable of playing. I played hurt a lot, not that I deserved any notoriety for that, but I did what I could to hold up my end of the bargain, and that's good enough for me.

I majored in business marketing and journalism. It was a pretty general education. I used to like to write a lot; I don't do it much anymore. The marketing end is so general that there's no exact application for it. In fact, when I was still in school, a journalist from Michigan, a real smartass, was doing a feature. He asked me, 'What are you studying?' And in the same breath, 'Phys ed?' Really snide.

I said, 'Oh no, something much simpler.'

He said, 'What could that be?'

I said, 'Journalism.'

Asshole.

I'VE BEEN VERY BLESSED. I've made a lot more money than I ever thought I would, done a lot more things, met a lot more people. The experience has been terrific, and I've managed to keep a pretty good sense of humor about everything.

I thought I might get into coaching, and I think I'm pretty good at it. The problem is with my wife and her position. I think it would be unfair to ask Lisa to move as much as is required. As she gets her medical practice established, she deserves a chance to thrive at what she does real well. At some point in time, I guess the only option would be either high school or pee-wees. I don't know if I'm ready for the pee-wees. What I did like about Ohio State is the players had enough grasp of the game that you could help them. You could talk about it theoretically. They understood what you said and had enough skill to grasp it. High school is not that way. Players in high school play for a lot of reasons. They play just for the camaraderie or the girls, so they're not compelled to get better. They don't have that inner drive. It's not that important to them. You can win in high school with just a couple of core guys who are really committed. I watch a high school game, and I see a trap play that doesn't look anything like a trap play. Whoa, I don't know what it started out as, but goddamn, what was that? It would drive me crazy.

Coach Hayes had this habit. It was very important to him to be with the team as much as he could, so he showered in the team's locker room, not the coaches' locker room. It drove everyone crazy, because if you were standing next to him, he'd ask you to wash his back. And everybody's just laughing their balls off. The shower facility was long and two-sided, and whatever side Coach Hayes was on, everyone would run to the other side. He'd be the only one over there. It got to the point where nobody, just nobody was going to wash his back. You'd have to go through too much shit, because then he'd feel compelled to wash your back. He'd say, 'Well, you washed my back; I'll wash your back.'

'Okay.'

This one guy, everyone else runs over to the other side of the room, but he doesn't. Sure as shit, 'You wash my back?'

He goes, 'Sure, Coach.'

We're all looking around: 'What the hell's he doin'?'

He's there washing old Coach's back. We can't figure out what he's doing. He's grinning from ear to ear. We look down. He's pissing on Coach's leg. You got to love it. The ultimate disrespect, but you got to admit, it's pretty funny. I don't know if anybody would want to hear that. People might take that one the wrong way. We laughed and laughed and laughed.

I HAVE NO REGRETS ABOUT ANYTHING. Coach Hayes always said, 'This's the most special time of your life. You will have more fun doing this and winning makes it even better, so let's make it better.'

I go back there today, and people will grab ahold of me, and say, 'Remember this game and when that happened?' I'm thinking, 'How can you remember that?' But it's important to them. A lot of us come back, and when I run into ex-teammates—even guys I didn't play with, guys like Fred Pagac, who love Ohio State, like Jim Stillwagon, he's always around, Champ—there's a great camaraderie. I don't take it for granted, and the longer I'm out of football, the more it flatters me. Someone like my wife, who had no knowledge of football, had no use for it, is astounded. It says a great deal about Ohio State football. She doesn't really like football, but she loves to go to Ohio State to a football game. It's the whole occasion. It's everything that's positive in sports. It's always an uplifting day. ”

OHIO
State

Tradition *and* *the* Individual Talent

"I WENT AFTER this one," John Cooper said when he became only the third football coach at Ohio State in nearly 40 years. "This is *the* Ohio State University. There are no others. What a tradition! I mean, Archie Griffin won two Heismans, and he works right down the hall!"

Cooper was 51 at the time, but he embraced the illustrious tradition of Buckeye football with childlike enthusiasm. He seemed never to consider that entering into such an intricate system of customs and beliefs was like inheriting a classic automobile—great-grandfather's Duesenberg or Pierce-Arrow—a vehicle impressive to drive but difficult and expensive to maintain. Along with the opportunity to win a national championship and to earn nearly a half-million dollars a year, the position brought with it certain venerated rituals—

"Script Ohio," Michigan Week, the ringing of the Victory Bell—and the inevitable necessity to confront the towering, omnipresent apparition of Woody Hayes. Just how demanding the Ohio State tradition can be John Cooper would soon learn.

Cooper himself came from a kind of tradition. In rural Tennessee, young men went to high school, found jobs, married, raised families. No Cooper had ever attended college, but the cocky, slender single-wing quarterback thought he'd be showered with scholarships after graduating. He didn't receive a single offer.

Caught in a deadend factory job, unable to afford college, Cooper joined the army. On leave, he married his high school sweetheart, and he spent much of his time overseas writing letters to coaches, still searching for a scholarship. He received a lukewarm invitation to come to Iowa State University after his discharge and became one of the Cyclones' "Dirty Thirty," so called because new coach Clay Stapleton ran off all but 30 players from the previous year's squad. Cooper was the team's MVP his senior season.

He remained at Iowa State, without pay, to coach the freshman team. While his pregnant wife worked to support them, Cooper began the obligatory odyssey of the major college coach.

He spent 15 years as an assistant at five schools before becoming head coach at Tulsa in 1977. He won five straight conference championships there, then took Arizona State to the school's first Pac-10 title. He was national coach of the year in 1986, when the Sun Devils beat Michigan in the Rose Bowl. He'd turned down numerous offers to head prominent programs, but Cooper accepted the Ohio State job without even visiting the campus. "When I was in high school," he said, "Ohio State was a powerhouse in college football—Hopalong Cassady, Woody Hayes. I thought everything was right for me to come here."

Everything seemed perfect when, in his first game as head coach, the Buckeyes beat Syracuse, 26–9, and Cooper rode from the field atop his players' shoulders, twirling a scarlet towel over his head. The celebration was short-lived, however. That team lost six of 11 games, the first losing season at OSU in 22 years and the school's worst Big Ten finish since 1959.

Cooper also defied custom. He appeared in advertisements for a supermarket chain and a hot tub manufacturer. He built a luxurious home on a $150,000 lot. Worst, he said his Rose Bowl squad at Arizona State was more talented than the Bucks. Cooper had maligned the hometown boys—violated a territorial imperative—and people resented him.

OSU continued to struggle, losing, at various times, five straight games to Illinois, four of five conference openers, and six of seven games to Michigan. Ohio State disappeared from Top 20 lists and lost in second-rate bowl games while Michigan went to three Rose Bowls.

The Buckeyes entered the 1993 Michigan game unbeaten, but were shut out by the 6-4 Wolverines before the largest crowd in NCAA history. "If I had known we were going to get beat 28–0, I'd have probably stayed home," Cooper said. Many wished he would do exactly that. Boos, jeers, taunts and chants of "Fire Cooper!" swirled around the Horseshoe. Calls to talk shows and letters to editors railed against him. His teams are undisciplined, they said; he runs the ball too much, they said; he throws the ball too much, they said; Gary Blackney or Glen Mason or Jim Tressel would do better, they said; all he cares about is money, they said.

Cooper kept hearing conditions—formal and informal—for keeping his job: Beat Illinois, win a bowl game, beat Michigan. However, even as he reached each goal, even as he kept the program free of scandal, even as he led the 1993 and '94 teams to a combined record of 19-4-1, the vituperation mounted. The movement to dump him reached its absurd nadir when, during Michigan Week in 1994, an injured Wolverine claimed that one of his team's motivations to beat Ohio State was to get Cooper fired.

John Cooper couldn't devise an effective game plan against his greatest rival. Each new Buckeye team was playing against an invincible opponent—against some idealized concept of past glories, against avatars of former teams. The tradition that, at least in part, had attracted Cooper to Ohio State and that could be of such use in recruiting—a section entitled "OSU Tradition" occupied 31 pages of the 1994 media guide—had turned on Cooper. (Coincidentally, one of the original meanings of *tradition* is "betrayal.")

"I think there's some looking back into the past," he said. "When Woody coached here, they didn't lose a recruit, and everybody loved Woody. That's not true at all." Cooper's greatest transgression—like that of his dour predecessor, Earle Bruce—was, quite simply, not being Woody Hayes. The irony is that Hayes and Cooper share so many characteristics: both country boys deeply attached to the hills in which they were raised; both fantastically resilient; both devoted to the game and aware of the need to graduate players; each a bit too frank for his own good; each bereft of the high gloss of sophistication—the insurance salesman's hustle—that has become so common among big-time coaches.

Even pictured on the cover of the media guide in a double-breasted suit, Cooper somehow retains the look of a misplaced country boy. His expression is perpetually one of pop-eyed surprise, as if he can't believe that a poor Appalachian kid has made this much money, become this famous or engendered this much antipathy. But whereas Hayes was eccentric enough to defy categorizing, Cooper's lack of cosmopolitan sheen seems to represent an aspect of themselves about which Ohio State fans are extremely touchy. Whatever the case, Columbus has clung stubbornly to its image of Woody, as if to accept Cooper—and for that matter, Bruce—were to reject Hayes and all he accomplished and stood for.

Oddly, Robert Smith, a player whose infamous disagreements with the coach are among Cooper's darkest moments at Ohio State, defended him against the constant encroachment of the rosy miasma of two or three or four decades ago. When a local sportscaster launched what amounted to a holy war against Cooper, based primarily on what the sportscaster saw as the death of tradition under Cooper's reign, Smith said, "People say Woody Hayes did this, Woody Hayes did that. I'm not one for the tradition thing, and personally I don't give a shit what Woody Hayes did. I don't think it's fair to compare coaches of different eras. It was a great era in Ohio State football. It's time for Buckeye fans to wake up and smell the coffee. Woody Hayes is dead."

"Some people say you have to be dead or be gone to be appreciated around here, and that may be true," Cooper said. "I'm not gonna tell you that I haven't had some times when I figured, 'I need this? How much more can I take?' But I came up the hard way; you gotta be thick-skinned to be the coach here, there's no question."

Past and present finally coalesced in Ohio Stadium on the final Saturday of the 1994 season. Hundreds of former Buckeyes lined up near the field gates to cheer the team as it took the field against Michigan for a game that everyone knew would decide Cooper's future. At halftime, in one of Hayes's trademark gestures, Cooper smashed his fist through a chalkboard. That afternoon, after OSU had beaten the Wolverines in Columbus for the first time in 10 years, after ABC had named Cooper its "Player of the Game," after his players had hoisted him again to their shoulders, after thousands of fans had swarmed the field, hands upthrust in rapturous salute, cries of "Cooop! Cooop!" rained down around John Cooper in a shower of forgiveness and acceptance and, perhaps, just a bit of embarrassment.

John Cooper

"I TELL PEOPLE I WAS RAISED so far out in the country that you had to come towards town to hunt. The little town I was raised in didn't have a high school. I went to high school in Powell, which is a suburb of Knoxville, Tennessee. Played all the sports in in high school—football, basketball, baseball. That's all they had. We didn't have track or anything else. I used to have to thumb a ride home after football practice because we didn't have a car. I didn't get any scholarship offers. I worked a year making thermostats. The plant was right next door to the University of Tennessee campus. As a youngster, I used to idolize Tennessee football. I sold Cokes at their stadium. I could tell you all the names of their players, their jersey numbers, how much they weighed, and their hometowns.

I was one of six children. My daddy was a carpenter, and in the little town I was raised in, nobody went to college. You got out of school, and you took whatever job you could find, and then you did that for the rest of your life. That's still pretty much commonplace in the hills of east Tennessee. When I got out, I was 5' 10", maybe 165 pounds, a blockingback/quarterback. We ran the old sidesaddle-T. The quarterback was a half-quarterback, half-blockingback. You lined up to the side, and you put your hands up under the center. You ran some T-formation plays, and you ran quite a few single-wing plays, so you were in between.

I got out of high school and thought I was good enough to play anywhere. I was cocky. I felt all the schools in the south should be after me, and they weren't. We had a city-county all-star game that summer after I graduated from high school, and out of 50 players or so who were in that game, probably half of them were going to SEC schools—Tennessee, Georgia Tech, Alabama, those kind of schools—and I was picked as the co-outstanding player in the game, but I didn't have any scholarship offers. I initially thought I was gonna walk on at Tennessee, but I didn't have any money, and my dad couldn't afford to pay my way, so I didn't walk on.

I worked that year, then I volunteered for the draft. I was dating my present wife, Helen Thompson. We dated her last year of high school, and then my cousin and I—Ralph Cooper; they called him 'Worry,' for 'worry-wart'—he and I went to uptown Knoxville and volunteered for the draft. The day Don Larsen pitched the perfect game in the World Series is the day we volunteered. There was no other opportunity. I was working; there was no future at that job for me. I didn't have any money. I wanted to go to college, but I wasn't getting any scholarship offers. I went in the service with my cousin and two other guys from my high school. Four of us went in together.

WE WENT TO FT. CHAFFEE, ARKANSAS, for basic training. We spent about five or six weeks at Ft. Chaffee, then we came home for Christmas, and when we came home for Christmas, I married my high school sweetheart. So, I'm married. Finished up basic training, and, of course, in the army, you have a preference whether you want to stay in the states or whether you want to go overseas or whatever. Obviously, I wanted to stay in the states because I was married. The other three guys wanted to go overseas because they were single. And you know what? They sent me overseas and kept those other three guys in the states.

I spent 15 months in Germany. When I was in Stuttgart, Germany, 7th Army Headquarters, I was playing a little service football. I was maturing, gaining weight. So, I sat down at the typewriter and wrote letters to about ten major schools around the country: Georgia Tech, Tennessee, Indiana. I get a letter from Lou McCullough, who wrote to me from Iowa State and said, 'Hey, if you can get out of the service at such and such a time, come to Ames, Iowa, and we'll give you a scholarship.'

So I got out of the service, came through Knoxville, picked my wife up, and came to Ames, Iowa. I played four years of football at Iowa State, graduated as the outstanding player on the football team, team captain, graduated in four years. I don't remember missing a class. My wife worked every day I was in college. We lived in married housing on the campus of Iowa State. When I graduated, I was gonna go back to east Tennessee and get me a high school coaching job. I went in and talked to Clay Stapleton, who was the head football coach at Iowa State. I never will forget it: I made an appointment, bought me a tie, went over to see the head coach. Back in those days, you didn't talk to the head coach unless you had some business, or he called you in on some discipline problems.

It was that spring before I was graduating. Made an appointment, walked in his office and told him that someday I wanted to be a head football coach, I wanted to be settin' in the same chair he was settin' in. He leaned back in his chair, loosened his tie and grunted, 'John, I think you'd be a hell of a coach.' He said, 'I want you to stay here next year and coach my freshman team.' He said, 'Now, you understand we can't pay you any money. You stay here and coach my freshman team, then we'll see what we can do.'

I went into graduate school that summer and coached the freshman team that fall at Iowa State. Now you would call it a 'graduate assistant.' Back in those days they didn't have grad assistants. I was just a student assistant or whatever. Didn't get paid a penny. My wife was working and she was pregnant with my son. Coach Stapleton asked me when the season was over, 'How would you like to coach at Oregon State?'

I said, 'Gee, that would be great.'

TO BE HONEST WITH YOU, I'd never heard of Oregon State. I thought I was going back to east Tennessee. Anyway, one night Coach Stapleton called me and said, 'If you're interested, Tommy Prothro wants you to call him.' So I called Tommy Prothro. My wife bought me a coat and a tie and a hat; we didn't have anything. I flew out to Corvalis, Oregon, and Coach Prothro offered me the job.

I think my wife cried all the way out there, because she thought we were going back to Tennessee. We're going *another* 2,000 miles away from home. The second year out there, Oregon State went to the Rose Bowl. Our staff moved to UCLA. The first year UCLA, we go to the Rose Bowl. So I'd been in coaching for three years and went to two Rose Bowls.

I started working my way back towards home. I left UCLA with Pepper Rogers. We were assistants together at UCLA. Pepper got the head job at Kansas, so I come with him. Our second year at Kansas, we won the Big 8 and went to the Orange Bowl. A couple of years after that, my daddy died of a heart attack at age 67. Mom was living at home by herself, and, again, I had the dream of coaching in the south and being back home. I left Kansas and went to Kentucky as the secondary coach to get back in this part of the country. Coached four years at Kentucky under Fran Curci, then the big break came. Out of the clear blue sky, I called Tulsa. We had a good team at Kentucky. Went to the '77 Peach Bowl, a real good football team. Later on, we went on probation because of some irregularities in recruiting. I wanted out of that program, to be honest with you. Anyway, the job opened in Tulsa. I didn't know a soul at Tulsa, and I can't remember if I'd ever been in Tulsa, Oklahoma.

Tulsa was a head coaching job. I was probably 38 at the time. I'd paid my dues as an assistant. Tulsa had Howard Twilley and Drew Pearson and Jerry Rhome and those kind of guys. We go out the first year, and we're three and eight. I figured, 'What in the world have I got myself into?' The next year, we turn that program around. We went from three and eight to nine and two, the nation's most improved football team. We did it with fundamentals, discipline, recruiting. We brought in six junior college players.

THE NEXT SEVEN YEARS I'M AT TULSA, we averaged eight wins a season. The response was fantastic. Until this day, I've probably got closer friends at Tulsa than any place I've been. I turned down a lot of jobs because I was happy there. I was athletic director and football coach. I ran my own program, scheduled the games. We beat a lot of teams on the road when I was at Tulsa. We beat Kansas, Kansas State, Texas Tech, TCU, Florida, Virginia Tech—road games. We got up one morning, had the pregame meal, flew to Lubbock, Texas, spent three hours or so at a Holiday Inn, bused to the stadium, beat Texas Tech 59–21, gave our players a box of Kentucky Fried Chicken, got on the plane, and came home. The most points that's ever been scored against Texas Tech. We didn't have the money to stay overnight. Anything under six hours, we bused. We'd bus halfway to Arkansas, eat a pregame meal, go on to Fayetteville, play the game, give 'em a box of Kentucky Fried Chicken, and come home. We spent eight great years at Tulsa.

Then I took the head job at Arizona State. I'd done what I wanted to do at Tulsa, and Arizona State was a great opportunity. Darryl Rodgers went to the Detroit Lions, and I got the job. Spent three years at Arizona State, and the first year, came real close to winning the championship. Arizona beat us the last game of the season by three points, 16–13. Kid kicked a 57-yard field goal. The next year, of course, we won it all. I spent one more year there, went to the Freedom Bowl, and came to Ohio State.

To be honest with you, I didn't care if I got the job or not. I had a good situation where I was. Nobody knew that I was talking to Ohio State at that time. I fly back home, and a week or so later, Jim Jones called and said they'd like for me to be head coach at Ohio State. Everything was attractive about the job. I came here thinking that this is the last move I'll make. Ohio State has the image out there nationally, of course. Great players, great tradition, great talent. You can win it all. I came here fully expecting that we were going to win the Big Ten and have a shot, at least, at the national championship. This is back in the part of the country I want to live in.

I THOUGHT EVERYTHING WAS RIGHT for me to come here and I fully expected to come in here and just continue the great legacy they've had. The first year was very, very disappointing. Let me tell you what I think has happened to Ohio State football. I'm not being negative, I'm being factual, when I tell you this—Woody Hayes coached here for years with one-year contracts. They hire Earle Bruce with a one-year contract, then hire a basketball coach, Gary Williams, and give *him* a five-year contract. Then they figure, 'Okay, we better do something for Earle.' Give Earle a three-year contract. The basketball coach has five, the football coach has three. The first year of that three-year contract, Michigan beat Ohio State. Ohio State missed a last-second field goal, and Michigan won. That's the Michigan team that we beat in the Rose Bowl. I've told some of these ex-players that if Ohio State kicks that field goal, then 'we beat *you* in the Rose Bowl.' Because we had a great team.

Now Earle has two years left on his contract. Ohio State wins the Cotton Bowl, if you remember; they beat Texas A&M. Earle was *that* close to taking the Arizona job. Rick Bay and the assistant coaches talked him out of it, and he thought he had a real good football team coming back, with Cris Carter, Tom Tupa, Kumerow, Spielman and all those guys. So Earle turns the job down. He's got two years left. Cris Carter got ruled ineligible, a couple guys flunked out of school. The next year,

Earle won six games. Iowa converts a fourth and a mile situation and beats him here, then, *boom*, Earle's fired.

I think what was happening, to be honest with you, is with a one-year contract, it was getting more difficult to recruit. The pressure is vicious. It was getting tougher to recruit nationally: 'We don't know if you're gonna be there. You don't have stability in the program.' High school football in this state is good, but all of a sudden, high school football in other areas, Florida particularly, is getting very good. Not a lot was being done to the facilities here. When Rick Bay came in, they built the Woody Hayes Athletic Center, which is state of the art.

UNDERSTAND WHAT I THINK HAPPENED. I think that a lot of good football players in this state were leaving. I think to be a national powerhouse now, you gotta not only control the state of Ohio, you gotta go to Florida, you gotta go to New Jersey, maybe Chicago. You gotta expand your recruiting base. You look at the powers in the country, other than Miami of Florida, a lot of their good players come from out of state. Southern Cal, for example. Penn State is getting players from all over the country. Michigan. Check their rosters. This has got me in trouble, but I'm being honest with you. The first thing people want to know when you come from the Pac Ten to the Big Ten is compare the talent here with the talent we had at Arizona State. That's not a fair comparison at all. We had great talent when I was coaching at Arizona State. If I'm not mistaken, about 11 of those players on those teams are starting in the National Football League. They're not playing in the NFL, they're *starting*. In the first three years I coached at Ohio State, we had five players that made an NFL roster.

Now, we've recruited well here, we really have. We're close to putting this program back to where it should be. But we're not over the hump yet. I never thought about the amount of pressure on the head coach here, because every place I've ever coached, I've gotten along with people. I haven't had a lot of enemies. At Tulsa, the whole community was behind me. At Arizona State, we had three great years, the games were sold out, everybody was behind the Sun Devils. I figured the same thing would happen here. I think it will happen here.

Don't take me wrong. We love living here. The difference here, in my opinion, is there's two, four, five percent of the people who are very, very vocal, very negative, and anti-anything. They were anti-Woody, they were anti-Earle, they were anti-Fred Taylor, they were anti-Eldon Miller. All four of those coaches have been fired. Ohio State doesn't have a great image nationally for the way they've treated coaches. It's impossible to please everybody here.

I really think if we won 12 games a year, shut out everybody and beat the point spread, I think there'd still be some people unhappy. I don't want to paint a negative picture, and, again, we love it here, and 95 percent of the people are great. Day after day after day, I hear the comments: 'Coach, good luck this fall'; 'We're behind you'; 'Win 'em all'; that kind of attitude. But there's a whole section of letters, for example, in the *Columbus Dispatch*, and, of course, they're negative. If they weren't negative, they wouldn't be in there. They want to criticize everything, from the size of the house you live in to the plays you run. The difference between Columbus, Ohio, and anyplace else is, here, there's Ohio State football, *period*. Basketball has done a great job, Gary Williams and Randy Ayers, but you don't have pro sports. It's Ohio State football, it's Ohio State football, it's Ohio State football. Columbus is located right in the middle of Ohio, and the hard thing about coaching here is uniting everybody in the state.

If you run an option play, they want you to throw the ball. If you throw the ball, they think you ought to be running the ball. Most of them are knowledgeable; most of them are great fans. Here's what I say: I'm not gonna let a small percentage of the people dictate what we do or run me out of here, to be honest with you. I'm not gonna do that. It's too good a place to live and coach. The great thing about Ohio State is you got a chance to be nationally competitive. If you do your job, if you do your recruiting job, you got a chance.

ARE THERE SOME THINGS I'D LIKE TO CHANGE? Absolutely. I think our coaching offices ought to be in Woody Hayes. This's is a nice office, but look around. The secretary is out in the hall. We got the worst assistant coaches' offices in football, period. We need to have an academic place on campus for our players to study. We have selective admission here now. It's tougher to get kids into school; it's tougher to keep players in school at Ohio State than it used to be.

My second year here—my first recruiting class—we got just about everybody in the state we went after. The next year, we got just about everybody in the state we went after. The next year, the contract controversy came up. I'd been here three years. I signed a five-year contract. I'd been here three years, then it came up, 'Are we going to extend his contract? Are we not going to extend his contract?' The newspapers loved it. It was finally decided, 'We're not going to extend his contract.' Which inferred there's some instability in the program. And then I lost four coaches that year. Bobby Turner was the offensive coordinator and got a $25,000 raise at Purdue. Ron Zook went to Florida with the feeling that he was gonna be defensive coordinator, which he is. The connotation was the coaches are bailing out; well, they all got better jobs. Then my recruiting coordinator went to Tennessee for a $15,000 raise. We're still living in the dark ages from the standpoint of paying assistant coaches. Our coaches here now are paid at the middle of the pack in the Big Ten Conference. This expectation level, of course, is that they're the highest. I lost four coaches this year. Two went to the National Football League and got $25,000 raises.

WELL, WOODY LOST COACHES, EARLE LOST COACHES, and I'm losing coaches. And I'll lose more coaches who have a chance to go someplace to a better position and a higher salary. That's a part of the business. A coach can leave here and go to a head coaching job, a coach can leave here and go to the National Football League, but a coach should not leave here to go to Florida because he'll make more money. That *shouldn't* happen.

It is happening because we need to upgrade the standards we're still living by. That third year, because of the instability in the program, in my opinion, we lost some good players in the state. This year, we came back and got virtually everybody in the state we wanted. Did the contract thing affect me? Yes, it affected me. It bothered me some, because the issue shouldn't've even been brought up. I didn't bring it up. I had never gone to the president or to the athletic director and asked that my contract be extended. I had never done that, contrary, maybe, to what you've read in the press. It was almost like, 'Cooper demanded an extension and didn't get it.' That wasn't it at all. I've been to Gordon Gee's office one time since I've been here. I've never been to his office demanding that my contract be extended, or even *talking* about the extension of my contract. I have not done that, and I won't do that.

Last year before the Michigan game, they offered me a three-year extension, and I went out and hired four coaches and had a great recruiting class, because of restoring the stability. Ohio State is a great program to sell. We got a lot to offer a young man: facilities, tradition, schedule, recognition, a great academic school, location. If you can cut out the negativism, you can build this program back.

I think there's some looking back into the past. You would think that Ohio State never lost a recruit. When Woody coached here, they didn't lose a recruit, and everybody loved Woody. That's not true at all. Anne Hayes has told my wife stories about when they piled Christmas trees in front of their door and they can't get out of their door after a bowl game, maybe after they lose a game; the banners that have been flown over the stadium during a game, 'Bye, Bye, Woody,' those kind of stories. Some people say you have to be dead or be gone to be appreciated around here, and that may be true, I don't know.

In spite of all those things, it's still a great place to live and a great place to coach. I'm not gonna tell you that I haven't had some times when I figured, 'Do I need this? How much more can I take?' But I came up the hard way; you gotta be thick skinned to be the coach here, there's no question.

WOODY TOLD IT. Woody wrote a book and called it *You Win with People*. The name of the game is recruiting. It's no secret. If we put this program back on the map, where it will be, we've done it recruiting. I think that's a strength I have. I think I'm a good salesman. I've had some great players play for me. Recruit the good players, and have a great winter conditioning program, teach the fundamentals, don't beat yourself, and you're gonna be successful.

I'm calling recruits right now. It's selling, it's hard work, it's perseverance, it's personality. First of all, you have to have a good product to sell, and, of course, we have it here. Second, you got to recognize its importance. Some coaches get carried away and think they're winning because they're out-coaching somebody when really that's not the case. You can call recruits, and they know Ohio State. I call a great running back in Minnesota; he's interested in Ohio State. I call a great linebacker in Pennsylvania; he's interested in Ohio State. Our job is very simple. We've gotta build a picket fence around Ohio, and we've gotta keep our players at home. Then we've gotta go to Florida and get a couple of speed guys. We gotta maybe go to New Jersey and get an Alonzo Spellman-type player, and then I think you can compete nationally.

The thing we haven't had that we have to do to get to the next level is 95 percent of your players gotta be good enough not to get you beat. Then, I think there's two or three guys who've got to win games for you. Desmond Howard won games for Michigan. Gary Beban, at UCLA, won the Heisman Trophy and put us in the Rose Bowl. A quarterback is usually that guy. We haven't had a, quote, great quarterback since I've been here. We've had some good ones, but we haven't had the great one. I've been criticized, as you know, by some people for taking Robert Smith back. But, see, Robert Smith might've been able to have taken us to that next level. I think that whole issue could've been avoided. It's a matter of communication, that's all. In my 30 years of coaching college football, I have never, nor will I ever, ask a young man to miss any kind of academic appointment—any kind—to come to football practice. I never have, and I never will, and I didn't in Robert Smith's case.

ROBERT AND ELLIOT UZELAC had a misunderstanding. Robert claims that Elliot told him that he wanted him at practice two days next week, and Robert had a class every day. So, for Robert to be at practice, then he had to miss class. Summer school was still going on. The unusual thing here is that we're on the quarter system. We play three games before school starts. So, Robert was taking a summer school class that met every morning, and he was missing the morning practice. So, Robert claims that Elliot told him to miss class, and Elliot claims that he didn't.

All Robert had to do was walk into my office, and it would've been settled just like that. Robert didn't do that. Robert bolted out of camp and then made some comments that he probably regrets. At least, since then, he said he's sorry that he made them. One thing led to another one, and he chose not to play.

Robert was all set to come back on this football team. I made the decision. I told the coaching staff, 'Hey, we're not having a debate about whether he's coming back or not. I'm the head coach, and I've made that decision, and if you can't live with that, then, fine, you need to get another job.' So, the decision was made for Robert to come back.

Robert and Elliot were gonna—the three of us—were gonna sit down and talk about what was gonna happen when he came back. We weren't gonna hold any grudges. We were gonna work him hard and treat him like everybody else. He was expected to do the things we asked him to do.

We sat at this same table. And Robert and Elliot, after I left the room, got to arguing, I guess, over 'You said this and I didn't say that.' That kind of situation. Robert, again, bolted out of the room. I made the decision to let Elliot go. He didn't do what I asked him to do. I asked him to patch it over, because I wanted the kid back on the team. Obviously, he felt like he didn't want the kid on the team. Those are some things that happen that you don't like.

THREE OUT OF FOUR YEARS I'VE BEEN HERE, we've played great games against Michigan, but we haven't beat Michigan. I'm reminded of that almost daily. When I was at UCLA, we played Southern Cal, 103,000 people, and the winner went to the Rose Bowl. It doesn't get any bigger than that. But the Ohio State-Michigan game, there isn't anything like it. It's a spectacle; it really is. That week is just different. Usually, the Big Ten championship and the Rose Bowl are on the line.

That first year, we were awful, and they were a pretty good football team. They're kicking us, I think, 20–0 at halftime. I'm thinking, 'Holy cow, we're gonna get embarrassed.' Then we came out in the second half and actually went ahead of 'em with, I think, about a minute or two left in the game. Kicked off to them, and they ran the kickoff back to the 40 yard line. Three out of the four games we've played with Michigan have been decided by the kicking game. Up until this year, we played 'em tough every year. Got beat by a field goal, got beat by a blocked extra point, got beat by a kickoff return. Michigan's had some great teams since I've been here.

Everybody says you could just beat Michigan and be okay, but Earle beat 'em his last year and still got fired. See, the thing that people don't accept in this league is that this league has changed. Iowa went 19 years without having a winning season, and Iowa's a pretty good football team. Everybody thinks you oughta go kick Indiana's butt. Indiana's a pretty good football team. They've made a commitment. The toughest times have been the Michigan losses.

The lowest point, probably, was the Air Force loss. The loser of the Ohio State-Michigan game has to go to Memphis. That's the way it was presented. There was 13,000 fans watching the game. That's when I lost four coaches. If I'm not mistaken, we were about three coaches short going into that game. It's almost like you can show up and beat Air Force. Well, I'm not sure people have enough respect for other teams here. Air

Force wasn't bad. Last year, they beat Mississippi State something awful in that same bowl game. With the Persian Gulf situation being what it was, and us heavily favored, we had everything to lose and nothing to gain. We went down there and got beat in a major upset. That's hurt us, there's no question whatsoever. Hey, we *should* beat Air Force. But the way everything was handled, with the loser has to go to Memphis and playing an Air Force Academy team that wasn't a great team—it was a good solid team that certainly had character and was well-coached and ran the wishbone, something we hadn't faced all year. We had the ball; all we had to do was score and go win the game, and we didn't do it. Quarterback threw an interception, game's over.

We've had some tough losses since I've been here, but I have no doubt in my ability to run this program. A lot of these people who are my critics don't know John Cooper. I've been coaching 30 years. I've been to most of the major bowls. I've been Coach of the Year. I've won 65 percent of the games that we've played. We won in Tulsa, we won at Arizona State, and we'll win here. If they'll leave us alone, if the administration will leave us alone, we'll put this program where it should be, and I think they'll do that. They've been supportive, except for the thing about the contract, and that should never have been brought up, and I think they realize that.

THE PRESS HERE IS TOUGH. I tried to deal with them like I have everywhere I've coached. I had open practices, and I was open and honest with them, granted them interviews, let 'em talk to me, let 'em talk to our coaches, let 'em talk to our players. That hadn't been done in the past, so I'm not sure they were ready for that. If you make a comment, *woo*, they're liable to take that thing and blow it way out of proportion. I'm settin' here now, wondering, 'Should I go back to my old ways and have open practices?' Last year, I closed them. This spring, I opened them again. Last year when they were closed, the press was complaining because they were closed. Well, Woody had 'em closed, Earle had 'em closed. And when you open them, your critics don't come to 'em. They don't know whether a football is puffed or stuffed. The two or three critics I have in this town won't come to practice once a year. Yet they're experts on everything.

I've never made a commercial, never done anything, to interfere with my coaching. Those commercials are done in the summertime, they're canned, and I'm at practice every day, staff meetings every day. Certainly, the hot tub was a mistake. There's no question about it. Looking back, if I could change that, I'd change that. I wouldn't do that hot tub commercial, because it wasn't worth it to me. The Big Bear commercials, the advertising—maybe that was a little over-exposed when I first came in here. But, again, people need to understand this is modern day. Coaches do commercials. See, what Woody was doing, people don't understand, Woody was writing books. How much time does it take you to write a book? It's liable to take you months to write a book, where a commercial, you go out and do it in an hour. I think I was over-exposed, to be honest with you, the first couple of years I was here. And all I did was just give the negative people something to be negative about.

I was accused of charging money to do alumni groups and do high school banquets. I have never in my life got a penny to do an alumni appearance. Alumni people don't pay you to do that. You might get a 'thank you,' and you may not. I've never charged a high school coach to do a banquet for him. Now, if I go do a banquet, they may give me a check for a hundred bucks or a couple hundred bucks, but I've never said, 'Hey, I'll come and do your banquet for $200.'

If I never coach another game in my life, I've had a pretty good run. How many coaches that came up the hard way like I have, that have chased this dream all over the country, have had a chance to coach in the Rose Bowl? How many of them have had a chance to coach at Ohio State? How many of them have been Coach of the Year?

I WAKE UP EVERY MORNING and thank the good Lord I have this kind of position, that I'm alive, that I'm healthy, that I have a beautiful family. I got so much to be thankful for. There's too many positive things out there for me to get carried away with the negatives. I'm not going to tell you that my wife hasn't regretted all the moving around, but it's worked out great for me. I think of all those people who've made that same set of moves who haven't had a chance to be a head coach. If I had thought I wasn't going to be a head coach, I would probably have settled down and coached high school football and been there the rest of my life.

I've been in more stadiums than any football coach in America, I guarantee you. I've been to probably 75 stadiums where we've taken a team in to play a game. I've bounced around. But I'm tired of bouncing. I'd like to finish up right here. I don't know if I can or not. I don't know if I will or not, but I'd like to. To do that, I think we gotta take the program to the next level. We gotta beat Michigan. We gotta win the Big Ten, maybe have a shot at the national championship. That's what I'd like to do. Can we do it? Yeah, I think we can, but it remains to be seen.

I think there's a lot more unsuccessful programs than there are unsuccessful coaches out there. So, I think, first, the administration had better make a commitment that, 'Hey, we're going to have a Big Ten competitive program or a nationally competitive program.' I think you gotta have entrance requirements where you can get the great athlete in school and, more important, you better be able to keep him in school. If he doesn't work at it, he doesn't belong in college. But if we let a kid in school, and he goes to class and does everything he can, then I think that kid oughta be able to get out. The important thing is not getting in, it's getting out.

I think we need to improve the academic facilities on this campus. To me, that is the number one thing we have to do athletically—to build an academic building where these kids can go during the day and have a place to study like all the other competitive teams in the country have, where they can go and have study cubicles, where they can have access to computers. We're getting some lip service about it, but we have all kind of cutbacks here, so, right now, I'd say all of that would have to be on hold. We needed that last year, three years ago.

I GREW UP INVOLVED IN ATHLETICS. Somewhere in my high school career I took a look at my high school coach and figured, 'Hey, this's a pretty good way to make a living.' As opposed to working in a factory, or as a laborer or a carpenter or a mechanic or something like my dad did. I figured it was a lot easier way to make a living than working.

I thought I'd be a high school coach; I thought I'd be a high school teacher. Everything beyond that's gravy. I could be happy living in a cabin and hunting and fishing all the time. I could be happy like that. I don't have to have a big house and a big car. Now, do I like those things? Yes, absolutely, but I don't have to have them. That's the reason I say I pinch myself every morning when I wake up.

I also don't know of anybody who's worked any harder to get where they are in the coaching profession than John Cooper. I don't know of anybody who's bounced around the country and taken the chances and sacrificed and worked any harder than I have. I'm humble, but I'm also very proud of where I am. I think I'm a good example of—and I'm not putting this the right way—of the American success story. The kid who came out of the hills of east Tennessee and has gone to the top of his profession. It can happen to you in America. I'm a good example.

There isn't anybody out there I don't like. I want everybody to like John Cooper. Why be unhappy? Life's too short to be unhappy. If anybody has an axe to grind with me, or if anybody doesn't like me, or anybody has something negative, come and visit with me. We can agree to disagree. We don't have to be disagreeable. You don't have to be somebody's enemy. You don't have to hate a guy not to agree with him, right? Maybe it's too simple, but that's me. Maybe I'm too simple. I don't have an axe to grind with anybody. I'm gonna compete, I'm gonna do the best I can, I'm gonna lay it on the line, and when the game's over, I'm gonna shake your hand and say, 'Hey, good luck.'

The other thing I think is very, very important—and we haven't done as good a job in this area as we will do—is the attitude I want to take: Nothing keeps you from being successful. I don't want to hear any excuses for why we can't win at Ohio State. I use this old country saying: 'Don't worry about the horse goin blind, load the wagon and pull the line.' Get the job done. We don't need to worry about injuries, or the weather, or the pre-game meal, or the bus ride, or the officiating. Don't look for reasons why you're not successful, just make it happen.

Recruit the best players you can, give 'em everything you possibly can to make 'em successful, and let 'em play. Sometimes you win, sometimes you lose. Sometimes you kick that field goal that wins the game, sometimes you don't get the breaks. I don't have any desire, at this time, to coach anyplace else. Now, you never say never, I don't suppose. But if things go as I hope they go here for me, this'll be it. ”

John Cooper
coach
Born July 2, 1937,
Powell, Tennessee

An outstanding high school athlete, he played four years of football at Iowa State, after two years in the army...Team captain and MVP...Began coaching career in 1962 as Iowa State freshman coach...Became assistant coach at Oregon State in 1963...In 1964, Oregan State won the Pac-8 title and went to the Rose Bowl...He followed Tommy Prothro to UCLA where the Bruins won the Pac-8 and he and Prothro returned to the Rose Bowl...After 1967 season, he became defensive coordinator at Kansas where in 1969 Kansas won the Big Eight title and played in the Orange Bowl...Cooper's last stop as assistant was in 1972 at the University of Kentucky...Recognized as one of the top assistants in the country, he went to Tulsa in 1977 as head coach...His 18-year tenure as head coach (136-66-6, .668) takes in Tulsa (1977-1984, .648), Arizona State (1985-1987, .722), and Ohio State (1988- , .666)...At Tulsa, he won five straight Missouri Valley Conference titles.

OSU: After a 4-6-1 record his initial year at Ohio State, he has moved the program back into the national spotlight...His last three teams finished second, first, and second in league play while compiling the best overall record in the Big Ten...The 1993 team, when the Bucks went 10-1-1, won a Big Ten co-championship—OSU's first since 1986—and a national ranking of 10th, was the most successful team since 1979...The 1994 team went 9-4 and beat Wisconsin and Michigan, losing a close decision to Alabama in the Citrus Bowl...Cooper has coached in several all-star games, including the Hula Bowl, the Japan Bowl, and the East-West Shrine game...He was national coach of the year in 1986 when ASU beat Michigan in the Rose Bowl and in 1993, he was head coach of the East Squad in the Shrine Game.

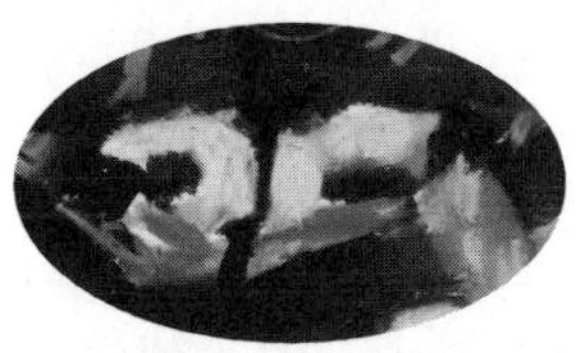

Tom Cousineau
linebacker
6' 3", 225 pounds
Born May 6, 1957,
Bloomington, Indiana
St. Edward (Lakewood, Ohio) High School
Ohio State, 1975-1978
Montreal Alouettes (1979-1981), Cleveland Browns (1982-1985), San Francisco 49ers (1986-1987)

One of nation's most recruited players at St. Edward High School in Cleveland where he was state finalist in wrestling as junior and senior...High school honor student.

OSU: Three-year starter, two-time All-America linebacker...His 211 tackles in 1978 is still OSU single-season school record...Also holds school record for most solo tackles in a single game, 16 against SMU in 1978...Second on all-time OSU tackle list with 569, three behind Marcus Marek...Defensive MVP of 1977 Orange Bowl and 1979 Hula Bowl...Bucks' MVP in 1978...Cleveland TD Club's Collegiate Player of Year for senior season at OSU...All-Big Ten in 1976, 1977, 1978.

Pro: NFL's No. 1 choice in the 1979 draft and drafted by Buffalo but signed with Montreal of the Canadian Football League...Played in CFL from 1979–1981 and described as best defensive player in last ten years...Alouette's rookie-of-year as well as outstanding defensive player in 1979 Grey Cup...In 1980, had 227 tackles, and named best defensive player in Eastern Division...Missed all but two games of final CFL season because of dislocated elbow...Traded to Cleveland and tested as best-conditioned Brown in offseason drills...Ran 4.65 forty...Despite rookie year strike, led Browns in 1982 with 72 tackles, 46 unassisted...In 1983, was first-team on USA Today All-NFL squad and UPI's All-AFC team...In 1984, was first-team All-AFC by UPI, second-team All-NFL by AP...In 1986, claimed by San Francisco off waivers and moved from inside to outside linebacker...Placed on injured reserve October 24 through end of season.

Tim Fox
defensive back
5' 11", 188 pounds
Born November 1, 1953, Canton, Ohio
Glenwood High School
Ohio State, 1972–1975
New England Patriots (1976-1981), San Diego Chargers (1982-1984), Los Angeles Rams (1985-1986)

Captained football, basketball and track teams at Glenwood High where he earned 10 varsity letters, including tennis...Was a gymnast, scored five touchdowns in one game, and long-jumped 22' 11".

OSU: Three-year starter, and named first-team All-America in 1975 by UPI, NEA, Kodak (American Football Coaches Association), Walter Camp Foundation, Sporting News...All-Big Ten first team by AP and UPI...defensive co-captain for 1975 team which had 11-0 regular season record...Recognized as one of hardest hitters on team...As senior led Big Ten in punt returns (22 for 256 yards, 1 TD) and ranked 12th nationally...Four-year letterman and played in 43 of 46 games (862 minutes) during college career, including four Rose Bowls...Defensive back coach Dick Walker called him the best athlete he ever coached...Fox could dunk a basketball, high jumped 6' 7", and broad jumped 22 feet...Played in Japan Bowl post-season all-star game.

Pro: 21st player taken in 1976 NFL draft, chosen with first-round choice from San Francisco in Jim Plunkett trade...One of three first-round picks by Patriots...After missing season opener with hip injury as a rookie in 1976, he made 91 consecutive starts for Patriots...Made both UPI and Professional Football Writers' all-rookie team in 1976...From 1977-1981 was top tackler in Patriots' secondary...Selected to Pro Bowl following 1980 season...Credited with 103 solo tackles in 1981...In 1983 made Sports Illustrated's All-Pro team, AP's All-Pro second team and alternate to AFC Pro Bowl squad...Chargers' field leader on defense until released during 1985 spring training camp...Signed by Rams and saw action in Rams' final six games and two playoff contests, including NFC Championship game...In ten years, he played in 127 games (116 starts) and had 26 interceptions.

Cornelius Greene
quarterback
6' 0", 172 pounds
Born January 21, 1954, Washington, D.C.
Dunbar High School
Ohio State, 1972-1975
Dallas Cowboys (1976), British Columbia Lions (1977)

Called "Flam" by high school teammates...Threw 23 touchdown passes as senior at Dunbar High where he was a three-sport All-American...Won nine high school letters, three each in football, basketball, and baseball.

OSU: Never lost to Michigan and went to four straight Rose Bowls, three as starting quarterback...Led Big Ten in total offense in 1974 when he set school record with 1,636 yards...All-Big Ten MVP in 1974 and1975...Presided over only two losing games in three years of regular season play...Bucks' MVP in 1975, which made teammate Archie Griffin the only Heisman Trophy winner who had not been his team's MVP...First Buckeye quarterback to win a Silver Football as the league MVP...Hula Bowl.

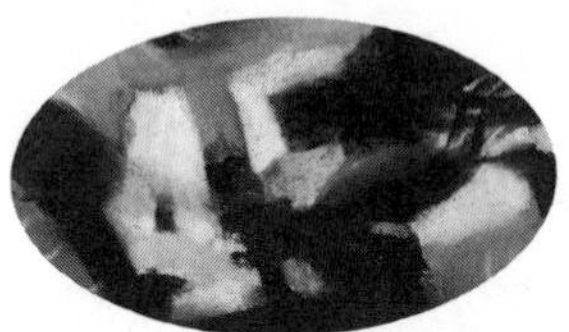

Archie Griffin
tailback
5' 9", 180 pounds
Born August 21, 1954, Columbus, Ohio
Columbus Eastmoor High School
Ohio State, 1972-1975
Cincinnati Bengals (1976-1983)

As All-Ohio, and Ohio High School Back of the Year, was one of most sought after prep players in the nation.

OSU: History's only two-time Heisman Trophy winner...In 1974, he was only the fifth junior to win it...One of four Buckeyes ever to be named All-American three times...Led OSU to 40-5-1 record and four Big Ten titles...In his first game as freshman in 1972, set what was then an OSU single-game rushing record with 239 yards against North Carolina...Rushed for 867 yards, then a freshman record...In 1973, became first OSU sophomore to ever rush for 1,000 yards (1,577)...Won Chigago Tribune's Silver Football as the Big Ten Player of the Year...In 1974, won second Silver Football and was UPI and Walter Camp Player of Year...In 1975, was again UPI and Walter Camp Player of Year...Still holds OSU record for career yards rushing, 5,589, as well as career rushing attempts, 924...Holds NCAA record for consecutive 100-yard games, 31...NCAA record for average yards per carry, 6.13...Fourth in NCAA rushing, 5,177 yards...Only player in collegiate history to start four Rose Bowl games...Hula Bowl...Played in the last College All-Star game in June of 1976...Ohio State University Athletic Hall of Fame...National Football Foundation Hall of Fame...Rose Bowl Hall of Fame...College Football Hall of Fame.

Pro: First round draft pick by the Bengals where he played with brother, Ray, a Berngal defensive back...Bengal captain, as well as being sixth on the Bengals all-time rushing statistics list with 2,808 yards for a 4.1 average...Also had another 1,607 receiving yards.

Wayne Woodrow Hayes
Coach
Born February 14, 1913, Clifton (Greene County), Ohio
Newcomerstown High School
Ohio State, 1951-1978

As an offensive tackle in 1934, he helped Denison University to a 6-1 record...Began coaching career as assistant at Mingo Junction High School in 1935...In 1947 and 1948 coached Denison University to back-to-back undefeated seasons...His second year at Miami University, the Redskins went 9–1 winning the conference title and upsetting Arizona State 34–21 in the Salad Bowl.

OSU: In his fourth season at OSU—1954—unbeaten Buckeyes won first of 13 Big Ten championships or co-championships, as well as the Rose Bowl and a national title...The 1954 squad won seven conference games, the first Big Ten team to do so since Chicago did it in 1913, the year Hayes was born...In 1968, Buckeyes win second national title after beating USC in Rose Bowl, 20-7...Last unbeaten team (his fourth) in 1973 when Bucks tie Michigan 10–10 for the Big Ten co-championship, and go on to beat USC 42–21 in Rose Bowl...Hayes's OSU teams went to the Rose Bowl eight times...His Bucks were 16–11–1 against Michigan...Coached 42 All-Americans...Under Hayes, Buckeyes went 205–61–10...His 28 seasons are surpassed in the Big Ten only by Amos Alonzo Stagg at Chicago (41) Bob Zuppke at Illinois (29), and Joe Paterno...Named top coach in country in 1957 and 1975...His 205 Big Ten wins are still first, trailed by Bo Schembechler's 194 wins at Michigan...Hayes's 238 career victories have been surpassed by only four major college coaches—Bear Bryant (323), Stagg (314), Pop Warner (313), and Joe Paterno (247)...During Hayes' tenure at OSU, the Bucks led the nation in attendance 21 times and were second in each of the other years...National Football Foundation Hall of Fame...Amos Alonzo Stagg Award from the American Football Coaches Association for long and meretorious service...Awarded an honorary doctor of humanities degree by Ohio State in 1986.

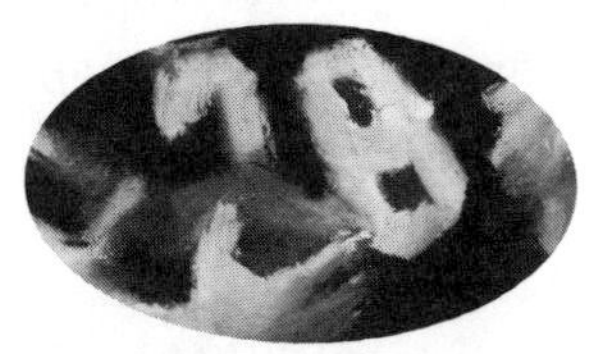

Harold R. "Champ" Henson, III
running back
6' 3", 240 pounds
Born June 1, 1953, Columbus, Ohio
Teays Valley (Ashville, Ohio) High School
Ohio State, 1971-1974
Cincinnati Bengals (1975)

OSU: Led nation in scoring—20 touchdowns— as sophomore...Never lost a yard rushing in his college career...Fumbled only once...Missed most of senior year with knee injury...His 44 carries against Northwestern in 1972 set school record which still stands...His four touchdowns in same game also tied a school record...College All-Star game.

Paul Hornung
sportswriter
Born July 18, 1915,
New Bavaria, Ohio
Holgate High School
Ohio State, 1934-1938

Began writing about OSU football for the Columbus Dispatch as campus sports correspondent in 1938, covering football and basketball practices...Hired fulltime in fall of 1940 and began writing about OSU football in 1941...After missing the second game of 1941 he covered 326 consecutive regular-season and bowl games, including nine Rose Bowls...String was broken in 1975 when he was assigned to cover the Cincinnati Reds in the World Series...Named *Dispatch* sports editor in 1956...Host of WBNS-TV's Woody Hayes Show...Wrote three books on OSU football...Charter recipient of the Robert C. Woodworth Award for meritorious contributions to the Big Ten and intercollegiate athletics...Retired in 1981.

Don Hurley
fan
Born Circleville, June 7, 1938
Walnut Township High School
Ohio State, 1957

Since 1948, Hurley has seen or heard 493 OSU football games: 67 in person, 145 on TV, and 281 on the radio.

Pete Johnson
fullback
6' 1", 246 pounds
Born March 2, 1954,
Peach County, Georgia
Peach County (Georgia) High,
Long Beach (New York) High
Ohio State, 1973-1976
Cincinnati Bengals (1977-1983),
San Diego Chargers (1984),
Miami Dolphins (1984)

Born Willie James Hammock, he changed his name to get extra year of high school eligibility—father's first name was Johnson; Pete came from neighborhood Peter Pan ice cream truck...Was All-Georgia and All-New York in high school, playing linebacker, defensive end, middle guard, halfback, and fullback.

OSU: Academic OSU All-America in 1976...All-Big Ten in 1975...Scored 58 touchdowns for OSU as Archie Griffin's running mate, which makes him the most prolific point-producer in school history...One of only 18 Division 1-A college players to ever score 50 or more career touchdowns...Gained 2,312 yards and set all Big Ten scoring records...Still holds Big Ten record for points (156 in 1975)...Was NCAA scoring champion in 1975 and 1976...Holds OSU single-game scoring record, with Keith Byars, 30 points, as well as season (156 points in 1975) and career (348)...Also holds touchdown records for game (5, against North Carolina in 1975, tied with Keith Byars), season (26 in 1975), and career (58)...Converted 54 of 74 third and fourth-down attempts in 1975...Played in Senior Bowl.

Pro: Picked by Cincinnati in 2nd round—49th player chosen—of 1977 draft...Started nine games as a rookie. Won $50 training camp wagers by dunking a basketball...Was Cincinnati's rushing leader each of his seven years there...Best season was Bengal Super Bowl campaign of 1981 when he had a club record 1,077 yards and 12 touchdowns... Also had career-best 46 receptions for another 320 yards...Pro Bowl selection in 1981. Holds Bengals' records for career and season touchdowns...Also second in all-time rushing yards and third in total career points...Acquired in September of 1984 from San Diego by Dolphins for 1985 second-round draft choice, and 12 hours after arriving in Miami—and learning plays in cafeteria—played in his first Dolphin game...In November 18 game against former San Diego teammates, Johnson tied Miami record for most consecutive games with rushing touchdowns—five...In eight years as a pro, gained 5,626 rushing yards for a 3.8 average, gained another 1,334 passing yards, and scored 82 touchdowns.

Rex Kern
quarterback
5' 11", 190 pounds
Born May 28, 1949, Lancaster, Ohio
Lancaster High School
Ohio State, 1967-1970
Baltimore Colts (1971-1973), Buffalo Bills (1974)

As prep all-star, was All-Ohio in football, basketball, and baseball... Also excellent golfer.

OSU: Buckeyes went 27-2 when he was quarterback...All-American in 1969 and still ranked as among greatest of OSU quarterbacks...Master of the fake and the broken play...Set OSU total offense record as junior, finishing career with 3,990 total yards...Had 1,586 yards rushing on 532 carries, and 24 touchdowns; 2,404 passing yards and another 19 touchdowns...MVP as sophomore in 1969 Rose Bowl win over O.J. Simpson-led Southern Cal...Finished fourth in Heisman Trophy ballots his junior year...Rose Bowl Hall of Fame...One of 12 scholar-athletes chosen by the National Football Foundation...Won Ernie Davis Memorial Award for Leadership at 1971...Coaches' All-American Game in Lubbock, Texas...Earned master's degree in Athletic Administration.

Pro: Drafted in 10th round of 1971 draft by Baltimore and played in every game his rookie season...Won starting job as cornerback in 11th game but career was hampered with injuries...Back injury and dislocated hand limited playing time in 1972...Picked up by Buffalo as free agent, Kern retired after failing his physical examination.

Ken Kuhn
linebacker
6' 2", 231 pounds
Born August 19, 1954,
Canton, Ohio
Louisville High School
Ohio State, 1972-1975
Cincinnati Bengals (1976)

All-Ohio and All-American in high school...Captain of his prep football and basketball teams...Won nine letters in high school where he still holds school shot put record.

OSU: Lettered as freshman at OSU in 1972...Played in four Rose Bowls...Defensive co-captain as senior...One of only two OSU linebackers to make the Academic All-Big Ten team twice.

Pro: Drafted in the seventh round in 1976...Missed rookie season after knee surgery following a pre-training camp injury; waived in 1977 pre-season.

Tom Matte
halfback/quarterback
6', 207 pounds
Born June 14, 1939, Pittsburgh, Pennsylvania
Shaw (East Cleveland) High School
Ohio State, 1957-1960
Baltimore Colts (1961-1972)

Outstanding all-around prep athlete in Cleveland...played hockey, football, basketball, and ran track...Once scored 36 points in a basketball game...

OSU: Began college career as halfback but pressed into duty as quarterback in 1959 (check) opener against Duke...Became OSU's top running quarterback, since Les Horvath...Was also excellent defensive player and as a senior punted 29 times for a 35.2-yard average...Buckeye MVP in 1960...All-Big Ten in 1960...College All-Star Game...Coaches' All-American Game...Named outstanding back in the East-West Shrine Game, in which his 10-yard touchdown pass resulted in the East's 7–0 win.

Pro: Drafted by Baltimore in first round of 1961 draft...Played in NFL Championship games, 1964 and 1968...In 1965, after injuries felled Johnny Unitas and Gary Cuozzo, Matte became the Colts's "instant quarterback," and with plays written on a wristband, inspired his teammates to a 20–17 win over the Rams, tying the Green Bay Packers for first place in the Western Conference...He then turned in a thrilling performance against the Packers in the playoffs before losing in sudden death...Pro Bowl, 1968 and 1969...Tied NFL Championship game records in 1968 in Cleveland for most touchdowns, game, 3, and most touchdowns, rushing, game, 3...In 1969, was NFL's third leading rusher with 909 yards and led league in combined rushing–pass receiving yardage (1,422)...Rushed for 4,646 yards for nearly a 4.0 average in 12-year career with the Colts and scored 56 touchdowns, 43 of them in four years...Added another 2,869 receiving yards, 1,367 in kickoff returns, and 246 passing yards.

Dave Mazeroski
fullback
6' 1", 227 pounds
Born March 20, 1954,
Cadiz, Ohio
Cadiz High School
Ohio State , 1972-1975

All-Ohio linebacker in 1971.

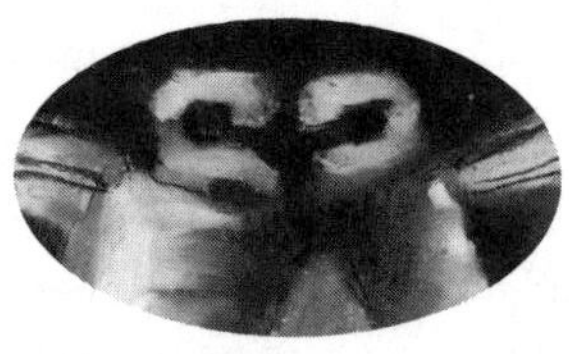

Jim Parker
guard/tackle
6' 3", 273 pounds
Born April 3, 1934, Macon,
Georgia
Scott (Toledo, Ohio) High
School
Ohio State, 1953-1956
Baltimore Colts (1957-1967)

Played last two years of high school football in Toledo, where Woody Hayes discovered him parking cars.

OSU: Was three-year starter and two-time All-American for OSU...During his varsity career, OSU won 23 of 28 games, won the 1954 national championship, and back-to-back Big Ten titles in 1954 and 1955...As a senior, he became the Bucks' first Outland Trophy winner...Played in East-West Shrine Game and Hula Bowl...College All-Star Game...Bucks' MVP in 1956...He is a charter member of the Ohio State Athletic Hall of Fame, a member of the College Football Hall of Fame, and still regarded as one of the finest offensive linemen ever to play college football.

Pro: Number one draft pick by Baltimore in the 1957 NFL draft...Known as exceptional blocker whose speciality was protecting the quarterback...Played half his professional career at guard, half at tackle...Played in eight Pro Bowls...In 1962, he was named All-Pro at both positions...All-NFL eight consecutive years, 1958-1965...Played in NFL Championship games, 1958, 1959, 1964...First fulltime offensive lineman named to the Pro Football Hall of Fame.

Daryl Sanders
tackle
6'5", 248 pounds
Born April 24, 1941, Canton, Ohio
Mayfield High School
Ohio State, 1959-1962
Detroit Lions (1963-1966)

Captain of his high school's first unbeaten, untied team...played tackle, end, and middle guard...

OSU: Paired with teammate Bob Vogel, OSU had one of best tackle duos in nation...honorable mention All-American...Played in North-South Shrine game, Senior Bowl, Coaches' All-America game, and College All-Star game...

Pro: Drafted number one by Detroit in 1963 NFL draft...Became starter at offensive tackle his rookie year where he was rated as one of the NFL's strongest linemen...Retired after fourth season to pursue business interests.

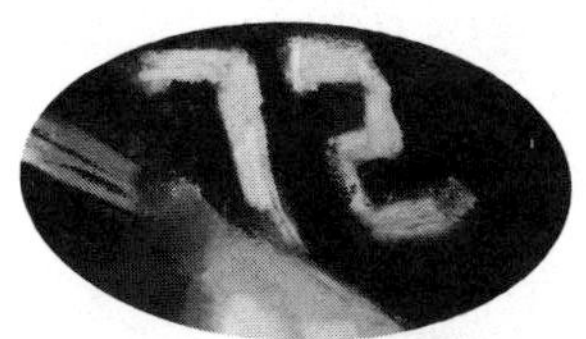

Kurt Schumacher
guard/tackle
6'3", 252 pounds
Born December 26, 1952, Cleveland, Ohio
Lorain High School
Ohio State, 1971-1974
New Orleans Saints (1975-1977), Tampa Bay Buccaneers (1978)

All-American, All-Ohio fullback and linebacker in high school...Good high school wrestler and discus thrower.

As sophomore, he learned his trade as backup to Outland Trophy winner John Hicks...Offensive tackle on the Sporting News College All-America team in 1974, as well as NEA first team All-American...All Big Ten in 1973 and 1974...Played in three Rose Bowls and the 1975 Hula Bowl, as well as the College All-Star game.

Pro: Chosen by New Orleans in first round of the 1975 NFL draft...Missed only one game in his three seasons in New Orleans.

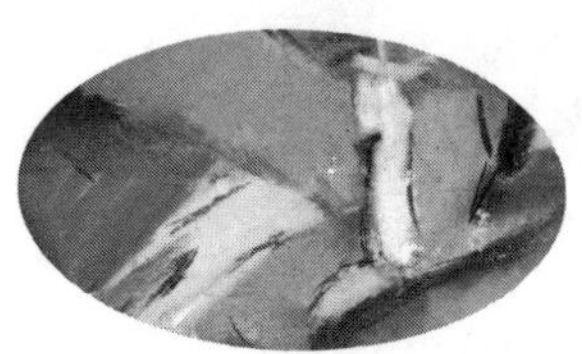

Tom Skladany
kicker
6', 192 pounds
Born June 29, 1955,
Bethel Park, Pennsylvania
Bethel Park High School
Ohio State, 1973-1976
Detriot Lions (1978-1982),
Philadelphia Eagles (1983)

While in high school, kicked a 43-yard field goal.

OSU: First kicking specialist ever recruited at OSU...One of only four three-time All-Americans at OSU...Brilliant on kickoffs and punts as freshman...In first nine games, his hang-time allowed Buckeye opponents only 25 yards in punt returns...20 of his 55 kickoffs were not returned...Broken ankle in Michigan game kept him out of Rose Bowl...Finest season was in 1975 when he punted for a 46.7 average, which set a Big Ten record and led the nation...Also in 1975, Skladany had a 68-yard punt and a 59-yard field goal, still fifth longest in the Big Ten...He's also still fifth in punting average in a season (46.7) in the Big Ten...His 52.3 average against Michigan in 1976 is currently an OSU record, while his 6,838 career punting yards is second on the all-time OSU list, as is his four-year average...And his 59-yard field goal at Illinois in 1975 remains the longest field goal in OSU history...Co-captain of the 1976 team, the only specialist ever so chosen at OSU...Played in Hula Bowl and Japan Bowl.

Pro: Drafted by Cleveland in second round of 1977 and touted as best punter to arrive in the NFL since Ray Guy came to Oakland...At Detroit, over five years, he punted for a 42.4 average (11,363 yards)...Led the NFC as a rookie in 1978, when he was named to the All-NFC squad...Was out much of 1979 with back injury...A 74-yard kick in 1981 was fourth-longest in Detoit history...Led NFL in 1981 in net average (37.3)...His best day was at Denver when he punted six times for a 50.0 average...Punted for the NFC in the Pro Bowl after that season...In 1983, his 268 punts ranked him third among all-time Lion performers...He punted for a 39.4 average during an additional year with the Eagles.

Game...College Football Hall of Fame...

Pro: First-round draft choice by Green Bay Packers but chose CFL where he was All-Eastern All-Star and All-Canadian All-Star, 1971, 1972, 1974...Played in 1971 Grey Cup.

Jim Stillwagon
middle guard
6', 240 pounds
Born February 11, 1949,
Mt. Vernon, Ohio
Augusta Military Academy
Ohio State, 1967-1970
Toronto Argonauts
(1971-1976)

Participated in football, lacrosse, basketball, wrestling, and track and field at Augusta where he won 14 letters.

OSU: Became first player to win the Outland Trophy and the Lombardi Award in the same year...Also won Knute Rockne Trophy as nation's best lineman...Three-year starter and two-time unanimous All-American...Twice All-Big Ten, in 1969 and 1970...With him at the heart of the defense, Buckeyes went 27-2, won three Big Ten championships, played in two Rose Bowls, and won a national championship...In 1969, Bucks' defense gave up only 93 total points...In 1970, only two opponents scored more than 13 points...Bucks' MVP in 1970...Hula Bowl (co-captain with Jim Plunkett)...Coaches' All-American

Bob Vogel
tackle
6'5", 248 pounds
Born September 23, 1941,
Columbus, Ohio
Massillon High School
Ohio State, 1959-1962
Baltimore Colts (1963-1972)

All-American end in high school where he won 13 letters in four sports...

OSU: One of top offensive tackles in collegiate football...Starter as sophomore...second-team UPI All-American...Played in the Senior Bowl, the Blue-Gray Game, the Coaches' All-America Game, the College All-Star Game, and the Hula Bowl...

Selected number one by Baltimore in 1963 NFL draft...Starting offensive left tackle as rookie...Sporting News NFL Western Conference All-Star teams, 1965-1969...All-Pro six of his ten years...Played in 1969 and 1971 Super Bowls.

1950s

Woody Hayes, in a controversial university decision, is named OSU football coach over popular favorite Paul Brown. Alumni petition governor to intervene. Hayes' salary: $12,500.

1952

Woody's first win over Michigan: a 27-7 upset. First OSU win over Michigan in eight seasons. First of 16 for Woody.

1955

OSU-Iowa game features nation's best two guards, OSU's Jim Parker and Iowa's Calvin Jones, both from Ohio. OSU wins 20-0. Bucks are Big Ten champions. Parker named All-American.

1956

Jim Parker wins Outland Trophy.

1957

OSU goes 9-1. Woody named coach of year by the American Football Coaches Association.

Jim Parker

1959

Junior halfback Tom Matte moved to quarterback at halftime of opener vs. Duke. Matte throws 22 yards for fourth-down TD and 14-13 come-from-behind win.

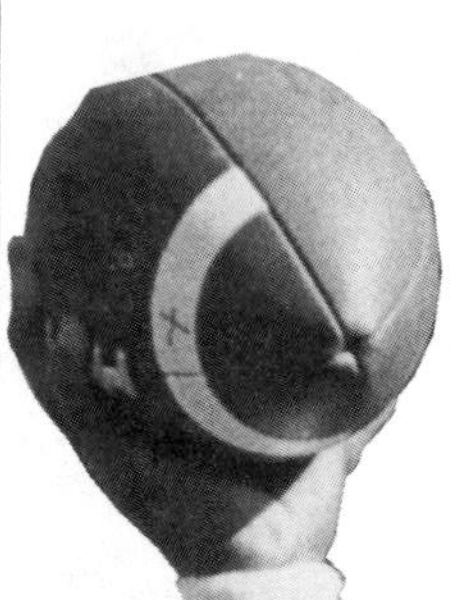

Woody's Boys, the timeline: 1951-1978

1955 Rose Bowl, 20-7 over USC, and national title.

1954 Michigan, with a first down on the OSU four-yard line, is finally stopped by a Jim Parker-led Buckeye defense one foot from the goal line, one of greatest moments in Buckeye football. OSU's 21-7 win gives 10-0 Bucks first undefeated, untied team since 1944;

1958 Rose Bowl, 10-7 over Oregon, and national title.

Cornelius Greene

1960s

1961

OSU beats Michigan 50-20 in Ann Arbor, OSU's 400th win, and finish season unbeaten. Faculty council votes no Rose Bowl; says OSU has become known as "football school." Students demonstrate at statehouse. Bucks named Football Writers's national champions. Matte drafted first by Baltimore.

1963

Tackles Bob Vogel (Colts) and Daryl Sanders (Lions) are first-round draft picks.

1964

Michigan wins only Big Ten title in Woody's first 18 seasons.

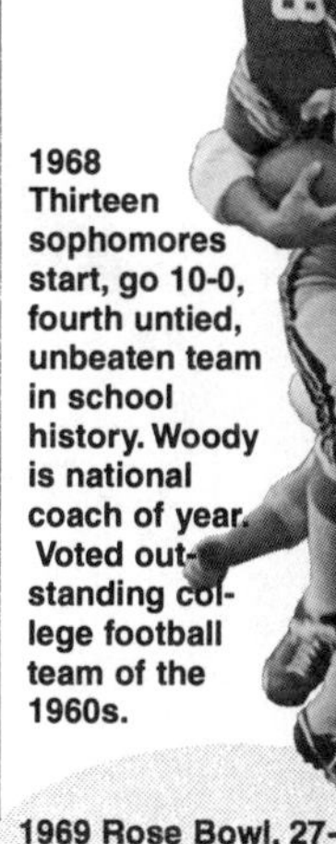

1968
Thirteen sophomores start, go 10-0, fourth untied, unbeaten team in school history. Woody is national coach of year. Voted outstanding college football team of the 1960s.

Champ Henson

1969 Rose Bowl, 27-16 over USC. Bucks win national title. Rex Kern Rose Bowl MVP.

1969

In home opener, Bucks beat TCU 62-0, widest victory margin for any game during Woody's 28-year tenure at OSU. Big Ten co-champions after 24-12 upset loss to Michigan on last day of season. Jim Stillwagon and Rex Kern named All-American.

Rex Kern

1970s

1970

OSU goes undefeated. Nose guard Jim Stillwagon wins Outland Trophy, the first Lombardi Award, and named All-American.

1972

Fifth-string tailback Archie Griffin debuts in Bucks' second game, against UNC; sets single-game rushing record—-239 yards. Sophomore Champ Henson leads nation in scoring.

1973

Sophomore Cornelius Greene starts opener at quarterback, Bucks score on four of first six possessions, beat Minnesota 56-7. Bucks go 10-0-1; considered best OSU team ever, outscoring opposition 413-64 and giving up only 4.3 points per game. Griffin named All-American and Big Ten MVP.

1974

Griffin, Tom Skladany, and Kurt Schumacher named All-American. Griffin wins Heisman Trophy.

1975

Tom Skladny sets school record with 59-yard field goal against Illinois. Pete Johnson sets Big Ten record with his 21st touchdown of the season. Griffin becomes the all-time major college rushing leader against Purdue, with 4,730 yards. Greene is Big Ten MVP. Griffin becomes only player to win two Heisman Trophies. Griffin, Fox, and Skladany named All-American. Schumacher is number one draft pick by New Orleans.

Kurt Schumacher

1971 Rose Bowl loss to Stanford, 27-17, is season's only defeat; costs Bucks chance at unanimous national title.

1973 Rose Bowl loss to USC, 42-17. Ranked 3rd by UPI.

1974 Rose Bowl, 42-21 over USC.Freshman fullback Pete Johnson scores three times; Greene is Rose Bowl MVP.

1975 Rose Bowl loss to USC, 18-17. Only defeat costs OSU national title.

1976 Rose Bowl loss to UCLA, 23-10; Bucks finish 11-1

1976

OSU goes 9-2-1; Big Ten co-champs and ranked No. 5 by UPI. Punter Tom Skladany becomes only specialty teams player in OSU history to be named co-captain, and OSU's fourth three-time All-American. Tim Fox drafted number one by New England, Griffin in first round by Cincinnati.

1977

Junior linebacker Tom Cousineau named All-American. Orange Bowl win, 27-10 over Colorado.

1978

OSU loses Sugar Bowl, 35-6, to Alabama.

1978

Linebacker Tom Cousineau sets OSU single game tackle record with 16 against SMU. He will be the first Buckeye to ever be the number one overall pick in the NFL draft. Woody gets last win November 18, at Indiana, 21-18. Bucks lose Gator Bowl to Clemson, 17-15, and Hayes fired after punching Clemson line-backer Charlie Bauman.

Tom Skladany

Former president Richard Nixon is one of 1,400 to attend services; 10,000 others show up next day for eulogy in Ohio Stadium. Nixon recalls their first meeting: "I wanted to talk football. Woody wanted to talk foreign policy. You know Woody. We talked foreign policy."

Tim Fox

March 12, 1987, Woody dies in sleep.

Pete Johnson

Index